Worldwide Destinations

Worldwide Destinations

The geography of travel and tourism

Fourth edition

Brian G. Boniface and Chris Cooper

ELSEVIER
BUTTERWORTH
HEINEMANN

AMSTERDAM   BOSTON   HEIDELBERG   LONDON   NEW YORK   OXFORD
PARIS   SAN DIEGO   SAN FRANCISCO   SINGAPORE   SYDNEY   TOKYO

Elsevier Butterworth-Heinemann
Linacre House, Jordan Hill, Oxford OX2 8DP
30 Corporate Drive, Burlington, MA 01803

First published as *The Geography of Travel and Tourism* 1987
Reprinted 1998, 1990, 1991, 1993
Second edition 1994
Reprinted 1994, 1995, 1996 (twice)
Third edition 2001
Fourth edition 2005
Reprinted 2005

British Library Cataloguing in Publication Data
A catalogue record for this book is available from the British Library

Library of Congress Cataloguing in Publication Data
A catalogue record for this book is available from the Library of Congress

ISBN 0 7506 5997 1

For information on all Elsevier Butterworth-Heinemann
publications visit our website at www.bh.com

Working together to grow
libraries in developing countries

www.elsevier.com | www.bookaid.org | www.sabre.org

ELSEVIER   BOOK AID
International   Sabre Foundation

Typeset by Newgen Imaging Systems (P) Ltd., Chennai, India
Printed and bound in Italy

Contents

Part One: The Elements of the Geography of Travel and Tourism

Part Two: The Regional Geography of Travel and Tourism

List of figures

List of tables

Preface

In the mid 1980s when we set out to write the first edition of *The Geography of Travel and Tourism* there was a pioneering feeling, as we followed in the footsteps of a very small band of geographers who had previously entered this new territory of tourism. Almost twenty years later, embarking on the fourth edition of *Worldwide Destinations: The Geography of Travel and Tourism*, the territory has been well and truly explored, not only by ourselves, but also by many other authors writing textbooks, reports and papers for specialist journals.

Indeed, writing the first edition presented real problems of sourcing accurate information and statistics about each country – yet for this edition the information is much more readily available, not only in print form but also on the Internet. This raises issues on the reliability of much of this material, and also the sheer quantity that is available creates information overload for students. Here the challenge is to transform that information into knowledge.

In the third edition we introduced case studies at the end of each chapter, to explore key issues and selected destinations at greater depth. To avoid being faced with an over-long textbook this time round, we have introduced a companion volume of case studies, *Tourist Destinations in Focus*, as a further learning resource for students and teachers. We also hope that the fourth edition has a less Eurocentric focus than its predecessors, by giving much more space to emerging destinations in Africa, Asia and the Americas. We have also updated the text to recognize the changing world and in particular the threat to international tourism in the wake of 9/11, by highlighting issues such as security and crisis management.

None the less, we have retained many of the ingredients of the previous successful editions. In particular, we have retained our comprehensive coverage of every country in the world, although some world regions have been altered in line with popular recognition, for example, Hawaii is included as part of North America in this edition. The regional chapters are written to a flexible template comprising tourism demand, supply, organization and resources. We make no apology for this comprehensive approach, as we feel that it is needed more than ever before in a subject area dominated by ever-increasing specialization, and it therefore complements the more detailed treatment of tourism found in the multitude of textbooks, reports and academic papers that deal with particular themes or regions.

For schools and colleges this specialization raises a real issue for library resources, and we hope that this book provides an all-embracing framework – supplemented by a good atlas – from which students can develop an understanding of most aspects of world travel and tourism. We feel that many tourism courses are requiring geographical knowledge, not only of the locations of routes and destinations – as traditionally recognized by the travel and tourism industry – but also for a systematic analysis of these destinations and the other supply elements of tourism. As in previous editions, we stress the demand-side of tourism, particularly where it concerns the world's most important generators of domestic and outbound travel. Geography can make a unique contribution to the study of tourism and this is often overlooked. Many tourism courses and modules have titles such as tourism impacts, sustainable tourism, tourism destinations, cultural tourism etc … Regardless of the title, they use geographical methods in analysing tourism. We therefore hope that a wide range of readers, including those with little geographical knowledge, will use this book.

As ever, a large number of family, friends and colleagues have assisted us, wittingly or unwittingly, in writing this edition. Maria Boniface helped with the research and the processing of e-mails exchanged between England and Australia. Robyn and Amy Cooper researched the list of destination websites; the library at the University of Queensland has been a comprehensive source of material; and our students, including those on distance learning courses from many countries around the world, have provided invaluable feedback and information on current trends in tourism. Sally North at Elsevier has been a supportive and most effective editor and, as always, a pleasure to work with.

Brian G. Boniface and Chris Cooper
Poole and Brisbane
July 2004

Part One

The Elements of the Geography of Travel and Tourism

Chapter 1

An introduction to the geography of travel and tourism

Learning Objectives

After reading this chapter, you should be able to:

- **Define and use the terms leisure, recreation and tourism and understand their interrelationships.**
- **Distinguish between the different forms of tourism – and the relationship of different types of tourist with the environment.**
- **Appreciate the importance of scale in explaining patterns of tourism.**
- **Identify the three major geographical components of tourism – tourist-generating areas, tourist-receiving areas and transit routes.**
- **Explain the push and pull factors that give rise to tourist flows.**
- **Appreciate the main methods used to measure tourist flows and be aware of their shortcomings.**

Leisure, recreation and tourism

What exactly is meant by the terms leisure, recreation and tourism and how are they related? *Leisure* is often seen as a measure of time and usually means the time left over after work, sleep and personal and household chores have been completed (Figure 1.1). In other words, leisure time is free time for individuals to spend as they please. This does, however, introduce the problem of whether all free time is leisure. A good example of this dilemma is whether the unemployed feel that their free time is in fact 'enforced' leisure, or whether volunteers at a sporting event see their activity as 'serious leisure'. This has led to the view that leisure is as much an attitude of mind as a measure of time, and that an element of 'choice' has to be involved. Of course, these relationships have

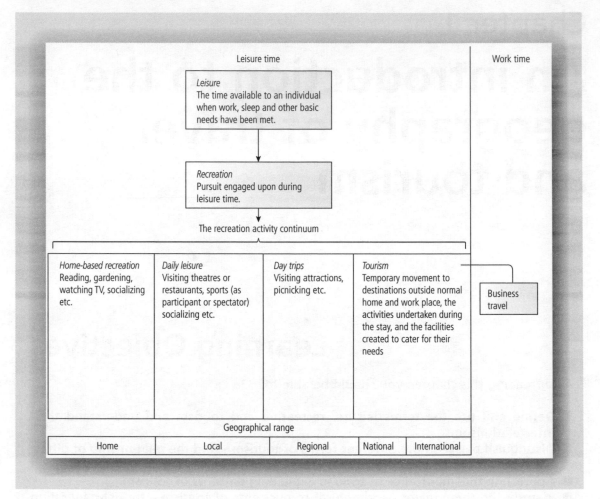

Figure 1.1 Leisure, recreation and tourism

changed over time – the Industrial Revolution for example brought about a sharp contrast between the workplace and the leisure environment, whereas in pre-industrial societies the pace of life is attuned to the rhythm of the seasons rather than 'clock time'.

Recreation is normally taken to mean the variety of activities undertaken during leisure time (Figure 1.1). Basically, recreation refreshes a person's strength and spirit and can include activities as diverse as watching television to holidaying abroad. We can make a useful distinction between physical recreation including sport, and other leisure pursuits that include the arts, cultural activities and entertainment.

If we accept that leisure is a measure of time and that recreation embraces the activities undertaken during that time, then *tourism* is simply one type of recreation activity. It is, however, more difficult to disentangle the meanings of the terms recreation and tourism in practice. Perhaps the most helpful way to think about the difference is to envisage a spectrum with, at one end, recreation based either at home or close to home, and at the opposite end recreational travel where some distance is involved and overnight accommodation may be needed. This is based on the time required for the activity and the distance travelled, and it places tourism firmly at one extreme of the *recreation activity continuum* (Figure 1.1). The idea of a spectrum is helpful as, for example, it allows us to consider the role of same-day visitors or excursionists. These travellers are increasingly a consideration in the geography of tourism – they visit for less than 24 hours and do not stay overnight. In other words, they utilize all tourism facilities except accommodation, and put pressure on the host community and the environment.

Clearly, tourism is a distinctive form of recreation and demands separate consideration. In particular, from the geographical point of view, tourism is just one form of 'temporary or leisure mobility', and in defining tourism it is therefore important to distinguish it from other types of travel. International debate as to the definition of tourism still continues, and there are many different interpretations. There are two ways to approach the problem:

- We can define tourism from the **demand side**, i.e. the person who is the tourist. This approach is well developed and the United Nations Statistical Commission now accepts the following definition of tourism: 'The activities of persons travelling to and staying in places outside their usual environment for not more than one consecutive year for leisure, business and other purposes'. This definition raises a number of issues:
  - What is a person's *usual environment*?
  - The inclusion of 'business' and 'other' *purposes of visit* demands that we conceive of tourism more widely than simply as a recreation pursuit.
  - Certain types of traveller are excluded from the definition. Of course, tourism itself is only one part of the spectrum of travel, which ranges from daily travel to work or for shopping to migration, where the traveller intends to take up permanent or long-term residence in another area.
- We can also define the tourism sector from a **supply side** point of view. Here the difficulty lies in disentangling tourism businesses and jobs from the rest of the economy. After 20 years of debate, the accepted approach is the Tourism Satellite Account (TSA), adopted by the United Nations in 2000. The TSA measures the demand for goods and services generated by visitors to a destination. It allows tourism to be compared with other economic sectors by calculating its contribution to investment, consumption, employment, the gross domestic product (GDP) and taxation.

Geography and tourism

When we study the geography of travel and tourism, three key concepts need to be considered:

- spatial scale
- the geographical components of the tourism system
- spatial interaction between the components of the tourist system.

Spatial scale

Geographers study the spatial expression of tourism as a human activity, focusing on both tourist-generating and tourist-receiving areas as well as the links between them. This study can be undertaken at a variety of scales, ranging from the world distribution of climatic zones, through the regional assessment of tourism resources, to the local landscapes of resorts. The issue of scale has become important in the global versus local debate. As the tourism sector embraces the tools of globalization – such as the forging of global airline alliances – we must never forget that the tourism product is delivered at the local scale, often by local people and within a local cultural context.

The idea of scale has been used to organize the material presented in this book because at each different scale a distinctive perspective upon, and insight into, tourism is gained. Simply, as a more detailed explanation is required, attention is drawn to increasingly smaller parts of the problem. This idea of scale, or geographical magnitude, keeps in focus the area being dealt with, and can be likened to increasing or decreasing the magnification on a microscope or the scale of a map. Flows of leisure tourism in Europe provide a good example of the importance of scale. At the international scale the dominant flow of tourists is north to south, but at the regional scale a variety of other patterns emerge, such as travel between cities, or out of cities to the coast and countryside, whilst at the local scale we can consider day-trip patterns, with people travelling relatively short distances from their accommodation to attractions in the holiday area.

The geographical components of the tourism system

From a geographical point of view tourism consists of three major components which are: first, the places of origin of tourists, or *generating areas*; second, the tourist destinations themselves, or *receiving areas*; and finally, the routes travelled between these two sets of locations, or *transit routes* (Leiper, 1979). These components are set within differing economic, environmental and social contexts. This simple model is illustrated in Figure 1.2 and the components form the basis for Chapters 2 to 5 in this book.

- **Tourist-generating areas** represent the homes of tourists, where journeys begin and end. The key issues to examine in tourist-generating areas are the features that stimulate demand for tourism and will include the geographical location of an area as well as its socioeconomic and demographic characteristics. These areas represent the main tourist markets in the world and, naturally enough, the major marketing functions of the tourist industry are found here (such as tour operation, travel retailing). Tourist-generating areas are considered in Chapter 2.
- **Tourist-receiving areas** attract tourists to stay temporarily and will have features and attractions that may not be found in the generating areas. The tourist industry located in this area will comprise the attractions, accommodation, retailing and service functions, entertainment and recreation facilities. In our view, tourist destination areas are the most important part of the tourism system, not only attracting the tourist and thus energizing the system, but also where the impacts of tourism occur and therefore where the sustainable planning and management of tourism is so important. Features of tourist destination areas are examined in Chapters 3 and 4.
- **Transit routes** link these two types of areas and are a key element in the system as their effectiveness and characteristics shape the volume and direction of tourist flows. Such routes represent the transport component of the tourist industry; they are considered in Chapter 5.

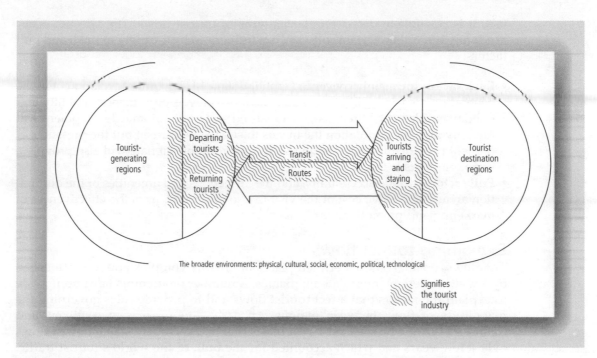

Figure 1.2 The tourism system
Source: Leiper, 1979

The differing contexts within which the tourism system is set pervade the characteristics of each component. For example, a tourism system in a developing country is likely to have a generating component more dominated by domestic travel than would be the case in a developed country. The external environment also affects the tourism system in terms of a range of issues – such as terrorism and security, and the need for all components to develop crisis and risk management plans. It is this connection with the real world that makes the geography of travel and tourism such an exciting and vibrant area to study.

Spatial interaction between the components of the tourist system

Tourist flows

While the study of the geography of tourism should include the three components identified above, there is a danger that, in conveniently dissecting tourism into its component parts, the all-important interrelationships are lost. The consideration of tourist flows between regions is therefore fundamental to the geography of tourism and allows the components of tourism to be viewed as a total system rather than a series of disconnected parts. An understanding of tourist flows is critical for managing the environmental and social impacts of tourism, securing the commercial viability of the tourism industry and for planning new developments.

Tourist flows are a form of spatial interaction between two areas, with the destination area containing a surplus of a commodity (tourist attractions, for example) and the generating area having a deficit, or *demand* for that commodity. In fact, it is possible to detect regular patterns of tourist flows. They do not occur randomly but follow certain rules and are influenced by a variety of push and pull factors:

- **Push factors** are mainly concerned with the stage of economic development in the generating area and will include such factors as levels of affluence, mobility and holiday entitlement. Often, too, an advanced stage of economic development will not only give the population the means to engage in tourism but the pressures of life will provide the 'push' to do so. An unfavourable climate will also provide a strong impetus to travel.
- **Pull factors** include accessibility, and the attractions and amenities of the destination area. The relative cost of the visit is also important, as is the effectiveness of marketing and promotion.

Explaining tourist flows

The flows, or interaction, between places are highly complex and are influenced by a wide variety of interrelated variables. A number of attempts have been made to explain the factors that affect tourist flows and to provide rules governing the magnitude of flows between regions. An early attempt was by Williams and Zelinsky (1970), who selected 14 countries that had relatively stable tourist flows over a few years and which accounted for the bulk of the world's tourist traffic. They identified a number of factors that helped to explain these flows. These included:

- distances between countries (the greater the distance, the smaller the volume of flow)
- international connectivity (shared business or cultural ties between countries)
- the general attractiveness of one country for another.

A second means of explaining tourist flows is offered by the *gravity model*, based on two main factors that influence flows. The first of these are the push and pull factors which generate flows, and the gravity model states that the larger the 'mass' (population) of country 'A' or country 'B', the greater the flow between them. The second factor, known as the friction of distance, refers to the cost (in time and money) of longer journeys, and this acts to restrain flows between the country of origin and more distant destinations.

Other, more complex, multivariate models based on travel itineraries can also be used to explain tourist flows. Four common types can be identified:

- point to point – 'there and back' trips
- point to point with an added touring circuit focused on one point
- a circular tour
- hub and spoke itineraries.

Measuring tourist flows

As tourism has become more prominent, national governments and international organizations have introduced the measurement of both international and domestic flows. There are three main reasons why tourism statistics are important:

- Statistics are required to evaluate the **magnitude of tourist flows** and to monitor any change. This allows projections of future flows to be made and the identification of market trends.

- Statistics act as a base of hard fact to allow tourism planners and developers to operate effectively and **plan for the future of tourism**.
- Both the public and private sectors use the statistics as a basis for their **marketing**.

There are three main categories of tourism statistics:

- **Statistics of volume** give the number of tourists leaving an area or visiting a destination in a given period of time and provide a basic count of the volume of tourist traffic. Volume statistics also include the length of stay of visitors at their destinations. A variety of methods are available to measure tourist flows.
  - For volume statistics, tourists can be counted as they enter or leave a country and immigration control will often provide this information. Obviously this is relatively straightforward for international flows, but much more problematical for domestic tourism. For destination areas, an alternative method is to enumerate tourists at their accommodation by the use of registration cards. This method is only effective with legal enforcement and normally omits visitors staying in private houses or 'VFR' tourists – those visiting (and staying with) friends or relatives.
  - Statistics of domestic tourism volume may be obtained by national travel surveys or destination surveys. National travel surveys involve interviewing a representative sample of the population in their own homes. Questions are asked on the nature and extent of travel over a past period and the results not only provide statistics on the volume of domestic tourism but also may include expenditure and the character of the flows. Examples of national travel surveys include the *UK Tourism Survey* (UKTS) and the *German Reiseanalyse*. In destination surveys, visitors to a tourist area, specific site, or attraction are questioned to establish the volume, value and characteristics of traffic to the area or site.
- The second category of statistics is that of **tourist characteristics**. While statistics of volume are a measure of the quantity of tourist flows, this second category measures the quality of the flow and will include information on types of tourist (such as gender, age, socioeconomic group) and their behaviour (such as structure of the trip, attitudes to the destination). It is not uncommon for statistics of tourist characteristics and volume to be collected together. Surveys of tourist characteristics have evolved from straightforward questioning, which gives basic factual information (for example, the age profile of visitors), to surveys that now concentrate on questions designed to assist the marketing and management of a destination, or to solve a particular problem. Statistics of tourist characteristics are obtained in a variety of ways. Additional questions can be added to accommodation registration cards, or border checks, but more commonly a sample of travellers is asked a series of questions about themselves, their trip, opinions of the destination, etc. (An example of this approach is the *UK International Passenger Survey* (IPS) which measures the volume and value as well as the characteristics of UK inbound and outbound tourism.)
- The third type is **expenditure statistics**. Tourist flows are not simply movements of people but they also have an important economic significance for the tourist system. Quite simply, tourism represents a flow of money that is earned in one place and spent in another. To make comparisons easier, expenditure is usually expressed in $US rather than the national currency. Measurement of tourist expenditure can be obtained by asking tourists directly how much they have spent on their holiday, or

indirectly by asking hoteliers and other suppliers of tourist services for estimates of tourist spending. For international expenditure statistics, bank records of foreign currency exchange may be used as another indirect method.

Despite the variety of methods available to measure tourist flows, it is not easy to produce accurate tourist statistics. In the first place, the tourist has to be distinguished from other travellers (e.g. returning residents) and, while internationally agreed definitions of tourists do exist, they are not yet consistently applied throughout the world. At the same time, until recently there has been no real attempt to coordinate international surveys. To add to these problems, survey methods change over the years, even within single countries, and comparisons of results from year to year are difficult. A further problem is that surveys count 'events', not 'people', so that a tourist who visits a country twice in a year will be counted as two arrivals. Those on touring holidays may be counted as separate arrivals in various destinations and will inflate the overall visitor arrival figures. The relaxation of border controls, especially within groups of trading countries – such as the European Union (EU) – compounds the tourist statistician's problem and makes it difficult to enumerate tourists.

Forms of tourism

The geographical components of tourism, allied to the idea of scale and tourist flows, combine to create a wide variety of different forms of tourism, which we can categorize according to:

- type of destination
- the characteristics of the tourism system
- the market
- the distance travelled.

Type of destination

Tourism can be classified according to the type of destination visited. Here, from a geographical point of view, an important distinction is that between international and domestic tourism:

- **domestic tourism** embraces those travelling within their own country
- **international tourism** comprises those who travel to a country other than that in which they normally live.
- International tourism can be thought of as:
  - *inbound tourism* – non-residents travelling in a given country
  - *outbound tourism* – involving residents of a particular country travelling abroad to other countries.

International tourists have to cross national borders and may well have to use another currency and encounter a different language. Clearly, the size of a country is important here. Larger countries are more likely to have a variety of tourist attractions and resorts and, quite simply, the greater physical distances may deter international tourism. This is exemplified by the volumes of domestic tourism in the USA (almost 90 per cent of all tourism) compared to the Netherlands (around 50 per cent). Increasingly, too, the distinction between these two forms of tourism is diminishing as movement between countries becomes less restricted.

Concern for the environmental impact of tourism has focused attention on ways of classifying tourists according to their relationship with the destination. Smith (1978), for example, groups tourists along a continuum ranging from explorers, with virtually no impact, to mass tourists where the impact may be considerable (see Table 1.1).

The characteristics of the tourism system

Here, we can consider forms of tourism based largely on the destination visited, but also where the destination visited will influence the other components of the tourism system – the market with its motivations to travel, and the means of transport used. In other words, the tourism product determines the nature of the tourism system. For example:

- rural tourism
- urban tourism
- spa tourism
- heritage tourism
- cultural tourism
- sport tourism
- ecotourism

The final form of tourism on the list – ecotourism – exemplifies this approach:

- In the *generating area* for example, the ecotourist characteristically will be motivated by the responsible consumption of nature-based tourism products and will be educated to an above average level.
- In the *destination area*, nature will be the main attraction and the ancillary services (accommodation, transport etc.) will be well managed, use local employees and be 'green' or 'environmentally friendly'.
- In the *transit zone*, the ecotourist will seek locally owned companies who attempt to minimize the impact upon the environment caused by their transport operations.

The market

A further basis for classifying forms of tourism relates to the market itself. This can be in terms of the purpose of visit of the tourist:

- **Holiday tourism** is perhaps the most commonly understood form, where the purpose of the visit is leisure and recreation. Holiday tourism can be divided into the 'sun, sea and sand' type, where good weather and beach-related activities are important, or the 'touring, sightseeing and culture' type where new destinations and different lifestyles are sought. Short breaks lasting up to three nights are usually distinguished from longer holidays for marketing purposes.
- **Common-interest tourism** comprises those travelling with a purpose common to those visited at the destination (such as visiting friends and relatives, religion,

Table 1.1 Smith's typology of tourists

Type of tourist	Numbers	Adapt to local destination	Tourist impact decreases	Tourist volume increases
			←	→
Explorer	Very limited	Accepts fully		
Elite	Rarely seen	Accepts fully		
Off-beat	Unknown, but visible	Adapts well		
Incipient mass	Steady flows	Seeks Western amenities		
Mass	Continuous influx	Expects Western amenities		
Charter	Massive arrivals	Demands Western amenities		

Explorer
These include academics, climbers and true explorers in small numbers. They totally accept local conditions, and are self-sufficient, with portable chemical toilets, dehydrated food and walkie-talkies.

Elite
Travelling off the beaten track for pleasure, they have done it all, and are now looking for something different. While they use tourist facilities, they adapt easily to local conditions — if they can eat it, we can.

Off-beat
Not as rich as the elite tourist, they are looking for an added extra to a standard tour. They adapt well and cope with local conditions for a few days.

Incipient mass
A steady flow of tourists but in small groups or individuals. They are looking for central heating/air conditioning and other amenities, but will cope for a while if they are absent, and put it down to part of the 'experience'.

Mass tourism
Large numbers of tourists, often European or North American, with middle-class values and relatively high incomes. The flow is highly seasonal, with tourists expecting Western amenities and multi-lingual guides.

Charter tourism
This is full blown, down-market, high volume tourism. It is totally dependent upon the travel trade. The tourists have standardized tastes and demands, and the country of destination is irrelevant. This type of tourism is less common in developing and undeveloped countries.

Source: Smith, 1978

health, or education reasons). Common interest tourists – especially the VFR category – may make little or no demand upon accommodation or other tourist facilities at the destination.

- **Business and professional tourism** makes up the final purpose of visit category. Included among business tourists are those attending trade fairs and conferences or participating in incentive travel schemes. The inclusion of business travel complicates the simple idea of tourism being just another recreational activity. Clearly, business travel is not regarded as part of a person's leisure time and cannot be thought of as recreation. Yet, because business travellers do use the same facilities as those travelling for pleasure and they are not permanent employees or residents of the host destination, they must be included in any definition of tourists (Figure 1.1). The business traveller, unlike the holidaymaker, is highly constrained in terms of where and when to travel. The differences are summarized in Table 1.2.

A further market-based approach is to consider segments. Here there are two aspects:

- The **nature of the tourists** themselves, such as
  - youth tourism
  - grey or 'third age' tourism – geared specifically to older travellers
  - gay tourism.
- The **type of travel arrangement** purchased, such as
  - an *inclusive tour*, where two or more components of the trip are purchased together and one price is paid
  - *independent travel arrangements*, where the traveller purchases the various elements of the trip separately
  - *tailor-made travel*, which is a combination of the two and increasingly common due to the use of the Internet to purchase travel.
- **Distance travelled** Here there are distinctions that are important in terms of aircraft operations and for marketing:
  - *long-haul tourism* is generally taken to mean journeys of over 3000 kilometres
  - *medium-haul tourism* means journeys of between 1000 and 3000 kilometres
  - *short-haul tourism* comprises journeys of less than 1000 kilometres.

Finally, in categorizing tourism it is important not to lose sight of the geographical components of the system. The areas generating demand, the destinations chosen and the transit routes used will be influenced in different ways by particular forms of tourism.

Table 1.2 Leisure and business tourism

	Leisure tourism	Business tourism	But …
Who pays?	• The tourist	• The traveller's employer or association	• Self-employed business travellers are paying for their own trips
Who decides on the destination?	• The tourist	• The organizer of the meeting, incentive trip,conference/exhibition	• Organizers will often take into account delegates' wishes
When do trips take place?	• During classic holiday periods and at weekends resulting in seasonal demand	• All year round, no seasonal fluctuations, but less demand at weekends	• Peak holiday months are avoided for major events
Lead time? (period of time between booking and going on the trip)	• Holidays usually booked a few months in advance; short breaks, a few days	• Some business trips must be made at very short notice	• Major conferences are booked many years in advance
Who travels?	• Anyone with the necessary spare time and money	• Those whose work requires them to travel, or members of associations	• Not all business trips involve managers on white-collar duties
		• Generally over 75% of business travellers are men	• In the USA women now account for half of all business travellers
What kinds of destination are used?	• All kinds: coastal, city, mountain and countryside	• Little choice of destination, except for conferences etc.	• Incentive destinations are much the same as for upmarket holidays
		• Largely centred on major cities	
How important is price in influencing demand?	• Sensitive to price, resulting in elasticity of demand	• Less sensitive to price – time is more crucial	• Economic recession can cause a downturn in demand or a switch to cheaper transport (e.g. from business to economy class)

Summary

Leisure has come to be accepted as a measure of free time, while recreation is seen as the activities undertaken during that time. Tourism is a distinctive form of recreation, including a stay away from home, often involving long distance travel and encompassing travel for business or other purposes.

The geography of travel and tourism focuses on three key concepts. First, tourism consists of three main geographical components; the tourist-generating areas, the tourist-receiving areas and transit routes. Second, from a geographical point of view, tourism can be considered from a number of scales, from the world scale, to the regional and local scales, depending upon the level of detail required. Finally, the spatial interaction that is generated between the components of the tourism system, and at different scales, is conceived of as tourist flows. Understanding of these flows is fundamental to the geography of tourism and can be achieved by considering the push and pull factors that give rise to these flows, and how they can be measured.

Different forms of tourism can be distinguished, based upon the destination chosen, components of the tourism system, the market, purpose of visit, the distance travelled and, not least, the nature of the tourists themselves.

Chapter 2
The geography of demand for tourism

Learning Objectives

After reading this chapter, you should be able to:

- Explain the term tourism demand and distinguish between effective and suppressed demand.
- Understand the concepts of travel propensity and frequency.
- Identify the motivations and determinants of demand for tourism.
- Explain the influence of stage in economic development, population factors, and political regimes on demand for tourism.
- Understand the influence of personal variables on the demand for tourism.
- Appreciate the main barriers to travel which lead to suppressed demand.

Leisure, recreation and tourism: a basic human right?

Leisure, recreation and tourism are of benefit to both individuals and societies. The United Nations (UN) recognized this as early as 1948 by adopting its Universal Declaration of Human Rights, which states that everyone 'has the right to rest and leisure including . . . periodic holidays with pay'. More specifically, in 1980 the World Tourism Organization declared the ultimate aim of tourism to be 'the improvement of the quality of life and the creation of better living conditions for all peoples'. Such statements would suggest that everyone has the right to demand tourism, but more recently the UN and WTO have tempered their views with the following considerations:

- The need to ensure that tourism is consumed in a sustainable manner. The WTO's 'Global Code of Ethics for Tourism' was endorsed by the UN in 1999 and designed to 'minimize the negative impacts of tourism on the environment and on cultural heritage, whilst maximizing the benefits for residents of tourism destinations' (WTO, 2003).
- The fact that tourism is perceived as an activity for the privileged and occurs in a socially divided world.
- The emergence of 'pro-poor tourism' is an attempt to redress this issue.

This chapter examines how participation in tourism differs between both nations and individuals and explains why, despite declarations to the contrary, tourism is an activity highly concentrated among the affluent, industrialized nations. For much of the rest of the world, and indeed many disadvantaged groups in industrialized nations, participation in tourism, and particularly international tourism, remains an unobtainable luxury.

The demand for tourism: concepts and definitions

Geographers define tourism demand as 'the total number of persons who travel, or wish to travel, to use tourist facilities and services at places away from their places of work and residence' (Mathieson and Wall, 1982). This definition implies a wide range of influences, in addition to price and income, as determinants of demand and includes not only those who actually participate in tourism but also those who wish to but, for some reason, do not.

We should distinguish between the 'effective' and 'suppressed' demand for tourism:

- **Effective or actual demand** comprises the actual numbers of participants in tourism, i.e. those who are actually travelling. This is the component of demand most commonly and easily measured and the bulk of tourist statistics refer to effective demand.
- **Suppressed demand** is made up of that section of the population who does not travel for some reason. Two elements of suppressed demand can be distinguished:
  - *potential demand* refers to those who will travel at some future date if they experience a change in circumstances, for example, their purchasing power may increase
  - *deferred demand* is a demand postponed because of a problem in the supply environment, such as the Severe Acute Respiratory Syndrome (SARS) epidemic of 2003.
- In other words, both deferred and potential demand may be converted into effective demand at some future date.

Additionally, there will always be those who simply do not wish to travel, constituting another category, that of **no demand**.

Effective demand

Travel propensity

In tourism, a useful measure of effective demand is travel propensity, meaning the percentage of a population who actually engages in tourism. Net travel propensity refers to the percentage of the population who take at least one tourism trip in a given period of time, while gross travel propensity gives the total number of tourism trips taken as a percentage of the population. Clearly, as second and third holidays increase in importance, so gross travel propensity becomes more relevant. Simply dividing gross travel propensity by net will give the travel frequency, in other words, the average number of trips taken by those participating in tourism during the period in question (see Box 2.1). The suppressed and no-demand components will ensure that net travel propensity never approaches 100 per cent and a figure of 70 per cent or 80 per cent is likely to be the maximum. Gross travel propensity, however, can exceed 100 per cent and often approaches 200 per cent in some Western European countries with many frequent travellers.

Determinants of travel propensity

Travel propensity is determined by a variety of factors which, for the purposes of this chapter, can be divided into two broad groups. First, there are the influences that lie at the national level of generalization and comprise the world view of travel propensity, including economic development, population characteristics and political regimes. Second, a personal view of variations in travel propensity can be envisaged in such terms as lifestyle, life cycle and personality factors. In fact, a third group of factors relating to the supply of tourist services is also important. This group encompasses technology, the price, frequency and speed of transport, as well as the characteristics of accommodation, facilities and travel organizers. These factors are dealt with in Chapters 3 and 5.

The world view

Stage in economic development

A society's level of economic development is a major determinant of the magnitude of tourist demand because the economy influences so many critical, and interrelated, factors. The economic development of nations can be divided into a number of stages, as outlined in Table 2.1 and Figure 2.1. Table 2.1 gives a more accurate picture than the over-simplified contrast between the 'First World' developed nations and the 'Third World' of developing countries (the 'Second World' referred to the planned economies of the former Eastern bloc countries in the Cold War era).

As a society moves towards a developed economy a number of important processes occur. The nature of employment changes from work in the primary sector (agriculture, fishing, forestry) to work in the secondary sector (manufacturing) and the tertiary sector (services such as tourism). As this process unfolds, an affluent society usually emerges and numbers of the economically active population increase from around 30 per cent or less in the developing world to 50 per cent or more in the high mass consumption stage of Western Europe or the USA. With progression to the drive to maturity, discretionary incomes increase and create demand for consumer goods and leisure pursuits such as tourism.

Box 2.1 Calculation of travel propensity and travel frequency

Out of a population of 10 million inhabitants:

3.0 million inhabitants take one trip of one night or more	i.e. $3 \times 1 = 3.0$ million trips
1.5 million inhabitants take two trips of one night or more	i.e. $1.5 \times 2 = 3.0$ million trips
0.4 million inhabitants take three trips of one night or more	i.e. $0.4 \times 3 = 1.2$ million trips
0.2 million inhabitants take four trips of one night or more	i.e. $0.2 \times 4 = 0.8$ million trips

5.1 million inhabitants take at least one trip   8.0 million trips
therefore:

$$\text{Net travel propensity} = \frac{\text{Numbers of population taking at least one trip}}{\text{Total population}} \times 100 = \frac{5.1}{10} \times 100 = 51 \text{ per cent}$$

$$\text{Gross travel propensity} = \frac{\text{Number of total trips}}{\text{Total population}} \times 100 = \frac{8}{10} \times 100 = 80 \text{ per cent}$$

$$\text{Travel frequency} = \frac{\text{Gross travel propensity}}{\text{Net travel propensity}} = \frac{80\%}{51\%} = 1.57$$

A further refinement to the above calculations is to assess the capability of a country to generate trips. This involves three stages. First, the number of trips originating in the country is divided by the total number of trips taken in the world. This gives an index of the ability of each country to generate travellers. Second, the population of the country is divided by the total population of the world, thus ranking each country by relative importance in relation to world population. By dividing the result of the first stage by the result of the second the 'country potential generation index' (CPGI) is produced (Hurdman, 1979).

$$\text{CPGI} = \frac{(N_e/N_w)}{(P_e/P_w)}$$

where N_e = number of trips generated by country
N_w = number of trips generated in world
P_e = population of country
P_w = population of world

An index of 1.0 indicates an average generation capability. Countries with an index greater than unity are generating more tourists than expected by their population. Countries with an index below 1.0 generate fewer trips than average.

Adapted from: Schmidhauser, H., 'Travel Propensity and Travel Frequency', pp. 53–60 in Burkart, A. J. and Medlik, S., *The Management of Tourism*, Heinemann, London, 1975; and Hurdman, L. E., 'Origin Regions of International Tourism', *Wiener Geographische Schriften*, **53/54**, 43–9, 1979.

Other developments parallel the changing nature of employment. The population is healthier and has time for recreation and tourism (including paid-holiday entitlement). Improving educational standards and greater access to media channels boost awareness of tourism opportunities, and transportation and mobility rise in line with these changes. Institutions respond to this increased demand by

Table 2.1 Economic development and tourism

Economic stage	Some characteristics	Examples
Traditional society Long-established land-owning aristocracy, traditional customs, majority employed in agriculture. Very low output per capita, impossible to improve without changing system. Poor health levels, high poverty levels	**The least developed countries of the Third World** Economic and social conditions deny most forms of tourism except perhaps domestic VFR	Parts of Africa and southern Asia
Pre-conditions for take off Innovation of ideas form outside the system. Leaders recognize the desirability of change	**The more advanced developing countries of the Third World** From the take-off stage, economic and social conditions allow increasing amounts of domestic tourism (mainly visiting friends and relatives).	South and Central America[a]; parts of the Middle East[a], Asia and Africa
Take-off Leaders in favour of change gain power and alter production methods and economic structure. Manufacturing and services expand	Outbound international tourism is also possible in the drive to maturity. Inbound tourism is often encouraged as a foreign exchange earner	Mexico; parts of South America
Drive to maturity[b] Industrialization continues in all economic sectors with a switch from heavy manufacturing to sophisticated and diversified products		
High mass consumption Economy now at full potential, producing large numbers of consumer goods and services. New emphasis on satisfying cultural needs	**The developed world** Major generators of international and domestic tourism	North America; Western Europe; Japan; Australia; New Zealand; parts of South-East Asia

Notes: (a) Countries which are members of the Organization of Petroleum Exporting Countries (OPEC) are a notable exception in these regions; examples include Algeria, Libya, Nigeria, Kuwait, Saudi Arabia, Ecuador and Venezuela.
(b) Other countries that merit a special classification are the former Eastern European and Soviet bloc countries, which are in the transition stage to market economies, and the centrally planned economies, although most are at the drive to maturity stage; examples include China and North Korea.

Source: Adapted from Chubb and Chubb, 1981, Cleverdon, 1979 and Rostow, 1959

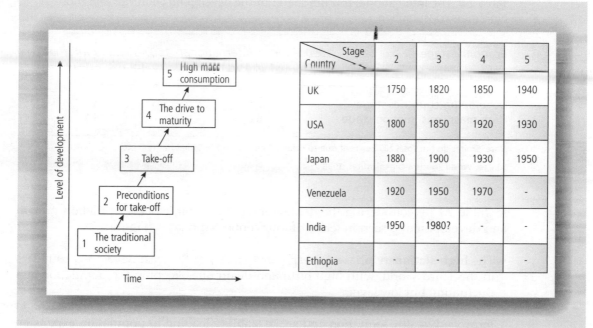

Stage Country	2	3	4	5
UK	1750	1820	1850	1940
USA	1800	1850	1920	1930
Japan	1880	1900	1930	1950
Venezuela	1920	1950	1970	-
India	1950	1980?	-	-
Ethiopia	-	-	-	-

Figure 2.1 Stages in economic growth
Source: Waugh, 1995: 574

developing a range of leisure products and services. These developments occur in conjunction with each other until, at the high mass consumption stage, all the economic indicators encourage high levels of travel propensity. Clearly, tourism is a result of industrialization and, quite simply, the more highly developed an economy, the greater the levels of tourist demand. For this reason the developing countries only account for a small proportion of the demand for international tourism, although a few – such as Brazil – in the drive to the maturity stage feature among the leading tourist-generating nations and China will be one of the leading generators by 2020. Even as tourist destinations, 'The combined share of developing countries in the global tourism market is still less than half that of developed countries in respect of arrivals, and only just in excess of one third of tourist receipts' (World Tourism Organization, 1995: 11). However, the share of the developing countries is increasing (Table 2.2). As more countries reach the drive to maturity or high mass consumption stage, so the volume of trade and foreign investment increases and business travel develops. Business travel is sensitive to economic activity, and although it could be argued that increasingly sophisticated communication systems may render business travel unnecessary, there is no evidence of this to date. Indeed, the very development of global markets and the constant need for face-to-face contact should ensure a continuing demand for business travel.

Population factors

Levels of population growth, distribution and density affect travel propensity. Population growth can be closely linked to the stages of economic growth outlined

Table 2.2 The international tourism shares of the developing countries and those at high mass consumption

Economic stage	1990 Share of international tourist arrivals (%)	1997 Share of international tourist arrivals (%)
Developing countries stage	28	31
High mass consumption stage	62	57

Note: Shares do not total 100 per cent due to other categories not included in the table.

Source: World Tourism Organization, 1998

in Table 2.1 by considering the demographic transition, where population growth and development is seen in terms of four connected phases (Figure 2.2).

- The **high stationary phase** corresponds to many of the least developed countries in the Third World, with high birth and death rates keeping the population at a fluctuating but low level.
- The **early expanding phase** sees high birth rates but a fall in death rates due to improved health, sanitation and social stability leading to population expansion characterized by young, large families. These countries are often unable to provide for their growing populations and as a result are gradually becoming poorer. Clearly, foreign travel is a luxury that most cannot afford, although some nations are developing an inbound tourism industry to earn foreign exchange: indeed low-income countries showed the highest growth in tourist arrivals in the 1990s.
- The **late expanding phase** sees a fall in the birth rate rooted in the growth of an industrial society and advances in birth control technology.

Most developing countries fit into the last two phases of population growth with a transition to the late expanding phase paralleling the drive to maturity.

- Finally, the **low stationary phase** corresponds to the high mass consumption stage of economic development. Here, birth and death rates have stabilized to a low level. At this stage, it is the changing characteristics of the population which have important implications for tourism demand because:
  - populations are ageing
  - these ageing populations have a high discretionary income
  - the 'baby-boomer' generation (born in the years immediately after the Second World War) are an important population cohort of experienced discerning travellers exercising 'grey' power and influencing demand
  - household composition is changing, with increased numbers of single and childless households and fewer families in the traditional sense.

Population density has a less important influence on travel propensity than has the distribution of population between urban and rural areas. The densely populated nations of South-East Asia have low travel propensities due to the level of economic development and the simple fact that the population is mainly dependent upon subsistence agriculture and has neither the time nor the income to devote to tourism. In contrast, densely populated urban areas normally indicate a developed economy with consumer purchasing power giving rise to high travel propensity.

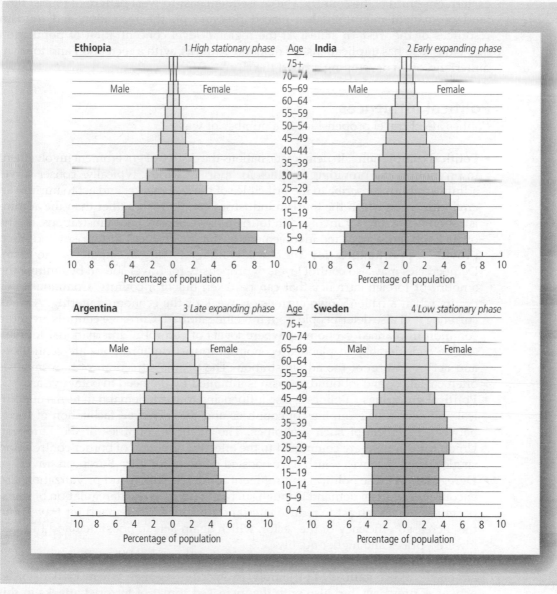

Figure 2.2 The demographic transition
Source: Demographic Yearbook of the UN, 1992

The urge to escape from the stress of the urban environment – 'to get away from it all' – is particularly strong in the large cities or conurbations of developed countries.

The trend to urbanization is also evident in the Third World, where vast numbers of poor rural migrants live on the periphery of major cities in shanty-towns without basic services. Even so, these people may well have greater access to employment, health care and education than in the countryside, and fertility rates are likely to decline, resulting in smaller families and less poverty.

The distribution of population within a nation also affects patterns, rather than strictly levels, of tourist demand. Where population is concentrated into one part of the country tourism demand is distorted. This asymmetrical distribution of population is well illustrated by the USA, where two-thirds of the population live in the eastern one-third of the country. The consequent east-to-west pattern of tourist flow (and permanent migration) has placed pressure on the recreation and tourism resources of the western states. At the regional level concentration of population into cities also has implications for demand patterns, with a recreation and tourism hinterland often developing around the city.

Political influences

Politics affect travel propensities in a number of ways:

- **Political complexion**   In democratic nations the degree of government involvement in promoting and providing facilities for tourism varies. Typically, 'conservative' administrations subscribe to the principles of the free market and act to nurture an environment in which the tourism industries can flourish, rather than the administration being directly involved in tourism itself. Socialist administrations, on the other hand, encourage the involvement of the government in tourism and often provide opportunities for the 'disadvantaged' to participate in tourism. Democracies may also control levels of propensity for travel abroad by limiting the amount of foreign currency that can be taken out of a country. Commonly this occurs when a nation's own currency is weak or the economy faltering. A weak currency will also deter people from travelling abroad. Currency controls are more common in planned economies, where levels of control of international tourism can be considerable. In planned economies tourist organizations are centralized and act as an arm of the administration. The people's freedom of movement is often curtailed, and inbound tourism is inhibited by the need to obtain visas.
- **Political groupings**   Politics is also influencing tourism demand in terms of political and economic groupings of countries and the increased facilitation of travel between members of such groupings. The member countries of the European Union for example, are committed to the effective abolition of border controls and single currency, moves which have boosted demand for intra-European travel.
- **Deregulation**   The political environment for deregulation and privatization also encourages tourism demand through such initiatives as the deregulation of transportation which can act to reduce fares and thus increase demand for travel; and the increased efficiency of the sector, which again acts to boost demand through lowered prices and higher quality.
- **Political instability**   In a more general sense, unstable political environments adversely affect tourism, not simply in specific regimes where civil disorder or war is prevalent, but also with the increased threat of terrorist attacks in this century, tourism demand has been adversely affected across the globe.

The personal view

Two sets of personal factors influence travel propensity and therefore act to condition access to tourism. The first group of factors can be termed *lifestyle* and include income, employment, holiday entitlement, educational attainment and mobility. A second group comes under the term *life cycle*, where the age and domestic circumstances of an individual combine to affect both the amount and type of tourism demanded. Naturally, these factors are interrelated and complementary. A high-status job is normally associated with an individual in middle age with a high income, above-average holiday entitlement, education and mobility. The interweaving of these variables, coupled with their rapid growth throughout the latter half of the twentieth century, have combined to make leisure, recreation and tourism a major force in the developed world.

Lifestyle determinants

Income
Tourism is a luxury, an expensive activity that demands a certain threshold of income before an individual can choose to take part. The key indicators are:

- **Gross income** The total amount earned gives little indication of the money available to spend on tourism.
- **Disposable income** The money that actually reaches the public's hands to dispose of as they please. However, demands on disposable income include essentials such as housing, food and clothing.
- **Discretionary income** The most useful measure of the ability to participate in tourism. Discretionary income is the income left over when tax, housing and the basics of life have been accounted for. Clearly, two households with the same gross incomes may have very different discretionary incomes.

The relationship between income levels and the consumption of tourism is an example of *elasticity of demand*. The demand for business tourism tends to be inelastic – it is relatively unaffected by changes in the cost of travel. Conventional leisure tourism on the other hand is sensitive to price; the elasticity of demand tends to be higher for Americans and Japanese than for Europeans on similar incomes (who respond to even a small reduction in prices by purchasing a proportionately greater number of holidays). A low discretionary income markedly depresses travel propensity. As discretionary income rises, the ability to participate in tourism is associated with the purchase of leisure-oriented goods, until, with a high discretionary income, travel may reach a peak and then level off as the demands of a high-status job, and possibly frequent business trips, reduce the ability and desire to travel for pleasure.

Employment
The nature of employment not only influences travel propensity by determining income and holiday entitlement but also has an effect upon the type of holiday demanded. A more fundamental distinction is between those in employment and those unemployed. The impact of unemployment on the level of tourism demand is obvious, but the nature of demand is also changed, with the threat of job insecurity among the workforce encouraging later booking of trips, more domestic and VFR holidays, shorter lengths of stay and lower spending levels.

Paid-holiday entitlement
A variety of holiday arrangements now exist worldwide, with most nations having a number of one-day national holidays, as well as annual paid-holiday entitlement by law or collective agreements. Individual levels of paid-holiday entitlement would seem to be an obvious determinant of travel propensity, but in fact the relationship is not straightforward. However, it is possible to make a number of generalizations:
- Low levels of entitlement do act as a real constraint upon the ability to travel, while a high entitlement encourages travel. This is in part due to the interrelationship between entitlement and factors such as job status, income and mobility.

○ As levels of entitlement increase, the cost of tourism may mean that more of this entitlement will be spent on leisure at home.
○ Patterns of entitlement are changing. Entitlement is increasingly used as a wage-bargaining tool and the introduction of flexitime, work sharing and long weekends will release blocks of time which may be used for short holiday breaks.

Social status and choice of lifestyle

Whereas in the period following the Second World War an individual's social class or socioeconomic group largely determined their use of leisure, in many developed countries the type of holiday demanded is increasingly related to an individual's choice of a particular lifestyle and the behavioural patterns associated with that lifestyle.

Other personal factors

Level of educational attainment is an important determinant of travel propensity as education broadens horizons and stimulates the desire to travel. Also, the better educated the individual, the higher his or her awareness and susceptibility to information, media, advertising and sales promotion. In addition, education enhances the ability to utilize technology and will facilitate demand for travel through access to the Internet. Personal mobility, usually expressed as car ownership, is an important influence on travel propensity, especially with regard to domestic holidays. This variable will be discussed in Chapter 5. Finally, other variables such as gender and belonging to an ethnic minority may condition access to tourism.

Life cycle determinants

The propensity to travel, and indeed the type of tourism experience demanded, is closely related to an individual's age. While the conventional measurement is chronological age, domestic age better discriminates between types of tourist demand and levels of travel propensity. Domestic age refers to the stage in the life cycle reached by an individual, and different stages are characterized by distinctive holiday demand and levels of travel propensity (Table 2.3). The concept of domestic age works well for Westernized, industrialized tourist generating countries and is therefore a useful generalization for the leading generators of tourism worldwide. However, it has its critics, as it:
○ is less well suited to other cultures
○ in the industrialized world, changing household composition and social norms mean that the concept has to be treated with care.

Personality factors

No two individuals are alike and differences in attitudes, perceptions and motivation have an important influence on travel decisions. Attitudes depend on an individual's perception of the world. Perceptions are mental impressions of, say, a place or travel company and are determined by many factors, which include childhood, family and work experiences. As perceptions will be influential in making the decision to travel,

Table 2.3 Domestic age and tourism demand

Adolescence/young adult
At this stage there is a need for independence and a search for identity. Typically, holidays independent of parents begin at around fifteen years, constrained by lack of finance but compensated by having few other commitments, no shortage of free time and a curiosity for new places and experiences. This group has a high propensity to travel, mainly on budget holidays using surface transport and self-catering accommodation. They are seen as opinion leaders and the tourism sector actively seeks their custom hoping to gain their loyalty in later years

Marriage
Before the arrival of children young couples often have a high income and few other ties giving them a high travel propensity, frequently overseas. The arrival of children coupled with the responsibility of a home mean that constraints of time and finance depress travel propensity. Holidays become more organizational than geographical with domestic tourism, self-catering accommodation and visiting friends and relatives increasingly common. As children grow up and reach the adolescence stage, constraints of time and finance are lifted and parents' travel propensity increases. In the industrialized countries this post-Second World War 'baby boom' group are the vanguard of the *new tourist* – discerning, experienced and seeking quality and value for money

Retirement
The emergence of early retirement at 50 or 55 years is creating an active and mobile group in the population who will demand both domestic and international travel. In later retirement lack of finance, infirmity, reduced personal mobility and often the loss of a partner act to offset the increase in free time experienced by this group. Holidays become more hotel-based and travel propensity decreases

---

it is important for planners and managers in tourist destinations to foster favourable 'images' of their locations in the public's mind.

Attitudes and perceptions in themselves do not explain why people want to travel. The inner urges, which initiate travel demand, are called travel motivators. It is important to understand these motivators as they help explain why some destinations fall in and out of fashion. An individual's personal needs help form motivations – the 'intrinsic' influences; whilst 'extrinsic' influences such as peer groups and fashion are a second set of influences. Gray (1970) has outlined a classification of travel motivators:

- **Wanderlust** is simply curiosity to experience the strange and unfamiliar. It refers to the basic trait in human nature to see, at first hand, different places, cultures and peoples. Status and prestige motivators would be included under this heading.
- **Sunlust** can be literally translated as the desire for sunshine and a better climate, but in fact it is broader than this and refers to the search for a better set of amenities for recreation than are available at home.

As tourist consumer behaviour has changed, there has been a shift away from sunlust to wanderlust motivators, partly driven by fears of the effects of the sun, but also by the desire to experience the culture fully as well as the physical attractions of the destination.

The interaction of personality attributes such as attitude, perceptions and motivation allow different types of tourist to be identified. One classification, by Cohen (1972), is particularly useful. He uses a classification based on the theory that tourism combines the curiosity to seek out new experiences with the need for the security of familiar reminders of home. Cohen proposes a continuum of possible combinations of novelty and familiarity and, by breaking up the continuum into typical combinations of these two ingredients, a fourfold classification of tourists is produced (Table 2.4).

Table 2.4 Cohen's classification of tourists

		Familiarity ↑
The organized mass tourist Low on adventurousness, he or she is anxious to maintain his or her 'environmental bubble' on the trip. Typically purchasing a ready-made package tour off-the-shelf, he or she is guided through the destination having little contact with local culture or people	**Institutionalized tourism** Dealt with routinely by the tourism industry — tour operators, travel agents, hoteliers and transport operators	
The individual mass tourist Similar to the above but more flexibility and scope for personal choice is built-in. However, the tour is still organized by the tourism industry and the environmental bubble shields him or her from the real experience of the destination		
The explorer The trip is organized independently and is looking to get off the beaten track. However, comfortable accommodation and reliable transport are sought and while the environmental bubble is abandoned on occasion, it is there to step into if things get tough	**Non-institutionalized tourism** Individual travel, shunning contact with the tourism industry except where absolutely necessary	
The drifter All connections with the tourism industry are spurned and the trip attempts to get as far from home and familiarity as possible. With no fixed itinerary, the drifter lives with the local people, paying his or her way and is immersed in their culture		↓ Novelty

Source: Adapted from Cohen, 1972

Suppressed demand

Potential demand

Throughout this chapter the concern has been to identify factors that influence effective tourist demand. Yet tourism is still an unobtainable luxury for the majority of the world's population, not just in undeveloped and developing countries but also for many in the developed world. Indeed, the concept of *potential demand* demonstrates that there are considerable inequalities of access to tourism, which are rooted in the personal circumstances of individuals. Lansing (1960) has identified five major reasons why people do not travel:

- expense of travel
- lack of time
- physical limitations (such as ill health)
- family circumstances
- lack of interest.

It is not uncommon for individuals to experience a combination of two or more of these barriers. For example, a one-parent family – or a person caring for a disabled relative – may find that lack of income and time will combine with family circumstances to prevent tourism. Obviously it is just these groups who would most benefit from a holiday, and tourism planners are increasingly concerned to identify these barriers and devise programmes to encourage non-participants to travel. Perhaps the best-known example of this is the *social tourism movement*, which is concerned with the participation in travel by people with some form of handicap or disadvantage, and the measures used to encourage this participation. In countries where state intervention is the norm the government and its agencies are largely responsible for social tourism; in some (such as Israel) the labour unions play an important role; while in others the participation of church groups and similar voluntary organizations is more significant.

Deferred demand

Of course, there are also barriers to travel based upon the supply environment, leading to deferred demand. The early years of the new millennium have seen a series of events that have markedly increased deferred demand around the world and reduced growth rates of international tourism. These events include:

- 9/11 (the terrorist attacks on New York and Washington on 11 September 2001)
- the war in Afghanistan
- the Bali and Mombasa bombings
- the outbreak of SARS
- the war in Iraq.

The effect on demand has been for tourists either to defer travel or to change the nature of their trip and:

- book later
- travel to 'safer' destinations closer to home
- use surface transport

- use 'flexible' booking channels such as the Internet
- consider the cost of travel carefully
- take shorter trips.

Summary

Tourism is a major contributor to the quality of life in the twenty-first century, and the demand for tourism is made up not only of those who participate but also those who do not travel for some reason. Travel propensity is a useful indicator of tourism participation, as it gives the proportion of a population who actually engage in tourism. Travel frequency refers to the average number of trips taken by those participating in tourism during a specified period. Travel propensity is determined by a variety of factors that can be viewed at two scales. At the world scale, those countries with a high level of economic development and a stable, urbanized population are major generators of tourism demand. The political regime of a country is also relevant here. At the individual scale, a certain level of discretionary income is required to allow participation in tourism, and this income, and indeed, the type of participation, will be influenced by such factors as job type, life cycle stage, mobility, level of educational attainment and personality. Even within the developed world, many are unable to participate in tourism for some reason. Demand for tourism is therefore concentrated in developed Western economies and predominates among those with high discretionary incomes.

Chapter 3
The geography of resources for tourism

Learning Objectives

After reading this chapter, you should be able to:

- Appreciate the nature of resources for tourism.
- Distinguish the methods used to classify and evaluate resources for tourism.
- Outline the main factors favouring the development of tourism resources.
- Understand the way that destinations evolve.
- Appreciate the need for tourism planning, marketing and sustainable development.

Introduction

Technology now allows tourists to reach most parts of the world, yet only a small fraction of the world's potential tourist resource base is developed. None the less, with a growing demand for tourism focused on a small resource base, tourist destinations are under pressure. In part this is because tourism does not occur evenly or randomly in space – pressure is focused seasonally and at special and unique places. This demands the effective planning and management of tourism resources and in particular the matching of appropriate types of tourists to particular types of resource. Of course, different types of tourism will have distinctive requirements for growth, and certain sites, regions or countries will be more favourable for development than others. This chapter examines tourism resources at three scales: the world, the national and the local.

Resources for tourism

Tourism resources have three main characteristics:

- The concept of tourism resources is normally taken to refer to tangible objects that are considered of economic value to the tourism sector. The sector, and indeed the tourist, therefore has to recognize that a place, landscape or natural feature is of value before it can become a tourism resource. For example, the combination of sun, sand and sea was not seen as a valuable tourism resource until the 1920s, when sunbathing became fashionable, while the increasing threat of skin cancer is now causing perceptions to change (see Chapter 4).
- Tourism resources themselves are often not used solely by tourists. Apart from resort areas or theme parks where tourism is the dominant use of land, tourism shares use with agriculture, forestry, water management or residents using local services. Tourism is a significant land use but rarely the dominant one, and this can lead to conflict. Tourism, as a latecomer, is 'fitted in' with other uses of land. This is known as *multiple use*, and needs skilful management and coordination of users to be successful.
- Tourism resources are perishable. Not only are they vulnerable to alteration and destruction by tourist pressure but, in common with many service industries, tourism resources are also perishable in another sense. Tourist services such as beds in accommodation, or ride seats in theme parks are impossible to stock and have to be consumed when and where they exist. Unused tourism resources cannot be stored and will perish, hence the development of yield management systems to maximize the consumption of resources.

Planning for tourism resources

Inevitably, tourism is attracted to unique and fragile resources around the world. In the period following the Second World War many countries sought international tourism as an ideal solution to economic problems. Tourism was seen as an 'industry without chimneys' which brought economic benefits of employment, income and development. However, this economic imperative overlooked the environmental, social and cultural consequences of tourism in many countries. In part, this was due to the ease of measuring economic impacts of tourism and the difficulty of quantifying other types of impact. However, there is an increasing awareness of the need for environmental and host community considerations to complement the economic need of destinations. Consumer pressure is shunning ethically unsound destinations and environmental impact assessments are being completed for major tourist developments. Since the late 1980s, sustainable tourism development has become the organizing framework, as mainstream concepts of sustainability have been applied to tourism. Bramwell and Lane (1994) see sustainable tourism development as a 'positive approach intended to reduce tensions and friction created by the complex interaction between the tourism industry, visitors, the environment and the community which are host to holiday makers'. A key priority is to translate the principles of sustainable development into action. For example, in the tourism industry, this is being done in a number of ways:

- codes of conduct and guidelines – providing the industry with practical measures for say, recycling

- accreditation and certification – inspecting and certifying businesses on the basis of sustainable practices
- licences – licensing businesses operating in environmentally sensitive areas
- best practice dissemination – educating and communicating sustainable tourism best practice to the industry.

Carrying capacity is a key concept of sustainable tourism – in other words, planners determine the levels of use that can be sustained by a tourist resource and manage to that level (see Table 3.1).

Table 3.1 Carrying capacity

The concept of carrying capacity has a long pedigree. It was originally developed by resource managers in agriculture and forestry to determine the cropping levels that pieces of land could sustain without nutrients and other food sources being depleted. Of course, in tourism the concept has a similar meaning. Quite simply, carrying capacity refers to the ability of a destination to take tourism use without deteriorating in some way. In other words, it defines the relationship between the resource base and the market and is influenced by the characteristics of each. One of the best definitions is by Mathieson and Wall (1982: 21): 'The maximum number of people who can use a site without unacceptable alteration in the physical environment and without an unacceptable decline in the quality of experience gained by visitors.'

This definition raises two key points:

- Carrying capacity can be managed and there is no absolute number for any destination. For example, *open heathland* can appear crowded with very few visitors present, while a *wooded area* can absorb many more visitors before appearing crowded.

There are different types of carrying capacity:
  - From the point of view of the resource:
    - *Physical carrying capacity* refers to the number of facilities available – aircraft seats or car parking spaces for example. It is easy to measure and can be calculated on a simple percentage basis.
    - *Environmental or biological carrying capacity* is more difficult to measure and refers to limits of use in the ecosystem. There is increasing interest in the capacity not only of the flora to take tourism use but also in terms of fauna – such as tourism based on whale or dolphin watching, or in the African game reserves.

From the point of view of the visitor:
    - *Psychological or behavioural carrying capacity* refers to the point at which the visitor feels that additional tourists would spoil their experience. This is less straightforward than may appear at first sight. For example, completely empty spaces are just as problematic as crowded ones, and the type of tourist also has an effect on perceptions of crowding.

And from the point of view of the host community:
    - *Social carrying capacity* is a measure of the ability of the host community to tolerate tourism. It is a more recent addition to typologies of capacity but is becoming an important issue. Indeed, one of the most important tests of a sustainable tourism destination is the level of involvement of the local community in plans and decisions relating to tourism development. Whilst there is a concern that local residents have a lack of knowledge about tourism, new techniques such as 'destination visioning' (where the locals determine the future of tourism), and 'limits to acceptable change' where they determine levels of future development, are increasingly being adopted and are a form of capacity management.

Tourism planning must be central to these issues. Such planning has evolved from an inflexible, physical planning approach to a flexible process which seeks to maximize the benefits and minimize the costs of tourism, whilst at the same time recognizing the 'holistic' nature of tourism – we must plan for the visitor as well as the resource. The benefits of tourism planning are clear (Table 3.2). Ideally, tourism planning:

- is based on sound research
- involves the local community in setting goals and priorities
- takes a holistic approach
- is implemented by the public sector in partnership with the private sector.

Despite the many approaches to tourism planning, the planning process can be reduced to six basic questions:

- What type of tourist will visit?
- What is the scale of tourism?
- Where will development take place?
- What controls will be placed upon development?
- How will development be financed?
- What will be government's role?

Table 3.2 The benefits of tourism planning

For those involved in delivering and developing tourism at the destination, tourism planning:

- provides a set of common objectives for all at the destination to follow
- coordinates the many suppliers of tourism at the destination
- encourages partnerships between stakeholders at the destination
- encourages effective organization at the destination
- provides an integrating framework for future actions and decisions.

For the destination itself, tourism planning encourages a high-quality tourism environment because it:

- optimizes the benefits of tourism to a destination
- minimizes the negative impacts of tourism on the economy, environment and host community
- encourages the adoption of the principles and practice of sustainable tourism
- provides a land-use-based plan for zoning areas for development, conservation and protection
- encourages design and other standards for the tourism sector to work to
- encourages careful matching of the development of the destination and its markets
- allows for the consideration of issues such as manpower and investment
- upgrades the destination environment
- encourages a monitoring system to be implemented at the destination.

The answer to these questions will depend, from place to place, on the government's approach to tourism and the importance of tourism to the economy. The planning process is summarized in Figure 3.1.

Unfortunately, despite the emergence of tourism planning as a profession, plans for tourism still either fail or are opposed. They may fail because policy changes, demand changes, unforeseen competition emerges, investment is not available or the plan was too ambitious or inflexible.

If tourism planning does not succeed then:

- the quality and integrity of the tourist resource are at risk
- the role of tourism in multiple land use may be threatened as other uses dominate
- the tourist suffers from a poor quality experience.

As we have become more sophisticated in the management of tourism, the emphasis has moved from the protection and preservation of resources to the management of the visitors and in particular the need to deliver an enjoyable, worthwhile experience. Figure 3.2 outlines the approaches used to manage visitors.

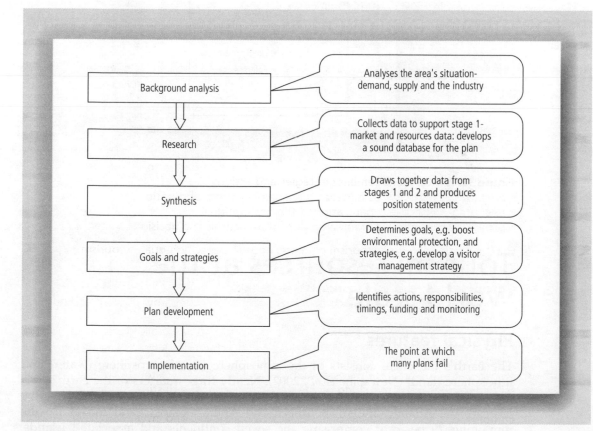

Figure 3.1 Tourism planning flow chart

Source: Based on Mill and Morrison, 1985

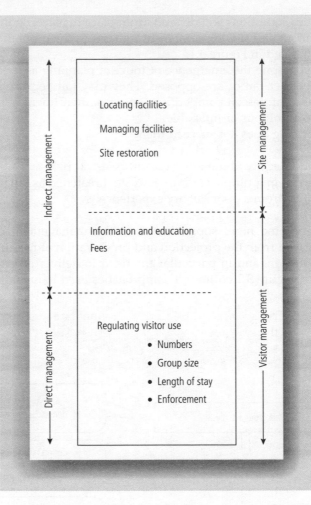

Figure 3.2 Visitor management strategies and actions

Tourism resources at the world scale

Physical features

The earth's biosphere consists of the atmosphere (air), hydrosphere (water) and lithosphere (land) (Newsome *et al.*, 2002). Nearly three-quarters of the earth's surface consists of sea, including the five oceans – namely the Pacific (by far the largest), the Atlantic, Indian, Southern and Arctic Oceans. Land makes up the remaining 29 per cent comprising the seven continents and associated islands, namely Asia (the largest both in land area and population), followed by Africa, North America, South America, Antarctica, Europe and Australasia. (Strictly speaking Europe is part of the greater landmass known as Eurasia.) Almost 40 per cent of the Northern Hemisphere, but less than 20 per cent of the Southern Hemisphere, is made up of land. This uneven distribution of land and sea has important implications for climate, population distribution, economic development, communications and, thus, tourism.

The land surface of the earth is composed of a variety of landforms which we can broadly group into four categories: mountains (areas of elevated, rugged terrain), more gently sloping hill lands, elevated plateaus and lowland plains. Within each landform category there are features resulting from natural forces and variations in the underlying rock. Volcanoes, crater lakes and calderas, lava formations, geysers and hot springs, are *geothermal* features caused by disturbances from deep within the earth's' crust. Even in areas where volcanic activity ceased long ago, springs rich in minerals have in turn given rise to the type of health resort known as a spa. Another important group of features is found in *karst* limestone areas, where surface streams have 'disappeared' underground to carve out impressive caves, sinkholes and gorges.

Mountains and hill lands account for 75 per cent of the land surface. Mountain ranges are found in every continent but are particularly associated with geologically unstable areas characterized by earthquakes and volcanic activity. This explains why some of the world's most spectacular mountains are situated in the 'Pacific Ring of Fire' close to the western and eastern margins of the world's largest ocean. Those mountain areas in middle latitudes affected by glaciation during the last Ice Age are particularly attractive for tourism development. This is due to the variety of scenic features, including spectacular peaks, glaciers, cirques, lakes and waterfalls, as well as the crisp clear air which encourages a range of activity and adventure holidays. Most of these involve limited numbers of visitors and are the concern of 'niche' tour operators dealing directly with their customers. In contrast, skiing, and more recently, snowboarding have attracted a mass following, and a major winter sports industry has burgeoned in most developed countries. Much of the demand is generated from densely populated countries where suitable resources are in short supply. This has resulted in the development of a multitude of ski resorts in the more accessible mountain regions: some of these are based on existing rural communities but a growing number are purpose-built at higher altitudes for the skiers' convenience. In summer these same regions attract tourists interested in sightseeing for a 'lakes and mountains' holiday. In southern Asia, the Middle East, Africa and Latin America mountain resorts cater more for health tourism, providing relief from the oppressive summer heat of the cities in the lowlands.

The sparse population of most mountain regions has made it easier for governments to designate areas as *national parks* for their outstanding natural beauty, unique geological features, wildlife or for their 'countryside capital' – the rural fabric such as buildings and landscapes. Nevertheless, few suitable areas are pristine wilderness, so that tourism has to compete with other demands on resources including forestry, pasture for grazing, hydroelectric power generation and mineral extraction. Since mountain areas have a limited carrying capacity, over-development involving the construction of roads and cableways is a matter of growing concern. This has led many authorities to discourage the more popular forms of tourism in favour of activities in harmony with the natural environment which will sustain the resource for future generations.

The coast continues to be the most popular location for holidaymakers worldwide. The beach, more than any other environment, appeals to all the physical senses and is associated in people's minds with carefree hedonism. Sandy beaches and sheltered coves providing safe bathing with a protective backland of sand dunes or low cliffs, will encourage tourism development and a wide range of recreational activities. More rugged and exposed coastlines might attract surfers, but would deter other water sports enthusiasts and families with young children. Although beaches have a high carrying capacity compared to most 'natural' environments, they are prone to pollution and erosion by winter storms. Small islands, and the coral reefs found along many tropical coastlines, are particularly vulnerable to the ecological damage caused by excessive numbers of tourists. Coastal plains are ideal for large-scale resort development, but such locations are also sought after as sites for major industries, and most would agree that oil refineries do not make good neighbours! Most destinations are now aware of the tourism potential of attractive beaches, so that the developers' attention has turned to the wetlands – estuaries, marshes, swamps and tidal mud flats, which are not valued as a tourist resource. Although ecologically important as a wildlife habitat – a fact recognized by the Ramsar Convention – the world's wetlands are increasingly under threat. In many tropical countries for example, mangrove swamps have been dredged to provide harbours and yacht marinas, or to expand the lucrative shrimp-farming industry. Elsewhere, wetlands have been reclaimed for use by airports, industry and intensive agriculture.

Inland water resources for tourism can be viewed as nodes (lakes, reservoirs), linear corridors (rivers, canals), or simply as landscape features (such as the Victoria Falls). Lakes are particularly numerous in recently glaciated areas such as the Alps, Northern Europe and North America. Where lakes are accessible to major cities they attract second-home owners and a wide range of recreational activities which may not be compatible (for example, anglers and jet-skiers). Spatial zoning and temporal phasing of these activities may be necessary to avoid conflict. Water pollution is also a problem, as unlike the tidal nature of the sea, lakes have no natural cleansing mechanism. Rivers are more widely available than lakes but, in most cases, tourism and recreation take second place to the needs of industry, commerce and agriculture. Even so, boating holidays on the inland waterways of Europe are growing in popularity, while rivers previously regarded as unnavigable are sought out by adventurous tourists for the challenge of whitewater rafting and canoeing.

The world's forest resources also deserve special mention. In most developed countries forests and woodlands are valued for recreation and wildlife protection, in contrast to the exploitation which occurred in the past. Multiple use is characteristic of such areas, and careful management is essential to protect the resource.

Cultural features

Tourists are interested in the differences between their country of origin and the peoples of the countries they visit, as expressed in terms of art and crafts, music, folklore and festivals, food, architecture and lifestyle generally. On a world scale, we can recognize a number of cultural regions where there is a broad similarity in lifestyles, architecture, agricultural systems and often a shared historical background and religion. These regions rarely correspond to continental divisions. For example, European or 'Western' culture since the Renaissance has spread well beyond the confines of Europe, as a result of overseas trade, colonial expansion, emigration and advances in technology. However, in most countries of Africa, Asia and in much of Latin America, 'Western' influence is superficial and strong cultural differences persist. This is evident in the Islamic countries of Africa and the Middle East, as well as the countries of South-East Asia where Buddhism has long been the dominant influence. Tourists need to respect these differences in lifestyle, and business travellers especially should be aware of the host country's social conventions and taboos to avoid causing offence. In many countries, so-called primitive tribal groups live outside the mainstream culture. Identified as the 'Fourth World' by some anthropologists (Graburn, 1976), these tribes are increasingly seen as a unique resource by tour operators and included on itineraries. Examples of such cultures might include the hill tribes of South-East Asia, the Andaman Islanders of India, the Aborigines of Australia and the Koi San (Bushmen) of southern Africa. Unfortunately, tourism could present another threat to a way of life which is already endangered.

Tourism thrives in the absence of barriers to communication, so the existence of a common language is an advantage – although the ubiquitous use of English poses a threat to other, minority languages. A shared religion can also encourage travel between countries. Most of the great religions have shrines or holy places, and some of these – Lourdes, Rome, Jerusalem and Mecca – annually attract millions of visitors worldwide. Pilgrimages, defined here as journeys with a religious motivation – were arguably the first form of organized mass tourism. Perhaps as a reaction to a secular, materialistic world, this type of tourism would appear to be on the increase. Travellers to 'secular shrines', such as the birthplace of a famous writer or national leader, are often described as pilgrims, but are more correctly cultural tourists. Such tourists are also attracted to destinations noted for their art treasures, historic sites and buildings. These visitors, including backpackers taking a *gap year* from work or college, are following in the tradition of those élite travellers who took the European Grand Tour in the eighteenth century, but on an altogether vaster scale in terms of their numbers and the extent of their travels.

Although *heritage* is a vaguely defined word, it has become the focus of a major form of tourism – *heritage tourism* – which has grown with tourists' curiosity about places, the past and nature. In its wider sense heritage includes those natural as well as man-made features which are considered worthy of preservation. Some features are so unique, spectacular or well known that they are of worldwide significance and their loss would affect humankind as a whole. For this reason the United Nations Educational, Scientific, and Cultural Organization (UNESCO) has designated most of these for special protection as World Heritage Sites. However, while this designation does bring with it management responsibilities, lack of the ability to enforce conservation means that some monuments are in a poor state of preservation.

Many tourists, especially those in the younger age groups, are less attracted by a country's past achievements than its contemporary culture, as reflected in sport, fashion and entertainment. Here, the influence of the media is evident. The national tourist organization of a country may have a large promotional budget, but this may have considerably less impact than the free publicity and exposure provided by a movie or television series seen by a worldwide audience.

Tourism resources at the national scale

At the level of individual countries, tourism development involves either finding suitable regions to develop or, in areas already established, alleviating problems of congestion or overuse. These activities demand accurate methods of classifying tourism resources and evaluating their potential.

Classification of resources for tourism

Tourist attractions

Attractions are the *raison d'être* for tourism; they generate the visit, give rise to excursion circuits and create an industry of their own. The simplest approach to identifying attractions in an area is to draw up an inventory or checklist, by defining the range of attractions, counting them and either listing or mapping the result. Swarbrooke (1995) has classified attractions into four main categories, which can be defined as:

- **natural** – including beaches, caves, scenic features and wildlife
- **man-made but not originally designed to attract tourists** – such as historic houses, castles and cathedrals
- **man-made and purpose-built to attract tourists** – includes museums, art galleries, exhibition centres, casinos and a growing range of leisure attractions for a 'day out' such as theme parks and water parks
- **special events** – these 'event attractions' differ from the others, which are 'site attractions', in that they occur only periodically and in some cases, change venues. The latter category includes sporting events, such as the football World Cup and the Olympic Games. These present unique opportunities to promote the host country and have a spin-off effect encouraging other attractions nearby. They also require considerable investment, planning and organization to safeguard the health, safety and security of both visitors and participants. Other event attractions include for example, markets, festivals, folklore events, ceremonies, pageantry and religious processions.

Quite clearly, different forms of tourism are based upon different types of attraction. The younger tourist, for example, is more likely to be attracted to theme parks with their emphasis on exciting rides and entertainment, than to most heritage attractions, such as 'stately homes', museums and cathedrals. Business travellers will also have different needs. They gravitate toward major commercial centres which are highly accessible, and offer facilities for conferences and trade exhibitions, as well as a range of complementary attractions and services.

Some attractions have a greater 'pulling power' than the rest, so that in most countries we can recognize a hierarchy of attractions. At the apex of the pyramid are those 'must see' attractions of international calibre; relatively few in number, they attract tourists worldwide. In the second tier are those that might be visited as part of an excursion circuit focusing on one or two major 'sights'. At the base of the pyramid are many minor attractions which currently draw their visitors from within the immediate region. Increasingly, tourist attractions and the tourism resource base in general, are suffering from increased use and need effective visitor management. This can only be achieved if these attractions are considered as an integral part of the tourism resource base rather than dealt with in isolation.

A broader view of the tourism resource base

The tourism resource base allows for hundreds of outdoor recreation activities, ranging from abseiling to zorbing. Some of these activities – notably skiing, golf and yachting – require specialized *facilities* as well as equipment and skills, whereas others – canoeing for example – are not associated with development on any scale. All types of sport and outdoor recreation are based on some kind of physical resource, that may be natural, man-made or a combination of both. The 'arts, culture and entertainment' sector of tourism is based more on a destination's human resources. It is worth emphasizing that access to a resource is not just about distance, journey time and the cost of transport, but is also about overcoming barriers such as disability.

One of the most useful ways of thinking about the total resource base for tourism is that of Clawson (Clawson and Knetsch, 1966). This sees resources as forming a continuum from intensive resort development at one extreme to wilderness at the other, and, therefore, incorporates both resource and user characteristics. Clawson's three basic categories are:

- **user-oriented** areas of highly intensive development close to population centres
- **resource-based** areas where the type of resource determines the use of the area
- **an intermediate** category, where access is the determining factor.

In Table 3.3 we relate a selection of recreation activities to Clawson's classification.

Another way of thinking about resources, related to Clawson's ideas, is to classify them into:

- **reproducible** – they can be replaced, for example, theme parks
- **non-reproducible** – they cannot be replaced, such as elements of the natural and cultural heritage mentioned earlier.

Evaluation of resources for tourism

Measurement of the suitability of the resource base to support different forms of tourism is known as resource evaluation. The main issue here is to include the varied requirements of different users. For example, pony-trekkers need rights of way, footpaths or bridleways, and attractive scenery. Combination of these various needs is the aim of a resource evaluation system which is often tabulated into a matrix or put on to data cards, each one of which relates to a location. They can also be combined into the so-called recreation opportunity spectrum.

The tourism product and destination marketing

An area may have tourism potential – a favourable climate, attractive scenery, hospitable people and a range of resources awaiting discovery. However, it will not become a viable tourist destination unless it has:

- at least one attraction that could be promoted as a unique selling proposition (USP)
- support facilities (accommodation for example)
- accessibility to the major tourist-generating countries
- favourable pre-conditions for development, which means the provision of basic infrastructure, a tourist organization and a measure of political stability.

Table 3.3 A classification of recreational resources

User orientated	Intermediate	Resource based
Based on resources close to the user. Often artificial developments (city parks, stadiums etc). Highly intensive developments. Activities often highly seasonal, closing in off-peak	Best resources available within accessible distance to users. Access very important. Natural resources more significant than user-orientated facilities, but these experience a high degree of visitor pressure	Outstanding resources. Based on their location, not that of the market. Primary focus is resource quality. Often distant from users, the resource determines the activity

Reproducible ←—————————————————→ **Non-reproducible**

Activity paramount ←—————————————————→ **Resource paramount**

Artificiality ←—————————————————→ **Naturalness**

←————————— **Intensity of development** —————————→

Proximity ←——— **Distance from user** ———→ **Remoteness**

Examples of activities:	Examples of activities:	Examples of activities:
Golf	Yachting	Sightseeing
Tennis	Windsurfing	Mountain climbing
Spectator sports	Boating	Trekking
Visits to theme parks, zoos, resorts, etc.	Camping	Safaris
	Hiking	Expeditions
	Angling	Surfing
	Field sports	Whitewater rafting
	Downhill skiing	Canoeing
	Snowboarding	Potholing
		Scuba diving
Typical resource:	**Typical resource:**	**Typical resource:**
Theme park	Heathland	Unique historical monument
		National park

These elements combine to provide the *tourism product* of a destination. Whilst individual enterprises within the tourism industry supply products to the consumer – hotels and airlines are notable examples, the tourism destination product is the sum of these many parts. The marketing of destinations – or places – demands a very different approach to the marketing of tangible products. First, the nature of the product is different. Destination tourism products comprise a set of tangible and non-tangible components based around an activity at the destination. That activity could be a skiing vacation, or a spa visit – and for each the mix of components will be different. We can therefore think of the destination product for a destination such as Innsbruck in Austria as being made up of the following components:

- the **core destination product** – the winter sports experience
- the **facilitating destination product** – the transportation services and accommodation in Innsbruck

- the **supporting destination product** – high quality shopping and restaurants in Innsbruck
- the **augmented destination product** – the overall ambience of Innsbruck communicated through the urban design and conservation of the old town (Kotler *et al.*, 2003).

Second, there is a range of destination stakeholders who feel they should have a say in the marketing of 'their' destination. Third, destination marketing is commonly done by a public sector agency, though they often lack marketing expertise and political considerations may override marketing issues. Finally, the real challenge for the destination marketer is to create 'differentiation' – in other words, to demonstrate that resort A is truly different from resort B.

Tourism resources at the local scale

For the tourism resource to be developed, someone or some organization has to act. These agents of development can be either in the private sector, or in the public sector – central government, state-funded organizations acting on its behalf and local authorities.

The public sector is involved not only in tourism development at the local scale, but at all levels, including the international. Developing countries receive assistance for projects through agencies such as the World Bank or the United Nations Development Programme. Many governments actively encourage tourism projects in their own countries by providing finance at generous rates and tax breaks to developers. Typically at the national and international levels government involvement is with the planning and coordination of tourism development. At the local level the role of the public sector is usually limited to providing the initial infrastructure; this includes all development on or below ground, such as roads, parking areas, railway lines, harbours and airports, as well as the provision of utilities. The importance of adequate water supplies, for example, needs to be emphasized, and where basic services have failed to keep pace with a spate of hotel building, a destination will suffer bad publicity regarding its standards of health and safety. The public sector is also responsible for ensuring adequate security against crime and terrorism. Even an isolated incident affecting tourists can receive widespread coverage by the media in the generating countries.

As tourism projects are costly, private sector developers typically provide the superstructure. This includes the accommodation sector, of which hotels are usually the most important component, entertainment, sport and shopping facilities, restaurants and passenger transport terminals. Clearly this division of responsibilities reflects the motives of the two sectors: the private sector looks for profit and a return on investment, while the public sector is anxious to provide the basic services in an environment favourable for tourism development. In some developed countries the *voluntary sector*, consisting of non-profit making organizations, plays a subsidiary role in the development process. As their main interest is conservation, they are much more likely to oppose large-scale tourism projects than to initiate development. The

National Trust is an outstanding British example, but it differs from most such organizations by being a major landowner.

At the local scale accessibility is all-important and may be the deciding factor in the success of a tourism project. Resorts in destination areas such as the Mediterranean owe much of their popularity to their location near an airport with direct flights to the major tourist-generating areas. However, accessibility is a relative term which is determined by cost as well as distance. Exclusive 'up-market' resorts are often located in areas away from the main tourist routes.

Other factors encouraging the development of tourism resources at the local level include land availability, suitable physical site attributes (soil, topography) and a favourable planning environment with zoning for tourism. Normally undeveloped *greenfield* sites are chosen, but there are an increasing number of tourism projects in inner city areas, often utilizing a waterfront location previously occupied by dockyards and industry. Such *brownfield sites* normally require costly treatment before building work can take place.

Finally, tourism development should take place with the consent of the local community. However, in most developing countries (and some developed ones) democratic structures of government are weak and even the ownership of land may be the subject of dispute. Local authorities may lack the expertise and financial 'muscle' to curb the activities of business interests from outside the region, such as multinationals, when these may have a negative social and environmental impact.

Tourist resorts and tourist centres

At the local scale the development of tourism resources leaves a distinct imprint on the landscape. This is particularly evident in the *resorts* of the developed countries which have evolved in response to the needs of tourists. They are distinct in layout and townscape from other urban and rural settlements. (In the USA the term resort usually means a hotel or leisure complex.) In Western Europe alone, over 400 resorts can be identified, including spas, winter sports resorts and cultural/historic centres, as well as coastal resorts of varying size, whose clientele ranges from the popular to the exclusive. Historic towns and cities are usually multifunctional, and tourism is a latecomer. Such places are *tourist centres*. In true resorts, tourism is the *raison d'être*, although other functions may be added later when the resort has reached maturity. Spa towns and holiday resorts are often characterized by eclectic styles of architecture in contrast to more workaday communities.

Typically you would find a concentration of tourist-orientated land and building uses close to the main focus of visitor attraction. This area of tourist-related functions is termed the *recreational business district* (RBD), distinct from the main office and shopping area, which in larger towns is termed the *central business district* (CBD). The RBD develops under the twin influences of the major access route into the resort and the central tourist feature. For example, in seaside resorts the RBD often develops parallel to the beach, behind a promenade (boardwalk in the USA) and contains premier hotels and shops. Beyond this, the intensity of tourist functions and land values decreases in a series of zones around the RBD (Figure 3.3). In the case of historic centres, the RBD usually corresponds to the ancient core of the town, which in most European examples is centred on a castle, university or cathedral. It is here that the efforts of conservationists are concentrated, and *interpretation*, using costumed guides or re-enactments of historical events, brings the 'heritage experience' to life for the tourist. However, as Ashworth and Tunbridge (1990) point

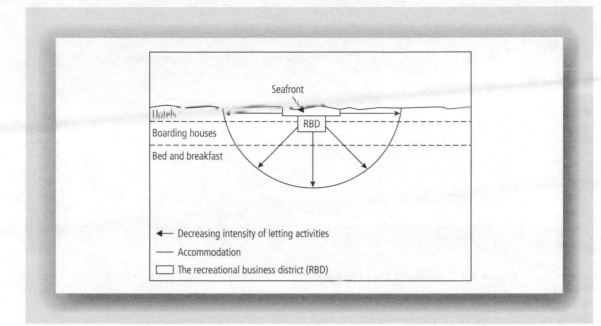

Figure 3.3 The recreational business district

Source: Wall, 'Car owners and holiday activities', in Lavery, 1971

out, 'the attraction may be medieval, but few tourists are prepared to sleep, eat and travel in medieval conditions', so modern support facilities, while necessary, may be an intrusive feature in the skyline of the historic city. In large cities, especially capitals such as London, the historic/cultural area is polycentric. Tourist facilities are more widely dispersed between a number of areas catering for different types of visitor (for example, Soho, Covent Garden), while the business traveller is attracted to the CBD with its range of financial and commercial services (in this example, the City of London).

The development of resorts over time is an important consideration for geographers concerned with tourism. Butler (1980) has suggested a tourist area life cycle where resorts evolve from discovery through development to eventual decline. Although the life-cycle approach has its critics – who feel it is difficult to operationalize – the main utility of the approach is as a way of thinking about resorts, an explanatory framework for their development; and as a means of integrating supply-side developments with the evolving market of a resort. After all, the type of tourist who visits at introduction will be very different from that visiting in consolidation or decline (Figure 3.4). The tourist area life cycle is as follows:

- **Exploration** – small number of adventurous tourists, main attraction is unspoilt nature or cultural features.
- **Involvement** – local initiatives provide facilities and some advertising ensues. Larger numbers of visitors, a tourist season and public sector involvement follows.
- **Development** – large numbers of tourists and control passes from locals to national or international companies. The destination begins to change in appearance. Overuse may begin.

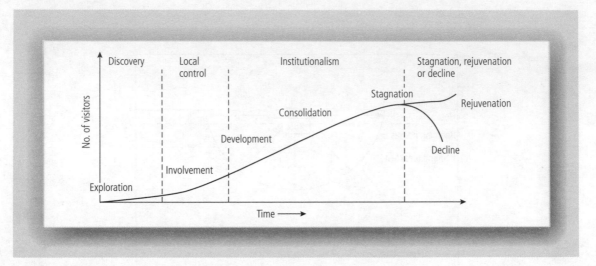

Figure 3.4 The tourist area life cycle

Source: Butler, 1980

- **Consolidation** – the destination is now a fully fledged part of the tourist industry; the rate of increase of visitors is reducing. A recognizable recreational business district has emerged.
- **Stagnation** – peak visitor numbers have been reached and the destination is unfashionable with environmental, social and economic problems. Major promotional efforts are needed to maintain visitor numbers.
- **Decline** – visitors now visit newer, rural resorts as the destination goes into decline. It is dependent on a smaller geographical catchment and repeat visits.
- **Rejuvenation** – here the authorities attempt to 'relaunch' the destination by providing new facilities, attracting new markets and re-investing.

Summary

Certain factors favour the development of tourism resources and this explains why the world pattern of tourism supply is uneven. Developed tourism resources are cultural appraisals, considered by society to be of economic value. They are usually shared with other users and are both fragile and perishable. As the negative impacts of tourism are realized, tourism planning for resources has become vital. Planning aims to minimize the costs of tourism and to maintain the integrity of the resource base. At the world scale both physical and cultural features are key factors influencing tourist development. Of the range of physical features in the world, coasts, mountains and inland water are the most popular locations for tourist development.

At the national scale, classifications of tourist attractions which include the whole tourist resource base are useful. Evaluations of the potential of the resource base to satisfy tourists' demands allow possible future areas for recreation and tourism to be identified. These evaluations can then be applied to the local scale where resultant resort developments have a distinctive morphology and mix of service functions. It is also possible to identify a cycle of resort development.

Chapter 4
Climate and tourism

Learning Objectives

After reading this chapter, you should be able to:

- Understand the importance of latitude and the distribution of land and sea areas in determining climatic differences.
- Be aware of the major climatic elements and explain how these affect the various types of recreational tourism.
- Understand the problems of classifying world climatic zones.
- Describe the distribution of world climates and their significance for tourism.

Introduction

We can view climate either as a resource encouraging the development of tourism or as a constraint limiting the appeal of a destination. Despite the widespread availability of air-conditioning and other forms of climate control, tourists are bound to spend much of their time in an outdoor environment, which may be considerably warmer or colder than their country of origin. As air travellers, with a limited range of clothing, we need accurate information on the climate of the destination. Many types of recreation, from sunbathing to skiing, are weather-dependent. On a world scale, the importance of climate is shown in the broad pattern of movement from the colder, cloudier tourist-generating countries to warmer, sunnier destinations; on a local scale it is seen in the decision of urban families to visit a nearby beach on a hot summer's day. For a destination, climate largely determines the length of the holiday season (although this is also influenced by external factors such as the timing of school holidays in the generating areas). Climate also determines factors such as a destination's development and operating costs; sales of beverages and leisure equipment are affected by weather changes, while the providers of tourist services have to cope with seasonal variations in demand. In most destinations, the problem of *seasonality* seriously affects profitability and employment in the tourism industry. Finally, the traditional relationship between climate and tourism may be changing as evidence linking skin cancer with exposure to sunlight is publicized and associated with issues such as global warming.

The world climate scene

Weather and climate relates to conditions in the atmosphere, the thin envelope of air surrounding our planet. Climate is characterized by long-term cycles, whereas the weather can change from day to day. Tourists usually need information on say, the average temperatures they can expect at a particular location, rather than the occasional extreme weather events that make headline news.

Climate is defined by three main factors: latitude, the distribution of land and sea areas and relief.

Latitude, or distance from the Equator, is the primary factor, as this determines the angle of the sun's rays at any given time of the year; if this is too oblique the sun's heating power will be limited. Due to the earth's rotation, the Northern Hemisphere is tilted toward the sun in June, when it is overhead at noon on the Tropic of Cancer (latitude 23.5° North). At high latitudes north of the Arctic Circle (66.5° North) there is daylight for at least 24 hours at midsummer, while Antarctica (south of 66.5° South) experiences continual darkness. By December, the sun's overhead path has moved south of the Equator to the Tropic of Capricorn (latitude 23.5° South). This marks the onset of summer in the Southern Hemisphere and, in contrast, a period of continuous cold and darkness north of the Arctic Circle. The low latitudes between the Tropics of Cancer and Capricorn enjoy a warm climate all year round as the sun is high in the sky for most of the day. The result of increasing distance from the Equator is a shorter summer and a greater difference in day length between the seasons.

The simple model of a steady decrease in temperature from the Equator to the poles is complicated by the fact that most of the world's landmass is concentrated in the Northern Hemisphere. Land surfaces heat and cool more rapidly than large areas of water. The oceans therefore act as a reservoir of warmth, so that windward coasts and islands have a *maritime* climate which is equable. Furthermore, warm ocean currents, notably the Gulf Stream and North Atlantic Drift, distribute some of the warmth of tropical seas to higher latitudes (see Figure 4.1). As a result, Britain and Ireland have a much milder climate than their position relatively near the Arctic Circle would suggest. Elsewhere, cold currents have a chilling effect, the most well-known example being the Labrador Current off the east coast of Canada. (Icebergs carried by this current caused the 1912 *Titanic* disaster.) The Pacific Ocean, because it is so much larger than any other body of water, has a worldwide influence on climate, as shown by the El Ninõ phenomenon. The heartlands of Eurasia and North America at similar latitudes to Britain are far removed from the influence of the sea and experience a *continental* climate, characterized by extreme variations in temperature.

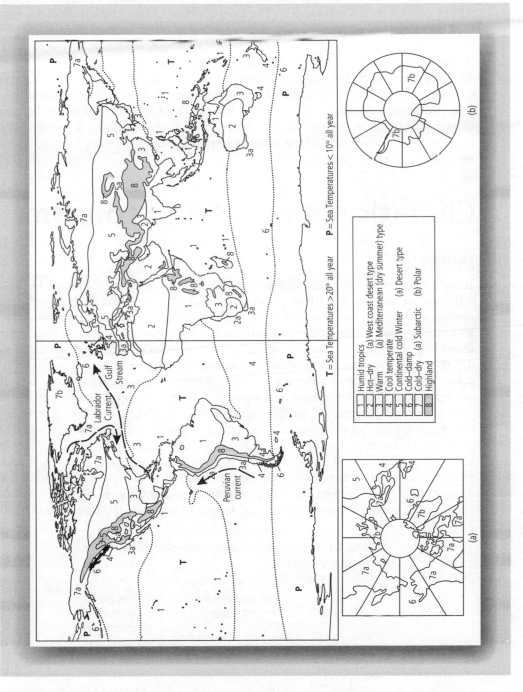

Figure 4.1 World climate zones; inset maps show (a) the Northlands and the Arctic Ocean, (b) the Antarctic

In many parts of the world, where there are high mountains, *relief* has a major effect on weather patterns. Climbers are well aware that air temperatures are considerably lower on the summit of a mountain. There is also a reduction of barometric pressure with increasing altitude; at 5000 metres the density of the air is less than 60 per cent of its sea-level value. The thinner atmosphere at such altitudes means that, although more solar radiation reaches the ground by day, heat is lost more rapidly to the sky at night. Because there is less oxygen in the air, physical exertion becomes more difficult. Great contrasts in temperature, moisture and sunshine are found within short distances in mountain regions, providing a variety of habitats for plants and animals. Mountain barriers profoundly modify the climates of adjacent lowlands since moist air from the sea is forced to rise over them, becoming drier and warmer as it descends. At a local scale, the position of a slope or valley in relation to the direct rays of the sun has important consequences for land use and resort development, as in the Alps.

Climatic elements and tourism

Temperature

Temperature is the element of climate that has the greatest influence on tourist *activity*, and the type of clothing worn (Table 4.1). Water sports such as swimming, surfing and diving are usually warm weather activities. At the beach, both the air temperature and the sea temperature (which is normally cooler during the daytime) should be above 20 °C. Water cools the body by conduction thirty times faster than dry still air at the same temperature – explaining why *wet suits*, and at colder temperatures *dry suits* made of neoprene – are essential for surfers. Land-based activities are less suited to high temperatures, especially when humidity is taken into account. This is normally expressed as the *relative humidity*, which measures the moisture content of the air as a percentage of the total amount it could contain at a given temperature. Thus tropical air at 35 °C can hold nine times more water vapour than cold air at 0 °C. A dry heat, where the relative humidity is less than 30 per cent, is widely recognized as being more tolerable than the humid heat typical of many tropical destinations. When moisture levels in the air are nearing saturation it is difficult to keep cool despite profuse sweating, and failure to maintain the body's heat balance

Table 4.1 Temperatures and clothing – holiday travel in January

	Average daytime temperature (°C)	Clos (units of thermal resistance)
Oslo	0	2.0
Paris	5	1.6
Alicante	15	1.2
Tenerife	20	0.8
Barbados	30	0.1

will result in heat exhaustion and, in extreme cases, heatstroke. A more common problem, due to the wearing of unsuitable clothing, is the skin condition known as 'prickly heat'. The effect of humidity on how hot the weather feels can be expressed as a value called *effective temperature* which also takes into account air movement, or more simply as the *apparent temperature*, as used in the bioclimatic chart (Figure 4.2). The importance of this for human well-being can be demonstrated if you compare conditions in Delhi and Aswan, as shown by the climographs on the chart, using average daytime values of temperature and relative humidity for each month of the year. The weather in Delhi would be more uncomfortable in August than in Aswan, although the actual air temperature is 5 °C lower.

Tourists do, however, vary considerably in their ability to acclimatize, according to their age, gender, body build, rate of metabolism and ethnic origin. Although the human body can adapt fairly readily to tropical conditions – by an increase in the

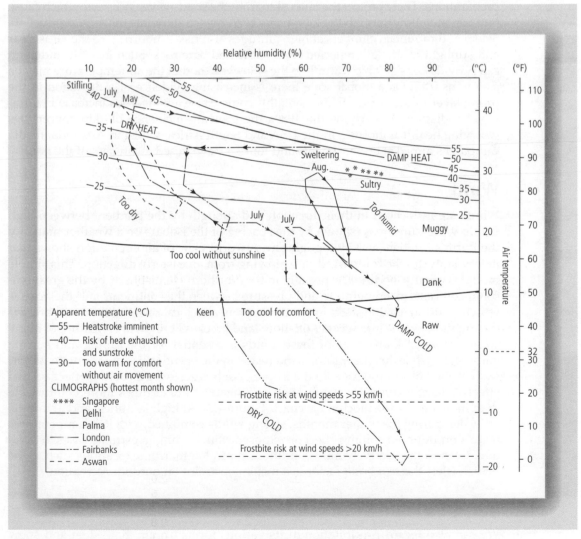

Figure 4.2 Bioclimatic chart

sweat rate, for example – much depends on alterations in patterns of behaviour and lifestyle. This is also true of severely cold conditions where the physiological response (such as shivering) is much less effective. Human comfort is also greatly influenced by factors such as radiant heat from the sun and air movement.

Sunshine

The effect of sunshine is particularly important at the seaside, where ultraviolet light is reflected from the water surface and the sand, adding to the heat load which the exposed skin is receiving from the sky. The British Isles, despite the advantage of having long summer days, experience a cloudy climate compared to that of southern Spain, where the sun shines for as much as 80 per cent of the daylight hours. Ultraviolet radiation is even more intense in low latitudes, although the duration of bright sunshine may be less than in the Mediterranean. The safe length of exposure to the sun will depend on the holidaymaker's skin type and the strength of suntan preparations. These protect the outer skin from the short-wave UVB rays, which cause burning but allow through the long-wave UVA rays to stimulate melanin production. Skiers and mountain climbers at high altitudes also risk sunburn since the air is clear and sunlight is strongly reflected from snow and bare rock. Such incident radiation can provide considerable warmth to the skin even though the air temperature may be as low as 0 °C. On a global scale there is increasing evidence of a depletion in the ozone layer in the upper atmosphere; this could cause a dangerous increase in ultraviolet radiation. As early as the 1980s the growing incidence of skin cancer was worrying health authorities in the USA and South Africa, whilst in Australia, media campaigns aimed at both residents and tourists have raised awareness of the issue.

Wind

Winds are influenced in their direction and strength by the gradient between high and low pressure areas (shown by the spacing of the isobars on a weather map), by the Earth's rotation, and by topography. A world view of air circulation shows that in low latitudes the trade winds are blowing from an easterly direction. This simple model is greatly modified, especially in the Northern Hemisphere, by the great seasonal contrasts in temperature and pressure between the continents and the oceans, which result in notable shifts in wind direction. At a local scale, onshore sea breezes during the daytime and weaker offshore land breezes at night are a feature of many coastal areas. A knowledge of these winds is essential for the sailing and surfing enthusiast, while the glider pilot is interested in the peculiarities of mountain winds, such as the Föhn of the Alps. In the tropics, sea breezes have a cooling effect, so that effective temperatures in islands such as Singapore are at times more comfortable than indicated by the bioclimatic chart (Figure 4.2). At high latitudes, and at middle latitudes during the winter months, strong winds combined with low temperatures have a pronounced chilling effect on exposed skin, leading in extreme cases to frostbite. Even in the relatively mild conditions typical of maritime locations such as the British Isles, this *wind-chill* factor is a major constraint on outdoor recreation.

Precipitation

We can also regard precipitation in its various forms of rain, hail, sleet and snow as a constraint. Much, however, depends on its intensity, duration and seasonal distribution. In the tropics there is usually a well-defined division of the year into 'wet' and 'dry' seasons. *Rain* typically falls in short heavy downpours, following strong convectional heating of the air and the build-up of cumulus clouds during the afternoon. In contrast, most of the rain that falls in Britain is cyclonic in origin; it may be smaller in total amount but is spread over many more rainy days.

We can view *snow* as an expensive hazard for transport or as a valuable recreational resource. Suitable locations for ski resorts are found mainly in accessible mid-latitude mountain regions, where there is adequate snow cover for at least three months of the year. As the provision of facilities for 'downhill' skiers is costly, the resort operator needs accurate information on the local climate, including temperature, sunshine, wind speeds and relative humidity. For example, where monthly average minimum temperatures are below −2 °C snowfalls are likely to be frequent. The type of cover is also important and 'powder' – loose, low-density snow – is favoured by skiers. Although the introduction of winter sports has brought economic benefits to remote mountain communities, it has also led to environmental degradation, especially in the Alps. Deforestation to create ski runs has increased the risk of avalanches, while the use of snow-making equipment to guarantee snow cover inhibits the growth of delicate alpine plants.

Air quality

Last but not least, the monitoring of air quality is increasingly crucial as part of the concern about environmental issues and the quality of life generally. The motor vehicle is well known as a major polluter, emitting nitrous oxide, hydrocarbons and ground level ozone (not to be confused with the ozone in the stratosphere). An older problem in most of the world's large cities, especially in the less developed countries, is the emission of sulphur dioxide from 'smoke-stack' industries. Smogs, or severe episodes of air pollution, are particularly common in regions where anticyclonic conditions, inhibiting air movement, prevail for much of the year. Examples would include the Mediterranean countries and California in summer, and the continental heartlands of North America and Eurasia in winter. An unpleasant cocktail of gases poisons the air of our cities, reducing visibility, blighting vegetation, eroding historic monuments and threatening the health of people suffering from respiratory problems. Moreover, the effects of 'acid rain' have degraded forests, lakes and monuments in many areas downwind of sources of industrial pollution in North America and Europe. Even the Arctic is under threat from pesticides and other pollutants carried north by winds and ocean currents; slow to break down at low temperatures, these contaminate the snow and poison the food chain.

World climate

Classifying climates

Even in a small country like Britain, temperatures, rainfall and exposure to wind or sunshine vary a good deal, resulting in many local climates. However, these differences are less significant on a global scale than those between, say, the South of England and the French Riviera. It is also true that areas of the world separated by vast distances have such similar features that they can be regarded as belonging to the same climate zone. Thus the climate of California resembles that of Spain, and the South Island of New Zealand shows broad similarities to England, once the reversal of the seasons in the Southern Hemisphere is taken into account.

It is relatively simple to draw a series of world maps showing the various elements of climate, but much more difficult to synthesize this information in order to determine the best overall conditions for tourism. A number of attempts have been made to classify climates from a human rather than an agricultural standpoint. Of particular relevance is the work of Lee and Lemons (1949), who devised a scheme relating temperatures to clothing requirements. Terjung (1966) utilized data on temperature and relative humidity to produce a Comfort Index for each month of the year for both day- and night-time conditions. This was further refined, where the data were available, to take account of the effects of wind-chill and solar radiation. Terjung's classification is the most comprehensive but has the disadvantage of producing an excessive number of climate zones, even when the features of the Comfort Index are summarized for the year as a whole. Another interesting approach is the 'climate code' devised by Hatch (1985). This is an index of overall climatic favourability ranging from 0 (abysmal) to 100 (idyllic), calculated from prorated monthly values of temperature, rainfall, sunshine and relative humidity. This index is particularly useful for assessing the suitability of a destination for beach tourism, as it is biased towards dry, sunny and warm climates.

The bioclimatic chart (Figure 4.2) was the starting point for our classification scheme. We can think of the world's climates as a continuum, from hot humid conditions at one extreme to cold and dry at the other. However, most parts of the world have climates which lie somewhere between these extremes, and which are characterized by distinct seasonal variations. This is shown by the climographs for Delhi, Palma, London and – in an extreme form – for Fairbanks, Alaska. Such climates are conventionally described in terms of their temperature and rainfall characteristics. They have been grouped into eight major climate zones, related more closely to human physiology. Figure 4.1 shows the distribution of world climates, but you should be aware that the boundaries drawn on the map indicate wide areas of transition rather than abrupt changes. A summary of these climates and their suitability for tourism is set out in Table 4.2.

World climate zones

The humid tropics (zone 1)

This is perhaps the most important zone, in view of its extent and potential for tourism development. Here the main problem is keeping buildings and their occupants cool, as temperatures rarely fall below 20 °C even at night, while humidity is generally high. Buildings should be designed to take advantage of any breezes; usually an open plan is adopted with rooms having access to a veranda. Sometimes buildings are elevated on stilts to capture any air movements above the vegetation. For the tourist, clothing should be lightweight, of open texture and made of absorbent materials. Most of the diseases for which the tropics are notorious are mainly due, not to the climate, but to the poor standards of sanitation prevailing in many Third World countries. Nevertheless, the hot moist environment favours the growth of harmful bacteria and parasites, while diseases such as malaria are carried

Table 4.2 World climates and tourism

Zone	Physical characteristics	Significance for tourism	Type location N = Northern Hemisphere S = Southern Hemisphere
(1) Humid tropics (a) Equatorial	Day and night equal in length year round. Extensive cloud cover and abundant rainfall. Temperatures in range 23–33 °C with high humidity. Weather enervating	Generally unfavourable. Scope for river-based expeditions	Amazonia
(b) Trade wind type	In Northern Hemisphere north-east trades bring heavy rainfall December–May; in Southern Hemisphere south-east trades bring heavy rainfall June–October. More sunshine than (a) especially in the 'dry season'	Generally favourable for beach tourism. Risk for cyclones/hurricanes during rainy season	Barbados (N) Mauritius, Tahiti (S)
(c) Tropical wet dry	Much greater seasonal variations, especially in rainfall. A long dry season often divided into the 'cool dry' (warm days and cool nights) and the 'hot dry' where the high temperatures are usually associated with low humidity. The rainy season typically lasts from June to November in the Northern Hemisphere and from December to May in the Southern Hemisphere. The parched landscapes of the dry season contrast with the lush vegetation resulting from the rains	Rainy season can be unpleasant due to sweltering conditions, while storms may disrupt communications Dry season suitable for sightseeing, safaris and beach tourism except during the periods of 'highest sun'	Goa, Bangkok (N) Darwin (S)
(2) Hot dry	Little or no rainfall. Great daily variations in temperature due to intense solar radiation and strong nocturnal cooling. Low humidity except in some coastal areas. In Northern Hemisphere the cool season lasts from November to March, in the Southern Hemisphere from April to September	The moderate temperatures and abundant sunshine of the cool season favour winter-sun tourism, especially in coastal areas. Summer conditions can be unpleasant. The desert environment attracts trekking expeditions	Aswan, Bahrain (N) Alice Springs (S)

Table 4.2 (Continued)

Zone	Physical characteristics	Significance for tourism	Type location N = Northern Hemisphere S = Southern Hemisphere
(a) West coast desert subtype	Moderate temperatures year-round but offshore dust-laden winds, especially at night	Less favourable. Scope for water sports, especially fishing	Tarfaia (N) Mollendo, Swakopmund (S)
(3) Warm	In Northern Hemisphere long warm season May to October, in Southern Hemisphere November to April	Highly favourable: weather permits outdoor recreation year-round. Summers ideal for beach tourism	
(a) Mediterranean type	Cool winters with moderate rainfall, warm to hot dry summers. Abundant sunshine		Palma, Los Angeles (N) Cape Town, Perth (S)
(b) Warm temperate humid summer type	Cool winters with moderate rainfall: in the Northern Hemisphere occasional outbreaks of cold weather. Summer tends to be the rainy season with much hot, humid weather		New Orleans, Shanghai (N) Buenos Aires, Sydney (S)
(4) Cool temperate	Mild to raw winters. Weather highly variable. Rather cool cloudy summers: in the Northern Hemisphere June to August, in the Southern Hemisphere December to February	Winters unfavourable. Short season for beach tourism; suitable for the strenuous types of outdoor recreation. All-weather facilities desirable at holiday resorts	Dublin, Vancouver (N) Wellington (S)
(5) Continental cold winter	Cold winters with extensive snow cover. Warm summers with moderate rainfall June to August. Pronounced seasonal changes	Winters suitable for skiing and other snow-based activities. Short season for beach tourism: lakes are likely to be more important for water sports than coastal areas	Chicago, Montreal. Stockholm, Sapporo (N)
(a) Mid-latitude desert type	Little or no rainfall due to the 'rain shadow' effect. Differs from the 'hot dry' in having very cold winters	Generally unfavourable. Scope for trekking expeditions in summer	Ulan Bator (N)

(6) Cold damp Subarctic Maritime (N) Subantarctic (S)	Raw winters, no real summer. Overcast skies and strong winds prevalent year-round	Unfavourable, but rich bird and marine animal life attracts nature-lovers	Faeroes, Aleutians (N) South Georgia (S)
(7) Cold dry (a) Subarctic continental	Very cold winters, spectacular spring thaws, short summers	Generally unfavourable. Winter temperatures below −20°C curtail outdoor recreation. Permafrost inhibits the construction of tourist facilities. Skiing and other snow-based activities possible in late winter; canoeing and fishing in summer	Fairbanks, Rovaniemi (N)
(b) Polar climates	Bitterly cold dark winter months with high wind-chill. Air temperatures in summer rarely rise above 10°C despite almost continuous daylight, poleward of latitude 70° from May to August in the Arctic and from November to February in Antarctica. Incident radiation from snow and ice-covered surfaces	Unfavourable – but scope for expeditions entailing a high degree of preparation. Cruising in Arctic and Antarctic waters during summer months	Spitzbergen (N) Deception Island (S)
(8) Highland climates (a) Tropical highlands	Great differences in temperature between day/night and sunlit/shaded locations. Intense ultraviolet radiation, low humidity, absence of dust and pollen at high altitudes above the cloud level. A mosaic of climates and life-zones at different altitudes. Permanent snowline above 4500–5000 metres	Very favourable at altitudes between 1500 and 3000 metres as the cool air gives relief from the heat of the tropical lowlands, encouraging the development of health resorts such as the 'hill-stations' of southern Asia. At higher altitudes increasing risk of 'altitude sickness' will restrict skiing and other activities to acclimatized individuals. Scope for trekking, climbing and nature study, but	Addis Ababa Quito Darjeeling (N) La Paz (S)

Table 4.2 (Continued)

Zone	Physical characteristics	Significance for tourism	Type location N = Northern Hemisphere S = Southern Hemisphere
		mountain ecosystems are vulnerable to the impact of tourism	
(b) Mid-latitude highlands	Much greater seasonal differences of temperatures than in (a). Cold snowy winters contrast with warm rainy summers, but weather is highly variable. Importance of mountain and valley winds. Life-zones include coniferous forest with alpine meadow above the tree-line. Permanent snowline above 2500–3000 metres	Generally favourable but conditions vary with altitude and aspect. A reliable snow cover in winter at altitudes of 1500–2500 metres encourages the development of ski resorts. Lack of air pollution favours health tourism and a wide range of outdoor activities in summer	St Moritz, Denver (N)

by insects which cannot thrive in cold temperatures. Visitors can protect themselves from malaria by taking prophylactic drugs and by preventative measures, such as not exposing legs and arms in the evenings when the mosquitoes are active. For other tropical diseases such as yellow fever, vaccination is essential. (It is worth noting that highland areas in the tropics not only enjoy a cooler climate but also are malaria-free.)

With the exception of the equatorial zone, most parts of the tropics have a 'dry season' of varying length when conditions are not unfavourable for tourism. It is then that the savannah grasslands, typical of much of Africa, provide the best conditions for game viewing or 'safari tourism'. In the beach destinations of the Caribbean, West Africa and southern Asia the dry season coincides with the winter months in North America and Europe, so that they are well placed to attract winter-sun seekers from the main tourist-generating countries. Tropical countries south of the Equator are less favoured as their best months coincide with summer in the countries of the Northern Hemisphere.

Extensive coral reefs fringing the coastline are a feature of many holiday destinations in the tropics (they cannot flourish where sea temperatures fall below 20 °C). These provide an ideal setting for water sports, particularly scuba diving. The exuberant vegetation and diversity of species found in the tropics is increasingly perceived as a resource for ecotourism. Here is it worth noting that tropical Africa is generally much richer in the 'big game' animals, sought by safari enthusiasts, than similar environments in South and Central America, southern Asia and Australasia. Each of these regions has distinct species occupying equivalent niches in the eco-system. Most tropical habitats are threatened by the growing pace of economic development in the Third World countries of the 'South', which is often geared to supplying raw materials for the developed countries of the 'North', such as Japan, the USA and the EU. The disappearing rainforests of the Amazon Basin and Indonesia are two well-known examples, with environmental consequences that may well be serious, not just for the tropical zone, but for the Earth as a whole.

The hot dry climates (zone 2)

Areas of constant drought account for about one-third of the Earth's land surface. They occur mainly in tropical and subtropical latitudes wherever the air is dry as a result of subsidence from the permanent high-pressure belts.

The hot dry regions include the sunniest places on earth – Upper Egypt and Arizona both receive more than 4000 hours of bright sunshine annually. They are also subject to extremes of temperature. Due to the intensity of the solar radiation, air temperatures often reach 45 °C by mid-afternoon in the summer but fall rapidly after dark as a result of radiation from the ground to the clear night sky. During the winter months frost may occasionally be recorded before dawn. The humidity is generally very low during the daytime. The main exceptions are coastal areas adjoining an enclosed sea where relative humidities are high due to evaporation from the water surface. Very little of this moisture is able to rise to produce rainfall, making the summer climate of places like Bahrain and Aden particularly oppressive. Other coastal areas, with a cold ocean current offshore, experience much cooler temperatures and a good deal of mist – the rainless Atacama and Namib Deserts are good examples.

The dryness of the air, aggravated by strong dust-laden winds, results in rapid evaporation from the skin and the risk of dehydration. The intense glare from the sky can cause eye disorders. The clothing most suited to the climate should be loose fitting, to allow evaporative cooling from the skin; the material should be of close texture and moderate thickness. It should also be light in colour to reflect radiation, and cover as much of the body as possible. A variety of shading and insulation devices are used by architects in hot dry regions to even out the daily variations of temperature and reduce the impact of solar radiation.

Areas of sand dune devoid of vegetation account for only a small proportion of the desert regions, which support a surprising variety of plant and animal life adapted to drought conditions. Strong winds and 'flash floods' after the sporadic rains have, over the millennia, produced many spectacular landforms by erosion. In the few places where ground water is available the vegetation can be luxuriant. Some of these oases can support large urban communities on the basis of complex irrigation systems.

The more accessible areas of the deserts are increasingly sought after by tourists, who value the space, the sunny winter climate and the scenery, which they can offer. At night, the stars shine with a clarity unusual in industrialized countries, which are subjected to *light pollution* from brightly lit urban areas and motorways. Some dry regions such as Arizona are perceived to have a healthy climate free of respiratory diseases, whereas in the irrigated areas of the Sahara and the Middle East there is a substantial risk of malaria. Development has taken place in those regions where adequate supplies of water and power can be provided at reasonable cost and where good external communications are available to the main tourist-generating countries. Coastal areas have the best prospects as water can be obtained from the sea by desalinization, although this is expensive.

The warm climates (zone 3)

Situated mainly between latitudes 25° and 40°, these regions come under the influence of air masses of tropical origin in summer and the westerly winds of middle latitudes in winter. Unlike the tropics, there is a definite cool season, but winters are rarely cold enough to prevent outdoor activities such as golf and tennis from being enjoyed in comfort. One standard layer of clothing (or 1 clo of thermal resistance, equivalent in insulation value to a business suit) is sufficient for winter temperatures that range between 10 °C and 20 °C. Most of the zone is, however, too cool for beach tourism in winter, despite the impression given by some 'winter sun' holiday brochures. The main exceptions are the Canary Islands, Madeira, Bermuda and southern Florida, which can be described as 'subtropical'.

Within this zone the Mediterranean climate, with its dry summers and abundant sunshine, provides the best all-round conditions for tourism and outdoor recreation. As the name implies, this climate is best developed around the Mediterranean Sea, which allows the influence of the Atlantic Ocean to penetrate as far as south-west Asia. It is also found in California and in equivalent latitudes of the Southern Hemisphere. During the autumn and winter months these regions lie in the path of depressions which bring a good deal of rain. The summers are very warm, although the afternoon heat is modified by sea breezes and fairly low humidities, while the nights are pleasantly cool. Lack of rain, however, causes problems in ensuring adequate water and power supplies to meet the needs of farmers, manufacturers and the tourism industry. The dry evergreen vegetation characteristic of these climatic conditions is frequently subject to devastating fires.

On the eastern margins of the continents in these latitudes the warm, temperate, humid summer climate has adequate rainfall throughout the year. In some areas, notably southern China and Japan, summer is the rainy season and winters are relatively dry, thanks to the monsoon. Summers can be oppressively hot due to the high humidity and there is generally less sunshine than in the Mediterranean. However, the prevailing warm moist conditions are very favourable for agriculture.

The cool temperate and continental cold winter climates (zones 4 and 5)

These climates of middle latitudes are significant mainly as generating areas for sun-seeking tourism. The main difference between the maritime climates of the western margins of the continents and the continental climates of their heartlands and eastern margins is the relative mildness of winter in the former compared to its severity in the latter. In Europe the westerlies and their associated depressions can penetrate far to the east, in the absence of any significant north-to-south mountain barrier. It is therefore difficult to draw any meaningful boundary between the maritime climate of Western Europe, best exemplified by the British Isles, and the continental climate of Eastern Europe. Indeed, anticyclones centred over Scandinavia can occasionally 'block' the westerlies and bring spells of very cold winter weather to parts of Britain. In North America high mountains run parallel to the west coast, shutting out the moderating influence of the Pacific Ocean and confining mild, moist climatic conditions to a narrow coastal strip. You may be surprised to find that the coastal areas of eastern North America and East Asia have a severe winter climate, but this is because the prevailing winds are offshore, bringing very cold air from the continental interiors. The Atlantic and Pacific Oceans do, however, have a slight warming effect, and this is sufficient to trigger heavy snowfalls in the mountains of New England and northern Japan. The situation is quite different at equivalent latitudes in the Southern Hemisphere, where there are vast expanses of ocean, interrupted only by the southern extremity of South America, Tasmania and New Zealand. These areas experience a maritime climate which is milder, more equable and much less prone to air pollution than that of the British Isles.

In the maritime or cool temperate zone, winter temperatures are generally in the range of 0 °C to 10 °C and there is little snowfall except on high ground. Two standard layers of clothing (1.6 clos) are normally sufficient for these conditions. However, the mild temperatures are often associated with overcast skies, drizzle, fog and strong winds. Due to the continual progression of warm and cold fronts, the weather is very changeable. There is generally adequate rainfall at all seasons, and it is often excessive on west-facing coasts and mountains. Summers tend to be rather cool and cloudy, with afternoon temperatures rarely exceeding 25 °C. Such a climate is invigorating, but it is not well suited to the more popular forms of outdoor recreation.

In the continental zone, winter temperatures are below 0 °C for one to five months, so that snow, icy roads and frozen waterways are to be expected – and dealt with – as a matter of course. Buildings are well insulated and in some regions have traditionally been designed to withstand heavy snowfalls. Winter clothing consists of three standard layers (equivalent of 2 clos) separated by 6 mm of trapped insulating air. An overcoat, adequate head covering and protection for the extremities are essential in these cold temperatures. However, the winter weather is generally more settled, due to the prevailing anticyclonic conditions, than in the cool temperate zone. This provides opportunities for a variety of snow-based activities such as cross-country skiing and snowmobiling. Summers are appreciably warmer than in the British Isles with daytime temperatures frequently exceeding 25 °C. Nevertheless, a good deal of rain falls during this season and hailstorms are frequent. Autumn in forested areas is a colourful season and is characterized by crisp, stimulating weather.

The cold damp climates (zone 6)

Small in terms of land area, these essentially maritime climates are dominated by the permanent low-pressure belts over the North Atlantic, North Pacific and Southern Oceans, which generate a great deal of stormy weather throughout the year. These regions receive less sunshine than any other part of the world, while temperatures rarely fall much below −5 °C in winter or rise much above 10 °C in summer. The climate is too cold and windy for tree growth and there is much boggy terrain due to the constant precipitation. Rain or wet snow can easily penetrate clothing, robbing it of its insulating qualities. Heat loss also occurs from the feet if these are not adequately protected from the wet ground, causing serious skin damage or 'trench foot'. Suitable clothing for these bleak conditions consists of material with small air spaces which prevents heat loss due to the wind and, at the same time, allows the skin to 'breathe' freely, plus a water-repellent outer layer which can be easily removed. The weather of the more exposed upland areas of Britain, so popular with hikers, approximates to these conditions for much of the year.

The cold dry climates (zone 7)

The cold climate regions account for a third of the earth's land surface, including 10 per cent (mainly in Antarctica and Greenland) which is permanently ice-covered. Although temperatures in the subarctic zone can reach 25 °C during the brief summers, the length and extreme severity of the winters is the dominant fact of life in high latitudes. In the Arctic zone the sun's rays are oblique even in summer, counteracting the advantage of continuous daylight at this season, while for several months the sun scarcely appears above the horizon. In the Southern Hemisphere, Antarctica has an even colder climate than that experienced by the northern lands adjoining the Arctic Ocean. Although the icy seas of both polar zones are surprisingly rich in marine life, the species representing the Arctic are distinct from those of the Antarctic. The Arctic supports a variety of land mammals as well as marine species, with the polar bear at the top of the food chain. In contrast, the interior of Antarctica is virtually sterile and only its coastal fringes provide a habitat for penguins and other bird life.

Provided the weather is calm, temperatures as low as −40 °C are bearable as the air is very dry. However, this causes dehydration, as moisture is lost from the body to the atmosphere in exhaled breath, and this, together with heat from vehicles and buildings, produces 'human habitation fog' in built-up areas. Extreme cold has a punishing effect on people and materials – for example, steel becomes brittle and shatters like glass. Under blizzard conditions exposed flesh can freeze in less than a minute, due to wind-chill. The extremities have to be protected from frostbite; the ears by a fur-lined hood and the hands and feet by two insulating layers. Arctic clothing tends to be bulky as several layers are needed under a windproof parka; with physical exertion large quantities of sweat are produced. The clothing should fit fairly loosely when active but be capable of being drawn in when at rest to trap insulating air. However, no amount of clothing will keep an inactive individual comfortable for long at temperatures below −15 °C.

Throughout the Arctic and most of the subarctic the summers are not warm enough to thaw more than the topsoil, so that the moisture beneath the ground remains frozen. This condition, known as *permafrost*, presents costly engineering problems. Buildings and even utilities must be insulated from contact with the ground, otherwise the permafrost would melt and the structure subside. Because moisture cannot drain down, there is much surface water in summer, which attracts swarms of biting insects. The southern part of the subarctic zone is dominated by vast, rather sombre forests of spruce, birch, or larch, which can withstand a short growing season and poor soils. As summer temperatures decrease, these are replaced by the stunted vegetation of the tundra and the polar deserts of the Arctic zone. Fur trapping has long been the only source of income for the native peoples of Alaska, northern Canada, Greenland and Siberia. Tourism offers them an alternative as guides and outfitters to groups of hunters, anglers and expeditioners from warmer climate zones. There is a growing interest in the wildlife and scenery of the northern lands surrounding the Arctic Ocean, now more accessible as Russia opens up to Western tourism. The cold climate zone will continue to appeal to only a small section of the travel market. However, there is evidence that even minimal numbers of tourists can have a damaging impact on the fragile ecosystems of the polar regions, even where tourist movements are strictly controlled, as in Antarctica. This is a problem simply because the ecosystem takes such a long time to recover from damage.

The highland climates (zone 8)

These are scattered throughout other zones wherever high mountains or plateaus rise more than 1500 metres above sea level, as this is the altitude at which the effects of reduced air pressure first become noticeable. Many important cities in Latin America, East Africa and the Himalayas are situated at altitudes of between 1500 and 4000 metres, where it is necessary for the tourist and business traveller to spend a few days adjusting to the rarefied air. Above 4000 metres acclimatization is more difficult and the symptoms of 'altitude sickness' may occur. Temperatures at these high altitudes are, on average, 20 °C lower than those recorded near sea level in the same latitude, although the seasonal rhythm is similar (see Figure 4.3). Ascending a high mountain in the tropics involves passing through a range of climates from warm to cold, depending on altitude, and with humid or dry characteristics according to exposure on windward or leeward slopes. At the highest levels the vegetation superficially resembles that of the Arctic tundra, but the climate of high altitudes differs from that of high latitudes in receiving a large amount of solar radiation throughout the year. Notable examples of a 'cold region where the sun is hot' would be Tibet and the Altiplano of Bolivia, where the Indian poncho is the garment best suited for the conditions. In the middle latitudes both the snowline and the treeline are at much lower altitudes than in the tropics and, as mentioned earlier, mountain regions in these zones are favourable for skiing in winter.

Summary

At the world scale, climate is one of the key factors influencing tourism development and holiday travel. Climatic conditions are determined by latitude, altitude and the interrelationship of coasts and mountains. Climate is made up of several

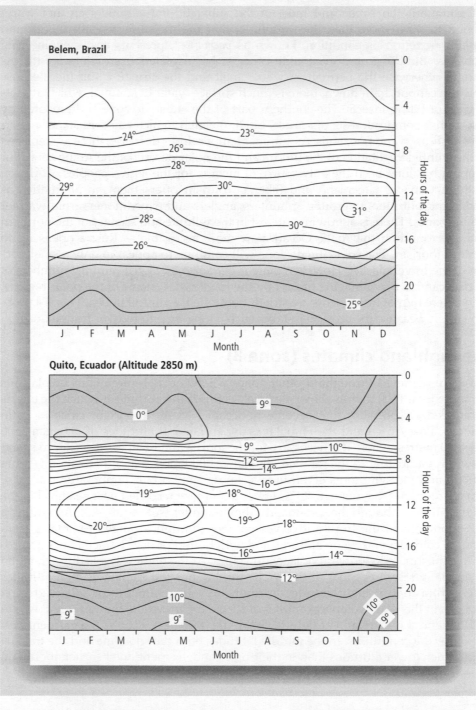

Figure 4.3 Tropical lowland and highland climates. The thermoisopleths (lines of equal temperature) indicate variations in temperature (°C) during the day throughout the year. As both Belem and Quito are situated at the Equator, seasonal variations in temperature are very small compared to the differences between day and night, with a rapid rise in temperature after sunrise

Source: Adapted from Trewartha, 1954: 243, 271

factors, of which temperatures and humidity are the most significant for human well-being, while others strongly influence particular types of recreational activity. Seasonal variation is an important characteristic of most climates and this is used as a basis for classification, so that useful comparisons can be made between different destinations. The optimal climate for tourism is the Mediterranean type.

However, tour operators are increasingly seeking out 'exotic' locations where conditions are much less favourable. The hot climates, formerly regarded as unhealthy, are now highly regarded as destinations for beach holidays. The cold climates of high mountain regions and high latitudes are attracting the more adventurous tourists who value the unpolluted, natural environment despite its hazards.

Like other tourism resources, climate is subject to change. It remains to be seen whether these changes will be beneficial to the tourism industry, or to tourists themselves. Some destinations will gain as a result, whereas others, dependent on beach tourism, will lose out. It is certain that tour operators and tourism generally will have to adapt, as the climate is beyond human control.

Chapter 5
The geography of transport for travel and tourism

Learning Objectives

After reading this chapter you should be able to:

- Appreciate the close relationship between tourism and transport.
- Understand the principles of spatial interaction between places and their importance to the geography of tourism.
- Describe the four main physical elements of any transport system.
- Identify the costs involved in running a transport system.
- Describe the distinguishing features of the main transport modes and recognize their particular contributions to tourism.
- Identify the Greenwich Meridian, the various time zones and the International Date Line and illustrate their importance for the traveller.
- Outline the characteristics of each mode of transport for the different types of traveller.
- Appreciate the environmental implications of different modes of transport.

Introduction

In Chapter 1, three components of tourism were identified: the tourist-generating area, the tourist-receiving or destination area and the linkages between them. This chapter introduces some of the basic principles of transport geography and illustrates their application to tourism.

Tourism and transport are inseparable. Tourism is about being elsewhere and transport bridges the gap between origin and destination. We need to consider transport for these reasons:

- In a historic sense transport has developed hand in hand with tourism. Improvements in transport have stimulated tourism and, in turn, tourism demand has prompted such transport developments as the growth of charter air services to serve the leisure market.

- Transport renders tourist destinations accessible to their markets in the tourist-generating areas. All tourism depends on access. Indeed accessibility, or the lack of it, can make or break a destination.
- Transport for tourism involves considerable public and private investment and represents a major sector of the tourism industry in terms of employment and revenue generated. Tourism then, is transformed by, and has helped to transform, the world communications map.

Moreover transportation is a major industry in its own right, with concerns extending well beyond tourism and influencing most aspects of everyday life. In effect, transport is civilization.

Principles of interaction

In Chapter 1 the basic principle of spatial interaction between two places was outlined in terms of a supplying area containing a surplus of a commodity and a generating area having a demand for that commodity. In geography this is known as spatial differentiation, with transport linking the two areas. Ullman (1980) has suggested that three main factors are necessary for spatial differentiation and transport development:

- **Complementarity**   This is a way of saying that places differ from each other and that in one place there is the desire to travel and in the other the ability to satisfy that desire. This complementarity of demand and supply will produce interaction between areas and a transport system will be required. Examples of complementarity are the flows of tourists from north-eastern states of the USA to Florida, or from north-west Europe to the Mediterranean.
- **Intervening opportunities**   While Ullman's idea of complementarity makes interaction possible there may be competing attractions. To take an example, for a resident of Munich wishing to take a summer holiday in a Spanish resort, mainland Spain is closer than one of the Canary Islands. Mainland Spain is therefore an intervening opportunity, even though perfect complementarity exists between Munich and the Canary Islands.
- **Transferability** or the friction of distance. This refers to the cost (in time and money) of overcoming the distance between two places. If the cost of reaching a destination is too high then even complementarity and lack of intervening opportunities will not persuade movement to take place.

The elements of transport

If interaction does take place a transport system will be needed. Faulks (1990) has identified four basic physical elements in any transport system:

- the way
- the terminal
- the carrying unit
- motive power.

For each *mode* or form of transport the characteristics of these elements vary and it is therefore useful to examine them in turn.

The way

The way is the medium of travel used by the various transport modes. It may be artificial, such as roads, railways, tramways and cableways; it may be a natural way, i.e. the air, the sea, lakes and rivers; or it can be a combination of the two, such as inland waterways. The following distinctions are important:

- If the way has to be provided artificially a cost is incurred.
- The cost of the way is influenced by a second distinction: whether the user shares the way with others (for example roads) or has the sole use of a specialized way (such as railways).
- Vehicles on roads and boats on inland waterways are controlled almost exclusively by their drivers or operators. In contrast, the movement of aircraft, trains and to some extent shipping is subject to traffic control, signalling or some other navigational aid.

The way is usually the responsibility of an organization that is independent of transport operators such as the airlines and bus companies. (Examples in the UK would include the Civil Aviation Authority and the Highways Agency.)

The terminal

A terminal gives access to the way for the users, while a terminus is the furthest point to which that system extends – literally the end of the line. Terminals can also act as interchanges where travellers transfer from one mode to another (for example from aircraft to coach/train at an airport, or in the case of the Channel Tunnel, from coach or car to the shuttle train). Terminals vary considerably in size, layout and the amenities they provide, as these are determined by the length and complexity of the journey, and the expectations of passengers. International airports are often showpieces of modern engineering design; this was also true of the monumental railway stations of London, Milan and New York, as well as the former terminals for the great ocean-going liners, for example Cherbourg. In contrast, a terminal for riverboat passengers in a Third World country might be little more than a landing stage.

The carrying unit

Each type of way demands a particular type of carrying unit – aircraft; ships and smaller vessels for waterways; cars, buses/coaches and other vehicles for the roads; and rolling stock for the railways. Aircraft have to be designed to particularly high specifications to ensure safety and comfort, and are therefore costly. Aircraft, ships and road vehicles are flexible to operate compared to trains, monorails and trams, where breakdowns on the track cause extensive delays.

Motive power

The historical development of motive power technology reads almost like a history of tourism, with a marked acceleration of the pace of change after the 1950s (see Table 5.1) Motive power combines with the 'way' and the carrying unit to determine the speed, range and capacity of the transport mode in question.

The motive power for most transport modes is now dependent on petroleum as the energy source. Geology determines that this natural resource is unevenly distributed, with the Middle East supplying almost two-thirds of the total world output. We are facing the possibility of an energy crisis even more severe than that of the early 1970s. Oil reserves are being depleted by competing demands not only from transport but the rest of the global economy. The USA is the world's largest consumer of petroleum, importing 50 per cent of its requirements, and is concerned to secure the flow of oil from the effects of political turmoil in the Middle East by tapping alternative suppliers in the Caspian Basin and the Gulf of Guinea. Heavy oil sources such as the tar sands of northern Canada are becoming commercially viable, but this would release unacceptably high levels of carbon dioxide into the atmosphere. In the meantime Japan and the EU are seeking to harness alternative energy sources, notably hydrogen, but as yet this is not a realistic prospect for transport on a large scale.

In terms of the capacity of a transport system, the most important consideration is to find the combination of carrying unit and motive power that can hold the maximum number of passengers while still allowing sufficient utilization of the transport system. Increasing size does bring its own problems. 'Jumbo jets' for example require longer runways and larger charter aircraft reduce the flexibility of tour operations.

Transport costs and pricing

Transport costs and pricing are fundamental to the geography of tourism. The distinctive cost structure of each mode influences consumer choice and thus determines the volume of traffic on a route. There are two basic types of transport cost:

- **Social and environmental costs** These costs are not paid for by the transport operator or user but are borne by the community. An example would be the unquantifiable cost of aircraft noise to residents living near an international airport.
- **Private costs** Those who operate the transport system pay private costs which are then passed on to the customer as fares. A basic distinction needs to be made here between fixed and variable costs:
  - Fixed costs (or overheads) are incurred before any passengers are carried or indeed before a carrying unit moves along the 'way'. These costs are 'inescapable' and include items such as interest on capital invested in the system and depreciation of assets. The most important feature of fixed costs is that they do not vary in proportion to the level of traffic on a route, the distance travelled or the numbers of passengers carried. For example the control tower of an airport must be manned irrespective of the number of aircraft movements at that airport.
  - Variable or running costs do depend on the level of service provided, distance travelled and the volume of traffic carried. Here costs include fuel, crew wages and maintenance. These costs are escapable because they are only incurred when the transport system is operating and can be avoided by cancelling services.

Table 5.1 The historical development of transport and tourism

Mode of transport	Pre-industrial era	1840–1920	1920–1940	1950	1960–1970	1980–2000	The future
Air			Propeller technology Civil aviation begins Travel expensive and limited Airships enjoy a brief period of acceptance Basic terminal facilities	Speeds of 400 km/h	Jet aircraft (B707) speeds 800 km/h Cheap fuel Rapid expansion of charter services Development of CRS and GDS	Wide-bodied jets (B747) Extended range Fuel efficiency No increases in speed except for Concorde Extensive terminal services	Hypersonic aircraft Space tourism Global alliances of airlines New generation jumbo jets with large capacity Increased deregulation
Sea		Steamships and packet boats	Sailing vessels	Ocean liners and cruisers Little competition from air Short sea ferry speed less than 40 km/h with very basic facilities No increase in speed for passenger liners	Air overtakes shipping on North Atlantic routes Hovercraft and hydrofoils being developed	Fly-cruise established Larger and more comfortable ferries Fast catamarans developed	Amphibious 'ground effect' craft Sub-marine tourism Themed cruising Increased use of boat for recreational use

Road	Horse-drawn carriages Unpaved roads	Cars achieve speeds of 55 km/h but remain unreliable Coaches develop from charabancs	Cars improve in speed and performance – 100–115 km/h Cars increasingly used for domestic tourism in place of public transport Roads improve, motorways introduced	Speed limits in USA Steep rise in car ownership rates Urban congestion Green fuel Improved coaches Re-introduction of trams	Urban gridlock Automated road systems Personal rapid transit Demand-responsive transport Resurgence of road-based public transport
Rail	Steam locomotive	'Golden age' of rail Speed exceeds that of cars	Electrification of rail networks Continuous welded tracks	High-speed networks develop in Europe Business products offered Dedicated rail tourism products developed based on nostalgia for steam	Development of medium-haul tourism products Enhanced motive-power technology

Source: Adapted from Cooper et al., 1998, p. 277

Because each mode has a different ratio of fixed to variable costs, the distinction is a very important one. Railways, for example, have to provide and maintain a track. This means that a railway system has to sustain a high proportion of fixed costs whereas for road transport the fixed costs are low. The outcome is that the cost per passenger-kilometre decreases rapidly for rail but more slowly for road transport. In other words, railways are uneconomic if they are only carrying a few passengers, as each one has to make an unacceptably large contribution to fixed costs.

On the other hand road transport is much more competitive as the greater part of the costs are variable, and fleets of buses, coaches or taxis can be deployed more readily to meet changes in demand.

In fact, the distinction between fixed and variable costs is blurred; for example costs of staffing and equipping a terminal may increase with the volume of traffic. These costs are known as semi-fixed. While we could say that wages are a variable cost, in reality crew have to be retained and paid irrespective of the utilization of the transport system in the short term. In the longer term, staffing can normally be adjusted to the volume of business.

The ratio of fixed to variable costs is an important consideration for transport operators in the tourism business. Compared to many activities transport has a high proportion of fixed costs. The product is also perishable, because if a seat is not sold on a flight it cannot be stored and sold at a later date. This means that operators must achieve a high utilization of their systems – if carrying units are idle for long periods they do not make a contribution to fixed costs. Finally, it is important to achieve a high *load factor* (i.e. the number of seats sold compared to the number available).

The link between load factor and pricing is clearly illustrated by the *marginal cost principle*. Using an air-inclusive tour as our example, marginal cost is the additional cost incurred by carrying one extra unit of output (in this case a passenger). The operator determines a load factor that covers the fixed costs of the journey and the variable cost of each passenger carried. If the flight is budgeted to break even at a load factor of 80 per cent, then every passenger carried over this level will incur a small marginal cost, because variable costs are low, and this represents a substantial profit for the tour operator. Unfortunately for the tour operator the opposite also applies – for every passenger below the 80 per cent level a loss will be incurred.

A related problem is the fact that tourism demand tends to be highly peaked on a daily, weekly and annual basis. This means that airline fleets may only be fully utilized at certain times of the year. Both in Europe and North America one solution to this was the creation of the winter holiday market in the late 1960s to utilize idle aircraft and make a contribution to fixed costs. Another solution is to use *differential pricing*. Here operators offer low fares for travel in the off-peak period to increase the traffic at those times. The trend in all transport modes is for fares to match distinctive market segments, each of which have their own travel requirements.

Transport modes, routes and networks

Modes

Each transport mode has different operational characteristics, based on the different ways in which technology is applied to the four elements of any transport system

(Table 5.2). Technology determines the appropriateness of the mode for a particular type of journey. It also ensures that some modes overlap in their suitability for the needs of travellers, and this may lead to competition between airlines and surface transport operators on some routes, such as London to Paris. In other cases transport modes are complementary, for example the road or rail links between airports and city centres. Another example would be fly-drive holidays, where the tourist has the advantages of air transport to reach the destination and the convenience of a hired car for touring the holiday area.

Routes

Transport routes do not occur in isolation from the physical and economic conditions prevailing in different parts of the world. Mountain ranges, extensive hilly terrain, deep river valleys, waterlogged ground and climatic factors influence their direction, as do the locations of major cities and political boundaries. However, not all modes of transport are equally affected by these factors. For example, mountains do not deflect air transport routes although they will influence the location of airports. In contrast railways are very much influenced by topographical features. These factors, combined with considerations of technology and investment, ensure that transport routes remain relatively stable channels of movement.

The fact that some modes of transport have a restricted 'way' – namely roads, railways and canals – will automatically channel movement. For navigational purposes those modes which use natural ways – the air or the sea – are also channelled and movement does not take place across the whole available surface of the earth. We can look at transport route systems at a variety of scales:

- At the world scale there is a network of inter-continental air routes, and those countries with a coastline are also linked by the long-haul sea routes (line routes), nowadays used mainly by oil tankers and to transport freight.
- At the regional scale, many countries have nationwide bus, coach and rail services.
- At the local scale there are excursion circuits based on a particular city or resort.

Networks

Each transport network is made up of a series of links (along which flows take place) and nodes (terminals and interchanges). The accessibility of places on a network is of particular interest to geographers as once a node is linked to another it becomes accessible. Scale is important here – at a local scale many places may be highly accessible but when viewed at the world scale they become relatively inaccessible. Geographers analyse these networks in a variety of ways:

- The most straightforward technique is a flow map, which shows the volume of traffic on each route. Examination of the map gives a rough indication of major nodes and links.
- A more accurate approach is to analyse the network using *graph theory*. However, before this can be done the transport network must be reduced to its basic structure of nodes and links on a *topological* map. Although such a map retains contiguity of relationships, it is not true to scale like the familiar topographic map of an area. A good example is the map of the London Underground system which shows stations in their correct sequence but disregards the actual distances

Table 5.2 Characteristics of transport modes

Mode	Way	Carrying unit	Motive power	Advantages	Disadvantages	Significance for tourism
Road	Normally a surfaced road, although 'off road recreational vehicles' are not restricted	Car, bus, or coach. Low capacity for passengers	Petrol or diesel engine. Some use of electric vehicles	Door-to-door flexibility. Driver in total control of vehicle. Suited to short journeys	Way shared by other users leading to possible congestion	Door-to-door flexibility allows tourist to plan routes. Allows carriage of holiday equipment. Acts as a link between terminal and destination. Acts as mass transport for excursions in holiday areas
Rail	Permanent way, with rails	Passenger carriages. High passenger capacity	Diesel engines (diesel/electric or diesel/hydraulic). Also electric or steam locomotives	Sole user of the way allows flexible use of carrying units. Suited to medium or long journeys, and to densely populated urban areas. Non-polluting	High fixed costs	In mid-nineteenth century opened up areas previously inaccessible for tourism. Special carriages can be added for scenic viewing, etc. Trans-continental routes and scenic lines carry significant volume of tourist traffic
Air	Natural	Aircraft. High passenger capacity	Turbo-fan engines; turbo-prop or piston engine	Speed and range. Low fixed costs. Suited to long journeys	High fuel consumption and stringent safety regulations make air an expensive mode. High terminal costs	Speed and range opened up most parts of the world for tourism. Provided impetus for growth of mass international tourism
Sea	Natural	Ships. Can have a high degree of comfort. High passenger capacity	Diesel engine or steam turbine	Low initial investment. Suited to either long-distance or short ferry operations	Slow. High labour costs	Confined to cruising (where luxury and comfort can be provided) and ferry traffic

between them. In theory, the more links there are in a network, the greater the connectivity of that network. In fact, even dense transport networks can be badly connected, making some cross-city or cross-country journeys difficult.

The remainder of this chapter provides a detailed consideration of transport systems for each mode and their relationship to tourist demands.

Air transport

Developments in civil aviation have done most to bring about far-reaching changes in the nature of international tourism and the structure of the travel industry since the Second World War. Few parts of the world are now more than 24 hours' flying time from any other part, and it is estimated by the World Tourism Organization that around 20 per cent of international tourists use air transport. The jet aircraft has opened up many formerly remote areas as holiday destinations. Here it is instructive to compare Concorde with the Boeing 747. Although the supersonic airliner captured the public imagination in the last quarter of the twentieth century, it had limited range and capacity, and the high fares ensured that it accounted for only a small share of the market for air travel compared to the wide-bodied jets. Concorde was in the last analysis unsustainable for environmental as well as economic reasons. Despite the current massive growth in air travel it is true to say that only a small percentage of the world's population have experienced flying, and even in developed countries surface modes of transport carry much greater volumes of traffic than the airlines.

The following are the main advantages of the air transport mode:

- The way allows the aircraft a direct line of flight unimpeded by natural barriers such as mountain ranges, oceans, deserts or jungles.
- Superior speeds can be reached in everyday service.
- Air transport has a high passenger capacity and is ideally suited to journeys of more than 500 kilometres, travel over difficult, roadless terrain (as in Papua–New Guinea) and journeys between groups of islands separated by stormy seas from the mainland (such as the Shetlands of Scotland).

Air transport does however have disadvantages:

- It needs a large terminal area that may be some distance from the destination it serves.
- It is expensive due to the large amounts of power expended and the high safety standards demanded.
- Payload restrictions mean that vehicles cannot be carried, in contrast to sea-going ferries and some rail services.
- It has negative environmental impacts. The true cost of air travel for the airlines and their passengers has been masked by the fact that the airlines, unlike other business enterprises, are exempt from certain taxes. The continued rapid growth of air traffic may not be sustainable, given the contribution of aircraft emissions to climate change. (It has been estimated that a passenger on a single transatlantic flight contributes as much to global pollution as the average motorist in a year's driving.)
- Air transport is particularly vulnerable to terrorism.

The world pattern of air routes

The shortest distance between two places lies on a great circle, which drawn on the surface of the globe, divides it into equal hemispheres. Aircraft can utilize *great circle routes* fully because they can ignore physical barriers, with the improvements in range and technical performance that have been achieved since the Second World War. For example, the great circle route between Britain and the Far East lies over Greenland and the Arctic Ocean. Aircraft can fly 'above the weather' in the extremely thin air, uniformly cold temperatures and cloudless conditions of the stratosphere at altitudes of between 10 000 and 17 000 metres. In middle latitudes pilots take advantage of upper air westerly winds that attain speeds as high as 450 km/h. These *jet streams* reduce the flying time from California to Europe by over an hour compared to the journey in the opposite direction.

However, air routes are influenced not only by the operational characteristics of jet streams but also by safety and security factors. The movement of aircraft, particularly over densely populated countries, is channelled along designated airways. The development of commercial routes is determined by three factors:

- the extent of the demand for air travel
- adequate ground facilities for the handling of passengers and cargo
- international agreements.

The Chicago Convention of 1944 defined five 'freedoms of the air' that are put into practice by bilateral agreements between pairs of countries (Figure 5.1).

- The first freedom refers to the privilege of using another country's airspace.
- The second freedom refers to the right to land in another country for 'technical' reasons.
- The third and fourth freedoms relate to commercial point-to-point traffic between two countries by their respective airlines.
- The fifth freedom allows an airline to pick up and set down passengers in the territory of a country other than its destination.

In many parts of the world these freedoms are greatly affected by international politics, but with the ending of the Cold War commercial considerations have become even more important. For example, as Russia and some other countries have tried to compete with established airlines to gain foreign exchange, new freedoms have emerged. The sixth and seventh freedoms allow an airline to pick up in a country other than the country of origin, take passengers back to its home base or 'hub' and then take them on to another destination. For example, the Dutch airline KLM may pick up passengers in London, then fly them back to Amsterdam where they change planes and are taken on to say, Quito or São Paulo. This is known as 'hub and spoke' operations and has encouraged the development of hub airports at a regional and intercontinental scale.

International agreements are becoming less important with the deregulation of the air transport system. This means that governments are no longer allowed to control routes, fares and volumes of traffic on flights within and across their borders. The first major country to deregulate was the USA in the late 1970s followed by the EU in the 1990s. Deregulation:

- encourages competition among airlines
- has led to the building of strategic alliances between airlines such as the 'Star Alliance' and the 'One World' alliance

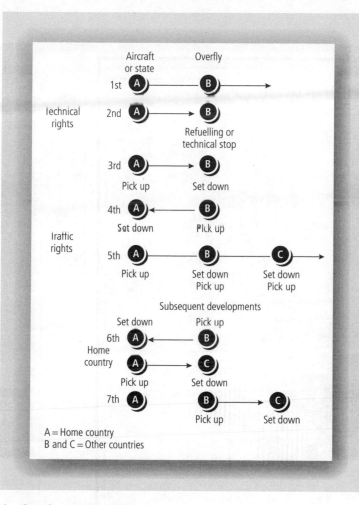

Figure 5.1 The five freedoms of the air

- encourages the growth of regional airlines and regional airports
- has favoured the development of 'budget' or low cost carriers (LCCs) on busy routes.

However, many countries have yet to agree to an 'open skies' policy for reasons of military security, or to protect the national 'flag-carrier' – usually state-owned and heavily subsidized – from foreign competition.

The routes and tariffs of the world's scheduled international airlines are, to an extent, controlled by the International Air Transport Association (IATA) to which most belong. IATA has divided the world into three Traffic Conference Areas for this purpose (see Figure 5.2).

Most of the world's air traffic is concentrated in three main regions – the eastern part of the USA, Western Europe and East Asia. This is due partly to market forces originating from their vast populations and partly because of the strategic location of these areas. The situation of London is particularly advantageous as it is at the centre of the earth's 'land hemisphere' in which over 90 per cent of the world's

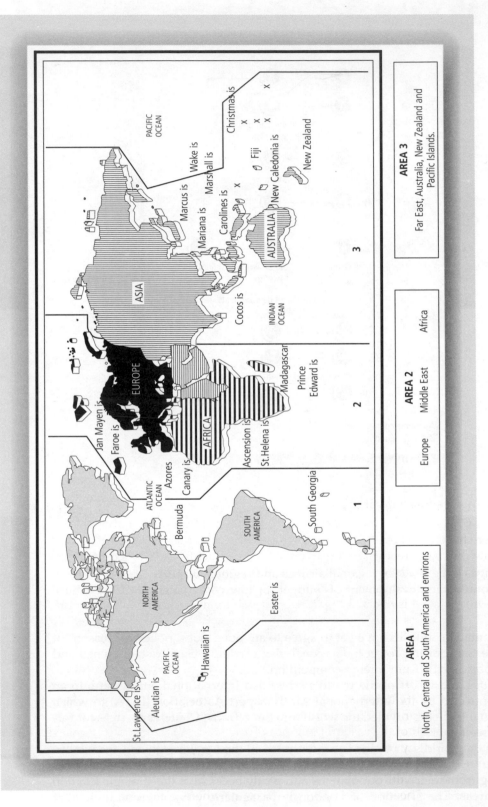

Figure 5.2 IATA traffic conference areas

AREA 1		
North, Central and South America and environs		

AREA 2		
Europe	Middle East	Africa

AREA 3		
Far East, Australia, New Zealand and Pacific Islands.		

Map labels:

St.Lawrence is
Aleutian is
PACIFIC OCEAN
Hawaiian is
NORTH AMERICA
Bermuda
ATLANTIC OCEAN
Azores
Canary is
Easter is
SOUTH AMERICA
South Georgia

Faroe is
Jan Mayen is
EUROPE
AFRICA
Ascension is
St.Helena is
Prince Edward is
Madagascar

ASIA
Cocos is
INDIAN OCEAN

PACIFIC OCEAN
Marcus is
Mariana is
Wake is
Marshall is
Carolines is
AUSTRALIA
New Caledonia is
Fiji
Christmas is
New Zealand

1   2   3

population – and an even greater proportion of the world's industrial wealth – are concentrated.

The 'air bridge' between Europe and North America across the North Atlantic is the busiest intercontinental route, linking the greatest concentrations of wealth and industry in the world. The capacity provided by wide-bodied jets and vigorous competition between the airlines has brought fares within reach of the majority of the population of these countries, while the Atlantic has shrunk, metaphorically speaking, to a 'pond' that can be crossed in a few hours.

Time zones

International travel usually necessitates a time change if the journey is in any direction other than due south or north. These differences in time result from the earth's rotation relative to the sun; at any given moment at one locality it is noon, while half the world away to the east or west it is midnight. The sun appears to us to be travelling from east to west and making one complete circuit of the earth every 24 hours. Viewed from space, the earth is in fact making a complete turn on its axis through 360 degrees of longitude. This means that for every 15 degrees of longitude the time is advanced or put back by one hour; places that lie to the east of the Greenwich Meridian have a later hour, those to the west an earlier hour due to this apparent motion of the sun.

Theoretically every community could choose its own local time. The development of the railways made standardized timetables essential, using an international system of time zones based on the Greenwich Meridian. Since 1884 the world has been divided into 24 time zones in which standard time is arbitrarily applied to wide belts on either side of a particular meridian, which is usually a multiple of 15 degrees. Often these correspond to political units rather than strictly following the meridians (for example Paris is one hour ahead of London despite being on the same longitude). A number of countries are too large for one standard time to be conveniently acceptable. Russia has the greatest west to east spread of any country, with no less than eleven time zones, followed by Canada with six, while the contiguous USA (excluding Alaska and Hawaii) has four – Eastern, Central, Mountain and Pacific. (In contrast China applies Beijing time to all its territory.) Countries in the Western Hemisphere have time zones that are designated with a minus number as so many hours 'slow' behind Greenwich Mean Time (GMT), which is the standard time on the Greenwich Meridian passing through London. Countries in the Eastern Hemisphere have time zones designated with a plus number as so many hours 'fast' on GMT. Only when it is noon on the Greenwich Meridian is it the same day worldwide; at all other times there is a 24 hour difference between each side of the 180 degree meridian. In 1884 the International Date Line (IDL) was established as the boundary where each day actually begins at midnight and immediately spreads westwards across the globe. By coincidence the IDL passes conveniently through the world's largest ocean and corresponds to the 180 degree meridian, except where deviations are necessary to allow certain territories and groups of Pacific islands to have the same calendar day. The calendar on the western (Asian) side of the IDL is always one day ahead of the eastern (American) side.

Whereas travellers by road or rail simply adjust their watches by one hour when crossing time zone boundaries, long-haul air travel presents more of a problem. For example, the time difference between London and Singapore is 7 hours and 30 minutes, and this needs to be taken into account when calculating the *elapsed flying time* (how long the flight actually takes between London and Singapore). Jet travel across a large number of time zones also causes disruption to the natural rhythms of the human body, which respond to a 24-hour cycle of daylight and darkness. The effect of *jetlag* varies considerably between individual travellers and appears to be more disruptive on long west–east flights than on westbound journeys.

The location of international airports

A major international airport acts as the primary *gateway* to a country or region for most foreign visitors, so that first impressions are important. Such an airport needs several passenger terminals, a cargo terminal, hotels with conference facilities and convenient interchange with long-stay car parks, bus and rail transport. It provides thousands of jobs in the retail, catering and transport sectors, and has all the problems associated with a large urban area. Also, security has been given a higher profile since 9/11.

The largest jet aircraft in operation need runways at least 3000 metres in length. In tropical countries, and especially at high altitudes, runways have to be even longer, as the lower density of the air means that jets have to make longer runs to obtain the lift to get airborne. A major airport therefore requires a great deal of land. The physical nature of the site is important; it should be as flat as possible with clear, unobstructed approaches. Such land is not abundant in the small islands that are popular with holidaymakers, or for that matter near many of the world's cities. In Rio de Janeiro, Osaka and Hong Kong airports have been built on land reclaimed from the sea. Runways are aligned so that aircraft can take off against the prevailing wind and airports are located up-wind of large concentrations of industry, which cause smog and poor visibility. The local weather record is therefore important.

At the same time the airport must be in a location that is readily accessible to the large centres of population it is primarily meant to serve. However, most are 20–30 kilometres distant, while Narita is 50 kilometres from the centre of Tokyo. Investment is needed to construct or improve rapid surface transport links with the city centre to minimize total travel time. This is particularly important for business travellers on short-haul flights. Generally there is a motorway link or in densely populated areas a dedicated high speed railway, separated from the main network.

The growth of air traffic has meant that many airports are now reaching, or have exceeded their passenger and aircraft capacity for safe and efficient operation. This is beginning to pose a real constraint on the development of air transport. Yet, despite their importance for tourism and the national economy, proposals for new airports, or for airport expansion, are fiercely opposed in developed countries. This is mainly due to the problem of noise pollution and because land is scarce, particularly in Western Europe. Consequently, on short- and medium-haul routes there is a definite role for short take-off and landing (STOL) aircraft. Helicopters require minimal ground facilities but are noisy and expensive to operate, and have only a limited range and capacity. The helicopter is, however, widely used for premium business travel, and in North America for sightseeing flights, or to reach remote mountain areas for hiking and skiing. There is possibly scope for new versions of seaplanes and even airships. Airships are slow but are ideally suited for luxury cruising, and unlike their ill-fated predecessors in the 1930s, they would use helium for motive power.

Land transport

Unlike air transport, which is truly worldwide in its scope, travel by road or rail is constrained to some extent by national boundaries. Although few borders are 'no go areas' like the Iron Curtain of the Cold War era, neither do they provide open access. Towns near designated border crossings benefit from spending by day visitors from neighbouring countries on shopping excursions. Following 9/11 surface transport was perceived as safe from terrorism, but this changed with the bombings of the Atocha rail terminal in Madrid on 11 March 2004, when the authorities realized that to implement security measures for surface transport is, if anything, more difficult than it is for air transport. Road and rail transport is subject to a greater degree of control by national governments than the airlines, and is therefore described in more detail in the regional chapters.

Road transport

The main advantage of road transport is the possibility in ideal conditions of door-to-door flexibility, and travel by other transport modes almost invariably begins and ends with a road journey. This, combined with the fact that road vehicles can only carry a small number of passengers and have a relatively low speed, makes them particularly suitable for short to medium-distance journeys. Also, the development of recreational vehicles (RVs) allows a form of motorized accommodation. The main disadvantage of road transport is that many users share the way and this can lead to congestion at periods of peak demand. As tourism is subject to annual and weekly peaks this can be a major handicap. Since the Second World War the private car has become the dominant transport mode for most types of tourism, while coach travel accounts for a much smaller share of the holiday market. Coach operations differ from scheduled bus services in that they are very much part of the tourism industry and provide higher standards of comfort and service (also note that in the USA 'coach' means economy class air travel). Coach travel not only provides a transfer service at airports and other terminals, but is also used for excursions from resorts, and for touring holidays as a product in its own right.

The main impetus toward an international system of highways has come about through the demands of an increasingly motorized population and the development of long distance coach services and road haulage. The popularity of the car is due to the fact that it can provide comfort, flexibility in timing, the choice of routes and destinations, and door to door service. The demands of the private car have resulted in a tourism landscape of motels and other drive-in facilities dedicated to personal mobility.

Current trends suggest that there will be 1 billion cars worldwide by 2030, with the largest increases taking place in China and other Third World countries. Nevertheless, car ownership in most developing countries is a luxury and public transport systems are often rudimentary. Passenger service vehicles may be improvised from former American school buses, jeeps or even trucks. Climatic conditions also affect road transport systems and the type of vehicles that may be used. In large areas of the tropics there are fairly extensive networks of roads made from the laterite sub-soil; these are viable during the dry season but impassable after the rains. In sub-arctic regions highways have a gravel surface which is less damaged by frost and thaw than tarmac. Many developing countries have by-passed 'the age of the loco-motive', investing heavily in road building to achieve national unity and economic progress. Brazil is one such example, with an extensive network of long-distance bus and coach services on offer. International road projects include the Pan-American Highway system in Latin America and trans-continental routes in Africa and Asia that can be used, when the political situation allows, by overland expeditions and the more adventurous traveller.

In Western Europe and North America a network of motorways or freeways – limited access highways – connects most major cities and industrial areas, though holiday resorts are sometimes less well served. Motorways have shortened journey times and appreciably reduced accident rates. Roads designed especially for sight-seeing have been built in scenically attractive coastal and mountain areas. However, too much road building and the development that invariably goes with it can destroy the very beauty the tourist has come to see.

The private car has brought about greater individual freedom, but at a cost to society. Some allege that the West is already characterized by 'hypermobility', implying that much leisure travel is unnecessary and could be reduced by a change in lifestyle. Car ownership is unlikely to decline in democratic countries, but car *use* can be reduced in urban areas in a number of ways (for example, 'park and ride') by improving access to bus and train services. It is clear however that more drastic measures are needed to curb car use in the world's major cities, such as road pricing or congestion charges, if traffic gridlock and episodes of severe air pollution are to be avoided. In the Third World antiquated diesel buses, 'collective taxis' and taxi-motorcycle combinations (such as the *trishaws* of South-East Asia) add to the traffic problems. Civic authorities worldwide are investing in 'rapid transit' – automated light railways with a high passenger capacity – such as Bangkok's 'Skytrain' – rather than building urban motorways.

Car use can also be controlled in rural areas by imaginative traffic management schemes. However, the most sustainable forms of transport are cycling and horse riding; these are growing in popularity as activity holidays, although artificial motive power is still needed to reach the destination area and provide logistical support to tour groups. In Europe a network of 'green routes', much of it utilizing disused railways, is being developed for the use of hikers, cyclists and riders. In some of the remote mountain regions of the Third World tourists on horseback are arguably preferable to those using four-wheel drive vehicles in terms of their impact on host communities.

Rail transport

In contrast to the road, the railway track is not shared and extra carriages can be added or removed to cope with demand. This is particularly important in holiday areas where special trains may be run. Also, special facilities can be provided on rolling stock such as dining cars or viewing cars on scenic routes. The railway's main disadvantage is that the track, signalling and other equipment has to be maintained and paid for by the single user of the way. Providing railway track is particularly expensive as the motive power can only negotiate gentle gradients. This means that engineering work for cuttings, viaducts and tunnels is a major cost consideration, especially on long routes and in mountain regions. Railways are therefore characterized by high fixed costs and a need to utilize the track and rolling stock very efficiently to meet these high costs. The railway's speed and capacity to move large numbers of passengers make it suitable for journeys of 200–500 kilometres between major cities.

In the nineteenth century the introduction of railways revolutionized transport and enabled large numbers of people to travel long distances relatively cheaply. The great trans-continental railways were built before 1914, when there was no serious competition from other modes of transport. The first was the Union Pacific between Chicago and San Francisco, completed in 1869, which opened up the American West to settlement and tourism. The introduction of the Pullman car at the same time allowed long distance journeys to be made in comfort. The Canadian Pacific was built for political as well as economic reasons, as to a large extent was the Australian Trans-continental linking Perth to Sydney. The world's longest line – the Trans-Siberian linking Moscow to Vladivostok – took 15 years to complete (1891–1905) and still remains the vital lifeline of Siberia.

After the Second World War the railways came under increasing competition from the airlines for long distance traffic and from the private car for short journeys. New railway construction virtually ceased in most countries, but improvements were made to track and steam was replaced as motive power by diesel fuel or electricity. The decline in passenger rail transport has been greatest in the Americas. In France, China and Japan, on the other hand, there has been considerable government investment in applying new technology to the development of high speed trains and upgrading the trunk lines between major cities. In Western Europe the Channel Tunnel between England and France has encouraged the development of rail-based tourism products such as the 'Eurostar' service between London and Paris/Brussels. There is also a niche market for luxury travel based on nostalgia for the 1920s, with products such as the revived 'Orient Express'. The growth of environmentalism and concern at a future energy crisis may yet prompt a modal switch from congested airspace and roads. It is perhaps ironic that high speed trains – namely the TGV in France – have themselves been opposed by environmentalists.

In mountain regions specially designed railways have long been used, as in Switzerland, to overcome the problem of steep gradients, and these are tourist attractions in themselves. However, aerial cableways are more versatile and cost-effective, as well as being faster in transporting large numbers of skiers and other tourists.

Water-borne transport

Water-borne transport is slow compared to air travel – an aircraft can make 20 crossings of the Atlantic in the time a ship makes one return journey. By the late 1960s most of the long-haul market on the North Atlantic routes had been lost to the airlines. Also many travellers are badly affected by the six types of motion that characterize a ship in heavy seas. However the advantage of this mode is that:

- Ships expend relatively little power.
- Ships can be built to much larger specifications than any vehicle or aircraft, to carry several thousand passengers at a time over long distances. Increasing size does bring safety and pollution problems.
- Ships can also provide a high degree of comfort. This has led to the development of the cruise market, which is travel for travel's sake in 'floating resorts'.
- Ships can be designed as roll-on roll-off ferries accommodating large numbers of motor vehicles – in effect 'floating bridges'. This has led to marketing directed at motorists using the short sea routes, such as those crossing the English Channel.

Technological advances are beginning to overcome some of the natural disadvantages of sea transport. For example, a conventional vessel has to displace a volume of water equivalent to its own weight. This can be partly overcome by vessels using the hydrofoil principle, where the hull is lifted clear of the water by submerged foils acting like aircraft wings, or hovercraft, where the entire vessel uses a cushion of air to keep it clear of the water. So far neither hydrofoils nor hovercraft are used on long ocean voyages due to their vulnerability in rough seas and strong winds, as well as their limited capacity and range of operation. They are successful on short sea crossings where their speed (up to three times that of a conventional ship), manoeuvrability and fast turn-round in port give them the advantage. Wave-piercing catamarans have proved to be more versatile than hydrofoils or hovercraft on some routes. As a result, hovercraft are being phased out of car ferry services, but their amphibious characteristics are well suited for specialist roles, such as transport in areas of marshy terrain. Hydrofoils cannot carry vehicles, but they have proven advantages operating on lakes such as those of northern Italy, and on the wide waterways of Russia. There is obvious potential for ocean-going high speed craft, combining the advantages of air and sea modes, currently under development.

The world pattern of sea routes

We must make a distinction between the long-haul or line routes plied by shipping and the short sea routes, especially those of Europe and the Mediterranean, where ferries provide vital links in the international movement of travellers by road and rail. Cruising is a separate category as it is essentially a type of holiday and not a point-to-point voyage.

Long-haul routes

Despite having the advantage of the freedom of the high seas outside a country's territorial waters, ships rarely keep to great circle routes. Instead they ply sea lanes determined by the availability of good harbours en route and which avoid sea areas characterized by storms and ice hazards. Economic considerations are foremost; the most important routes are those linking Europe with its main trading partners. Many ports on the long-haul routes, including Liverpool and Valparaiso, have declined as a result of changing patterns of trade. Tourists and legal emigrants now account for only a small fraction of the business due to competition from the airlines and the high labour costs involved in operating a passenger liner. (Some cargo liners do take up to 12 passengers, and voyages on these ships attract a significant niche market in the USA.) The Panama and Suez Canals are vital links between the oceans on the line routes, avoiding a much longer voyage around Cape Horn or the Cape of Good Hope. Generally speaking, international regulations on shipping have been less effective than for civil aviation. Many ship owners operate under 'flags of convenience' to avoid strict adherence to safety standards and labour laws in their countries of origin.

Short sea routes

Passenger traffic on the short sea routes is increasing rapidly throughout Western Europe largely as the result of the popularity of motoring holidays and the growth of trade between the countries of the EU. The introduction of roll-on roll-off facilities has enabled ports on these routes to handle a much greater volume of cars, coaches and trucks, and most ferries now operate throughout the year with greatly improved standards of comfort and service. The opening of the Channel Tunnel in 1994 caused shipping companies to transfer investment to the western English Channel. Ferries are often the only transport option available to groups of small or remote islands where airports may be few and far between. In the case of the Aegean Islands of Greece, a popular holiday destination, large capacity ferries provide a link to the mainland ports, while smaller vessels offer an inter-island service, especially during the peak summer season. Services making greater use of hydrofoils connect the many islands along the Adriatic coast of Croatia. In the case of Hawaii, however, inter-island ferries have long been replaced by air services. In island nations of the Third World such as the Philippines, ferries are popular due to their low fares, although safety standards are below those considered acceptable in Western countries. Ferries are not widely used by business travellers for whom time is money; one notable exception is the jetfoil service linking Hong Kong to Macao.

Cruising

The chartering of ships for inclusive tours began in the 1860s. Prior to the Second World War such cruises typically lasted for several months and catered exclusively for upper income groups with abundant leisure and wealth. The sea voyage, often undertaken for health reasons, was more important than the places visited. Faced with increasing competition from the airlines in the 1950s, ship owners diversified from operating passenger liners into cruising, although this was not an easy transition as the ships were often unsuitable. Few ports of call can accommodate 30 000 tonne vessels.

The introduction of *fly-cruising* in the 1960s was important as it allowed the cruise ship to be based at a port in the destination region, so that clients no longer had to make a long, possibly stormy voyage from a port in their home country. The cruise market has proved resistant to recession with a loyal, repeat clientele. There has been massive investment in large purpose-built cruise ships, designed with a great deal of open deck space for warm water voyages. As well as a high standard of service and accommodation, a variety of sports, activities and entertainment are available. At the same time prices have fallen and there are more passengers in the younger age groups, so that cruising is less of a 'grey market' than in the past. Themed and special interest cruises are increasingly promoted. Whale and dolphin watching are popular activities in many parts of the world, but these are controversial in view of their possible ecological impact.

The Caribbean is the most popular cruising destination, due to its location close to the North American market, the warm climate and the wide variety of scenery offered by the islands. The two other main cruising destinations are the Mediterranean and the Far East/Pacific. The North European market dominates cruising in the Mediterranean, where many ports of great cultural, historic and natural interest can be visited on shore excursions. The western Pacific and South China Sea are mainly popular with the Australians and the Japanese.

Areas for summer cruises include the Baltic and Norwegian coast in northern Europe and the even more spectacular coastline of British Columbia and Alaska in North America. New cruising routes are being pioneered in South America, Antarctica and the Arctic Ocean.

Ports

There are relatively few seaports with deepwater harbours, and most ports are located on river estuaries where improvements are necessary to accommodate modern shipping. For example, the English Channel port of Poole boasts one of the world's largest natural harbours and has shown impressive growth as a container port and ferry terminal. However, shipping is restricted to a narrow channel less than 10 metres in depth that requires constant dredging. Ports need considerable investment in terminal facilities and improved transport links with major cities in the hinterland. The popularity of leisure sailing may involve conflicts of use, justifying the development of purpose-built marinas, where yachts can be safely moored and serviced in a location separate from the commercial activities of the port.

Inland waterways

In pre-industrial times rivers were used wherever possible by merchants and other travellers in preference to the hazards of the road. Improvements to these natural waterways, and the development of canals in the eighteenth century, provided cities located in the interior with a commercial route to the sea, but locks and other engineering devices were needed to ensure constant water levels. Most inland waterways are now used as a recreational resource (such as the narrow canals of Britain). Waterbuses have an important role in a few places with an extensive river or canal waterfront. At the regional scale some of the world's great rivers serve as a lifeline for many communities. Cruises on the Volga and the Yangtze are promoted to attract Western tourists and earn foreign exchange for Russia and China. Cruises on the Rhine, Danube and the Nile have been part of the international tourism scene since the nineteenth century.

Transport integration

Travellers on complex journeys suffer from the lack of coordination between transport operators as regards timetables and the siting of terminals, and this causes frequent delays. An integrated transport system would make travel much more convenient. In a wider sense transport needs to be more closely integrated with other issues affecting tourism in policy-making. At the international scale airlines are seldom concerned with the environmental impact of their operations, although British Airways' 'Tourism for Tomorrow' awards are a notable exception. At the national scale few countries have an agency that coordinates policies on, say, highway planning with the demands from the tourism industry. At the local scale transport facilities should be designed as part of the leisure environment; the monorail serving the Darling Harbour project in Sydney is a good example.

Summary

Transport satisfies a need for spatial integration between two places, which can be explained by the principles of complementarity, intervening opportunity and transferability. A transport system consists in general terms of four basic physical elements – a way, a terminal, a carrying unit and motive power. There are as yet few alternative sources to petroleum as an energy source. Increased mobility is an advantage to the individual and the economy, but transport development takes place at a cost to the community. The fixed and variable costs of the transport system are borne by the operators and the users, while the cost structure determines the suitability of a particular transport mode for different types of journey. Transport routes are determined by economic considerations, the nature of the way, or navigational convenience.

The development of rapid means of communication, especially in civil aviation, has done much to revolutionize the scale and structure of the travel industry. It has also meant that almost all countries have adopted a system of time measurement based on the Greenwich Meridian. Airports are closely integrated with surface forms of transport, but the expansion of major international airports leads to demands on scarce land, energy and human resources that are increasingly difficult to resolve. Airlines and shipping are part of worldwide networks that are based on market forces and which need to be examined on an international scale. This is less true of road and rail transport operators which are subject to more scrutiny by national governments and therefore best dealt with on a country by country basis. The private car is the dominant mode in domestic tourism, while coaches and some forms of rail transport have significant roles in reducing the environmental impact of car use. In shipping we need to distinguish between the long-haul routes that have long ceased to carry much passenger traffic, and the short sea routes used mainly by holiday motorists. Some forms of transport such as the hydrofoil have highly specialized roles, while cruising is a type of holiday rather than a means of transport in the true sense.

Part Two

The Regional Geography of Travel and Tourism

Chapter 6
An introduction to the tourism geography of Europe

Learning Objectives

After reading this chapter you should be able to:

- Appreciate why Europe continues to dominate world tourism.
- Understand the major patterns of tourism demand in Europe.
- Be aware of the major physical and social features in Europe and their implications for tourism.
- Appreciate the role of the European Union and the euro in tourism organization and development.
- Recognize the major geographical influences on the distribution of tourism resources in Europe.
- Recognize the role of improvements in transport infrastructure in encouraging a freer movement of tourists throughout Europe.

Introduction

Physical features prescribe Europe's boundaries, yet within these boundaries Europe is a region of immense economic, social and cultural diversity. In part this diversity explains why Europe continues to be a crucible of conflict, with two world wars in the twentieth century, which ended with a civil war in the Balkan region. Europe is also under economic pressures from both North America and the newly industrializing countries of South-East Asia. Here, Europe's failure to perform as a region is brought into clear focus when shares of international tourism are examined:

- In 1960 Europe accounted for 72 per cent of international tourism arrivals.
- By 2000 this share had fallen to 58 per cent.

Nonetheless, Europe continues to dominate world tourism. This is despite the fact that Europe accounts for less than 10 per cent of the world's population and an even smaller share of its total land area. In 2000 it received over 400 million of the world's 697 million international tourist arrivals, and accounted for almost 50 per cent of the world's receipts from international tourism. The strong economies in the region account for most of the world's top tourist generating countries, dominating the outbound flow of international travel, and are also estimated to generate massive demand for domestic trips.

Europe is pre-eminent in the world's tourism system for the following reasons:

- Most of the region's economies are in the high mass consumption stage, or in the drive to maturity. The population, though ageing, is in general affluent, mobile, and has a high propensity to travel.
- Europe consists of a rich mosaic of languages, cultural resources and tourist attractions of world calibre.
- The adoption of the single European currency, the Euro, in many European countries in 2002 has facilitated tourism.
- Europe comprises many relatively small countries in close proximity, encouraging a high volume of short international trips.
- The region's climatic differences are significant, leading since the 1950s to a considerable flow of sun-seeking tourists from northern Europe to the south.
- Europe's tourism infrastructure is mature and of a high standard.
- The tourism sector throughout most of the region is highly developed, and standards of service – though not the best in the world – are good.
- Most European governments have well-funded, competent tourist authorities with marketing and development powers.

With a few striking exceptions, Europe's political and economic structures are stable, providing a safe environment for investment in tourism. Since the 1980s, the dismantling of the Iron Curtain and the opening up of Eastern Europe, along with the advent of the Single European Market and the adoption of the Euro, have removed barriers to tourism movement within Europe. On 1 May 2004 eight former Eastern bloc countries along with Malta and Cyprus were admitted to the European Union, continuing the process of integration.

The setting for tourism

Physical features

Physically, but not culturally, Europe is in effect a western extension of Asia, a peninsula surrounded on three sides by sea. The eastern boundary is much more indeterminate, being marked by the not very impressive Ural Mountains, the Caspian Sea and the narrow waterways linking the Mediterranean and Black Seas. A glance at the map will show that this boundary is in fact straddled by two important nations – Russia and Turkey. Within Europe we can distinguish two major physical/climatic divisions – north and south – separated by a series of mountain ranges such as the Alps.

The dominant feature of Northern Europe is a plain, crossed by many rivers, and extending from southern England to Russia, with the remnants of worn-down mountain systems along its periphery. It is on this plain that the major industries and cities are located, and therefore it acts as the source of many tourists to the rest of Europe. Southern Europe on the other hand is hilly or mountainous, containing only small pockets of fertile lowland, and with few inland waterways of any length.

Europe's mountain ranges act as a major influence on weather systems, in the past were barriers to communications, and nowadays are seen as a recreational and tourism resource for both winter sports and 'lakes and mountains' summer holidays. The most important are:

- **The Alps** A series of high mountain ranges extending in an arc from southeastern France to Austria and Slovenia. Their great height is due to geologically recent earth movements, while the valleys were widened and deepened by glaciers during the last Ice Age. A number of large lakes were formed as a result of moraines – accumulations of glacial debris – blocking the valleys.
- **The Pyrenees** The mountain ranges extending from the Bay of Biscay east to the Mediterranean, and forming the boundary between France and Spain.
- **The Balkan mountain ranges** form a very rugged peninsula in south-eastern Europe bordered by the Adriatic, Aegean and Black Seas. Earthquakes are frequent in this region. There is a striking contrast between the coastlands that enjoy a Mediterranean climate, and the interior that experiences harsh winters.
- **The Carpathians** A series of mountain ranges forming a crescent around the Danubian Plains in the heart of Europe.
- **The Caucasus** lies far to the south-east, between the Black Sea and the Caspian (which is not really a sea, but a vast, partially saline lake). These mountains rise to even greater altitudes than the Alps.
- **The Kjolen Mountains** The spine of the Scandinavian Peninsula. These mountains differ from the other ranges in being geologically stable. The remnants of a much older mountain system than the Alps, over the ages they have been worn down to a series of high plateaus rather than rugged mountain peaks.

Europe's seas also deserve consideration in view of the importance of coastal tourism – in most countries with a coastline more than two-thirds of the accommodation stock is found at the seaside. Tourism is however only one of many uses of the coast, with the result that pollution and degradation of the marine ecosystems are serious problems, particularly in the following:

- **The Mediterranean**, although virtually an inland sea, is the focus of much of Europe's tourism. Not only are there a number of large industrial cities on the coast but the Mediterranean also attracts over 120 million holidaymakers each summer, far in excess of any other body of water of similar size. In other words, the Mediterranean accounts for only 0.7 per cent of the world's sea area but its shoreline attracts almost 20 per cent of the world's international tourism arrivals. Over 500 rivers flow into this enclosed sea, carrying all manner of pollutants. The natural cleansing action of the sea is reduced by the weakness of the tides, and the water is changed only once in every 90 years, through the Mediterranean's only outlet – the Straits of Gibraltar – to the Atlantic Ocean. The scope for international cooperation to mount clean-up operations and prevent further pollution is limited, and less than half of the shoreline belongs to EU countries.

- **The Baltic Sea** is a major focus for tourism but also the repository of many rivers and much industrial waste, particularly from the countries of the former Eastern bloc, where environmental controls are less stringent than those of Scandinavia.

Climatically, Europe is very varied – on the western fringes of the European plain Atlantic influences keep the climate mild, but unpredictable, whilst the further east one travels, the more extreme are the temperatures in both summer and winter. In the mountains long periods of high pressure bring clear skies and excellent visibility, whilst the Mediterranean climate is judged to be just about perfect for most tourism activities, with hot sunny summers and mild winters.

Cultural features

Europe does not represent a homogeneous population or society – there is a mosaic of languages, traditions and cultures. To Asian or African eyes, there are many cultural similarities between the countries of Europe, but these are much less obvious to a North American, or for that matter a British tourist, visiting the Continent. These cultural differences are rooted in history and partly determined by language and religion. The most striking differences in lifestyles, cultural traits and perhaps national temperaments are:

- Those between northern Europe and the 'Latin' south-west, so called because its languages – notably French, Italian, Portuguese and Spanish – are derived from Latin, the language of the Roman Empire, which once dominated southern Europe, and later the language of the Roman Catholic Church. Whereas the Protestant Reformation of the sixteenth century came to dominate most of northern Europe, it failed to take root south of the Alps.
- Those between Western and Eastern Europe. The differences here go much further back in time than the Cold War division of Europe between Russia and the Western powers between 1945 and 1989. Whereas Roman Catholicism dominated Western Europe in the Middle Ages, the eastern part of the continent was much more influenced by the Orthodox version of Christianity based at Constantinople, and disrupted by mainly Muslim invaders from Asia. The differences between east and west are shown in their starkest form in the former Yugoslavia in the conflict between Catholic Croatia and Orthodox Serbia. In contrast, in Western Europe the tensions between Catholics and Protestants have, to a large extent, disappeared, with the notable exception of Northern Ireland.
- Many of the mountain regions of Europe contain communities that are culturally different from those of the surrounding lowlands. Their former isolation helped preserve traditional lifestyles, but these are now increasingly under threat, partly as a result of tourism and second home development by affluent city-dwellers.

A complex history of interaction between the different cultures spanning more than two millennia has left a rich architectural heritage throughout Europe that is now an important tourist resource. At least as far as Western Europe is concerned, we can distinguish the following stages of cultural development as expressed by those monuments that survive:

- **Prehistoric** This is the long pre-literate period, embracing the Stone, Bronze and Iron Ages, from which date Stonehenge and similar megalithic structures in Minorca, Brittany and Malta.

- **Greco-Roman**   The heritage of the Romans – which in turn was influenced by ancient Greece – as expressed in their engineering achievements such as bridges and aqueducts as well as their temples, baths and arenas, can be found throughout the Roman Empire, which stretched from Hadrian's Wall to Palestine, and from the Rhine and Danube to the edge of the Sahara Desert in North Africa.
- **Romanesque**   The so-called 'Dark Ages' which followed the break up of the Roman Empire and the invasions of barbarian peoples from northern and eastern Europe, eventually produced the Romanesque style of architecture, expressed mainly in churches and monasteries of a simple but robust design. In the eastern Mediterranean, centred on Constantinople, the more elaborate Byzantine style developed, which eventually spread to Russia and other parts of eastern Europe.
- **Gothic**   In the twelfth century the Romanesque was replaced by the Gothic style of architecture, which originated in Northern France at the time of the Crusades, when the Catholic Church was at the height of its power. It is characterized by an emphasis on the vertical – notably soaring spires – and by an abundance of stained glass.
- **Renaissance–Baroque**   The Renaissance (rediscovery of classical learning), which started in Italy in the fifteenth century, was inspired by the design of ancient Greek and Roman temples. This was followed by the Baroque style of architecture, which emphasized colour and exuberant ornamentation.
- **Industrial Revolution**   The technological changes that took place in the nineteenth century resulted in the use of mass-produced building materials, and this was an age of great engineering achievements, particularly applied to transport.
- **Post-Industrial**   During the twentieth and twenty-first centuries, social as well as technological changes have led to a great emphasis on individuality of design in architecture and experimentation with new materials, often in the public buildings and tourism symbols of Europe – exemplified by Bilbao's stunning Guggenheim Museum.

Within contemporary Europe there are striking regional differences in economic development. Geographers have identified a core region extending from Birmingham to Milan where there is a pronounced concentration of industrial wealth, aided by excellent communications. The contrast between this central axis and the peripheral regions may become less evident in the future, and a secondary axis of development is already in evidence along the 'sunbelt' – the north shore of the Mediterranean from Barcelona to Genoa.

Demand for tourism

Europe's population exceeds 500 million people and represents a major tourism market for both the region and elsewhere in the world. There are a number of demographic trends impacting upon tourism:

- decreasing propensity to marry
- increasing diversity of lifestyles and living arrangements
- a trend to marrying later in life
- a decline in fertility
- an increase in the number of divorces
- an increase in immigration.

This means that the traditional family holiday will no longer be the norm in many countries, the elderly will become an important consideration in tourism. Also, the European market is not growing as fast as other regions of the world; to some extent, the rise of the eastern European market will offset the slower growth characteristic of Western Europe.

These social and demographic factors have resulted in a complex pattern of tourism demand in Europe, although the methods of collecting tourism statistics do differ between countries, making comparisons difficult. Western Europe takes the lion's share of international tourism, with about 35 per cent of arrivals, followed by southern Europe, with a share of over a quarter. However, there are clear signs that the traditional flow of tourists from the northern industrial areas to the south is diminishing for the following reasons:

- consumers are tiring of the inclusive-tour format
- the Mediterranean is becoming increasingly polluted
- traditional 'sun, sea and sand' holidays are less popular, as people become more aware of the risk of skin cancer
- competing destinations for other forms of tourism have become increasingly available
- new destinations are opening up in the east of Europe
- long-haul destinations are growing in popularity
- the adoption of the Euro has made what had been reasonably-priced destinations, such as Spain, more expensive.

The bulk of tourism in Europe is generated from within the region and only the USA is a major market from outside it, although 9/11 has significantly reduced travel from North America. Most countries are important destinations in their own right but Spain, Italy and France are clearly in the lead, not just for the region but also for the world as a whole. Estimates suggest that two-thirds of European international tourism is for leisure purposes, around 20 per cent is business travel and 15 per cent is VFR. The car is the dominant mode of transport because of the many short, cross-border trips, followed by air travel.

Of course, international tourism is an important feature of the European economy with a redistribution of wealth from north to south, which varies in significance from country to country. For example, in Spain and Portugal tourism is a significant source of export earnings in the form of foreign exchange, yet for the major generators of tourism (such as the Netherlands and Germany) tourism represents only a small percentage of the expenditure on imports, despite the volume of outbound travel. Tourism is therefore a vital ingredient in Mediterranean economies and the fall in arrivals is a major problem for these countries, demanding imaginative solutions. It is also these countries in southern Europe – particularly Portugal, Spain and Greece – which still have low levels of holiday-taking by populations who are less urbanized, and more family-centred than other parts of Europe. Seasonality is a major issue in European tourism, fuelled not only by climate but also by traditions. Although beach tourism (increasingly augmented by sports and activities) still dominates the European product, other sectors of tourism are on the increase. These and other trends include:

- Europeans continue to take more, but shorter tourism trips.
- Short-break city and cultural tourism is growing rapidly.

- Traditional north–south holidays are still a significant feature of European tourism, but east–west and west–east travel is growing rapidly.
- Significant market segments for the growth of tourism will be those aged over 55 years and those aged under 25 years of age.
- Intra-regional flows of tourism continue to dominate Europe's international tourism but their share is decreasing.
- The market is moving increasingly towards holidays that involve active pursuits, and/or exposure to local society and culture.
- The popularity of the car for leisure-based trips is decreasing, with an increase in the use of air travel, encouraged by the growth of budget airlines.
- Demand for business tourism in Europe will continue to be strong despite the growth of communication technologies.
- Capacity ceilings are being reached in some Western European countries, whereas countries in eastern and southern Europe have considerable growth potential.

Supply of tourism

Transport

The transport sector in Europe has been heavily influenced by deregulation.

- For air transport, deregulation has encouraged the development of regional airports and airlines and is taking pressure from the very busy routes between major cities, and from the north to southern holiday destinations. There are three key trends evident in the air transport sector in Europe:
  - the rapid growth of budget airlines is one result of increased competition on routes and they are taking passengers away from the traditional charter airlines
  - congestion in the skies over Europe is likely to become acute, necessitating a more unified system of air traffic control
  - the impact of 9/11 has been severe on Europe's national scheduled airlines.

Although deregulation also applies to surface modes of transport, its impact is less obvious, but other events will be important. The cross-Channel ferry industry, for example, has moved its activities to the western Channel to counter the effect of the Channel Tunnel; the European rail network is investing in high-speed routes which will eventually link the major European countries and could conceivably extend into Eastern Europe. Indeed, the continued investment in rail transport will see a gradual switch from road and air to rail travel. Although this is being done partly for environmental reasons it is not clear whether these lines will be cost-effective and they may even create their own pollution problems. For road transport, the disappearance of border controls, which will extend across the region as more countries are drawn into the European Union, will encourage international travel. There is already a network of Continental highways bearing the 'E' designation (for example, E1 running from Le Havre to Sicily and E2 from Paris to Warsaw via Nuremberg). Mountain ranges act as a constraint on overland transport, although the Alps separating northern and southern Europe are no longer a formidable barrier, with a number of tunnels and passes allowing year-round travel. However, any further road developments in the Alps will exacerbate the environmental problems, which are already acute.

On the supply side in Europe there are trends towards:

- A more deregulated and liberal environment for transport and other tourism sectors, although this has been set back by the need for the public sector to support the airlines following 9/11.
- Improved quality of existing provision of tourism supply in the former countries of the Eastern bloc.
- Diversification of products in established destinations, such as coastal resorts.
- Special interest, city-based, activity-centred developments growing at the expense of traditional beach resorts.
- Consumer and government support for sustainable tourism products and destinations.
- Cruising combined with special interest activities as a growth area.
- Expansion of business tourism facilities in the former Eastern bloc.

Attractions

The range of tourist attractions in Europe is impressive and many are of a high quality. Despite the drive to a unified Europe, very significant differences exist between the constituent countries, and this very diversity in a small area is a major part of Europe's attraction to tourists. A division can be seen in physical and cultural terms between the countries north and south of the Alpine ranges, and between those of Eastern and Western Europe.

- Southern Europe is the most climatically favoured area with a *pleasure periphery* of resorts in almost every country fringing the Mediterranean. Add to this the cultural and heritage attractions of many of these Mediterranean countries – for example, Greece and Italy – and the classic mix of a tourist destination is created. The climate is ideal for tourism, with hot and sunny summers followed by mild winters. It is therefore doubly tragic that the pollution and low-cost development in much of the Mediterranean has detracted from these natural and cultural attractions.
- The mountains of Europe, extending from the Pyrenees to the Carpathians, are also a major summer and winter destination. They are complemented by the uplands of northern Europe which tend to cater for a regional or local, rather than an international, market for outdoor recreation.
- The lowlands of Europe offer fewer natural attractions for tourism, but many of Europe's major cities are located here so business tourism and short sightseeing breaks are popular. It is also here that we see the development of theme parks and other market-based attractions. Examples include Disneyland Paris, Parc Asterix and Futuroscope in France; Warner Bros Studios and Port Aventura in Spain; and Legoland in England.

Accommodation

The accommodation and catering sectors are mainly characterized by small businesses throughout Europe; in the UK over one-half of accommodation establishments are independently owned, and in the Netherlands two-thirds have less than 16 rooms. There is, however, a trend towards dominance by large hotel chains such as the French group Accor. These can take advantage of the opportunities offered by globalization and an expanding EU to extend their operations all over Europe, including the former Eastern bloc countries.

Organization

The organization of tourism in Europe is complex. Each country has its own distinctive administration and traditions that influence both the public and private sector in tourism. Every country in Europe has a national tourism organization, supported by both regional and local organizations. Generally, the functions of these organizations are to develop and promote tourism, although in some cases their powers are more wide-ranging and include the registration and grading of accommodation as well as education and training. There is an identifiable trend towards devolution of tourism powers from the national level to regions, and a move to involve the private sector in the activities of the tourist boards. The individual organizations and their powers are described in the relevant chapters, but since the early 1980s, the European Union has also become involved in the organization and administration of tourism.

Summary

Europe is pre-eminent in world tourism, representing over half of international world arrivals, and has a large outbound and domestic tourism industry. This is because most of the region's economies are either in the high mass consumption stage or the drive to maturity, so the population, though ageing, is in general affluent, mobile and has a high propensity to travel. Europe also comprises many relatively small countries in close proximity, encouraging a high volume of short international trips. The region's climatic differences are significant and have led to a flow of tourists from the industrialized countries of northern Europe to the south. In terms of the organization of tourism in Europe, most governments have well-funded, competent tourist authorities with marketing and development powers and, as the region attempts to compete with other world destination regions, the role of the EU will become increasingly important to tourism. Europe's tourism infrastructure is mature and of a high standard, with a fully developed transport network. The tourism industry is also highly developed, with the largest regional concentration of accommodation in the world. Europe's rich mosaic of culture and physical features produces many tourist attractions of world calibre.

Chapter 7

An introduction to the tourism geography of Britain

Learning Objectives

After reading this chapter, you should be able to:

■ Appreciate that socioeconomic, technological and institutional factors present a powerful force in British society enabling the demand for tourism to be realized.

■ Be aware of changes in domestic tourism in Britain, and the factors that have brought about these changes.

■ Appreciate the volume and scope of both British residents' domestic tourism and tourism overseas, and the factors that have brought this about.

■ Understand the recent influences upon the volume of inbound tourism to Britain and the nature of the overseas market.

■ Recognize the importance of physical geography in influencing the tourism resource base.

■ Demonstrate a knowledge of the key components of tourism supply in Britain.

■ Understand the way in which tourism is administered in Britain.

Introduction

Geographically, Great Britain and Ireland are the two largest islands in the group known as the British Isles, lying off the north-west coast of Europe. They include two sovereign states – the United Kingdom of Great Britain and Northern Ireland (UK) and the Republic of Ireland. *Britain* comprises the three nations of England, Scotland and Wales, and so excludes Northern Ireland, which we cover along with the Republic in Chapter 10. The islands of Guernsey, Jersey and the Isle of Man are semi-independent states associated with the UK, but for geographical convenience we include the Channel Islands with England in Chapter 8 and the Isle of Man with Scotland and

Wales in Chapter 9. Although only a narrow stretch of water separates Britain from the Continent of Europe, this has been sufficient to give the British:

- a strong maritime outlook with interests extending to all corners of the globe, while the naval heritage is an important part of Britain's tourist appeal
- a cultural identity quite distinct from other west Europeans, the 'Narrow Seas' are often stormy and in the past have acted as a barrier against invaders from the European mainland.

The British, with their long tradition of travel and exploration, invented holidays in the modern sense, since Britain was the first country to experience the consequences of the Industrial Revolution. The importance of tourism is clearly illustrated by these statistics for the beginning of the twenty-first century:

- Overseas arrivals to the UK exceeded 24 million.
- The British took 58 million trips abroad.
- The British took 160 million domestic trips.
- Tourism was estimated to support over 2 million jobs directly and indirectly, and contribute almost 4.5 per cent of gross domestic product (GDP).

The setting for tourism

Physical features

Although Britain is relatively small in land area it offers great scenic variety as the setting for tourism, which can be categorized into three physical zones:

- The highland zone includes Central and North Wales, the Southern Uplands and the Highlands and Islands of Scotland. Here rocks are older, often impermeable, and high rainfall gives leached, infertile soils. The population is thinly scattered and land use is dominated by livestock rearing.
- The upland zone includes Exmoor, Dartmoor, the Brecon Beacons, the Black Mountains and the Pennines; and in Scotland, Caithness, Sutherland and the Orkneys. Here the rocks are younger, landforms more rounded, and distinctive regional differences are apparent (contrast the Yorkshire Dales with Dartmoor). Britain's national parks are mainly in the highland and upland zones where they have been designated for their natural beauty and characteristic landscapes.
- The lowlands nowhere exceed 300 metres in altitude and encompass much of southern and eastern England. The lowlands are warmer and drier, with intensive agriculture and sprawling conurbations dominating land use.

The coasts are of major importance, particularly for domestic tourism. The western coasts are deeply indented and rugged, with sandy coves and many offshore islands, in contrast to the east and south, where smooth, low-lying coasts are typical, with long beaches, spits, chalk cliffs, or dunes. Most of the more attractive stretches of coastline have been given protection as 'Heritage Coasts'.

Climate and weather

The latitudinal extent of the British Isles (from 50° North to 60° North) gives a diversity of climatic influences and conditions. Their location off the coast of mainland Europe does mean that the climate is tempered by maritime influences, especially in the south-west of England, where moist, mild conditions predominate. The British Isles are a battleground of different air masses and conditions are dependent upon either the nature of the dominant air mass at the time or the wet and stormy weather which results from the 'fronts' where the air masses meet. Low-pressure systems are constantly coming in from the Atlantic, and the western highlands and uplands bear the brunt of these systems, sheltering the lowland zone.

In winter, temperatures are lowest in the north-east of the British Isles and mildest in the south-west, but in summer the gradient changes to west–east, with cooler temperatures in the west, although sea temperatures are often lower along the North Sea coast, as the prevailing westerly winds are offshore. In the summer, too, sunshine figures are a source of keen competition between resorts. The south coast has the highest average duration of bright sunshine, with the number of sunshine hours decreasing inland, to the north, and with altitude.

If sunshine is the goal of many holidaymakers, precipitation is to be avoided (apart from snow in winter sports resorts). The highest precipitation is found over the higher ground of the west (the Lake District, Wales and the Scottish Highlands) which, at 2500 millimetres per year, is about four times as much as parts of eastern England. Precipitation falling as snow is more common in the highland and upland zones, and the colder east. In the Cairngorms in Scotland snow can lie for more than 100 days of the year and this has led to a major development of winter sports in the Aviemore area. Climate statistics can be deceptive and the variety of influences upon weather in the British Isles means that there are considerable differences from the average experience.

Changes in British society since the Second World War

Demand for tourism and recreation in Britain has grown at a phenomenal rate since 1945, not only in terms of volume but also in variety. The cause of this growth is rooted in the social and economic development of Britain since the Second World War; specifically, two major influences can be identified: social/economic and technological.

Social and economic influences

Social and economic changes in Britain have combined to boost demand for both domestic and international tourism. Since 1945 rising per capita incomes have brought higher purchasing power. The 1960s were a particularly prosperous period of high employment in which the first real stirrings of mass demand for holidays abroad were experienced. The following decades suffered the setbacks of energy crises, recession, and unemployment, but even so, real household disposable incomes per head have increased steadily, fuelling demand for tourism.

The dramatic increase in *car ownership* has played its part in revolutionizing holidaying habits. Car ownership has increased rapidly over the period and, in 2001, car ownership stood at over 25 million vehicles, and facilities for motorists have grown accordingly. For example, in 2001 the length of British motorway exceeded 3400 kilometres, bringing many holiday destinations within reach of the conurbations.

As a consequence of these developments, the number of passenger-kilometres driven increased considerably. However, rising concerns about the environmental impact of traffic have slowed government road building schemes and attempts are being made to curb the use of the car, especially in the cities, as in London with the introduction of a 'congestion charge' in 2003.

Increased affluence and personal mobility have been paralleled by an increase in both educational levels and access to education, and as a consequence there has been a heightened awareness of opportunities for tourism. In 2001 5 million students were in full-time higher or further education.

The *time available* for holidays has also grown with increased holiday entitlement, three-day weekends and various flexible-working arrangements providing blocks of time for trips away from home. Through the 1960s, for example, industry and services (such as retailing and banking) moved towards a five-day working week. This in itself is significant for the shorter-holiday market, but for the traditional long holiday, it is the annual entitlement that matters, and this has greatly increased since the Second World War. Since the 1990s, legislation at the European level has increased workers' entitlement to holiday and leisure time.

Perhaps surprisingly, the increase in demand for tourism and recreation has come more from changes in society brought about by the above factors than from any large increase in the population itself. Indeed, between 1951 and 2001 the population in Britain grew by less than 20 per cent, despite large-scale immigration. More important to tourism is the changing composition of the population. For example, the post-Second World War baby boom produced a generation that demanded tourism and recreation from the late 1970s onwards. Similarly, people are healthier and living longer than previous generations, and almost one-third of the population will be over the present retirement age (60/65) by 2030. This raises the question whether older people will be able to afford an active, leisured and affluent lifestyle, and the options available to government and society generally, faced with the situation of a declining birth rate and fewer economically active citizens, are a topical area of discussion.

Technology

These changes in society have gone hand in hand with technological innovations (aside from transportation, which we looked at in Chapter 5). For example:

- Breakthroughs in product design have brought a range of leisure goods within reach of the majority of the population (such as fibreglass boats, mountaineering equipment and specialist outdoor clothing).
- Technology, too, through the media and the Internet, has brought awareness of holiday and recreational opportunities to all, specifically through newspaper and magazine travel sections, television and radio programmes featuring holiday opportunities, the guidebooks produced by tourist boards and motoring organizations, and many websites featuring tourism destinations.
- The Internet and computer reservation systems have empowered both the tourism industry and the consumer to allow the assembly of tailor-made travel itineraries and rapid response to consumer demand.
- Finally, not only has technology released the workforce from mundane tasks as microprocessors and robot engineering are introduced, but labour-saving devices have also helped to reduce the time spent on household chores and released that time for leisure and tourism.

Demand for tourism

Inbound tourism

Britain is a major recipient of international tourists in the global scene while nationally tourism is an important earner of foreign currency. Overseas visitors come to Britain for heritage, culture, the countryside and ethnic reasons. The ebb and flow of tourist movements in and out of Britain is due to the relative strength of sterling against other currencies, the health of the economy, special event attractions, the impact of international and national crises and the marketing activities of both public and private tourist organizations.

The historical trend

- **The 1960s**   The early 1960s saw between 3 and 4 million overseas visitors coming to Britain, but with the devaluation of sterling in 1967 Britain became a very attractive destination.
- **The 1970s**   The number of overseas visitors had increased to almost 7 million visits by 1970. By the mid-1970s the weakness of the pound against other currencies made Britain the 'bargain basement' of the Western world and arrivals leapt to 11 million. This boom in inbound travel easily outpaced the depressed demand for overseas travel by British residents, and Britain enjoyed a surplus on its balance of payments travel account: in other words, spending by overseas visitors to Britain was greater than spending by British residents overseas. This was compounded by the Queen's Silver Jubilee in 1977, which increased arrivals to 12 million. By 1978 sterling was a stronger currency and Britain was experiencing high inflation.
- **The 1980s**   These latter two factors had the effect of increasing the real price of tourism services and goods in Britain and increased taxation on goods in the early 1980s led to a 'price shock' for overseas visitors. Britain was no longer a cheap destination and both visitor numbers and spending (in real terms) declined accordingly. This led to a deficit on the balance of payments travel account, the first for many years. World economic recession also depressed visits in the early 1980s but an upturn began in 1982, caused by a weaker pound and allied to economic recovery in the main generating areas of Western Europe and North America. Only in 1986 was this growth rate checked by the Libyan bombing, the Chernobyl disaster and the weakening of the US dollar.
- **The 1990s and the new millennium**   The period saw significant events that have profoundly influenced the trend of tourism to the UK. The opening of the Channel Tunnel changed the mode of transport of visitors to the UK and took market share from both air and sea arrivals, whilst deregulation of air travel within Europe and the emergence of budget airlines encouraged the growth of arrivals to regional gateways. In addition, world events – notably 9/11 – depressed international travel in 2001, while the outbreak of foot and mouth disease in the British countryside also had a negative impact. By the late 1990s, overseas visits to the UK had grown steadily to reach a peak of almost 26 million, but by 2001 they had fallen back to 23 million. Recovery began in 2002 with over 24 million arrivals. In the new millennium we can recognize the following trends for incoming tourism:
  - The origin of overseas visits to Britain is changing. Not only are the sources of travel becoming more diverse, but also visits from all major source areas have increased steadily. Visits from Western Europe form the majority of the market

at around two thirds of the total but are declining. Visits from North America have remained relatively stable at between 15 and 20 per cent of the total whilst new markets such as Eastern Europe have made a major contribution to arrivals over the decade. In the rest of the world, the major markets are Australia, New Zealand, the Middle East and Japan.

○ Length of stay is decreasing.
○ Independent travel is increasing.
○ Visitor spend is increasing.

Visitor characteristics

Aggregate figures conceal variations in the different segments of incoming tourism:

- Holiday visits grew rapidly up until 1977 (to almost half of total arrivals), but have declined slowly since that date, with considerable annual fluctuations, to reach 30 per cent by 2002.
- Visiting friends and relatives is a reliable and growing segment that has reached a plateau at 25 per cent of total arrivals. This is a particularly important sector of the Scottish market.
- Business travel has also grown steadily, accounting for 30 per cent of total arrivals in 2002.

Within the UK, both the geographical and seasonal distribution of overseas visitors is very concentrated. Geographically, almost 90 per cent of visitors are to England, with Scotland (7 per cent) and Wales (4 per cent) taking much smaller shares. Even within England, the pattern is concentrated on London, which as the capital, international gateway and world business centre receives almost half of all overseas visits, especially first-time arrivals. However, tourist authorities are anxious to spread the benefits of this spending to other areas by encouraging motoring and touring holidays (especially from Western Europe). Equally, encouraging traffic through the English Channel and North Sea ferry terminals, the Channel Tunnel and regional airports may reduce the dominance of London. Indeed, there is evidence that these measures are meeting with some success, with Glasgow and Edinburgh increasing their share of overseas visits. Seasonality is less of a problem than before, but the third quarter of the year still accounts for the highest percentage of overseas visitors to Britain.

Around 70 per cent of visitors to Britain arrive by air and less than 20 per cent by sea, with 12 per cent arriving through the Channel Tunnel. The share of sea-borne visits is declining due to:

- competition from the Channel Tunnel
- growth of budget airlines and regional air services
- deregulation of Ireland/UK air services.

British residents' demand for tourism

Britain's tradition of tourism has led to a high level of travel propensity in the population. Around 60 per cent of the British take a holiday in any one year, but, taken over a period of 3 years, this figure rises to 75 per cent as some enter and others leave the market in a particular year. Even so, there is a hard core of those who do not travel, especially the poor and the elderly.

The main growth in tourism has been overseas travel at the expense of the domestic long-holiday market. For the British tourism market as a whole the underlying factors fuelling growth – leisure spending, holiday entitlement and mobility – continue to rise. However, whilst outbound tourism continues to grow, domestic tourism can only share in this growth through the trend towards leisure day trips and shorter holidays.

Demand for domestic tourism

Although domestic tourism accounts for about 6 per cent of consumer spending, it contrasts sharply with international tourism out of Britain in the following ways:

- The length of stay is shorter.
- The level of spending is lower.
- It is more difficult to measure – in 1989 the four UK national tourist boards launched the United Kingdom Tourism Survey (UKTS), replacing previous surveys.

The historical trend

Holidays in Britain are inextricably linked with disposable income and general economic health:

- **The 1970s** The decade began with strong demand for domestic holidays in Britain. However, over the decade demand fluctuated and, in the face of changing economic factors, the share of domestic tourism experienced an absolute decline as that of overseas tourism by British residents increased.
- **The 1980s** Recessions adversely affected demand for domestic tourism and a number of factors came into play. First, domestic tourism is dominated by those in the lower socioeconomic groups who are more sensitive to price and changes in income or economic circumstances. Second, the industrial heartlands of the North, the Midlands, Scotland and South Wales, which traditionally generated high levels of demand for holidays at home, were particularly badly hit by the recessions. As a consequence, demand for holidays in Welsh and northern resorts fell. Finally, not only did inflation push up the cost of a holiday at home but also, at the same time, recession bred uncertainty about employment and holiday decisions were delayed. The mid-1980s saw a significant upturn in domestic tourism due to the increased cost of travel overseas, a weak pound and vigorous promotion of holidays in Britain. Hopes for the continuation of this increase were dashed in the late 1980s/early 1990s as recession and the Gulf War severely reduced domestic volumes and spending across the whole of the UK.
- **The 1990s and the new millennium** Whilst world events in the new millennium might have been expected to keep the British to holidaying at home, the outbreak of foot and mouth disease rendered large parts of the British countryside out of bounds. Nonetheless, the volume of domestic trips grew to over 160 million in 2002. Since the 1990s there have been important structural changes in the domestic tourism market:
  - a continued decline in length of stay
  - growth in the market for short holidays
  - growth of business and conference tourism

○ a shift away from traditional coastal destinations towards towns and countryside
○ a response by the coastal resorts to upgrade and reposition their facilities
○ an increased volume of trips to friends and relatives.

Visitor characteristics

Aggregate totals do disguise differences between the various sectors in Britain, but an important distinction in the domestic market is between a long holiday (four nights or more) and a short holiday (one to three nights). For some time, the general trend has been a gradual decline in domestic long holidays and an increase in short, often additional, holidays. Clearly, many short holidays are taken as 'additional' holidays to complement the 'main' holiday (which may be taken in Britain or overseas). The generation of domestic holiday trips is broadly proportional to the distribution of population across the British Isles. However, some areas have a relatively high holiday-taking propensity (London and the South-East of England) while others are comparatively low (Scotland, the North-West of England).

England is the dominant domestic holiday destination for the UK, with 80 per cent of mainland trips in 2002. Scotland accounts for 11 per cent of trips and Wales 7 per cent, with Northern Ireland approaching 2 per cent of the market. Within England, the West Country is by far the most popular destination. Britain's holiday islands – Guernsey, Jersey, the Isle of Man and the Isles of Scilly – account for over 2 million trips a year from the mainland.

Of course, holiday choices are difficult to explain and are subject to the vagaries of changing tastes and fashion. However, the basic principle of spatial interaction is in operation in the domestic market, with a supplying area containing a surplus of a commodity and the tourist-generating area possessing a demand for that commodity. For example, the South of England and the West Country are perceived to be sunny and warm, with their added advantages of an attractive coast, established resorts with a range of amenities and opportunities for touring. But set against these attractions is the problem of overcoming distance to reach the holiday destination from home.

Domestic tourism demonstrates a clear pattern in time as well as space. The trend towards short, additional holidays has gone some way towards reducing the acute seasonal peaking of domestic holidays, rooted in the timing of school and industrial holidays. Around 40 per cent of long holidays begin in July or August, but for short holidays, this figure falls to 20 per cent.

The business and conference sector of the domestic market has grown steadily, representing 12 per cent of total trips, but 15 per cent of total expenditure. Resorts, towns and cities hotly compete for this lucrative sector across Britain for these reasons:

○ It is not concentrated in the summer peak.
○ Business and conference tourists tend to use serviced accommodation.
○ This type of visitor spends much more per capita than the average holiday-maker.

Demand for outbound tourism

The UK consistently features among the world's top five tourist-generating countries. Indeed, the greatest market growth in tourism has been in trips overseas, which exceeded 58 million trips in 2001. Since the 1950s, the holiday sector in particular has exhibited strong growth, especially inclusive tourism to short-haul (mainly Mediterranean) destinations. This growth has been fuelled by:

- competitive pricing of inclusive tours
- the growth of budget airlines
- a strong consumer preference for overseas destinations
- an increasingly experienced outbound market.

In the future, growth in the market will be by an increase in travel frequency, rather than through newcomers to overseas travel attracted by the low fares offered by budget airlines.

The historical trend

Growth in the holiday sector stems from economic factors, but the activities of the travel trade since the 1950s have brought a holiday overseas within reach of a large percentage of the population. What has happened is that the increased organization of the travel industry coupled with the growth of travel intermediaries, such as travel agents and tour operators, has taken much of the responsibility of organizing a holiday away from the tourist. Add to this sophisticated marketing, pricing, reservations systems and the Internet, and it is clear that the travel industry has done much to convert suppressed demand into effective demand for holidays overseas. Taking the critical 20 years when growth was at its height, in 1970 only one-third of the population had ever taken a holiday overseas; by 1990 this figure was well over two-thirds. Clearly, this has implications for both products and destinations as the market matures.

- **The 1970s**   Between 1965 and 1972 the real price of inclusive tours fell by 25 per cent, due to increased use of jet aircraft, fierce price competition and the increased availability of winter holidays. This encouraged demand, only to see it dashed by the oil crisis of 1973/1974 and the bankruptcy of a major tour operator. The mid-1970s saw fluctuations in the numbers of holidays taken overseas as higher oil prices, weak sterling, economic recession and higher holiday prices took their toll. In the late 1970s, a strong pound, cheaper holidays/air fares and vigorous marketing increased demand to a growth rate of 20 per cent per annum. At the same time, high inflation pushed up the price of a domestic holiday, and with the British beginning to view the annual holiday as a priority, overseas holidays grew in popularity.
- **The 1980s**   The decade of the 1980s saw virtually uninterrupted growth in overseas holiday trips. Four key underlying causes can be identified:
  - thanks partly to North Sea oil, Britain was a wealthier country with a relatively strong currency *vis-à-vis* popular holiday destinations
  - real discretionary income rose for those sections of the population with a preference for overseas travel (the young, the upwardly mobile and the higher socioeconomic groups)
  - a sophisticated tour operation and distribution system, allied to high spending on promotion, made overseas travel accessible also to lower socioeconomic groups
  - competitive pricing of inclusive tours.
- **The 1990s and the new millennium**   The market continued to grow into the twenty-first century, despite the setbacks of 9/11 and other world events, leaving a considerable deficit on the UK's travel account. The outbound market is

influenced by a number of factors:

○ acquisition and merger in the tour operator/travel agency sector leading to an increased concentration of capacity in the hands of a few companies
○ the deregulation of European airlines, blurring the distinction between charter and scheduled services and allowing the growth of budget airlines
○ opening of the Channel Tunnel leading to a response by the ferry companies in terms of new ships and routes in the western English Channel
○ effective devaluation of the pound in 1992 when the UK left the European Monetary System
○ introduction of a tax on air passenger departures
○ introduction of the Euro as European currency
○ competitive pricing of long-haul destinations such as Florida and the Far East.

Visitor characteristics

The level of spending on overseas trips confirms the high priority given to overseas travel by the British. Examining the reason for the visit, holiday tourism is growing, representing two-thirds of trips; business tourism accounts for 15 per cent and VFR for 12 per cent of trips.

In total, almost three-quarters of trips are by air, compared to 16 per cent of trips by sea while almost 10 per cent use the Channel Tunnel. The modal split changed in the 1990s due to the influence of the Channel Tunnel (which provided the first fixed link to the Continent) and European airline deregulation. Holiday arrangement – inclusive tour or independent – has also changed with a growth in independent travel, as the relative share of inclusive tours shrinks (just over one-third of all trips in 2001). The fact that a large majority of the British population has experienced a holiday overseas has led to an increased number who feel confident to travel independently. For these travellers, France is the most important destination. However, this new breed of experienced travellers now travels further and to a greater range of countries.

In the new millennium the most popular destinations continue to be Spain, France, Ireland, North America, Italy and Greece. Clearly, Western Europe dominates, with the USA the only non-European country with considerable drawing power. In line with this and recent trends worldwide, long-haul destinations are a sector showing considerable growth. Business trips have remained buoyant over the decade and trade with EU member states generates a significant volume of surface travel for business purposes.

Three key influences will determine the volume and nature of the UK market for travel overseas in the future:

• prospects for the UK economy and relationships with Europe and the Euro
• changes in consumer habits and attitudes, particularly with regard to green issues
• the growing maturity of leisure markets in terms of the products offered and the response of consumers.

Supply of tourism

This section examines the various components of tourism in Britain from a geographical viewpoint. Those involved in the industry now have an organization – the Tourism Alliance – that can represent their views to the government.

Transport

Travellers entering Britain can do so through a variety of gateways, but in fact both air and surface transport networks focus on the south-east of England.

- **Air** Over 80 per cent of international passengers travelling by air are channelled through the London airports and airlines are reluctant to move out from these gateways. Manchester has been identified as the UK's second major airport and Glasgow's international status has stimulated major growth. Airports on Guernsey, Jersey and the Isle of Man complete the network, and although holiday traffic to these islands is not inconsiderable, it has a highly seasonal pattern. Overall, Britain's major airports handled around 142 million passenger movements in 2001.
- **Sea** For sea traffic, there is again a concentration of passengers in southern England due to the dominance of cross-Channel ferry routes. Elsewhere there is a diversification of routes such as those from Hull and Harwich on the east coast. A second concentration of routes is from the west coasts of mainland Britain to the Republic of Ireland and Northern Ireland. On the sea routes the upgrading of ships and the introduction of high-speed 'catamarans' is a response both to the threat of the Channel Tunnel and the rise in the expectations of travellers.
- **The Channel Tunnel** The 'Channel' opened in 1994 and has not only stimulated new traffic, but also taken traffic from both air and especially sea services to Europe. Its impact is expected to continue as high-speed rail links are developed on the English side of the Tunnel. Interestingly, the response of ferry operators to develop routes in the western English Channel has been less successful than hoped. Other responses have been mergers on the short sea routes, closure of some routes (Newhaven to Dieppe for example) and price competition.
- **Land transport** In the domestic holiday market, and for overseas travellers touring Britain, road transport dominates. Since the Second World War the use of the car has become more important than either rail or coach services, as road improvements have been completed and the real cost of motoring has fallen. The 1980 Transport Act revolutionized bus/coach operations in the UK by deregulating services. Coach travel poses a very real alternative to the railways on journeys of up to 400 kilometres and the new generation of luxury coaches have increased passenger numbers for this type of public transport. Privatization of British Rail in the mid-1990s resulted in train services being operated by a multiplicity of companies while the permanent way and terminals remained the responsibility of a separate organization. There has been much private sector investment, particularly on some inter-city routes and those serving coastal and inland holiday areas. There are also over 40 small private railways outside the network which are tourist attractions in themselves, trading on nostalgia for the 'age of steam'.

Attractions

It is in areas such as national parks and the hinterlands of major resorts that the most successful point tourist attractions lie. Since the 1990s, tourist attractions in the UK have received a major funding boost from the Heritage Lottery and Millennium funds, which have directed money to develop new attractions and improve many existing ones. Indeed, these initiatives have begun to transform the leisure landscapes of Britain. The UK has some 6400 tourist attractions and their very diversity of size, type and ownership makes classification difficult but Patmore (1983) has identified three basic types:

- Many attractions simply result from the opening of an existing resource – an ancient monument, stately home or nature reserve.
- Some attractions have begun to add developments (such as the motor museum and monorail at Beaulieu Palace) to augment the attraction and broaden their appeal. The varying shades of provision in the English and Welsh *country parks* mean that they should also be included in this second category.
- The third type of attraction is one artificially created for the visitor, including theme parks such as Alton Towers, the London Zoo, or heritage attractions such as 'Wigan Pier'. The government and the tourist boards are anxious to improve the professionalism of tourist attractions and to diversify the range on offer – which now includes coal-mining museums – capitalizing on Britain's rich industrial heritage.

Accommodation

Although the major cities account for much of the stock of serviced accommodation, around 40 per cent of beds in hotels and guest houses are located at the seaside, especially on the south and south-western coasts of England, and in North Wales. However, much of this accommodation is in outmoded Victorian and Edwardian buildings – establishments that do not meet the aspirations of contemporary holidaymakers. Both the public and private sectors are trying to remedy this problem and ensure that accommodation supply matches demand. The real change in holiday tastes has been for self-catering accommodation; between 1951 and 2001 the proportion of main holidays in England based on self-catering rose from 12 to over 30 per cent. Self-catering developments were initially in holiday camps, later in caravan parks, and more recently in purpose-built leisure complexes with provision for a range of sports and other activities. The first of these all-weather complexes was opened by the Dutch company Centre Parcs in Sherwood Forest. This has since expanded its operations as well as taking over the Oasis holiday village in Whinfell Forest on the edge of the Lake District National Park, which was originally established as a competitor. At the same time the holiday camps, pioneered by Butlin before the Second World War, have had to upgrade their facilities and reposition themselves in the marketplace as tastes have changed. In major towns and cities, demand from business and overseas travellers keeps bed occupancy rates high. Here provision tends to be in the larger, expensive hotels (often with more than 100 bedrooms).

Accommodation is also dispersed along routeways and in rural areas. Initially, board and lodging for travellers was found on stage-coach routes and later, during the nineteenth century, at railway termini and major seaports. More recently, airports and air terminals have attracted the development of large, quality hotels (as at Heathrow and in west London) and motorway service areas now also offer budget accommodation – the equivalent of the old coaching inns. In rural areas accommodation is concentrated in south-west England, Scotland and Wales. There is a growing demand for farm holidays, self-catering cottages and 'time-share' developments. It is also the rural areas that bear the brunt of second-home ownership, with social consequences for declining village communities.

Organization

Public agencies with responsibility for tourism in Britain play a vital role in shaping the tourist 'product', through their promotional activities and advice to business enterprises. Increasingly, government is 'devolving' these functions from national level to regional and local organizations.

National level

In Britain the 1969 Development of Tourism Act formed three statutory national tourist boards (English, Scottish and Wales Tourist Boards) and the British Tourist Authority (BTA) which was given sole responsibility for overseas promotion and any matters of common interest between the national tourist boards. The Scottish and Wales Tourist Boards (STB and WTB) reported to the Scottish Office and the Welsh Office respectively. The Northern Ireland Tourist Board predates these bodies, having been created in 1948.

In the 1990s the administration of tourism throughout mainland Britain was reorganized as a result of changes in the perception of the role of the public sector, and with the devolution of power to Scotland and Wales in 1999 their tourist boards could undertake overseas promotion. In England, the focus has been changed to be more strategic and less operational, and in 1999 an ambitious national strategy – 'Tomorrow's Tourism' – was designed to coordinate government actions affecting the sector. This coincided with the creation of the English Tourism Council (ETC) from the English Tourist Board, followed by the merger of the ETC with the BTA in 2003 to form VisitBritain, which is primarily a marketing agency for both domestic and international tourism. At ministerial level the Department for Culture, Media and Sport oversees the work of VisitBritain. In Ireland a similar degree of change is under way as 'Failte', an all-Ireland agency has been created. Guernsey, Jersey and the Isle of Man each continue to have small, relatively independent boards reporting directly to their island governments.

Regional and local level

The increasing emphasis on devolution is shown by the regional development agencies, which receive tourism funding for development, and across the UK there is a structure of regional tourist boards (RTBs). There are ten RTBs in England, and three regional tourism companies in Wales. In Scotland, a major restructuring at the regional level has given rise to 18 Area Tourist Boards, with enterprise agencies taking responsibility for development. At the local level throughout Britain, county and district councils have considerable powers that they can use for tourism promotion and development.

Tourism resources

Britain's tourism resource base is remarkably diverse, including a number of national parks and other areas subject to varying degrees of protection under planning law. In England and Wales national parks are required both to preserve their landscapes and to enhance their enjoyment by the public. It is not always easy to balance these objectives, as unlike those of North America and Africa, Britain's national parks contain sizeable communities, and to a large extent their landscapes have been modified by farming and mining activities over the centuries. Multiple use is also characteristic of the areas managed by the British Forestry Commission, whose primary aim is to reduce the country's dependence on timber imports. The Commission is charged with opening up the forests for recreation and tourism, and it has developed self-catering cabins in holiday areas for this purpose. 'Community forests' have also been designated on the edge of conurbations on land previously used for agriculture and industry.

Britain also boasts many scenic lakes and reservoirs, but demand for their recreational use outstrips supply. This has led to intensive management of lakes such as Windermere and Lake Bala as well as the Norfolk Broads. Other linear features include rivers and canals, both of which are extensively used for recreation, as are the Heritage Coasts and national hiking trails, such as the Pennine Way. Government provision for tourism and recreation is complemented by conservation trusts and charities, notably the National Trust (NT) which has purchased extensive areas of attractive coast and countryside, as well as a large number of historic buildings.

Regional landscapes and character often feature in the novels of British writers and the marketing of a particular area often capitalizes on these literary associations; for example South Tyneside has been promoted for many years as 'Catherine Cookson Country' and Carmarthenshire in Wales as 'Dylan Thomas Country'. However, association with a celebrity (for example Bedfordshire as 'Glenn Miller Country'), a well-known TV series, or a feature film are perhaps less easy to justify.

The tourist regions of Britain are covered in detail in Chapters 8 and 9.

Summary

Britain is a major generator of both domestic and international tourism. Demand for tourism has grown rapidly since the Second World War for social and economic reasons. Around 60 per cent of the British population now take a holiday in any one year, but, even so, there is a hard core of those who do not travel. The long-established pattern of domestic holidays spent at the seaside is changing with the trend towards shorter holidays. The demand by residents of Britain for holidays abroad has increased steadily since the Second World War and the UK is consistently one of the world's top tourist generators. A combination of economic circumstances and the response of the travel industry has converted suppressed demand into effective demand for holidays abroad. Britain is a major recipient of overseas tourists on the global scene and this demand is influenced by the relative strength of currencies, the health of the economy, special events, external world events such as 9/11 and the marketing activities of tourist organizations.

Britain offers a rich variety of landscapes and weather conditions, broadly categorized into the highland zone, the uplands, and the lowlands, but the climate is everywhere tempered by maritime influences. The main components of tourist supply in Britain are a diversity of attractions from national parks to purpose-built theme parks; a wide accommodation base focused on the coasts and the major cities; and a comprehensive internal transport network, as well as international gateways of global significance, including the major innovation of the Channel Tunnel. Tourism in Britain is administered by a newly reorganized structure of organizations involving the private as well as the public sectors.

Chapter 8
The tourism geography of England and the Channel Islands

Learning Objectives

After reading this chapter, you should be able to:

- Demonstrate a knowledge of the main tourist regions in England.
- Understand the distribution and importance of England's coastal resorts and resources, especially for domestic tourism.
- Recognize the role of the industrial and naval heritage in defining England's tourism product.
- Recognize the appeal of the English countryside to tourists.
- Understand the importance of London and other major cities as centres for business and leisure tourism.
- Characterize the tourism resources of the offshore islands.

Introduction

England offers the tourist a great variety of scenery; this is partly due to differences in geology – for example the contrast between chalk downlands, sandstone or limestone ridges, and clay vales. These have not only influenced the shape of the countryside but also the traditional building materials used in rural communities. However, much of the English countryside we see today was the creation of the Enclosure Acts of the eighteenth century. This important resource is increasingly under threat as a result of changes in farming practices, such as the removal of hedgerows.

As well as the countryside, England's heritage resources include the following:

- Many ancient monuments and historic buildings from medieval times, such as castles, abbeys and cathedrals.

- The great country houses of the landowning class. Many of these 'stately homes' are now major tourist attractions.
- Fine examples of Georgian and Regency architecture from the eighteenth and early nineteenth centuries in England's spas, seaside resorts, market towns and cities.
- Maritime heritage, especially that related to the Royal Navy's role in the defence of the realm. This was given wide publicity in 2003 through the feature film *Master and Commander*.
- The legacy of the Industrial Revolution, which, particularly in the Midlands and the North of England, has recently undergone a re-appraisal and forms the basis of a growing number of heritage attractions.

Separate government agencies are involved in the protection of the countryside and the conservation of historic buildings/monuments – where English Heritage rivals the National Trust as a provider of opportunities for history-based tourism. However, in focusing on heritage, it is easy to overlook the major contribution to tourism made by England's contemporary arts, culture and entertainment industries, as well as sports events.

Tourism resources of England

For convenience, we have divided England for tourism purposes into a number of geographical regions. These are based on the areas covered by the regional tourist boards, but sometimes regional boundaries are arbitrary and the historic counties have greater significance for both visitors and local communities.

The South

Aside from London, two regional tourist boards – the South-East and Southern – cover the south of England. The South is the UK's main gateway region for all modes of transport, and is also a major concentration of population, wealth and commercial activity. As a consequence, this part of England suffers more than other region from the problems of economic growth, including congestion on air and surface transport routes. These problems are particularly evident in London and the adjacent Home Counties for the following reasons:

- London is the focus of national communications, including the main railway termini, the Channel Tunnel terminal, a major coach interchange, and the busiest motorways. It is circled by airports (Heathrow, Gatwick, Stansted, London City Airport and Luton) which are fundamental to the international network of air services.
- London is one of the world's great cosmopolitan cities with a population of well over 7 million, attracting overseas and domestic tourists as well as day visitors.

London offers the ceremonial and architectural heritage of Britain's imperial past, world-class tourist attractions, shopping and nightlife. As well as the great showpieces of Church and State – notably St Paul's Cathedral, the royal palaces and the Houses of Parliament – most of the nation's leading museums and art galleries are located here. Since the 1990s a range of new attractions have been developed, some as a result of Millennium funding, including:

- the FA Premier League Hall of Fame, showcasing soccer
- the London Aquarium
- Churchill's Cabinet War Rooms, commemorating his leadership in the Second World War
- Rock Circus
- the Millennium Wheel – now the London Eye. (Like the Eiffel Tower in Paris a century earlier, this was not originally meant to be a permanent attraction, but very soon became a much-loved feature of the city's skyline, in contrast to the Millennium Dome)
- the Millennium Bridge, enhancing the appeal of the river Thames
- London Zoo's Millennium Conservation Centre.

Tourism does add to the capital's traffic problems, especially in the central area, where most of the attractions and quality hotels are situated. This area includes:

- the City of London, which was the original trading nucleus on the north bank of the Thames, and is now a major centre of international finance. Since it has only a small resident population, it is almost traffic-free at weekends. The annual Lord Mayor's Show is a reminder of the traditions of 'The City' and its separate identity.
- the City of Westminster, which was once the seat of royal power, and is now the nation's administrative centre, including most of the 'West End', where luxury trades and entertainment originally developed to serve the court and the aristocracy.
- the Royal Borough of Kensington and Chelsea, with its quality shopping and world-class museums.

Tourist pressure is a particular problem for London's historic buildings, but set against this is the fact that tourism contributes to London's economy through spending and jobs. It also helps to support the West End theatres, department stores and other amenities that Londoners enjoy.

Following the abolition of the Greater London Council based at County Hall in 1986, it was difficult to coordinate the tourism policies of the 33 London boroughs. With the formation of the Greater London Authority (GLA) in 1999 there is once again a single body, with an elected London Assembly and mayor, to implement strategies for tourism and transport covering the metropolitan area. Here the London Development Agency which is responsible for promotion and the London Tourist Board plays an important role. Even so the GLA has a limited budget for tourism compared to say, New York City. A congestion charge was imposed in 2003 to price out non-essential traffic from the central area, and Trafalgar Square was partly pedestrianized. Efforts have been made to 'spread the load' of tourist pressure to lesser-known attractions outside central London, such as Islington, Greenwich and the former dock area to the east. London Docklands is one of the world's largest examples of inner city regeneration, involving the redevelopment of almost 90 kilometres mainly for residential or commercial use. There are facilities for water sports and attractions based on London's historic role as a great port. To the west of London there is a cluster of well-established attractions, including Hampton Court, Kew Gardens (now a World Heritage Site), the Thames at Richmond and the London Wetlands Centre.

London is the setting for many special events in the sporting and arts calendar which draw hundreds of thousands of visitors, notably the Notting Hill Carnival, Wimbledon (tennis), Twickenham (rugby union), soccer finals and cricket test matches. London was the first city to stage an international trade exhibition (in 1851), and continues to attract business and conference tourism on a vast scale. While there are a number of purpose-built facilities – ExCel, the Barbican Conference Centre, the Queen Elizabeth II Conference Centre, Olympia and Earl's Court – much of the activity takes place in the capital's larger hotels that have world class facilities for meetings. Even with the 200 000 beds presently available, there is a shortage of accommodation in London. There are new developments to address this problem, notably in the budget hotel sector and in converted buildings such as the former County Hall.

The countryside of the Home Counties has been protected by a 'green belt' from the sprawl of Greater London. This includes two Areas of Outstanding Natural Beauty (AONB) – the Chilterns to the north-west of London and the North Downs in Surrey – where country parks, picnic sites and trails focus visitor pressure. The range of tourist attractions includes:

- St Albans Cathedral
- 'stately homes' such as Blenheim Palace (Churchill's birthplace), Clandon Park, Knebworth, Luton Hoo, Polesden Lacey and Woburn Abbey – one of the first to appeal to the mass market by providing additional attractions to the house and gardens
- Whipsnade Wild Animal Park
- the Grand Union Canal, one of England's most popular waterways.

The Thames flows through several towns that feature prominently on the *milk run* – the standard excursion circuit for foreign tourists. In Oxford the university's historic colleges, libraries and museums are the main attraction; here the conflict between tourist pressure and the historic townscape is recognized but as yet unresolved. Windsor, further downstream, is a classic example of the tension between tourism and local interests. Windsor's key attractions – associated with royalty over the centuries – are the Castle and St George's Chapel. This small town is inundated with coaches in the summer months and has introduced a strict management regime. Henley is famous for its regatta, in an area noted for boating activities. Other attractions in the Thames Valley include the historic site of Runnymede, Ascot racecourse and new developments such as the Lookout Discovery Centre and the Roald Dahl Gallery. A number of theme parks – Legoland, Thorpe Park and Chessington World of Adventures – have been located in the Windsor/north Surrey area to take advantage of the motorway ring around London and the access this provides to a major concentration of demand. The city of Guildford is also well situated as a focus for business tourism and tourism education.

To the south-east of London, **Kent** is both the 'Garden of England' – with its orchards, hop farms and country houses – and the historic gateway for visitors from the Continent. As a result it has been the focus of considerable development pressure in association with the Channel Tunnel and its rail link to London. It is also the focus of the demand for 'out of town' shopping, where new developments include the Bluewater leisure and shopping centre – the largest in Europe. The Channel ports, notably Folkestone, have declined in the face of severe competition from the Channel Tunnel. To mitigate the loss of jobs, Dover has developed a major themed attraction – 'The White Cliffs Experience' – highlighting its dual role as gateway and fortress from Roman times to the Second World War. Although many of the coastal towns of Kent are attractive centres of tourism (Broadstairs, Ramsgate, Whitstable, Herne Bay) or historic and important resorts (Margate), the industrialization of the south side of the Thames estuary conflicts with tourism, while the improvement in communications is a mixed blessing, as the area now faces competition from northern France as a destination for Londoners. The Historic Dockyard at Chatham is an example of how England's naval heritage has been adapted to become a popular tourist attraction, while Rochester has capitalized on its associations with Charles Dickens.

Kent boasts many historic buildings, of which the most famous are Hever Castle and Leeds Castle –a major heritage attraction and conference venue. The following market towns are important tourist centres:

- Ashford, now given added importance as a Channel Tunnel rail terminal
- Tonbridge, with its Norman castle
- Royal Tunbridge Wells, with its chalybeate spa
- Canterbury, the spiritual capital of England and of the worldwide Anglican community; the cathedral and the themed 'Canterbury Tales' exhibition, recalling its importance as a centre of pilgrimage in medieval times, are a major attraction for domestic and overseas visitors.

Westwards along the coast in **Sussex**, historic towns such as Rye compete for attention with the large well-established resorts of Eastbourne, Brighton, Hove, Littlehampton, Worthing, and Bognor Regis. Brighton in particular has been successful in attracting a younger clientele while other resorts have declined. It has good transport links to London and is arguably more sophisticated than other English seaside resorts, with a readiness to accept alternative lifestyles. Brighton has the usual holiday attractions (except for a good beach) but it can also offer a unique architectural fantasy (the Royal Pavilion), a purpose-built marina and conference centre, and it is the stage for cultural events such as the Brighton Film Festival. In a bid to attract new markets, Hastings has developed themed attractions – the 1066 Story, Smugglers' Adventure, the Shipwreck Heritage Centre and a Sealife Centre. Although much of the Sussex coastline has been overdeveloped, significant natural features such as the Seven Sisters are protected by the National Trust and through designation as Heritage Coast. A short distance inland, the South Downs AONB owes its character as open, rolling grassland to centuries of farming practice, and many fear that designation as a national park will increase visitor impacts and antagonize local farmers. Historic towns in the area include Chichester with its cathedral and Festival theatre, and Arundel, which features a castle and a cathedral in a spectacular setting.

The counties of Dorset and Hampshire form a major part of the area covered by the Southern Tourist Board, and of the vaguely defined region known as **Wessex**, which is loosely based on the Anglo-Saxon kingdom of that name and the novels of Thomas Hardy. The two counties offer a variety of resources for tourism, including:

- A number of harbours with facilities for sailing, such as Christchurch, Lymington, Poole, and Cowes – with its famous yachting Regatta. The Solent, separating the Isle of Wight from the mainland,. is one of Europe's finest coastal waterways.
- Large areas of unspoiled countryside, particularly Cranborne Chase and the much visited New Forest. The New Forest is an environmentally sensitive area with a unique landscape under severe pressure from tourism and recreation. Today, the landscape, flora and fauna are conserved under a variety of pieces of legislation which give it national park status in all but name. Visitor pressure in the Forest arises from the adjacent Bournemouth and Southampton conurbations, and the fact it is easily accessible through the national motorway network. Managing the growing numbers of visitors is vitally important, given their possible impact on local communities and the sensitive wildlife habitats that visitors find so appealing. This will be achieved by the tourism strategy for the New Forest.
- The Dorset coast is a classic fieldwork area for geographers and geologists, attracting many educational visits to the fossil beds near Lyme Regis, Chesil Beach and Lulworth Cove. Careful management is needed to reduce the impact of visitors on the Dorset Coastal Path and at popular sites such as Studland and Lulworth Cove.
- England's naval heritage is the focus of a maritime leisure complex regenerating Portsmouth's harbour area, where visitors can inspect historic ships from different eras, namely Henry VIII's *Mary Rose*, Nelson's *Victory* and *HMS Warrior*. The adjoining seaside resort of Southsea has invested in attractions such as the Blue Reef aquarium, the Pyramids leisure pool and the D-Day Museum, which highlights Portsmouth's role in the Second World War.
- Southampton also has an important maritime heritage relating to the era of the great ocean liners, but this tends to be eclipsed by the city's role as a regional administrative and shopping centre.
- The Bournemouth conurbation (embracing Poole and Christchurch) is the region's major holiday destination with one of the largest concentrations of tourist accommodation outside London. It is also a major provider of English language schools, so that the spend of foreign students contributes significantly to the local economy. Bournemouth has successfully adapted to change, updating its former genteel image, to attract the youth market with a vibrant club scene, and at the same time has retained its appeal to the family market and senior citizens. Although Bournemouth's beachfront remains less commercialized than other major resorts, the council has invested in a major international conference centre among other attractions, and has been foremost in launching sports events and festivals. To some extent Poole has been overshadowed by Bournemouth, but the redevelopment of its historic quay should raise its tourism profile significantly.
- Weymouth is both a historic seaport and one of England's oldest seaside resorts. Regeneration initiatives include the 'Timewalk' exhibition and speciality shopping at Brewer's Quay.
- Swanage is a small family resort in an attractive setting backed by the Purbeck Hills.
- Winchester is the most important of the region's historic towns. At one time a royal capital, with a famous castle and cathedral, it has moved with the times as shown by INTECH 2000 – an interactive learning centre. Other tourist centres include Dorchester, with its Thomas Hardy associations, Wimborne, Sherborne and Bridport.
- The Isle of Wight is an important holiday destination in its own right, offering a choice of family resorts such as Ryde, Shanklin and Ventnor, and is responding to

the challenge of its competitors with attractions based on local finds of dinosaur fossils. The island is linked to Lymington, Portsmouth and Southampton by car and passenger ferry services.

The West Country

The area covered by the West Country Tourist Board includes the counties of Cornwall, Devon, Somerset and Wiltshire. The **South West Peninsula** corresponds geographically to the major part of the region, offering two attractive coastlines, fine scenery – including two national parks – and a mild, relatively sunny climate (which has given rise to such advertising slogans as 'The Cornish Riviera' and more recently 'The English Riviera'). The M5 motorway and increased car ownership have made the region much more accessible and ensured its continued popularity with the domestic market. Tourism is important for employment and income generation in a largely rural region with few alternative industries, although seasonality is a problem.

The countryside is a major tourism resource throughout the region, encouraging farm stays and activity holidays. Many of the picturesque villages with their craft workshops are linked by themed routes for cycling, hiking or riding. Perhaps the best known of these is the 'Tarka Country' trail in north-west Devon, which is held up as a classic example of sustainable tourism. As the West Country largely escaped the Industrial Revolution, many of the market towns have preserved a rich architectural heritage and some now act as regional tourism centres – for example Truro, Barnstable, Taunton, Marlborough and Salisbury. However, the coast of the South West Peninsula is the best-known feature, through the experiences of successive generations of British holidaymakers since Victorian times. Most of this varied and often beautiful coastline is protected by National Trust ownership or Heritage Coast policies, which effectively prevent the encroachment of industry or insensitive tourism development. The coast provides many recreational opportunities, notably surfing off the more exposed beaches, sailing in the sheltered estuaries, and long-distance paths for hiking.

Cornwall epitomizes the beach tourism product of south-west England, but it is different in character from other parts of the region – with its granite cliffs and Celtic heritage, where the Cornish language is recalled by the distinctive place names. As a peninsula, Cornwall has the advantage of both an Atlantic and Channel coastline, but a peripheral location is also a disadvantage in terms of accessibility and possibilities for touring. The county also faces high unemployment with the decline of its traditional mining and fishing industries. A number of attractions are based on this maritime and industrial heritage, while the small fishing ports of the south coast, such as Fowey, Looe, Mevagissey and Polperro, have preserved much of their character. Cornwall's tourism resources also include:

- the surfing beaches along the Atlantic coast, focusing on the resorts of Bude, Newquay and Polzeath
- the large family resorts of Falmouth and Penzance
- the impressive coastal features of Land's End and St Michael's Mount
- the mild climate that has made possible an ambitious garden restoration project – the Lost Gardens of Heligan, with their sub-tropical vegetation
- the Eden Project, backed by Millennium funding, is another example of reclamation – in this case a former china clay pit has been transformed into a series of climate-controlled domes representing the world's major ecosystems

- Tintagel and Bodmin Moor, associated with the legends of King Arthur
- the county's dramatic landscapes and seascapes have been an inspiration to writers and artists; St Ives in particular is a well-established 'artists' colony', with a branch of the Tate Gallery and the Barbara Hepworth Museum attracting many visitors.

With the exception of Dartmoor, Devon and Somerset are characterized by a gentler, more wooded landscape, where dairy farming is the predominant land use. Areas of Outstanding Natural Beauty account for a large part of the two counties, while the two national parks differ greatly in character. Dartmoor is a bleak, treeless moorland punctuated by granite masses known as 'tors'. Exmoor is visually appealing and has been romanticized for tourism promotion as 'Lorna Doone Country'.

The maritime heritage includes reminders of the Elizabethan age of overseas expansion, in which the small ports of north Devon – Appledore and Bideford – played an important role as well as Bristol, Dartmouth and Plymouth. There is a wide choice for beach holidays; in south Devon the large resorts around Torbay – Brixham, Paignton and Torquay – are distinct in character and cater for different market segments, yet are promoted together as the English Riviera. They have been the focus of a tourism development plan and share the English Riviera Conference Centre, with the purpose of diversifying their product to attract new clients. In East Devon, Exmouth is typical of a number of smaller resorts that cater for the traditional family market. The North Devon coast offers more spectacular scenery and good surfing beaches; Ilfracombe is a major resort. Clovelly is an example of a picturesque village that has become a popular 'honeypot' for swarms of day-trippers, and where a new visitor centre should ensure that residents are less exposed to the tourist gaze. Further along the Bristol Channel in Somerset, Minehead has the themed accommodation development of Somerwest World, based on a former Butlin's holiday camp, while Weston-super-Mare has invested in new initiatives such as the controversial Tropicana Pleasure Beach.

Other tourism resources of the West of England worth investigating include the following:

- Bath, which reached its zenith as a spa resort in the eighteenth century, although the Romans had recognised the value of a geothermal resource unique in Britain. Spa tourism is expected to revive with a new state of the art facility, but Bath is mainly visited for its cultural heritage, fine Georgian architecture (earning UNESCO designation as a World Heritage City), event and shopping attractions.
- Bristol, on the other hand, is a major commercial centre with a functioning port at Avonmouth. Its tourism industry is based on business travel; transport heritage – particularly that associated with the great Victorian engineer, Brunel; the city's role in the expansion of the British Empire; and contemporary museums (for example At-Bristol and Science World);
- Wells is a small historic town noted for its cathedral and other medieval buildings.
- The Mendips nearby offer impressive limestone scenery, featuring Cheddar Gorge and show caves such as Wookey Hole with their stalagmite and stalactite formations.
- Glastonbury has been regarded as a sacred site since ancient times, when the imposing hill known as Glastonbury Tor was an island amid the marshes of the Somerset Levels. In the Middle Ages the abbey attracted pilgrims as the burial

place of King Arthur. The town has now become a destination for 'New Age' - devotees and the Glastonbury music festival also attracts a wide youth following.
- Exeter is the county town of Devon, featuring an imposing cathedral and Roman remains among its attractions.
- Plymouth promotes its naval heritage, focusing on the Hoe, the historic Dockyard and the *Mayflower* connection. The large natural harbour of Plymouth Sound is ideal for sailing, while the Aquarium is a long-established tourist attraction.

The chalk downland of **Salisbury Plain** is a dominant feature of Wiltshire. This area is particularly rich in prehistoric remains, the best known being Avebury and Stonehenge – both World Heritage Sites and subject to tourist pressure. Responsibility for Stonehenge is shared between English Heritage and the National Trust, while much of the rest of Salisbury Plain is used by the Ministry of Defence for military training. For Stonehenge to retain its mystique it needs effective traffic and visitor management. Contrasting attractions in Wiltshire include Longleat – a stately home with a popular safari park attached; the National Trust village of Lacock Abbey – associated with one of the pioneers of photography; and the restored Kennet and Avon Canal.

East Anglia

Facing the North Sea and within easy reach of London, East Anglia is well placed to attract Continental visitors through Stansted Airport and the ports of Harwich and Felixstowe. In medieval times the region was the most prosperous part of England thanks to the wool trade with the Low Countries, and this explains the rich architectural heritage of small towns such as Lavenham. East Anglia largely escaped the developments of the Industrial Revolution and has preserved much of its rural character. Predominantly low-lying, the landscape is none the less varied, including the former marshlands of the Fens to the north-west, the sandy heaths and forests of Breckland in west Suffolk, and the fertile countryside along the river Stour in east Suffolk, an area made famous by Constable's paintings. The following are important tourist centres:

- Cambridge, where the university's historic colleges are located in a beautiful riverside setting.
- Ely, famous for its cathedral dominating the Fens
- King's Lynn – once a major port, now featuring the 'North Sea Haven'
- Norwich, the regional capital, with many historic buildings
- Colchester, with a heritage dating back to Roman times.

The north Norfolk coast, with its low cliffs of boulder clay, and the sandy coast of east Suffolk are quite different in character. Both have been designated as Heritage Coasts, and the latter boasts an internationally renowned bird reserve. North Norfolk has a number of small resorts – Cromer, Hunstanton, Sheringham and Holt, which are linked by a coastal steam railway. The Essex coast is characterized by marshes and river estuaries, on which are situated the yachting centres of Burnham on Crouch and Maldon. Essex resorts illustrate different approaches to tourism; for example Clacton has developed to attract the mass market, while neighbouring Frinton has banned any commercialization of its seafront. Southend, boasting the world's longest pier, is primarily a day trip destination for Londoners.

Great Yarmouth is one of eastern England's largest and oldest resorts, and is also the gateway to the **Norfolk Broads**. These shallow lakes of medieval origin are Britain's best-known area for water-based recreation and holidays. There are over 200 kilometres of navigable waterways and over 2000 powered craft are available for hire. However, the commercial success of tourism has been achieved in competition with agriculture, which makes heavy demands on water supplies in an area with a relatively low rainfall, and at a cost to the environment, for example:

- Detergents, human sewage, discarded fuel and a lowered water table have upset the ecological balance.
- Banks are eroded and wildlife disturbed by the wash from the boats.
- The sprawl of boatyards and other development despoils the landscape.

In an effort to balance the conflicting demands of tourism, agriculture and wildlife this unique wetland area is now carefully managed by the Broads Authority as a national park in all but name.

The Midlands

The Midlands are usually associated more with industry than tourism, presenting the tourist boards covering the west and east of the region with an image problem. However, imaginative theming of short breaks, investment in attractions and accommodation and effective marketing is attracting tourists and day visitors to the countryside, historic towns and industrial heritage of the region. The Midlands boasts two of Britain's most popular theme parks – Alton Towers and the 'American Adventure' near Ilkeston, which take advantage of the national motorway network. For both domestic and overseas tourists, the Cotswolds are famous for their mellow limestone buildings in tourist centres such as Broadway and Chipping Campden. In comparison, Cannock Chase scarcely ranks as a tourist destination but is an important recreational resource for the region, as it is located near the West Midlands conurbation. Other countryside areas in the west Midlands include the Malverns and the Shropshire Hills, while the Wye Valley near the Welsh border attracts canoeing and other activity holidays.

Of the many historic towns, the best known is Stratford-on-Avon, which is popular with overseas visitors for its literary associations, underlined by the Royal Shakespeare Theatre. Other important tourist centres in the west Midlands are:

- the cathedral cities of Gloucester, Hereford and Worcester, which host the Three Choirs Festival celebrating the music of Elgar
- the elegant spa town of Cheltenham
- Warwick and its castle, which has become a major themed attraction
- Shrewsbury and Ludlow, which in the Middle Ages were fortress towns of the Welsh Marches (the border country with Wales) and preserve a rich architectural heritage; Ludlow is also noted for its quality restaurants.

The industrial heritage of the West Midlands is undergoing radical change, with the restoration of canals for recreation and a new breed of museum such as:

- the Ironbridge complex which interprets the beginnings of the Industrial Revolution

- the Potteries Museum at Stoke-on-Trent and 'Ceramica' at Burslem showcase the ceramics industry of north Staffordshire
- the Black Country Museum at Dudley portrays life and work in this former area of heavy industry.

Modern engineering industries are still thriving in the West Midlands conurbation, which includes Birmingham, Coventry and Wolverhampton. The National Exhibition Centre and National Arena at the heart of the motorway system enhance Birmingham's importance as a centre for business tourism and event attractions. This is complemented by the redeveloped Bull Ring shopping complex in the city centre, the Jewellery Quarter focusing on Birmingham's speciality trades, and new attractions such as 'Think Tank' – an interactive discovery museum, Cadbury World of Chocolate, and the National Sealife Centre. For many people Coventry and its cathedral symbolize urban recovery after the Second World War, but the city's museums also showcase its contributions to transport technology, while Millennium Place is a new outdoor arena.

The East Midlands region includes the Lincolnshire coast, with the resorts of Skegness, Mablethorpe and Cleethorpes providing traditional seaside recreation for the industrial cities of Derby, Leicester and Nottingham. Lincoln is a major tourist centre with a magnificent cathedral dominating the city's skyline. Nottingham has exploited its association with the legendary Robin Hood, while Leicester has downplayed its heritage in favour of the National Space Centre. Countryside areas for recreation include Charnwood Forest, the Vale of Belvoir and Sherwood Forest, while the artificial lake known as Rutland Water is an important resource for water sports.

The North

The northern part of England, which includes four regional tourist boards, is one of contrasts, from industrial heartlands, through the spectacular scenery of national parks, to its bustling resorts. The region also forms an important gateway to Britain for Scandinavian, German and Dutch tourists who enter through the ports of Newcastle and Hull. The scenery of the area is evidenced by the fact that it contains five national parks – which are the focus of tourism and day trips – and a number of areas of outstanding natural beauty, such as the Solway Firth – noted for its golf courses – and the Eden Valley and North Pennines – which are popular with anglers.

In many rural upland areas EU and British regional funds are supporting the development of farm-based tourism. Tourism and recreation brings income and jobs, supports rural services and stems depopulation, but herein also lie seeds of conflict, as some argue that tourism interferes with farming operations and destroys the very communities that tourists visit. This may occur through the purchase of second homes and the reorientation of rural services towards weekend and summer visitors. The opportunities for outdoor recreation and the threats from tourist pressure are greatest in the national parks:

- The **Lake District** is intensively managed for tourism and recreation with 'honeypot' areas designed to take pressure, for example Ambleside and Bowness, along with traffic management and car parking schemes. Access to the park from the north is through the market town of Penrith, and from the south through the historic town of Kendal. Keswick is the major tourist centre for the park, and there is a national park centre at Brockholes. There are attractions based on the literary associations with Wordsworth and Beatrix Potter, but the Lake District is mainly popular for active tourism and recreation – walking, water sports, outdoor pursuits and mountaineering. In the past these activities have interfered with the upland farming regime of the area, but management schemes run by the park's authorities have solved many of these problems. The landscape is on a human scale with attractive towns and villages, *fells* (low moorland hills) and lakes, each with its own character. Windermere, for example, is intensively used, while remoter lakes and tarns are little visited.

- The **Yorkshire Dales** National Park is characterized by a gentler landscape than the Lake District. It is criss-crossed by limestone walls and dotted with field barns (some converted to shelters for walkers). Touring centres in the park include Richmond, Skipton and Settle, and popular villages such as Malham, with its cove and tarn which are spectacular relics of the Ice Age. In and around the park are literary sites linked to the Brontes and also locations associated with a popular drama series on British television. Like its southern neighbour, the Peak District National Park, the dales are popular for outdoor pursuits and field studies. The Settle/Carlisle Railway is a major scenic route linking two national parks.

- The **Peak District** is the most visited of Britain's national parks due to its proximity to the industrial cities of both the North and the Midlands, with some valleys, notably Dovedale, experiencing visitor pressure. The White Peak is the southern and central area of limestone dales and crags with important centres such as Matlock and Castleton. The Dark Peak in the north is a more rugged and spectacular area with a number of lakes and reservoirs. Some caverns and mines are open to visitors and the industrial heritage is featured in attractions such as the Crich National Tramway Museum. At Matlock Bath the Heights of Abraham is a country park with theme park attractions. The main touring centres are Bakewell, Ashbourne, Matlock and Holmfirth – home of another popular television series. The spa town of Buxton has revived its opera house and conference facilities. Hardwick Hall in Chesterfield is one of Britain's foremost Elizabethan country houses, while Chatsworth is one of its most visited stately homes.

- The **North York Moors** National Park is characterized by heather-covered, rolling countryside with picturesque villages. It also offers a spectacular coastline, summits such as Roseberry Topping, and natural features such as the Hole of Horcum, popular with hang-gliders. The North Yorkshire Moors steam railway runs through the park from Pickering to Grosmont.

- The **Northumberland** National Park lies on the Scottish border and contains Kielder Forest and Kielder Water, both recent additions to the landscape. Hadrian's Wall to the south is of unique historic interest as a Roman military achievement, with associated archaeological attractions, but in places under intense tourist pressure. Hadrian's Wall runs from Hexham westwards to Carlisle, which is an important regional centre and historic gateway to Scotland.

The coasts of northern England include both major resorts and areas of scenic interest that have been conserved as Heritage Coast or as wildlife sanctuaries, such as Spurn Head and the Farne Islands. Many of the North's resorts have faced the problem of declining traditional markets in nearby industrial cities by investing in new facilities, upgrading accommodation and marketing aggressively to attract new market segments. Holidaymakers have the following choice of resorts:

- Blackpool's 'Golden Mile' is a classic example of a RBD (recreational business district), where the famous Tower is jostled by a townscape of tourist facilities and small guest-houses. The Pleasure Beach is one of the most visited attractions in Britain. Blackpool introduced 'The Illuminations' as an early attempt to extend the holiday season, and has constantly developed new attractions, such as the Sandcastle Centre. Blackpool hopes to be the main beneficiary of government proposals to liberalize gambling laws, and thus re-invent itself as 'Britain's Las Vegas'.
- Scarborough is one of Britain's oldest resorts, an elegant town situated between two bays, offering a Sealife Centre among its modern attractions. The redeveloped Spa Conference Centre adds a business dimension to its market.
- There is a range of smaller resorts, such as Bridlington, Hornsea, Whitby and Filey on the North Sea coast and Morecambe on the less bracing Irish Sea coast.
- Day trip resorts close to conurbations include New Brighton and Southport serving Merseyside, and Whitley Bay for Newcastle.

The North of England is mainly known for its great industrial cities and their role in sport and popular culture, but the region can also boast many historic buildings and sites of national importance, which increasingly attract overseas tourists as well as day visitors. These include the following:

- A large number of castles, particularly in areas close to the Scottish border. Alnwick and Bamburgh are good examples.
- Reminders of pre-Reformation England in abbeys such as Fountains and Rievaulx in Yorkshire, and the pilgrimage centre of Holy Island (Lindisfarne) off the Northumberland coast.
- Stately homes like Castle Howard, which has been used as a location for costume dramas.
- More modest buildings from different parts of the region have been brought together on one site at the Beamish North of England Open Air Museum in County Durham.
- The spa towns of Buxton, Ilkley and Harrogate – now a major conference venue.
- The historic centres of Beverley, Chester, Durham, Lancaster and York. Chester has significant Roman remains, but tourism focuses on 'The Rows' – medieval shopping arcades. Durham boasts an impressive castle and Romanesque cathedral, reflecting the power of its prince-bishops in the Middle Ages. However **York** is outstanding, for these reasons:
  - it has retained its medieval walls, city gates and street pattern
  - York Minster is one of Europe's largest Gothic churches
  - the Jorvik Viking Centre has transformed an archaeological site into a visitor attraction featuring 'authentic' sights, sounds and smells.

York has also exploited its part in the Industrial Revolution through the National Railway Museum, although the industrial heritage is more obvious in larger, less historic cities. Bradford, for example, has shown an imaginative approach to tourism based on its woollen textile industry, but also utilizing its proximity to 'Bronte Country' and the contribution of the large Asian community to contemporary culture, particularly food. Indeed, the resurgence of tourism, sport and leisure-related projects on 'brownfield' sites reclaimed from industrial use characterizes most northern cities. Regional centres such as Hull, Leeds, Newcastle, Liverpool and Manchester have major tourist developments leading their drive for reinvestment. For example, in Merseyside the Liverpool Garden Festival and Albert Dock schemes were designed to attract investment in other sectors of the economy. As a result the city now features the Tate Liverpool Art Gallery and museums celebrating its maritime and musical heritage, as well as an impressive collection of civic buildings from the Victorian era. Manchester raised its international profile by hosting the Commonwealth Games in 2002 and its city centre was redeveloped following an IRA terrorist attack. At Castlefield there is now an urban heritage park and a new exhibition venue – the GMex Centre. Further along the Ship Canal there is the Lowry Centre at Salford Quays, celebrating one of the region's most famous artists. Manchester has set out to attract particular markets – for example, sport tourism, music lovers, youth tourism with a vibrant club scene and gay tourism. Developments elsewhere in the North West include Wigan Pier – a themed heritage attraction based on life in Victorian England, and at Preston, the National Football Museum and the Riversway dock redevelopment project.

On the other side of the Pennines, Newcastle has expanded its leisure and shopping attractions, while the Baltic at Gateshead is at the cutting edge of the contemporary art scene. In Yorkshire and Humberside the following tourism developments are of significance:

- Wakefield's National Coal Mining Museum in a former colliery, celebrating one of England's major industries prior to the 1980s.
- The Royal Armouries Museum and the Thackray Medical Museum in Leeds.
- Sheffield is developing special event tourism and boasts the Meadowhall leisure and shopping complex – one of Europe's largest – and the Ski Village with dry slopes and other facilities for winter sports.
- 'The Earth Centre' at Doncaster – a major environmental project for the Millennium.
- Rotherham's 'Magna' is a visitor attraction based on the achievements of British industry.
- Hull hosts 'The Deep', an exhibition interpreting the life of the oceans and the nineteenth-century whaling industry. Similarly, Grimsby's trawlermen are celebrated in the National Fishing Heritage Centre. These attractions have helped to alleviate the loss of jobs and income caused by the decline of the North Sea fishing industry.

The offshore islands

Britain's offshore island destinations include the Channel Islands, which are geographically much closer to the Cherbourg Peninsula in France than to southern England, and the Isles of Scilly, lying some 50 kilometres to the south-west of Cornwall in the Atlantic Ocean.

The Channel Islands

The Channel Islands capitalize on their favourable climate – boasting more sunshine than other parts of the British Isles, Norman-French traditions and culinary attractions.

Jersey and Guernsey are officially dependencies of the British Crown, with their own parliaments, postal services and fiscal systems offering low rates of tax, which attracts business visitors, an influx of retired people and duty-free shoppers. The islands have attractive coastal scenery and fine beaches (although the strong tides are hazardous to bathers). The Channel Islands were the only part of the British Isles to be occupied by Germany during the Second World War, and the Occupation features in a number of heritage attractions. Tourist facilities are well developed, with a range of accommodation (other than camping). Jersey and Guernsey are linked by air, fast ferry and shipping services to ports in northern France and southern England. Tourism has helped to boost an economy once largely dependent on dairy farming and horticulture, but hotels depend to a large extent on imported labour (from Portugal for example) and visitors' cars add to the pressure of traffic on the islands' road networks.

The tourist centre of Jersey is the capital, St Helier, which features Elizabeth Castle in the bay and the Fort Regent Leisure Centre above the town. The waterfront includes a marina development, illustrating the importance of the yachting market. The island's history is interpreted at a number of sites, particularly the Living Legend themed attraction. Other key attractions are Jersey Zoo, beaches such as St Brelade's and the sweep of St Ouen's Bay, and a number of secluded coves. Jersey has lost market share to Mediterranean destinations; however the island's tourist board has developed an imaginative strategy to claw back tourists, facilitated by the introduction of budget-priced air services.

Guernsey's tourist industry is on a smaller scale than that of Jersey but offers similar attractions. These include a number of craft centres and museums based on the island's literary associations, while the introduction of gambling casinos may attract higher spending visitors. The focus of tourism is the capital, St Peter Port.

The smaller Channel Islands can be visited on day excursions from Guernsey or Jersey. Sark boasts spectacular coastal scenery, and along with Alderney, Herm and Jethou, can offer a limited amount of accommodation.

The Isles of Scilly

The Scillies consist of 200 small islands, of which five are inhabited. They belong to the Duchy of Cornwall, and tourism, along with other matters affecting the islanders, is the responsibility of the Council of the Scillies based at Hugh Town on the island of St Mary's.

The main attractions are the mild climate (as shown by the subtropical gardens of Tresco), the unspoilt maritime scenery and bird life and the many shipwreck sites for divers. St Mary's provides boat services to the other islands, and is linked to Penzance on the mainland by air and shipping services.

Summary

England, with the Channel Islands and the Isles of Scilly, is well endowed with most types of tourist attractions and an increasingly professional approach to their management is evident. Each region comprises a variety of attractions and resources for tourism, which blend to give a distinct product. However we can identify common themes, such as the growth of heritage attractions which are often based on declining industries; the increasing use of rural resources for tourism and recreation; and the growth of what we may broadly describe as cultural as well as recreational tourism to cities in addition to London (such as Birmingham, Bradford and Sheffield), that until recently were associated solely with commerce and industry. In the meantime, the resorts that traditionally provided an English seaside holiday are re-investing in improved facilities to attract new markets.

Chapter 9

The tourism geography of Scotland, Wales and the Isle of Man

Learning Objectives

After reading this chapter, you should be able to:

■ Demonstrate a knowledge of the main tourist regions in Scotland, Wales and the Isle of Man.
■ Understand the distribution and importance of coastal resorts and resources in Scotland, Wales and the Isle of Man.
■ Recognize the increasing role being played by heritage resources and attractions in these countries.
■ Recognize the importance of rural resources in Scottish and Welsh tourism.
■ Understand the importance of the major cities of Scotland and Wales as business and leisure tourism centres.

Introduction

Scotland, Wales and the Isle of Man occupy the north and west of Britain, and form part of the 'Celtic fringe' of Western Europe. Despite centuries of dominance by England, they have retained their separate national identities, expressed in sport, language and culture, and have now regained most of their former independence.

Scotland

The Romans never conquered Scotland, and it retained its independence until the Act of Union in 1707. However, a form of the English language became dominant except in the more remote western and northern parts of the country, where the Gaelic language and culture still survive. The Scots developed a separate legal system and with the Reformation their own Church, while styles of architecture were influenced by France rather than England. Outside the conurbations of Glasgow and Edinburgh, Scotland is a much less crowded country than England, with plenty of space for outdoor recreation. Two-thirds of the country is mountainous, and the Highlands are one of the largest areas of unspoiled mountain and lake scenery in Europe. Many potential visitors are deterred by the reputation of the climate such that, outside of the Central Lowlands, leisure tourism is very seasonal. However, the west coast of Scotland in fact enjoys more spring sunshine than most parts of Britain. Apart from the fine scenery, Scotland can also offer a wealth of folklore and a romantic history – re-interpreted by Hollywood films in the 1990s.

Since devolution of power to Scotland in 1999, Scottish tourism is administered by the Scottish Tourist Board (VisitScotland), EventScotland and a range of regional and local agencies, while the Scottish Tourism Forum represents the industry to government. Tourism is important economically, directly supporting almost 200 000 jobs and accounting for 5 per cent of GDP. The Scottish tourism product is delivered primarily by small businesses and this places a question mark over the quality of the product at times, and has also held back investment in the sector; for example there are few all-weather developments. Scottish tourism is based on scenery, cultural heritage and the large ethnic market formed by the descendants of emigrants, especially in Canada. Special interest and activity holidays are also important – particularly those based on fishing, whisky and golf. Scotland's tourists come mainly for leisure purposes, as the country was a late entrant into the conference and exhibition market. The overseas market has remained healthy for Scotland, with the USA and Continental Europe providing most of the demand. Most visitors arrive by air, as Scotland has no direct ferry access to mainland Europe. Scotland also attracts domestic tourism, of which around one-half originate from within the country. Increasingly, Scotland faces a dilemma: the traditional image of lochs, tartan and heather is inappropriate for the newer forms of tourism, based on short city-break products as developed in Glasgow and Edinburgh.

Tourism resources

Three main tourist regions can be identified in Scotland, based on differences of geology and culture:

- The Southern Uplands, mainly high moorlands with only a few pockets of lowland.
- The Central Lowlands, which is actually a rift valley formed between two faults or lines of weakness in the earth's crust. Although this region occupies only 10 per cent of the total area, it contains 80 per cent of Scotland's population of 5 million.
- The Highlands and Islands of the north and north-west, where ancient rocks form rugged mountains and a magnificent coastline, and the nearest there is to true wilderness in the British Isles.

The Southern Uplands

The Southern Uplands lie between the Cheviots on the English border and the southern boundary fault of the Central Lowlands, which approximates to a line drawn between Girvan in Ayrshire to Dunbar. Granite is the rock most commonly found in Galloway in the west, forming a rugged landscape. To the east of Dumfries the hills are more rounded and broken up by areas of lowland, the most extensive being the Merse of the Tweed valley. The Southern Uplands as a whole are thinly populated, and the towns are quite small. There are few roads or railways and the main lines of communication with England keep to the valleys.

This area forms the gateway to Scotland and tourist developments at Gretna have exploited this, although the centuries of border warfare and cattle raiding have been less publicized than the clan warfare of the Highlands. The main tourist attractions in the Border Country to the east include:

- the abbeys at Jedburgh, Kelso and Melrose, immortalized by Sir Walter Scott
- the spa town of Peebles
- the textile weaving towns of Hawick and Selkirk.

On the route west to Galloway, Dumfries has a 'Burns Trail' celebrating its associations with Scotland's national poet. Galloway has a milder climate and gardens are an attraction. The area has facilities for sailing and other activity holidays, and there are important archaeological sites and the Galloway Forest Park. Stranraer is a major ferry port for Northern Ireland.

North of Galloway the Ayrshire coast has notable seaside resorts such as Girvan, and Ayr has one of Scotland's few all-weather facilities at Haven Holiday Park. There are also golf courses, as at Troon. Northwards towards the central lowlands are the attractions of:

- Traquair House
- the Scottish Museum of Woollen Textiles near Peebles
- Chatelherault hunting lodge
- New Lanark industrial village.

The Central Lowlands

Despite the name, the Central Lowlands include a good deal of high ground, since the formation of this rift valley was accompanied by extensive volcanic activity. The isolated 'necks' of long-extinct volcanoes can still be seen, the crag on which Edinburgh Castle is built being a good example. The Ochils and Sidlaws to the north of the estuary known as the Firth of Forth, and the Pentland Hills to the south, rise to 500 metres – high by English standards. Parts of the eastern Lowlands are quite fertile, notably the Carse of Gowrie in Fife and the Lothians around Edinburgh. The western part of the Lowlands has a damper climate. The coastline is deeply indented by three great estuaries – the Firths of Forth, Clyde and Tay, on which are situated Scotland's major ports, Leith (for Edinburgh), Glasgow with its outport at Greenock, and Dundee.

The Central Lowlands contain by far the greater proportion of Scotland's industry and population. The main centres – Glasgow, Edinburgh, Dundee and Stirling – are linked by a good communications system, which has involved bridging the Forth and Tay. Here too are the main international and domestic air gateways to Scotland. Both Edinburgh and Glasgow have shuttle services to London, while Glasgow Airport has developed international services since the deregulation of air services in Scotland and the demise of Prestwick. Budget airlines also operate to Dublin, Luton and regional airports in the British Isles.

The region is dominated by the two rival cities of Glasgow and Edinburgh. Both are significant cities for tourism but have very different products and approaches. Each has its own tourist board and tourism strategy.

Edinburgh, as the capital of Scotland, is home to the Scottish Assembly and is a major cultural centre, attracting a large number of overseas visitors, especially to the International Festival and Military Tattoo. The old city is built on a narrow ridge on either side of the 'Royal Mile' connecting the Castle to the palace of Holyrood House, and is crammed full of picturesque buildings. It is separated from the 'New Town' to the north by the Norloch Valley, now occupied by public gardens and the Waverley railway station. The New Town, built according to eighteenth-century ideas of planning and architecture, contains Princes Street, a major shopping area, but other speciality shopping streets now compete with Princes Street's multiple stores. In particular, the area to the north of Princes Street, the Grassmarket area in the old town and Stockbridge, abound with restaurants and speciality retailing. Edinburgh has a wealth of historic buildings and national attractions such as the Royal Scottish Museum and the newly developed 'Dynamic Earth' story of the planet. The Edinburgh International Conference Centre has been a major boost to business tourism. There are also many attractions on the outskirts, including:

- Edinburgh Zoo
- the Forth road and rail bridges
- Dirleton, Tantallon and Crichton Castles
- Linlithgow Palace, associated with Mary Queen of Scots
- the restored Royal Yacht Britannia
- Ocean Terminal at Leith
- the Scottish Mining Museum.

Across the Forth Estuary lies Dunfermline, a former capital of Scotland. The Fife coast has a string of picturesque fishing villages – Elie and Crail – and the historic university town of St Andrews with its golf course. Dundee is the regional centre and has the twin attractions of the royal research ship *Discovery* at Discovery Point and a Science Centre. Perth is another former Scottish capital and acts as the gateway to the Highlands.

Glasgow is a much larger city than Edinburgh, having developed mainly during the nineteenth century as Scotland's major port and industrial centre. Glasgow's renaissance as a city was well publicized in 1990 with its selection as European City of Culture. With the vision of the local authority and the Greater Glasgow Tourist Board and Convention Bureau, a fine Victorian city now has a wealth of attractions, accommodation, restaurants and tourist facilities. In particular:

- the Burrell Collection in the art gallery and museum
- the People's Palace
- St Enoch Shopping Centre
- the Scottish Exhibition Centre
- the refurbished Pollok House
- the Clyde Auditorium
- the Gallery of Modern Art
- the Glasgow Science Centre.

Stirling with its strategically located castle played a major role in the Scottish Wars of Independence, given worldwide recognition by the film *Braveheart*.

The Highlands and Islands

Geologically speaking, the Highlands include the whole of Scotland to the north of a line drawn from Helensburgh on the Firth of Clyde to Stonehaven on the North

Sea coast, which represents the northern boundary fault of the Central Lowlands. The region is made up of very old, highly folded rocks, and was severely affected by glaciation during the Ice Age, which formed its landscape of rugged mountains (the highest in the British Isles), lochs and broad, steep-sided glens. Most of the forests of Scots pine which formerly covered much of the Highlands have disappeared, with the significant exception of the Cairngorms area, leaving a treeless, heather-covered landscape.

The Highlands are divided into two by Glen More, the great rift valley extending right across Scotland from Fort William to Inverness, which is followed by the Caledonian Canal. The north-west Highlands to the west of Glen More are more rugged than the Grampians to the east. The Atlantic coast from Kintyre to Sutherland is deeply indented by sea lochs and is fringed by innumerable islands, with very little in the way of a coastal plain. Along the North Sea coast the coastline is more regular and less spectacular; there are fairly extensive lowlands in the north-east 'shoulder' of Scotland between Aberdeen and the Moray Firth, where the climate is drier and better suited to farming.

By comparison with other mountain regions of Europe, such as the Alps, most parts of the Scottish Highlands are sparsely populated, for historical reasons. Despite a difficult climate and poor soils, the glens, the coastal lowlands and islands once supported substantial communities whose way of life was quite different from that of the Lowlands. The Highlanders spoke Gaelic and had a strong feeling of loyalty to the clan or tribal group. In the nineteenth century many such communities were evicted in the Clearances to make way for large private sheep farms and reserves for field sports. Traditionally, many Highlanders have gained a living from 'crofting' – a self-sufficient type of agriculture on smallholdings supplemented by fishing. In some localities weaving and whisky distilling have been important activities.

Tourism has become an important source of income and provider of jobs. In 1965 the Highlands and Islands Development Board was set up by the British government to encourage public and private investment in the seven 'crofting counties' (Argyll, Inverness, Ross and Cromarty, Sutherland, Caithness, Orkney and Shetland). In the past this area was very short of quality accommodation, so the Board financed new hotels and self-catering accommodation. In 1991 it became the Highlands and Islands Enterprise Network which is also concerned with investigating ways of extending the short tourist season, and ensuring that tourism does not damage the beauty of the scenery.

The main tourism centre for the Highlands is Inverness, where the majority of accommodation and services are found. South of the town, Loch Ness has a tourist industry based on the world famous 'monster' with visitor centres at Drumnadrochit.

Transport is a problem in the Western Highlands on account of the deeply indented coastline; so wide detours have frequently to be made to get from one place to another. With the exception of Skye, the Hebrides are particularly isolated, although some of the small scattered communities are linked by 'air taxi' services and ferry connections to the mainland. The ports of Ullapool, Kyle of Lochalsh, Mallaig and Oban are the main bases for visiting the Hebrides. Islands have a great attraction for holidaymakers, despite in this instance the unpredictable weather and lack of facilities.

- Skye is popular because of its historical associations with the clans and the 1745 Jacobite rising, as well as the magnificent mountain scenery of the Cuillins.

- Iona is a place of pilgrimage.
- Staffa is noted for its basalt sea caves.
- Crossing the Minch, the Outer Hebrides or Western Isles have a bleaker environment. Harris is noted for its tweed, cloth handwoven into distinctive patterns, while Lewis has a major prehistoric site at Callanish.
- The Orkneys and the Shetlands, separated from mainland Scotland by some of the stormiest seas in Europe, were once ruled by Norway – and in the Shetlands the Scandinavian influence remains strong even today (one manifestation being the 'Up Helly A' festival in Lerwick). The Orkneys are fairly low-lying and fertile, and contain unique pre-historic sites at Skara Brae and Maes Howe. The magnificent harbour of Scapa Flow was once an important naval base. The Shetlands lie 140 kilometres further north and are bleaker and much more rugged. Oil has brought wealth to a community where fishing has traditionally been the mainstay of the economy and the distinctively small, hardy island sheep and ponies are reared. These northern islands are linked by regular air services from Edinburgh and Glasgow as well as ferries from Scrabster (near Thurso) and Aberdeen.

The scenic attractions of the Grampians are more readily accessible to the cities of the Lowlands than the Western Highlands. This part of Scotland was made fashionable as a holiday destination by Queen Victoria, and the Dee Valley west of Aberdeen is particularly associated with the British royal family. More recently, Hollywood films based on Scottish heroes have also stimulated renewed interest in the area. During the nineteenth century a number of hotels were built, notably on the shores of Loch Lomond, in the Trossachs (an area of particularly fine woodland and lake scenery now designated as a national park), and at Gleneagles near Perth, which is a noted centre for golf. The Spey Valley (famous for its whisky and salmon fishing) was another area that particularly benefited from Victorian tourism. It has good road and rail communications to Glasgow and London. After the 1960s, this area became important for winter sports, since the Cairngorms can provide a suitable climate and terrain.

Skiing takes place from December to April in the Coire Cas, a corrie or cirque that acts as a 'snowbowl', located high above the treeline on the northern slopes of Cairngorm Mountain. The Aviemore Centre in the valley below is a purpose-built resort offering a full range of services. Conferences are held in spring and autumn, while in summer the Centre is used as a base for activity holidays, including pony-trekking and nature study – for which the Cairngorms nature reserve is probably unrivalled in Britain. Unlike other Scottish resorts, Aviemore has a year-round season and adequate wet-weather facilities, so that it can take full advantage of tourism. Elsewhere, new winter sports facilities are being developed near Fort William and at Glen Shee. However, proposals to expand ski facilities have received considerable opposition from environmentalists, concerned about the fragile nature of the mountain ecosystem.

Wales

Wales has maintained a separate national identity despite the union with England imposed by King Edward I and later reinforced by Henry VIII. This is evidenced by:

- the survival of the Welsh language, especially in the mountainous north and west of the country
- the Celtic heritage, expressed in a strong literary and musical tradition, and the national gatherings known as *eisteddfods*
- the strength of Nonconformist Christianity, with simple chapels featuring in the landscape rather than imposing cathedrals, and the world famous choirs
- the importance of rugby football as a showcase of national identity.

In the course of the twentieth century, the Welsh language and culture have been encouraged by the British government, although Wales has not yet achieved the same degree of devolution as Scotland. Overall tourism policy and product development is the responsibility of the Wales Tourist Board, a public body reporting the Welsh Assembly. A ten-year tourism strategy has been drafted to take the industry to 2010.

Tourism resources

Three tourist regions can be identified in Wales, based on both geography and culture.

North Wales

North Wales, consisting of the counties of Gwynedd and Clwyd, is scenically the most interesting part of the country. Gwynedd is the most important tourism region in Wales. It is often regarded as the cultural 'heartland' of Wales, where the people continue to speak Welsh as their first language. The traditional culture has persisted partly because the region is isolated to some extent by the rugged mountains of Snowdonia, which rise abruptly from the coast. North Wales contains Britain's largest national park and castles dating from Edward I's conquest of Gwynedd in the thirteenth century. A number of these castles – Conwy, Harlech, Beaumaris and Caernarfon – are World Heritage Sites.

The mountains of Snowdonia form the core of the Snowdonia National Park. They have a craggy appearance quite different from the rounded outline of the Cambrian Mountains to the south and the Hiraethog or Denbighshire moors to the east. Radiating from Snowdon itself are a number of deep trough-like valleys carved out by the glaciers of the Ice Age – examples include the Llanberis Pass and Nant Ffrancon, which contains a number of small lakes. In such a valley is Lake Bala, offering facilities for water sports and fishing. The beautiful scenery has encouraged touring and activity tourism in such centres as Beddgelert, Llangollen and Betws-y-Coed. For the less active, the Snowdon Mountain Railway takes visitors to the summit of the highest mountain of Wales from Llanberis, but visitor pressure has caused serious erosion.

Tourism dominates the economy of North Wales and takes advantage of both the rural and industrial heritage. Most of the high land in North Wales is of little agricultural value. In the upper valleys there are isolated sheep farms, with their characteristic stone buildings and small irregular fields separated by roughstone walls. As in northern England, hill farms cater for tourists as a way of supplementing their incomes. The other major industry is based on mineral resources; large areas near Bethesda, Llanberis and Ffestiniog are the sites of slate quarries, some of which have become important tourist attractions – as at Llechwedd. In Llanberis the Welsh Slate Centre interprets this once important industry for the tourist. Other industrial features that are now tourist attractions are the narrow-gauge railways, promoted as 'the Great Little Trains of Wales'. Today, Wales is a source of both power and water for England and these resources are also used for tourism, as the power stations welcome visitors. In contrast to these examples of Victorian and modern industry, the Centre for Alternative Technology at Machynlloth is an important attraction, with true 'green' credentials.

The coastline of North Wales is particularly attractive and easily reached from the conurbations of Merseyside and Manchester. There are a number of popular seaside resorts along the coast east of the estuary of the Conwy:

- Llandudno is perhaps best known as a conference venue, but boasts a fine beach situated between two headlands – the Great and Little Orme
- Colwyn Bay is the site of the Welsh Mountain Zoo
- Rhyl with its all-weather 'Sun Centre' and Sea Life Centre has undergone substantial redevelopment; much of the narrow coastal strip around Rhyl accommodates large caravan sites.

These resorts, and particularly Llandudno, have benefited from the upgrading of the A55, traditionally the route from the conurbations of North-West England, although this does mean that day visitors now easily outnumber staying holidaymakers.

Anglesey and the Lleyn Peninsula are less commercialized, with smaller resorts, such as Pwllheli, devoted to sailing or other 'activity' holidays. Bardsey Island off the coast is a nature reserve. In parts of North Wales the purchase of country cottages as 'second homes' by visitors from outside the region is controversial (partly because it is felt to weaken the Welsh language and culture). Although some villages (for example, Abersoch on the Lleyn peninsula) are dominated by second homes, others argue that the rural area benefits economically by bringing business to local suppliers. Holyhead, with its marina and important ferry service to Ireland, is the only significant commercial centre.

Mid-Wales

Mid-Wales is also mountainous and thinly populated, except for the narrow coastal plain around Cardigan Bay, and the upper valleys of the Wye and the Severn. Around Cardigan Bay Welsh culture is strong, while much of Powys has been English-speaking for centuries. North–south communications are difficult, especially by rail, and there are no large towns. There are a number of small seaside resorts on Cardigan Bay, such as Aberdovey and Aberystwyth, which are popular with visitors from the English Midlands. Inland, there are some small market towns, such as Newtown, Llanidiloes and Welshpool, and a number of former spas, such as Builth Wells. These have become centres for touring the Cambrian Mountains, but are important historic towns in their own right; Montgomery, for example, has many Georgian buildings. Other attractions in Mid-Wales include Powis Castle, Lake Vyrnwy and the Glywedog Gorge.

South Wales

South Wales contains the majority of the Welsh population of almost three million and most of the industries. The region is separated from the rest of Wales by the

Black Mountains and the Brecon Beacons, but is easily accessible from southern England via the two Severn road bridges. In the centre of the region lies the South Wales coalfield, which is crossed from north to south by a number of deep narrow valleys, including those of the Taff, Rhondda and Rhymney. Mining communities straggle almost continuously along the valley bottoms, and the landscape was formerly disfigured by spoil heaps, tips and abandoned workings. Both British and European Union initiatives have transformed this landscape of dereliction with:

- landscaped country parks
- the development of a museum of coal mining at Big Pit, Blaenavon
- the Rhondda Heritage Park.

A similar transformation has occurred in the two main urban centres of Wales. In Swansea dockland areas have been redeveloped as a maritime quarter with water sports, retailing, restaurants and hotels. West of Swansea, the Gower Peninsula is an Area of Outstanding Natural Beauty with good beaches. **Cardiff**, as the capital of Wales and seat of the Welsh Assembly, is the location of major developments such as:

- the Millennium Stadium
- the Wales Millennium Centre for the Performing Arts
- a major redevelopment of Cardiff Harbour with museums – such as Techniquest – restaurants and hotels
- national institutions such as the Welsh Folk Museum at St Fagan's, the National Museum of Wales and the refurbished Cardiff Castle.

On the outskirts, Penarth is a small resort, Barry Island has a major pleasure park, Llanelli is developing a coastal park and Castell Coch overlooks the city. The city is served by Cardiff Wales Airport.

Historically, the region has a great deal to offer. There are important Roman remains at Caerwent and Caerleon; and in this area too the Normans built many castles to control the coastal plain, and the valleys leading into the mountains of Mid-Wales. Near the Welsh border, Tintern Abbey, Monmouth, with its fortified bridge, and Chepstow Castle are notable examples of heritage attractions.

The Brecon Beacons National Park rises to over 900 metres at Pen-y-Fan, while to the west is the old hunting ground of Fforest Fawr, in the north-east the broad valley of the river Usk and to the south spectacular waterfalls and caves. Hay-on-Wye is the touring base for the park, the centre for the second-hand book trade and inspiration for the 'book city' concept. On the Usk, Abergavenny is also a touring and trekking centre. East of Brecon, Llangorse Lake is developed for water sports and is an important centre for naturalists.

In Dyfed in the south-west, the National Botanic Garden for Wales is an attraction of international significance. The Pembrokeshire Coast National Park is Britain's only linear national park, extending from Pen Camais in the north to Amroth in the south and including some offshore islands. Notable here is Caldey Island, where tourists can visit the monastery, and the bird reserves on Skokholm and Skomer. One outstanding cultural attraction is St David's, which was a major place of pilgrimage in medieval times. Around the park runs the 269 kilometre coastal path, taking in resorts such as Tenby and Saundersfoot, and features such as Manorbier Castle, the lily ponds at Bosherston and Pendine Sands, famous for attempts on the world land speed record.

The Isle of Man

The Isle of Man – 50 kilometres long and 20 kilometres wide – is situated in the Irish Sea, midway between Ireland, England and Scotland. The island is often described as 'northern England' in miniature, but it is culturally distinct, with a Celtic and Viking heritage. It has its own language, postal service, parliament (Tynewald) and an independent fiscal system which has allowed it to develop as an offshore finance centre. In Victorian times holidaymakers reached the Isle of Man by steamship, sailing out of Liverpool, Heysham, Belfast and Dublin. In recent years fast catamarans have also been introduced, but the success of the island's airline – Manx (now a subsidiary of British Airways) made it an important carrier for business and leisure passengers. The island's airport, Ronaldsway, is linked to many regional airports in the UK, Ireland and the Channel Islands.

The island can provide a variety of attractions:

- **Douglas**, with its sweeping Victorian promenade of guest houses and terraced hotels, is the capital and major seaport of the Isle of Man, featuring the Manx Museum and 'The Story of Mann' exhibition. It represents the main concentration of bed spaces, and offers a range of restaurants and entertainment facilities that are used by residents and visitors alike, such as the Summerland casino and leisure centre. Other coastal towns, each with a range of small visitor attractions, craft workshops and accommodation, include Port Erin, Peel, Ramsey and Castletown.
- The **cultural heritage** includes many historic buildings, for example the castle and cathedral in Peel and Castle Rushen at Castletown, which was the former capital. The best-known feature is the world's largest working waterwheel at Laxey. There are a number of museums and craft centres, while the Cregneash Folk Village interprets the crofting way of life of islanders in the past.
- The **natural heritage** provides the setting for special interest holidays, and both walking and cycling trails are available.
- The **transport heritage** includes horse-drawn trams and narrow gauge railways, but the most famous attraction is the annual Tourist Trophy (TT) motorcycle races, which started in 1904 as a way of extending the holiday season. This event takes place on a road circuit around the island and fills hotels to capacity during 'TT Week' in June.

The Isle of Man has a varied accommodation base, ranging from luxury country house hotels to value-for-money guesthouses. The Manx government has a long-standing scheme to assist the accommodation sector both to adjust to the demands of the contemporary holidaymaker and to attract new accommodation stock. The tourism authorities also operate a compulsory registration and grading scheme for accommodation. By 2002 there were almost 7000 bed spaces available on the island, mostly in serviced accommodation.

The Department of Tourism and Leisure has responsibility for both the promotion and development of tourism on the island as well as leisure and public transport. The Isle of Man has had to adapt its tourism product to the tastes of twenty-first century holidaymakers. The island's traditional markets sought an English seaside product, and while this still forms part of the island's appeal, other elements of the destination mix are now seen as more important in attracting visitors. The Isle of Man is therefore an excellent example of a destination that has successfully repositioned itself to become more competitive.

Summary

Scotland, Wales and the Isle of Man are well endowed with a wide variety of tourist attractions. Both Scotland and Wales can be divided geographically into three tourist regions, each with its own unique blend of natural and cultural resources. However, common themes include the growth of attractions stressing the Celtic and industrial heritage; the increasing use of rural tourism to boost the economy in remoter areas – often based on farm tourism or specialist products such as fishing; and the growth of tourism in towns and cities – in terms of both cultural and short-break tourism and business travel. In both the traditional resorts of Wales and in the Isle of Man, the authorities are reinvesting to attract new markets. Scotland, Wales and the Isle of Man now have the autonomy to carry out tourism development and promotion for their own areas.

Chapter 10
The tourism geography of Ireland

Learning Objectives

After reading this chapter, you should be able to

- Demonstrate a knowledge of the main tourist regions in the Republic of Ireland and Northern Ireland.
- Understand the distribution and importance of tourism resources in the Republic of Ireland and Northern Ireland.
- Recognize the increasing role being played by heritage resources and attractions in the various regions.
- Recognize the importance of rural resources in Irish tourism.
- Understand the importance of the major cities of the Republic of Ireland and Northern Ireland as business and leisure tourism centres.
- Recognize the effect of the peace process in bringing about tourism initiatives and a unified tourism organization for the whole of Ireland.

Introduction

As an island situated at the western periphery of Europe, Ireland is geographically isolated from the rest of the EU and the world's main tourist-generating countries, with the exception of Britain. Since 1922 it has also been a divided island. The Republic of Ireland chose independence and neutrality in the Second World War, whereas the Province of Northern Ireland (made up of six out of the nine counties of Ulster) remained part of the United Kingdom. This partition never achieved widespread support among the Catholic population, who form a substantial minority in Northern Ireland. In 1969, the outbreak of violence in Northern Ireland proved detrimental to both its tourism industry and that of the Republic. The division of Ireland, based largely on religious differences between Catholics and Protestants, and historical memories of British rule, remains an unresolved problem. However, on-going peace initiatives have made considerable progress toward ending 'the troubles' and have led to the coordinated development of tourism on both side of the border with a newly created 'all-island' agency, 'Failte Ireland'.

Despite the impressive economic development that has taken place since the 1970s, Ireland remains more rural than other West European countries, with few major cities. The low population density, uncrowded roads, unspoiled countryside and slower pace of life make Ireland an appealing destination. The people have a reputation for hospitality and conviviality and the legendary *craic* is itself an attraction. It is therefore no accident that Irish 'themed' pubs are now found all over the world, while Irish music and dance have gained an international following.

The central feature of Ireland is a low-lying plain, dotted with drumlins – rounded hills of glacial origin – lakes and expanses of peat bog. This is almost encircled by mountains, which are not particularly rugged, and breached by both the valley of the Shannon in the west and the coast around Dublin in the east – traditionally the gateways for visitors. Ireland's reputation as the 'Emerald Isle' is due to the mild, damp climate, which favours the growth of lush dairy pasture throughout the year, and in the south-west, subtropical vegetation. However, the unpredictable weather, particularly cool cloudy summers, is one of Ireland's weaknesses as a holiday destination.

Ireland is poor in natural resources compared to Britain, and until recently, many of its young people emigrated to seek greater economic opportunities. In the eighteenth century, the Protestant 'Scots-Irish' from Ulster played a major role advancing the frontier of settlement in North America. Following the Great Famine of the 1840s much larger numbers, mainly from the Catholic south and west, were forced to emigrate overseas. The descendants of those emigrants in the USA, Canada, Australia and Britain are now many times more numerous than the population of Ireland itself. Ethnic tourism and genealogy (tracing family roots) is therefore a lucrative business in both the Republic and Northern Ireland. The epic theme of emigration also plays a major role in the heritage attractions of both countries.

Ireland's heritage is an important part of its tourism industry, though Catholics and Protestants in Northern Ireland interpret this differently. The following themes can be identified:

- **Religion in Ireland as the 'Land of Saints and Scholars'** Many of Ireland's religious monuments – Celtic crosses, monasteries and 'round towers' – together with works of Celtic art such as the Book of Kells, date from the so-called Dark Ages when Ireland was a centre of Christian missionary endeavour to the rest of Europe. The Rock of Cashel in County Tipperary is a remarkable example of this religious heritage in a magnificent setting.
- **Nation building** The Gaelic language and Celtic heritage are seen as central to Ireland's national identity. However, the great majority of the population are English-speaking, due to the long period of domination from Britain. The Anglo-Irish ruling class left a legacy of great country houses that are now important tourist attractions. In their time, these were viewed as symbols of oppression, so that the struggle for independence, particularly the 1798 rebellion, is a major theme in heritage interpretation.
- **The literary and artistic heritage** Ireland has produced many of the great writers and dramatists of the English-speaking world, and tourist trails and guides are available.

Transport

The mode of travel to Ireland has changed since the 1970s as budget airlines and aggressive marketing have seen air transport increase at the expense of the ferry services. The only direct sea routes to Ireland from the Continent are:

- Cork/Roscoff
- Rosslare/Cherbourg.

There is a wide choice of sea routes from Britain:

- Rosslare/Fishguard or Pembroke
- Dun Laoghaire/Holyhead
- Dublin/Liverpool
- Belfast/Liverpool
- Belfast/Douglas and Heysham
- Belfast/Stranraer or Cairnryan.

On many of these sea routes operators are investing in state of the art vessels, including high-speed catamarans, and are also cutting fares in a bid to regain market share from the airlines. Deregulated airlines have also reduced fares, sparking a price war, and opened up access to Ireland's regional airports. Ryanair for example, pioneered the budget airline as a business model and the development of regional airports – supported by EU funding – namely Waterford, Kerry (Farranfore), Galway, Sligo, Donegal (Carrickfinn) and Horan International (formerly Knock). The four main airports are Belfast, Dublin, Shannon and Cork. Dublin is the international gateway to the Republic of Ireland, and the hub for Aer Lingus, the national carrier. Belfast City Airport is the gateway to Northern Ireland, and is well served by routes to the rest of the UK (including a shuttle service to Heathrow) and the Continent. The expansion of air services has encouraged the growth of business and conference traffic. Ireland's location on the western periphery of Europe does give it the advantage of uncongested skies and, with the development of route networks between European regional airports, the authorities intend that Ireland will become less isolated from its tourist markets. Road transport is much more important for domestic tourism than the limited railway network. Some measure of integrated travel is possible through Coras Iompair Irelandann (CIE), which operates coach/bus services throughout the Republic.

The Republic of Ireland

Demand for tourism

Domestic and outbound tourism

The propensity for, and frequency of, holiday-taking has increased in recent years particularly for overseas travel. The strength of the Irish economy allied to airline competition has encouraged the growth of overseas tourism, and over 4 million trips overseas are made each year. The most popular destinations are the United Kingdom (with around half of all trips) and mainland Europe, but with budget and charter flights to long-haul destinations, a greater range of destinations are in evidence. There is also a substantial volume of cross-border traffic by road and rail between the Republic and Northern Ireland. Factors differentiating the nature of tourism demand in Ireland from that in Britain include the following:

- There is a much higher proportion of young people in the population, resulting in an expanding market for family holidays.
- Although the role of the Roman Catholic Church has diminished since the 1980s, popular devotion remains strong, as expressed in pilgrimages to religious shrines such as Lourdes. The most important of these in Ireland itself is Knock in County Mayo, which even has its own airport.

Nonetheless, domestic tourism remains the mainstay of Irish tourism, with almost 6 million trips in 2002. The south-west is the most popular region, and holiday trips are growing at the expense of business and VFR.

Inbound tourism

In contrast to the UK, Ireland achieved only very slow growth in overseas tourist arrivals over the decade of the 1970s, and high inflation and unfavourable exchange rates led to slight reductions in arrivals in the early 1980s. However, deregulation of Ireland/UK air services and the development of regional airports increased arrivals to approach 7.5 million in 2000, although they fell back to almost 6 million in 2002 as a result of world events. Substantial investment in the Irish tourism product, improved marketing and the prospects for peace in Northern Ireland have boosted arrivals – particularly from North America. Features of the Irish inbound market include:

- A heavy dependence on the British market (almost 60 per cent of arrivals).
- Dependence on the peace process in Northern Ireland.
- The increasing domination of the airlines has led to a response by the ferry companies to improve quality and introduce faster services.
- Acute seasonality in the market.
- A high percentage of 'ethnic' visits, especially from Britain and the USA; dependence on the US market leaves Ireland vulnerable to events such as 9/11.

Supply of tourism

The Republic of Ireland's tourism industry employs 7 per cent of the economically active population, and is characterized by small businesses. The country's tourism resource base includes three national parks, a number of forest parks and an extensive system of inland waterways. Among the most important linear attractions are the Grand Canal and the Wicklow Way, a long distance footpath. Tourism products include:

- rural tourism that not only supports the local economy and helps to stem depopulation from the more remote parts of the country, but also keeps alive traditions and handicrafts such as embroidery and knitwear
- activity holidays, including fishing, golf, sailing and horse riding
- cultural activities based on the theatre, folk museums and international festivals
- ethnic activities based around the many centres of genealogy
- English language schools in competition with the UK
- culinary activities.

The tourism sector has received considerable assistance from the government and the European Union, providing Ireland with a competitive edge in the twenty-first century.

In the Republic of Ireland the policy-making body for tourism is the Department of Arts, Sport and Tourism, supported by the national tourist organization – Failte Ireland. The original tourist board for Ireland, Bord Failte, was established in 1955 with promotion (both domestic and overseas) and development functions. Unlike the situation in most of the UK, hotels and guesthouses are classified under a statutory registration scheme, while the government's business expansion scheme supports tourism enterprises. In the 1980s the Irish government re-evaluated the importance of tourism to their economy and instituted a review of the role of Bord Failte. This led to Bord Failte contracting out much of its operational work to focus on international marketing. At the same time, a five-year planning framework for tourism was put in place with the aim of increasing both tourist volume and spending. The review was closely integrated into a successful bid for investment from the European Regional Development Fund and the European Social Fund. These were applied to programmes to extend and upgrade the range and quality of tourist facilities. Three priority areas were identified:

- tourism infrastructure
- tourism facilities
- marketing/training.

The investment was focused on 'population' and 'spatial' areas:

- the population areas include Dublin and Killarney, Wexford and Sligo, Castlebar and Dingle, Kilkenny and Cobh, and Ballybunion and Bundoran
- the spatial areas include touring areas (Ring of Kerry, Boyne Valley), special-interest areas (The Burren, Western Lakes), developmental areas (Shannon and the canals), and product areas where local communities can support a saleable product such as handicrafts.

The injection of money into the tourism sector has led to greater professionalism, widened the product range and improved quality generally. It has also had the effect of changing the distribution of tourism across Ireland. While tourism is evenly spread compared to most other European countries, the west and the south-west have lost market share to Dublin.

With the new millennium and the apparent success of the peace process in Northern Ireland, Failte Ireland, an all-island marketing body was created in 2003. The functions of the new body comprise:

- international and domestic marketing
- product development and promotion
- improving the quality of accommodation
- managing the tourism product development scheme.

Tourism resources

Although the Republic of Ireland is organized in seven regional tourist boards, we prefer to divide the country for tourism purposes into three main tourist regions, based on the historic provinces of Leinster, Connacht and Munster:

- Dublin and the East
- Western Ireland
- The South-West.

Dublin and the East (Leinster)

Dublin is not only the capital of the Republic of Ireland and home to a third of its population, but has also become one of the world's great tourist cities, with a major airport and ferry access through the port of Dun Laoghaire. The Dublin region has seen the largest growth of tourism in Ireland, so that by 2002 the city received 3.3 million overseas visitors and almost a million domestic tourists, supporting 25 000 full-time jobs.

The main tourism resources of Dublin are linked by a series of themed trails and include:

* the city's role in Irish history, recalled by Dublin Castle (the seat of government under British rule), Kilmainham Gaol and the General Post Office (associated with the 1916 Easter Rising); this history is brought to life in the multi-media exhibition at City Hall and a number of museums
* literary heritage, showcased in the Dublin Writers' Museum, featuring the lives and works of Joyce, Sheridan, Wilde and other celebrities, and the Abbey Theatre, where many of their plays were first performed
* the architectural heritage of fine eighteenth century buildings and squares
* the Genealogical Office, an important resource for the ethnic tourist market retracing their Irish roots
* the Guinness Storehouse, a themed experience based on Dublin's most famous product.

The river Liffey divides the city into the *northside* and the *southside* and was the focus for city-wide initiatives to celebrate the millennium. The southside of Dublin contains Trinity College, Ireland's oldest and most famous university, and Temple Bar, an exciting 'left bank' district that has emerged since the early 1990s. This is now one of the city's most popular tourist areas, offering a wide range of leisure facilities and entertainments. The northside include O'Connell Street, Phoenix Park and a cluster of cultural attractions.

The capital is a good base for tourism circuits that include some of the most attractive scenery of **eastern Ireland** – the granitic Wicklow Mountains with their steepsided glens. The narrow coastal plain is fertile, with a relatively dry and sunny climate. The Vale of Avoca is famous for the beauty of its landscape, and the village of Avoca attracts many visitors as the setting for a well-known TV series. The main tourist centres include the holiday resorts of Bray and Tramore; Waterford, famous for its glassware; and Wexford, which hosts an international opera festival. New Ross is one of many small towns that have capitalized on ethnic links with the USA – in this case the Kennedy family. Kilkenny has a fine medieval heritage, also supported by international festivals. New Grange to the north of Dublin is one of Europe's most important prehistoric sites.

Western Ireland (Connacht and Donegal)

The Irish government has encouraged tourist facilities to locate in the west, which is a much poorer region economically, with a high dependence on traditional peasant farming. Special incentives are available in the Gaeltacht – those areas where the people still speak the Gaelic language as their mother-tongue. This is because the west is regarded as the true repository of Irish national culture, rather than the Anglicized south and east. Local communities have encouraged tourism with farmhouse holidays and by providing self-catering accommodation in the form of traditional style cottages.

Galway is the recognized capital of the west and its airport has developed rapidly in line with Ireland's other regional airports. It is the southern gateway to the Connemara area and, with its adjoining resort of Salthill, is an important centre for touring holidays and conferences. The main touring circuits are:

- to the north, the Great Western Lakes – Corrib, Mask and Caarra
- to the west, a superb indented coastline and the Connemara Mountains
- to the south-west, the Aran Islands – famous in Irish literature and folklore – can be reached by sea or air
- to the south are the cliffs of Moher and the Burren area of limestone scenery in County Clare, which is of great interest to botanists as well as geologists; a modern visitor centre interprets this heritage, helping to reduce the impacts of tourism on these sensitive natural areas.

Donegal in the north-west is geographically part of the historic province of Ulster. Here a rugged coastline is interspersed with fine beaches and a number of attractive fishing harbours such as Killybegs.

The South-West (Munster)

The south-west includes the most attractive scenery in Ireland, and three of its main tourism centres – Killarney, Cork and Limerick. The major tourism resources are:

- Killarney, which was recognized as a holiday resort of international significance in the nineteenth century. Nowadays it is an ideal touring centre, including the famous scenic road known as the 'Ring of Kerry'. Killarney has the largest concentration of bedspaces outside the capital, and its airport at Farranfore is positioned to attract the short-break market from the UK. Nearby are the lakes and mountains of the Killarney National Park, Muckross House and some of the best golf courses in Europe.
- Tralee has an important festival, deliberately promoted to attract participants claiming Irish descent from all over the world.
- Cork is the second city of the Republic and the centre of a development zone that includes:
  - Kinsale – a long-established important sailing and fishing centre, finding a niche market in culinary short-breaks
  - Blarney – world famous for its castle featuring the stone which confers the gift of eloquence
  - Cobh – was historically important before the jet era as the principal staging point for passenger liners and millions of emigrants to the United States, most of whom would have travelled in steerage class; the quayside has been restored with attractions recalling its role in Ireland's social and transport history, including the voyage of the *Titanic*.
- The Limerick/Shannon area has a range of high-quality accommodation and provides good access to other areas. Shannon Airport until the 1960s was a compulsory stop on transatlantic flights and pioneered the 'duty-free' concept of airport shopping shortly after the Second World War. The river Shannon is now more important as a tourism resource for sailing and fishing than as a commercial waterway, with Athlone and other smaller centres providing facilities. North-west

of Limerick is Bunratty Castle, which pioneered the medieval banquet theme so popular with North Americans. Bunratty has now expanded its heritage attractions into a folk park and shopping complex.

Northern Ireland

The province of Northern Ireland is much smaller than the Irish Republic, with a population of over 1.6 million in 2001. It is, however, more urbanized, with almost one-third of the inhabitants living in the capital, Belfast. The Province has frequent air and shipping services to Scotland and England, and a good road and railway network. Northern Ireland's main tourism resource is the scenery of limestone uplands, lakes and the basalt plateau of Antrim. The distribution of tourism is tied to the coast, with the exception of the Fermanagh Lakeland. Tourism promotion and development are the responsibility of the Northern Ireland Tourist Board (NITB), which was one of the first statutory tourist boards to be set up (in 1948). The NITB works closely with Failte Ireland and VisitBritain. There are also a number of regional tourist associations.

Tourism resources

Belfast
During the nineteenth century Belfast became an important port and shipbuilding centre (the *Titanic* was launched here), due to its location on a deep, sheltered estuary. Since 1969, the threat of terrorism has severely curtailed tourism, especially from Britain, but with the peace process the city is receiving an increasing number of visitors and attracting investment, assisted by the formation of the Belfast Visitor and Convention Bureau in 1999. Belfast remains a deeply divided city, but even at the height of the troubles the sectarian murals of certain areas attracted sensation-seeking groups of foreign tourists. More conventional attractions include the city's rich industrial heritage, the redeveloped area around the cathedral, which now rivals Dublin's Temple Bar district for shopping and nightlife, the Odyssey Project – a large-scale education, science and sport development; and ECOS – an environmental education centre. Belfast also hosts a variety of international events such as the Cutty Sark Tall Ships Race. Attractions on the outskirts of the city include Hillsborough Castle, Carrickfergus Castle and the Ulster Folk and Transport Museum at Cultra.

The North
North of Belfast lies the Antrim Plateau, where the basalt rock gives rise to impressive scenery, including:

- the Giant's Causeway, perhaps Ireland's most famous natural attraction, and because of its unique character, a World Heritage Site
- the nine glens of Antrim – deep wooded valleys sloping down to the sea which were carved out of the basalt by fast-flowing streams; Glenariff is the best-known of these, and at the foot of the glen one of the many *feiscanna* (festivals) of the region is held

- the spectacular coastline between Larne and Portrush; Portrush, Ballycastle and Coleraine are the main resorts on the Antrim coast, which have reinvested to improve facilities for family holidays and golf tourism.

The West

To the west is Londonderry (Derry), set on a hill on the banks of the Foyle Estuary. This is divided for sectarian reasons, with the Protestant community occupying the walled town that withstood a historic siege in 1689. South-east of Londonderry are the touring circuits of the Sperrin Mountains, where attractions include the Sperrin Heritage Centre, Springhill House and the historic town of Moneymore. To the south is the Ulster-American Folk Park of Omagh, one of the increasing number of folk museums in the Province, which explores Scots–Irish links with the USA.

Fermanagh Lakeland

In the centre of Ulster the river Erne links a number of large lakes to provide an important resource for water-based recreation, nature lovers and fishing holidays – which have long been popular with Dutch and German tourists. Castle Archdale on Lough Erne is the main centre for sailing and hire cruising on this extensive system of inland waterways. Castle Coole and Florence Court are significant attractions run by the National Trust. Enniskillen is a historic garrison town on the river Erne.

The South

This area includes the historic city of Armagh, which is the spiritual capital of Ireland with its two cathedrals. South-east of Armagh rises the granite mass of the Mournes, rounded mountains sweeping down to the sea. On the coast, Newcastle is a seaside resort and a sailing and golf centre. Other resorts at the foot of the Mourne Mountains are lively Warrenpoint and the quieter Rostrevor, both on Carlingford Lough. The Ards Peninsula is a scenic area within easy reach of the resort of Bangor and the city of Belfast. Attractions on the peninsula include Castle Ward, Mount Stewart and Kearney Village. The Ards Peninsula is separated from the rest of County Down by Strangford Lough, providing a bird sanctuary and the setting for the Strangford Stone, erected for the Millennium. Around the Lough are the abbeys of Inch, Grey and Comber, and to the south, the cathedral town of Downpatrick, with a new visitor centre interpreting the legacy of St Patrick.

The Border Region

This area, between Northern Ireland and the Republic, is the focus of considerable tourism investment in the wake of the peace process. Local authorities on both sides of the border are cooperating under the aegis of Interreg (the European Structural Fund's assistance for border regions) and other EU schemes.

Summary

Despite the political and religious divisions, Ireland is well endowed with many types of tourist attractions. It can be divided geographically into a number of tourism regions, each with a particular blend of natural and cultural resources. We can however identify a number of common themes. These include the use of European funds to develop tourism; the growth of themed heritage attractions – particularly those stressing the Celtic contribution; the increasing use of rural tourism to encourage the economy in remoter areas – often based on farm stays; and the growth of urban tourism in terms of both short holidays based on cultural attractions and business tourism. The unified development of tourism across Ireland is also a significant innovation.

Chapter 11
The tourism geography of Scandinavia

Learning Objectives

After reading this chapter, you should be able to:

- Describe the major physical regions and climate of the Scandinavian countries and understand their importance for tourism.
- Understand the nature of Scandinavian economies and society, and their significance for tourism demand.
- Outline the major features of demand for both domestic and international tourism in Scandinavia.
- Describe the major features of the Scandinavian tourism industry, including transport, accommodation and promotion.
- Be aware of the importance of ecotourism in the Scandinavian environment.
- Demonstrate a knowledge of the tourist regions, resorts, business centres and tourist attractions of Scandinavia.

Introduction

Strictly speaking, Scandinavia consists of only three countries – Denmark, Norway and Sweden. However Finland is usually included. Although they are geographically isolated in the North Atlantic, Iceland and the Faroe Islands (which belong to Denmark) have been added, as they share with the other countries a similar culture and outlook, while Greenland is regarded as part of North America. All these countries are members of the Nordic Council (Norden), which is responsible for a high level of cooperation in policies affecting transport, tourism, education and the environment. The Scandinavian airline SAS, which is jointly owned by the governments of Denmark,

Norway and Sweden, is one such example of international cooperation, and was the first to develop transpolar routes to North America and the Far East. Despite limited natural resources, a rigorous climate and a peripheral location in Northern Europe, the Scandinavian countries have achieved economic prosperity and stability with health and social welfare services among the best in the world. High environmental standards are maintained, both in the cities, which are free of litter and graffiti, and in the countryside. Compared to the crowding which afflicts most of Europe, Scandinavia can offer vast areas of sparsely populated coast and countryside, with almost unrestricted access to a range of recreational resources. Public transport systems are usually integrated and provide a viable alternative to touring by car.

The Scandinavian landscape still bears the imprint of the glaciers of the last Ice Age. The glaciers eroded the valleys of western Norway into deep troughs and scraped bare the ancient plateau surfaces of Finland and Sweden. Here the ice sheets left masses of boulder clay, which are now covered by coniferous forest dotted with lakes and outcrops of rock. Nevertheless, the region contains a great diversity of scenery. The lush farmlands of Denmark are in marked contrast to the lunar volcanic landscapes of Iceland, or the forests of northern Scandinavia. The climate also varies from cool temperate in Jutland to subarctic in Northern Scandinavia. Most of the region has a continental climate, with severely cold winters and warm summers. The main negative feature affecting the development of tourism is the shortness of the summer season and the darkness of winter, due to the northerly latitude.

The Scandinavian countries have shared similar cultural features since the Viking era (approximately 800 to 1100 AD). Historically, Denmark, and later Sweden, were the dominant countries in the region – with the result that they now have a more impressive heritage of historic buildings than the other three countries. Also, the Lutheran Church has provided a measure of cultural unity since the Reformation in the sixteenth century. Nevertheless, each country has developed a strong national identity and the differences extend to international politics. Sweden, for example, has pursued a policy of neutrality for the past two centuries. However, in 1995 it joined the EU along with Finland, following the example of Denmark, whereas Norway and Iceland have decided to stay out.

The Scandinavian countries have a total population of only 24 million, which is mainly concentrated in the towns and cities of the southern part of the region. The climate as well as social and economic conditions combine to make Scandinavia one of the major generating areas in the world for holiday tourism, especially to winter-sun destinations. The people enjoy a high standard of living, but at the same time place great emphasis on leisure, active participation in outdoor recreation and the quality of life; levels of education are also high and typical annual leave entitlement is five weeks or more. Add to this a well-developed and efficient travel trade throughout the region, and it is no surprise that levels of both domestic and foreign holiday-taking are much higher than the average for Europe. Holidays abroad represent around one-third of all holidays taken by residents of Norway, Sweden and Denmark and, in consequence, these countries have a deficit on their international travel account. A large percentage of these holidays are to other countries in the region, facilitated by the abolition of passport controls for inter-Scandinavian travel. This does mean, however, that statistics for international travel between Scandinavian countries are not collected, making it difficult to measure regional tourism flows. In domestic tourism there is a growing trend for short second holidays, especially those based on winter sports and other types of outdoor recreation.

On the other hand, the relatively high cost of living, high levels of taxation and strong currencies combine to make Scandinavia an expensive destination for foreign visitors. The majority of tourists are from other parts of Europe, especially Germany. There is a widespread perception that Scandinavia is not only more expensive but also less accessible than other destinations, involving long journeys by road and car ferry, or expensive air travel. The completion of a number of bridges and tunnels connecting the Danish Islands to the mainland is greatly improving transport by road and rail between Scandinavia and the rest of Europe. With deregulation under the EU, air fares are falling, while Copenhagen is rapidly becoming a major hub for long-haul as well as inter-regional air services. Inbound tourism to Scandinavia should also increase as interest in 'green tourism' gathers momentum. The tourism products offered by the Scandinavian countries are generally more 'environment friendly' than those available in the Mediterranean and other 'sunlust' destinations. They include:

- camping and self-catering holidays in the countryside
- a range of activity and 'wilderness adventure' holidays.

Denmark

The smallest and most densely populated of the Scandinavian countries, Denmark lacks wilderness areas and spectacular scenery (the highest point is only 170 metres above sea level). Denmark's appeal lies in its neat, gently rolling countryside and picturesque towns and villages, immortalized by Hans Christian Andersen. Consisting essentially of 100 inhabited islands and the Jutland Peninsula, with only a short land border with Germany, no part of the country is far from the sea. It is therefore not surprising to find that sailing is a popular pastime and that the Danes have the highest rate of yacht ownership in Europe. They also have one of the highest rates of ownership of second homes (known locally as 'summer houses'). Much of the demand is generated from the capital, Copenhagen, where most families live in apartments. Cycling is also very popular – the topography is ideal even if the weather is unpredictable, and this greenest of transport modes is encouraged by a nationwide system of bikeways. Danes have the reputation for being more informal and 'continental' than other Scandinavians, with a quality of life expressed by the Danish word *hygge* (roughly translated as 'cosy'). This is experienced in the traditional inns, as drinking laws are more relaxed than elsewhere in Scandinavia. Copenhagen is particularly renowned for its exuberant nightlife and tolerance of different lifestyles.

Demand for tourism

Domestic and outbound tourism
Danes enjoy up to six weeks' annual holiday entitlement and two-thirds of the population take a holiday away from home every year. Almost half of these holidays are domestic as the Danes increasingly holiday at home. People prefer to stay with friends and relatives, or in owned and rented 'summer houses' or use camping sites in preference to serviced accommodation. Along with other Scandinavian countries,

Denmark encourages the principle of 'tourism for all' or social tourism for those people who for various reasons find it difficult to take a holiday. Under 'tourism for all', retired people on limited incomes can even take state-subsidized holidays in the Canary Islands during the winter months, which at least reduces the cost of heating bills. Taking the population as a whole, over half of all holidays are taken abroad. Other Scandinavian countries are less popular with Danish holidaymakers than Spain and Germany.

Inbound tourism

With over 2 million arrivals annually, Denmark is heavily dependent upon Germany and the rest of Scandinavia for international arrivals. These are highly seasonal, with most concentrated between May and September.

Supply of tourism

Transport

Apart from Kastrup Airport, serving Copenhagen, there are an increasing number of budget airlines offering flights to regional airports such as Aarhus, Esjberg and Billund. Surface transport is also excellent, with good road, rail and ferry links to the UK and the rest of Europe. Transport within Denmark is mainly by private car using a well-developed internal and international road system with ferry connections between the islands. Stena and DFDS Seaways operate international ferry services to the rest of Scandinavia, Germany and the UK. However, the ferries will decline in importance as a result of the completion of a number of bridge and tunnel projects. These must rank as some of the world's most spectacular engineering feats; they include the Great Belt Bridge linking the islands of Funen and Zealand, and the Oresund Bridge and Tunnel connecting Zealand to Sweden. The Oresund link, positioned close to Copenhagen, is already enhancing the city's role as the gateway to Scandinavia. Another project – the Fehmarn Belt Tunnel – will provide a more direct route between Copenhagen and North Germany.

Accommodation

The majority of Denmark's accommodation capacity is self-catering, including summer homes and campsites, and this is where most of the growth has occurred. Hotels, inns and youth hostels are widely available, with the highest occupancy levels in Copenhagen, and, during the summer peak, on the island of Bornholm. Stays on Danish farms are popular with British families, often as part of a package deal with the ferry operators.

Organization

The Danish Tourist Board is the national body responsible for the marketing and travel trade development of Denmark as a destination, while domestic tourism is the responsibility of the regional and local authorities.

Tourism resources

The advantage of a small country like Denmark is that tourists can follow the scenic 'Marguerite Route' and see virtually all the key attractions in the course of one short touring holiday, starting with the Jutland Peninsula. Much of the peninsula is covered with pine forest and large tracts of heathland, interspersed with peat bogs, which have yielded fascinating evidence from prehistoric times. Interest in Denmark's rich and varied heritage is widespread, forming the basis of a number of folk museums with buildings and traditional crafts preserved in an authentic setting, or in reconstructed Iron Age villages, where students re-enact the lifestyles of the remote past. The preserved 'old town' of Aarhus is another heritage attraction, which can be enjoyed alongside a vibrant modern city. Denmark is also well equipped with activity parks for children known as 'Sommerlands', but the most popular attraction is undoubtedly Legoland at Billund. Jutland's west coast has fine sandy beaches backed by dunes, but bathing is often unsafe due to the changing winds and tides. The fishing port of Esbjerg is a major centre, with ferry connections to Harwich in England and the islands of Fano and Romo. It is also close to the medieval town of Ribe with its Viking Centre.

The islands of the Danish Archipelago to the east offer different landscapes and attractions:

- Bornholm, situated in the Baltic Sea 200 kilometres east of Copenhagen, is particularly appealing with its rocky granite scenery, but it is somewhat remote from the rest of the country.
- Funen, known as the 'Garden of Denmark', is especially well equipped for tourism.
- Odense attracts many American tourists as the birthplace of Hans Christian Andersen.
- Zealand is probably the most interesting for the foreign visitor; at Roskilde there is much evidence of Denmark's Viking past and 'longship cruises' are even available. There are a number of important historic buildings, the best known being Frederiksborg Castle, and Kronborg Castle at Helsingor, famous for Shakespeare's *Hamlet*. Above all, Zealand contains Copenhagen, which is a long-established city breaks destination and a major cultural centre. With its copper-sheathed roofs and spires, harbour and pedestrianized shopping streets, the Danish capital has a particular appeal. Specific attractions include the Tivoli Gardens, Europe's oldest amusement park, with its theatres and summer festivals, the Danish Royal Ballet, the Louisiana Museum of Modern Art and the Carlsberg Brewery. Unlike most European capitals, Copenhagen has fine beaches and resort attractions within easy reach by public transport from the city centre.

Norway

Of all the Scandinavian countries, Norway is probably the best known. Since the nineteenth century tourists have visited the fjords in the western part of the country, attracted by the breathtaking combination of mountain and coastal scenery. The land is rugged and only 3 per cent can be cultivated, so Norwegians throughout their history have turned to the sea for their livelihoods. Norway has the longest coastline in Europe, deeply cut by the fjords, with chains of offshore islands providing a sheltered coastal waterway for shipping. Norway has a substantial merchant navy and is important in the cruise market, while sailing is a popular pastime for Norwegians. The heritage of seafaring and exploration, from the Viking longships to Amundsen and Thor Heyerdahl (of *Kon Tiki* fame) is greatly valued. The former isolation of many areas, separated by mountain and fjord, explains why

Norway, in contrast to Denmark, has retained much of its traditional culture, including the wearing of colourful regional costumes on special occasions. Norway's huge resources of hydroelectric power are vital to the economy, but concern about the impact of the power industry on the environment has led to demands for more areas to be set aside as national parks.

There are substantial variations in climate in such an elongated country, as the North Cape is almost 2000 kilometres by air from Kristiansand in the south. Temperatures on the coast are much milder than might be expected for such high latitudes, due to the influence of the Gulf Stream. The fjords and shipping lanes remain ice-free in winter and it is possible to grow fruit and cereals as far north as Tromso, 300 kilometres inside the Arctic Circle. True Arctic conditions can be experienced further north, in the Svalbard archipelago. It is worth emphasizing that the midnight sun in summer, can only be seen, weather permitting, north of the Arctic Circle; at the North Cape there is continuous daylight from mid-May to the end of July. Exposed coastal areas like Bergen receive an excessive amount of rain, while the sheltered heads of the fjords are much drier, sunnier and warmer in summer – but cold in winter. In the mountainous interior, heavy snowfalls are frequent, making it possible to ski year-round in areas like the Hardangervidda east of Bergen. The Norwegians claim to have invented skiing – although as a means of travel rather than as a sport – and they probably have the world's highest participation rate in skiing, with ski trails even in cities such as Oslo.

Demand for tourism

The prosperity of the Norwegian economy, thanks largely to North Sea oil revenues, explains why travel propensities are high. However, holiday patterns are changing as the traditional long summer holiday gives way to shorter, more frequent trips.

Domestic and outbound tourism

Most Norwegians take holidays within their own country, largely because the ownership of holiday chalets is widespread. Many of these are situated in the *saeter*, the high summer pastures above the treeline, and are a reminder of the pastoral lifestyle of the past. Hiking is a popular activity in summer and skiing in winter. With over 4 million overseas trips yearly by Norwegians, there is a deficit on the country's travel account. Only a small number of trips are to other Scandinavian countries, as Norwegians prefer instead to travel to the UK, southern Europe, North Africa and the Canary Islands.

Inbound tourism

Norway experienced a growth of inbound travel following the Lillehammer Winter Olympics, but numbers have gradually declined since then. Norway's foreign visitors come largely from Denmark, Germany and Sweden, but those from outside Scandinavia, such as the British and Americans, tend to stay longer and spend more. There is a pronounced peaking of demand during the short summer season.

Supply of tourism

Transport

In such a mountainous country, getting around can be a problem – it takes over a week to travel the length of Norway by car – so air transport is important.

International air passengers are served by Oslo's two airports, boosted in recent years by budget airlines such as Ryanair. Domestic air services – such as those operated by Braathens SAFE – link almost fifty destinations. However, the majority of foreign visits and domestic trips are by private car, taking advantage of the improved 80 000 kilometre road network and ferry links across major fjords (although the ferries are crowded during the summer peak). The rail network run by Norwegian State Railways is more limited, since it terminates in Bodø, leaving Northern Norway without a rail service. The Bergen to Oslo railway does offer the tourist one of Europe's most scenic journeys, and it played a major role in opening up Norway for tourism. However, it is the shipping services that have traditionally provided the country with a lifeline. Tourists can travel on the Norwegian Coastal Express fleet from Bergen to Kirkenes on the Russian border. Ships call at some thirty-five ports to take on or unload passengers and cargo throughout the year. The round trip takes 12 days and is an interesting alternative to the summer holiday cruises available to the Western Fjords and 'the Land of the Midnight Sun'. Large numbers of visitors also use the ferry services operated by Fjord Line, DFDS Seaways and Stena which link Norway to the UK and Denmark through the ports of Bergen, Stavanger, Oslo and Kristiansand.

Accommodation

In the peak season the majority of accommodation is in camping, although other types of self-catering have grown in popularity, leading to a shortage in the supply of holiday cabins. Other accommodation is available on farms and in *rorbus* – fishermen's winter cabins built on stilts over the water's edge. Relatively few tourists, other than business travellers, use hotels although these are generally open year round. Even so, there is an acute shortage of accommodation capacity in the popular tourist areas in the peak summer and Easter periods.

Organization

The Norwegian government recognizes the importance of the industry in aiding rural communities, transport operators and the accommodation sector, and has therefore attempted to reduce the acute seasonal and geographical concentration of visits. In an attempt to boost the volume of tourism in Norway and to develop professionalism in the sector, the Norwegian Tourist Board has been created as an independent, commercial agency, jointly supported by the Norwegian government and the tourism industry. It is licensed by the Ministry of Trade and Industry.

Tourism resources

Western Norway

Western Norway is the most popular area for foreign visitors since it includes the five most spectacular fjords (Hardanger, Sogne, Nord, Geiranger and Romsdal), the highest mountains, and the largest glacier in mainland Europe the Jostdalsbreen. Less well known is a cultural resource unique to Norway – the *stave* churches, built entirely of wood and with Viking features in their design. The historic port of Bergen, situated between the two longest fjords – the Hardanger and the Sogne – is the gateway for exploring this region by ship, road or rail. The Geiranger Fjord is generally recognized to be the most attractive, with its towering rockfaces and myriad waterfalls. Of the many villages lining the shores of the fjords, Laerdal,

Olden and Ulvik are the most popular resorts, while Balestrand has retained much of the ambience that attracted British tourists in Victorian times. A short distance inland lies the Jotunheim National Park, Norway's most visited wilderness area, and a favourite with hikers and climbers.

Southern Norway

Southern Norway offers a gentler coastline of sheltered coves and beaches that are popular with domestic holidaymakers. Although a modern city compared to Bergen, Oslo is an established destination for cultural tourists. The main attractions are the museums celebrating Viking and maritime heritage, and the Vigeland sculpture park. Oslo is the gateway to Norway's main skiing areas, and a number of resorts have developed along the railways linking the capital to Bergen and Trondheim. Lillehammer, venue for the 1996 Winter Olympics, is the most important.

Northern Norway

Northern Norway beyond the Arctic Circle is different from the rest of the country, not least because the interior is occupied by people of an age-old, distinct culture – the *Sami* (formerly known as Lapps). Lapland also includes part of Northern Sweden, Finland and Russia, but the Sami of Finnmark have retained their semi-nomadic way of life, based on reindeer herding, to a greater extent than elsewhere. Tourism provides a welcome source of income but, as with all such indigenous peoples, represents a potential disruption to a culture that is in delicate balance with the harsh environment. The coastal communities, such as those on the Lofoten Islands, largely depend on the fishing industry and tourism is of secondary importance. The regional capital Tromso boasts the world's most northerly university and brewery. It is called 'the gateway to the Arctic' as so many polar expeditions set out from here. Most tourists then proceed to the North Cape, which ranks as a mass tourism destination by Arctic standards, attracting several thousand visitors daily during the summer. Svalbard, Norway's Arctic archipelago, is situated 1000 kilometres further north. Spitzbergen, the largest island, is noted for its dramatic landscape of fjords, ice-sculpted mountains and glaciers, as well as for the variety of wildlife that has adapted to an inhospitable environment. Despite its location in the High Arctic of 75° North latitude, the west coast is accessible to cruise ships. Activities include trekking, mountain climbing, adventure/wildlife tourism and survival training/ leadership courses.

Sweden

Although it is the largest of the Scandinavian countries, Sweden lacks the clearly defined image presented by Norway and Finland. Although it shares the Kjolen Mountains with Norway, the scenery tends to be less spectacular on the eastern slopes. With 50 per cent of its area under forest, and boasting innumerable lakes, rivers and rapids, Sweden has the largest area of unspoiled wilderness in Europe. However the country is known mainly for the quality of its industrial products, from motor vehicles to furniture, rather than for any specific tourist attractions.

Sweden has a varied coastline on two seas, lakes and mountains, forests, inland waterways and a rich cultural heritage. It was the first country in Europe to develop a system of national parks to protect its wilderness areas from exploitation by the important mining, timber and wood pulp industries. Public access to the countryside is guaranteed by the traditional law known as *Allemansrätt* (every man's right), which allows the visitor to camp overnight, hike, ride, cycle and picnic on private land. Although winters are severely cold, with abundant snow, summers are warm and sunny, especially along the Baltic coast. Midsummer Day is the occasion for festivities throughout the country.

Demand for tourism

With a very prosperous economy the majority of Swedes have at least five weeks' annual holiday entitlement and the Swedes not only have one of the highest travel propensities in the world, at almost 75 per cent, but also they are more likely to take a second holiday than the European average.

Domestic and outbound tourism

The private car accounts for the majority of holiday trips taken by Swedes, but escalating costs have reduced the amount of touring. Self-catering accommodation is favoured, especially summer cottages. There are some 600 000 of these and they are often owned by people who have migrated to the cities but wish to retain a link with their rural homeland. Domestic business travel is focused on Stockholm, Gothenburg and Malmö.

With their level of prosperity, the Swedes are important generators of international travel, with over 12 million trips taken annually. Foreign destinations popular with Swedish holidaymakers include other Scandinavian countries, Germany, Spain, Greece, Cyprus and the UK, while long-haul travel is increasing in popularity.

Inbound tourism

The volume of inbound overnight visitors to Sweden is around 11 million, but day trips from other Scandinavian countries are substantial at around 130 million visits annually. For overnight visitors, the main generating countries are the rest of Scandinavia, Germany, the UK, the Netherlands and the USA.

Supply of tourism

Transport

International air transport is served by Stockholm Arlanda, Gothenburg and Malmö Airports and domestic flights are operated by SAS and Braathens SAFE to some twenty destinations. However most holiday tourists arrive by car and ferry, or hovercraft, via the main routes from Denmark and Germany. Car travel is expensive in Sweden and government policy is to favour public transport by imposing controls on car use. Swedish railways have therefore received considerable public investment to provide high-speed routes between the major cities. There is also a nationwide system of cycle routes.

Accommodation

Sweden's serviced accommodation stock has grown since 1997, though it is still dominated by small businesses. Demand for hotel accommodation by domestic tourists is small, with the exception of business travellers. In the past acute shortages of suitable hotels in cities like Stockholm has led to the development of company apartments. Self-catering accommodation in the form of summer cottages and log cabins is in demand for holiday tourism; timeshare and multi-ownership schemes are being developed, as are high-quality campsites.

Organization

In 1992, the state-owned Swedish Tourist Board was replaced by a private sector initiative, the Swedish Travel and Tourism Council. The Council is jointly owned by the private sector and the Swedish government, and its mission is to promote Sweden as a tourist destination. It is supported by an independent network of 22 regional organizations. Another agency – the Swedish Tourism Authority – is publicly funded and has the remit of coordinating tourism activity in Sweden.

Tourism resources

The main tourist areas are found in the south, along the Baltic and North Sea coasts, and in the central lake district west of Stockholm. These three areas are linked by the Gota Canal. This is a linear attraction, 190 kilometres in length, which connects Gothenburg to Stockholm and the three largest lakes – Vänern, Vättern and Mälaren. The canal was built in the nineteenth century to provide a short cut for shipping. Although it has lost most of its significance as a commercial waterway, some of the original vessels have been adapted for summer cruises.

The North Sea coast

Gothenburg is Sweden's major North Sea port but offers many cultural attractions and the Liseberg theme park, one of the largest in Scandinavia. The 'golden coast' of Bohuslän nearby is popular with Swedish families, especially the resort of Tanum Strand, which is an excellent base for exploring the many offshore islands. Scania in the extreme south of Sweden has lowland landscapes similar to those of Denmark and its capital Malmö, very close to Copenhagen, is a major business centre.

The Baltic coast

On the Baltic coast, the island of Gotland with its white sandy beaches and strange rock formations has a special appeal. The well-preserved medieval city of Visby is a World Heritage Site as well as being a lively summer holiday resort.

The Central Lake District

Lying close to the Norwegian border, the provinces of Värmland and Dalarna offer scenic lake and forest landscapes, and are ideal for activity holidays, including fishing, canoeing and whitewater rafting in summer. Mora on Lake Siljan has hosted international downhill ski events, but is mainly noted for the Vasaloppet, a cross-country ski race which attracts thousands of participants each March. Dalarna is regarded as the cultural heartland of Sweden, offering picturesque folk customs, heritage museums and innumerable handicraft outlets. However, the most interesting place for the foreign visitor is undoubtedly Stockholm. The capital is attractively situated on a number of islands at the entrance to Lake Mälaren, while thousands more islands scattered along the Baltic coast provide ideal sites for summer homes. The well-planned modern city contrasts with heritage attractions such as Gamla Stan (the preserved old city), the Vasa Ship Museum and Skansen, Scandinavia's oldest folk museum. Stockholm's main event attraction is the Water Festival in August.

The North

Norrland, the sparsely populated northern half of Sweden, includes part of Lapland. Tourism in Swedish Lapland began in the late nineteenth century and is growing in importance because of interest in ecotourism and green issues. It is one of the largest areas of unspoiled wilderness in Europe, including six national parks. It is Europe's most northerly developed ski area, offering skiers and snowboarders the novelty of practising their sport until late June under the midnight sun. Tourists also visit to experience the Sami (Lapp) culture, centred on Jukkasjarvi and Jokkmokk, where the old ways continue to flourish and silver and leather handicrafts are sold. Jukkasjarvi also offers a unique winter attraction – the Ice Hotel – promoted as the 'world's largest igloo'.

Finland (Suomi)

Culturally, Finland is different from the other Nordic countries due to its language and the cultural links with Russia to the east. Finland offers the visitor vast expanses of lakeland blending almost imperceptibly with forest, a unique landscape associated with the music of Sibelius. The marketing campaigns of the Finnish Tourist Board emphasize unspoiled nature and the absence of air and water pollution. Of the total area no less than 10 per cent is inland water – lakes, marshes, rivers and rapids – while forests of conifers and birch make up the other two-thirds. Eskers, long sinuous ridges of material laid down by glaciers in the last Ice Age, separate the lakes and are a distinctive feature in a landscape which is for the most part lowland. Winters are long and severe, but the Finns are adept at dealing with them; fleets of icebreakers keep open the shipping lanes and a whole range of winter sports, including ice hockey and snowmobile rallies, are popular during the cold season.

Much of Finland's prosperity is derived from its seemingly inexhaustible forest resources which provide timber, wood pulp and furs. The exploitation of these in the past has caused concern among environmentalists, but as in Sweden, the timber is now harvested on a sustained yield basis. The forests and lakes are much valued as a recreational resource. Many families in Helsinki and other cities own a lakeside cabin as a second home, usually with a sauna attached. In Finland the sauna is as much a social institution as a means of relaxation.

Demand for tourism

Around 50 per cent of the population take a holiday of four nights or more away from home. The proximity of Finland close to the weak economies of the former Soviet Union, allied to devaluations of the Finnish mark, meant that the tourism sector suffered from overcapacity in the 1990s. In turn this led to reductions in prices and a formerly expensive destination became much more affordable. Finland therefore experienced considerable increases in inbound travel in the 1990s, and volumes have stabilized to around 4 million arrivals annually with an additional 1.5 million day trips. As Finland recovered from this economic crisis and began to share in the EU's prosperity, including adoption of the Euro, outbound tourism has grown to approach 6 million trips annually. Even so, this is less than the volume of domestic tourism, as Finns prefer to visit their second homes at the coast and beside the lakes.

Supply of tourism

Transport

Swedish and Norwegian visitors arrive mainly by sea, in preference to the long road journey around the Gulf of Bothnia, through the ports of Helsinki, Turku and Maarianhamina in the Aland Islands. Visitors from other West European countries can take the more direct ferry route from Travemünde in North Germany. Air transport has grown steadily in importance, with Helsinki acting as the gateway and Finnair as the national airline. Domestic transport arrangements are excellent, with broad all-weather highways, an improved rail system and a network of domestic air services to more than twenty destinations.

Accommodation

Motels and hotels are concentrated in the major cities (Helsinki, Turku and Tampere) where business travel means they can maintain a high annual occupancy rate (up to 75 per cent in Helsinki). Finland can also provide low-density holiday villages, which are mainly concentrated in the central lakeland area, holiday cottages, farm accommodation and campsites. Seasonality is high, with the majority of foreign tourists arriving between May and October with a peak in July. In consequence, roughly one-quarter of the accommodation stock is only open for part of the year. A conscious effort has been made to extend the season by developing conference and winter sports tourism. Partly because of Finland's post-Second World War neutrality in world politics, Helsinki has become a major international conference centre, offering facilities such as Finlandia Hall and first class hotels.

Organization

Finland has pursued an aggressive tourism policy, spearheaded by the Finnish Tourist Board, which reports to the Ministry of Trade and Industry. Tourism is seen as a means for regional development in the rural areas, and also for diversification of the national economy.

Tourism resources

Finland's appeal to foreign visitors lies in its uncrowded natural resources and it has capitalized fully on the growth of ecotourism.

Finnish Lapland

Finnish Lapland especially offers scope for wilderness adventure holidays, both for independent travellers and for package tourists. Summer activities include rafting, canoeing, gold panning and mountain-biking; while in winter 'reindeer safaris' involving a stay in a Sami encampment and dog-sled expeditions are on offer. Charter flights are available in December from Britain to Rovaniemi, the main tourist centre, which has been promoted with considerable success as 'the home of Santa Claus' and now has a theme park – Santa Park. As a result Finland has a larger share of winter visitors from the UK than any other Nordic country. Skiing 'under the midnight sun' is available in the far north near Lake Inari, where the forest at last gives way to barren fells and tundra.

Saimaa Lake District
The best opportunities for outdoor recreation are to be found in the Saimaa Lake District in the south-east of the country. The lakes offer 50 000 kilometres of shoreline and are forested down to the water's edge; not surprisingly, this is a popular area in summer. The main tourist centres are Lapeenranta for summer cruises, and the spa town of Savonlinna which has an international opera festival. The Karelia forest region bordering Russia is culturally distinct, as shown by the many Orthodox churches.

The coasts
Both the southern and western coasts of Finland are characterized by clusters of offshore islands which provide opportunities for sailing. Seafaring traditions are particularly important in the Aland Islands, which are Swedish-speaking and have the status of an autonomous region. For this reason they are popular with Swedish as well as Finnish holidaymakers, not least for the duty-free shopping available on the ferries. Other places of interest include the resort of Hanko, favoured by the Russian aristocracy prior to the 1917 Revolution, the Moominland theme park, and Helsinki. Finland's capital is noted more for its fine modern architecture than for historic buildings. It is a convenient starting-point for excursions to St Petersburg and Estonia.

Iceland

Promoted as 'a land of ice and fire', exposed to the raw forces of nature, Iceland is geologically unique. This large island is located on one of the major fault lines in the Earth's crust and contains over 200 volcanoes – major eruptions and earthquakes occur on average every five years. Although one-fifth of the country is covered by glaciers, Iceland is by no means as cold as its western neighbour Greenland, thanks to the warming influence of a branch of the Gulf Stream. However, its location close to the Arctic Ocean does mean that the weather is highly unpredictable, and in winter 'abysmal' (as defined by Hatch's climate code mentioned in Chapter 4). The tourist season is short, even by Scandinavian standards, and summer temperatures rarely exceed 20 °C (although it may feel warmer as the air is unpolluted and remarkably clear). Iceland's abundant geothermal resources are harnessed to heat swimming pools, buildings and greenhouses. One well-known example is the so-called 'Blue Lagoon' outside Reykjavik, which is actually an effluent reservoir from a power plant. Agriculture is largely restricted to sheep farming and the landscape is for the most part treeless. Nearly all the population lives in or near the coast, while the interior is made up of desert-like lava plateaux or rugged volcanic mountains.

With few resources other than the dominant fishing industry, Iceland is anxious to encourage tourism. Promotion is the responsibility of the Icelandic Tourist Board assisted by the national carrier Icelandair. Because Iceland is an expensive destination and relatively difficult to reach, the volume of inbound tourism is small (around 300 000 annually), although growing and significant given the country's sparse population. Visitors come mainly from the USA, Germany and the UK. Outbound tourism is constrained by the scant leisure time available to many Icelanders (who have to 'moonlight' at a second job to maintain their high living standards).

The bulk of the air transport services from Western Europe and Scandinavia are provided by Icelandair, Iceland Express and SAS, while the international airport at Keflavik is often used as a stopover on transatlantic flights. Access by sea is much less convenient and comprises ferry services from Bergen, the Shetlands and Esbjerg. There is an extensive domestic air network which is necessary in view of the fact the Iceland has no railways and the least developed highway network of any country in Europe (Albania excepted). In fact, most of the roads, especially in the rugged interior, are suitable only for four-wheel drive vehicles. Iceland's accommodation stock comprises hotels, guesthouses, youth hostels, farms and campsites.

Iceland's tourism appeal lies in its unspoiled natural scenery and the scope for adventure holidays. Pony trekking for example, is a successful product utilizing the native breed of horse which is small and uniquely adapted to the rugged terrain. Other activities include bird watching, whale watching, snowmobiling across glaciers, rafting and camping expeditions. Skiing facilities on a modest scale are available near Reykjavik and Akureyri.

The most popular tourist attractions are located in the 'Golden Circle' east of Reykjavik, including the Gullfoss waterfall, the Great Geyser and the Thingvellir National Park – a spectacular natural amphitheatre where Iceland's parliament was held in Viking times. Another cluster of natural attractions in the north of the country includes Lake Myvatn and Dettifoss, Europe's largest waterfall. Considering that Iceland has less than 300 000 inhabitants, it has made a remarkable contribution to European culture in literature, namely the Viking sagas, also in architecture and popular music. Unlike most capitals, Reykjavik is a close-knit community characterized by low rise, brightly coloured wooden buildings, but it does contain 60 per cent of the country's population and most of its high-class accommodation. The city's vibrant clubbing culture increasingly attracts the youth tourism market on short breaks from North America and the UK.

Some allege that Iceland's green credentials have been damaged by the decision in 2003 to resume commercial whaling, and the project to construct an aluminium smelter in the north-east of the country.

The Faroes

The Faroes consist of 18 inhabited islands in the stormy North Atlantic, halfway between the Shetlands and Iceland. They are a self-governing nation within the Kingdom of Denmark, but they have stayed outside the EU. As yet, tourism is much less important than the fishing industry, which may explain why the Faroese have rejected calls from the world's environmentalists that they should give up their whaling traditions. The excessively wet and windy climate is a major constraint on tourism, but the islands can offer some of Europe's most spectacular cliff scenery and vast colonies of seabirds. The capital, Thorshavn, is accessible by scheduled flights from Copenhagen and by summer ferry services from Esbjerg, Bergen and Iceland.

Summary

Scandinavia's climate is typified by severely cold, long winters and warm, sunny summers. The varied landscapes include forested countryside dotted with lakes, indented coastlines with fjords and islands, and the volcanic features of Iceland. Social and economic conditions have combined to make Scandinavia one of the major generating regions in the world for holiday tourism, delivering a deficit on the travel account for the region. Inter-Scandinavian travel has been particularly popular, facilitated by the abolition of passport controls.

Accommodation capacity in the short summer season is dominated by the self-catering sector as serviced accommodation is in short supply. The majority of international tourists arrive by car using the many ferry services available, though international air links are comprehensive. Internal travel will be facilitated by new tunnels and bridges, and is typified by rapid intercity rail links, broad, surfaced highways, and extensive domestic air and sea links. The most important of Scandinavia's tourism resources are the uncrowded, unpolluted countryside, the spectacular scenery of the mountains and many coastal regions, the islands and holiday beaches, and the Scandinavian culture and outdoor way of life on show in the capitals and major cities of the region.

Chapter 12

The tourism geography of the Benelux countries

Learning Objectives

After reading this chapter, you should be able to:

- Describe the physical regions and climate of the Benelux countries and understand their importance for tourism.
- Understand the relationship between the individual Benelux countries and be aware of their linguistic differences.
- Appreciate the scale of demand for both domestic holidays and holidays abroad, and the nature of that demand.
- Outline the main features of the tourism industry in the Benelux countries.
- Demonstrate a knowledge of the tourist regions, resorts, business centres, and tourist attractions of the Benelux countries.

Introduction

Three small countries in Western Europe – Belgium, the Netherlands and Luxembourg – have a much greater economic, cultural and political significance we might expect from their size. Historically known as the Low Countries, the Netherlands and most of Belgium are made up of lowland plains adjoining the North Sea, while flat-topped uplands are characteristic of southern Belgium and Luxembourg. Areas of heathland separate the coastal lowlands from the uplands of the Ardennes, which rise to just over 600 metres above sea level. The region has a cool maritime climate similar to that of England. Near the coast the cloudy weather is unpromising for tourism, with moderate rainfall throughout the year, whereas inland the maritime influence begins to fade; winters are colder, with enough snow in the Ardennes for skiing, while summers are warmer.

Culturally the Benelux countries are interesting for their heritage of historic buildings and art treasures, a reminder that the region has played a major role in European history. However their economic prosperity has frequently led to conflict with powerful neighbours, with the result that after the Second World War Belgium, the Netherlands and Luxembourg led the way to European unity with the formation of a customs union. This means that restrictions on movement between the three countries are minimal. With a combined population of 27 million, the Benelux states are the most densely populated countries in Europe. Not only does this lead to intense competition for land use, but it also places pressure on the environment to the extent that any proposed tourism developments are very closely scrutinized. The economies of the three countries have grown steadily since the Second World War, giving rise to increasing demands for both domestic and foreign tourism. Expenditure on overseas travel exceeds the receipts from inbound tourism in all the countries of the region. Annual holiday entitlement averages five or more weeks and a typical working week is less than 40 hours.

The Netherlands

The Netherlands Board of Tourism promotes the country as 'Holland', although the name strictly applies to just two of the eleven provinces that united to resist Spanish rule in the sixteenth century. Holland has a strong identity; its landscapes and cultural features are known worldwide. The Dutch contribution to art, with painters like Rembrandt, Frans Hals, Vermeer and Van Gogh, has been immense. Dutch achievements in seamanship, agriculture and engineering have also been remarkable. Much of the country, especially in the west, is made up of flat *polderlands* reclaimed from the sea. The story of this reclamation and the constant battle against the sea is proudly told in exhibitions and museums, as well as in the many engineering works (such as the Delta Plan) which are tourist attractions in themselves. The countryside is criss-crossed by dykes and canals, although relatively few windmills now survive along with the *meers* (lakes) resulting from early drainage schemes. However much of the east and south of the Netherlands is scenically different, with extensive areas of heath and woodland.

The Netherlands can also offer cultural diversity. For centuries the Dutch ruled a major overseas empire, with colonies in the Caribbean, South America, South Africa and Asia. The influence of their most important former colony – Indonesia – is evident for example in the buffet-style *rijstaffel*. Perhaps because of their maritime outlook and the pressures of living in a small, crowded country, the Dutch have a reputation for both tidiness and tolerance, and it is probably this which has attracted young tourists from all over the world. In contrast, some of the formerly isolated fishing communities around what was once the Zuider Zee (now the Ijsselmeer) have retained a strong religious outlook, along with the wearing of the traditional costumes that attract tourists. In contrast to its image, the Netherlands is a major industrial nation. High living standards, urban pressures, excellent transport systems and an unpredictable climate have combined to encourage the development of theme parks, zoos and innovative ideas in leisure. The best known examples are the De Efteling Family Leisure Park near Breda, and the Center Parcs accommodation concept, which uses advanced technology to create an all-weather leisure environment in an attractive woodland setting.

Demand for tourism

The level of economic development has fuelled the demand for leisure and tourism. Throughout the 1990s the domestic market declined, with the Dutch taking more foreign holidays, so that the Netherlands has a growing deficit on its travel account.

Domestic tourism

Domestic holidays (particularly short trips) and day excursions are an important sector of the Dutch tourism industry and recreation is becoming a major part of the Dutch lifestyle. The majority of domestic holidays are concentrated in July and August, leading to congestion in popular holiday areas. A nationwide programme to stagger holidays was introduced in 1983 to help ease seasonal congestion, while a trend to more winter holidays may also help combat the problem. Most people taking domestic holidays use the private car and tend to stay in self-catering accommodation (such as 'summerhouses', caravans, campsites, or holiday villages) rather than in hotels. Despite the prevalent use of the private car, the Dutch rarely take touring holidays, preferring instead single-centre stays in their small and crowded country. Business and conference tourism is an important sector of the domestic market. Good-quality conference facilities are dispersed throughout the country in both purpose-built centres and in hotels, motels and holiday villages. International conferences are seen as a growth area, especially given the Netherlands' central position in Europe.

Outbound tourism

As the Dutch have one of the highest holiday propensities in Europe – they take more holidays abroad than in their own country – the Netherlands is a major generator of international tourists on a world scale. This trend is enhanced due to the affluence of the country and a generous social welfare system which means all levels of society can travel abroad. Moreover the introduction of the Euro will enhance outbound travel as the Dutch will be able to compare prices more easily across Europe. Although one might expect South Africa to be a leading overseas destination, in fact it has only received substantial numbers of Dutch tourists since the ending of apartheid in the 1990s. There is an increasing trend for the Dutch to take winter holidays, particularly for skiing. The small size of the country encourages day excursions and cross-border trips (around two-thirds of all foreign trips are to neighbouring countries). In the early years of the twenty-first century the Dutch took around 14 million outbound trips.

Inbound tourism

With the new millennium the Netherlands received between 9 and 10 million visitors annually, but this still leaves a substantial deficit on the travel account. The majority of tourists are from Western Europe, dominated by arrivals from Germany. Inbound tourism to the Netherlands showed modest growth in the 1990s, partly due to a range of special events (such as major art exhibitions) and the Dutch tourism authorities' promotional campaigns, but has stabilized in the early years of the twenty-first century, with no major events in prospect. The international short-break market is important in the Netherlands, with most foreigners only staying for two to three nights on average. However, in contrast to the domestic market, they tend to use serviced accommodation. In consequence, hotels and foreign visitors are concentrated in a few centres; Amsterdam alone accounts for around 50 per cent of the commercial bednights spent in the country.

Supply of tourism

Transport

Schiphol, Amsterdam's international airport, is not only the major gateway to the country, but also a serious competitor to London Heathrow as an inter-continental hub, and now with a fifth runway, its services are expanding. Likewise KLM, the national carrier, is one of the world's leading airlines and dominates the industry in the Netherlands. It serves both domestic passengers and those travelling to neighbouring countries, with an aggressive pricing policy encouraging European short breaks. Martinair and Transavia are the main tourist charter airlines. Other international gateways are Maastricht Airport and the ferry terminals at Vlissingen, Europoort and the Hook of Holland, mainly handling passengers from the British Isles. Surface transport arrangements are excellent throughout the Netherlands and also into neighbouring countries, with 90 000 kilometres of road and a comprehensive intercity rail network. There is a fully integrated public transport network of buses, trams and trains. Cycling is encouraged with a nationwide system of dedicated routes.

Accommodation

Accommodation in the Netherlands is dominated by self-catering with campsites, holiday villages and a network of 'trekkers' huts' for cyclists and walkers. This sector of the accommodation market is well developed in the Netherlands to meet the demand for inexpensive family holidays, but with increased affluence preferences are switching to hotels and motels. Also, given the extensive water resources of the Netherlands, marinas are an important source of accommodation.

Organization

Tourism promotion, both domestic and international, is the responsibility of the Netherlands Board of Tourism and Conventions with responsibility for domestic and inbound promotion. The board is backed by regional, provincial and local promotion, as well as by the Netherlands Congress Bureau. The government is improving tourist infrastructure by investing in 'bungalow parks', hotels, marinas and tourist attractions. Promotional themes focus on waterland, cultural/historic heritage, cities and the seaside. This reflects the fact that each of the provinces of the Netherlands has special appeal for foreign visitors (except maybe for Flevoland, which is almost entirely polders reclaimed from the Zuider Zee in the 1930s).

Tourism resources

Most foreign tourists are attracted to the western half of the country, particularly to the cities of the **Randstad**. This is a ring of urban development that contains almost half the population of the Netherlands, but on just 15 per cent of its land area. Development in the Randstad is therefore carefully planned to preserve its so-called 'green heart' – an area of attractive countryside inside the ring that includes the world-famous bulbfields between the historic towns of Haarlem and Leyden. The Randstad includes the following major tourist centres:

- The Hague (Den Haag), the diplomatic capital of the Netherlands; attractions nearby include
- Madurodam – 'Holland in miniature', Delft – famous for its ceramics and associations with Vermeer; and the resort of Scheveningen
- Utrecht – celebrated for its music festivals
- Rotterdam – Europe's largest port, at the mouth of the Rhine; whereas other Dutch cities tend to promote their heritage attractions, Rotterdam was rebuilt after the Second World War and is thoroughly modern in its outlook and architecture.

Amsterdam is also located in the Randstat. It is the commercial capital of the Netherlands, and one of the world's top five tourist centres. Most of the historic area dates from Amsterdam's 'Golden Age' in the seventeenth century, when the city was the hub of a vast trading empire, and there was little expansion or rebuilding in the long period of subsequent decline. The merchants' houses, with their intricate brickwork, stepped gables and narrow frontage along tree-lined canals, now form one of the world's most picturesque urban landscapes.

Amsterdam boasts an excellent transport infrastructure that includes the famous trams, a network of cycleways and a metro system that provides improved access to Schiphol Airport. The *Grachtengirdle* – the concentric ring of canals – is now mainly used for sightseeing excursions.

Compared to London or Paris, Amsterdam has few individual buildings that are internationally renowned as tourist attractions. The floating flower market on the Singelgracht and the Ann Frank House – a reminder of the city's important Jewish community – are among the most popular with foreign visitors. Art lovers are attracted to the Rijksmuseum and the Van Gogh Museum. However, the main appeal of Amsterdam lies in its street life, shops, cafes and entertainment facilities. These include the theatres around the Leidseplein, the smoke-filled 'brown bars' of the Jordaen district and the De Wallen area near the Eastern Docks, which has a long-established sex industry.

Amsterdam faces a number of problems in competing with other European cities as a tourist destination, namely:

- Tourism development is often given a low priority by the city government, whose policies are aimed at maintaining a large resident population in subsidized housing in the historic centre.
- Long-established perceptions of the city relate to a particular time period – the seventeenth century – which make change and diversification difficult, whereas
- Since the 1960s a very different image – of Amsterdam as a city of drugs and sex – has become deeply ingrained in the popular culture, especially among young tourists. This has led in some areas to an ambience of sleaze, litter and drug-related crime that provides an unwelcome contrast to the traditional Dutch obsession with cleanliness and public order. In 2003 the authorities imposed strict regulations on drug sales partly in response to pressure from the governments of neighbouring countries.

The **North Sea coast**, with its sandy beaches backed by dunes, is served by a string of resorts, which attract large numbers of German holidaymakers (mainly from the

Ruhr conurbation), as well as the Dutch themselves. The busiest resorts are:

- Zandvoort – noted for its motor racing circuit
- Noordwijk – renowned for its flower gardens
- Scheveningen – Holland's best-known seaside resort.

After a long period of decline, Scheveningen was transformed by an ambitious scheme of re-investment in exciting new leisure facilities, and it has become a major conference venue, as a well as a classic example of the rejuvenation stage of the tourism area life cycle. Between the resorts there are conservation areas where further development is strictly prohibited. This is because the dunes, which play a vital part in Holland's coastal defences, are very vulnerable to visitor pressure. To the south lies the province of Zeeland, originally a group of islands at the mouth of the Rhine, now joined up by the Delta Plan to create an environment suitable for a wide range of water sports. In contrast, the medieval towns of Middelburg and Veere have much to attract the heritage tourist.

In the north-east, the province of **Friesland** offers a more tranquil environment of small rural communities where the Frisian language is still spoken. The main attraction here is the Frisian Lake District around the resort of Sneek that offers facilities for boating and sailing. Separated from the mainland by the extensive mudflats of the Wadden See, the Frisian Islands such as Texel provide fine beaches, self-catering accommodation and a number of important nature reserves.

Gelderland in the east of the country is under-populated by Dutch standards, and large expanses of heath and woodland have been designated as the Hoge Veluwe National Park. The city of Arnhem was the scene of a major battle in the Second World War, as the bridging point over the River Rhine close to the German border, and now offers a number of museums and attractions focusing on the region.

The province of **Limburg** in the extreme south is the only part of the Netherlands that can be described as hilly. Partly for this reason the resort of Valkenburg, with its casinos and golf courses, is very popular among domestic tourists. The attractive city of Maastricht has taken advantage of its location on the borders of three countries to become an important venue for international conferences.

Belgium

It can be difficult to define the tourism product of Belgium compared to neighbouring France, Germany and Holland. This is largely because the country is divided in language and culture between the Dutch-speaking Flemings in the north, the French-speaking Walloons in the south, and the German speakers of the districts of Eupen and Malmedy in the east. Scenically too, the flat farmlands of Flanders and the heaths of the Kempen are quite different in character from the hills and forests of the Ardennes. Moreover Belgium as an independent nation did not exist until 1830. In the Middle Ages, cities such as Bruges, Ghent, Antwerp and Liège were to a large extent independent, and grew wealthy on the profits of the cloth trade. However lack of political unity led to the region being dominated by the great powers of the time, namely Burgundy, France, Spain and the Austrian Empire. Unlike the Dutch, the Belgians were generally ready to accept foreign rule and remained strongly Roman Catholic in religion after the Reformation in the sixteenth century. This is shown by the abundance of religious art and impressive Baroque architecture in cities such as Brussels. Because of its location, Belgium was the 'cockpit of Europe' in the frequent wars between France and other countries. Some of the many battlefields have become historic sites on the tourist itinerary, notably:

- Waterloo just south of Brussels (the Napoleonic Wars)
- the cemeteries and war memorials around Mons and Ypres – with its Flanders Fields exhibition (the First World War)
- the 'Battle of the Bulge' museum at Bastogne in the Ardennes (the Second World War).

Although it can offer beaches, attractive waterways and fine scenery, Belgium's appeal is mainly cultural, in the widest sense. Like the French, the Flemish and Walloons take food and drink seriously, and the country produces little wine but over 400 different kinds of beer. As this is a predominantly Catholic nation, the tourist can also enjoy many interesting festivals, although by no means all are religious in character. As in the Netherlands, theme parks are popular, which attract large numbers of tourists from neighbouring countries such as France.

Demand for tourism

Belgian travel propensities are very high, with 80 per cent of the population taking a holiday in any one year and the rise in the number of holidays abroad has outstripped growth in the domestic market; equally expenditure on travel overseas is greater than receipts from inbound tourists.

Domestic and outbound tourism

For domestic holidays the most popular form of transport is the car, and self-catering accommodation (holiday villages, caravans, and camping) is increasingly used, as serviced accommodation declines in popularity. Social tourism is important in the Belgian domestic market. The Ardennes and the coast are the most popular holiday regions. Belgium is an important generator of international tourists, with the majority of main holidays taken abroad. Most trips are to neighbouring countries, but Italy and Spain are also important destinations. As in the Netherlands, the high number of trips abroad leaves a deficit on the travel account.

Inbound tourism

The performance of Belgium as an international tourist destination is modest, with around 6.5 million arrivals in the early years of the twenty-first century. The majority of foreign visitors are from other European countries – particularly the Netherlands. However, visits from neighbouring countries tend to be short compared to those from, say, the UK or the USA. Business trips are concentrated into Brussels (particularly as it hosts the European Commission), and Antwerp; whilst international conferences are attracted to the seaside resorts of Ostend and Knokke, as well as to new facilities in Liège and Bruges. Apart from these business travel centres, visits elsewhere in the country tend to be for holiday purposes.

Supply of tourism

Transport

Both external and internal transport links are highly developed. Brussels is the gateway to Belgium for the great majority of air travellers, although the airports at

Antwerp, Liège and Ostend do have some international services. More significant from the viewpoint of price-conscious British tourists are the ferry services to Ostend and Zeebrugge, including a fast catamaran connection. The Channel Tunnel is providing competition for the ferry operators and the airlines, so that the Eurostar fast train service from London to Brussels has gained a large share of the lucrative business travel market. Belgium has an extensive motorway network for such a small country (over 1250 kilometres). The environmental impact has been considerable, but it does mean that no part of the country is more than 3 hours' drive from the coast, and Belgium's traditional role as 'the crossroads of Europe' has been enhanced. The Belgian railway network is less convenient for touring the country, as it is focused on Brussels.

Accommodation

In the serviced accommodation sector low occupancy rates mean that few new hotels are being built and, despite government assistance schemes, little investment is occurring in the existing hotel stock. Most hotel guests are business travellers while demand for self-catering accommodation comes from holidaymakers. Campsites, holiday villages, chalets and apartments are available.

Organization

The small size of the tourism industry in Belgium has meant that government policy for tourism is low on the priority list and lacks clear objectives. There are separate promotional commissions for the French-speaking and Flemish regions, both with head offices in Brussels, while the Belgian Tourist Office oversees the promotion of Belgium abroad.

Tourism resources

The tourist resource base is very diverse for a country of this size. These resources may be summarized as:

- the coastal resorts
- the art cities of northern Belgium
- the Ardennes.

The **North Sea coast**, like that of Holland, is sandy, flat and backed by dunes. However flooding has been less of a problem in the past than the silting up of ports such as Bruges, which now lies a considerable distance inland. The coast is only 60 kilometres in length and it has suffered from over-development and lack of planning, as shown by the ribbon development of high rise apartments and holiday villas. However the beaches are well maintained, colourful windbreaks provide protection from the constant breezes, while the resorts provide many amenities. A tramway linking all the resorts offers a safe alternative to the car in an area where traffic can reach saturation point in peak season. In addition to domestic tourists, the coast is popular with Germans, while Ostend has long been an established favourite with the British. The resorts differ a good deal in size and character:

- De Panne, with its wide expanse of beach, can offer sand yachting as an activity for the young affluent visitor

- Zeebrugge caters more for families
- Ostend and Blankenberge are the busiest resorts, providing a sophisticated holiday product including casinos
- Knokke-Heist near the Dutch border is definitely upmarket.

The main attractions for foreign tourists are the **art cities**, mostly situated in Flanders within easy reach of the coast. These are ideal for short breaks, or as part of an extended tour taking in Northern France and the Rhineland. The heritage of Gothic and Renaissance art and architecture is a reminder not only of the power of the Church but also the wealth and prestige of the merchant guilds from the four-teenth to the sixteenth centuries.

- Bruges (Brugge in Flemish) is one of the best preserved medieval cities of northern Europe. For this reason it has become a popular short-break destination as well as a long-established attraction on European touring circuits. Unlike modern conur-bations, the townscape of Bruges is on a human scale – a picturesque composition of red-brick gabled buildings, church spires, cobblestone streets and squares, and tranquil waterways set in the green Flanders countryside. Bruges is often described, somewhat misleadingly, as the 'Venice of the North'.
- Ghent is perhaps more typical, as it has moved with the times and remained a major centre of commerce.
- Antwerp on the River Scheldt is Europe's second port and rivals Brussels in its nightlife and range of museums and exhibition centres. It was the birthplace of the painter Rubens and was designated European City of Culture in 1995. The import-ant diamond industry owes a great deal to the city's close links with Belgium's former colony in the Congo.
- Brussels has the advantage of being the capital, not only of the Flanders region and of the country, but also, in a sense, of the European Union. Flemish, French and – increasingly – English are in use throughout the city. It contains the European Commission that has spawned a high-spending bureaucracy and encouraged many multi-national corporations to set up their head offices near the centre of power. Brussels boasts one of the finest groups of Baroque buildings in Europe – around the Grand Place, and in contrast, the modernistic Atomium.
- Liège is the most important city in French-speaking Wallonia and is famous for its glass and gun-making industries. It is close to the Ardennes holiday region. Much of the Sambre-Meuse area to the west was blighted by heavy industry in the nine-teenth century, and is now undergoing economic regeneration.
- Namur, in an attractive setting at the confluence of the rivers Meuse and Sambre, is the official capital of Wallonia.

The **Ardennes** uplands, with their forests, limestone gorges, winding river valleys and picturesque chateaux, are Belgium's scenic resource; much of the region was, until recently, comparatively remote and sparsely populated. Field sports have been important in the past, but nowadays a wide range of activities are catered for such as riding, cycling, rock-climbing, caving and canoeing. The Ardennes attract large numbers of Dutch tourists as well as domestic visitors, but this popularity has put increasing pressure on its resources. In the areas most accessible to the conurbations of Belgium, the Netherlands and Germany, the unplanned proliferation of second homes has caused social and environmental problems. Greater control over devel-opment and more effective visitor management are needed, and for this reason part of the Upper Ardennes has been designated as a National Park.

Many of the villages and market towns of the region have become resorts, the most important being Dinant, in an attractive setting on the River Meuse. Specific tourist attractions include the caves at Han-sur-Lesse, the castle at Bouillon, and Orval Abbey – noted for its beer. One other resort deserves special mention, as it has given its name to similar attractions elsewhere; this is Spa, where the mineral springs set the fashion for 'taking the waters' to the rest of Europe. Like other health resorts, it offers a range of cultural and sporting activities. It is also the venue for the Belgian Grand Prix motor racing event.

Luxembourg

The Grand Duchy is the smallest member of the European Union, but the largest of the six 'mini-states' of Europe, which have somehow survived since medieval times. Since 1839 it has been closely linked with Belgium and the Belgian franc is legal tender. Due to its size (slightly less than the county of Dorset or the US state of Rhode Island), inbound tourism is of far greater importance to Luxembourg than it is to Belgium. The annual number of visitor arrivals is almost double the resident population, but the impact of tourism is less than you might expect for these reasons; the length of stay is short, and many visitors are business travellers to Luxembourg City. Others are transit passengers taking advantage of Luxembourg's low cost international flights, while most holidaymakers tend to be campers from the neighbouring conurbations in France, Belgium, the Netherlands and Germany. Tourism has a major impact on the economy and is Luxembourg's third foreign currency earner after financial services (banking and insurance) and steel exports. The majority of visitors are from Europe, with almost half originating from Belgium and the Netherlands. Seasonality is high, with most tourists arriving between June and September.

Transport facilities are excellent for a small country made up largely of rural communities. In addition to the international airport at Findel, close to the capital, there are 270 kilometres of railway network and 5000 kilometres of road.

Most of Luxembourg's accommodation capacity is on campsites. Although more nights are spent in campsites than in hotels, it is the latter which are most important in terms of tourist spending. However, this is affected by the nature of the business travel market, which can afford the high tariffs.

Tourism is the responsibility of the Ministry of Tourism backed by the National Tourism Office. The promotion of conference tourism is given a high priority; helped by the fact that the country has three official languages and its people are proficient linguists and supporters of European cooperation.

Luxembourg's tourist appeal lies in its capital city and attractive countryside. **Luxembourg City** is an important financial centre as well as hosting the Secretariat of the European Parliament and other EU organizations. The city has an attractive setting on a series of hills and valleys linked by viaducts. Although most of the massive fortifications were torn down and replaced by boulevards long ago, enough remains to explain why Luxembourg was once called 'the Gibraltar of the North'.

The country's other attractions lie mainly in the **Oesling** region in the north, which forms part of the Ardennes. They include Vianden, a noted beauty spot with an impressive castle; Clervaux, famous for its abbey; and Echternach, a pilgrimage centre, which is of unique interest for its Whitsun dancing processions.

The Germano-Luxembourg Nature Park nearby is an outstanding example of international cooperation in conservation. The **Bon Pays/Gutland** region in the south of the country is less impressive scenically, but it does contain the spa town of Mondorf-les-Bains, which has been rejuvenated to meet contemporary leisure demands.

Summary

Physically, the Benelux countries comprise three regions – the lowlands of the coast, the intermediate plateaux zone and the uplands. The Benelux countries were joined by a customs union in 1947 and this close integration is now enhanced by their adoption of the Euro. Demand for tourism and recreation is high, but this does place pressures on the environments of these small, densely populated countries. In each country demand for overseas travel is high and there is a deficit on travel accounts. The majority of foreign tourists are from other countries of Western Europe. Transport facilities are comprehensive and the region's position in Europe attracts many transit passengers. Accommodation provision is dominated by self-catering capacity, particularly campsites and holiday villages, although affluence is seeing a shift in preference towards hotels. There are three main areas of tourist attraction. First, the historic towns and cities attract business and holiday tourists alike; second, the resorts of the North Sea coast are major holiday and day-trip centres; and third, the uplands and countryside are important holiday destinations for campers.

Chapter 13

The tourism geography of Austria, Germany and Switzerland

Learning Objectives

After reading this chapter, you should be able to:

■ Describe the major physical regions and climates of Austria, Germany and Switzerland and understand their importance for tourism.

■ Recognize that the strength of the economies of the three countries encourages demand for outbound tourism but their reputation as expensive destinations deters inbound tourism.

■ Recognize the special contribution of Austria and Germany to world culture and the importance of the cultural heritage.

■ Appreciate the importance of winter sports tourism to the Alpine region and its environmental impact.

■ Understand that stagnating demand for tourism to Austria, Germany and Switzerland has led to a restructuring of the national tourism organizations.

■ Describe the main features of the tourism industries in the three countries.

■ Demonstrate a knowledge of the tourist regions, resorts, business centres and tourist attractions of Austria, Germany and Switzerland.

Introduction

The countries of Austria, Germany and Switzerland occupy a key position in Central Europe. Both Austria and Germany were historically great empires, whereas Switzerland has always been a small country owing much of its importance to its strategic location astride the major passes over the Alps.

Apart from Germany's short North Sea and Baltic coasts, the area under consideration in this chapter is landlocked. Three major physical regions can be identified:

- The North German Plain and the coast are of relatively limited importance for tourism.
- The Central Uplands, which include areas such as the Rhineland and the Harz Mountains in Germany, the Mittelland plateau in Switzerland and the Danube Valley in Austria, are more significant.
- The Alpine region is of major importance for international tourism. It includes most of Austria, half of Switzerland and the south of Bavaria in Germany.

Forests, lakes and mineral springs are major recreational resources in all three countries.

With the exception of the North Sea coast, the region has a continental climate, with winters getting colder the further one travels east, but also as a result of altitude. In the mountains the climate is bracing, with clean air and brilliant sunshine, but the weather varies with aspect and altitude and fogs are frequent in some valleys during the winter. The cold winters bring the snow which made possible the development of winter sports, yet the resorts on the shores of the more southerly lakes bask in almost Mediterranean temperatures. The *Föhn* wind frequently blows down some of the south-facing valleys of the Alps bringing unseasonal warmth and excessive dryness during the winter months.

Despite their very different historical backgrounds, all three countries are federal republics, with considerable devolution of powers (including tourism responsibilities) to the states in Germany, provinces in Austria and cantons in Switzerland. Major population concentrations include the Rühr conurbation of Germany, Vienna in Austria and in Switzerland, Zurich, though not the capital, is the largest city. German is the dominant language throughout the region, but in Switzerland, French, Italian and Romansch are also official languages.

The economies of the three countries are highly developed and industrialized with a high standard of living and quality of life. This is reflected in the widespread demand for environmentally sound tourism. Both Germany and Austria are members of the European Union, while Switzerland – in line with its historic tradition of neutrality – has no political affiliation. A central geographic location and good communications mean that levels of outbound tourism are high in all three countries. However, high prices do limit the number of inbound tourists. In Austria and Switzerland the annual holiday entitlement is four weeks or more, and in Germany entitlement is five or more weeks. In Austria there is a 35–40 hour working week, in Germany 40 hours is the norm, but in Switzerland working hours are relatively high and attempts are being made to reduce them.

Austria

Austria is a small country with a capital that is larger than might be expected, due to the historical fact that Vienna ruled the vast Hapsburg Empire until 1918. The lavishly decorated Baroque churches, monasteries and palaces are part of that heritage. Austrian composers – notably Mozart and Schubert – made an immense contribution to the world of music and are now celebrated through annual music festivals. But for most people, the abiding image of Austria is its scenic countryside of lakes and mountains, while its reputation as one of the world's major winter sports destinations has tended to overshadow the many cultural attractions.

Tourism plays a major role in Austria's economy, accounting for 5 per cent of the gross national product. Austria has the benefit of both a summer and a winter season – the winter sports market has grown steadily since the late 1950s and is now more significant in terms of tourist spending than summer tourism, although it remains smaller in volume. Skiing helped to restore national pride following the disaster of two world wars, and ski-racing is a major spectator sport. For many years Austria was in the top position as a skiing destination, having overtaken Switzerland in the 1950s, but more recently France has relegated it to second place. Much of the resort development took place in the years following the Second World War as part of the reconstruction of Austria's economy.

Demand for tourism

Domestic and outbound tourism

The travel propensity of Austrians is increasing (over two-thirds of the population take a holiday) of which domestic holidays account for the majority of trips. There is a growing move towards taking more than one holiday, particularly in the form of short breaks to events in Austrian cities, and this is spreading the holiday pattern away from July and August. Farmhouse stays have been successfully promoted to encourage tourism throughout the rural areas, but there is still a concentration of holidays in the Tyrol, creating considerable congestion, with visitors outnumbering the inhabitants in many villages. Austria is a major generator of international tourists on a world scale, though the majority of trips are to neighbouring countries, emphasizing Austria's favourable location in Europe. The majority of holidays abroad are to Mediterranean countries – particularly Italy, Greece and Croatia.

Inbound tourism

Austria attracted around 18 million international visitors in the early years of the twenty-first century, giving Austria a surplus on its travel account. The majority are on a holiday visit and there is no doubt that proximity to Germany is important to Austria as that market accounts for well over half of all arrivals. The next two countries, the Netherlands and the UK, are also important sources of tourists but together only account for a small proportion of overnights. New markets in Eastern Europe, coupled with marketing initiatives also mean that Austria is receiving an increasing number of visits from this region. In addition to their proximity, Germans are attracted to Austria because there is no language barrier, their currencies have similar buying power, and yet Austria, with its more relaxed lifestyle, is sufficiently different from Germany to give a feeling of being in a foreign country. This reliance on one market does leave Austria vulnerable in times of recession and the concentration of visits determined by holiday periods in Germany causes congestion at the borders. In popular holiday areas many resorts become totally geared to the German market.

Supply of tourism

Transport

With the German market so dominant, the majority of tourists arrive by car on the 18 000 kilometre road network and experience traffic congestion at the beginning and end of the main holiday periods. The tortuous nature of some of the roads emphasizes the difficulty of transportation in this elongated and mountainous country, yet the network reaches into the most remote parts, and includes Europe's highest road to the summit of the Gross Glockner. There are over 6000 kilometres of railway including 20 private railway companies, and these are well integrated with rural bus services reaching the most remote communities.

With six airports of international standard in Austria, this is the main mode of travel for outbound tourism, although some argue that a restrictive policy on inbound flights to Vienna in the past has held back the development of the tourist industry and compounded Austria's dependence on the German market. On the other hand Austrian Airlines is expanding its international network, with Vienna as the hub, in partnership with the charter airline Lauda Air.

Accommodation

The majority of Austria's bedspaces are in serviced accommodation and except in the cities, these are mainly small, family-run hotels and guesthouses. The authorities are improving the quality of accommodation as a means of boosting both domestic and foreign tourism. Although business travel is relatively unimportant in Austria, the small conference market is being developed, particularly in Vienna, Linz, Salzburg, Innsbruck, Graz and Villach, as well as in the larger *schlosshotels* (castles and palaces formerly owned by the aristocracy) which have been converted into hotels.

Organization

Each of the nine Austrian provinces has responsibility for tourism administered by the provincial government and a tourist board. At national level tourism is the responsibility of the Ministry of Economic Affairs. Promotion of Austria is the responsibility of the Austrian National Tourist Organization, a joint public/private agency with funding from the government and the Chamber of Commerce. The organization has undergone a restructuring to ensure an overtly marketing focus in the face of stagnant demand from the international market. The tourism authorities in Austria are upgrading tourist infrastructure generally, particularly in the area of sports and facilities for activity holidays, and extending the network of ski lifts and funiculars. Nevertheless some resorts (such as Mayrhofen) have halted further development in line with Austria's green image and this may have persuaded potential skiers to choose France instead.

Tourism resources

Austria contains 35 per cent of the Alpine area (compared to Switzerland's 15 per cent) and the country is famed for its lake and mountain scenery, winter sports facilities and picturesque towns and villages. Trending east–west across the country and separated by the deep valley of the river Inn, the mountains are Austria's main attraction. Here tourism is often the only economic land use and is seen as a remedy for the problems of a declining agriculture. However, this is not without environmental costs, such as forest hillsides and meadows scarred from ski-lift development or villages marred by insensitive building.

Each of the Austrian provinces can offer distinctive attractions:

- **The Tyrol** is by far the most popular destination for foreign visitors, containing the most spectacular Alpine scenery and the greatest number of ski resorts.

Tyrolean folklore and costumes are the best known of Austria's traditional cultures. Most of the resorts have been developed from farming villages situated in the tributary valleys of the river Inn – the Otztal and Zillertal for example – at altitudes of between 1000 and 1800 metres. Traditional building styles, based on the chalet that is well adapted to heavy winter snowfalls, provide a pleasant ambience for holidays. Summer activities in the Tyrol include hiking and gliding, while most villages are equipped with a swimming pool and facilities for tennis and other sports. Tourist centres include the following:

○ Innsbruck, which is not only the capital of the Tyrol but an important cultural centre. The many Renaissance buildings are a reminder of its former role as a summer residence for the Hapsburg emperors. Along with the ski resorts on the slopes nearby, the city has twice hosted the Winter Olympics.

○ St Anton, Kitzbühl, Söll, Seefeld and Mayrhofen are also ski resorts of international significance.

- **The Vorarlberg** to the west of the Arlberg Pass is similar to the Tyrol, but also has some affinity with neighbouring Switzerland. Lech and Zürs offer up-market skiing, while Bregenz on the Boden See is a popular lake resort and venue for music festivals.

- The tiny independent principality of **Liechtenstein**, which is better known as a tax haven than as a winter sports destination, has strong historical ties to Austria but uses the same currency as Switzerland.

- The **province of Salzburg** and the **Salzkammergut area** (so called because of the historically important salt mining industry) offer gentler lake and mountain scenery. St Wolfgang is the most popular of the resorts in summer, but its entertainment scene is subdued compared to Söll or Kitzbühl in winter. Other attractions include the Krimml waterfalls in the Hohe Tauern National Park, the Dachstein ice caves and the spas of Bad Ischl and Bad Gastein.

- Domestic tourists mainly favour the forested 'green province' of **Styria**, although the city of Graz was designated as the 'European capital of culture' for 2003 by the EU Council of Ministers. **Carinthia** is increasingly popular with foreign visitors as a summer holiday destination, where the warm sunny climate and lakes such the Wörther See, offering many facilities for water sports, are the main attractions.

- The remaining provinces of Austria, occupying **the Danube Valley**, are scenically less attractive, with large areas of lowland supplying most of the country's agricultural needs. The Burgenland is similar in its steppe landscapes to neighbouring Hungary (to which it historically belonged), while the shallow Neusiedlersee is an important nature reserve. Both the provinces of Upper and Lower Austria contain vineyards, monasteries (such as Melk) and castles (such as Dürnstein) and it is possible for the tourist to see these on a Danube river cruise from Vienna.

Whereas Graz, Linz and Innsbruck are important regional centres, only two of Austria's cities – Vienna and Salzburg – attract huge numbers of visitors from all over the world, thanks to their heritage of music and architecture:

- **Vienna** is full of reminders of its imperial past. These include the monumental buildings lining the Ringstrasse encircling the old city, and the art treasures housed in the former palaces of the Hofburg, Belvedere and Schönbrunn. Music and dance are as much a part of the city's social and entertainment scene as they were in the time of the 'Waltz King' (Johann Strauss) in the nineteenth century. The State Opera House and St Stephen's Cathedral are also part of this musical heritage. Although Vienna trades on nostalgia for its tourist appeal, the city is an efficiently run modern conference venue, with an international role as a United Nations centre, while geographical location makes it the recognized gateway to Eastern Europe.

- **Salzburg** has a flourishing tourism industry based on:
  - The summer music festival, which was further boosted in 1991 by the Mozart bicentenary celebrations. During festival time, accommodation in this relatively small city is at a premium.
  - The '*Sound of Music* connection'. Classical music lovers are outnumbered by those tourists who are attracted to the city and the scenic countryside of lakes and mountains nearby, through their associations with this popular film.
  - Its unique heritage of Baroque architecture – probably unrivalled outside Spain or Italy – which was brought into being by the powerful Prince–Bishops who once ruled Salzburg.

Switzerland

Switzerland is poor in natural resources and contains a diversity of languages and cultures. Yet its people have achieved a degree of political stability and economic prosperity that is envied by the rest of the world. Swiss industrial products, based on a high input of skill in relation to the value of the component raw materials, have an international reputation for quality. Similarly, the country's scenic attractions – arguably the most spectacular in Europe – have been intelligently exploited by a hospitality industry that is renowned for its professionalism. Historically, the country developed as a loose federation of cantons – small mountain states – fighting to preserve their independence from foreign domination, and in many respects the cantons still play a more important role in Swiss politics than the federal government in Berne. At the local level the communes also determine tourism planning and development to a large extent, in line with the Swiss tradition of direct citizen participation in politics.

Tourism in Switzerland has a long history, and the industry was already well established in the late nineteenth century. Its development came about as a result of a number of factors:

- From early times, Switzerland was a transit zone for invading armies, merchants and pilgrims, and later had to be crossed by wealthy travellers undertaking the Grand Tour. The Swiss were in demand as guides, as there were no serviceable roads and the Alpine passes were often hazardous. Accommodation was also needed for travellers, the most famous example being the hospice on the St Bernard Pass.
- As a result of the Romantic Movement in art and literature at the close of the eighteenth century, the mountains were no longer seen as a barrier to be feared, but as a resource to be valued. For example, Byron and Shelley stayed for a considerable time by Lake Geneva, and summer resorts gradually developed for well-off tourists around other lakes in Switzerland.
- From the middle of the nineteenth century the demand for tourism in Switzerland grew as the result of the Industrial Revolution in Western Europe, the improvement in road and rail communications and the growth of the middle class, particularly in countries like Britain, where Thomas Cook did much to popularize the country.

The more adventurous tourists sought the challenges of mountain climbing, following Whymper's ascent of the Matterhorn in 1865. More remote areas of the Alps were progressively opened up to tourism with the construction of funicular and cog railways, and hotels were built at what was then the edge of the Alpine glaciers, such as the Aletsch.

- Although Switzerland had been known for its spas since Roman times, substantial development of health tourism occurred in the late nineteenth and early twentieth centuries as a result of the spread of tuberculosis in the industrial cities of Europe. The pure mountain air in spas such as St Moritz Bad and Arosa was believed to provide a remedy for the disease.
- Skiing and other winter sports were introduced to St Moritz and the resorts of the Bernese Oberland by wealthy British tourists at the close of the nineteenth century. At first, the existing mountain railways – now operating year-round – were used to transport the skiers to the slopes, but as demand grew from the 1930s onwards, they were largely superseded by faster, more efficient aerial cableways.
- International trade had long been important to Swiss cities such as Geneva. The strict neutrality of Switzerland and its multi-lingual character encouraged the growth of all kinds of business and conference tourism. Starting with the Red Cross, Geneva became the venue for many international organizations, while Zurich is a financial centre of worldwide significance. Berne and Lausanne – the headquarters respectively of the Universal Postal Union and the Olympic Committee – also provide important conference functions.

Demand for tourism

Domestic and outbound tourism

The Swiss have one of the highest holiday propensities in the world, with around 75 per cent taking a holiday of at least four nights. Holiday-taking is at its highest among upper-income groups, the middle-aged and those living in the larger towns or cities. Demand for domestic tourism has grown in the past five years with the high frequency of holiday-taking meaning that most domestic holidays are second or third holidays.

Domestic holidays contrast with those taken abroad as they tend to be winter sports or mountain holidays, many taken in the months of January to March. Swiss holidays abroad are concentrated into the summer months of July to September and the most popular destinations are Italy and France.

Inbound tourism

Demand from foreign visitors to Switzerland has stagnated since the 1990s (although the travel account remained in surplus) for the following reasons:

- the strength of the Swiss franc, which has given Switzerland a reputation as an expensive country to visit as is reflected in the increasingly short lengths of stay of foreign visitors
- declining levels of service
- an old-fashioned image of Switzerland.

As in Austria, Germans account for the majority of visitors. Around 40 per cent of bednights occur in the winter season (November to April), a figure boosted by the Swiss participating in winter sports.

Supply of tourism

Transport

The private car dominates travel in both the domestic and foreign travel market. As in Austria, the transport networks are tortuous and the topography often demands major engineering feats – the 18 kilometre tunnel under the St Gotthard being an outstanding example, while the roads over the Alpine passes are spectacular. Even so, roads in the High Alps are often blocked by snow from November to June. While the road network brings many remoter parts of the country within reach of day visitors, this has created congestion in holiday areas. Imposition of tolls may alleviate this congestion.

The Swiss Federal Railways and the private railway companies operate 5000 kilometres of track (1400 kilometres are narrow-gauge) and there are many mountain railways, funiculars and rack-and-pinion systems which are often tourist attractions in themselves. Although the cost is high, tunnels and snowploughs allow the railways to operate throughout the year.

There are three international airports – at Zurich, Geneva and Basle. Swissair – the former national airline – was a casualty in the wake of 9/11, and was replaced by Swiss International Air Lines, financed by the private sector. Other features of the Swiss transport system, which is highly integrated, include the postal coaches – which penetrate the remotest villages – bicycle hire at many rail stations, and lake ferries.

Accommodation

The development of accommodation since the 1970s has led to an excess of supply over demand. About a third of the serviced accommodation capacity is only available in the winter season, particularly in the high ski resorts (such as St Moritz and Arosa). Most hotels are small with the few larger hotels found mainly in Zurich and Geneva. Hotels and holiday chalets (mainly catering for groups of skiers) are highly dependent on foreign labour. 'Supplementary accommodation', including holiday chalets, apartments, holiday villages and camping/caravan sites, provide a lower-cost alternative to hotels for foreign visitors, but they are also popular with domestic holidaymakers.

Organization

In the face of declining international demand for Switzerland in the 1990s, the Swiss National Tourism Organization was renamed 'Switzerland Tourism' in 1995 and underwent restructuring and a refocusing of priorities. It is responsible to the Federal Department of Public Economy and formulates and implements national tourism policy. Switzerland's maturity as a destination is reflected in the long tradition of tourist associations and information services at local and regional levels. There are also many specialist organizations such as the Swiss Travel Bank that was founded to give less privileged workers the chance to go on holiday.

Tourism resources

The most popular area is the Alpine zone, attracting over half of all visitor arrivals. Here lie the majestic snow-capped peaks, glaciated valleys and winter sports developments that are Switzerland's trademark. However, tourist development has placed pressures upon the society and environment of the area and the integration of tourism into the agricultural and forest economies has needed sensitive handling.

Each of the Swiss cantons has its own range of attractions, but several major tourist areas stand out.

- **The Bernese Oberland** The most spectacular Alpine scenery is found here, south of the lake resort of Interlaken. An excellent network of funicular railways and cableways provides access to the snowfields and glaciers, the most famous ascending the slopes of the Jungfrau and Eiger. At Lauterbrunnen there is a classic example of a glaciated valley with spectacular waterfalls. Long popular with British tourists, the area preserves Swiss rural traditions and at the same time has some of the most sophisticated ski resorts in Europe, notably Gstaad, Wengen and Grindelwald.
- **The Valais** This includes the upper Rhone valley as far as the Simplon Pass and a number of small historic towns. The most well-known resort is Zermatt, with its views of the Matterhorn, but the most popular ski area is Crans-Montana, where considerable development has taken place.
- **Lake Lucerne and the Forest Cantons** The fjord-like Lake Lucerne is arguably the most beautiful body of inland water in Europe. The cantons around it, especially Schwyz, are historically important as the cradle of Swiss independence. Lucerne is a picturesque city, famous for its medieval Chapel Bridge.
- **The Grisons** In some respects this is the most traditional part of Switzerland. In the villages of the Engadine Valley the Romansch language is still spoken and a pastoral type of rural economy persists, protected by government subsidy. This canton also contains the Swiss National Park where endangered alpine species such as the *chamois* are protected. In contrast are the number of spas and ski resorts catering mainly for wealthy tourists, the most famous being St Moritz, Davos and Klosters.
- **Lake Geneva** This French-speaking area attracts a wealthy international clientele to its schools, the festival resort of Montreux and the shopping and nightlife of Geneva. This city's role as a United Nations centre is showcased by the Palais des Nations.
- **The Ticino** The Italian-speaking Ticino enjoys the warmest climate in Switzerland due to its sheltered location and the moderating effect of Lakes Lugano and Maggiore. The landscape has Mediterranean features such as palm trees, lemon orchards and colourful towns and villages. Travellers from northern Europe appreciate the contrast most in early spring, when they emerge from the cold and gloomy weather prevailing north of the St Gotthard into the warm sunshine of the Ticino Valley. Locarno, Lugano and Ascona are important holiday resorts and major conference venues.
- **The Mittelland** Most of the Swiss population lives outside the Alps in the plateau region to the north and west, and the important industries are located in the Basle–Winterthur–Zurich triangle. Basle on the Rhine has a historic university and is a major cultural centre, while Zurich contains the Swiss National Museum, but Berne is probably the most interesting city from a tourist viewpoint. The picturesque old town, with its medieval shopping arcades and Clock Tower, is a World Heritage Site.
- **The Jura** The western boundary of Switzerland lies along the forested Jura Mountains. Less spectacular than the Alps, this region accounts for only a small percentage of tourist overnights. The small towns of the region, such as Les Chaux de Fonds, are noted for traditional Swiss crafts such as watchmaking.

Germany

Unlike Austria or Switzerland, Germany lacks a well-defined tourism image, with many people regarding it as a destination for business rather than holiday travel. This is not surprising as Germany is the world's third largest economy. Yet the country is well endowed with a variety of beautiful scenery and cultural attractions, particularly those based on music and the applied arts and sciences. The Cold War political division of Germany between East and West has tended to obscure the long-standing physical and cultural differences between the Protestant northern part of the country and the predominantly Catholic south and west. Regional differences are also a legacy of the time, prior to the nineteenth century, when Germany was a patchwork of small, virtually independent states forming part of the so-called Holy Roman Empire. As a result Berlin has strong rivals in several other major cities, which act as world class cultural and business centres.

The development of tourism in Germany has also been complicated by the fact that from 1945 to 1990 the country was divided, along with the city of Berlin. The two Germanies that resulted from this division had widely differing political and economic structures, and a continuing legacy:

- West Germany, officially known as the Federal Republic of Germany or BRD, prospered under a democratic style of government and a free market economy.
- East Germany, officially called the German Democratic Republic or DDR, was compelled by its Soviet masters to adopt Communism and a centralized command economy. Tourist enterprises such as hotels were nationalized and the whole industry was subject to state control. East Germans were discouraged from visiting other countries, with the exception of those in the Eastern bloc, such as Romania and Hungary. Visits from West Germans were virtually prohibited while tourism from other Western countries was subject to many restrictions.

This structure changed rapidly after 1989 with the removal of the Berlin Wall and the reunification of Germany a year later. This meant that Germany could offer a range of new tourism products and domestic markets for tourism. For example, there has been a flood of West German tourists into East Germany, attracted by the low cost of accommodation. East Germans now have the freedom to travel abroad, but it will be some time before they have the financial resources to do so in large numbers. The economy of the former DDR was badly depressed because it was based on industries that could not compete with foreign products without the protection of state subsidies, a pattern repeated in other countries of the former Eastern bloc (see Chapter 18). The cost of reunification also contributed to the downturn in the German economy as a whole after the late 1990s. The former West Germany comprises 80 per cent of the population, and dominates both tourism supply and demand in the new Germany.

Demand for tourism

Domestic tourism

The Germans have been amongst the world's greatest spenders on travel and tourism for many years and they attach great importance to their annual holiday, even in times of recession. Generous holiday entitlement means that travel frequencies are high and holiday propensities reach almost 75 per cent, though this does vary according to age, socioeconomic status and place of residence. Residents of the former East Germany also have high holiday propensities but these are still mainly expressed in domestic trips. The domestic market accounts for the great majority of bednights and so dominates the industry. Domestic holidays are particularly concentrated into the summer months and in the south of Germany and on the coast. Business travel is important in the domestic market. Germans are very health-conscious and over 200 spa resorts based on abundant mineral springs have long been developed to meet this demand. These cater for a wide cross-section of the population, and have been supported by generous state-sponsored health insurance schemes. Most spas are located in the uplands of the Mittelgebirge in the central part of the country. Hiking is popular and Germany was the first country to provide a nationwide network of youth hostels. Since the 1980s there has been considerable investment in theme parks and other purpose-built visitor attractions, such as the Bremen Space Centre.

Outbound tourism

Germany was for many years the most important generator of international tourists in the world until the 1990s, when it was overtaken by the USA. Around two-thirds of all holidays are taken abroad, and the majority of trips are to Mediterranean countries (particularly Italy and Spain) and to neighbouring Austria. Many trips are package tours sold by the highly organized travel industry that has grown up to meet the demand for holidays abroad. Spain is by far the most important package holiday destination; Germans take roughly the same number of holidays in Spain as the British, but they are much more likely to take a second holiday in their own country. Long-haul travel is also important to a wide range of destinations.

Inbound tourism

The high volume of travel abroad keeps Germany's travel account in considerable deficit, even though in the early years of the twenty-first century there were around 18 million arrivals. The main countries of origin are Germany's neighbours – now more numerous as a result of reunification – and excursionists form a significant tourism flow into Germany. Generally, average lengths of stay are short – around two days – and this does mean that foreign visitors contribute only a small percentage of the bednights in the country. Business travel is important in the inbound market, exceeding the volume of holiday traffic from abroad.

Supply of tourism

Transport

The car is the most important form of tourist transport. The road network is excellent with *autobahns* (high-speed motorways) and also specially designed scenic routes for visitors. A major problem is seasonal congestion both en route to, and in, the popular holiday areas. Rail travel is the second most popular form of travel, with promotional fares and inclusive package holidays available; plans for a high-speed train network (ICE) are well advanced. The larger cities have a fully integrated public transport system of trams, buses, 'U' Bahn (underground), and 'S' Bahn (fast suburban trains).

Air travel is served by ten international airports, all well connected by rail with the urban areas they serve. The national carrier, Lufthansa, is based at the main gateway and hub at Frankfurt. Tourists arriving by sea can use ferries from Harwich to Hamburg, from Trelleborg in Sweden to Sassnitz, and from Roby Havn in Denmark to Puttgarten. Cruises are also popular on the Rhine and the other major rivers, the canals that link these natural waterways and on the Boden See (Lake Constance).

Accommodation

Domestic business travellers and most foreign visitors are accommodated in hotels in towns and cities. Demand for self-catering accommodation exceeds supply, as does that for most types of accommodation in the peak season. There is a concentration of hotels and guesthouses serving the holiday market in Bavaria and Baden-Württemburg, and a shortage of accommodation throughout most of the former DDR, although many hotel chains are now developing properties in this part of Germany. Holiday parks (groups of chalets around a pool and other leisure facilities) are popular with German families.

Organization

Tourism in Germany suffers from a long history of having no representation at senior level in the federal government. Tourism responsibilities are in the hands of the *länder* (states) who have considerable independence to promote and develop tourism but this does result in considerable fragmentation. There is, for example, no national tourism policy as tourism is low on the list of government economic priorities and little federal aid is available for the industry; this is mainly used to boost accommodation in less-developed areas and to stimulate farm tourism. The states provide funds for both upgrading accommodation and for season-extension developments (such as indoor swimming pools) in resorts.

The German National Tourist Board (Deutsche Zentrale für Tourismus – DZT) is the major marketing agency for Germany, with responsibilities for both domestic and international promotion. It is mainly financed by the federal government and aims to boost visitor arrivals and revenue, and to reposition Germany as a multi-faceted, attractive destination.

Tourism resources

Each of the sixteen *länder* has a historical identity, but they vary greatly in size and tourism potential. For example the Saarland and Schleswig–Holstein compare unfavourably with Bavaria's scenic variety. Germany's cities on the other hand have world-class facilities for music and the performing arts. These will become more prominent in the tourism sector, as the generous state subsidies to cultural institutions have been scaled down owing to the stagnation of the economy.

Northern Germany

This region includes the states of Schleswig–Holstein, Lower Saxony, Hamburg, Bremen, along with Mecklenburg–West Pomerania in the former DDR. In this part of Germany the main tourist attractions are found on or near the coast. Inland, there are large areas of forest, heathland, and lakes – such as those of Holstein and Mecklenburg, providing some variety in the otherwise featureless expanse of the North European Plain. The North Sea is colder and rougher than the Baltic, and the coast is low-lying, with large areas of mudflats exposed at low tide. However, the North Frisian Islands have fine beaches, the most popular being those of Sylt, which is linked to the mainland by a causeway. The resort of Westerland attracts fashionable holidaymakers as well as German families, and it was here that naturism – known in Germany as *freikorpskultur* (FKK) first appeared on the holiday scene in the 1920s. The tideless Baltic coast is scenically more attractive, with sandpits enclosing extensive lagoons. With the exception of Kiel, a major yachting centre, and Travemünde, most of the Baltic resorts were situated in the former DDR. These flourished serving a captive domestic market, but their outdated facilities and substandard service practices left them ill-equipped to face the competition following German reunification and the introduction of a free market economy. They are now being 'rediscovered' by West German holidaymakers, who are attracted by the lack of commercialization – caused by decades of neglect under Communism. This is particularly true of the island of Rügen, with its cliffs, deeply indented coastline, beaches and beautiful countryside. Its chief resort, Warnemunde, attracted the German elite in the late nineteenth century. The National Socialist regime developed the island for a regimented form of 'tourism for the people' in the 1930s as part of the 'Strength through Joy' movement. The East German government adopted a similar policy after 1945 under a very different political system.

Many of the cultural attractions of northern Germany date back to the Middle Ages, when the powerful Hanseatic League of merchants from Hamburg and other cities dominated trade throughout northern Europe. This heritage is exploited for tourism in the picturesque port of Lübeck, with its well-preserved city walls and gates, church spires and red-brick merchants' houses. Similar examples, but less commercialised, can be found in Rostock, Wismar and Stralsund.

The major cities of the region – Hamburg, Bremen and Hanover – are primarily business centres with tourism playing a secondary role. Hanover, the capital of Lower Saxony, has historical associations with Britain, but is mainly known for its trade fairs. Hamburg deserves special mention for the following reasons:

- It is one of Europe's major ports, with worldwide trading connections, and a special economic role in relation to Eastern Europe and the countries of the former USSR.
- It is a major cultural centre, with publishing as one of its major industries.
- The picturesque setting of the old city, between the harbour and the Alster Lakes, appeals to visitors.
- It is known for the vitality of its nightlife, centred on the Saint Pauli district and the notorious Reeperbahn.

Central Germany

To the south of the North German Plain rise the forested uplands of the Mittelgebirge. For the most part they are not high or rugged enough to be regarded as mountains, but they are ideal hiking country. The towns of Hesse and the Weser Valley are rich in legendary associations, notable examples being Hamelin and the castle at Sababurg immortalized by the Brothers Grimm. The German Tourist Office has promoted a tourist route from Bremen south to Marburg based on these resources as the 'Fairy-Tale Road'.

To the east, the Harz Mountains are renowned for their beautiful scenery and waterfalls. During the Cold War division of Germany this region was bisected by the Iron Curtain, which severely disrupted all communications to the detriment of its tourism industry. Although the barriers have long gone, the picturesque medieval towns such as Goslar on the western side of the former boundary are thriving more than those in what was once the DDR (such as Wernigerode and Quedlinburg).

The Rhineland

Western and southern Germany contain the areas most popular with foreign visitors. Its people tend to be more pleasure-loving – Carnival or *'Fasching'* is an important festive event in many of the towns and cities, especially in the Rhineland. The Rhine is Europe's most heavily used inland waterway, and river cruises have been popular with tourists since the beginning of the nineteenth century. The most scenic stretch of the river is between Bingen and Koblenz, where it is confined in a narrow gorge. Here the Rhine, followed closely by the autobahn and railway, meanders between terraced vineyards and steep crags crowned by romantic castles which feature prominently in German legend. The northern Rhineland is less attractive as it includes the heavily industrialized Rühr Valley conurbation. This area is now undergoing regeneration, with the transformation of polluting factories and mines into heritage museums, theme parks and leisure centres, and much has been done to 'green' the landscape. The many important centres in the Rhine valley include the following:

- Rüdesheim is the most popular of the wine festivals in the region.
- Dusseldorf is the commercial hub of the region and is a 'must' for the serious shopper as well as business travellers.
- Cologne (Köln) boasts Germany's most famous cathedral and is an important venue for trade exhibitions. Phantasialand – one of Germany's major theme parks – is situated nearby.
- Bonn was a small university town, famous as the birthplace of Beethoven, when it was chosen as the capital of the new Federal Republic in 1949. This status gradually became defunct following the 1991 decision of the Bundestag (Parliament) to reinstate Berlin as capital of a united Germany.
- Aachen lies close to the border with Belgium and the Netherlands, and is an example of international city promotion, in partnership with Liège and Maastricht. It is historically important as the city chosen by Charlemagne to be his capital when he founded the Holy Roman Empire – the forerunner of the German state, and in a sense, of the European Union.
- Trier in the wine-producing Moselle Valley, is rich in historical monuments dating back to Roman times.
- Other important historic cities in the Rhine Valley are Mainz, Wörms and Speyer, similarly located near vineyards.
- In contrast, Frankfurt on the River Main emphasizes its modern role as the financial capital of Germany, rather than any particular heritage attractions. Its airport is one of the world's busiest, and it lies at the 'crossroads' of the autobahn network.

Southern Germany

South Germany comprises the states of Baden-Württemberg and Bavaria. Baden-Baden is Germany's most noted spa town, while the famous old university town of Heidelberg is a 'must' on the international tourist circuit. In contrast, Stuttgart is the centre of the German motor vehicle industry and attracts a good deal of business travel for this reason. Bavaria is the most popular state with domestic and foreign tourists, since it can offer a great variety of scenery and is noted for its folklore, which has much in common with the Austrian Tyrol. Major attractions of Southern Germany include:

- **The Black Forest**, a scenic area of pine-covered uplands, waterfalls and picturesque villages rising to the east of the Rhine, which offers ideal opportunities for skiing in winter and hiking in summer, with the world's oldest long-distance footpath – the *Westweg*. The region is also famous for its folklore and clock-making industry, carried on in small towns such as Triberg.
- The '**Romantic Road**', Germany's best-known tourist route, linking a number of well-preserved medieval towns, including Würzburg, Bamberg and Rothenburg.
- Nuremberg is a major cultural centre. It was the birthplace of Durer, Germany's most famous painter, contains the German National Museum, and is also celebrated for its Christmas market. The Zeppelin Field and Congress Hall are a reminder of the city's role in more recent times as the setting for the National Socialist Party rallies.
- Regensburg on the Danube was at one time capital of the Holy Roman Empire.
- Bayreuth is celebrated for the Wagner music festival.
- The **Bavarian Alps** provide spectacular lake and mountain scenery and picturesque villages. Tourist centres include Garmisch-Partenkirchen, which is a leading ski resort, and the village of Oberammergau, which is world famous for the Passion Play staged every ten years by the community.
- The romantic castles built by King Ludwig II of Bavaria in the nineteenth century are very popular with visitors, the best known example being Neuschwanstein.
- **Munich**, the capital of Bavaria, has a wealth of Renaissance architecture and is a favourite with art and music lovers. It is also a thoroughly modern city with facilities provided for the 1972 Olympics. Its beer gardens and annual *Oktoberfest* attract many foreign visitors.

Eastern Germany

Prior to 1990 this region, consisting of the states of Brandenburg, Saxony, Saxony-Anhalt and Thuringia, formed the bulk of the DDR. It is crossed by the river Elbe, and cruises are now available from Hamburg to the scenic area known as the 'Saxon Switzerland' near the border with the Czech Republic. Unfortunately, much of Saxony south of the Elbe has suffered severe pollution from obsolescent heavy industrial plant using low-grade coal. Only investment on a vast scale can bring environmental standards up to the level of those in West Germany. In contrast, the state of Thuringia is a forested upland region and has more tourist appeal, containing a number of historic towns, notably Weimar – important for its associations with Göethe, Germany's greatest poet – and Eisenach, where Martin Luther initiated the Protestant Reformation. As in other parts of the former DDR, there is a shortage of tourist accommodation.

Three cities in the region are major tourist centres: namely Leipzig, Dresden and Berlin.

- **Leipzig** hosts an international trade fair twice a year and has played a leading role in the cultural life of the nation, especially music, with its associations with J.S. Bach.

- **Dresden** is a beautiful Baroque city that was reconstructed after its devastation in 1945 (Dresden porcelain is actually made in the town of Meissen 30 kilometres away).
- **Berlin** exerts a special fascination for tourists because of its place in recent history. The city first became important in the eighteenth century as the capital of Prussia, the most militaristic of the German states, under the leadership of Frederick the Great, and in 1871 it became the capital of a united Germany. In the 1920s Berlin was notorious for its cabarets. During the Cold War era, the Berlin Wall and 'Checkpoint Charlie' epitomized the confrontation between NATO and the Soviet Union. West Berlin was an 'island' of democracy and free enterprise surrounded by Communist East Germany (although it was heavily subsidized by the federal government in Bonn), whereas East Berlin was the capital of the DDR. West Berlin's shopping and nightlife contrasted with the greyness and restrictions of life in East Germany. Shortly after the fall of the Berlin Wall, the administrative functions of a re-united Germany gradually moved from Bonn to Berlin, a process symbolized by the opening of the new Reichstag (Parliament Building) in 1998. East Berlin in particular became the focus of one of the world's greatest urban regeneration projects. This has led, however, to an oversupply of hotel accommodation, as the demand for conference tourism was less than anticipated. Berlin offers the cultural tourist a number of world-class museums and music venues, while the legacy of Frederick the Great includes the Brandenburg Gate, the elegant avenue known as the Unter den Linden, and the royal palaces at Charlottenburg and Potsdam.

Summary

Apart from the short German coast, Austria, Switzerland and Germany are land-locked countries. Physically, three regions can be identified: the coastal lowlands, the central uplands and the Alps. Highly developed economies and standards of living have resulted in a considerable demand for tourism and recreation. Of particular note is the importance of Germany as one of the world's leading generators of international tourists and the social, political and economic issues raised by the reunification of Germany. Austria and Switzerland are both significant destinations for tourists from the rest of Europe. The stagnation of international demand since the 1990s has led to the restructuring of the region's national tourism organizations. Transportation in the three countries is well developed but has to overcome the harsh physical conditions and topography of the Alps. The federal organization of the three countries has led to considerable devolution of tourism powers to the states in Germany, provinces in Austria and cantons in Switzerland.

The main tourist regions are: the coast of northern Germany, with its islands and resorts; the central uplands of Germany, including the Rhineland and the Black Forest; and the Alpine area of all three countries, with its opportunities for both winter and summer tourism. The towns and cities are important for sightseeing and as business travel centres.

Chapter 14
The tourism geography of France

Learning Objectives

After reading this chapter, you should be able to:

- Appreciate the social and economic changes that have taken place in France and understand their importance for tourism.
- Recognize the contribution of France to world culture and the importance of the cultural heritage.
- Recognize the variety of physical features and climates in France and understand their significance for tourism.
- Be aware of the major role played by the public sector in the organization and planning of tourism in France.
- Understand the importance of transport infrastructure in the development of tourism.
- Recognize the major components of the French holiday market and the scale of inbound tourism to France.
- Be aware of the importance of the regions in supplying distinctive tourism products.
- Be aware of the importance of rural tourism and measures to protect the French countryside.
- Demonstrate a knowledge of the tourist regions, resorts, business centres and tourist attractions of France.

Introduction

For many years France has been the world's top tourist destination in terms of visitor arrivals, and one of the leading countries in terms of tourism receipts. This means that tourism is important in the economy, representing 7 per cent of GDP and directly and indirectly generating over 2 million jobs. France was one of the first countries to recognize the importance of the industry, setting up a national tourism office as early as 1910. It is no coincidence that much of the vocabulary used in tourism is of French origin, particularly as regards the hotel and catering sectors.

Among the factors contributing to France's success in tourism are:

- It is the largest country in Western Europe, boasting a natural resource base which includes an extensive coastline facing three seas, some of Europe's finest rivers – the Loire, Rhône, Seine and Garonne – and mountain areas such as the Massif Central, the Alps, Jura and Pyrenees – the last three forming natural boundaries.
- France is also unique among European countries in its latitudinal and altitudinal range, which gives rise to a variety of climates and landscape features. Mediterranean conditions are found in Provence, Languedoc–Roussillon and Corsica. A long dry summer with abundant sunshine, combined with mild winters, allows for a prolonged tourism season in world-famous resorts such as Nice and Saint-Tropez. The Atlantic and Channel coasts have less sunshine and a climate favouring the more active types of recreation. Eastern France has a continental climate with cold winters, while in the mountains, snow cover is uneven and variable – especially in those ski resorts situated at low or middle altitudes.
- French culture has been widely emulated, starting in the Middle Ages with the Gothic style of architecture and the ideal of chivalry. In the seventeenth century, Louis XIV's court and palace at Versailles was the role model for the upper classes throughout Europe, and despite subsequent wars and revolutions, France remained pre-eminent in the world of *haute couture* and fashion. In the late nineteenth and early twentieth centuries, French artists and architects were responsible for many innovations, such as impressionism, cubism, art nouveau and art deco.
- French is one of the most widely spoken world languages. Even in the post-colonial era, France extends beyond Europe to embrace far-flung 'Overseas Départements and Territories' (DOM-TOM) in the Americas, Indian and Pacific Oceans, which are described in later chapters. Cultural and business ties between Metropolitan France and the former colonies remain strong, determining the pattern of long-haul tourist flows to a large extent.
- France is one of the world's leading economic powers, and has been at the forefront of technological advance. However, most of this industrial development has taken place since the Second World War, and many city dwellers retain close links with the countryside. France has the largest agricultural sector in Western Europe, offering the tourist a landscape that owes much of its charm to the prevalence of small-scale mixed farming, using fairly traditional methods of production.
- France can offer a wide variety of tourism products based on these resources. For example:
  - Special interest holidays, including wine tasting tours of Burgundy and culinary short breaks for gourmets – *foodies* – in Normandy.
  - The Club Méditerranée holiday village concept in beach and sport tourism.
  - Spa tourism: most of the numerous spas in France developed in the nineteenth century on the basis of mineral springs, while others on the coast offer *thalassotherapy* – seawater treatments. Some spas have upgraded their facilities to meet changing demands, but the sector has generally declined since the Second World War, in contrast to the situation in Germany and Italy.
  - The importance of pilgrimages in a country where, although secularism has long been official policy, 90 per cent of the population are, at least nominally,

Catholic. Some shrines such as Mont St Michel in Normandy, Le Puy in the Auvergne, Rocamadour in Aquitaine and Vezelay in Burgundy, were well-established in medieval times, acting as 'gathering points' on the major pilgrim routes to Santiago de Compostela in Spain. In contrast, Lourdes and Lisieux became pilgrimage centres in the nineteenth century.

○ Winter sports are offered in the mountain resorts of the Alps, Pyrenees and the Massif Central. France has been an innovator in ski instruction (the short ski method), and in the development of purpose-built ski resorts above the tree line to guarantee a longer snow season. It has overtaken Austria and Switzerland as Europe's leading winter sports destination.

○ Sailing is another major activity, which has spawned a massive investment by the public and private sectors in coastal marina developments. In 2001 France boasted 466 such *ports de plaisance*.

○ Other activity and adventure-based types of tourism include:
  – boating on the superb network of rivers and canals
  – canoeing on fast-flowing rivers, such as the Ardèche
  – horse riding
  – cycling – here two influences are perhaps at work: the trend toward 'green tourism' and the role of the Tour de France in raising the international profile of the sport
  – surfing along the Atlantic coast
  – diving, along parts of the Mediterranean coast such as Corsica
  – mountain climbing in the Alps and Pyrenees
  – caving in the Dordogne region
  – hiking on the network of *grandes randonées* (long-distance waymarked trails) which penetrate the scenic areas of France
  – golf, which is a fast-growing market, with developments in the coastal resorts of northern France.

In some of these products France has few rivals. However, the country's flair for style and innovation has not always been matched by effective marketing.

Demand for tourism

The French tend to take their holidays in France, due to the country's range of tourism resources, and also the tradition of spending the summer in the south. As a consequence, the propensity of the French to travel abroad is lower than for most other west Europeans. However, this may change with the introduction of the Euro, cheap flights and increased leisure time. Yet, as recently as 1958, only 25 per cent of the French took a holiday. Both domestic and foreign tourism have since increased, and by the early years of the twenty-first century 60 per cent of the population took a holiday away from home.

Domestic tourism

The changing economic and social geography of France has had implications for participation in tourism. Demographic changes since the Second World War have boosted the population by 19 million (to over 59 million), restored the imbalance between males and females and replenished both the low numbers of young people and the toll of two world wars. However, as early as the 1970s, France was experiencing an increased number of old people and a decrease in average family size. At the same time, France was transformed from an essentially rural society into an industrial economy with people leaving the countryside for urban manufacturing and service centres. Accompanying these changes has been a growth in the numbers employed in the service sector, increased car ownership, social tourism initiatives and substantial rises in both disposable and discretionary incomes. This has led to an expansion of leisure spending as recreation and tourism have become a significant part of the French lifestyle.

In this respect, an important enabling factor has been the increased leisure time available to the French. Successive reductions of working hours resulted in a statutory working week of less than 40 hours. Also, the minimum school leaving age has been raised to 16 years and there is continuing pressure for early retirement. Since its introduction in 1936, annual paid holiday entitlement has grown to five weeks and many workers have six or more weeks. The fact that at least two of the weeks have to be taken between May and October has led to congestion in this peak holiday period. With the new millennium the working week was reduced to 35 hours – the lowest in Europe, further increasing the leisure time available, with the result that short breaks have trebled in popularity in subsequent years. The downside of the social legislation affecting labour is that employers may be reluctant to recruit staff, resulting in a high rate of unemployment compared to the USA or the UK.

France has a very high proportion of domestic holiday taking, with trips demonstrating a number of characteristics:

- They are lengthy, often three or four weeks, although there are signs that the traditional month away in August *en famille* is decreasing.
- They are concentrated into the peak summer months (the majority of holidays are taken in July and August) although efforts are being made to spread the load with promotional campaigns, staggering of school holidays and the growth of winter holidays.
- In a country with such varied holiday opportunities, a wide distribution of holiday destinations is evident, though a general movement from north to south, as well as to the periphery, can be discerned, with a concentration in the mountains, and more so at the coast, which accounts for 40 per cent of all overnight stays.
- The car is the most common means of domestic holiday transport.
- Self-catering, second homes and visiting friends and relatives account for the majority of holidays, simply because their cost commends them to families in peak season.
- The majority of holidays are arranged independently, but works councils and other non-profit making organizations play an important role. These range from professional organizations, who own fully-equipped holiday accommodation and rent to members at competitive rates, to those involved in social tourism.

Social tourism represents a very strong movement in France and is significant for French domestic patterns of demand. There was a spectacular growth in social tourism initiatives in the 1960s, and in the late 1990s the government established a new fund to allow the unemployed and poorer citizens to take a holiday, using spare capacity in the coastal resorts. Examples of social tourism initiatives include:

- children's hostels – *colonies des vacances*
- family holiday villages – *villages vacances familiales* (VVF)

- government schemes such as the *cheque vacances* to boost holiday opportunities for the disadvantaged groups in society.

Second homes – *residences secondaires* – continue to play an important role in domestic travel, accounting for a fifth of both summer and winter overnight stays. The high incidence of second home ownership (estimated at 3 million) and the wide distribution of these homes throughout the country are reminders that most city dwellers have rural roots. Improvements in transport have resulted in the growth of a second home belt within a 100–150 kilometres radius of the major cities.

Outbound tourism

Almost 20 million trips are taken abroad, mainly to Spain or Italy. This represents a growth in foreign tourism since 1945 that is rooted in the changing social and economic circumstances of France. Spending abroad by French nationals is low compared to receipts from inbound tourists and France therefore runs a surplus on its travel account. Inclusive tour holidays account for a smaller percentage of French travellers abroad than is the case in Britain or Germany, and most foreign travel is by car. However, long-haul tourism has shown consistent growth, with the USA and French-speaking destinations tending to be the most popular. The French travel trade is mainly concerned with outbound tourism, and in contrast to the UK is made up of many small and medium-sized enterprises. For example, the top ten operators in France generate one-third of the total turnover in this sector, compared to Britain where the equivalent figure is well over two-thirds. The most well-known tour operators are Nouvelles Frontières for package holidays, and Club Méditerranée, which pioneered the all-inclusive concept in tourism, and has over a hundred holiday villages worldwide.

Inbound tourism

France ranks as one of the world's most popular tourist destinations with around 75 million arrivals annually in the new millennium. This has been helped by developments such as the Channel Tunnel and Disneyland Paris, as well as a number of sports events that attracted worldwide TV coverage. The majority of visitors are from other countries in Western Europe, although new generators, such as Eastern Europe, are growing in significance. Germany, Belgium, the Netherlands and the UK account for most of the visits to France, attracted by the ease of road and ferry access and the range of French tourism resources. Most British tourists travel independently by car and tend to fall into two distinct types:

- day visitors to the Channel ports such as Calais, where shopping in the hypermarkets for wine and beer is the main objective
- those on a touring holiday or visiting their second homes in France. This type of visitor is attracted by the cultural differences between the two countries as expressed by the *charcuterie*, the bistros and the café lifestyle.

The geographical position of France does mean that it attracts a large number of day excursionists. Also, a large percentage of international tourists arrive in June, July or August to exacerbate the already acute concentration of French domestic holidays. However, the growing popularity of winter holidays and the German trend to take second holidays in France in the off-peak may help to alleviate the problem.

France has always been popular for conventions and sales meetings and a government-run conference bureau coordinates the promotion and development of conference activities. Business travel is an important sector of French tourism, typically concentrated in major urban centres and using higher category hotels:

- Paris has for long been the world's leading conference destination, offering a range of venues, with the added incentive of a short-break holiday before or after the business trip
- Nice now boasts Europe's largest conference venue with its 'Acropolis Centre'
- other important conference cities are Lyon, Marseille, Cannes and Strasbourg.

Event attractions have also played an important role as a 'pull factor' for foreign tourists. They include:

- the 1989 celebrations for the Bicentenary of the French Revolution
- the 1992 Winter Olympics at Albertville in the French Alps
- the 1994 celebrations of the 50th anniversary of the D-Day landings in Normandy
- the 1998 football World Cup.

Supply of tourism

Tourism is a fragmented industry in France, comprising many small, often family-run, enterprises. It is therefore difficult to gauge levels of employment in the industry. Official figures estimate half a million jobs in hotels and catering, official tourist offices and agencies, but this figure clearly falls short of the real total. A further 1.5 million jobs are attributed as an indirect result or 'spin off' from tourism.

Transport

Transport by car dominates tourism in France, accounting for two-thirds of inbound tourists and almost 80 per cent of domestic holidays. This reflects the demand for self-catering and informal holidays, as well as the asset of a road system that ranks among the best in Europe, including 9000 kilometres of motorway and 28 500 kilometres of *routes nationales* (first-class highways). There are few long-distance bus services in France, so the rail system handles a high proportion of inter-city travel, competing effectively with the private car and domestic air services. The state-owned railways authority (SNCF) has invested in the electrification of main line services and in high-speed trains – the famous TGVs. These run mainly on dedicated track at speeds of 270 kilometres per hour, linking Paris to Lyon, Lille, Nantes, Bordeaux and Nice. The rail network continues to be focused on Paris, so that it is usually necessary to transfer between termini to make inter-regional connections. However, an overnight through-train runs between Calais and the French Riviera all year round, and between Calais and Languedoc in summer.

International air connections are comprehensive, with three airports serving Paris, while Air France is one of the world's leading airlines. Air Inter provides domestic services from Paris to over 40 destinations. Although opposed by the

French government, the air transport sector has undergone deregulation as part of the European Commission's liberalization of air transport, allowing new airlines to enter the market.

Cross-Channel ferries are the preferred transport mode for tourists from Britain. The former wide choice of routes has diminished as the car-carrying *Le Shuttle* train service through the Channel Tunnel becomes an established alternative, having overcome widely publicized safety and operational problems. Similarly the airlines' share of the lucrative business travel market is being reduced through competition from the *Eurostar* train service between London and Lille/Paris. Trans-Mediterranean ferry connections to Corsica, Sardinia and North Africa are provided by SNCM (*Société Nationale Maritime Corse-Mediterranée*) from the ports of Marseille, Toulon and Nice. The 9000 kilometres of inland waterway are now mainly used for recreation and have become a tourist attraction in their own right, the most well-known being the Canal du Midi between Toulouse and Sète, built in the reign of Louis XIV to link the Atlantic and the Mediterranean. Converted barges called *peniches* and hotel-boats provide an interesting way of viewing the French countryside.

Accommodation

The bedstock in France is concentrated in Paris and in the coastal resorts, and is comprehensive in terms of both self-catering and serviced accommodation:

- Although serviced accommodation dominates, there is an increasing trend among holidaymakers toward self-catering. In total, self-catering accounts for about 3 million bedspaces, mainly concentrated in the southern and western parts of France:
  - Camping and caravanning are popular among foreign as well as domestic tourists, and the number of sites – especially at the top end of the market – has increased. Most campgrounds are located on or near the coast, where demand can exceed supply at the height of the summer season – particularly on the Côte d'Azur.
  - British holidaymakers have shown an interest in *gîtes*, which combine the advantages of self-catering with living in a small rural community. Typically these holiday homes are converted farm buildings which are surplus to their original purpose. In the past, *gites* were subsidized by the state as part of a campaign to stem rural depopulation; nowadays, they are self-financing but still subject to controls by the local authorities and the non-profit-making 'National Federation of Gîtes de France'. Some of the ferry operators and the British motoring organizations have been active in marketing this type of tourism.
  - In addition, large numbers of British, Dutch and German holidaymakers own second homes, particularly in Provence, the Dordogne and the Ardèche regions.
- In terms of serviced accommodation, only a small percentage of domestic nights are spent in hotels, so these increasingly rely on business travellers and foreign tourists. Despite this, hotel building, especially in the two-star and budget categories, has continued – both to attract the foreign market and also under social tourism schemes. Hotel capacity is concentrated in Paris, the Rhone–Alps region and in Provence–Côte d'Azur. The hotel sector is very fragmented – less dominated by international chains than in most European countries, although the French-owned Accor is one of the world's leading hotel groups. The hotel stock

includes a large number of small, budget-priced hotels (*logis de France*), inns (*auberges*) and converted chateaux (*relais-chateaux*).

Organization

The Ministry of Tourism and the state promotional and marketing agency – La Maison de la France – represent tourism in France at the national level. Since 1982 there has been some decentralization of policy-making from Paris to the 22 regions, each of which has a Comité du Tourisme (Regional Tourism Council), with more scope than other public sector organizations to carry out development. At local level, the 95 *départements* into which France has been divided for administrative purposes since the Revolution have never achieved the same popular acceptance as the counties of the UK, and although each *département* has its own tourism committee, they vary considerably in resources and effectiveness. Tourism illustrates the importance of the 'mixed economy' in France, with the public and private sectors cooperating at regional level on the regional councils and at local level in the *syndicates d'initiatives* – which in most French towns provide information for travellers (there are over 5000 offices nationwide). Where resorts have development potential but lack private initiative, a government-run *office du tourisme* can be set up to carry out promotion and development. At national level there is some degree of coordination between the various government departments and agencies involved in tourism through the Commission Interministerielle d'Amenagement du Territoire (the Interministerial Commission for Land Development).

Since the time of Louis XIV, there has been a tradition of state intervention in the economy of France, with a tendency to favour large-scale projects. The re-planning of Paris by Napoleon III in the 1850s and the public works carried out by President Mitterand in the 1980s are the best-known examples. The Languedoc–Roussillon project is a good example of the state taking direct responsibility for large-scale tourism development. In 1963 the government set up an interministerial commission to coordinate the work of various public agencies and local chambers of commerce in developing seven new resorts on the western Mediterranean coast. The objectives were:

• to take pressure off the congested Côte d'Azur
• to divert holidaymakers who might otherwise go to Spain – in other words, to act as an intervening opportunity.

The state financed the necessary land acquisition and preparation for development, including mosquito eradication from the coastal marshes, as well as a new motorway to improve access. Mixed economy companies – bringing together the private and public sectors – carried out the infrastructure works for each resort. Private developers then provided the accommodation and other facilities under the direction of an architect charged with giving each resort 'unity' and 'style'. Although Languedoc–Roussillon is one of the world's most ambitious tourism projects, many of the jobs created are seasonal, and there is a danger that the region could become as over-dependent on tourism as it had previously been on agriculture.

Similarly on the Aquitaine coast a management plan was inaugurated in 1967, with the aim of maximum use of the dune, lagoon and forest resources of the area for recreation. Nine 'tourist unities' were to be created, based primarily on existing resorts, to provide 760 000 bedspaces in hotels, guest houses, campsites and marinas. However, this project has not achieved the success of Languedoc–Roussillon due to insufficient public funding, lack of enthusiasm from some of the communities affected, and opposition from environmentalists. Since the 1980s tourism policy has moved from large-scale initiatives toward smaller, local projects where environmental considerations are taken into account. These initiatives are spearheaded by the regional councils with financial support from central government.

Tourism plays an important role in regional development, enabling the economic regeneration of stagnating rural areas such as those of the Massif Central. Government grants, loans and subsidies not only encourage the upgrading of accommodation in spas and seaside resorts throughout France, but provide much of the funding for conservation. The government showed little concern for countryside conservation until 1960, when the first national park was designated. This was due to the country's low population density, compared to say the UK, so that the need for protection was seen as less pressing, and also the French passion for field sports. The majority of France's most scenic areas now have protected status as national parks or regional nature parks, under the overall control of the Ministry of the Environment.

The national parks are managed by a state agency with the primary objective of conserving the natural flora and fauna, and the impact of visitors is controlled by a system of zoning:

- Tourism is encouraged in the outer zone, with information points, accommodation and recreational facilities – for example, there are a number of ski resorts in the Vanoise National Park.
- A second zone supports traditional rural activities, subject to regulations on field sports and activities that might be detrimental to the natural environment.
- The inner zone severely restricts entry to give maximum protection to individual species and eco-systems.

Although the Port-Cros marine park is off the Mediterranean coast, and the Parc des Cevennes is part of the Massif Central, three of the national parks are situated in the Alps and one is in the Pyrenees. The Vanoise is linked with the Gran Paradiso National Park in Italy, while the Parc des Pyrenees Occidentales adjoins Spain's Ordesa National Park.

The regional nature parks generally consist of landscapes that have been greatly modified by human intervention and where multiple use management of resources is necessary. Unlike the national parks, the 25 regional nature parks are widely distributed throughout France, and are more accessible from the major cities. Examples include St Amand Reismes near Lille, the Camargue and the Parc d'Armorique in Brittany. The Corsican regional nature park has the triple aims of nature conservation, providing for tourism, and preserving rural life and traditions in an attempt to stem the movement of population from the mountainous interior to the coastal resorts.

Conservation of the built heritage has a longer history in France, although there is no real equivalent to the English National Trust. The French tend to take a more robust approach to the conservation of historic buildings, with an emphasis on full-scale restoration. Notable examples include:

- the chateaux of the Loire, which were ransacked during the French Revolution
- the medieval city of Carcassonne – which is actually a nineteenth century reconstruction
- the port of St Malo, destroyed in the Second World War and subsequently rebuilt complete with the medieval fortifications.

Tourism resources

Tourism in France is more evenly distributed than in most European countries, with the interior sharing the benefits to a greater extent than is the case in Spain, for example. This is because the French countryside and the many historic towns are significant tourism resources, ideally suited to touring holidays. Nevertheless, there are important differences between the regions of the south and west, which attract a large international as well as domestic market, and the climatically less-favoured regions of the north, where the resorts along the Channel coast have suffered a decline since the Second World War.

Northern France

As far as the majority of sun-seeking tourists from northern Europe are concerned, most of northern France is a zone of passage on the routes south to the Riviera, Italy and Spain, while its heritage attractions and gentle landscapes are overshadowed by the more dramatic scenery of the south and west. A major exception is the Paris region, known historically as the **Île de France**, which is in fact the part of the country most visited by foreign tourists, for the following reasons:

- The city of Paris offers a complete range of cultural attractions, many of which are world famous – such as the Eiffel Tower, Notre Dame, the Arc de Triomphe and the Louvre. Then there are the romantic associations evoked by the River Seine and its bridges, and the city's reputation as a centre of high fashion and stylish entertainment. Compared to most world capitals, the townscapes of central Paris within the *peripherique* (ring road) consist of low-rise buildings and broad tree-lined boulevards forming a harmonious whole. Some of the historic *quartiers* (districts) have preserved their specific character – although areas like Montmartre have become commercialized as a result of tourism. Nevertheless, a considerable amount of urban renewal has taken place since the 1970s, including such exciting examples of modern architecture as the Louvre extension, the Beaubourg (Pompidou) Centre, the Bastille Opera and La Défense. The Musée d'Orsay is an example of an old building with an obsolescent function (railway station) revitalized as an impressive art gallery. For many years Paris has been the most popular city-break destination and this is likely to continue, given its improved accessibility as a result of the Channel Tunnel to the UK. However, its share of the market declined during the 1990s largely due to competition from the 'newcomers' in Eastern Europe, such as Prague.
- The French capital offers the opportunity of excursions to the former royal palaces at Versailles and Fontainebleau, or to the historic towns of Orleans, Chartres and Beauvais.
- The tourism industry of Paris was boosted in 1992 by the opening of the largest theme park in Europe – Disneyland Paris (operated by Eurodisney) to the east of the city. This is an interesting example of cooperation between the public sector and a foreign-owned private corporation, with the French government providing the dedicated rail link from Roissy–Charles de Gaulle Airport. After initial teething troubles, due in part to the wide cultural gap between French and North American tastes and expectations (shown, for example, in drinking and service attitudes), Disneyland Paris has established itself as the leading theme park in

France, with over half of its estimated 12 million visitors from abroad. Much more than a theme park, it is a resort in its own right, adding 10 000 beds to the accommodation stock in the Paris region. Faced with this competition, the Asterix Park to the south of Paris has managed to retain its share of the market, basing its appeal on traditional French themes.

- Paris is also a major destination for business travellers, and this is reflected in the availability of modern conference facilities and top quality hotels (half of the 'de-luxe' class of French hotels are located in the capital).

The North

Consisting of the historic provinces of Artois and Picardy, this region contains Calais, the major gateway to France for British tourists travelling by car, coach or train. Dunkirk also handles a significant volume of ferry traffic, but Boulogne has lost its ferry link, and like Dover across the Channel, has had to diversify, investing heavily in the 'Nausicaa' marine-life attraction. Inland, parts of the region have been adversely affected by nineteenth-century heavy industry, but Lille has become a major transport hub and business centre thanks largely to the Channel Tunnel. Lille's cultural attractions, along with those of historic towns such as Arras and Douai, are now more widely appreciated for short break holidays. The 'Opal Coast' south of Boulogne, particularly the attractive resort of Le Touquet, was fashionable with British holidaymakers before the Second World War. It continues to be popular with Parisians and golf is providing the impetus for rejuvenation.

Normandy

Normandy's history has been closely linked with that of England, as shown by the Bayeux Tapestry commemorating the Norman conquest in 1066 and the battlefields of the Hundred Years War. In more recent times, the Normandy beaches at Arromanches were the launch-pad for the Allied campaign to liberate Europe in the Second World War. Visitors are drawn to its attractive countryside and a number of historic towns such as Caen and Rouen, but in summer the seaside resorts provide the main appeal. The Côte Fleurie between Caen and the Seine estuary remains popular with domestic holidaymakers. A creation of the late-nineteenth-century *belle époque*, Deauville continues to be visited by fashion-conscious Parisians, although it has invested heavily in a marina and other modern facilities. Other resorts such as Trouville are more family-oriented and suffer from competition from self-catering complexes, a surplus of hotel accommodation and changing holiday tastes. The port of Cherbourg, usually a brief staging point for British and Irish tourists on their way south, has invested in the *Cité de la Mer* project, whereby the former ocean terminal has been transformed into a marine life exhibition. Normandy also boasts one of France's most unique and most visited heritage attractions – the medieval abbey of Mont St Michel, which is daily separated from the mainland by some of the world's strongest tides.

Brittany

With its Celtic heritage – including the Breton language – and maritime outlook, the peninsula of Brittany, with its rugged, deeply indented coastline, has long been peripheral to the mainstream of French economic and social life. Yet these characteristics have considerable tourism potential, for this region with its distinctive folk costumes and religious traditions has long attracted French artists to picturesque fishing ports such as Pont-Aven, and more recently has appealed to a growing British market. Over a third of France's marinas, for example, are located on the Brittany coast. The main holiday area focuses on the part of the north coast – the Côte Emeraude – which includes the resort of Dinard and the historic seaport of St Malo. Efforts are being made to disperse tourism away from these established centres to the more rugged coastal areas of western Brittany and the neglected interior, which, unlike Normandy, is a poor area agriculturally.

Western France

Consisting of the regions of La Vendée, Poitou–Charentes and Aquitaine, western France has a mild but sunny Atlantic climate, some of the best beaches in Europe and is regarded by the French themselves as the land of gastronomy and good living. On **the coast** there are old-established resorts such as Biarritz and Arcachon, which have adapted to modern trends such as surfing and camping. The Aquitaine coast also boasts the highest sand dunes in Europe and extensive lagoons backed by pine forests. North of the Gironde estuary there are a number of offshore islands where the number of summer visitors greatly outnumbers the local inhabitants. The interior is also well-endowed with scenic and cultural attractions, which include:

- the **Loire Valley**, one of the best-known touring areas, where the main attractions are the chateaux and palaces associated with French royalty in Renaissance times, notably Chambord and Chenonceau, where history is brought to life by *son et lumière* performances during the summer months
- the caves of the **Dordogne**, which contain outstanding examples of Ice Age art; at the most famous of these – Lascaux, which was not discovered until 1940 – a replica cave has been opened to protect the original paintings, which otherwise would have deteriorated from the impact of visitors
- the wine-producing area around **Bordeaux**, a city which is also famous for its eighteenth century Grand Theatre
- Futuroscope near Poitiers, a science theme park showcasing the film industry
- Toulouse, which is the centre of the French aero-space industry, showcased by the European Space Park.

The Massif Central

This mountain and plateau region in south central France offers scope for a wide variety of recreational activities, including hang-gliding, mountain biking and whitewater rafting. The landscapes include deep limestone gorges, extensive forests and the strange remnants of extinct volcanoes known as *puys*. Geothermal activity is evident today in the large number of mineral springs – as a result, the Massif Central contains more than a third of French spas. The volcanic landscapes of the Auvergne provided the inspiration for the Vulcania 'science park' near the industrial city of Clermont Ferrand. This project has attracted private sector funding from Michelin and Volvic, both major commercial enterprises based in the region. Agrotourism has been encouraged to stem depopulation from one of France's poorest farming regions, by integrating holiday villages and second homes with rural communities. There has also been some development of winter sports tourism for the domestic market.

Vichy is probably the best-known of French spas, although it now attracts fewer wealthy foreign clients than in the era prior to the Second World War. The hotels, bathing establishments, casino and opera house are grouped around the Parc des Sources, which is the major focus of the resort. Like other European spas, Vichy has adapted to changing demands by:

- diversification of the product into conferences, exhibitions and festivals
- modernization of spa treatments to appeal to today's busy executives rather than the traditional three week 'cure'
- the provision of sports facilities to attract young tourists.

Eastern France

The vast swathe of France extending from the Ardennes to the Jura mountains has for centuries been a zone of passage for trade and invading armies and is now well suited for touring holidays. Resources include:

- the rolling countryside of the **Champagne** region, which includes Reims, historically important as the religious capital of France
- **Lorraine**, which, although more industrialized, boasts one of the best examples of eighteenth-century town planning in the city of Nancy
- German-speaking **Alsace**, which has more to offer the visitor with its picturesque half-timbered villages and an important wine route based on Colmar; its regional capital, Strasbourg, has acquired a major international role as a seat of the European Parliament and other EU agencies.

Burgundy, lying astride the routeways connecting the Rhine to the Rhône, and thus linking northern Europe to the Mediterranean, played a major role in European history in the Middle Ages. Its rich cultural heritage includes the Romanesque abbeys of Citeaux and Cluny, and the historic cities of Dijon and Beaune, although Burgundy is best-known for the wines of the Côte d'Or and Beaujolais districts.

Lyon deserves special mention as the second city of France, which became of major importance through its silk weaving industry and strategic location at the junction of the rivers Rhône and Saône. In addition to a fine architectural heritage, the city is increasingly recognized as a short break destination and for its culinary attractions.

The South of France

For the tourist travelling overland, the Rhône Valley south of Lyon provides the introduction to the region known by the French as Le Midi. The South of France is distinguished by its Mediterranean climate, but more tangibly by the colourful landscapes, and the quality of its light, which have attracted many world famous artists. Regional lifestyles also differ from those of northern France, while the popularity of bull fights in Nîmes, Perpignan and Arles, and the use of the Catalan language in Roussillon, reflect the influence of Spain. The South includes two major tourist regions: the Languedoc–Roussillon coast, which we mentioned earlier as an example of large-scale planning, and the French Riviera.

In **Languedoc–Roussillon** the coastal resorts have tended to draw tourists away from the interior, which includes such scenically attractive areas as the Corbières and the Cevennes. During the summer months the new resorts such as Cap d'Agde, with its Mediterranean village ambience, and La Grande Motte, distinguished by its pyramid-shaped apartment blocks, are full of activity. They provide a contrast to the historic cities of the interior, notably Montpellier with its university, Carcassonne and Nîmes, which boasts a well-preserved Roman arena and the Pont du Gard aqueduct.

In **Provence** the rural areas have been more successful in attracting tourists and second home owners. The cities of the region are also important tourist centres, with a wealth of heritage attractions dating back to Roman times, and a calendar of cultural events such as music festivals. The best known are Aix en Provence, which is a major artistic centre, Arles and Avignon – where the Palace of the Popes is a reminder of the city's former importance as a political and religious centre. However tourism is of secondary importance in Marseille, due to the dominance of industry and commerce and its reputation for crime. Provence can also offer a number of contrasting natural attractions such as the wetlands of the Camargue and the gorges of Verdon.

The **French Riviera** is the Mediterranean coast of eastern Provence, extending almost 200 kilometres from Toulon to the Italian border. The western Riviera is backed by the Esterel and Maures mountains, while the Côte d'Azur, the section between Cannes and Menton, is sheltered by the much higher Maritime Alps to the north. This was the first area to be developed – for winter tourism and the European elite – in the nineteenth century. In the 1920s sunbathing became fashionable, so that the Riviera changed to be a summer destination. Although some resorts continue to be an international playground for the rich and famous, most of the coast has been a popular holiday area for the French domestic market since the 1950s. It is easily accessible through the international airport at Nice as well as the French rail and motorway network, while the resorts of the Côte d'Azur are linked by the contour-hugging *corniches* that must rank among Europe's most scenic highways. The Riviera offers many event attractions, the best known being the Carnival in Nice, the Cannes Film Festival and the Monaco Grand Prix. Saint-Tropez is the leading resort of the western Riviera, with good beaches compared to those of the Côte d'Azur. Along with Cannes and Antibes, it has retained a stylish and exclusive image. Nice, on the other hand, is a large commercial city, with a range of accommodation to suit even the budget-conscious tourist and a rich cultural heritage. The tiny independent principality of **Monaco** is famous for its yacht harbour and the casino at Monte Carlo, but there are also a number of visitor attractions and conference/exhibition venues.

Corsica

Known to the French as 'the island of beauty', Corsica offers some of the most spectacular scenery in the western Mediterranean. From the deeply indented western coast rise high mountains covered with forests of pine and chestnut and sweet-smelling *maquis*. Tourism has underlined the differences between the coastal towns, which have always been more outward-looking, and the remote interior, where traditional lifestyles prevailed until recent times. The main resorts – Calvi, Ile Rousse and Porto Vecchio – lie on the west coast and offer facilities for water sports such as sailing and diving, while the island's capital – Ajaccio – has capitalized on its fame as the birthplace of Napoleon. Development plans for the island seek to redress the imbalance between the coast and the interior, although continuing to recognize the key role of tourism, which provides about 25 per cent of jobs. Attention is focused on the flatter east coast, where development is taking place in a more orderly way than in the past. Improved transport links to the mainland, and the growth of inclusive tours, will ensure a greater role for tourism in Corsica. However, tourism must be seen to benefit the local population, who are keen to preserve their cultural identity.

The French Alps

The traditional economy of this mountain region was based on pastoralism, with the livestock being moved to the high pastures above the treeline in summer and back to the villages in autumn. The economy is now dependent on tourism, including winter sports and, in summer, lakes and mountains holidays. Most of the development has taken place in the north, where the mountains are higher, yet more accessible. Mountain climbing has been a major activity at Chamonix since the early nineteenth century, due to its proximity to Mont Blanc and the spectacular glacier known as the Mer de Glace. It has now become a major ski resort. Villages at lower altitudes – in the so-called Pre-Alps – are less used for skiing due to the unreliable snow cover, but are much in demand for second home development, while Aix les Bains and Evian rank among France's most noted spas.

Full-scale development for winter sports tourism began in the 1960s, involving public sector investment under the *Plan Neige*. Purpose-built resorts were planned at high altitudes above the treeline, where glacial cirques provided maximum snow cover. These were to be veritable 'ski-factories' of a uniform design appealing to sports-minded tourists, with apartment blocks sited to give direct access to the lift system. Resorts such as Tignes have been criticized for their lack of human scale, severely functional design and their impact on the fragile alpine environment. Overall, the majority of the development has been in the northern Alps, where the 15 major resorts account for over three-quarters of the industry's turnover. In the 1990s there has been something of a reaction favouring smaller resorts of a more traditional design.

The French Alps have become Europe's most popular winter sports destination, attracting domestic and foreign skiers alike, for the following reasons:

- proximity to the areas generating the demand: thanks to the Channel Tunnel, British skiers have a wide choice of routes and modes of transport to the resorts; in addition to airports at Nice (serving the southern resort of Isola 2000), Lyon, Grenoble, Chambery and Geneva, there are Eurostar ski-trains, and 'ski-drive' arrangements are available for motorists using the excellent road network
- good infrastructure, including the most extensive lift system in Europe
- suitability for a wide range of markets, from family holidaymakers to young singles and snowboarders
- an extensive range of accommodation, from first class hotels to family-run *auberges*, serviced chalets, and self-catering studio apartments.

The French Pyrenees

Winter sports play a less important role in the Pyrenees than in the Alps, and the region attracts fewer foreign skiers. Although the mountain peaks are not as high, remoteness from Paris and transport problems retarded the development of tourism. Nevertheless, a number of spas function as ski centres during the winter months. In summer, visitors are attracted by the unspoiled scenery – notably the Cirque de Gavarnie, a spectacular natural amphitheatre resulting from glacial erosion – and the opportunities for ecotourism and adventure sports. The major tourist centre of the region – **Lourdes** – is in fact one of the world's leading attractions and deserves special consideration:

○ This small town – with less than 20 000 inhabitants – annually hosts over 6 million visitors (compared to 2 million in the 1950s), and is second only to Paris in hotel capacity. With over 400 hotels and a number of campsites on the outskirts, Lourdes can accommodate more than 100 000 visitors at peak times.

○ Its fame as a tourist centre is based not on a tangible physical resource, but on the visions of St Bernadette. The Grotto of Massabielle, where these occurred in 1858, subsequently became the focus of pilgrimage. Miraculous cures are attributed to the spring water in the grotto and although a Medical Bureau scrutinizes these claims, Lourdes is not a spa in the conventional sense (unlike nearby Cauterets).

○ Lourdes was the first pilgrimage centre to be created by modern means of transport and communication, which explains its rapid growth, and it has become a role model for similar developments in other countries.

○ One-third of the visitors to Lourdes can be described as true pilgrims. More than 500 organized group pilgrimages take place every year, brought in by charter flights, coaches and special trains equipped by SNCF to carry the large numbers of sick and disabled. This involves considerable organization, in which volunteer carers play a major role.

○ The distinction between the religious and secular aspects of pilgrimage is not always clear, but in Lourdes there is some geographical separation of the two. Religious activity is centred on the Domain of the Sanctuaries, covering an area of 20 hectares. This includes the esplanade – a vast open space for processions – and a number of large churches grouped around the entrance to the Grotto. The devotion of the pilgrims provides a stark contrast to the commercialism of the town centre, with its array of shops displaying what many would regard as tasteless religious souvenirs.

Summary

Changing economic and social conditions in France since the Second World War have encouraged participation in tourism. The majority of French tourism is domestic, characterized by long-stay holidays concentrated in the peak summer months. Domestic holidays are widely distributed throughout France, and tend to be organized independently, although social tourism is important. The majority of French holidays abroad are to Spain and Italy, although long-haul destinations are becoming more popular, spearheaded to some extent by Club Méditerranée. Incoming tourism is more significant, and France is one of the world's most popular destinations.

The tourism industry in France is fragmented, comprising many small businesses. A wide choice of accommodation is available, with self catering traditionally the preferred option for domestic holidaymakers, leaving the hotel sector largely dependent on the business and inbound tourism markets. Tourism benefits from comprehensive air, rail and road networks. Tourism tends to be centralized at government level, with the state also initiating major development projects, although both regional and local organizations are now playing a more important role.

France can offer a great diversity of tourism resources and products, based on its countryside, coastal resorts and cultural heritage, and ranging from winter sports and adventure tourism in the Alps to sightseeing in Paris and the Loire Valley. Each region can offer different attractions, although tourism tends to play a more significant role in the coastal and mountain areas.

Chapter 15
The tourism geography of Spain and Portugal

Learning Objectives

After reading this chapter you should be able to:

■ Describe the major physical features and climates of the Iberian Peninsula and the islands belonging to Spain and Portugal, and explain their significance for tourism.

■ Trace the development of Spanish tourism and understand the reasons for Spain's success as a tourist destination.

■ Appreciate the nature of tourism demand in Spain and Portugal.

■ Appreciate the cultural differences between Spain and Portugal, and contrast the nature of tourism development in the two countries.

■ Outline the major features of the tourism infrastructure in Spain, Portugal and Gibraltar.

■ Outline the main features of tourism administration in Spain and Portugal.

■ Demonstrate a knowledge of the tourist regions, resorts, business centres and tourist attractions of the Iberian Peninsula and the islands belonging to Spain and Portugal.

Introduction

The Iberian Peninsula, the Balearic and Canary Islands and Madeira have been favourite holiday destinations for north Europeans since the availability of inclusive tours in the 1960s. By the early years of the twenty-first century tourist arrivals in Spain and Portugal had exceeded 60 million. Spain was one of the first countries in the world to enter the mass inclusive tour market, taking advantage of its sunny climate and long Mediterranean coastline. With the new millennium Spain faces increasing competition from other destinations that can offer similar attractions to north Europeans, but at lower prices. Spain has attempted for many years to promote products other than beach tourism, but this is proving difficult for the following reasons:

- Most of the tourism development is well established on the Costas – the resort areas of the Mediterranean coast of Spain – and the Balearic and Canary Islands.
- Spain's image of 'sun, sand and sangria' is firmly engrained in the popular culture of northern Europe.

Portugal, on the other hand, entered the international tourism scene later than Spain. It not only made a determined effort to avoid some of its neighbour's worst excesses of tourism development, but also attempted both to control tourism's impact on the country and to attract the more affluent tourist from the outset.

Spain

In area, Spain is the second largest country of Western Europe after France, and occupies the greater part of the Iberian Peninsula. This can be a consideration in planning a holiday itinerary, as it is almost 1000 kilometres by road from Bilbao or Santander on the north coast to Málaga in the south. The dominant feature of the Iberian Peninsula is a high plateau – the Meseta – separated by rugged mountain ranges or *sierras* from the narrow coastal strips where most of the tourism development has taken place. Because of this, only the Balearic Islands and the south and east of Spain have a typically Mediterranean climate. The northern coast from Vigo to San Sebastian is not called 'Green Spain' without reason; summers are cooler and rainier and it enjoys less sunshine than the Mediterranean coast. The Meseta experiences a more extreme climate, with rather cold winters and hot summers. These physical contrasts are reflected in the country's great cultural diversity, with regional languages such as Basque, Catalan and Galician flourishing alongside Castilian Spanish.

The rugged nature of much of the Iberian Peninsula has also helped to isolate Spain from the rest of Europe. Even today, the Pyrenees are crossed by very few roads and railways. In the south, only a narrow stretch of water separates Spain from North Africa and its Islamic culture. In fact almost the whole of Spain – except for Asturias and Galicia – was at one time under Arab domination. The struggle to oust the 'Moors' lasted from 718 to 1492. This forged the religious fervour and devotion to the Roman Catholic Church that still characterizes much of Spain, and explains the ambivalent attitudes of Spaniards today towards their Muslim heritage and the issue of large-scale immigration from North Africa. Despite the impressive economic development, and social changes (in the role of women for example) that have taken place since the 1960s, Spain differs from other West European countries in the following ways:

- the greater persistence of craft industries, notably ceramics and Toledo metalwork
- the *fiestas*, *ferias* (fairs) and *romerías* (pilgrimages), which play such an important role in the life of many communities; these provide an opportunity to display Spain's rich heritage of regional dances and colourful costumes

- aspects of the lifestyle, for example the traditional afternoon siesta, whereas dining and social activity takes place very late into the night.

Spain has achieved outstanding success as one of the world's top five destinations, and can offer well over one million bedspaces in serviced accommodation alone. There is no doubt that tourism has contributed greatly to the transformation of the Spanish economy from that of a developing country to one of Europe's major industrial nations since the 1950s. By the beginning of the twenty-first century tourism supported 1.5 million jobs, contributed one-third of the country's export earnings and accounted for 12 per cent of GDP. However, this success has been achieved at a cost to society and the environment, for example:

- Spain's rich cultural diversity has been set aside in favour of a commercialized version of *flamenco* for tourist consumption in the resorts.
- The demands of the tourism industry have affected family life in some areas.
- Uncontrolled resort developments mar part of the Mediterranean coastline and bring pollution.
- Tourism has sharpened regional contrasts, particularly between the developed coastal areas and the interior.

Yet the Spanish beach product is still guaranteed a loyal repeat market, and tourism is likely to continue as a vital sector of the economy. Spain's success in tourism is due to a variety of factors:

- There was a growth in demand for holidays in the sun from countries in northern Europe once they had recovered from the effects of the Second World War.
- Spain was well placed to benefit from the development of civil aviation and changes in the structure of the travel industry, especially the introduction of low-cost air inclusive tours.
- Spain's relatively late entry into the European tourism market allowed it to evaluate the competition and offer lower prices than those of established destinations such as Italy and the French Riviera.
- The Spanish government responded positively to the opportunities tourism offered, in the following ways:
  - abolishing visa requirements for most European tourists in the late 1950s
  - maintaining a favourable rate of exchange for the tourist by successive devaluations of the peseta
  - providing advantageous credit terms to developers
  - regulating the industry to protect the consumer
  - creating a new Ministry of Tourism in 1962 to provide more effective co-ordination and promotion.

Arguably, the tourism industry was able to benefit from the long period of political stability under the authoritarian rule of General Franco (1939–1975), as industrial unrest was outlawed. The views of local communities on tourism development were also frequently ignored in the interest of economic expediency. However, although the Franco regime tried to isolate Spain from the social changes taking place in Western Europe, tourism, through the demonstration effect, played a major role in bringing about the liberalization of Spanish society.

Demand for tourism

Domestic and outbound tourism

Before the 1960s only a relatively small minority of the Spanish population could afford to take holidays away from home. The middle and upper classes escaped the summer heat of the cities by visiting spas in the mountains, the beaches of the east coast or the northern coastal resorts such as Santander and San Sebastián. The economic progress which took place after 1960 increased personal incomes and boosted car ownership, so that tourism propensity is now around 60 per cent. Despite the social changes brought about by industrialization, family ties remain stronger than in most other European countries, although the present low birth rate gives cause for concern over the future. Leisure is highly valued, and the public holidays celebrating national and religious festivals are sometimes linked by a practice known as *puente* (literally 'bridge') to increase the number of 'long weekends' in the year.

The pattern of holiday-taking by Spaniards also contrasts with that of foreign visitors. Although the coasts are popular with both, many Spaniards visit the rural areas of the interior, often retracing their family roots. Domestic tourism in Spain has the following characteristics:

- almost 80 per cent of trips are by private car
- only 20 per cent of overnight stays involve hotel accommodation, as two-thirds of domestic tourists stay with friends or relatives, or in second homes
- the most popular month is August, when one in four Spaniards is on holiday.

Around 90 per cent of holidays taken by Spaniards are in their own country, and it was not until the 1990s that they began to view a foreign holiday as an annual event. The most visited destinations are neighbouring France and Portugal, although touring holidays in northern Europe, Morocco and long-haul destinations are becoming more popular. Spending per capita by Spanish tourists is higher than the European average, demonstrating the country's new-found prosperity. History, culture and education are important features sought by the Spanish abroad, with guidebooks stressing the culinary attractions of a destination. Day trip volumes to neighbouring Portugal, France and Andorra are estimated to be around 25 million a year.

Inbound tourism

Although Spain is now the second most popular tourism destination in the world, it was a relative latecomer to the international tourism scene. It did not usually feature on the Grand Tour, since the generally poor state of the roads and the inns tended to deter all but the more adventurous travellers. A major improvement in the situation took place after 1928, when the government-sponsored *Patronato Nacional de Turismo* began to set up a chain of state-run *albergues* (inns) and *paradores* offering a high standard of accommodation. The small numbers of foreign visitors to Spain before the Civil War (1936–1939) were attracted by the country's picturesque traditions and not by sun, sand and sea, unlike most of today's tourists. For example, the American writer Ernest Hemingway was largely responsible for publicizing bullfighting and Pamplona's Fiesta de San Fermín, which continue to attract a wide international following.

Tourism growth on a large scale began in the early 1950s with the influx of French followed by British holidaymakers to the Costa Brava, spreading to the Balearic Islands and the other Costas as soon as the introduction of jet aircraft made these areas more accessible in the mid-1960s. By the early 1970s Spain had become the leading holiday destination for most of the North European tourist-generating countries. However this has left Spanish tourism vulnerable to the effects of recession in these countries, with the result that demand stagnated during the 1980s and early 1990s. This prompted the search for new markets – such as the USA and Japan – and volumes recovered in the mid- to late 1990s to exceed 40 million staying visitors and 20 million excursionists (the latter including cruise passengers and day visitors from France and Portugal). By the early 2000s, they had grown further to exceed 50 million overnight arrivals.

The most important tourist-generating countries continue to be the UK, Germany, France, the Benelux countries and Italy, which together account for around 80 per cent of arrivals. The German market has declined as tourists desert Spain in favour of less expensive destinations such as Turkey, Croatia and Bulgaria. This is of particular concern for Spanish tourism as Germans tend to be higher spenders and their visits are spread over a longer period of the year than other nationalities. Surprisingly, although you might expect the Spanish-speaking countries of Latin America to be a major source of tourists, they account for less than 2 per cent of all foreign arrivals.

Despite the efforts of both national and regional governments, tourism in Spain is highly concentrated both seasonally and geographically. Well over half of foreign visitors arrive between June and September, coinciding with domestic holiday demand, and creating congestion in the resorts. The Canaries do not have this problem because of their subtropical climate, but other areas – notably the Costa Daurada and Costa Brava – are overwhelmingly dependent on summer visitors. Seasonality creates a problem for businesses as many find it uneconomic to remain open out of season, whereas those that do reduce their staff and add to seasonal unemployment in the community. The public sector too is affected as services – such as water and power supplies – must have the extra capacity to cope with the peak demand, but are under-utilized at other times of the year. One solution to the problem is to encourage 'third age' tourism in which Spanish senior citizens stay in resort hotels at reduced rates outside the peak season.

Geographically the distribution of tourism is very uneven. Over two-thirds of Spain's hotel capacity is concentrated in just four of the autonomous regions, namely the Balearic Islands, Catalonia, Andalucia, and Valencia, which contain the most popular coastal areas. At the other extreme the interior regions of La Rioja (famous for its wine industry), Navarra, and Extremadura each have less than one per cent of hotel capacity, and the ratio between tourists and residents here is very low compared to the coastal resorts and islands. This means that the benefits of tourism are not spread widely throughout the country, and it has led to a migration of labour from the less developed areas to the resorts. Tourism could therefore be said to have contributed to the massive exodus from Spain's rural areas, where many villages are now virtually deserted. Agro-tourism has grown in popularity in recent years and may help to stem further rural depopulation, but this in turn leads to another problem – loss of cultural identity – if villages simply become second homes for north European expatriates seeking 'the good life'.

The very nature of tourism demand to Spain has reduced the economic benefits. Spanish tourism is dominated by the demands of the major north European tour operators who provide high volumes of visitors yet demand low-priced accommodation. This encourages low-cost, high-rise hotel and apartment development in the coastal resorts and reduces the contribution of each tourist to the economy.

The anti-social behaviour of some of the youth element in mass tourism has resulted in costs to local communities. These problems are concentrated in a few weeks during July and August in resorts dominated by the British or the Germans, such as Magalluf and Arenal in Mallorca (Majorca), Playa de las Americas in Tenerife and San Antonio in Ibiza.

Supply of tourism

Transport

Around two-thirds of all visitors to Spain arrive by surface transport, especially by road through the eastern Pyrenees. The inclusive tour market ensures a constant supply of tourists arriving mainly on charter airlines, owned in most cases by the major north European tour operators. However, their share of the holiday market is being eroded by the low cost 'no frills' airlines that can offer greater flexibility in travel arrangements for the increasing numbers of visitors staying in second homes, or in rented apartments and villas. Many independent travellers touring Spain use the national carrier Iberia and its subsidiaries. Although Madrid and Barcelona are important international gateways, most north European holidaymakers fly to one of the regional airports serving a particular holiday area, namely:

- Girona for the Costa Brava
- Reus or Barcelona for the Costa Daurada
- Alicante or Valencia for the Costa Blanca
- Murcia for the Costa Cálida
- Málaga for the Costa del Sol
- Palma, Ibiza and Mahon for the Balearic Islands
- Las Palmas, Tenerife Sur and Arrecife for the Canary Islands.

Touring Spain by car has been facilitated by the massive improvement of the road network that has taken place since the 1980s, including some 6000 kilometres of motorways. The most important of these are the Autopista de Levante (east coast motorway), and the routes linking Madrid with the regional centres of Seville, Valencia and Zaragoza. The rail system under Spanish State Railways (RENFE) is tightly focused on Madrid and therefore touring by train is less convenient. The break of gauge at the borders with France and Portugal also affects most international train services. However, plans are now well advanced to integrate Spain with the rest of the European rail network, and high-speed trains link Madrid with Seville, Barcelona and San Sebastián. The 'golden age' of rail travel is recalled by the luxury *Al Andalus Express*, which allows the visitor to see the countryside and cities of southern Spain in style.

Accommodation

Spain offers a variety of accommodation, from luxury resort hotels to simple *hostales* (pensions). Hotel classification is based on the facilities provided rather than the quality of service. Sol-Meliá is the largest Spanish-owned hotel chain in a sector dominated by independent establishments and small groups, which have little bargaining power with foreign tour operators on pricing. In addition to the private sector, there are 100 state-owned *paradores*, situated away from the main tourist centres and providing accommodation in traditional Spanish style (often in converted castles, palaces or monasteries). As such, they are favoured by independent travellers touring the 'real Spain' (as distinct from the Costas) by car. Although hotels account for two-thirds of stays by foreign tourists, their share has declined since the 1990s, and there are problems of over-supply in some areas such as the Costa del Sol. Self-catering accommodation, in the form of apartments and holiday villas, is mainly found in the resort areas of eastern and southern Spain. An almost continuous series of *urbanizaciones* – second home developments, often dominated by a particular nationality – now stretches from Denia to Estepona. Campsites are concentrated in those locations that are most accessible from France, such as the Costa Brava and the Valencia region.

Organization

Spain's organization of tourism has attracted attention from countries around the world and many have adopted the Spanish model. Tourism became the responsibility of a cabinet minister in 1951 and the national tourism plans since 1953 have set the institutional and public service framework for Spain's growth and continued presence in the world tourism market. At national level, the Ministry of Trade, Tourism and Small and Medium Sized Businesses is responsible for tourism policy and promotion. Generally the government is anxious to provide an environment within which tourism can flourish and a variety of grants and incentives are available for developers, in addition to direct investment by the state. There are also two specialist national agencies, one to promote conferences and the other to manage state-owned accommodation, restaurants, hunting reserves and tourist routes.

Until 1978 tourism was firmly administered by central government from Madrid. The Spanish Constitution of that year gave the new autonomous regions (*communidades autónomas*) wide powers as part of the post-Franco democratization of the country. Tourism is therefore administered by 17 regional governments who have the power to approve developments and determine policy. At the local level, the *municipios* (town councils) also take on the responsibility for some aspects of tourism and can impose taxes to finance projects in their area. This may well mean that tourism receives more favourable treatment in some areas than others. In the largest resorts there are associations of business people – *centros de iniciativas* – who promote their destination and local facilities; as in other areas of Spanish politics much depends on the personality and connections of those in power.

Although the authorities are aware that the mass inclusive tour market for beach tourism still represents the majority of demand, attempts are being made to develop new holiday styles in order to reduce seasonality, spread tourism more evenly throughout the country and encourage higher spending visitors. The market continues to become more sophisticated and independent travellers from countries such as Britain now outnumber those on inclusive tours. Changes in the pattern of demand means that as much as 10 per cent of the accommodation stock needs to be taken off the cheaper end of the market, especially in Mallorca. The main objectives of the Spanish Tourist Office are:

- to increase awareness of the lesser-known areas, mainly from the cultural viewpoint
- to upgrade standards for those seeking beach holidays on the Costas and the islands.

In line with this policy, conferences and activity holidays are being promoted. Many Mediterranean resorts are now well equipped with marinas for the high-spending yachting enthusiasts, and some have invested in aqua-parks to attract the family market. Winter sports facilities have been developed in the Pyrenees, the Sierra de Guadarrama near Madrid and the Sierra Nevada, although as yet these cater mainly for domestic demand. The remaining coastal areas are being opened up for international tourism, although under more stringent environmental controls than was the case in the 1960s.

Promotional campaigns by the Spanish NTO, such as 'Spain – Passion for Life' and 'Spain Marks' have highlighted the appeal of the Spanish lifestyle and the cultural heritage, with an emphasis on the different regions.

Tourism resources

Northern Spain

Dominated by the Cantabrian Mountains and overlooking the Atlantic Ocean to the west and the Bay of Biscay to the north, the coastlands of northern Spain are characterized by a green countryside of meadows, woodlands and orchards. Appropriately enough, the attractions of coast, countryside and mountains have been promoted by the regions of Galicia, Asturias, Cantabria and the Basque Country under the banner of *España Verde* (Green Spain). For an increasing number of foreign visitors, usually travelling independently by car, the appeal lies in this 'real Spain' of unspoiled scenery, rich folk traditions and distinctive regional cuisines, in contrast to the bland international food and artificial attractions of the Mediterranean beach resorts. However, parts of Asturias and the Basque Country offer a less attractive hinterland, where declining 'smokestack industries' provide the impetus to expand tourism as a means of regenerating the area.

The region of **Galicia** in the west has much in common with other areas on the 'Celtic fringe' of Europe. Although the Galicians speak a language similar to Portuguese, the folk traditions and misty landscapes are reminiscent of Ireland. This is one of the poorest areas of the Peninsula as the pocket-sized farms cannot provide a decent livelihood, so that in the past large numbers of Galicians have emigrated, particularly to South America. There is an important fishing industry based on ports such as Vigo and La Coruña, where the *rias* (drowned river estuaries) provide excellent harbours. Although there are many fine beaches facing the Atlantic, few seaside resorts of significance have developed, while the region's fishing and tourism industries suffered a major setback with the *Prestige* oil spill disaster in 2003. The most important tourist centre – Santiago de Compostela – lies some distance inland.

The scenery becomes more rugged in **Asturias** and **Cantabria**, culminating in the spectacular Picos de Europa National Park. The area is ideal for activity holidays such as hiking and canoeing, and a number of spas and picturesque seaside resorts have developed along the fine beaches fronting the Bay of Biscay, including Laredo and Castro Urdiales. By far the best known is Santander, with its festival attractions, and growing in importance along with Bilbao as a gateway to Spain for British tourists arriving by ferry from Plymouth or Portsmouth. The region's heritage attractions include the medieval town of Santillana de Mar and the Altamira Caves – known as 'the Sistine Chapel of Stone Age art' – now protected by an award-winning replica and museum.

The **Basque Country** actually extends into the south-west corner of France. The three Spanish Basque provinces, known locally as Euskadi, lie between Bilbao and the western end of the Pyrenees. The region is marked off from the rest of Spain by its people, who speak a language unrelated to any other in Europe, and by their passion for gastronomy and unusual pastimes – notably *jai alai* or *pelota*, an exciting ball game which has gained an international following in the Americas. Many Basques are not content with autonomy, and have given support to the ETA separatist movement. Despite the threat of terrorism, there are two tourist centres of international standing, namely:

○ **San Sebastián** (Donostia), with its wide sweep of beach between two protecting headlands, festivals and fashionable shops, is the premier resort of northern Spain, although it is no longer the summer capital of the country

○ **Bilbao**, in contrast, is primarily a port and industrial centre, which until recently had little to recommend it for tourists. This has now changed, thanks to the ultra-modern Guggenheim Museum, showcasing international art, which has transformed the waterfront area.

Eastern and Southern Spain

The majority of foreign tourists to Spain head straight for the Mediterranean coastal resorts where summer sunshine is guaranteed. For this reason the numerous cultural attractions of the regions of Catalonia, Valencia, Murcia and Andalucia tend to be overshadowed by the pull of the beaches. Barcelona, Seville and Granada are the most notable exceptions.

The region of **Catalonia** has its own language, culture and a strong sense of national identity. Historically the Catalans have been more outward-looking and progressive than other Spaniards and they have made their capital, Barcelona, one of Europe's great seaports and centres of industry and commerce. **Barcelona** has also attracted avant-garde artists and architects and is pre-eminent in fashion design. The 1992 Summer Olympics focused world attention on the host city and gave the impetus for many civic improvements, notably the regeneration of the run-down waterfront area. Major sightseeing attractions in the city include:

○ the street life and floral displays of the Ramblas

○ the Pueblo Español (Spanish Village), showcasing architectural styles and regional crafts from all over Spain

○ The cathedral and its quaint medieval district – the Barrio Gótico

○ The Basilica of the Sagrada Familia, the unfinished masterpiece of the Catalan architect Antonio Gaudí.

Barcelona is also a good centre for touring other places of interest in the hinterland of Catalonia, notably Montserrat – a monastery and place of pilgrimage in a spectacular setting.

Catalonia includes two major holiday areas – the Costa Brava to the north-east of Barcelona and the Costa Daurada to the south-west:

○ The **Costa Brava**, the rugged coastline between Blanes and Port Bou on the French border, was the first area to be developed for mass tourism in the 1950s and 1960s. The scenic beauty of this coast – pine-covered hills, red cliffs and sheltered coves – had earlier attracted artists and fashionable holidaymakers to picturesque Tossa and the resort of S'Agaró, purpose-built for tourism in the 1920s. Some resorts – notably Lloret de Mar – have been given over to the package holiday market and their natural assets buried under concrete. The Costa Brava no longer appeals to a mass market experiencing 'destination fatigue', and in 2004 it was dropped from the programmes of a leading British tour operator. Nevertheless, some stretches of coastline – as at Begur and Cadaqués – remain unspoiled, and increasing numbers of independent holidaymakers are seeking out the cultural attractions of this part of Catalonia. These include the Salvador Dalí Museum at Figueres and the picturesque medieval city of Girona.

○ The **Costa Daurada** is characterized by long beaches of golden sand and extends beyond Barcelona as far as the Ebro Delta. Its appeal is reduced by the proximity of industry in some areas. Sitges is the most attractive resort and one that is popular with Spaniards, but like others on this coast it is moribund out of season. Salou is the most popular resort with foreign holidaymakers, and has experienced a revival in its fortunes following the opening of the Port Aventura theme park in 1993.

Likewise tourism plays an important but not exclusive role in the economies of the **Valencia** and **Murcia** regions. Despite its dry climate, the narrow eastern coastal plain is one of the most productive agricultural regions of Spain, thanks to sophisticated irrigation techniques. The landscape includes citrus orchards, the villages with their blue-domed churches, the date palm plantation at Elche and the rice fields around the Albufera lagoon. These features contrast markedly with the barren mountains to the west and Europe's only desert to the south, which is a favourite location for producers of low-budget 'western' movies. The city of Valencia is primarily a seaport and industrial centre, and its tourism appeal lies not so much in historic buildings but in that well-known culinary product *paella* and the spectacular *Las Fallas* festival, which culminates in the burning of elaborate papier-mâché effigies. The city's go-ahead outlook is shown by the impressive 'City of Arts and Sciences' – a science park commemorating the Millennium – and a model civic tourism administration. The Costa de Azahar to the north consists of a string of resorts, including the historic town of Peñiscola.

The **Costa Blanca** between Denia and Alicante is one of Spain's most popular holiday areas, due in large measure to Benidorm. In 1960 this was a mere fishing village but a progressive *alcalde* (mayor) provided the impetus for its transformation into a high rise mega-resort or 'leisure factory' designed specifically for the mass market and capable of absorbing 6 million visitors a year, with as many as 350 000 arriving in the first two weeks of August. Benidorm boasts an average year-round occupancy rate of 90 per cent, thanks to a loyal domestic and international clientèle, with 'third age' tourists filling the hotels during the winter months. Benidorm's success is due to its sheltered position, two fine sandy beaches, proximity to Alicante Airport, and – not least – an uninhibited entertainment industry catering for most tastes, age groups and nationalities. It has readily adapted to changes in demand, with the opening of the Terra Mitica theme park and the state of the art Hotel Bali – one of the largest in Europe – as the flagship of a new drive to attract conference business and 'four star' tourists. Elsewhere on the Costa Blanca development tends to be low-rise, but arguably extensive villa developments have a greater social and environmental impact than 'skyscraper' hotels, as they generate large volumes of car traffic, directly compete with local agriculture for land, power and water resources, and require greater resources in policing. Even the coastline of the dry south-east corner of Spain has been developed for golf tourism and water sports as the 'Costa Cálida', focusing on the resort of La Manga and the Mar Menor lagoon.

The region of **Andalucia** for many people epitomizes Spain, with its warm, sunny climate, easy-going lifestyle and picturesque villages. Moorish rule persisted for much longer in this part of Spain, and their heritage is particularly evident in the traditional architecture. Yet this region has had more than its fair share of social and economic problems, as much of the land is dominated by large estates given over to olive production, unemployment is high and the gypsies, who have inspired flamenco as an art form, remain a marginalized element in society. Rural tourism is growing in importance, while horse riding and trekking are popular holiday activities in the mountain areas. The many picturesque small towns and villages known as the *pueblos blancos* are accessible from the bustling resorts of the Costa del Sol, and yet a world apart. Nevertheless tourism is mainly focused on the major cities of the region and the coast:

○ **Seville** is the regional capital and was historically Spain's gateway to the Americas in the colonial period. The city achieved international acclaim as the host city for the 1992 World Expo. Tourists arrive in great numbers each spring for the awe-inspiring spectacle of the Holy Week processions, followed a few weeks later by the colour and excitement of the April *Feria*.

○ **Córdoba** under Muslim rule was Europe's largest city in the tenth century, and contains one of the most outstanding relics of that era – the Mezquita, now a cathedral. The new Arab-style public baths epitomize the revival of interest by Spaniards in their Moorish heritage. Córdoba is also noted for its colourful patios.

○ **Granada** is world-famous for an exquisite example of Moorish architecture – the Alhambra Palace. The adjoining gardens of the Generalife, with the snow-capped mountains of the Sierra Nevada in the background, provide an incomparable setting for festivals of music and dance. The Albaicín district nearby is also a World Heritage Site and has become an artists' quarter containing many Moroccan-style tea houses.

○ **Jerez** is the centre for the production of one of Spain's most celebrated exports, the fortified wine known throughout the English-speaking world as sherry. The city is also renowned throughout Spain as a showcase for equestrian skills in a region devoted to horse riding and the bullfight.

○ Jerez is the gateway to the **Costa de la Luz**, Andalucia's Atlantic coastal region, which has some of the best beaches in Spain. This is a popular holiday area for the Spanish but has attracted little attention so far from foreign tour operators. Most of the development has been grafted on to existing seaports. Cadiz, once the leading commercial city of Spain in the colonial era and now celebrated for its Carnival, is a tourist centre of growing significance, while Tarifa is noted for windsurfing.

○ North of Sanlucar, mass tourism is in conflict with conservation in one of Europe's most unique wetland environments – the Coto Doñana National Park – where the ecosystems depend on the maintenance of the water table. This is already under intense pressure from large-scale agro-business and mining activity to the north. Further expansion of the resort of Matalascanas would tip the balance still further. The national park has attracted opposition for its strict management policies, which have allowed local communities little share in decision-making or the profits to be made from ecotourism.

The **Costa del Sol** extends for 300 kilometres from Gibraltar to Adra, and is the holiday area that has shown the most spectacular growth since the 1960s, with resorts such as Torremolinos having experienced the various stages in the tourist area life cycle from 'discovery' to 'decline'. The location of the Costa del Sol in the extreme south of Spain is advantageous for the following reasons:

○ The Sierra Nevada and other mountain ranges protect this south-facing coast, guaranteeing warmer temperatures and more sunshine in winter than elsewhere in western Europe, and making it possible to cultivate sugar cane and other sub-tropical crops.

○ The Costa del Sol can offer the tourist an exceptionally wide range of outdoor activities, including golf, tennis, horse riding and sailing, while skiing can be enjoyed in the Sierra Nevada, where the snow cover lasts from December to May.

○ The coastal resorts provide easy access to the many cultural attractions of southern Spain.

This part of Andalucia has long been a winter destination for wealthy tourists, starting with Málaga in the nineteenth century, while the picturesque mountain town of Ronda served as a summer retreat for British officers stationed in Gibraltar. The development of the Costa del Sol for mass tourism did not get underway until after the opening of Málaga airport in 1962. The completion of the E340 coastal road improved access to the resorts, but it soon acquired a reputation as the 'highway of death', as high-rise ribbon development extended from Málaga to Estepona. Tourism has largely replaced fishing and farming as a source of employment for local people, and greatly improved living standards. However, in some of the villages – Mijas is a notable example – expatriates from the countries of northern Europe now make up almost half the population.

The section of the Costa del Sol to the east of Málaga contains fewer resorts and most of the development consists of holiday villas designed to blend in with the local landscape. Most of the hotel accommodation is found in the large resorts to the west of Málaga, which include:

○ **Torremolinos,** which has become a byword for the ills of mass tourism and speculative development. However, this former fishing village was an upmarket, fashionable resort with a handful of luxury hotels in the late 1950s and early 1960s. This was followed in the 1970s by a massive expansion of accommodation in the form of high-rise hotels and apartments, using cheap mass-produced materials, to cater for an ever-growing demand from the tour operators of northern Europe. We could say that Torremolinos, along with its neighbours Benalmadena and Fuengirola, plays a vital role in concentrating vast numbers of holidaymakers in a small area, providing them with familiar food and entertainment, and thereby saving the villages of Andalucia from some of the negative impacts of mass tourism.

○ **Marbella** first became fashionable in the 1920s, and has been more successful than the other resorts on the Costa del Sol in retaining an image of sophistication, based on a large number of five-star hotels, a wealthy expatriate community, yacht marinas such as Puerto Banus, golf and cultural activities. But even Marbella experienced a period of stagnation, if not decline, in the 1980s, caused by its association with sleaze and drug-related crime. Under energetic leadership, the resort has invested in improved facilities on its beach front, more efficient policing to ensure visitor security, and the diversification of its product to attract conferences and foreign business enterprise based on high-tech industries to the 'California of Europe'.

○ **Málaga** differs from the other tourist centres of the Costa del Sol in being primarily a working seaport and commercial city. It has been shunned by the hordes of package holidaymakers heading straight from the airport to the beach resorts, but has the potential to attract tourists seeking a genuine Spanish ambience. Málaga has done much to renovate its waterfront and city centre, as well as restoring such important examples of Moorish heritage as the Alcazaba citadel. The city also hopes to promote its cultural appeal as the birthplace of Picasso. Along with Algeciras, Málaga provides ferry services to Morocco. Here it is worth noting that the cities of Ceuta and Melilla on the North African coast are administratively part of Spain but enjoy free port status. Their role in the growing problem of illegal immigration and the presence of a large Muslim minority makes them a potential flashpoint for terrorism after '11-M' (the Madrid bombings of 11 March 2004).

The Spanish Heartlands

The Meseta dominates central and northern Spain and presents an austere landscape, where the many historic towns, castles and monasteries provide the main attractions for the cultural tourist. The northern Meseta gave rise to the warlike kingdom of Castile, which strove for centuries to dominate the Iberian Peninsula, and whose language became modern Spanish. A number of tourist routes have been promoted to link the principal places of interest, namely:

- El Camino de Santiago (The Way of Saint James) has been followed since the early Middle Ages by pilgrims from all parts of western Europe, and experienced a major revival in the 1990s. The Spanish section of the route links the historic cities of Pamplona, Burgos and León and some of Spain's finest examples of Romanesque and Gothic architecture to the shrine of St James in Santiago de Compostela. Numerous hostels provide accommodation for pilgrims travelling on foot, horseback and bicycle.
- The 'Silver Route' links northern and southern Spain and includes Salamanca, home to Spain's most famous university. It crosses the region of Extremadura, land of the *conquistadors* – who colonized the Americas in the sixteenth century.
- The 'Don Quixote Route' crosses the region of La Mancha, famous for its windmills and associations with the best known figure in Spanish literature.

Tourism in central Spain focuses on **Madrid**, and Barajas Airport is the gateway to Europe for many visitors from Latin America. Madrid became the capital of Spain in 1560, and is a latecomer compared to other Spanish cities. Although the Madrid region accounts for only 5 per cent of overnight stays by foreign visitors in Spain, the capital is firmly established as a short break destination. The following features give Madrid its special appeal:
  - The altitude of 700 metres makes it Europe's highest capital, with the benefits of clear skies for most of the year and invigorating mountain breezes from the Sierra de Guadarrama.
  - The Prado is one of the world's finest art collections, including masterpieces by Goya and Velázquez.
  - The city has a range of restaurants offering the best of Spain's regional cuisines, speciality shopping and first-class sports facilities.
  - The city has a vibrant nightlife, with much of the action taking place in the historic core of the city between the Plaza Mayor and the Puerta del Sol.
  - The city makes an ideal base for a touring holiday.
Cultural attractions recognized by UNESCO as World Heritage Sites within easy reach of Madrid include:
  - the university town of Alcalá de Henares
  - Toledo, the religious capital of Spain, which has preserved its medieval character
  - Avila, famous as the birthplace of the great visionary St Teresa; the town still retains its medieval walls, making it a favourite location for film-makers
  - El Escorial, the austere monastery-palace built by Philip II as the nerve-centre of the Spanish empire, contrasting with the gardens of Aranjuez, the former summer palace of the Bourbon kings of Spain

○ Segovia, featuring a Roman aqueduct and the romantic Alcázar Cuenca, noted for the picturesque 'hanging houses' overlooking the river Jucar and its reputation as an artists' resort.

The region of **Aragón** to the east of the Meseta also played a crucial role in Spanish history, where for centuries Moors and Christians co-existed to create the *Mudejar* style of architecture. Its capital Zaragoza is a major centre of communications and one of the great cathedral cities of Spain.

The Spanish Pyrenees

The mountains along the French border include the Aigüestortes and Ordesa National Parks, spas and winter sports developments, notably in the Aran Valley. Wildlife and traditional lifestyles, for long protected by isolation, are threatened by improvements in the transport infrastructure such as the Somport Tunnel, power projects and the growth of summer recreation.

Tourism has been most successful in the principality of **Andorra**, which is a small Catalan-speaking independent state. Duty-free shopping attracts over 8 million day visitors and over 3 million overnight visitors annually from France and Spain, but the great majority of these are concentrated in the capital, Andorra-la-Vella and only a small proportion spend more than a few hours in the principality, thus safeguarding its rural landscapes and traditions. Andorra's budget prices attract skiers in the winter months to resorts such as Arinsal and Pas de la Casa.

The Spanish islands

The two groups of Spanish islands – the Balearics in the western Mediterranean and the Canaries in the Atlantic – are different in many respects from Peninsular Spain, so that we are justified in regarding them as separate holiday destinations.

The Balearic Islands

The Balearic Islands, consisting of Mallorca (Majorca), Menorca, Ibiza and Formentera, account for a quarter of all tourism to Spain – Mallorca alone has more hotel beds than Portugal, and tourism is estimated to account for almost 60 per cent of the regional economy. The islands are of limestone formation with few surface streams, but they are generally well cultivated, mainly with tree crops such as almonds, olives and citrus. Agriculture has to compete for supplies of ground water with the tourism industry, which has to cater for a massive influx of summer visitors. Each island has distinctive landscapes, architecture and dialects.

- **Ibiza** is relatively small in terms of area and population, and it is here that the impact of tourism has perhaps been greatest. The island was also much poorer economically in the pre-tourism era than Mallorca or Menorca. Ibiza has passed through the following stages of tourism development:
  ○ The initial period of 'discovery' by hippy-style travellers in the early 1960s, who were attracted by the island life-style that was perceived to be more tolerant than the rest of Spain at that time. Some of these visitors later became permanent residents, and Ibiza remains something of an artists' community.
  ○ The introduction of direct charter flights to Ibiza airport shortly after led to the growth of the inclusive tour market, mainly from Britain, catering for family beach holidays.

○ Since the 1980s there has been a growing emphasis on the international youth market and the all-night clubbing culture. The binge drinking and 'hooliganism' of some north European tourists has attracted unfavourable publicity in the media, which in turn has deterred holidaymakers from the older age groups from visiting Ibiza.

The major impacts of mass tourism are mainly confined to San Antonio, which is a noisy high-rise 'tourist ghetto' catering for the lower end of the market. The island's capital Eivissa (Ibiza Town) has managed to retain some of its character as a historic Mediterranean seaport and offers nightlife that is more reputable and expensive. However, Ibiza's best beaches are often located at a distance from the resorts. There is concern that the traditional way of life based on agriculture has all but disappeared, while the island is reaching saturation point as far as tourism is concerned due to problems of water supply.

- **Formentera** is the smallest of the Balearics. It is comparatively barren, sparsely populated, and scenically low-key. It does however have some good beaches, and because it is featured by few tour operators, and can only be reached by ferry from Ibiza, attracts holidaymakers seeking relative seclusion.
- **Menorca** is scenically and culturally much more diverse, and its economy is less dependent on tourism. The island authorities have managed to secure greater control over tourism development than was the case in Ibiza, with well-planned holiday villages at Binibeca and Fornells catering for upmarket tourists. The island's main tourism resource are its fine harbours, which provide an ideal environment for yachting. The largest of these – Mahon – was an important base for the British navy in the eighteenth century, when it replaced the old city of Ciudadela as the island's capital.
- **Mallorca** is much the largest of the Balearic Islands, with a coastline 550 kilometres in length and mountains rising to over 1000 metres in the northwest. Between these and a lower range in the east lies a fertile plain meeting the sea in a number of fine bays. Most of the high-rise hotels and apartments are concentrated in the south-facing coastal strip extending from Paguera to Arenal, within easy reach of Palma airport, which in summer is one of Europe's busiest. Even here, the worst excesses of sun, sea and sand tourism are confined to Magalluf–Palma Nova, with its 500 or so pubs, fast food outlets, discos and souvenir shops. The rugged west coast is little developed for tourism although it was the beauty of this area which attracted writers such as Robert Graves, artists and celebrities to Deya and Formentor in the 1930s, when it took the best part of three days' travel to reach Mallorca from Britain. The east coast, indented with numerous small coves, is given over mainly to villa developments. Mallorca can cater for both the mass market and selective tourism, and has much to offer the sightseer, including:
  ○ the Caves of Drach, an outstanding example of a geological feature that has become a showpiece attraction
  ○ the island's industries, notably the manufacture of artificial pearls
  ○ Palma, the regional capital, which is one of the leading seaports of the Mediterranean, with ferry services to the mainland and the other islands; it boasts an imposing cathedral and castle among its heritage attractions, and except for one small district, has been relatively unaffected by mass tourism.

Since the early 1990s the Balearic regional government has followed a policy of sustainable tourism; a third of the island's area has been designated for conservation, while steps have been taken to improve the environment of the most overcrowded resorts. However, it is a moot point whether the further development of golf courses is truly 'green' tourism in view of their demands on water supplies, while the buying up of rural properties, mainly by Germans, has implications for the social balance of the Mallorcan countryside.

The Canary Islands

While the Balearics are essentially summer sun destinations, the Canaries have the advantage of a sub-tropical climate, which favours beach tourism throughout the year. Winters are pleasantly warm, while the cool ocean current moderates summer temperatures; but this also means that sea temperatures are too cold for bathing for much of the year. The islands are of volcanic origin and contain some magnificent scenery, but on the other hand there are relatively few fine beaches. Situated some 1000 kilometres to the south-west of Cadiz, they are much closer geographically to Morocco and the Western Sahara than to mainland Spain. The location of the islands, on important shipping routes, resulted in the 'discovery' of Tenerife and Gran Canaria as winter destinations by wealthy British travellers and returning colonial officials in the nineteenth century. Large numbers of cruise ships still call at the ports of Santa Cruz and Las Palmas, which offer duty-free shopping as their main attractions. Since the 1960s the great majority of visitors have arrived on charter flights and are drawn from a wider range of countries and socioeconomic groups. Most north European tourists still arrive during the winter months, whereas Spanish holidaymakers from the Peninsula are more evident in summer.

- **Tenerife** is the largest of the islands and offers the greatest variety of scenery and climate, due to the effect of the spectacular peak of Teide on the prevailing trade winds. The strange volcanic landscapes of Las Cañadas National Park in the centre of the island contrast with the desert-like south and the fertile valley of Orotava, with its woods and banana plantations to the north. In this part of the island, Puerto de la Cruz is a well-established resort catering primarily for the older age groups. This is because its position on the windward slopes of Teide means that sunshine cannot be guaranteed, and its lack of beaches is only partly compensated by a magnificent lido. The south coast has the climatic advantage, where hotels and time-share apartments line beaches within easy reach of the international airport. Playa de Las Americas – a creation of the tourist boom of the 1970s – is now the most popular resort on the island. The capital, Santa Cruz, is enhancing its cultural appeal with a Carnival to rival that of Rio de Janeiro and a magnificent new auditorium.
- **Gran Canaria** has on balance more to offer mass tourism than Tenerife, particularly in the fine sandy beaches of its southern coast. This supports a tourist concentration second in size only in Benidorm, consisting of the resorts of Playa del Inglés, San Agustín and Maspalomas, attracting mainly German and lesser contingents of British, Scandinavian and Spanish holidaymakers. Some of the man-made attractions – 'wild west shows' for example – have no Spanish connection, the emphasis being purely on international-style entertainment. Away from the resorts, the interior of Gran Canaria has been described as 'a continent in miniature' offering spectacular contrasts in scenery.
- **Lanzarote** is still volcanically active, and the craters of Monte del Fuego in the Timanfaya National Park are a major attraction. Development was carefully planned by the architect Cesar Manrique to enhance a landscape of lava spreads dotted with white villages. Upmarket tourists are catered for at Costa de Teguise and sports enthusiasts at La Santa, while Puerto del Carmen is the most popular resort.

- **Fuerteventura** is the driest of the Canary Islands, due to its closeness to the Western Sahara, and is the most sparsely populated. Persistent trade winds provide ideal conditions for windsurfing and surfing, while the vast beaches attract jeep safaris and are popular mainly with German tourists.
- **Gomera, La Palma** and **Hierro,** the three western islands, have remained relatively untouched by mass tourism due to their relative isolation, lack of good beaches and the rugged topography. The prospects for tourism are most promising in La Palma, where the main attraction is the beautiful mountain scenery, culminating in one of the world's largest volcanic craters – the Caldera de Taburiente. There is also the appeal of a more traditional lifestyle, based on agriculture and handicrafts such as cigar-making rather than tourism.

Gibraltar

Although Gibraltar is one of Britain's few remaining colonies, it is physically attached to Spain, while the people are a mixture of Mediterranean cultures and equally fluent in English and Spanish. Britain's interest in Gibraltar was primarily due to its strategic location guarding the entrance to the Mediterranean. Nowadays its military role is less significant and the Royal Navy dockyard has closed, forcing the colony to develop other roles as an offshore financial centre and tourist destination.

Gibraltar is a small territory, only 6 square kilometres in area, dominated by the great limestone mass of the Rock, which towers 400 metres above the densely packed town and busy harbour on its western flank. Since 1985, when the frontier with Spain was re-opened, Gibraltar has attracted millions of Spanish excursionists, as well as cruise passengers and much smaller numbers of staying tourists, mostly from Britain. The Spanish are motivated by curiosity and the lure of shopping bargains, while the British, many of whom are first time visitors overseas, are reassured by the familiar language, food, currency, British-style 'bobbies' and pubs, combined with Mediterranean sunshine. Apart from these, the colony's main attractions include:

- the world famous Rock, which is honeycombed with caves and 'galleries' constructed for military purposes, is better known as a habitat for Europe's only ape colony
- the duty-free shopping in Main Street
- the historical associations with the British army and navy
- the relics of the Moorish and Spanish occupations
- the facilities for water sports, including a yacht marina, although there are only a few small beaches in the shadow of the Rock
- its proximity to Morocco, using the hydrofoil and ferry service to Tangier
- its proximity to the holiday resorts of the Costa del Sol; prior to the 1960s, Gibraltar was the gateway to this part of Spain, and since 1985, growing numbers of British visitors have again been using it as a base for touring Andalucia.

However, the expansion of tourism in Gibraltar faces a number of problems, namely:

- the shortage of land for development
- the threat posed by the erosion of the Rock, caused by massive tunnelling in the past

- the accommodation stock consists of a small number of hotels, guesthouses and self-catering complexes that need to be upgraded and extended
- The restricted site of the airport that lies on 'neutral territory' with its runway on land reclaimed from the Bay of Gibraltar. To the south the airport is hemmed in by the sheer face of the Rock, while the Spanish frontier lies immediately to the north, which brings us to the most deep-seated problem
- The continuing political difficulties with Spain.

Although Gibraltar has been British since 1703, Spain has never relinquished its claim to sovereignty. During the last major dispute, which lasted from 1969 to 1985, telecommunications were cut, the land border was closed and the ferry service to Algeciras was severed by the Spanish government. Cut off from its natural hinterland, Gibraltar was forced to develop its own tourist attractions and recruit labour from Morocco. Another bone of contention is Gibraltar's alleged role in smuggling contraband from North Africa to Spain. The response of the Spanish authorities has been to subject motorists crossing the border at La Linea to lengthy delays. Spain's recent willingness to consider 'joint sovereignty' with Britain is rejected by the great majority of Gibraltarians.

Portugal

Portugal is a much smaller country than Spain, both in population and land area. Due to its long Atlantic coastline, Portugal's climate is milder and more humid, and the landscape generally greener, than is the case in most of Spain. In culture and temperament, the Portuguese differ from the Spanish in a number of ways; for example, the music form – *fado* – is full of the melancholy or *saudade* which is part of the national character and the Portuguese bullfight is an altogether gentler affair than the Spanish *corrida*. Portugal's contacts with its former colonies, particularly in Asia, are reflected in its cuisine and the ornate decoration of its churches and country houses.

Although agriculture, fishing and textiles still dominate the Portuguese economy, tourism has made a major contribution, supporting 6 per cent of jobs and 8 per cent of GDP. Portugal has one of the lowest standards of living in the European Union, and this is reflected in the continuing high rate of emigration (whereas Spain has become a prime destination for immigrants from North Africa, South America and Eastern Europe).

Demand for tourism

Domestic and outbound tourism
Holiday propensities at around 50 per cent are lower than those of Spain; fewer trips are taken abroad and budget accommodation is generally sought.

Inbound tourism
Inbound tourism, in contrast, has grown steadily since the 1960s, with the exception of a downturn in the mid-1970s following the April Revolution which introduced democracy and industrial unrest. This affected the hotel industry, which also had to

cope with a massive influx of refugees from Angola and Mozambique. The early 1990s were a second period when international arrivals were depressed, partly as a result of over-pricing. This prompted a fierce debate as to a future strategy for Portugal and resulted in major changes in the organization and approach to tourism, as outlined later in this chapter. This new strategy was successful and by the early 2000s arrivals of foreign tourists exceeded 12 million, although volumes could have been higher but for 9/11. Most visits are for holiday purposes; however, day visitors are around 16 million – Spaniards crossing into Portugal for shopping, or cruise passengers visiting Funchal and Lisbon on shore excursions. The Euro 2004 football championship also boosted visitor numbers. Spain is by far Portugal's largest market, accounting for most of the visitors arriving by road, but visitors are usually short stay. Portugal's other main markets of Britain, Germany and France have different characteristics:

- air-inclusive tours are the norm
- there is a marked summer peak in demand
- visitors stay longer
- spending per capita is higher than is the case with Spanish visitors.

Supply of tourism

Transport

Portugal's location in the south-west corner of Europe necessitates a long journey if road or rail are used as travel modes. This has prompted a major road upgrading programme and also explains why air transport is the dominant mode for tourists arriving from northern Europe. Fly-drive arrangements are important for those staying in self-catering accommodation in the Algarve. The national airline, TAP, underwent a programme of privatization to take it into the millennium and the major scheduled and charter airlines operate flights into Lisbon, Faro (for the Algarve), Oporto and the island of Madeira.

Accommodation

As in Spain, villas used as second homes or retirement properties have created a long-stay market, particularly in the Algarve and Madeira. Around two-thirds of visitors to Portugal use hotel accommodation, although an increased preference for cheaper forms of accommodation has become evident as more Spaniards visit Portugal and use campsites or stay with friends. None the less, Portugal's accommodation stock is well developed, with a concentration of larger hotels in the Algarve, at Estoril, and on Madeira (both catering for inclusive-tour clients), and in Lisbon, where business travel is important. The government owns a chain of hotels – *pousadas* – similar in concept to the Spanish *paradores*. Camping and caravanning is important on the Algarve, especially around Faro, and attracts German, French and Spanish visitors, while the many sites around Lisbon are a popular and cheaper alternative to the capital's hotels. The British and Dutch patronize apartments, again mainly in the Algarve.

Organization

The importance of tourism as a 'safety net' against a decline in demand for Portugal's traditional products in agriculture, fishing and textiles was reflected in the government's response to depressed arrivals figures in the 1990s. The organization of tourism was changed by merging government departments to create *Investimentos Comercio e Turismo de Portugal* (ICEP) in 1992. This new body has put into place a successful new tourism strategy to:

- diversify source markets
- introduce quality controls
- reduce bureaucracy
- establish a new image for Portugal stressing historic and cultural resources
- use the *fundo de turismo* (tourism fund) to create new products and upgrade existing ones

In addition, Portugal is anxious to control the impacts of tourism on both the environment and Portuguese society. There are a number of national nature reserves and management plans exist for national parks, as well as the estuaries and coasts in the more popular recreational and tourist areas. Impacts are also reduced by Portugal's emphasis on the upper and middle sectors of the tourism market, in contrast to Spain's domination by mass market tourism, and this is reflected in the generally higher quality of the Portuguese tourism product compared to Spain. Portugal is also attempting to spread the load of tourism more evenly, both seasonally and geographically (well over a half of foreign arrivals are between June and September). The Algarve is already nearing saturation in terms of tourist development, and contrasts with the more remote interior provinces – such as Tras-os-Montes – which see few foreign tourists. Counter-attractions are being developed in the Oporto – Espinho area in the north and at Setubal, south of Lisbon. Finally, Portugal is diversifying its tourist product by encouraging activity holidays, conference tourism and sport tourism, with Lisbon hosting the 2004 European football championship.

Tourism resources

Southern Portugal

The Algarve is Portugal's most popular holiday region, thanks to an exceptionally sunny climate, fine sandy beaches, rocky coves and picturesque fishing villages. Tourism did not develop until the mid-1960s when Faro Airport was opened and the April 25 Bridge across the Tagus from Lisbon greatly reduced travel times by road to what had been a remote region. In the late 1990s, a second bridge – the Vasco da Gama – opened, giving a further boost to tourism south of Lisbon. Many of the resort developments (for example, near Lagos, Albufeira and Portimão) are in the form of self-contained holiday villages. Sports facilities (above all, golf courses) have been important in attracting investment from northern Europe. However, not all the development has been of a high standard – the haphazard growth of Quarteira compares unfavourably with nearby Vilamoura, planned around its yacht marina. Tourist development is extending westwards towards Cape St Vincent following upgrading of the coastal road, whereas the low-lying coast east of Faro remains largely undeveloped with the exception of the resort of Monte Gordo. The cultural heritage of the Algarve is relatively neglected; this includes the medieval walled town of Silves of Moorish origin, traditional handicrafts and markets, and Sagres, with its associations with Prince Henry the Navigator and the great age of Portuguese exploration.

In contrast to the Algarve, **The Alentejo** in the interior of southern Portugal has been neglected for tourism. This region is characterized by wide plains, large country estates and extensive forests of cork oak trees – a resource threatened by changes in the international wine trade. The only tourist centre of significance is Evora with its important Roman heritage, but it is likely that a major power project on the river Guadiana will be the catalyst for large-scale development near the Spanish border.

Central Portugal and Lisbon

Tourism in central Portugal around Lisbon has been established for much longer, and there is a wealth of attractions available for the cultural tourist as well as the sun-seeker. **Lisbon**, on the wide Tagus estuary, is one of Europe's major seaports, while Portela Airport is a hub for international flights to Europe, South America and Africa. The capital is rich in reminders of Portugal's maritime history, notably the Tower of Belem and Jeronimos Monastery. Tourism received a boost with Expo '98, which involved the regeneration of the waterfront area, and Lisbon is becoming a popular short break destination, with its mix of old fashioned trams, quality shopping and exuberant nightlife. There are several tourism resources close to Lisbon:

- The strip of coast to the west of Lisbon known as the **Costa de Estoril**, after its most well-known resort, has good beaches, hotels, a casino and facilities for sport and entertainment, especially at Cascais.
- South of the Tagus, the coastline around Setubal underwent considerable development during the 1980s with much self-catering accommodation.
- North of Lisbon, and extending from Peniche almost to Oporto, the **Costa de Prata** is mainly popular with Portuguese holidaymakers. Its long sandy beaches are, for the most part, exposed to the Atlantic surf. The most important resorts are Nazaré (famous for its traditional fishing industry) and Figueira da Foz.

Away from the coast, this part of Portugal boasts many places of interest, readily accessible from Lisbon. They include:

- Sintra, in a scenically beautiful location overlooking the capital, once favoured as a health resort by Portuguese royalty and wealthy foreigners
- Caldas da Rainha, a spa town noted for its ceramics
- Obidos, a picturesque medieval town
- Fatima, a world-famous shrine rivalling Lourdes in significance; in May each year vast numbers of pilgrims are attracted to the Basilica for candle-lit processions
- Coimbra, an attractive university town noted for its contribution to *fado* music.

The North

Tourism development is being encouraged in northern Portugal, assisted by regional development schemes and upgraded road transport. Resources include:

- **Aveiro**, with its large sheltered lagoons, ideal for water sports, is known as the 'Venice of Portugal'.
- **Oporto** (Porto) at the mouth of the River Douro is Portugal's second city, its major commercial centre and gateway to the northern region. Oporto's main claim to fame is its association with the port wine industry, although the actual vineyards are located 150 kilometres upstream and the picturesque barges are no longer used to transport the wine. Oporto's nomination as European capital of culture in 2001 has helped to boost its tourism industry.
- Stretching from Oporto north to the Spanish border lies the **Costa Verde**, which is attracting increasing numbers of foreign visitors, travelling independently by car

rather than using inclusive tours. Espinho, Povoa de Varzim, and Viana do Castelo are the chief resorts in this area.

- The Peneda Geres National Park on the Spanish border offers wild granite mountain scenery. The small historic towns of the **Minho** region are interesting places to visit, notably Braga, the religious centre of Portugal with its spectacular Bom Jesus shrine, and Guimarães, celebrated as the cradle of Portuguese independence.

The Portuguese islands

In addition to mainland Portugal, there are two groups of islands in the Atlantic that we can treat as separate destinations – Madeira and the Azores. They are both of volcanic origin and since 1975 they have enjoyed a degree of autonomy from Lisbon. In view of the limited resource base of the islands, and with fewer opportunities than in the past for the islanders to emigrate to the Americas or South Africa, tourism should play an important role in the economy. However, tourism has been much more successful in Madeira than in the Azores, and this is largely due to differences in accessibility.

Madeira

Madeira is situated 800 kilometres south-west of Lisbon and slightly nearer to Casablanca. Of greater significance is the position of the harbour of Funchal on the main shipping routes from Europe to South America and South Africa. It was largely for this reason that Madeira became a fashionable winter destination for well-to-do British travellers in Victorian times. The island was able to broaden its appeal after 1964 when the international airport was opened east of Funchal, and the number of visitors increased fivefold between 1970 and 1990. However, mass tourism in the way it has occurred in the Canary Islands is ruled out by:

- the impossibility of extending the airport, which is not capable of handling wide-bodied jets
- the shortage of land for development generally, on this mountainous but densely populated island
- the absence of beaches, except on the small and otherwise barren island of Porto Santo some 50 kilometres away from Funchal.

The regional government of Madeira has therefore aimed at promoting quality tourism. Foreign visitors are attracted by the beautiful scenery of mountains, coastal cliffs and sub-tropical vegetation and the almost ideal climate – winter is still the peak season for the British, Germans and Scandinavians. Hiking trails follow the intricate network of *levadas* (irrigation channels), which carry water from the mountains to the pocket-sized farms. The road network is being improved to make the interior more accessible, sports facilities are being developed to attract a younger market and traditional craft industries such as embroidery are encouraged.

The Azores

The Azores are situated 1500 kilometres west of Lisbon and 3500 kilometres east of New York. Their mid-Atlantic location was important in the early years of trans-atlantic flight when Faial and Santa Maria acted as staging points, but with the introduction of longer-range aircraft the islands have been by-passed. Although the

Azores have three international airports – Santa Maria, Lajes (on the island of Terceira) and Ponta Delgada (on Saõ Miguel) – no foreign airlines as yet operate scheduled services, and charter flights from Europe are discouraged by the Portuguese government. The islands are dispersed over 800 kilometres of ocean, making it difficult to organize multi-centre holidays. Unlike Madeira, the Azores are not regarded as a winter-sun destination because, although the climate allows the cultivation of sub-tropical produce such as tea and pineapples, sunshine amounts compare unfavourably with the Mediterranean. There are few beaches and the islands' main appeal is the spectacular volcanic scenery, the best-known examples being the crater lakes, hot springs and geysers on Saõ Miguel. Yachting, whale watching (replacing the traditional whaling industry) and sea angling also offer prospects for the growth of tourism.

Summary

The Iberian Peninsula and the holiday islands of Spain and Portugal are among the world's major tourist destination areas. This is partly due to Spain's early entry into mass tourism in the 1960s based upon its holiday resources of an extensive Mediterranean coastline and accessibility to northern Europe. Portugal was a later entrant into the tourism market and is attempting to avoid mass tourism, focusing instead on more affluent markets.

Tourist accommodation is concentrated at the coast, on the islands and in the major cities. The principal resort areas are served by a well-developed transport infrastructure. However, in Spain uncontrolled resort development has caused environmental damage, deepened regional contrasts and affected Spanish lifestyles to such an extent that many other countries – including Portugal – have been anxious to avoid these negative effects of tourism. The attractions of both countries are mainly based on the coastline and there are major resort concentrations on the islands, the Spanish Mediterranean Costas and the Algarve. Other attractions include winter sports in the Pyrenees and the Sierra Nevada, the cultural attractions of the historic cities of Spain and Portugal and the natural appeal of the landscapes of the Iberian Peninsula and the islands, although ecotourism has yet to become an important sector of the market.

Chapter 16
The tourism geography of Italy

Learning Objectives

After reading this chapter you should be able to:

- Explain the special appeal of Italy as a tourist destination.
- Describe the major physical features of Italy and understand their importance for tourism.
- Appreciate the nature of the demand for inbound, outbound and domestic tourism.
- Outline the major features of tourism infrastructure, especially the differences between North and South Italy.
- Appreciate the public sector organization of tourism in Italy.
- Demonstrate a knowledge of the tourist regions, resorts, business centres and tourist attractions of Italy.

Introduction

As a tourist destination, Italy for many people means sunshine, good food, music and, perhaps, romance. Others are attracted by the style and quality of Italian fashion and engineering products. Tourism in Italy has a long pedigree. Domestic tourism was certainly flourishing at the time of the Roman Empire, when the wealthier citizens of Rome had holiday villas in resorts such as Baia on the Bay of Naples. As far as international tourism is concerned, during the Middle Ages Rome was the destination for hordes of pilgrims from all over Europe. They were followed as a result of the Renaissance by what we might call cultural tourists, attracted to Italian cities such as Florence and Venice, then at their zenith as the 'cutting edge' of European civilization. Shakespeare was strongly influenced by Italian culture and a host of writers and artists from northern Europe – among them Milton, Göethe and Shelley – visited Italy for inspiration. It became the custom for wealthy young men to go on the 'Grand Tour', which involved a stay of at least a few months in Italy. Here they completed their education – in more ways than one – buying classical sculptures (not all genuine) and paintings as souvenirs of their travels, while on their return, they renovated their country houses in the style of Italian architects such as Palladio. In a sense, the expansion of the railways allowed entrepreneurs such as Thomas Cook to popularize the idea of a European tour, bringing Italy within the reach of the expanding middle class of Victorian Britain.

Even today, most tourism to Italy is to an extent cultural, and the country is among the world's top five tourism destinations. It is likely to retain this position because of the appeal and variety of its tourism products, although the marketing and organization of these could in many cases be improved. Italy's tourism products include:

- short city breaks and longer touring holidays, appealing mainly to art lovers
- music festivals, usually associated with a particular composer's hometown, such as Pesaro (Rossini) and Torre del Lago near Lucca (Puccini); Italy originated opera as an art form and there it enjoys widespread popular support
- seaside holidays
- summer lakes and mountains holidays in the Alps
- winter-skiing holidays in the Alps
- health tourism, based on Italy's abundant geothermal resources – spas such as Ischia, Montecatini Terme and Abano have an excellent international reputation
- religious pilgrimages to the shrines of Rome, Assisi, Loreto and Padua
- rural tourism, including stays in farms and villas that vary in size from the modest to the magnificent; the government agency, Agriturist, has done much to promote rural tourism as a means of stemming the depopulation of the countryside
- trade fairs and exhibitions; notably Milan, Genoa, Bologna and Turin
- sport tourism, focusing particularly on football and motor racing
- activity holidays, for example, hiking and climbing in the Dolomites.

With some notable exceptions, such as the Gran Paradiso in the western Alps and other National Parks, Italy's environmental record has been relatively poor compared with the countries of northern and central Europe, and ecotourism is not well developed. Conservation of the nation's cultural heritage is also a major problem, given the vast number of art treasures and historic sites, and the inadequate public funding available.

The setting for tourism

Physical features

Italy is separated from Northern Europe by the high mountain barrier of the Alps and has a long coastline facing both the Adriatic and the western Mediterranean. Another chain of mountains – the Apennines – forms a rugged spine down the boot-shaped Italian Peninsula, and is a formidable obstacle to east–west communications. Between these mountains and the Alps lies an extensive area of fertile lowland – the North Italian Plain – that includes most of the regions of Piedmont, Lombardy, Veneto and Emilia-Romagna. This area contains some of Europe's largest and most prosperous industrial centres. Central and southern Italy are hilly or mountainous, and geologically unstable – as witness the 1997 Assisi earthquake, the frequent landslides in the Apennines and the volcanic activity evident in the Naples area and Sicily. The landscape becomes drier and more neglected south of Rome, and it is here in the Mezzogiorno that we find some of the poorest regions of Europe.

Social and cultural features

The Italian lifestyle has always been an attraction for visitors from the more reserved countries of northern Europe. The people enjoy public displays, as you can see in the evening *passegiata* or parade in every town. Italy now has one of the lowest birth-rates in Europe due to the economic and social changes that have taken place since the Second World War; however it is still true that family ties are very strong. The Roman Catholic Church continues to play an important role, although it is no longer the all-powerful patron of the arts it was in Renaissance times. Italian culture is characterized by great regional variety, as expressed, for example, in food specialities, handicrafts and dialects. This is due largely to the fact that Italy became a united country only in the nineteenth century – before that it was a collection of small states largely under foreign domination. Italians continue to have stronger loyalties to their city or region than to the state as a whole. One of the biggest obstacles to national unity is the long-standing negative attitude of North Italians toward the South, which they regard as socially backward and a burden on the economy.

Demand for tourism

Domestic and outbound tourism

Despite Italy's appeal to the foreign visitor, it is the large domestic market which dominates and sustains the tourism industry, accounting for about 60 per cent of all overnight stays. Italians have a legal entitlement to at least four weeks' annual leave, and well over half the population take at least one holiday away from home. The domestic market is highly seasonal with three-quarters of trips in July and August and average lengths of stay are falling as the three- or four-week vacation becomes less popular. Domestic tourism is more evenly spread geographically than is the case with foreign tourists, who tend to be concentrated in a few cities, resorts and regions; nevertheless seasonality is a problem. Although participation in winter sports and activity holidays is growing, summer beach holidays remain the most popular type of domestic tourism. Whereas some of the resorts of the Adriatic coast and Liguria favoured by Italians are also very much part of the international tourism scene, many of the small seaside resorts of Tuscany, Lazio and the South see few foreign holidaymakers.

An increasing number of Italians are travelling abroad, especially to long-haul destinations, and in fact Italy is among the world's top ten tourist-generating countries. However, it is only relatively recently that the country has become sufficiently affluent to generate a massive demand for foreign travel, and since there is a wealth of holiday attractions nearer home, the Italian domestic market remains important. In consequence, Italy has a substantial surplus on its travel account and tourism accounts for 6.5 per cent of gross domestic product.

Inbound tourism

Italy is one of the leading receivers of international tourism in Europe. During the late 1980s and much of the 1990s the tourism industry stagnated, due to unfavourable publicity regarding:

- overcrowding and environmental conditions in the main resorts
- high prices
- high crime rates, terrorist bombings and Mafia trials
- obsolescent hotel stock, where facilities compared unfavourably with those in other Mediterranean countries such as Spain.

However, in the late 1990s tourism recovered, only to be checked by the impact of 9/11. Although there is a considerable volume of business travel to cities such as Milan and Turin, holidays are the main reason for visiting Italy. Germany is by far the most important market in terms of arrivals and overnight stays, on account of the good road access (most German tourists arrive in their own cars). The most popular destinations for German tourists are:

- Venice
- the Alto Adige region (which is German-speaking) for skiing
- Campania for camping
- Sicily for beach holidays.

Other important markets are the USA, France, UK, Japan and Austria. The French and Austrians typically arrive by car and visit the beach resorts and historic cities. In contrast, British tourists are less inclined to be independent travellers, with over half arriving by air, although the proportion using charter airlines is less than for other Mediterranean destinations such as Spain and Greece as budget airlines take market share from the traditional charter carriers. For British visitors, Venice, Tuscany, Campania (particularly the Sorrento Peninsula) and Emilia-Romagna (especially Rimini and Cattolica) remain the most popular destinations – a pattern that has changed little since the 1960s. The USA and Japan are the most important long-haul markets. Visitors from the USA are commonly touring Europe and consequently spend only a short time in Italy, which is just one of the countries visited. The main attractions for North Americans are the well-known art cities. Not surprisingly, most of Italy's luxury hotels are concentrated in Rome, Florence and Venice. For the year of the Holy Jubilee (millennium year, 2000) record numbers of visitors had to be accommodated.

Supply of tourism

Transport

Domestic and international tourist travel is mainly by surface transport.

Roads

Italy has an excellent road network, including over 6500 kilometres of *autostrada* (motorways). This is effectively linked to the wider European system, despite the bottlenecks (caused mainly by excessive numbers of trucks) which do occur on the approaches to the Brenner Pass and other routes through the Alps. It is possible to drive at high average speeds from Flensburg on the German–Danish border to the southern tip of the Italian Peninsula. The Autostrada di Sole from Milan to Reggio di Calabria is therefore used by hordes of sun-seeking tourists from Germany and the countries of northern Europe. The engineering problems involved in building the autostrada in mountainous terrain are shown, for example, in Liguria, where there are more than 100 tunnels, and almost the same number of viaducts in a distance of less than 100 kilometres.

Rail

The rail network is also extensive and generally offers travellers an efficient service with some of the lowest fares in Europe, although it does suffer from overcrowding in the summer. Italian State Railways (FS) own most of the network, apart from a few narrow gauge lines. A number of high speed trains are in service between the major cities, including the *Direttissima* from Florence to Rome. Although the system is in state ownership, most of the funding for these high-speed rail projects comes from the private sector. Italian State Railways also own the major tour operator, CIT, and by catering for both holiday and business tourists have done much to revive the demand for rail travel.

Sea

Italy's long coastline and location in mid-Mediterranean has encouraged a long sea-faring tradition. Genoa, the birthplace of Columbus, is one of the most important ports in the Mediterranean. Although few tourists arrive by sea, cruise ships operating in the Mediterranean usually call in at Italian ports, such as Venice or Naples. A number of Italian ports such as Civitavecchia (serving Rome), Ancona and Brindisi are essential nodes in a network of coastal shipping services and international ferries linking various parts of the Mediterranean, not just neighbouring Corsica, Tunisia, Croatia and Greece, but as far afield as Turkey, Egypt and Israel. High-speed hydrofoils operate on the short sea crossings between the mainland and the smaller islands such as Capri; they are also used for sightseeing excursions on the lakes of northern Italy.

Air

Italy is well served by international airports, the most important being Fiumicino (Rome) and Linate (Milan), which rank among Europe's busiest. Alitalia, the national airline, is active in tourism promotion, working closely with CIT and the national tourism organization. Alitalia and its subsidiary ATI provide a network of domestic flights to over thirty destinations, while a number of charter airlines link the islands and resort areas to the tourist-generating areas. A growing network of budget airline services links Italy with regional airports across Europe.

Accommodation

Italy has almost 4 million beds distributed across hotels, campsites, pensions and *locande* (inns), which are favoured by Italian tourists. Hotels are concentrated in the north-east of the country, and across Italy most hotels are small family concerns – large hotel chains are less of a feature in the resort scene than elsewhere in Europe. There is a trend toward greater use of self-catering accommodation, and campgrounds are numerous, especially along the Adriatic coast. Holiday villas are owned or rented by the more affluent. A number of holiday villages are also available, run on similar lines to Club Méditerranée by the Italian tour operator Valtur.

Organization

There is a clear demarcation between public sector tourism support at the national and the regional level.

National level

Italian governments since the Second World War have been weak coalitions lasting on average less than a year, making it difficult to implement clear policy objectives on, for example, tourism development. In contrast to a flourishing private sector, much of the public sector is characterized by inefficiency and widespread political corruption. This has resulted in one of the largest 'black economies' in Europe. The Italian State Tourist Office (Ente Nazionale Industrie Turistiche – ENIT), which was set up as long ago as 1919, has tried to remedy this situation. However, in 1993, the Ministry of Tourism and Performing Arts was disbanded and replaced by a small department of tourism located in the Prime Minister's Office. The Italian State Tourist Office's main purpose is promotion and research, and it is particularly attempting to diversify Italy's tourism product away from beach holidays and the 'big three' historic cities – Rome, Florence and Venice – towards other forms of tourism. At the same time ENIT is hoping to achieve a more balanced spread of visitors by including less well-known cities in the classical tours, promoting the ski resorts in the eastern Alps, and by developing tourism in the Mezzogiorno – aided by INSUD, the public sector agency promoting tourism to the South. With reduced public sector commitment to tourism ENIT is involved in cooperative marketing with the private sector and the airlines.

Regional level

Each of Italy's 20 regional governments has responsibility for tourism, although some – notably the autonomous regions of Sicily, Sardinia, Valle d'Aosta and Trentino-Alto Adige – have been more active than others in planning, development and promotion. None the less, it is at the regional level where most activity is occurring, with funding based on the number of inhabitants in the region, rather than the number of tourists visiting.

At local level voluntary associations known as 'Pro Loco' draw on the civic pride of the people living in the historic towns of central and northern Italy. They work closely with tourist offices to organize festivals, revitalize traditional craft industries and enhance the appeal of the community.

Tourism resources

Italy's tourist attractions are so diverse and numerous that it is impossible to provide more than a short list of those we consider to be of major importance or to be unique in some way. As this is a large country by European standards, we have divided it for convenience into the following tourist regions:

- northern Italy – including the Italian Alps, the North Italian Plain and Liguria
- central Italy – including Tuscany, Umbria and Rome

- southern Italy – including Naples
- the islands of Sardinia and Sicily.

Northern Italy

The Alps

The Italian Alps are generally sunnier than the mountains of Austria and Switzerland, but this does mean that the ski season tends to be shorter. We can divide the Alps for convenience into central, western and eastern sections.

The **central Alps** are dissected by long transverse valleys that end in a number of large lakes of glacial origin. Because of their long-established importance as a holiday destination we need to treat the Italian Lakes as a separate entity. The central Alps include a number of skiing resorts, such as Bormio, Livigno and Madessimo, which are popular with price-conscious foreign skiers and accessible from airports at Milan and Bergamo.

The **western Alps** include the highest mountain peaks in the system, and are popular with foreign, as well as Italian skiers. The most important resorts in the area are located within easy reach of Turin, such as Sauze d'Oulx and Sestrière. The Valle d'Aosta region has a French-speaking population and its government has done much to promote tourism in an effort to stem rural depopulation. Cervinia on the slopes of the Matterhorn (Monte Cervino) is an important resort in this area along with Courmayeur near Mont Blanc. Both resorts form part of international ski circuits – Cervinia with Zermatt in Switzerland, and Courmayeur with Chamonix and Mégève in the French Alps.

Much the same can be said of the **eastern Alps**, although here, the scenery, and to a greater extent the cultural features, are different. Although the Dolomites are by no means the highest part of the Alps, the limestone rock has been sculptured by erosion into a breathtaking array of spectacular landforms. This area is a paradise for walkers and skiers alike, with one of Europe's longest ski circuits, the Val Gardena, and one of its most stylish resorts, Cortina d'Ampezzo. The nearest airports are at Venice and Verona. The eastern Alps include the German-speaking South Tyrol (Alto Adige), where the villages and folklore are reminders that this area formed part of the Habsburg Empire for more than six centuries, before becoming part of Italy after the First World War.

The Italian Lakes owe their elongated shape, and their great depth, to glaciation of the mountain valleys during the most recent Ice Age (Lake Como for example is over 400 metres deep, which means its lowest point is 300 metres below sea level). The southern ends of the lakes open out into relatively flat countryside, while their northern sections are hemmed in by mountains. The vast quantities of water stored in the lakes, and a location sheltered from northerly winds, result in a milder, sunnier climate than the Lombardy Plain to the south. The most important lakes for tourism are, from east to west, Garda, Como, Lugano and Maggiore, each having its specific attractions:

- **Lake Garda** is the largest of the lakes. Its western shoreline is studded with so many resorts offering high-class accommodation, that it is often described as a 'Riviera'. Some 40 per cent of visitors are foreign tourists, and of these two-thirds are German. The best beaches are on the south shore where the picturesque spa town of Sirmione is situated.
- **Lake Como** is only 60 kilometres from Milan and is therefore popular with day-visitors; also its southern fringes have been affected by industrial development.

Bellagio, at a scenic location between two arms of the lake, is the most stylish of the resorts. Most tours of the lake feature a visit to the villas built by wealthy landowners in the eighteenth century, which are admired by garden-lovers worldwide.

○ Most of **Lake Lugano** falls within Switzerland. The resorts on the Italian side are little more than villages, with the exceptions of Porlezza and the gambling centre of Campione.

○ **Lake Maggiore**'s northern tip is also Swiss territory. Much of the development is on the western shore, where Stresa is the most popular resort. Growth was rapid after the opening of the Simplon Tunnel in 1906 greatly improved access to the area.

The Italian Lakes appeal to a wide variety of visitors, including water sports enthusiasts, families travelling independently and older holidaymakers on 'lakes and mountains' package holidays. The larger resorts such as Riva del Garda and Stresa boast conference facilities of international standard, and feature music festivals among their attractions.

The North Italian Plain

In comparison with the Alps, the North Italian Plain stretching from Turin to the Adriatic Sea is scenically unattractive. It has a continental, rather than a Mediterranean climate, with cold, often foggy winters and hot rainy summers. Its main river, the Po, has changed course many times over the centuries, and is held in check by an extensive system of artificial embankments. Rice fields are a feature of the landscape in some areas, and this is Italy's main food-producing region. The main tourist attractions lie in the many historic towns, where, despite industrialization, the art treasures and buildings of medieval times have been preserved. The most important of these are:

- **Venice**, which is truly unique, a city without the motor car, in which all transport is on foot or by water, due to its island setting in the middle of an extensive shallow lagoon. It is not so much individual attractions that define this city's appeal, but the townscape and canal network that have changed remarkably little over the centuries. The Republic of Venice, known as *La Serenissima*, was once a great power in the eastern Mediterranean, using the profits from the trade in silks and spices from Asia to employ the best artists of the day in embellishing merchants' palaces, churches and other public buildings. Tourism mainly focuses on St Mark's Square, the Byzantine-style St Mark's Basilica and the Doge's Palace. Event attractions such as the Venice Carnival and the *Regatta Storica* (gondola race) on the Grand Canal are an important part of the city's traditional image, while Venice's contemporary role as a centre of art and culture is exemplified by the film festival held in Lido di Venezia, the city's beach resort on the Adriatic.

- **Milan** is Italy's second largest city and main business centre, world famous for its fashion industry. More important in terms of employment are the car industry and engineering, and the skyline is dominated by office buildings. Nevertheless, this brash, bustling city has much to attract cultural tourists, including its magnificent multi-spired cathedral and the Teatro Alla Scala, home of the world's greatest opera company.

- **Turin** is the capital of Piedmont and a major cultural centre. It is best known as a centre of the car industry, including the Fiat empire. The cathedral is a focus for pilgrimages due to 'The Shroud', venerated as a relic of Christ.

- **Verona** has one of the world's best preserved Roman arenas. Capable of seating 20 000 spectators, this forms an atmospheric setting during the summer for one of Europe's most popular opera festivals. Many tourists are also attracted to this beautiful city because of its association with the legendary Romeo and Juliet.
- **Bologna**, along with the other cities of Emilia-Romagna, has been overshadowed by the cultural centres of Venice and Tuscany. It is better known as a focus of Italy's railway system and for its food industries. Nevertheless it has much to offer the tourist, including its medieval shopping arcades and leaning towers to rival those of Pisa.
- **Ravenna** is famous for its Byzantine art treasures, a reminder that this city served as capital of the Roman Empire during its final decline.
- **Trieste** has potential as a short-break destination. During the Cold War the city's peripheral location on the border with eastern Europe was a disadvantage, but this will change with the accession of Slovenia and Croatia to the EU. Trieste was historically important as the main port of the Austro-Hungarian Empire.

For less culturally inclined holidaymakers, the extensive sandy beaches of the northern Adriatic coast offer safe bathing and a wide range of facilities appealing to families as well as the young. Scenically, most of the coastline from Trieste to Cattolica is flat. The type of development is also not particularly attractive, consisting of high-rise apartments and hotels, separated by extensive camping areas. Rimini, with more hotel beds than any other Italian tourist centre, is the gateway and chief resort of the 'Adriatic Riviera', catering for mass tourism from the industrial cities of Lombardy. Along with Cattolica and Lido di Jesolo, it is also popular with foreign holidaymakers on package tours, while Riccione is more upmarket. As in Italy as a whole, most beaches are privately owned and well maintained, with catering concessions in the hands of family businesses.

The Italian Riviera

The coast of **Liguria**, sometimes known as 'the Italian Riviera', is very different in character. Mountains to the north offer protection from the weather and it was the mild climate that initially attracted foreign as well as domestic tourists in the nineteenth century. It is generally divided into two sections:

- ○ the Riviera de Ponente, between Genoa and the French border, which has the better beaches
- ○ the Riviera di Levante, lying to the south-east of Genoa, which is for the most part rocky.

Of the many resorts along this coast, San Remo is probably the best known and remains highly fashionable, with an important yacht marina. Portofino, once a small picturesque fishing village, has become a very exclusive (and expensive) yachting centre due to its location on the most attractive stretch of the Riviera di Levante. Most of the other resorts, such as Alassio, have seen better days and are suffering from over-development and overcrowding in summer, now that much of the coast is highly accessible by motorway as well as by rail from the industrial cities of Piedmont and Lombardy.

Central Italy

South of the Apennines the landscape changes and is scenically much more attractive than the plains of Lombardy and Emilia-Romagna. It is characterized by small farms, vineyards, olive groves and rolling hills crowned by a small town or village which, on first impressions, appears to have changed little since medieval times. The picturesque countryside largely explains the appeal of Tuscany and, to a lesser extent, Umbria and the Marche region, for rural tourism. In fact, the area of Tuscany near Siena has attracted so many British second home-owners that it has been nick-named 'Chiantishire' after the well-known local wines. The rather flat coastline of Tuscany gets less attention from foreign holidaymakers despite the fine beaches, with the exceptions of the lively resort of Viareggio, and the island of Elba, famous for its associations with Napoleon. However, it is the cities, rather than coast or countryside, which have made central Italy, and especially Tuscany, one of Europe's most popular destinations. Cities that have received wide international recognition for their tourist attractions include:

- **Florence**, on the river Arno, is the capital of Tuscany and since medieval times has been one of Italy's leading cultural centres. Thanks to its wealth and the power of its ruling family – the Medicis – during the Renaissance, Florence was able to attract the leading artists of the day, including Leonardo da Vinci, Michelangelo and Botticelli. As a result, the city can boast three of Europe's finest art collections. The skyline is dominated by the dome of the cathedral, which was a major architectural achievement for the fifteenth century. Other attractions include the famous covered bridge known as the Ponte Vecchio. The city is also famous for its luxury trades, notably high-quality leather and jewellery. Unfortunately, Florence has suffered from pollution and overcrowding due to its popularity as a tourist destination.
- **Pisa** would probably not be included on the international touring circuit were it not for the world famous 'Leaning Tower', actually one of a number of medieval buildings around the cathedral square. Pisa's international airport is the gateway to Tuscany.
- **Siena** is a fascinating medieval city, with narrow streets opening onto the Piazza del Campo, where the Palio horse race in medieval costume is held every August. Facing the Campo are two spectacular buildings – the cathedral, beautifully designed in black and white marble, and the medieval city hall.
- **San Gimignano** is a small hilltop town famous for its towers, built by rival families in the Middle Ages and a reminder of the strife that characterized Tuscany in those times. It is a favourite location for film-makers and for music festivals.
- **Assisi** is the most visited town in Umbria, the 'green heart of Italy'. Assisi's fame as a place of pilgrimage is due to its association with two great religious leaders – St Francis (nowadays widely regarded as the patron of ecology) and St Clare. The magnificent Basilica of San Francesco is actually two churches on one site.
- **Urbino** in the Marche was once a major cultural centre and is famous as the birthplace of Raphael. This mountainous region in the Appenines is noted for its picturesque hill towns. Of these **San Marino** is the most visited, mainly because of its curiosity value as an independent republic surviving from the Middle Ages. The Adriatic coast of Marche is scenically attractive, with a number of important resorts such as Pesaro and Gabicce Mare.

Rome is known as the 'Eternal City' because it has been a centre of civilization for the best part of 3000 years. With the new millennium, exceptional numbers of tourists were accommodated from all over the world for the Holy Jubilee. This is mainly because Rome includes Vatican City, a tiny independent state ruled over by the Pope, who is the spiritual head of the world's 900 million Roman Catholics. The main gathering place for pilgrims is St Peter's Square, which provides a magnificent approach to the world's largest church – St Peter's Cathedral. This adjoins the celebrated Sistine Chapel with its paintings by Michelangelo. Rome was given a makeover in the seventeenth century by the architect and sculptor Bernini, and many of the city's monuments, fountains, public squares and historic buildings date from that period. Traces of the ancient city, however, can still be seen, as reminders of the grandeur of the Roman Empire. They include:

- ○ the Colosseum, where the populace spent much of their leisure time watching subsidized entertainment that included fights to the death between gladiators and other 'Roman Games'
- ○ the Forum which was the 'nerve-centre' of the empire
- ○ the Baths of Caracalla, which are a reminder of the importance of public bathing as recreation in ancient Rome
- ○ the Pantheon, which is the best-preserved Roman temple, largely because it was converted early on into a Christian church

With so much history, it is easy to forget that Rome is no museum piece, but a bustling modern capital, with acute traffic problems. With Rome so dominant as a tourist centre it is also easy to overlook the other attractions of its region – Lazio. These include lakes of volcanic origin, summer retreats such as Tivoli, and the seaside resorts of Ostia, Sperlonga and Terracina.

Southern Italy

The Mezzogiorno or 'land of the noonday sun' tends to be more traditional than the North in its outlook and way of life, with a much larger proportion of its people dependent upon agriculture. Because of widespread poverty and lack of resources, the region has experienced two great waves of emigration:

- to the New World – mainly the USA and Argentina in the early 1900s
- mainly to northern Italy during the economic boom of the 1950s and 1960s.

The Italian government after 1950 made great efforts to redress the economic disparity between north and south through the Cassa de Mezzogiorno, which initiated development projects and improved transport infrastructure. Funding was made available for hotel building and upgrading along with other tourist facilities. In 1984 the role of the Cassa was largely taken over by the seven regional governments, which include Sicily and Sardinia. The South is now largely dependent on financial assistance from the EU, INSUD and private investors. Yet, despite the efforts of the agencies concerned, the South has not attracted foreign tourists on a large scale, with the exception of well-established areas such as the Neapolitan Riviera. Also the stranglehold of the secret societies on local businesses and politicians, particularly in Naples and western Sicily, has tended to discourage long-term investment in tourism as well as other industries.

None the less, southern Italy can offer the tourist large stretches of almost empty beaches, combined with spectacular mountain scenery in Calabria – 'the toe of Italy' – and many historic towns that remain 'undiscovered'. There are also curiosities such as the *trulli* – strange beehive-shaped dwellings in the villages of Apulia, 'the heel of Italy' – and the cave dwellings of Matera, excavated from the soft volcanic tufa. Matera is now designated as a World Heritage Site but was formerly notorious for its poverty. The Abruzzi National Park contains some of the finest scenery in the Apennines.

Campania

Campania is popular because it includes the Neapolitan Riviera, the name given to the coastline and islands of the Bay of Naples. As the most visited region of southern Italy it deserves closer study. As mentioned earlier, the area is subject to volcanic activity and near Pozzuoli there is an area known as the Phlegrean Fields, with numerous hot springs, steam jets and emissions of sulphurous gases. In 79 AD the towns of Herculaneum and Pompeii were destroyed by an eruption of Vesuvius. The excavated buildings provide a fascinating glimpse of many aspects of life in Roman times and Pompeii is very much on the tourist circuit.

Most of the resorts are situated in the **Sorrento Peninsula** that forms the south side of the Bay of Naples. Beaches are in short supply and the main attractions, especially to the older foreign visitor are:

○ the superb scenery of the coastal road from Sorrento to Amalfi
○ the picturesque resorts of Positano and Ravello
○ the easy-going lifestyle.

Excursions are also available from Sorrento to the island of Capri – world famous for its Blue Grotto – and Ischia, which is renowned for its therapeutic radioactive springs. Both Capri and Ischia attract fashion-conscious Italians as well as large numbers of excursionists.

Although Sorrento is the largest holiday resort, **Naples** is the gateway to the region. Unfortunately, as Italy's third largest city and busiest port, Naples has a reputation that tends to deter visitors rather than attract them. Once the capital of an independent kingdom, the city has had more than its fair share of problems, notably chronic unemployment. Naples deserves to be better known for its contributions to Italian culture. These include:

○ the street life of the Santa Lucia district, inspiration for the sentimental popular music which to many tourists epitomizes Italy
○ the Teatro San Carlo, the nation's oldest opera house
○ one of Europe's best archaeological museums
○ numerous Baroque churches.

The Italian islands

The Italian islands, because they are widely scattered, are less important in the tourism scene than those of Greece, Croatia or Spain. With the exception of Capri, Ischia and Elba, most of the smaller islands see few foreign tourists. One example is Ponza, with its spectacular rock formations, despite a location on the coastal shipping route between Civitavecchia and Sorrento. The two largest islands – Sicily and Sardinia – are each almost the size of Belgium.

Sicily

Although Sicily is separated from the mainland by only a narrow stretch of water – the Straits of Messina – it is very much a region apart from the rest of Italy. This is due to the island's closeness to North Africa and its extraordinary history under the domination of many different civilizations. Although Sicily's former overlords left a rich architectural heritage, the natural environment has suffered from centuries of exploitation, resulting in widespread deforestation. Many of the tightly packed hill towns and villages of the interior rise out of a parched landscape and they depend upon one industry – agriculture. They have a neglected, somewhat forbidding appearance – Corleone (of *The Godfather* fame) is a typical example. Tourism has made more headway on the coast, where a number of fishing villages have become beach resorts.

Sicily has much to offer the tourist. The climate is generally warm and dry, although the heat of summer is often oppressive when the Sirocco wind blows from North Africa. The rich cultural mix, which includes Spanish, Arab and Greek contributions as well as Italian, is evident in the Sicilian dialect, food specialities, handicrafts and folklore, and the religious intensity of Holy Week. The two major cities are not particularly attractive to tourists, although they are ports of call for cruise ships:

- Palermo is the gateway to the western half of Sicily
- Catania is the gateway for the east.

Ferries serve the island from Genoa, Livorno and Naples, as an alternative to Reggio, so shortening the long road journey down the Italian Peninsula. Sicily will become even more accessible once the controversial project of a fixed link between Messina and Reggio goes ahead.

Sicily's natural attractions include Mount Etna, one of the world's largest active volcanoes; you can approach the crater rim by road or by cable car. The Lipari Islands off the north coast are also volcanic and offer interesting scenery as well as opportunities for scuba diving; Stromboli is the most impressive of the group.

Sicily's heritage attractions include:

- an array of temples and theatres built by the ancient Greeks, which rival anything to be found in Greece itself; the most outstanding example is the Valley of Temples at Agrigento and other important sites from this period (*c*.300 BC) can be seen at Syracuse, Segesta and Selinunte
- the cathedral at Monreale near Palermo, which is a blend of Norman and Arab styles
- Taormina, which in its spectacular setting with Mount Etna as a backdrop is Sicily's most sophisticated and fashionable resort; many cultural events are staged in the beautiful theatre overlooking the sea, which was built by the ancient Greeks and added to by the Romans
- Cefalú, which caters more for families and is favoured by foreign tour operators as it has an asset that Taormina lacks, namely a fine beach; it also boasts an impressive Norman cathedral and picturesque fishing port.

Sardinia

Tourism is an important part of Sardinia's economy. Because of its relative isolation, tour operators feature the island as a separate destination; certainly a greater number of foreign tour operators feature Sardinia for beach holidays than Sicily. Until the 1960s the island was a remote backwater outside the mainstream of Italian culture, while the sparsely populated interior had a reputation for lawlessness. Nowadays, four-wheel drive wildlife safaris are available in the mountains, and rural tourism is well developed, including a scheme run by a women's cooperative movement. Most of the development, however, has taken advantage of the white sandy beaches. One of the first areas to be developed was the Costa Smeralda, north of Olbia, which includes some of the most expensive hotels and holiday homes to be found anywhere in the Mediterranean, and yet blending perfectly with the natural scenery. Most of Sardinia is much less exclusive, and Alghero in particular caters for package holidays. Sardinia is well connected by charter flights to northern Europe and by ferry services to the mainland of Italy, Corsica and mainland France.

Summary

Italy has a long pedigree as a tourism destination, with a dominantly cultural tourism product, based on the country's past civilizations and contemporary lifestyle. Physically, Italy is characterized by two mountain chains – the Alps and the Apennines, with extensive lowland plains and long Mediterranean coastlines. Public sector support for tourism has waned since the 1990s, and most of the activity takes place at the regional level. Small family hotels dominate the accommodation supply, and surface transport is the most important means of travel both to and within the country. Italy's tourism market is dominated by domestic travel, although more Italians are travelling abroad. Inbound tourism is heavily dependent upon the European market and the USA.

Italy's attractions and tourism resources are varied and of international importance. In northern Italy, the Alps are a region for winter sports and summer touring holidays, while the North Italian Plain comprises a number of towns, such as Milan and Venice, which are important for both cultural and business tourism. The northern Italian coasts have a number of important resorts such as Rimini. Central Italy has both rural tourism and city tourism products. For the latter, Florence and Rome are world-ranked tourist cities. In the South, efforts are being made to develop tourism to counterbalance the economic dominance of the North. Here coastal resorts complement the volcanic landscapes of the Bay of Naples. The Italian islands of Sicily and Sardinia are tourism destinations in their own right.

Chapter 17

The tourism geography of Malta, Greece and Cyprus

Learning Objectives

After reading this chapter you should be able to:

- Explain the special appeal of Greece and the Greek Islands.
- Appreciate the cultural and economic ties that link Cyprus and Malta to other countries.
- Describe the major physical features and climate of these countries and understand their importance for tourism.
- Appreciate the tradition of tourism in Greece and the more recent entry of Malta and Cyprus to the holiday market.
- Appreciate the role of shipping and air services in the development of tourism in Greece, Malta and Cyprus.
- Understand the nature of tourism demand to the region.
- Appreciate the administration of tourism in the region.
- Demonstrate a knowledge of the tourist regions, resorts, business centres and tourist attractions of Greece, Malta and Cyprus.

Introduction

Apart from their location in the eastern half of the Mediterranean, we think there is justification for including Malta, Greece and Cyprus in the same chapter. Although Greece is not an island-nation like the other two countries, most of its popular tourist areas are islands and the country has a strong maritime outlook. All three countries have developed tourism industries based on Mediterranean beach holidays, serving the North European market. Cultural tourism is also important, and part of their attraction to visitors is a heritage that is a blend of Western and Middle Eastern influences. During the period of Turkish expansion, Malta, the Greek Islands and Cyprus were often in the front line in the struggle waged by the Republic of Venice and the Knights of St John in the defence of Christian Europe. There are also cultural ties linking Greece to Cyprus that go back thousands of years. In more recent times, there is the connection between Britain and its former colonies of Malta and Cyprus – both countries remain members of the Commonwealth and their people are to a large extent English-speaking.

Malta

The Maltese islands, small in size and poor in natural resources, are strategically important because of their location, midway between the Straits of Gibraltar and the Suez Canal, and between Europe and Africa. The main island – Malta itself – was a valuable prize for foreign invaders, the last being Britain, which used the Grand Harbour at Valletta as a base for the Royal Navy. The smaller island of Gozo was neglected and remains something of a backwater compared to Malta, although it is greener and scenically more attractive. The first impression of Malta is an apparently barren landscape of small terraced fields, separated by drystone walls and dotted with villages built from the honey-coloured rock. Because of the limestone formation of the islands and the rather dry climate, water supply is a major problem and tourism has to compete with other uses for this scarce resource.

Demand for tourism

Before independence from Britain in 1964, Malta was not a major tourist destination. The departure of the British armed forces meant that the government had to transform the country's economic base, by concentrating on the service sector, including tourism. Tourism to Malta rapidly expanded in the 1970s, reaching 700 000 by 1980. In the first half of the 1980s visitor numbers declined, but have grown steadily to reach over one million arrivals at the beginning of the twenty-first century. Malta's entry into the European Union in 2004 should assist the country's economic fortunes and boost tourism in the long term. The tourist authorities are concerned at Malta's dependence on a few markets – the UK represents almost half of all arrivals, followed by Germany, Italy and France. The national carrier, Air Malta, also operates services to Libya and Egypt, demonstrating the importance of the Arab market in business travel. The capital Valletta has been successfully promoted as an international conference venue and financial centre, yet despite this the majority of arrivals to Malta are holidaymakers. About a quarter of Malta's visitors are cruise passengers, spending up to 24 hours on the island, with much smaller numbers – mainly Italians – arriving on ferries from Sicily and Naples. However, Luqa Airport is the main gateway, with large numbers of holidaymakers arriving on charter flights operated by North European tour operators. Most of these are on package holidays, but other passengers are 'flight only' visiting their second or retirement homes on the island.

Supply of tourism

Accommodation

Malta has a large stock of hotels (supplying over 40 000 bedspaces) and self-catering accommodation, with the lower end of the package holiday market being concentrated in Sliema and a number of new resort developments by international companies responding to the government's upgrading strategy. In contrast, Gozo's tourism industry is much less developed since it is highly dependent on day visitors, using the ferry services linking it to the main island.

Organization

Government commitment to tourism is evidenced by the fact that in 1999 the Malta Tourism Authority (MTA) was created with the mission of marketing and planning Maltese tourism and upgrading the product. The MTA is anxious to maintain Malta as a competitively priced destination, but it faces a number of problems. These include:

- water shortages – desalinization is an expensive solution
- the social and economic imbalance between Malta and Gozo; to encourage tourism and employment prospects for young Gozitans, inter-island ferry services need improvement
- development pressures, on an island that already has one of the world's highest population densities
- poor standards of accommodation.

These problems have led to restrictions on further development in St Paul's Bay, Sliema and in the south-east of the island. There is also the realization that if Malta has reached saturation point in terms of tourism development, then the only way the industry can expand is to use the spare capacity in the off-peak months and to attract a higher sending clientèle.

Tourism resources

Malta's main appeal for holidaymakers lies in its warm sunny climate, with sheltered, unpolluted bays and harbours providing an ideal environment for sailing, windsurfing and scuba diving. However, sandy beaches are mainly restricted to the north-west of the island, where a number of resorts have developed, such as Bugibba–St Paul's Bay and Mellieha.

Malta's unique heritage also attracts cultural tourists. Although the Maltese people are service-oriented, used to dealing with foreigners, they have retained their traditional culture that has some Middle Eastern influences as well as being characterized by a strong devotion to the Roman Catholic Church. Each village has its *festa* (festival) and elaborately decorated church. The main attractions include:

- Valletta and the Three Cities built by the Knights of St John to defend the finest natural harbour in the Mediterranean from the Ottoman Turks. Some of the Renaissance palaces have found a new role as conference centres or luxury hotels, while St Johns Co-Cathedral is outstanding for its works of art. The *dghajsas* used to ferry tourists across the Grand Harbour are similar to Venetian gondolas.
- The prehistoric temples at Tarxien built by a mysterious early civilization.
- The medieval walled town of Mdina, the former capital, known as the 'Silent City' in contrast to the bustle of Valletta.

Greece

The location of Greece on the periphery of the European Union, and its relatively weak economy, have tended to obscure the unique contribution that this small country has made to European culture.

- Greece is seen as the birthplace of European civilization. The Minoan culture of Crete flourished at the same time as ancient Egypt (*c*. 2000 BC) and was in some respects more advanced. It was followed by the more warlike Mycenean culture on the mainland, which formed the basis of legends such as the Iliad, the Odyssey and Jason's Argonauts. Greece as 'the land of gods and heroes' has inspired a good deal of European art and literature.
- Later (after 500 BC), Classical Greece under the leadership of Athens developed many of the ideas and institutions which became central to the Western heritage, such as democracy and the Olympic Games. Architectural achievements, such as the Parthenon, continue to provide inspiration, and the dramas of Sophocles are still performed for modern audiences in the original open-air theatres as at Epidauros. Hellenic culture was spread far beyond Greece particularly by Alexander the Great, and strongly influenced the Romans.
- After the fall of the Roman Empire in the West, the torch of civilization was carried on by the Greek-speaking Byzantine Empire, based in Constantinople (now Istanbul). The Greek Orthodox Church spread to much of eastern Europe and Russia, strongly influencing religious art (for example, the use of ikons) and architecture.

Geographically, Greece forms part of the Balkan Peninsula, and has a cultural outlook different from Western Europe. It shares with other countries in the region:

- Orthodox Christianity, rather than Roman Catholicism
- the Cyrillic rather than Roman alphabet
- a history of centuries of domination by the Ottoman Empire.

Greece is also situated at the threshold of the Middle East, and Greek communities have long been a feature of the Levant – the eastern shore of the Mediterranean – from Alexandria to Asia Minor. Middle Eastern influences are evident in many aspects of modern Greek culture, including food and music. However, relations with Turkey have often been strained, with emotional responses based on historical grievances getting in the way of international cooperation that would benefit tourism in both countries as well as in Cyprus. The entry of Turkey into the European Union should reduce these tensions. The geographical proximity of Greece to some of the world's 'trouble spots' in the Balkans and the Middle East has also had a negative impact on the country's tourism industry. For example, the Western media have alleged lack of security at Athens Airport on several occasions.

The country's geography also explains why Greece has a maritime outlook extending well beyond the Mediterranean. The 16 000 kilometre-long coastline is deeply indented and has many islands, while the interior is, for the most part, mountainous – in Greece the sea and the mountains are never far away. The landscape has been devastated by soil erosion (largely due to deforestation) and good agricultural land is scarce. Not surprisingly, Greeks have been seafarers throughout their history, while Greece today has one of the world's largest shipping fleets and is active in cruise tourism. Due to the lack of economic opportunity there has been a great deal of emigration, particularly from the Aegean islands, to countries such as Australia or the USA. In fact, the Greeks of this overseas diaspora far outnumber the population of Greece itself. As far as tourism is concerned, the multiplicity of islands and harbours provides an ideal environment for sailing holidays and cruising, while the clear water of the Aegean favours diving.

Tourism is vital to the Greek economy, since it accounts for about 8 per cent of GDP and is a significant source of foreign exchange, compensating for nearly half the country's international trade deficit. The hosting of the Olympic Games in 2004 is set to increase the economic benefits of tourism to Greece and has prompted major infrastructure and facility developments.

Around 10 per cent of the workforce are employed in the tourism industry during the peak summer months, according to official figures. However, the contribution of tourism to job creation is even higher if we consider the 'black economy' of unregistered businesses, which is a fact of life in Greece as in other south European countries. Tourism is also responsible for facilitating economic and social development in areas where other opportunities for wealth-creation are lacking. Tourism has stemmed the tide of emigration from the Aegean islands, and there is now a reverse flow, including entrepreneurs from the mainland (which is not always to the advantage of the island economy).

Demand for tourism

Domestic and outbound tourism
Although nearly half the population engage in tourism, only a small percentage of trips are to foreign countries, mainly due to the economic problems in Greece in the new millennium and also concerns for safety. In some of the Greek islands, notably Rhodes, domestic tourists are far fewer than foreign holidaymakers, and their length of stay tends to be much shorter. Domestic tourism includes summer excursions to the coastal resorts and islands, winter skiing in the mountains, and pilgrimages to Orthodox shrines, such as Tinos in the Aegean.

Inbound tourism
Cultural tourism has a long history in Greece, and although the country was not included in the Grand Tour, it was visited by writers like Lord Byron, who did much to promote the cause of Greek independence in the early nineteenth century. However, organized tourism did not take place on any scale until the 1950s. Along with other Mediterranean destinations, Greece developed rapidly during the 1970s largely on the basis of price and the attractions of the Greek islands. By the early years of the twenty-first century, arrivals for the country as a whole were exceeding 14 million. The majority of tourists to Greece nowadays are visiting for recreational rather than cultural reasons – in search of sun, sand, sea, the nightlife and for a substantial number of visitors – the so-called 'Shirley Valentines' – romance. The Greek tradition of hospitality known as *philoxenia* (literally love of strangers) has probably been an asset in developing a vast service sector dominated by small family-run enterprises. Britain and Germany each supply about 25 per cent of the total number of visitors, most of whom arrive on inclusive tours. Italy, the Netherlands, Austria and the Scandinavian countries are also major generators of tourism to Greece. Large numbers of tourists also come from the USA, attracted mainly by the heritage of Classical Greece.

Supply of tourism

Transport

More than three-quarters of visitors to Greece arrive by air, encouraged by the growth of budget airline services across Europe. The most important gateways are Athens, serving southern and central Greece, and Thessaloniki for the north. The national carrier Olympic Airways and its associate Olympic Aviation operates a network of domestic air services based on Athens throughout this fragmented country, although it no longer holds the monopoly. Quite a few Greek islands can be reached by direct charter flights from the cities of northern Europe, the most significant being Corfu (Kerkira), Cephalonia, Zante (Zakinthos), Crete (Iraklion and Chania), Mykonos, Rhodes and Kos. Greece receives around 5 per cent of its visitors from cruise ships plying the eastern Mediterranean. Overland travel by road or rail is also available, but it is time-consuming as it involves:

- ferry crossings from Ancona or Brindisi to Patras if the visitor is arriving via Italy, or lengthy delays at border crossings if the visitor is travelling through the republics of the former Yugoslavia. Before the break-up of that country and the subsequent wars in Croatia, Bosnia and Serbia (1991–99) this was the preferred route, but it remains potentially unsafe given the likelihood of a further crisis in the Balkans.

The rail network within Greece, operated by Hellenic Railways (OSL), has suffered from chronic under-funding and many of the lines are single-track, reducing capacity and speed. However, fast inter-city services do link Athens to Thessaloniki and Patras. Much of the road system is also poor by European Union standards, especially on the islands where the accident rate among moped-users for example, is unacceptably high. On the other hand, Greece has one of the world's most extensive networks of coastal shipping services. However, the system is not ideal from a tourism viewpoint, as most ferries operate from the hub of Piraeus, the port of Athens, inter-island connections can be infrequent, and shipping companies are reluctant to provide an integrated service. 'Island-hopping' is part of the attraction of Greece for many tourists, but it requires patience and an element of planning. Ferries are subject to delays and even cancellations, especially in the Aegean, when the *meltemi* wind blows during the summer months. In good weather, the more remote islands can be reached by *caiques* (converted fishing boats).

Accommodation

The accommodation and catering sectors are well represented in Greece, and consist mainly of small and medium-sized enterprises (SMTEs). The official stock of hotels and self-catering villas, apartments and studios is considerable (over 300 000 beds in serviced accommodation alone), but it is exceeded by unregistered accommodation known collectively as *parahoteleria*, amounting to perhaps one million bedspaces. Most of the establishments offering rooms to let to visitors arriving in the Greek islands fall into this category. A large number of campsites are also available.

Organization

The importance of tourism is recognized by the government. The Ministry of Tourism shares responsibilities with the Greek National Tourism Organization (GNTO) for promotion, planning, the implementation of policies at both national and regional levels and coordination of the public and private sectors in tourism development. Government involvement currently is less than in the 1970s when it took a direct role in encouraging tourism, itself building facilities on a considerable scale, and offering a wide range of incentives to private developers. Tourism is included in the Five Year Plans for economic and social development, supplemented by European Union funding.

The GNTO faces a number of problems brought about by both the nature of tourism to Greece and the vulnerability of many of the country's resources. They include:

- Seasonality – the emphasis on 'summer sun' tourism does mean that there is a major problem, as 75 per cent of tourist arrivals are concentrated in the months May to September. This forces those employed in the tourism sector to work excessively long hours, to the detriment of the traditional family values characteristic of the Greek way of life.
- Geographical concentration – tourism development is mainly restricted to Athens, the coastal resorts and some of the islands. This makes it difficult to spread the benefits of tourism more evenly throughout the country, and to provide adequate accommodation and other facilities to cope with demand.
- Negative social impact of mass tourism – during the off-season, the islands are almost crime-free, but health and police services are stretched to the limit in some popular resorts during the peak summer months to cope with the effects of alcohol and drug abuse by some north European holidaymakers. This type of behaviour is offensive to the host community but is tolerated because tourism brings in much-needed income.
- Overdependence on foreign tour operators – attempts by hoteliers to introduce higher standards and prices mean that the mass market no longer sees Greece as an inexpensive destination, while high-spending tourists are deterred from visiting the popular resorts and the country faces competition from cheaper destinations in the region.
- Environmental degradation – the development of tourism has often been characterized by unplanned, haphazard building that has blighted the landscape. The rapid development of tourism, and its concentration in the dry summer season, has placed severe pressure on water supply systems. Marine pollution has been caused by inadequate sewage treatment and waste disposal. Noise pollution is a feature of the popular resorts, and has contributed, for example, to the decline of an endangered species of turtle on the island of Zakinthos. It is estimated that two-thirds of the forest fires that afflict Greece each summer are deliberately carried out to clear land for development.

These issues do mean that, while Greece is endowed with superb tourism resources, the country's tourism industry does not always fulfil its potential.

Tourism resources

We can divide Greece for tourism purposes into:

- the Greek mainland, which consists of a number of regions, the most important being the Peloponnese, Sterea Hellas (central Greece, including Athens) and Macedonia in the northern part of the country
- the Greek islands, which includes Crete and a number of separate groups or archipelagos. The most popular of these are the Ionian Islands lying to the west of the mainland, the Cyclades in the central Aegean and the Dodecanese to the south-east.

Mainland Greece

The mainland of Greece is divided into two by the Corinth Canal, itself a major engineering achievement. To the south is the **Peloponnese**, where mass tourism has as yet made little impact, largely due to the absence of good beaches. Tolon and Naplion are significant holiday resorts, within easy reach of Athens. The government has encouraged the revitalization of traditional communities such as the Mani in the extreme south, famous for its fortified villages. This formerly remote area has been opened up for walking and special interest holidays, which include Mystra, an important city in the Byzantine era. The Peloponnese contains some of Greece's most important archaeological sites. Some of these are included in classical tours based on Athens, such as:

- Olympia – site of the original Olympic Games
- Mycenae – associated with the legends of the Trojan War
- the well-preserved theatre at Epidauros, dating from the fourth century BC, which is still used for cultural events.

Tourism in **Athens** has declined significantly since the 1970s, when it was still the centre *par excellence* for sightseers. This has come about partly as a result of the growth in popularity of the Greek islands, at the expense of cultural tourism. Ugly urban sprawl and severe air pollution resulting from motor vehicles and factory emissions have also diminished the sightseeing experience. As a solution, the civic authorities have regularly banned private vehicles from the city centre, usually on a rota basis, in an attempt to reduce the *nefos* (smog) which endangers both health and historic monuments. The 2004 Olympics was the catalyst for urban regeneration, with infrastructure improvements such as a new airport and metro system. Two- and three-star hotels have been upgraded, while manufacturing industries have been given incentives to move out of the city. Nevertheless, the decision to stage some of the water events at Marathon – the scenic location of the Greek victory over the Persians in 490 BC – aroused opposition from environmentalists.

The capital's main attractions include:

- the Acropolis, the fortified hill which was the core of ancient Athens, containing a number of important temples such as the Parthenon, as reminders of the glory of Ancient Greece
- the Agora, once the marketplace of Athens in Classical and Roman times, which has only partly been excavated; there are plans to unite all these sites as one archaeological park
- to the east of the city lie a number of beach resorts – the so-called 'Apollo Coast' – which are mainly visited by domestic tourists and day trippers
- to the south of Piraeus are the Argo-Saronic Islands, the most popular being Aegina, while Spetses is perhaps the most attractive, providing a welcome relief from the extreme summer heat and congestion of Athens
- to the north-west is the classical site of Delphi in its beautiful mountain setting – this was an important place of pilgrimage as the site of the famous Oracle in ancient times.

In **northern Greece**, the well-wooded Halkidiki Peninsula with its fine beaches has been developed for recreational tourism, with yacht marinas, golf courses and holiday villages. The area is close to Thessaloniki, which is second in importance only to Athens as a business centre. Elsewhere, the emphasis has been on selective tourism to:

- stem rural depopulation
- revive traditional village industries
- conserve the region's natural and cultural heritage.

Attempts to develop winter sports tourism in the Pindus Mountains as a means of reducing seasonality have not been particularly successful, and northern Greece is mainly visited for its national parks – the Vikos gorge is outstanding – and its cultural attractions – such as the monasteries of Meteora in their spectacular setting.

The Greek islands

Of the hundreds of Greek islands, relatively few are served by regular ferry or hydrofoil services, and an even smaller number have been developed for international tourism. Each of these islands offers a unique product on the basis of its scenery and cultural heritage, rather than the quality of its beaches.

Crete is the largest by far of the islands, with a mountainous interior where the traditional lifestyle has persisted to a greater extent than elsewhere in Greece, contrasting with the well-developed international tourism scene along the north coast. Mallia has borne the brunt of mass tourism, while Aghios Nikalaos, with its attractive harbour has remained more upmarket. Crete can offer those tourists looking for more than beaches and nightlife:

- the heritage of Venetian rule in towns such as Chania
- the Samaria Gorge, one of the most impressive examples of its kind in Europe; unfortunately, its very popularity with hikers has caused ecological damage to this national park and disruption to its wildlife
- the impressive remains of the Minoan civilization at Knossos; this too is popular with tourists on day excursions from the nearby resorts; Phaestos on the less visited south coast is an uncrowded alternative.

The Cyclades are generally rather barren in appearance, and the small island communities are characterized by their white cube-shaped buildings, interspersed with tiny blue and white chapels. On these and other Aegean islands, we can usually identify two types of tourist centre, which are complementary in terms of the facilities they provide – the port and the *chora*, the traditional focus of island life – often situated some distance inland. The most popular islands in the group are the following:

- Mykonos perhaps most closely resembles the tourist stereotype of a Greek island, but it is in fact a sophisticated resort, with expensive bars and boutiques, and a large gay clientele.
- Paros as a hub of the Aegean ferry network is ideal for the independent traveller.
- Ios likewise attracts swarms of young backpackers during July and August, on account of its fine beaches and non-stop nightlife.
- Naxos contains more scenic variety and is the most fertile of the islands. Until the completion of a new airport with European Union funding in 1990, tourism took second place to agriculture and is still relatively low-impact in nature.
- Santorini (Thira) is undoubtedly the most spectacular of the Greek islands. It features prominently on cruise itineraries, thanks to its unique volcanic scenery – the harbour is the centre of a huge caldera – and the remains of the Minoan city of Akrotiri, buried by a volcanic eruption circa 1500 BC.

The most popular island in the group known as **the Sporades** in the north-west Aegean is Skiathos, thanks to a combination of pine-covered landscapes and fine beaches. Skyros, in contrast, has developed a niche market in 'holistic community' holidays as a solution to the stress of modern life.

The islands of the **north-east Aegean** include Lesbos, Samos and Chios. Here, agriculture and shipping continue to be the mainstays of the local economy, rather than tourism, which is dominated by the domestic market.

The Dodecanese are a group of islands situated far from the Greek mainland and close to the coast of south-west Turkey. Their cultural heritage is different from other Greek islands as they were ruled successively by the Knights of St John, the Ottoman Empire until 1912 and then by Italy until the Second World War. For the most part they are relatively undeveloped for tourism, with the exceptions of Kos and Rhodes where mass tourism has made a major impact. By the late 1990s Rhodes had a capacity of 50 000 registered bedspaces or 10 per cent of the stock for Greece as a whole. This large island offers natural attractions such as the 'Valley of the Butterflies' at Petaloudes, and many heritage sites, as well as a number of cultural events, festivals and *son et lumière* shows bringing history to life. The old town of Rhodes retains its medieval walls, castle and hospital built by the Knights of St John. The main touring circuit is along the east coast to the picturesque town of Lindos which has been carefully preserved, and where almost all the accommodation consists of rented rooms with local families or self-catering accommodation in traditional village houses. In contrast, Faliraki is characterized by unplanned hotel and self-catering development, and has acquired notoriety as a resort catering primarily for the British youth market. Rhodes needs to diversify its markets to reduce its dependence on package tours and overcome the problem of seasonality.

The Ionian islands include three popular destinations – Corfu (Kerkira), Cephalonia and Zante (Zakinthos). They are mountainous but fertile, with a softer climate than the Aegean islands and a greener landscape. Their cultural heritage reflects a long period of rule by the Republic of Venice, and also British occupation (from 1815 until 1864).

Corfu has for long been a favourite with British holidaymakers, and a large number of resorts have developed, particularly along the east coast, although the west coast has the best beaches. Mass tourism has had an adverse effect on Corfu, particularly in Ipsos and Benitses, which have become mass-market resorts, while Kavos is very much an enclave for the youth market, attracted by its throbbing nightlife. In contrast, the town of Corfu has a number of cultural attractions.

Cephalonia and Zante have less to offer in this respect, as they were badly affected by an earthquake in 1956 and underwent subsequent rebuilding. Zante is the more popular of the two and much of the development for the package holiday market has been insensitive, especially in the resort of Laganas. The island is a good example of the struggle between environmentalists, who want part of the coast to be designated as a marine national park, and local hotel developers and boat operators eager to increase their profits. Tourism to Cephalonia has been boosted by the popular film *Captain Correlli's Mandolin*.

Cyprus

Cyprus is the third largest of the Mediterranean islands, offering a great variety of coastal and mountain scenery and the heritage of many civilizations. Yet it is a divided island, occupied by two different ethnic groups – the Greeks and the Turks – separated by language, religion, history and since 1974 by a military/political frontier – the Green Line – which also divides the capital, Nicosia. The Greek-speaking Republic of Cyprus occupies two-thirds of the island, contains 75 per cent of its population and accounts for perhaps 95 per cent of its tourism industry. The Turkish Republic of North Cyprus (TRNC) on the other hand is not recognized by the international community. It was hoped that the admission of Cyprus to the European Union would reduce these divisions. The location of Cyprus, only 200 kilometres from Beirut, has meant that tourism is affected not only by the long-running dispute between Greece and Turkey over the island itself, but also by the uncertain political situation in the Middle East. In the 1990/1991 Gulf War, for example, tourism suffered badly.

Demand for tourism

Inbound tourism

Before Cyprus gained independence from Britain in 1960, few tourists visited the island. In the late 1960s it was 'discovered' by British tour operators, since Cyprus (along with Gibraltar and Malta) was part of the 'sterling area' and not subject to the strict currency exchange controls imposed by the British government at that time. After the invasion and occupation of the northern part of the island by the Turkish army in 1974, there was a drastic decline in tourist numbers, as most of the hotel stock was destroyed in the conflict. However, a major investment in tourism facilities in southern Cyprus followed, including the opening of a new airport at Larnaca to replace Nicosia, and the rapid development of Ayia Napa as a resort for the mass market. In the early years of the twenty-first century international tourist arrivals grew to over 2.5 million, four times the Greek Cypriot population of the island. The British inclusive tour market remains important to the island's tourist industry, using charter flights to the airports at Larnaca and Paphos. There are also substantial numbers of independent British visitors travelling to their holiday villas and retirement homes on the island. As is the case in Greece, the Cyprus government discourages seat-only charters.

Domestic tourism

There is a considerable internal demand for the island's recreational resources, generated not just by the Cypriots themselves, but also by the United Nations peacekeeping force in Nicosia, and the British armed forces stationed at the Sovereign Base of Akrotiri.

Supply of tourism

Transport and accommodation

The Republic of Cyprus has a varied resource base for tourism, supported by a good infrastructure and a considerable stock of accommodation of international standard, although there are relatively few first class hotels to attract the top end of the market. Before the 1974 invasion, Famagusta (Magusa) and Kyrenia (Girne) in northern Cyprus, were the major resorts of the island. They are much less popular nowadays as few Western tour operators are prepared to risk retaliation by the Greek or Greek Cypriot authorities by including the TRNC in their programmes. Nevertheless, the best beaches of Cyprus are in the Turkish-occupied zone, and there is also scope for cultural tourism, as the mountains near Kyrenia contain a number of monasteries and castles dating from the time of the Crusades. Apart from Turkish visitors from the mainland, a small but growing number of British and other west European tourists are attracted to the TRNC, arriving on Turkish Airways flights at Erkan Airport via Istanbul or Izmir.

Organization

Tourism is represented at ministerial level in the Republic of Cyprus as it is so important to the economy (accounting for over 20 per cent of GDP). This over-dependence upon tourism also causes concern regarding the industry's use of scarce resources and its social and environmental impacts. The Cyprus Tourism Organization (CTO) has promotion, development and licensing responsibilities. In this respect, the CTO is very concerned about the risks of over-development of the coastline – already evident in resorts such as Limassol and Ayia Napa – and is aiming for high quality, high-spending tourism by upgrading the tourism product. It has successfully promoted the island as an all-year-round destination and as a result the Scandinavian countries and Germany have become important generators of tourism to Cyprus. The CTO is also actively seeking new markets, notably Russia, Israel and the Arab states of the Middle East.

Tourism resources

We can summarize the main tourism products of the Republic of Cyprus as follows:

- Beach tourism is based on major resort developments at Paphos, Limassol, Larnaca and Ayia Napa. The trend is to go upmarket with the provision of golf courses and yacht marinas, although Ayia Napa is likely to appeal mainly to the mass market, particularly young tourists interested in the vibrant club scene.
- Conferences and incentive travel are catered for by the larger resort hotels and a conference centre in Nicosia.
- Agro-tourism in the rural villages, which are being carefully restored to attract visitors to the 'traditional Cyprus'.
- Ecotourism, specifically birdwatching in the Akamas National Park, the one remaining undeveloped stretch of coastline in the south-west of Cyprus.
- Skiing during the winter months in the pine-covered Troodos Mountains. During the summer, resorts such as Platres continue to be visited by Cypriots escaping the intense summer heat of the plains around Nicosia. There are a number of small country hotels.
- Business tourism in Limassol and Larnaca (which is being positioned as a hub for air services to the Middle East). Tourism in Nicosia is discouraged by the political situation, but the city has nevertheless become an important communications and financial centre for a large part of the Middle East.
- Cultural tourism based on the heritage of Cyprus includes Ancient Greek theatres at Kourion (now used for music festivals) and Amathus; Byzantine monasteries; Crusader castles; and Islamic monuments from the Ottoman Empire.
- Cruises to the Greek Islands, Israel and Egypt from the port of Limassol.

The Republic of Cyprus was admitted to the European Union in 2004, but the future growth of tourism will depend to a large extent on the reunification of the island under a federal system of government with the agreement of Turkey. In the meantime a limited amount of cross-border traffic is taking place.

Summary

Greece has a long tradition of cultural tourism, while Malta and Cyprus are comparative latecomers to the industry. All three countries have benefited from their accessibility to the tourist-generating countries of northern Europe and the demand for 'sun, sand and sea' holidays, but large-scale tourism had to await the introduction of air-inclusive tours in the 1960s. Outbound and domestic tourism are much less significant than incoming tourism. The hosting of the 2004 Olympic Games in Greece has arguably stimulated that country's tourism industry, whilst the membership of the European Union across all three countries should encourage investment in tourism and boost demand.

The primary resources are the attractive island and coastal environments, while the Mediterranean climate is ideal for recreational tourism. The islands in particular have a rich cultural heritage, blending south European and Middle Eastern influences; however, cultural tourism nowadays takes second place to beach holidays. Cultural attractions include well-preserved archaeological sites, religious buildings, castles and festivals. Malta, Greece and Cyprus have a long maritime history, and as a result their people are service-oriented and used to dealing with foreign visitors. The tourism sector is well developed, and characterized by small family enterprises so that the benefits of tourism are spread widely through the economy.

One of the main problems facing tourism is a pronounced summer peak in demand, especially in Greece. Attempts to develop winter tourism have met with little success, with the notable exception of Cyprus. The domination of the industry by foreign tour operators makes it difficult for local entrepreneurs to respond with new quality products as the markets are price-sensitive. After a long period of neglect, there is a growing awareness by the authorities in each country of the need to protect the coastal environment and the cultural heritage from the impacts of mass tourism.

Chapter 18

The tourism geography of Eastern Europe, Russia and the Commonwealth of Independent States (CIS)

Learning Objectives

After reading this chapter, you should be able to:

■ Describe the major physical features and climates of the region and understand their significance for tourism.

■ Understand the role of Communism in promoting social and economic change in Eastern Europe and the former Soviet Union.

■ Be aware of the emergence of countries in the region as market economies and the consequent effects on the organization of tourism and on tourist flows.

■ Recognize the importance and social character of domestic tourism in these countries.

■ Understand that outbound tourism has been mainly directed toward other destinations within the region, but that since the collapse of Communism travellers are venturing further afield.

■ Appreciate the role of inbound tourism in boosting national economies.

■ Recognize the problem of pollution in many areas due to the legacy of relying on outdated heavy industry.

■ Appreciate that, with the collapse of the Communist system, the cultural differences between the various countries are now more important than the similarities.

■ Demonstrate a knowledge of the tourist regions, resorts, business centres and tourist attractions of Eastern Europe, Russia and the other countries of the CIS.

Introduction

Eastern Europe is the name given to the great tract of land, over a million square kilometres in area, extending from the Baltic to the Black Sea. It has acquired a special identity mainly for political reasons since 1945, but its historical background puts it definitely in the mainstream of European culture. Russia, on the other hand, includes vast Asian territories and most of the former USSR lies outside Europe. In such an extensive region there is great scenic and climatic variety. However, it is generally the case that, except in a few favoured coastal areas, the climate is definitely continental, with much colder winters than are experienced in the same latitudes in Western Europe.

Between 1945 and 1989 the countries of Eastern Europe could be said to form a political and economic region sharply differentiated from those on the western side of the 'Iron Curtain'. With the exception of Albania and the former Yugoslavia, these countries were closely associated with the Soviet Union (USSR) as the Eastern bloc. However, this impression of unity was, to a large extent, imposed by the Soviet Union following the Second World War and concealed the deep-seated differences between the many and varied ethnic groups which make up the population of the region. In the long historical perspective, the countries of Eastern Europe had found their progress towards nationhood, stability and economic prosperity retarded by their location in the path of invading armies, many originating in the steppes of Central Asia. Most countries had substantial ethnic minorities at variance with the majority culture, and all had experienced periods of foreign rule, forming part of various empires with their centres outside the region. The Ottoman Empire, based in Istanbul, imposed its cultural stamp on the countries of the Balkan Peninsula. These came to be less advanced in their economic and social development than the lands to the west of the Dinaric Alps and the Carpathians, which fell under the sway of the Habsburg Empire based in Vienna, or even those of the Russian Empire to the north-east. Thus a case can be made for dividing 'Eastern Europe' and the former Soviet Union into three sub-regions:

- The first group of countries – the Czech Republic, Slovakia, Hungary, Poland and the Baltic States – are the most advanced economically and have long had a strong cultural orientation towards the West, and the same is true of Slovenia and Croatia in the former Yugoslavia.
- The second group consists of the countries of the Balkan Peninsula where the influence of the Orthodox Church and Islam have been dominant in the past, namely Romania, Bulgaria, Albania, Serbia and the other republics of the former Yugoslavia.
- The third group extends well beyond Europe to the Pacific Ocean in northern Asia – this includes Russia and the other countries that make up the Commonwealth of Independent States (CIS).

Nevertheless, the adoption of Communism as the political and economic model, first by Russia after 1917 and then by the countries of Eastern Europe after 1945, has had a profound effect on tourism in the region. Communism, which entails the state ownership of the means of production and distribution, influenced both the nature of the demand for tourism and recreation and the type of facilities that were on offer. Governments in the so-called 'socialist' or 'people's republics' had virtual monopoly control over all aspects of tourism from strategic planning to owning and managing accommodation. Public institutions were closely involved in 'social tourism' or 'trade union tourism' by subsidising workers' holidays and providing tourist facilities. The type of holidays on offer differed fundamentally from commercial mass tourism as it developed in the West.

History of tourism demand and supply

Some East European countries had well-developed tourist industries before 1939, but, with the notable exception of Czechoslovakia, the majority of the population were too poor to afford holidays. Following the Communist takeover, the luxury hotels in spas, seaside resorts and cities were nationalized and put to other uses. Concern for leisure and tourism revived in the 1960s when the economic restructuring was well under way, and considerations of housing, education and health care were less pressing. The rights of all citizens to recreational opportunities had been recognized in the constitutions drawn up by the new republics. Pressure for longer holidays and two-day weekends coincided with the growing movement from the rural areas to the industrial cities. Demand also grew for the introduction of leisure goods, including cars, although long waiting lists meant that ownership levels remained at only a fraction of those in the West. Domestic holidays were customarily spent at the seaside or in spas, where rather spartan accommodation was provided, often in the form of holiday villages or workers' sanatoria, provided by the government-controlled trade unions. However, the *nomenklatura* – the Communist Party elite and other favoured groups – had access to more luxurious facilities, including, in some cases, private beaches and hunting reserves. In the cities, the government provided generous subsidies to the arts and cultural attractions that to some extent compensated for the restrictions and consumer shortages that made everyday life drab for most citizens. The rich folklore of the various ethnic groups was also encouraged as a tourist attraction.

Demand for outbound international tourism grew slowly due to currency and visa restrictions. Inevitably, most outbound travel was to other socialist countries and its volume was regulated by bilateral agreements between the governments of the region. Inbound tourism from the West was initially viewed with suspicion, but in most countries was actively sought from the 1960s, as it earned hard currency to purchase much-needed imports from outside the COMECON trading bloc. Indeed, Western visitors had privileges denied to most of the population, as they could buy goods from so-called 'dollar shops', which accepted only hard currencies. Giving preference to group travel, which could be carefully supervised, was one way of ensuring favourable publicity for 'socialist achievements'. However, low standards of service, outdated infrastructure and bureaucratic controls inhibited the growth of international tourism, while the simple lack of bedspaces held back domestic tourism.

The dramatic political changes which have taken place in Eastern Europe and the former Soviet Union since 1989 have had a profound effect on the pattern of tourism development. The state tourism organizations, which were, in effect, tour operators and travel agencies like the USSR's Intourist, lost their monopoly position. Changes have been most rapid in those countries such as the Czech Republic, Poland and Hungary which had a flourishing tourism industry before 1939, and where there is a strong entrepreneurial tradition. A flurry of tourism plans and significant investment in tourist infrastructure and accommodation has been evident as the countries of the region bring their tourism sector up to international standards.

On the other hand, the switch to a market economy has had a damaging effect on social tourism. In some countries domestic tourists were priced out of international hotels, where previously they had been charged very preferential rates. The introduction of democracy has given the peoples of Eastern Europe and the former Soviet Union much greater freedom to travel to the West, and this flow will increase as the economic outlook of the countries in the region continues to improve. The admission to the European Union of some countries in Eastern Europe will also accelerate this trend.

Since the mid 1990s East Europeans and Russians have been frequent visitors to the Mediterranean coastal resorts and the ski slopes of the French Alps. The Poles and Czechs arrive by car, coach or charter flights and use budget self-catering accommodation. Most of the Russian tourists on the other hand are high-spending members of the former *nomenklatura* or new business class. In contrast to these affluent visitors, many so-called tourists are in fact would-be immigrants in search of a better life in the West. The unacceptable face of this new mobility is the trafficking in women and girls, duped or coerced into supplying the sex industry.

The surge in car ownership in Eastern Europe, and the growth in demand for touring holidays in the region, has necessitated massive investment in road improvement schemes to meet West European standards, while public transport has been relatively neglected. However the economic situation of these countries means that governments have been less able to deal effectively with the region's already numerous environmental problems, such as those caused by the smokestack industries of Silesia and Transylvania. There is also concern over nuclear power plants in Bulgaria and elsewhere. Unless these problems can be addressed, inbound international tourism demand will suffer as the 'new tourists' express their concerns for these issues by 'voting with their feet'.

Tourism resources of Eastern Europe

Eastern Europe is rich in tourism resources, although these are of a kind more likely to attract visitors with cultural or special interests than the mass market. Beach tourism is well established on the Adriatic, Black Sea and Baltic coasts. The mountain ranges, such as the Carpathians, provide opportunities for winter sports, although facilities rarely attain the standard of the ski resorts of the Alps. Thanks to the growing interest in healthier lifestyles in the West, the numerous spas of Eastern Europe are undergoing a revival. All the countries of the region have designated national parks or reserves, but considerable land use conflicts need to be resolved if the wildlife resources are to be adequately protected. The region's great rivers offer scope for recreational tourism, especially the Danube. The main attraction of most countries is likely to be the heritage of past cultures, exemplified in historic cities such as Dubrovnik and Krakow, and the colourful peasant folklore of the rural areas. Cities and countryside alike reflect the strong national differences to be found within Eastern Europe.

In detailing the resources and the type of development that has taken place in each of the countries of the region, we start with the Czech Republic, Slovakia and Hungary, three countries that consider themselves to be part of Central rather than Eastern Europe, and where German is the second language.

The Czech Republic

In January 1993 the Federal Republic of Czechoslovakia was dissolved with the Czech Republic and Slovakia henceforth following separate paths. The Czechs of Bohemia and Moravia differ from the Slovaks not only in language but also in cultural traditions. Before Czechoslovakia was established in 1918 the Czech lands were part of the Austrian Empire, whereas Hungary had for many centuries ruled Slovakia. The Czech Republic is not only much larger than Slovakia, with twice the population, but is also disproportionately wealthier. Since the 'Velvet Revolution' of 1989 it has attracted considerable foreign investment as a result of its drive to a free market economy, and in 2004 it became a member of the EU. Although the Czech Ministry of Economics does not have a strong tourism policy, the Czech Republic has a well-established tourism industry which contributed 5.5 per cent of GDP in 2001.

Tourism demand and supply

The Czech Republic has long been famous for its therapeutic springs and spas. Karlovy Vary (formerly Carlsbad) and Marianske Lazne (Marienbad) in Bohemia were the favourite meeting places for the statesmen and the wealthy of Europe in the early 1900s. Under Communism the luxury hotels were taken over by labour unions and fell into neglect, but since 1990 there has been something of a revival. With developments spearheaded by the Czech Tourist Authority (CTA) and Cedok, the former state tourism organization and now the largest hotel and travel company, a wide range of products are available to today's foreign visitor, including city breaks, spa treatments, sporting holidays, stays in lake and mountain resorts, and touring holidays.

After the 1989 revolution, tourist numbers more than doubled to exceed 20 million in the early years of the twenty-first century, while Prague has become one of the world's most visited cities. However, the majority of these are day excursionists, mainly from neighbouring Germany and Austria and the number of staying visitors is around 5 million.

The country's new found popularity highlighted the shortage of accommodation, especially the three- and four-star hotels favoured by Western tour groups, and the need to upgrade standards is one of the most pressing needs of the tourism sector. Until recently, most of the demand has come from other East European countries where expectations are lower, and this has resulted in a proliferation of low-cost camping sites. The situation is improving as a result of joint ventures by Cedok with Western corporations for the larger hotels and privatization of the smaller hotels and pensions, with new hotels opening in Prague and a programme of renovation of older properties.

Domestic tourism is important as an advanced industrial economy has given most Czechs comparative affluence by East European standards. Sport and an interest in physical fitness and the outdoor life had been fostered by the *Sokol* movement even before 1918. This has resulted in a growing demand for a wide range of outdoor recreation activities and for second homes in the countryside.

Tourism resources

The Czech Republic offers scenic variety and a physical environment that is generally favourable for tourism. The large number of rivers and small lakes make up to some extent for the lack of a coastline. Forests cover 20 per cent of the country and are particularly extensive in the mountain ranges along the national borders. These forests are managed as a recreational resource, with nature reserves, waymarked trails and areas set aside for hunting – an important earner of foreign currency. Skiing is popular during the winter months in the resorts of Harrachov in the Giant Mountains and Spicak in the Sumava Mountains. Southern Bohemia and Moravia also boast spectacular limestone caves among their natural attractions.

A rich natural and cultural heritage is given a considerable degree of environmental protection, with the establishment of a 400 kilometre-long 'green corridor' linking Prague to Vienna, designed for hiking, riding and cycling holidays, or leisurely touring by car. This tourist route includes some of the historic towns of southern Bohemia – notably Cesky Krumlov, with its unique Baroque theatre – and a number of castles. Cedok has converted some of these to luxury hotels, while others are being restored to their former aristocratic owners after a long period of neglect under Communism. Interpretation of the heritage is achieved through open-air museums. Despite these initiatives, the Czech Republic has its share of conservation problems. These include:

- serious pollution from smokestack industries using lignite, in north Bohemia and north Moravia–Silesia
- lack of government funding often means that historic buildings continue to fall into disrepair, while art treasures illegally acquired from the country's churches find their way to the international market.

Of the cities of the Czech republic, a number have received UNESCO listing as World Cultural Heritage Sites and **Prague** has achieved worldwide significance as a tourist centre. Prague's cultural appeal is due to:

- a strong musical heritage, including associations with Mozart and the Czech composers Smetana and Dvorak
- a unique architectural heritage (which escaped destruction in the Second World War), with outstanding examples of buildings in the Gothic, Baroque and Art Nouveau styles
- a vibrant contemporary arts scene attracting a large expatriate community, particularly from the USA.

As Prague has more than one historic centre, tourist attractions tend to be clustered in three distinct areas, namely:

- Hradcany, the original fortress-capital on a hill overlooking the river Vltava. This contains Prague Castle, seat of Bohemian kings, Holy Roman emperors and Czech presidents, St Vitus Cathedral, and the picturesque street known as Golden Lane.
- The Old Town on the east bank of the river, which is linked to Hradcany by the highly decorative Charles Bridge. Two of the finest masterpieces of Gothic

architecture in the Old Town are Tyn Church and the clock tower in Old Town Square.

○ The New Town, which was actually planned as early as the fourteenth century but rebuilt in the nineteenth century. It is centred around Wenceslas Square, the setting for some of the key events in Czech history, nowadays lined with hotels, apartment buildings, restaurants and shops. Many of these are decorated in the Art Nouveau style associated with the great Czech artist Alfons Mucha.

Tourism has brought economic benefits to Prague, including international funding of much-needed restoration work. However, the enormous influx of visitors, especially of tour groups and young backpackers from all over the world, is threatening to turn the city into another Florence.

Other cities are mainly important as centres for business travel, namely:

* Plzen (Pilsen) and Ceske Budejovice (Budweis) are famous for their brewing industries
* Brno, the capital of Moravia is noted for its engineering industries, and as an important venue for trade fairs.

Slovakia

Slovakia has made less progress with free market reforms than the Czech Republic and consequently tourism is not as developed. Before the Second World War, it had a predominantly agrarian economy, and it suffers from the legacy of dependence on the heavy industries introduced under Communism. Slovakia is a country with great tourism potential, and whilst it has benefited from the share-out of federal assets following its 'divorce settlement' with the Czech Republic, significant investment in tourist infrastructure is needed. It now has both its own national airline and national tourist organization – the Slovak Tourist Board – with marketing and development powers, although the CSA airline continues to play an important role in promoting the country's attractions. A new bridge across the Danube on the border with Hungary will boost tourist activity between the two countries.

Tourism resources

The main appeal of Slovakia for foreign visitors lies in its beautiful mountain scenery rather than the attractions of the capital, Bratislava. Unlike the Czech Republic, this is a wine rather than beer drinking nation, with some cultural similarities to neighbouring Hungary; for example, gypsy folk music is an important part of the entertainment on offer to foreign tourists in both countries. Slovaks take even greater pride in their rural peasant traditions than the Czechs, and a considerable variety of village architecture has been preserved. Other heritage attractions include medieval mining towns, the castles of the former Hungarian nobility and, in eastern Slovakia, Orthodox churches are a reminder of the region's proximity to Romania and the Ukraine.

Tourism is mainly focused on the following areas:

* The High Tatras on the border with Poland, which contain the highest peaks of the Carpathians; apart from the superb lake and mountain scenery, the area can provide some of the best skiing to be found in Eastern Europe.

- The karst limestone region of eastern Slovakia, which boasts the spectacular UNESCO-listed Dobsina ice cave as well as waterfalls and rock formations.
- The spas of western Slovakia, the most important being Piestany, which attracts large numbers of wealthy Arab and German tourists.
- Bratislava and southern Slovakia, which forms part of the Danube Plain. Bratislava is known primarily as a modern industrial city and its cultural attractions have been overshadowed by those of Prague; it is now a major port, thanks to the controversial power project on the Danube at Gabcikovo which, in taming the river, also threatens to destroy the wetland environment of the area.

Hungary

Hungary is a small landlocked country in the centre of Europe, marked off from its neighbours by the complex Magyar language, its history as a major power and the spicy cuisine. The bulk of the country consists of a great plain in the middle of the Carpathian Basin, crossed by the rivers Danube and Tisza; only in the north and west are there highlands rising to, at most, 900 metres. Winters are cold and cloudy, but summers approach Mediterranean conditions in heat and sunshine.

Tourism demand and supply

Tourism has become an important part of the economy, accounting for 5 per cent of GDP and over 6 per cent of employment. This is due partly to the successful marketing of Hungary's two main attractions, namely the capital Budapest and Lake Balaton, which together account for the majority of foreign visitors. The tourism strategy is now to focus on quality and high yield tourism rather than mass tourism, which requires improvements in the infrastructure.

Even under Communism, Western tourists were encouraged by the removal of restrictions, and a limited amount of foreign investment in hotels was permitted. During the 1980s the number of visitors from the West almost trebled, whereas those from other socialist countries actually declined. This was largely due to the low value of the Hungarian *forint* relative to Western currencies, whereas it was over-valued compared to the non-convertible currencies of the Soviet bloc. Hungary's success in attracting international tourists continued in the 1990s with volumes approaching 32 million arrivals in the early years of the twenty-first century.

The majority of tourists arrive by car and are short-stay, particularly the Austrians, who cross the border on shopping forays to towns such as Sopron and Szombathely. The gateway for air travellers is Budapest's Terihegy Airport, while large numbers of excursionists use the hydrofoil service on the Danube from Vienna. A high proportion of the accommodation stock is in campsites or private homes. There has been significant investment in hotels, both within and outside of Budapest, with the major chains represented.

Before 1989 the state-owned Ibusz company handled both inbound and outbound tourism, but it has since been reorganized as part of the new government's policy of economic liberalization, and faces competition from a multiplicity of independent travel agencies. The industry is managed by the Tourism State Secretariat of the Ministry of Economy and Transport, supported by the Hungarian National Tourist Office and tourist boards responsible for marketing at regional level.

As visa and currency restrictions have been relaxed, and the economic position has improved, increasing numbers of Hungarians are travelling abroad, with Spain and Greece as popular destinations and a small, but growing long-haul market. Although annual holiday entitlement averages 20 days, effective demand for domestic tourism is reduced by the widespread practice of 'moonlighting' at several jobs to make ends meet so that holiday propensities languish at around 33 per cent. The majority of domestic tourists stay with friends or relatives, or in cottages in the countryside.

Tourism resources

Hungary's tourism resources include:

- Numerous spas based on the thermal springs that underlie the Carpathian Basin. These not only provide rest and recuperation for Hungarian workers, but also attract much-needed hard currency from long-stay Western visitors – and are becoming venues for meetings and conferences.
- Excellent facilities for activity holidays, such as horse riding, cycling and water-sports.
- Cultural attractions appealing more to the older tourist. These include the traditional peasant dances and crafts – notably embroidery – of the villages of the Great Hungarian Plain where rural tourism is growing, whereas the country's art treasures are mainly found in the capital.
- **Budapest**, which is one of Europe's most attractive capitals. Formed from what were two separate cities – Buda, picturesquely situated on the hills above the Danube, and Pest, the commercial centre on the river's left bank – it contains many reminders of its pre-1918 role as the joint capital of the Austro-Hungarian Empire. These include the following:
  ○ the magnificent neo-Gothic Parliament Building in Pest and the Fisherman's Bastion in Buda are the city's two major landmarks
  ○ the Hungarian State Opera is a reminder that Budapest vies with Vienna as a centre of art and music
  ○ the shopping boulevards, café society and vibrant nightlife
  ○ spa establishments such as the Hotel Gellert, and the Szechenyi Baths, with year-round bathing in the open air
  ○ business opportunities – in the new climate of economic liberalism Budapest has attracted an international business community and the city is growing in importance as a conference venue.

Budapest is close to the other main tourist areas of Hungary, namely:

- The Danube Bend, where the great river changes its course between mountain ranges, is a popular excursion zone. It contains some of Hungary's most historic towns including Szentendre, with its *skansen* or museum of Hungarian rural life.
- Lake Balaton is one of Europe's largest at 77 kilometres in length, but averaging only 3 metres in depth. Its shores are fringed by beaches, modern hotels and campsites, while a number of areas have been designated as nature reserves. Demand for accommodation in summer frequently exceeds supply and the threat of pollution from intensive agriculture has to be constantly monitored.
- Heviz is the most well-known of a number of spas in the vicinity of Lake Balaton, due to its unique thermal lake.

- The Great Hungarian Plain, where the *pusztas* or vast, treeless pasturelands east of the Danube provide Hungary with many of its characteristic landscapes and traditions, such as the *csikos* (cattle herders), whose displays of horsemanship are a tourist attraction. Many of the *csardas* (country inns) feature the traditional folk music and dances that inspired Liszt and other Hungarian composers. Ecotourism is being promoted in areas such as the Hortobagy National Park near Debrecen where aspects of the traditional culture and the steppe ecosystem have been carefully preserved.

Poland

Poland is one of the largest countries of Europe, with a population of almost 40 million. Its exposed situation on the North European Plain between Germany and Russia has resulted in a history of invasion, fluctuating boundaries and periods of foreign domination. The Roman Catholic Church has long been identified with Polish nationhood and resistance, particularly to the Communist regime. Largely as a result, less than 20 per cent of Poland's farms were collectivized after 1945. At the same time, massive industrialization brought about the Solidarity free trade union movement that did so much to inspire opposition to Communism during the 1980s. In some respects, Poland was better placed than most East European countries to make the transition to a market economy after 1989.

Demand for tourism

Until the early 1990s, tourism played only a minor role in the Polish economy. The majority of visitors originated from the former socialist countries and tended to be short-stay. This market has declined in importance now that more appealing destinations are available to the Russians, Czechs and East Germans and Poland's inbound tourism has suffered as a result. However, to a greater extent than other East European countries, Poland can attract a large ethnic market in North America, the UK and other countries of Western Europe. Most of the tourism from these countries has been for VFR or business purposes, but increasing numbers are visiting Poland on inclusive tours or on tailor-made holiday arrangements, primarily for cultural reasons. The recovery of Poland from the economic crisis of the early part of the 1990s has also led to considerable growth in domestic and outbound tourism.

Supply of tourism

A much greater choice of accommodation is now available to Polish holidaymakers than was the case in the past. Tourism's higher profile has led to a change in government policy, with the State Sport and Tourism Administration's responsibilities in marketing being taken over by the new Tourism Development Agency in 1999. This organization is staffed by tourism industry professionals and is funded by the government and the regional administrations. It aims to stimulate further investment and growth in the sector, in line with the government's National Development Strategy, and is involved in tourism training initiatives with West European countries. Orbis, the national tourism organization, has been privatized, although it remains one of Poland's major tour operators and hotel companies.

Tourism resources

The main tourist areas of Poland are situated near its southern and northern borders, and a fair distance from Warsaw, the capital and gateway for air travellers. The tourist areas include the following:

The **Baltic Coast** is by far the most popular area, accounting for a third of all holiday overnights. On offer are 500 kilometres of sandy beaches and coastal lagoons, backed by pine forests, but the climate is often cloudy and windy, with temperatures rarely getting much above 20 °C. From Miedzyzdroje at the mouth of the Oder to Hel and the Amber coast along the Gulf of Gdansk, a string of resorts attract Swedish as well as domestic holidaymakers. Sopot is a popular and relatively sophisticated resort adjoining the historic seaport of Gdansk (Danzig). Two of Poland's most important recreational resources lie a short distance inland from the Baltic coast, namely:

- the lake country of Pomorze (eastern Pomerania), which includes the medieval fortress of Malbork (formerly Marienburg) built by the Teutonic Knights, a reminder of the former German domination of this region
- the Mazurian Lake District, an area of forests, lakes and low hills of glacial drift, which is popular for sailing, canoeing and camping.

The border country of **southern Poland** offers more interesting scenery and facilities for winter sports. To the west lie the Sudeten Mountains, adjoining Bohemia, where a number of spas have long been established. Further east, the Carpathian Mountains, culminating in the Tatry and Beskid ranges adjoining Slovakia, rise to over 2000 metres and account for a fifth of all holiday overnights in Poland. Zakopane in the Tatry Mountains is a well-developed resort with a year-round season. In addition to skiing, organized walking tours and whitewater rafting through the gorge of the Dunajec river are available. Tourism has greatly benefited the economy of this formerly remote and poverty-stricken mountain region.

The flatlands of **central and western Poland** are scenically less attractive, but the countryside does provide opportunities for fishing and riding holidays, often based on the manor houses of the former Polish aristocracy. On the eastern border with Belarus the Bialowieza National Park provides a refuge for rare animals such as the European bison.

Poland's **cultural attractions** are mainly to be found in the cities, although most of these suffered wholesale destruction in the Second World War. The historic cores have generally been meticulously restored, and provide a welcome contrast to the bleak industrial suburbs. The most important cities from the viewpoint of tourism are Warsaw and Krakow, whereas others such as Poznan, Lodz and Wroclaw are primarily business centres:

- **Warsaw** is one of the world's most impressive examples of urban reconstruction. The old city was painstakingly rebuilt *as it was* in Baroque style, on the basis of old paintings, photographs and plans, as hardly a building was left standing at the close of the Second World War. As a short break destination, the Polish capital is popular with art and music lovers, especially Chopin enthusiasts. One of Warsaw's most impressive – if not best loved – landmarks is the Palace of Culture and Science built during the Stalinist era.
- Warsaw is surpassed as a tourist centre by **Krakow**, Poland's former royal capital and religious centre, which has been designated as a World Heritage Site and

European City of Culture. The city, which largely escaped wartime destruction, has retained its medieval atmosphere, and has attracted world-wide interest due to its association with Pope John Paul II. The major attractions include the impressive Market Square, the Cloth Hall and Wawel Castle. Unfortunately, the restoration programme has difficulty in keeping pace with the ravages of pollution from the steelworks at Nowa Huta nearby. Krakow is conveniently near the ski resorts and scenic attractions of the Carpathian Mountains. In addition, a tour based on the city might include:

○ the salt mines of Wielisza, which have been worked for many centuries
○ the shrine of the Black Madonna at Czestochowa, which is Poland's most important pilgrimage centre
○ the former concentration camp at Oswiecim (better known by its German name of Auschwitz), one of many established in Poland during the Nazi occupation. It is regarded by the international Jewish community as the main site of the Holocaust and as a place of national martyrdom by the Poles.

The Baltic States

Like most of Poland, the three small countries of Lithuania, Latvia and Estonia on the eastern shore of the Baltic Sea formed part of the Russian Empire from the eighteenth century to 1918. Between the two world wars they enjoyed a brief period of independence before being annexed by the Soviet Union in 1940. The Baltic States have much closer cultural ties with Scandinavia and Germany than with Russia (although there are large ethnic Russian minorities), and since regaining their independence in 1991 they have sought economic association with those countries and see tourism as an important source of foreign currency. In 1993, all three states agreed to cooperate in the sphere of tourism policy and promotion.

The scenery is low key, the highest point reaching only 300 metres above sea level, but is made attractive by the combination of pastureland, forest and a myriad lakes. The sandy beaches of the Baltic have been adversely affected by pollution in this shallow, largely enclosed tideless sea, into which flow the industrial wastes of eastern Germany, Poland and Russia.

During the period of Soviet rule the coastal resorts were popular with Russian tourists, and Intourist developed some of its best hotels in the area. The Baltic States are now attracting short-break Western tourists, and direct flights now link the capitals Vilnius, Riga and Tallinn with cities in Western Europe. Outbound tourism has increased dramatically since 1990 and Estonia has benefited from improved ferry services to Finland. All three countries are noted for their music festivals and folklore, in which national identity was nurtured during the long period of foreign domination.

Lithuania

Lithuania was united with Poland for much of its history and is likewise staunchly Roman Catholic. The impressive 'Hill of Crosses' on the outskirts of Siauliai is the country's most famous religious site. The capital Vilnius (Vilna) is a major cultural centre with many fine Renaissance buildings, and has a famous university. Trakai, with its mediaeval lakeside fortress was the ancient capital. Lithuania has a much shorter coastline than its neighbours but boasts fine beaches along the Neringa, a 100-kilometre sand-spit separating the Kursia Marios lagoon from the Baltic Sea.

Latvia

In Latvia the former German influence is particularly evident in the seaports of Courland in the western part of the country. The capital, Riga, is the industrial hub of the Baltic States and an important cultural centre. The city's elegant Art Nouveau buildings are a reminder of the period before 1914 when Riga was the leading port of the Russian Empire. Similarly, Jurmala on the Gulf of Riga was then a fashionable resort, but facilities will need upgrading for it to become once more the 'Baltic Riviera'. The Gauja National Park in eastern Latvia is an important area for winter sports.

Estonia

Estonia shows many reminders of Swedish and Danish rule and has close affinities with Finland. The capital, Tallinn, a former Hanseatic port, is one of the best-preserved medieval cities of northern Europe. It is also a major yachting centre, stemming from its role in the 1980 Olympics. To the west, Saaremaa is the largest of Estonia's many offshore islands. The Lahemaa National Park in the east of the country is noted for its lakes and waterfalls. Estonia would prefer to reduce its dependence on the Finnish day visitor market – mainly attracted by cheap alcohol – by promoting itself as a cultural destination for British and other West European tourists.

The Balkan countries

Compared to Poland and the Baltic States, the Balkan countries of south-eastern Europe are well endowed with tourism resources. However, they have suffered from a long history of misgovernment that has inhibited economic progress. During the era of Soviet domination, the Black Sea beaches of Romania and Bulgaria were, in some respects, the eastern equivalent of the Spanish costas, attracting sun-seeking tourists from the more developed socialist countries of Poland, East Germany and Czechoslovakia.

Romania

Romania is the largest country in the region, with a population of over 23 million. The Romanian people regard themselves as different – Latins surrounded by Slavs – but although in language and temperament they are akin to Italians, their religion is Orthodox and the climate is definitely continental rather than Mediterranean. The forested Carpathian Mountains divide the country in a great horseshoe-shaped arc, separating picturesque Transylvania from the broad plains of Wallachia to the south and the rolling plateau of Moldavia to the east. Whereas Wallachia and Moldavia were separate principalities on the fringes of the Ottoman Empire until 1858, Transylvania was part of Hungary until 1918. As a result, Transylvania has substantial Magyar and German minorities who differ in religion as well as language from the Romanians. There are also perhaps 2 million gypsies who form a marginalized group in society (as elsewhere in Eastern Europe) but who play an important role in Romanian folklore.

After the Communist takeover in 1947, Romania experienced considerable industrialization and urbanization. Nevertheless, traditional peasant lifestyles persist, despite the attempts by Ceausescu in the 1980s to create a 'new socialist man' by replacing villages with apartment blocks. Domestic tourism is said to have increased tenfold between 1965 and 1987, although it is probable that much of this was group travel, including youth organizations.

During the 1960s the Romanian government embarked on a major investment programme for the Black Sea coast, creating a number of new holiday resorts. In 1971 a Ministry of Tourism and Sport was established and the state tourism organization ONT and its subsidiary Carpati set out to increase numbers of visitors from the West as well as from other socialist countries. During the 1970s they were successful in attracting Western tour operators. However, after 1979 the economic situation in Romania deteriorated and the Ceausescu regime became increasingly repressive. As a result, tourism receipts fell by 40 per cent between 1981 and 1986. The violent overthrow of Ceausescu in December 1989 was followed by a slow progress toward economic reform. In a bid to upgrade standards and facilities by attracting investment, the Romanian Ministry of Transport, Construction and Tourism implemented a 'master plan for tourism' covering key elements of the industry. These mainly focus on two contrasting areas; the Black Sea coast and the Carpathian Mountains in the north-west of the country.

The flat **Black Sea coast** is scenically the least interesting part of Romania, but with its broad gently shelving beaches and a holiday season lasting from mid-May to September it has become the main destination for foreign holidaymakers and accounts for the majority of all bedspaces. Mamaia is the largest resort, situated on a sandspit between the sea and an extensive lagoon. Like the tourist complexes of Aurora, Jupiter, Neptune, Venus and Saturn, it offers a variety of accommodation and sports facilities. The older resort of Eforie with its mud-bathing establishments is well known for health tourism. Further north, the Danube Delta is a wetland environment over 4000 square kilometres in extent, teeming with wildlife and now protected as a nature reserve and a UNESCO Biosphere Reserve.

The spas and resorts of the **Carpathians Mountains** have not received as much investment as those of the Black Sea. Neither as high nor as rugged as the Alps, they form a number of separate massifs, of which the most impressive are the Bucegi and Retezat Mountains, noted for their lakes and glaciated landforms. Exploitation of the region's forest resources has gone hand-in-hand with tourism and there are a large number of dispersed mountain chalets to supplement hotels and campsite accommodation in the resorts. Before the Second World War Sinaia attracted Romanian royalty, but nowadays the main resort is Poiana Brasov, purpose-built for winter sports, but also a centre for hiking and adventure holidays. Between the mountain ranges lies the fertile Transylvanian Plateau, where the rural communities preserve much of their traditional culture. The historic towns have a strong German influence in their architecture. The 'Gothic' ambience of towns such as Sibiu and the castle of Bran, in its picturesque mountain setting, are inevitably associated with the Dracula legend.

Moldavia's main tourist attractions are the unique painted monasteries of the Bucovina region; amazingly the exterior frescoes have survived since the fifteenth century.

Bucharest, Romania's capital, lies in the rather less appealing plains of Wallachia bordering the Danube. The city, with its spacious boulevards, was known before the Second World War as 'the Paris of the East' but it has little to offer the tourist nowadays. This is due to the destruction of many churches during the Ceausescu era to make way for the dictator's grandiose projects such as the 'House of the Republic'. The Herastrau Village Museum, however, is one of the best of its kind.

Bulgaria

Bulgaria is a small country in the heart of the Balkan Peninsula, which is best known in Western Europe for budget-priced beach and skiing holidays. It does, however, offer a great variety of scenery and is rich in the remains of many civilizations. The country is traversed from east to west by several thickly forested mountain ranges, rising to over 2000 metres, which attract heavy snowfalls in winter. Between the mountains lie fertile valleys enjoying a warm sunny climate which have given Bulgaria its reputation as 'the market garden of Eastern Europe', producing fine tobacco and the famous perfume known as 'attar of roses'. Before the violent break-up of Yugoslavia, the country received a good deal of transit tourism due to its location on the E5 route from Belgrade to Istanbul. Proximity to Turkey in the past was a disadvantage, resulting in Bulgaria being submerged in the Ottoman Empire for several centuries. It regained its independence, with Russian help, in 1878, a fact commemorated by the elaborate Alexander Nevsky Cathedral in Sofia. Despite the presence of Turkish and Pomak (native Muslim) minorities, the Islamic contribution to the cultural heritage has been neglected. Restoration projects have focused instead on the 'museum towns' such as Veliki Turnovo, which played a major role in the medieval period or in the National Revival leading to independence.

The country was one of Europe's poorest and most underdeveloped before the Second World War, with over 80 per cent of the population employed in agriculture. The development of an industrial economy since the 1950s has greatly improved living standards, while the introduction of the two-day weekend encouraged the ownership of second homes, which are situated mainly around the capital Sofia and on the Black Sea coast. As in other East European countries, spas play an important role, the most popular being Sandanski, Kustendil, Hissarya and Velingrad. However, throughout the 1990s the country suffered a severe economic crisis, which has depressed the demand for domestic as well as outbound tourism, although inbound tourism has grown steadily to around 3 million international trips annually.

Bulgaria recognized the importance of tourism as a source of hard currency in the 1960s and concluded agreements with a number of Western tour operators. Balkantourist was the state agency responsible for international tourism, owning most of the large stock of hotel accommodation, particularly on the Black Sea coast. As a result, most Western visitors are on low-budget inclusive packages and the rate of return per individual tourist is small. Since the collapse of the Zhivkov regime in 1989 Bulgaria has moved towards a free market economy, encouraging joint ventures with Western hotel and banking enterprises and encouraging investment in transport and tourism infrastructure. The Ministry of Economy implements tourism policy working with the Bulgarian national tourist board and various industry organizations. They are supported by a regional and local network of tourist organizations.

We can identify three resources Bulgaria can offer the visitor.

The **Black Sea coast** of Bulgaria receives the majority of tourists in the country and is the location of almost two-thirds of the bedstock. It is scenically more varied than the coast of Romania with fine beaches that are ideal for family holidays. Resort development has centred around Varna in the north – where Zlatni Pyasatsi (Golden Sands), Albena and Drouzhba are the main resorts – and Bourgas in the south – where Slunchev Bryag (Sunny Beach) is the most popular centre. Most of these resorts offer international entertainments and are rather characterless; however, the holiday village of Dyuni has been developed in a more traditional style.

Bulgaria is also a winter sports destination, with major resorts at Borovets and Bansko in the Pirin Mountains, Aleko on Mount Vitosha, which caters for large numbers of weekend skiers from nearby Sofia, and Pamporovo in the Rhodope Massif. However, facilities, although improving, are not as sophisticated as those of the Alps, and the Balkans cannot offer the high-altitude skiing favoured by Western tour operators.

There is more scope for future development in promoting **special interest holidays**. These include 'eco-paths', spas, wine tours, musical folklore (the country is noted for its fine choirs), archaeology (the Thracian civilization was probably the earliest in Europe) and caving. Bulgaria is also noted for its monasteries, often situated in remote mountain settings where the Orthodox Church preserved the national identity during the centuries of Ottoman rule. The most famous of these are those of Rila to the south of Sofia and Boyana on the outskirts of the capital. For such cultural tourism to be successful, more attention needs to be paid to improving accessibility and visitor management facilities to a standard appropriate for Western tourists.

The republics of the former Yugoslavia

The pre-1991 Yugoslavia has been described as an experiment to unite many peoples of widely differing languages (including two alphabets), religions and historical backgrounds. It was a federation of six republics – Serbia, Croatia, Slovenia, Bosnia-Herzegovina, Macedonia and Montenegro – and two autonomous regions – Kosovo and Vojvodina. This complex arrangement was made to work largely through the authority of Marshal Tito, who ruled the country from 1945 to 1979. Furthermore, Yugoslavia set out earlier to attract foreign investment and was far more successful than Bulgaria or Romania in attracting package holidaymakers from Western Europe. In 1960 Yugotours was set up to market the country and in 1965 restrictions on the movement of foreign visitors were removed. In the same year the Adriatic Highway was completed with Western aid, permitting the development of resort facilities along the coast from Istria to Montenegro. By 1988 Yugoslavia was attracting 9 million foreign visitors annually, but these were highly concentrated geographically on the Adriatic coast, while the former West Germany accounted for a third of the total. Although domestic tourism was mainly accommodated in low-cost holiday villages away from the main Adriatic resorts, Yugoslavs were not discouraged from contact with Western tourists at home and had greater freedom than other East Europeans to travel to Western countries.

However, the communist system of 'worker's control' in practice caused problems in hotel administration and marketing, and did little to encourage private enterprise. The ending of the Cold War also brought about the revival of nationalism and ethnic rivalries, initiated by Serbia. This caused the break-up of the Federation, swiftly followed by a series of wars that lasted throughout most of the 1990s. Needless to say, this has been disastrous for the tourism industries of the former Yugoslavia, although the republics of Croatia and Slovenia have recovered some of their former popularity. As the following survey shows, tourism resources are far from evenly distributed throughout the region.

Croatia

In contrast to the other republics, Croatia can offer the visitor a wealth of natural and cultural attractions and a well-established tourism industry. The country is fortunate in occupying some 1500 kilometres of Adriatic coast, including the greater part of the Istrian Peninsula and the scenic, island-studded Dalmatian region. The coast is protected from the cold winters experienced in the capital, Zagreb, by the parallel ranges of the Dinaric Alps, so that it enjoys a typically Mediterranean climate. However, where there are gaps in the mountains, the blustery *Bora* wind can be disruptive in spring and autumn.

Croatia accounted for over 80 per cent of tourist nights in registered accommodation in the former Yugoslavia during the late 1980s. With the apparent resolution of the ethnic strife in Bosnia and Kosovo, the country has regained its position as a major holiday destination. This was spearheaded by the Ministry of Tourism through a privatization policy which has attracted a flow of investment into the tourism sector since 2000.

Tourism has particularly benefited the economy of the Dalmatian islands and stemmed out-migration, which was a problem in the early part of the twentieth century. Some islands – such as Brioni – are protected as national parks, while others – notably Hvar, Korcula and Rab – have been developed as holiday resorts. A network of shipping and hydrofoil services provides access to the mainland, where most of the major resorts are located. Some of these have a long history. For example, Opatija, which has good road and rail links to Central Europe, was a favoured resort for the Austrian and Hungarian elites before the First World War. Most of the development, however, has taken place since the 1960s, much of it in the form of self-contained hotel complexes, as for example on the Babin Kuk peninsula near the historic city of Dubrovnik. Makarska is Croatia's nearest equivalent to a typical Mediterranean resort, with big hotels and a range of entertainment. The numerous sheltered deep water harbours have encouraged cruising and sailing, while the clear unpolluted sea is ideal for diving and bathing. A disadvantage for family holidays is the lack of good sandy beaches. Croatia since the 1960s has been more liberal than most Mediterranean destinations in its attitude towards naturism, which continues to be favoured by German holidaymakers.

The coast can offer a rich cultural heritage, including:

- Important Roman remains, such as the arena at Pula, and the impressive palace of the Emperor Diocletian at Split.
- The architecture of the coastal towns and islands, showing the influence of Venice, which was a major power hereabouts in medieval times.
- Dubrovnik, an almost perfect example of a medieval seaport, complete with city walls and pedestrianized streets and squares. Most of the buildings damaged by the Serbian bombardment of 1991/2 have been meticulously restored while the international summer festival continues to be a major attraction.

The interior of Croatia consists of the plains of Slavonia – similar to those of neighbouring Hungary – to the east, and mountains in the west. These contain some of the best examples of karst limestone scenery in Europe, culminating in the lakes and waterfalls of the Plitvice National Park. Zagreb is an attractive historic city as well as being an important business centre, hosting international trade fairs and sports events.

Slovenia

With a small area of 20 000 square kilometres and a population of only 2 million, Slovenia has nevertheless a broad tourism appeal and the government has implemented an ambitious tourism marketing and development strategy, boosting international arrivals to over one million by 2001. The country was economically advanced compared to most of the former Yugoslavia, and its state carrier, Adria Airways, has energetically promoted business travel from Western Europe to replace the loss of Yugoslav markets for its products.

Austrian influence is particularly evident in the attractive capital, Ljubljana, and in the mountain villages of the Julian Alps, which resemble those of the Tyrol. Winter sports facilities have long been established at Kranjska Gora, Bovec and Rogla, while the lake resorts of Bled and Bohinj provide a range of summer activities. Although Slovenia has only a short stretch of Adriatic coastline this includes the popular resort of Portoroz and the seaports of Piran and Koper with their Venetian-style architecture. Other attractions include the spectacular and much-visited network of caves at Postojna, the equestrian centre at Lipica and a number of themed touring routes.

The Yugoslav Federation

Montenegro and Serbia are the only republics remaining in the Yugoslav Federation. Their respective governments in Podgorica and Belgrade do not always see eye to eye, and they can be considered here as separate countries.

Montenegro (Crna Gora) has one of the finest stretches of Adriatic Coast, including some good beaches and the magnificent fjord-like Gulf of Kotor. International-style resorts were developed in the 1960s at Budva, and Sveti Stefan – which is unique in being a one-time fishing village converted to a luxury hotel complex. The interior of Montenegro, with its stony mountains, deep gorges and 'eagle's nest' villages, is very different from the lush greenery of the coast. The former capital, Cetinje, is a reminder that Montenegro was an independent kingdom before the First World War, and this small city, approached by a spectacular road, is one of the curiosities of the Balkans.

Inbound tourism has suffered from the effects of the sanctions directed at the regime in Belgrade and the Kosovo refugee crisis in 1999, but in the early years of the twenty-first century there are signs of a recovery.

Serbia has seen an increase in its tourist arrivals but the tourism industry has been handicapped by its landlocked situation, and throughout the 1990s by international ostracism, economic sanctions and the NATO bombings in 1999. Previously, Belgrade was a major business and conference centre and Serbia received a large volume of transit traffic en route to Greece or Turkey. Winter sports facilities were developed at Kopaonik and Zlatibor, but these attracted little attention from foreign tour operators. Serbia's cultural heritage includes a number of medieval Orthodox monasteries – Studenica and Sopocani are World Heritage Sites – but again these are little appreciated in the West compared to the art treasures of Croatia. The future of tourism will depend to an extent on political stability and the curbing of extreme nationalist movements.

Provisionally known as FYRM – the **Former Yugoslav Republic of Macedonia** – in deference to Greece, this small country was the poorest region of Yugoslavia before independence. The re-opening of the Greek border has allowed Macedonia to develop its trade and fledgling tourism industry. This is based not so much on Skopje the capital, which was rebuilt after a major earthquake in 1963, but on Ohrid, which is scenically located on the deepest lake in Europe.

Bosnia-Herzegovina

Bosnia's war-ravaged economy and refugee crises have allowed even less scope for tourism than the other republics and considerable reconstruction is needed. The 1995 Dayton Agreement secured an uneasy peace on the basis of power-sharing between the three principal ethnic groups – the Muslims, the Croats and the Serbs, but in effect the country has become a United Nations protectorate. In the former Yugoslavia, Bosnia's diversity of cultures and religions was no small part of its appeal for foreign visitors, most of whom were based in Dubrovnik and other holiday resorts on the Adriatic coast. Tourists were particularly attracted to the old Turkish quarter of Sarajevo, and the picturesque Turkish bridge over the river Neretva at Mostar. The federal government also invested heavily in Sarajevo as the venue for the 1984 Winter Olympics, as part of its policy to spread the benefits of tourism from the coast to the mountainous interior. The only type of tourism that continues to flourish, despite a lack of government encouragement, are the pilgrimages to Medjugorje. Since 1981 this obscure Croat village in Herzegovina has attracted well over 30 million Roman Catholics from all over the world.

Albania

A small mountainous country, known to its people as Shqipri (land of the eagles), Albania is different in language and culture from its Greek and Slav neighbours. It is also the poorest and least developed of the East European states. In 1991 the government envisaged ambitious plans for tourism development, under a new Ministry of Construction and Tourism. There is little doubt that the country has considerable potential, including an extensive and as yet unspoiled Mediterranean coastline where ramshackle developments are now being cleared away, spectacular lake and mountain scenery, and potential ecotourism based on the great biodiversity of the country with its bears, lynx and golden eagles. None the less, Western-style tourism has been held back for the following reasons:

- The historical legacy of the hard-line Communist regime established by Enver Hoxha between 1945 and 1989, which imposed a policy of economic self-sufficiency, closed mosques and churches, and isolated the Albanian people from contacts with foreigners.
- Inadequate infrastructure. The road network is poorly developed, with horse-drawn vehicles impeding the traffic flow. Many mountain villages remain inaccessible by road. External transport links by road, air and ferry are limited, there are constant power cuts, and water supplies are of poor quality.
- Lack of investment due to the poor state of the economy. The collapse of get-rich-quick 'pyramid' investment schemes in the 1990s discredited government attempts to introduce a free market economy.
- Political instability. In the northern part of Albania there has been a recrudescence of the tribal feuding that characterized much of the country's pre-1945 history, and visitor safety cannot be guaranteed.

By the early twenty-first century inbound arrivals were growing, to exceed 350 000 in 2001 and domestic tourism was a significant growth sector. To provide for this market, the European Bank for Reconstruction and Development (EBRD) is closely involved with the funding of facilities suitable for Western tourists, such as hotels, holiday villages and campgrounds and the bedstock has grown to approach 8000. Most of the development will be on the coast, particularly south of Vlore. The EBRD would like developers to concentrate on a relatively few upmarket projects. However, the Albanian government desperately needs the foreign exchange earnings from tourism to modernize the country's infrastructure, and some observers fear that this will put pressure on Albania's unique ecological and cultural resources. These include:

- The archaeological sites at Apolonia and Butrint – the 'lost city' of the ancient Illyrian civilization, and one of the best-preserved classical sites in the Mediterranean. Because of its accessibility from the beach resort of Ksamil and Corfu, Butrint may have to cope with visitor numbers well beyond its present capacity.
- The mountains of the interior. These contain a number of medieval fortress-towns which played a major role in the Albanian struggle for freedom against the Ottoman Empire; of these Berat, Gijrokastro and Kruje are the most important.
- The lakes on the border with Macedonia.

The changes that have taken place in Albania since the fall of Communism are mainly evident in the capital, Tirana. Under Hoxha the city was effectively a car-free zone, but it now has traffic problems, while the private sector, often with Italian financial backing, is providing hotels and restaurants in competition with Albturist, the state travel organization.

Tourism resources of the Commonwealth of Independent States (CIS)

Russia was very clearly the dominant country in the former Soviet Union. Its role is much less evident in the loose grouping of republics known as the Commonwealth of Independent States (CIS) that replaced the USSR in 1991. Russia's economic power is also increasingly challenged by the West in Transcaucasia and Central Asia. We will look first at the tourism resources of the vast Russian Federation and then at three geographical groupings of the other independent states: the western and southern republics, and those of Central Asia.

Russia (The Russian Federation)

Physical features

Although much smaller than the USSR, the Russian Federation is still almost twice the size of the USA and spans eleven time zones. In other words, a difference of half a day separates Kaliningrad on the Baltic coast, from Petropavlovsk on the Bering Sea, 12 000 kilometres to the east. As one would expect, there is a great range of climatic conditions in a landmass that also extends across nearly 40° of latitude, and we can broadly distinguish the following life zones, starting in the north:

- treeless boggy tundra bordering the Arctic Ocean from the Kola Peninsula in the west to the Bering Straits in the east, very sparsely occupied by groups of reindeer herders
- the wide zone of the *taiga* – the world's largest forest – covering 8 million square kilometres of northern Russia, including the greater part of Siberia; due to the harsh sub-arctic climate and poor soils this is almost entirely dominated by a few tree species such as birch, firs and larch
- a belt of mixed forest, typifying the more varied landscapes of central Russia
- a zone of treeless grassland or steppe in the south, although most of this now lies in an independent Ukraine and Kazakhstan; much of this zone has very fertile 'black earth' soils and was the 'bread-basket' of the USSR, but it is often prone to devastating droughts
- the high mountains along part of the southern border, namely the Caucasus and Altai ranges
- landscapes and climates comparable to those of the Mediterranean, although these are found only in sheltered pockets along Russia's short Black Sea coastline.

The continental climate that characterizes almost the whole of Russia is a major constraint on tourism development. Winters are severe, for example: snow lies on average for 150 days in Moscow and 160 days in St Petersburg. Some 7 million square kilometres of northern Russia are affected by permafrost, which in parts of Arctic Siberia reaches a depth of 1000 metres or more.

Cultural features

The cultural diversity of the Russian Federation is greater than the variety of its landscapes. The country is a mosaic of over 300 ethnic groups, although Russian Slavs account for perhaps 80 per cent of the population of around 150 million. There are 21 autonomous republics and 11 autonomous regions that represent the principal non-Russian minorities. As a result of *glasnost* (the policy of open government), religion and nationalist feeling, previously suppressed under Soviet Communism, revived in the late 1980s. The Russian Orthodox Church has regained some of the prestige it enjoyed under the Tsars before the 1917 Revolution. There is also an important Muslim minority, particularly in Tatarstan and the northern Caucasus, where the Chechens have been in revolt against the Russian government since the early 1990s, and have been implicated in terrorist attacks in Moscow.

Transport

The sheer size of Russia, the difficult climate and terrain of most of the country and the undeveloped nature of surface transport means that aviation has long played a major role. Many communities in Siberia are only really accessible by air, since they lie more than 1600 kilometres from the nearest railhead, the earth roads are impassable during the spring thaw and the autumn rains, while the rivers are ice-free only in the brief summer.

In the former USSR the state-owned Aeroflot had a monopoly of domestic air services, making it the world's biggest airline. With the break-up of the Soviet Union it was likewise divided up between the various republics and separate national airlines emerged. Aeroflot-Russian International Airlines, reorganized as a joint-stock company in 1992, now provides two-thirds of Russia's international air services, with a worldwide network like its Soviet predecessor. However, its network within the CIS is a far cry from the 1980s, with flights to only 40 or so cities now, compared to 3600 destinations then, and it faces competition from a number of private airlines. Air fares remain relatively low, even for foreign tourists paying in US dollars. On the other hand, flights can be irregular due to recurrent fuel shortages, staff morale is affected by low pay, and aviation experts allege that safety standards are below those considered acceptable in the West.

As mentioned in Chapter 5, Russia has the world's longest railway – the Trans-Siberian – which provides the major west to east transport link. Although the journey from Moscow to Vladivostok – a distance of almost 10 000 kilometres – takes over a week, and the trains make few concessions to tourism, the Trans-Siberian has become one of Russia's most sought-after travel experiences. On the other hand, the Bolshoi Express, with carriages designed for the Soviet ruling elite, is a luxury product aimed at high-spending foreign tourists. Most rail services are cheap by Western standards but also slow, and security on the trains is a problem. Road transport is even less efficient, and the standard of road maintenance, even between major cities in European Russia, is well below Western standards. On the other hand, Russia has a very extensive network of inland waterways. These link the great rivers Dnieper, Don and Volga (which have played a major role in Russian history) to the Baltic, White and Black Seas. In the summer months, fleets of hydrofoils ply the waterways with large numbers of domestic passengers, and Russian expertise in the field of hydrofoil design may yet see a new role for this type of vessel elsewhere. River cruises on more conventional ships are becoming increasingly popular with Western tourists, especially those linking St Petersburg to Moscow via Lakes Ladoga and Onega, which provide a leisurely way of absorbing the timeless quality of Russia's countryside.

Tourism demand and supply

Domestic tourism under the Soviet system was mainly the responsibility of the state-controlled trade unions. Health care and rest from labour was provided in a network of sanatoria and purpose-built holiday centres which provided groups of workers with a subsidized, if somewhat regimented, two week vacation. Only a small proportion of this accommodation was allocated to families, while children were catered for by the Young Pioneer camps. The transition to a market economy after 1990 dealt this system of subsidized domestic tourism a severe blow. *Perestroika* (the restructuring of the economy) was accompanied by rampant inflation and devaluation of the rouble. The consequent rise in the prices of food and other essentials drastically reduced the amount of discretionary income available to the average citizen. The Ukraine and Georgia, which contained most of the Black Sea resorts, were now independent countries. The funding for subsidised holidays from public sector organizations was considerably reduced. As a result tourism propensities are now very low compared to the European average. Although outbound travel has grown considerably since 1990, domestic tourism has declined. On the other hand, *glasnost* encouraged rising expectations, fuelling a demand for independent holidays on the Western model.

Activity holidays have grown in popularity, especially canoeing, camping and cross-country skiing. Russians on a touring holiday prefer to use *tubaza* (tourist bungalows), which provide cheap but basic accommodation, as they are paid for in roubles rather than US dollars, unlike Western-style hotels. Although half the workforce are entitled to paid holidays of 24 days, most Russian city dwellers have to be content with a stay nearer home, in a *dacha* (country cottage) in one of the villages on the outskirts, which they may own themselves, part-own through a garden cooperative or rent.

The trend for independent holidays will increase as car ownership levels rise – at present these are low by Western standards. After the near-collapse of the economy in 1998, the situation has improved with the rise in oil prices, growth in industrial output and stronger leadership. Nevertheless huge gaps remain between the *nouveaux riches* 'New Russians' who have benefited most from the market economy, and the mass of the population, whose living standards and even life expectancy have actually declined since 1990.

Inbound tourism contributed only a small proportion of the Soviet Union's foreign exchange earnings, and attitudes towards foreign visitors have been ambivalent since the times of the Tsars. Bureaucracy, an obsession with state security and travel restrictions characterized Russia even before the 1917 Revolution, and seem likely to persist long after the demise of Communism. Large areas were officially closed to foreign visitors until the early 1990s, tourists had to follow approved itineraries and stay only in officially designated accommodation. The Soviet authorities saw tourism as a means of promoting the achievements of the world's first socialist state, and in 1929 Intourist was founded as an all-purpose agency to serve foreign visitors. Although most tourists were travelling for cultural rather than ideological reasons, official itineraries included visits to factories and collective farms. In 1957 international youth travel to the USSR became the responsibility of the Sputnik organization, part of the Komsomol (League of Young Communists), with a network of camps and low budget hotels. From 1966 onwards investment in tourism infrastructure and training became part of the government's Five Year Plans. Additional impetus was given by the choice of Moscow as the host city for the 1980 Olympic Games.

With the demise of the Soviet Union, Intourist lost its state monopoly and was privatized, along with Sputnik. As a commercial organization it has advantages over its competitors, with offices in 14 countries outside the CIS, as well as an established network of agencies in all the countries of the former Soviet Union. It still owns and manages hotels and restaurants, arranges surface transportation for clients, organizes excursions and tickets for cultural events, and supplies guides and interpreters. In the public sector tourism is closely linked to physical culture and sports, and is regulated by the 1996 Tourism Law. There is a strong organization at city level that recognizes the fact that most Western tourists to Russia spend at least part of their stay in the cities of St Petersburg and Moscow. Indeed the lack of tourism infrastructure elsewhere is a major constraint on visitation.

Since the late 1980s the appeal of Russia has broadened, tourist arrivals and receipts have increased, although much of this increase is from former Soviet republics, and a diversity of products are available for foreign visitors. By the early years of the twenty-first century international arrivals exceeded 21 million, more than double those recorded in 1990 for the whole of the Soviet Union. Exploiting nostalgia for the Cold War, Western tourists are invited to participate in a James Bond theme, operate Soviet military hardware and visit a space research centre. Other options include hunting expeditions, river cruises, conference tourism, adventure holidays and homestays with Russian families. However the growth of Western-style tourism faces a number of problems, namely:

- the language barrier
- the lack of nightlife; although casinos are springing up in many cities throughout Russia, they are not always reputable
- a continuing shortage of accommodation, particularly in the major centres, where hotels are pre-booked by the travel companies
- tour itineraries still need to be pre-booked and paid for in hard currency, leaving the independent traveller at a disadvantage
- foreign investment in the tourism industry, as in the economy generally, is deterred by the absence of a reliable banking system, bureaucratic inertia and corruption, and uncertainty over the laws relating to private property
- the lack of small and medium-sized business enterprises
- the prevalent low standards of service in hotels and restaurants.

On the other hand, the younger generation in the workforce is well educated and eager to adopt Western-style methods.

Tourism resources

Russia's tourism resources are primarily cultural, with a major concentration in the cities of Moscow and St Petersburg.

- **St Petersburg** is probably the most beautiful city in Russia, and occupies a special place in the country's history for these reasons:
  - It was founded as the capital of the Russian Empire in 1703 by the modernizing Tsar Peter the Great as Russia's 'window on the west'. No expense was spared to import the best European architects of the time to design a city on classical lines, with broad streets, canals and impressive public buildings.
  - The attack on the Winter Palace in October 1917 brought Lenin and the Communist Party to power in Russia (for this reason the city was renamed Leningrad during the Soviet era).
  - It endured an epic siege from 1941 to 1943, epitomizing the almost unimaginable sacrifices made by the Russian people during the Second World War.
  - Because of its northerly latitude St Petersburg is best visited during the season of the 'white nights' (from May to July). Among its many cultural attractions, the following are of special significance:
    - the Hermitage, one of the world's largest art collections, occupying the former Winter Palace of the Tsars
    - the Maryinsky Theatre, home of the renowned Kirov Ballet
    - the former palaces of the Tsars on the outskirts of the city, which were restored by the Soviet government at enormous cost after the Second World War.
  - St Petersburg is also convenient for excursions to the well-preserved medieval city of Novgorod and the island-monasteries in Lakes Ladoga and Onega.
- **Moscow** is a much older city than St Petersburg, and is now a sprawling metropolis of 9 million people. The historic nucleus is the Kremlin – the walled inner city of the Tsars, and later the seat of power of the rulers of the USSR and the Russian Federation. It is adjoined by Red Square and Russia's most familiar building – St Basil's Cathedral, with its distinctive onion-shaped domes. Under Stalin, the city

acquired its Metro system – with ornately decorated stations – and 'wedding-cake' skyscrapers, one of which accommodates the University of Moscow. After the fall of Communism, a dynamic mayor embellished the capital with some impressive new projects, including the reconstructed Cathedral of Christ the Saviour – symbolic of the revival of the Russian Orthodox Church after 70 years of official atheism. Other attractions include:

- the Bolshoi Theatre, world famous for its touring ballet company
- the Moscow State Circus with some 16 000 performers
- the Pushkin and Tretyakov art collections
- the Exhibition of Economic Achievements, showcasing technology
- the Izmaylovo market where the tourist can buy antique samovars, icons and Soviet memorabilia.

Moscow also has one of the world's largest hotels – the Rossiya – and conference centres – the Palace of Congresses in the Kremlin. The international airport at Sheremetyevo was expanded for the 1980 Olympics but has since acquired an unenviable reputation among foreign business travellers for bureaucratic delays and indifferent service, problems to be addressed by a redevelopment programme.

Moscow is a good base for excursions to the following places of interest in **central Russia**:

- the 'Golden Ring' of historic towns to the north-east of the capital, including Rostov the Great, Vladimir, Sergiev Posad and Suzdal; these have preserved much of the Old Russia of wooden churches, fortified *kremlins*, colourful Byzantine-style monasteries, traditional craft industries and *troika* rides during the winter months.
- the country houses of Tchaikovsky at Klin, and Tolstoy at Yasnaya Polyana for lovers of Russian music and literature.
- Star City, the centre of Russia's space programme.

The other tourist attractions of Russia are widely scattered, although the river Volga provides a major tourist route linking a number of important centres, including:

- Kazan, which is not only the capital of the largely Muslim Tatar republic, but also one of the holy cities of the Russian Orthodox Church
- Ulyanovsk, famous as the birthplace of Lenin
- Volgograd (formerly Stalingrad), scene of one of the epic battles of the Second World War.

In **northern Russia**, Archangel is the base for visiting the island monasteries of Solovetsky in the White Sea. Murmansk, despite its location well to the north of the Arctic Circle, is one of Russia's few ice-free ports and a 'boom town', thanks to the natural gas fields of the Barents Sea. Environmentalists are concerned at the threat to the marine life and the international fishing industry.

In the extreme west the Russian enclave of **Kaliningrad**, faced with the decline of its military importance, hopes to become a trading gateway to the EU, once the problem of transit through Lithuania has been resolved. It is also exploiting its German heritage for tourism (until 1945 the city of Kaliningrad, then known as Königsberg, was part of East Prussia).

Russia's **Black Sea coast** has long been a major holiday destination thanks to its agreeable climate. In the Soviet era this formed part of a much more extensive 'Russian Riviera' that included the Crimea and part of Georgia. In the 1980s Sochi alone attracted 6 million tourists from all over the USSR to its beaches. Russia's principal Black Sea resort is now repositioning itself as a destination for Western holidaymakers.

In the **northern Caucasus** a number of skiing and mountain climbing centres have developed alongside spas dating from the late nineteenth century. From the viewpoint of international tourism these are uncomfortably close to the republic of Chechnya, one of the world's major trouble spots.

Siberia comprises the vast expanse of the Russian Federation lying to the east of the Urals. Since the seventeenth century Russians have regarded the territory with its wealth of furs and minerals as a land of opportunity, but this has been overshadowed by a fearsome reputation as a place of exile for dissidents. Since the early 1990s Siberia has been open to Western business enterprise and tourism, although for reasons of climate and accessibility most of the development has taken place in the south, based on the cities linked by the Trans-Siberian Railway. There are now opportunities for special interest tourism undreamed of in the old Soviet Union, including:

- whitewater rafting and ecotourism in the Altai Mountains, an area of unspoiled wilderness bordering Kazakhstan and Mongolia
- visits to the sites of the former *gulags*, the notorious labour camps of the Stalin era, where untold millions of political prisoners died as a result of the appalling conditions
- summer cruises on the great rivers – the Ob, Yenisei and Lena – that flow northwards for 4000 kilometres to the Arctic Ocean.

Two of Siberia's natural attractions deserve special mention because of their unique character:

- **Lake Baikal**, which is the world's biggest natural reservoir of fresh water, due to its extent, purity and immense depth (over 1700 metres). The lake also supports a remarkable variety of species, making it a fascinating area for ecotourists. As early as 1916 Russia's first nature reserve was established here, and in the 1960s it was the birthplace of the country's fledgling environmentalist movement. This came about as a consequence of industrial development, and Baikal's ecology continues to be threatened by effluent from pulp mills, fertilizers and acid rain.
- **Kamchatka**, despite its raw, foggy climate and poor communications, has considerable ecotourism potential, with the ending of Cold War travel prohibitions, as it is geographically close to Alaska on the other side of the Bering Sea. The peninsula contains no less than 33 active volcanoes and a large number of geysers and hot springs, and is also known for its salmon fisheries and abundant wildlife.

The cities of Siberia are of less interest to tourists, except for those that have preserved the traditional wooden buildings of the pre-Soviet era, such as Tobolsk and Irkutsk. Others worth mentioning include:

- Ekaterinburg in the Urals is visited mainly because it was here that the last of the Romanov Tsars, Nicholas II, and his family were murdered in 1918
- Novosibirsk with its modern industries and universities is the business capital of Siberia, while the scientific community of Academgorok nearby is a centre for space research.

The mining communities of northern Siberia face an uncertain future as the government in Moscow can no longer afford to heavily subsidize transport and other public services. On the other hand the non-Russian indigenous peoples can continue an age-old way of life that is better adapted to the rigorous climate, and some, like the Yakuts, may enjoy a cultural renaissance as a result of tourism.

The Russian **Far East** region adjoining China and North Korea has benefited from the free market economy. This includes the naval port of Vladivostok and the island of Sakhalin which are free enterprise zones open to foreign, mainly Japanese, investment. However, this has a downside in that the region's monsoon forests and unique wildlife – including the rare Siberian tiger – are under threat from illegal hunting and the logging industry, while ecotourism is as yet undeveloped.

With the Cold War a distant memory, the **Russian Arctic,** Russia's sector of the Arctic Ocean, is now opening up to the Western market for ecotourism. Only a small number of locations feature on Arctic cruise itineraries, such as the bird colonies of Franz Josef Land, and access to these is highly dependent on the extent of pack ice and fog. At the present time Russia's strategic Northern Sea Route is navigable only with a fleet of icebreakers during the brief shipping season. Global warming would shorten the sailing time from Europe to the Far East by a week, dramatically increasing the route's commercial viability, but also posing a serious threat to Arctic ecosystems.

The other republics of the CIS

The western republics

Ukraine, Belarus and Moldova continue to have close business ties to Russia. Progress toward a market economy has been slow, while unemployment and poverty are major problems with the decline of state-run industries.

Ukraine

The Ukraine is better known for its agricultural and industrial resources than for tourism. Winters are less severe than in Russia, with snow lying an average of 80 days in Kiev. This attractive capital on the river Dnieper was historically the nucleus of the first Russian state before its destruction by the Mongol invasions in the thirteenth century. The surviving medieval heritage includes the Caves Monastery and the Cathedral of Saint Vladimir. The western Ukraine formed part of the Austro-Hungarian Empire prior to 1918, and Lvov, its principal city, has many Baroque buildings as reminders of that heritage. The principal focus of tourism is the southern part of the Crimea Peninsula, where the warm climate and beautiful coastal scenery – in contrast to the uniformity of the Ukrainian steppes – made it a favourite of the Russian nobility before the 1917 Revolution. Under Communism resorts such as Yalta were made available to all Soviet citizens, and following the collapse of the Soviet Union, to foreign tourists with hard currency to spend. The battlefields of the Crimean War (1854–56), near the fortress of Sevastopol, provide a secondary attraction for British and French visitors. Further to the west, the elegant port city and resort of Odessa features prominently on Black Sea cruise itineraries.

Belarus

Belarus exemplifies the problems faced by the former Soviet republics in promoting a tourist image and identifying a unique selling proposition (USP). At first sight the resource base is not particularly promising; the country has been overshadowed by Poland and Russia and repeatedly invaded throughout its history. On the other hand it can offer the largest remaining area of the unmodified mixed forest that once covered most of Europe, interspersed with marshes and peat bogs. There is potential here for ecotourism as well as hunting and fishing trips as currency earners. The forest also produces the raw materials for the traditional craft industries that have largely disappeared elsewhere.

As for the cities, Brest and Minsk lie on the main route from the West to Moscow, and although transit tourism is important, there is little to persuade visitors to stay for longer periods.

Moldova

Moldova shares much of the culture and history of neighbouring Romania, although there is a large Russian minority with separatist ambitions. This small country has the advantage of a warm, sunny climate that favours large-scale wine production. As is the case with other cities of the former USSR, theatre companies from the capital, Chisinau, are touring the West to earn much-needed foreign exchange and perhaps gain publicity for the country's cultural attractions.

Transcaucasia

The three countries to the south of the natural barrier formed by the Caucasus Mountains have more in common with the Mediterranean region or the Middle East than with Russia. They have great tourism potential – a favourable climate, spectacular scenery, a rich cultural heritage going back to ancient times, and peoples with a tradition of hospitality and business enterprise. Yet the prospects for tourism have been blighted since the late 1980s by inter-communal violence, for example the war between Armenia and Azerbaijan over the enclave of Nagorno-Karabagh, and the separatist movements in Georgia. The failure to resolve these disputes by peaceful means is an obstacle not only to regional cooperation in tourism promotion but also to the exploitation of the oil resources of the Caspian Basin and the development of trade links with the West.

Georgia

We can best describe the situation of tourism in Georgia by looking at some of its component regions, including its two autonomous republics:

- **Abkhazia** in the north-west used to attract millions of Russians to the Black Sea resorts of Sukhumi, Gagra and Pitsunda. In 1991/2 the tourism industry here was devastated by the civil war between the central government in Tblisi and Abkhazian separatists. This breakaway state is not recognized by the international community and tourism has not recovered.
- **Adzharia** in the south-west has fewer beaches but offers lush subtropical landscapes featuring tea plantations and lemon orchards. Batumi, the capital of the autonomous republic, is a port of call for cruise ships and a base for excursions to other parts of Georgia. In 2004 tensions rose with a new reformist government in Tblisi, and this may well have repercussions for trade and tourism.

The **High Caucasus** includes the skiing and trekking resort of Gaudari, but further development in the mountains is hindered by poor communications and ethnic unrest in the South Ossetia region.

Tblisi and **Kutaisi** are the main tourist centres in Georgia. This part of the country is noted for its wines and a strong culinary tradition (in contrast to the mediocre catering which is characteristic of most of the former USSR).

Armenia

Tourism in Armenia has been overshadowed by the effects of the 1988 earthquake, the country's landlocked situation with two hostile neighbours, and historical memories of the 1915 genocide of a million Armenians. The snow-capped peak of Ararat is a holy mountain and national symbol for Armenians, dominating the horizon in the capital, Erevan, yet it is virtually inaccessible as it lies across the border in Turkey. The economy is dependent on remittances from the millions of ethnic Armenians living in the USA, Canada, France and Russia, who also account for the majority of the 30 000 or so international tourist arrivals. Armenia can claim to be the world's oldest Christian nation, and hoped to boost tourism by staging celebrations for the 1700th anniversary in 2003. In fact the country's main attractions are the ancient churches and monasteries in a spectacular lake and mountain setting. Armenia's physical isolation as a high plateau separated by mountain barriers from its neighbours is reinforced by border tensions and the lack of rail, road and even air links with Azerbaijan and Turkey.

Azerbaijan

Azerbaijan has immense oil resources and for this reason it has attracted a much greater amount of foreign investment than Armenia and Georgia combined. A good deal of this money has gone into hotel building in the capital, Baku for a new wave of business tourists. This is a predominantly Muslim nation, with religious and language ties to Iran and Turkey respectively. Some of the oil wealth is being used to conserve the rich cultural heritage and create a system of national parks that will eventually cover 10 per cent of the national territory. Although Baku has been an oil boom town – in the early years of the twentieth century – much remains from earlier periods, and the well-preserved historic quarter has a strong Middle Eastern ambience with its minarets and bazaars. Azerbaijan has considerable biodiversity from mountain and desert landscapes in the west to the subtropical coastlands along the Caspian Sea in the east, while ecotourism has an important role to play in stemming the depopulation of small rural communities.

The Central Asian republics

Most of Central Asia east of the Caspian Sea consists of desert and steppe, fringed by mountains to the south and east. Russian rule did not begin until the late nineteenth century, and was imposed on civilizations that had developed over thousands of years. The Muslim religion and heritage are dominant throughout the region, and the Russian influence is relatively slight, except in Kazakhstan and the modern cities of Tashkent and Almaty, which were massively industrialized during the Soviet era. The Soviet authorities were responsible for most of the environmental problems in the region. The best-known example is the shrinkage of the Aral Sea, which was brought about by vast irrigation projects for cotton cultivation in the desert. This has resulted in a deterioration of the local climate, with salt and sand-laden winds blowing in from the dried-up lake bed. The effect of 9/11 and the war in Afghanistan in 2001 has been to align the Central Asian republics with the USA, to counter the threat of Muslim fundamentalism to their secular, authoritarian regimes.

There are important differences between the individual republics and these are reflected in the extent of tourism development:

- **Uzbekistan** offers the richest heritage in the region, and has a well-developed tourism industry, but one that still discourages independent travel. Its capital, Tashkent, is the major air hub of Central Asia and an important conference venue. However, tourism is mainly concentrated in the oasis cities of Khiva, Samarkand and Bokhara, which served as staging points on the 'Silk Road' – the ancient overland trade route linking the Mediterranean and China via Persia. Of these:
  - ○ Samarkand is the best known as it boasts one of the world's most striking Islamic monuments – the Registan, resplendently decorated in blue tiles and gold leaf
  - ○ Khiva is a perfectly preserved 'museum-city'
  - ○ Bokhara is a hive of activity, with bazaars similar to those of the Middle East.
- **Kazakhstan** is a vast expanse of steppe and desert, except where it includes parts of the Tian Shan and Altai mountain ranges. Tourism possibilities include whitewater rafting on the river Ili and trekking in the mountains. The former capital Almaty (Alma-Ata) is the second largest city of Central Asia, with direct air links to Western Europe. The nearby resort of Medeo is an important centre for skiing and ice skating. **Baikonur** is a major centre of space research.
- **Kyrgystan** is dominated by the glaciated Tian Shan mountains, and has as its main attraction the lake of Issik Kul, which is a destination for health tourism.
- **Tajikistan** is the smallest, the most mountainous, and throughout the 1990s the most politically unstable of the Central Asian republics, and this has held back the development of its tourism industry.
- **Turkmenistan** includes some of the hottest and driest locations in Central Asia. The country is noted for the traditional carpet weaving industry based in Ashqabad and Merv. In ancient times, Nissa was the power base of the Parthians, who were the Romans' great rivals for control of the Middle East. With vast reserves of natural gas at its disposal, the present autocratic regime has seen little need to encourage leisure tourism.

Summary

A long period of state control over tourism, amounting to 40 years in Eastern Europe and 70 years in the former Soviet Union, have left a legacy which differentiates these countries strongly from those of Western Europe. Since 1989 this has been followed by a strong liberalizing trend, characterized by economic restructuring, foreign investment, privatization and the encouragement of local initiative. Western involvement in the development of tourism has greatly increased. Entry, exit and currency restrictions were severe under the Communist regimes but have eased with their demise. The former regimes encouraged social tourism linked to health and education, but as incomes rise with the successful transition to a market economy, Western-style domestic tourism will increase in significance. Outbound tourism is showing more rapid growth as the region's economy improves. Entry to the European Union by a number of countries in the region will also be a significant boost to tourism.

The removal of Communism has improved the image of the region in Western eyes. This needs to be reinforced by each country emphasizing its individual attractions.

The differences between countries were previously concealed by the grey uniformity of Communism and are now much more evident. There is increasing scope for innovation in tourism products and niche marketing. Some countries, notably the Czech Republic, have made much more progress than others.

Tourism planning is widespread across the region but there is a danger that the encouragement of mass tourism might well result in the region becoming a cheap playground for West Europeans. This is particularly true of Romania and Bulgaria, which have long depended on a captive regional market that is now free to travel to other 'sunlust' destinations. Environmental problems are already widespread, and ecotourism is in its infancy. Transport systems need to be improved, to cope with rising car ownership levels and the expectations of Western tourists. Future growth in tourism could also be severely constrained by these negative factors:

- Political instability and ethnic strife
- Rising crime levels, as economic growth fails to meet people's expectations
- Poor standards of service, and mediocre products – once the novelty of visiting a previously 'forbidden' destination has faded.

Chapter 19

The tourism geography of The Middle East

Learning Objectives

After reading this chapter, you should be able to:

- Describe the major physical features and climates of the Middle East and understand their importance for tourism.
- Account for the fact that, due to political unrest, the region's tourism potential is largely unfulfilled despite its closeness to the tourist generating markets of Northern Europe.
- Appreciate the continuing importance of religion in the everyday culture of the region, and the impact of religious fundamentalism and sectarianism on the political stability of many of these countries and the safety of foreign tourists.
- Appreciate that inbound tourism to the region encompasses beach holidays, cultural tourism and business travel.
- Recognize that the Middle East is an important generator of international tourism.
- Identify the major features of tourism infrastructure in the region.
- Demonstrate a knowledge of the tourist regions, resorts, business centres and tourist attractions of the Middle East.

Introduction

For the purposes of this book, our definition of the Middle East differs from that of the World Tourism Organization by including Turkey and Iran, and excluding Libya. It comprises the countries along the eastern seaboard of the Mediterranean, sometimes known as the 'Near East' or Levant, as well as the other countries of south-west Asia. Vast petroleum resources and the Arab–Israeli conflict have brought the Middle East under the international spotlight since the Second World War, culminating in the Gulf War of 1990–1991 and its sequel the Iraq War in 2003. However, these are but recent episodes in a history of trade, migration and conquest that goes back at least to the third millennium BC. The Middle East is strategically located at the crossroads of trade routes linking the Mediterranean to the Indian Ocean and the Far East – and at the interface of three continents – Europe, Asia and Africa. The component countries share many physical and cultural features. Similarities in religion, language, architecture, food specialities and other aspects of lifestyle, plus a shared historical experience, link almost all of the countries in the region, together with those of North Africa.

The setting for tourism

Cultural features

Significant cultural similarities are that:

- All but three of the countries in the region (Israel, Iran and Turkey) are Arabic-speaking.
- All of these countries (except for Iran) at one time formed part of the Ottoman Empire based in Constantinople (now Istanbul). During much of the twentieth century, Britain exercised various forms of control over most of the countries in the region while France was active in Syria and Lebanon. Events in the new millennium have confirmed the USA as the dominant power in the Middle East.
- The Middle East is predominantly Muslim in religion, except for Israel and Lebanon. However the Muslim world is as divided on sectarian lines as Christendom, with the Sunni branch of Islam dominant in most Arab countries while the adherents of Shia are more numerous in Iraq and Iran.
- There are substantial ethnic as well as religious minorities in most countries of the region (Iraq is a classic example), while the Kurds – 'a nation without a state' – are divided between Turkey, Iraq, Iran and Syria.

Western perceptions of Islam have been strongly influenced on the one hand by historical memories of the Crusades and the threat posed to Europe by the Ottoman Empire, and on the other by highly romanticized images of the region created by European writers and artists in the nineteenth century. More recently, unfavourable publicity in the Western media has been a reaction to the growth of Muslim fundamentalism. Although it is true to say that, in this secular age, religion plays a greater role in everyday life in Muslim countries than in most other parts of the world, the influence of Islam does in fact vary greatly in strength from country to country. Only a few governments, for example, impose *sharia law* based on the Koran, rather than Western legal systems. Attitudes towards the status of women and towards foreign tourists also range from the strict (for example, Saudi Arabia) to the relatively liberal (Jordan, Lebanon and Turkey). We should take into account the following aspects of Islam as they influence the tourist experience and business practice:

- The obligation of Muslims to pray five times a day with special emphasis on Friday (the Muslim Sabbath). The mosque with its distinctive minaret forms a dominant feature in the skyline, but as figurative art is discouraged by the Koran, the decorative features of traditional architecture tend to be limited to abstract patterns or inscriptions in Arabic.

- The requirement to fast between sunrise and sunset during the month of Ramadan, the fifth month of the Muslim year. As this is based on a lunar calendar the timing of Ramadan varies from year to year.
- At least once in a lifetime, Muslims should make the pilgrimage or *haj* to the holy city of Mecca, the birthplace of the prophet Muhammad. The haj takes place during the twelfth month of the Muslim year, resulting in a mass movement of people that is concentrated both in time and space. The pilgrim routes extending to all parts of the Muslim world became important for trade, and were therefore well supplied with inns (known as *khans, fonduks* or *caravanserais*). Some of these traditional types of accommodation still survive (although the camel caravan has long since been replaced by motorized transport).

Another important cultural feature of the region is the contrast between the cities and the countryside, where settled and nomadic lifestyles appear to have changed little since biblical times. Even in the cities, the older districts have a seemingly chaotic street pattern while the colourful *souks* and bazaars retain many traditional features. These are essentially covered markets with whole sections devoted exclusively to a particular trade or type of merchandise. Traditional domestic architecture is characterized by rooms opening off an enclosed courtyard, allowing privacy for the extended family and protection from the sun. The major cities have well laid-out, modern districts similar to those of Europe – Tel Aviv is a good example here – very different in character from the adjoining Arab town of Jaffa with its maze of twisting, narrow streets.

Physical features

There is no clear physical break (the Suez Canal and Red Sea hardly count) and, as seen above, no distinct cultural boundary between Africa and Asia. Most of the Middle East region forms part of the arid climate zone, and irrigation is essential. Agriculturally, productive land is restricted to a few areas that in turn have attracted the great majority of the population, which is concentrated in these areas at densities similar to or exceeding those of Western Europe. They comprise:

- the coastal plains adjoining the Mediterranean, Aegean, Black and Caspian Seas, which enjoy relatively good rainfall
- a narrow strip along the river Nile in Egypt
- the alluvial plains of the rivers Tigris and Euphrates, which link up with the Mediterranean coastal plain in Syria to form the so-called 'Fertile Crescent'.

To the east of the coastal strip, mountain ranges and high plateaux prevent rain-bearing winds from penetrating further into the interior. Often the dividing line between the desert 'wilderness' and the cultivated area is very distinct. Not surprisingly, water supply and distribution is a major problem in the Middle East, and this precious resource is the subject of local and even international disputes.

Most of the region is characterized by extremes of heat in summer, and even the Mediterranean coast can be oppressive. In winter, the weather is usually mild or pleasantly warm, with the important exception of some mountain areas that experience heavy snowfalls. Conditions are particularly severe in Kurdistan, where temperatures are comparable to those of Russia. Cold, overcast weather is not uncommon – even as far south as Amman and Jerusalem, which are situated at quite high altitudes – in contrast to the subtropical warmth and sunshine of the Red Sea coast.

Tourism demand and supply

Considering its location and resources, the Middle East region accounts for a relatively small share of world tourism – some 3 per cent of arrivals. The countries of the Middle East are close enough to the inclusive tour markets of north-west Europe to have developed a tourism industry based on sun, sea and sand. This is a logical extension of the coastal resort developments of Mediterranean Europe, facilitated by improvements in air transport. However, the response to this opportunity has been uneven. Most countries with the potential to enter the market have only done so since the 1980s – Turkey is a notable example. Long before the expansion of mass tourism, Israel and Egypt had based their tourism industries on the attractions of the Holy Land and the relics of ancient civilizations. More recently, the oil-based prosperity of Saudi Arabia and the Gulf States has attracted a large business travel market. There is also a considerable volume of travel between countries in the region, involving business tourism, returning migrant workers visiting relatives, pilgrimages and health tourism.

Contrary to popular belief in the West, only some of the countries in the Middle East have become affluent on oil resources, so that foreign exchange earnings from tourism are needed to even out regional imbalances. The population, as in most developing countries, contains a high percentage of young people and tourism is seen as a means of providing much-needed employment. In fact, since the 1980s economic development has not kept pace with population growth, with a consequent decline in living standards. With only modest progress in education, telecommunications and access to information technology, most countries in the region are ill-equipped to meet the challenge of globalization. Nevertheless foreign investors as well as national governments have provided much of the infrastructure needed for international tourism, including good roads, a large number of airports of international standard, and hotel development in the major cities and coastal resorts. You would expect external transport links to be efficient as the region is a crossroads between Europe, Africa and Asia and its airports are important as staging points for business on the long-haul routes between Western Europe and the East Asia–Pacific region. Although most tourists visiting the Middle East arrive by air, movements within the region are predominantly by road. The main exception is the Arabian Peninsula, due to the vast distances and difficult terrain. Throughout the Middle East, rail networks are poorly developed, and there are few international services. Given the abundance of cheap oil, an ever-growing demand for car ownership, even in the poorer countries, and a lack of environmental awareness, this situation is not likely to change.

Tourism resources of the Middle East

The Middle East has many strengths as a destination region, with opportunities for further development, but these are constrained by a number of serious problems. We can summarize the tourism resources of the region as:

- A wealth of cultural attractions, due to the fact that this region gave rise to the world's earliest civilizations and three major world religions – Judaism, Christianity, and Islam. Successive invaders, including the Greeks and Romans in ancient times, followed by Crusaders from western Europe defending the pilgrim routes to the Holy Land, have all left their mark. Some of the best known of these sites can be visited on a Mediterranean cruise. However, overland cultural tours, taking in several countries, have not developed to the same extent as in Europe, due to the political situation in the region.
- A generally favourable climate for beach tourism, although in some countries this is restricted by cultural and religious attitudes. A growing number of tourists now visit the region purely for the sake of recreation and relaxation. Resorts have developed to meet their needs, but with the exceptions of Turkey, Israel and Dubai, facilities are generally not to the same standard as those of the western Mediterranean.
- There are opportunities for winter sports in some of the mountain ranges of the region. At present, resorts have developed to meet the needs of the small domestic market and are generally not well equipped by international standards. Many mountain areas, such are Kurdistan, are relatively inaccessible.
- There is also scope for adventure holidays in the more accessible mountain and desert areas. Ecotourism has made little progress, except in Israel and Jordan.

The main threats to tourism in the region are twofold:

- First, the political situation has been a major factor in preventing the region realizing its tourism potential. Since the Oslo initiatives in 1994, tourism has ebbed and flowed to the region depending upon the prospects for peace. The region is still torn by internal unrest – often provoked by religious fundamentalism – and, since 2001, by the war on terrorism, culminating in the Iraq War in 2003. Terrorism by groups such as Hamas in the Israeli-occupied territories and the PKK (Kurdistan Workers Party) in south-east Turkey has resulted in much negative publicity. Most governments in the region have a poor or indifferent record on human rights. In consequence, tourism has suffered, despite the region's accessibility and its wealth of natural and man-made attractions. The Gulf War of 1990/91, for example, not only disrupted tourism throughout the Middle East, but disturbed world tourism flows, although the actual hostilities were highly localized.
- Second, the unique appeal of the region lies in its antiquities and cultural sites. These need careful management and have a limited capacity to receive visitors. This implies that there is a limit to the numbers of tourists that the region can absorb if these attractions are to remain available for future generations. The heritage is also under threat from the widespread trafficking in artefacts from archaeological sites, and from industrialization, such as dam building projects on the upper Euphrates.

Egypt

In many ways, Egypt typifies the contrasts found in the Middle East. It is a meeting place of East and West; it is mysterious and yet highly accessible. Cairo is the hub of the air routes between Europe, Asia and Africa, while the Suez Canal is one of the world's most important shipping routes. Egypt is the most populous of the Arab countries and a cultural centre for the Arabic-speaking world. Its people are the inheritors of an ancient civilization that flourished many centuries before the rise of Islam, and in many respects, the way of life of the *fellahin* (peasant farmers) along the Nile has changed little since the time of the Pharaohs. The Nile is also a reminder that Egypt has strong connections with sub-Saharan Africa to the south.

The bulk of Egypt's territory is desert, but we should make a distinction between the dune-covered expanses of the Western Desert extending into Libya, and the rugged scenery of the Eastern Desert and Sinai Peninsula. In between, lies the narrow green ribbon of cultivated land along the Nile, widening in the north as the Nile Delta. Just as in ancient times, Egypt is 'the gift of the Nile', highly dependent on the river's vagaries. Although it is the most highly industrialized of the Arab countries, Egypt is not self-sufficient in petroleum and its economy cannot provide enough jobs for a population exceeding 70 million. In this context, the contribution made by tourism is crucial as it filters down to the lowest levels of society and employs 12 per cent of the workforce. The government recognizes this and has had a long involvement in tourism. The first formal tourist authority was established in 1935, and the present Ministry of Tourism dates from 1967. In addition, the Supreme Council for Tourism, chaired by the Prime Minister, acts to coordinate public sector actions in tourism. The aim of the Ministry is to upgrade tourism infrastructure, improve the image of Egypt and diversify to include new products such as golf tourism.

Tourism demand and supply

Travellers from the West have visited the Pyramids at least since Roman times, although modern tourism did not begin until the late nineteenth century. To a large extent, this was due to the British travel company Thomas Cook, who inaugurated steamship services on the Nile, luxury river cruises and the development of Luxor as a winter resort. Since the 1960s tourists from other Arab countries, visiting primarily for recreational rather than cultural reasons, have formed a growing share of the Egyptian market. Arab visitors tend to stay during the summer months, when the Mediterranean coast around Alexandria is cool by comparison with the stifling heat of the Arabian Peninsula. Most Western sightseers arrive during the winter season, which is pleasantly warm and much drier than other Mediterranean destinations.

Egypt is the dominant destination for international tourists in the Middle East. In the 1950s there were fewer visitors but they stayed for an average of one month, and even in the 1980s, the main reason for visiting was to view the cultural sites. However, recreational tourism has become increasingly important and international arrivals rose steadily in the 1990s, despite the setbacks of terrorist attacks and the Gulf War, and approached 5 million by the early years of the twenty-first century, comprising both Western and Arab markets. Although there are few charter services, most tourists arrive by air in Cairo. Domestic tourism is also significant and this includes social tourism as well as travel by a relatively affluent middle class.

Most of Egypt's 5,000 hotel rooms are found in the capital or to a lesser extent, in Alexandria and Luxor. The government encourages investment in the accommodation stock by both Egyptian and foreign companies, and tourism is given priority at the highest levels of government. The Tourism Development Authority was set up to identify potential areas for growth. Egypt is therefore attempting to widen its resource base by encouraging conferences and special interest tourism. The objective is to tempt tourists away from the Nile Valley, where the tourism industry is competing with other economic sectors for scarce water, power and land resources. This is problematic as Ancient Egypt – notably the Pyramids and the Valley of the Kings – is the subject of worldwide interest, probably to a greater extent than any other bygone civilization.

To develop its full potential tourism in Egypt has to overcome a number of problems, not the least of which is the country's infrastructure, particularly overloaded water and power supplies and an inadequate road system. Environmental considerations are also important, especially along the Red Sea coast where there is concern for the ecology of the coral reefs. But perhaps the main problem is the uncertain political climate of the region, which causes severe fluctuations in tourist arrivals, especially from the USA. Although the government is pro-Western and was the first Arab state to normalize relations with Israel, Egypt suffers from acute social and economic tensions. This has contributed to the rise of fundamentalism among the poorer classes in society, which is causing concern for the future stability of the country and the future of its tourism industry.

Tourism resources

Most Western tourists stay firmly on the cultural circuit, the highlights of which are:

- the Pyramids of Giza just outside Cairo – the unique survivors of the 'Seven Wonders' of the ancient world
- the temples and other antiquities near Luxor, which is the main centre for touring Upper Egypt; these include the world-famous Valley of the Kings
- the temple at Abu Simbel near Aswan, which UNESCO campaigns saved from inundation by the Aswan High Dam project.

Although the very dry climate of the Nile Valley has ensured the survival of artefacts for over four thousand years, safeguarding the monuments from pollution for future generations is a matter of concern. Tourist pressure on the Pyramids has led the government to implement drastic conservation measures, including attempts to curb the activities of unauthorized guides and entrepreneurs. A popular way of visiting the sites in Upper Egypt is by a river cruise on the Nile, as an alternative to road transport or domestic air services from Cairo. In fact, Nile cruises have long been Egypt's best known tourism product.

The emphasis on the relics of the Pharaohs has obscured the fact that Egypt has a more recent heritage and many other attractions. This is particularly true of Cairo, although the congestion in this city of over 15 million people can be a traumatic experience. In addition to early Islamic buildings such as the Citadel of Saladin, there are Coptic churches, a reminder that this early form of Christianity was flourishing in Egypt centuries before Islam. But for most tourists, the main attraction is shopping in the bazaars for an assortment of souvenirs.

Other tourism resources include the following:

- The Fayyum oasis, 100 kilometres to the west of the Nile Valley is culturally interesting and a good deal less hectic than Cairo. A number of hotels have been built in this area.
- Sailing in a traditional *felucca* on the Nile offers a more authentic experience of rural Egypt than a luxury cruise in a 'floating hotel'.
- Trekking in the Sinai Desert includes a visit to St Catherine's Monastery with its biblical associations.

The greatest potential for attracting a wider market lies in the development of Egypt's coastal resorts where a year-round season is possible, and there are good facilities for water sports.

- **The Mediterranean coast** west of Alexandria has long attracted well-off domestic tourists. Egypt's second city is a cosmopolitan seaport with Greek and French cultural influences, but much of its former elegance faded after the 1952 revolution which overthrew the monarchy and brought Nasser to power. Almost nothing remains of the ancient city of Roman times, although there are exciting proposals for the world's first 'marine archaeological park' in the harbour, centring on the long-lost palace of Cleopatra.
- **The Red Sea coast** has clear water and coral reefs that are a major attraction for divers. It is now an established holiday destination for Western tourists, and includes the resorts of Hurghada, Nuweiba and Sharm al Sheikh.

Israel

Israel has a significance out of all proportion to its size. Within an area equivalent to the US state of New Jersey, two nations have so far failed to find a formula for peaceful co-existence. And yet this strife-torn country can offer an almost unrivalled variety of scenery and climate, including the snows of Mount Hermon in the north, the sub-tropical fertility of Galilee and the heat and aridity of the Dead Sea, the lowest place on Earth.

People's perceptions of the country are largely coloured by their political or religious beliefs, for example:

- to Jews, a nation dispersed in exile since Roman times, Israel is their homeland. Jewish religious observance plays an important role in this otherwise secular state
- to Christians the world over Israel is largely synonymous with the Holy Land, containing many of the most significant places associated with the Bible
- to Muslims a number of these sites are also of great religious significance; many regard Israel as an intruder and are sympathetic to the cause of the Palestinian Arabs.

Since the founding of Israel in 1948, the Jewish state has been under siege from its Arab neighbours. Internal security is also threatened by the Palestinians in the occupied territories of the Gaza Strip and the West Bank (Cisjordan), which Israel

acquired aft[...] [O]slo agreement in 1994 laid the
foundation[...] [autono]my to Gaza and most of the West
Bank. However the [...] since 2001 has been a major set-
back to the peace process and tour[...] [developme]nt. The Palestinian Authority was
unable to restrain terrorist activity, while the Israeli government, faced with the
problem of absorbing large numbers of immigrants from the former USSR, had permitted the growth of Jewish settlements in the occupied territories. In response to
the threat from Palestinian *shaheeds* (suicide bombers), Israel has implemented a
security barrier around the West Bank. This, together with the existing military
checkpoints, has effectively fragmented Palestinian territory and disrupted the
tourism-based economy of Bethlehem and other Palestinian communities.

Demand for tourism

Despite these problems, Israel attracted over 2 million international tourists in the
Millennium year, although numbers decreased significantly due to subsequent
events and the industry is currently in crisis. The USA, which has a special relationship with Israel, is a major generator of demand. European countries, including
Britain, have become important markets since the liberalization of charter flights in
1976. The Israeli Ministry of Tourism endeavours to develop new markets, such as
Japan, in close cooperation with the national carrier El Al – indeed the majority of
arrivals are by air. There is also a health spa authority to coordinate this important
sector of tourism, particularly foreign visitors seeking treatment for psoriasis. As
regards outbound tourism, Israelis are avid travellers, with over 3 million trips in
the early years of the twenty-first century, leaving a deficit on the international
travel account. However, they are prevented from visiting most countries in the
Middle East, with the exceptions of Egypt, Jordan and Turkey. Security problems at
home have favoured the growth of outbound travel at the expense of domestic trips,
although this suffered a setback as a result of the Mombasa bombing in 2002.
Surprisingly, given its small population, Israel is well represented in the tourist
arrivals for many long-haul destinations.

Tourism resources

Israel can offer a great variety of tourist products including:

- summer holiday resorts along the Mediterranean coast at Herzliya and Netanya
  north of Tel Aviv, and at Ashkelon to the south
- Eilat, Israel's outlet to the Red Sea, a popular winter sun destination, with facilities for underwater photography, diving and water skiing
- spa tourism around picturesque Lake Kinneret (better known as the Sea of
  Galilee), and in a more spectacular setting on the shores of the Dead Sea, utilizing
  the unique resource provided by the mineral-rich lake and its microclimate
- working holidays on a *kibbutz*, the uniquely Israeli experiment in communal living –
  however, some *kibbutzim* have departed from their socialist ideals by providing
  guest house accommodation to paying tourists.
- adventure holidays, including desert trekking
- cultural tourism based on the large number of archaeological sites, many of which
  are mentioned in the Bible; Galilee and Jerusalem attract large numbers of
  Christian pilgrims, with a peak in demand during the Easter holidays, while

Herod the Great's hilltop fortress at Masada is a shrine to the Jewish struggle for freedom
- the attraction of seeing a nation in the making, composed of Jewish immigrants from all over the world; Israel's achievements in making the Negev Desert productive are particularly interesting.

Business travel gravitates to the three major cities:

- **Tel Aviv** is the business and financial centre of the country. The city is very much a creation of the twentieth century, with a good deal of nightlife.
- **Haifa** is Israel's largest seaport, catering for tourists arriving by ferry from Greece, Cyprus and Turkey as well as cruise passengers.
- **Jerusalem**, the capital of ancient Judea and since 1967, of the modern state of Israel, is an important venue for conferences. It is a world class tourist attraction as the meeting place for three major religions, and also a potential flashpoint for disputes involving Christian, Jewish and Muslim fundamentalists. Some allege that the Israeli authorities have insensitively handled hotel expansion in the old Arab quarter of East Jerusalem. Major points of interest for the visitor include:
  - Yad Vashem – Israel's major memorial to the Jewish Holocaust of the Second World War
  - the sites associated with Christ's Passion, including the Mount of Olives, the pilgrim route known as the Via Dolorosa and the Church of the Holy Sepulchre
  - the Temple Mount, an area sacred to Christians, Jews and Muslims alike. The Al Aqsa Mosque is the holiest site in Islam after Mecca and Medina. The Western Wall is all that remains of the Jewish Temple after its destruction by the Romans in 70 AD
  - the nearby Arab town of Bethlehem is a major centre for Christian pilgrims, attracted to the Church of the Nativity.

Jordan

Without significant oil resources and consisting largely of semi-arid plateaux and desert, Jordan is a small and relatively poor Arab country. The population includes two very different communities – the Palestinian refugees, mainly concentrated in the capital Amman, and the Bedouin tribes of the desert. However, the country has remained politically stable thanks to the statesmanship of King Hussein, who ruled from 1953 to 1999.

Tourism plays an important role in the economy, with around one million international arrivals annually. However, over-reliance on the attractions of East Jerusalem, Bethlehem and Jericho meant that most of Jordan's appeal, as well as its hotel stock, were lost when Israel occupied those territories (the West Bank) in 1967. Jordan had then to redevelop tourism east of the river Jordan, on a less promising resource base. The major attractions now include:

- Petra – an ancient city in a unique setting, concealed in a deep valley; this accounts for a substantial part of Jordan's tourism revenue, and has encouraged hotel development in the area
- the desert scenery of Wadi Rum, where ecotourism is being developed

- the eastern shores of the Dead Sea, where spa tourism is being developed
- the Crusader castle at Kerak
- the well-preserved Roman city of Jerash with its annual festival
- the pilgrim sites on the east bank of the River Jordan
- the beaches and water sports of Aqaba on the Red Sea coast, which has been developed as a rival to Eilat.

Tourism has been restricted by the lack of infrastructure and good hotels, although the Middle East peace initiatives have encouraged hotel investment, particularly in Amman, Aqaba and by the Dead Sea. Most hotels are located in Amman although a network of formerly government-run 'rest houses' (now privatized) provides accommodation in the areas likely to be visited by tourists. The normalization of relations with Israel after 1994 enabled Jordan to benefit from the Millennium year tourist boom with the easing of restrictions on travel between the two countries. The Ministry of Tourism and Antiquities has encouraged sustainable tourism and community tourism projects as at the award-winning Taybeh-Zaman tourist village close to Petra, where visitors can see local craft skills in action and stay in traditional rural houses.

Syria

Unlike Jordan, the regime that has ruled Syria since 1971 has done little to encourage foreign investment or Western tourism, although since the Gulf War the country is no longer shunned by the international community as a 'pariah state'. Relations with the USA have improved, if not with Israel. Roughly the size of England and Wales, Syria comprises a large section of the Fertile Crescent, contrasting with the stony Syrian Desert in the south-east. Poor infrastructure, such as unreliable power supplies, is a major constraint on tourism development. Nevertheless the country has major tourism potential with international arrivals in the early years of the new millennium exceeding 3 million (although most of these are from Lebanon and Jordan). The economic potential of tourism is taken seriously by the government with a Ministry of Tourism and a 'High Council of Tourism' that has a coordinating role under the prime minister. Most of the limited development has taken place in the western part of the country, focusing on the historic cities of Aleppo and Damascus. There are beach resorts on the Mediterranean coast north of Lattakia as well as mountain resorts taking advantage of the cooler climate of the Anti-Lebanon, but these are visited almost exclusively by domestic tourists. Of greater appeal to Western sightseers is Syria's cultural heritage, represented by:

- the capital Damascus, reputedly the world's oldest city; it is famed for its association with St Paul and contains the Ommayad Mosque and numerous bazaars
- the ruins of the ancient trading city of Palmyra in the Syrian Desert
- the Krak des Chevaliers, the most spectacular of the castles built by the Crusaders.

Most of Syria's 15 000 hotel beds are geared to the business market, being concentrated in the major cities of Damascus, Aleppo and Lattakia. As yet, few tour groups from European countries visit Syria. Although Damascus airport is an important regional gateway, most visitors arrive overland from neighbouring Arab countries and their length of stay tends to be short. There seems little scope for expanding holiday tourism until the international situation in the Middle East improves.

Lebanon

Although Lebanon is a small mountainous country its people have been involved in overseas trade since at least the first millennium BC, when the Phoenicians from Tyre and Sidon dominated the Mediterranean sea routes, and Lebanese communities are now found all over the world. Lebanon is a classic example of a multi-cultural society peopled to a large extent by successive waves of refugees from other parts of the Middle East. Until 1975, when civil war broke out between the two main communities – the ruling Maronite Christians and the various Muslim groups, including Palestinian refugees, Beirut was not only the financial capital of a large part of the Arab world but also its main entertainment centre. Arab tourists came to Lebanon not only for relief from the intense summer heat of their own countries, but also to escape the prohibitions on gambling and nightclubs imposed by a strict interpretation of Islam. Since the end of the conflict in 1991 the economy has made a slow recovery and Beirut is no longer a divided city. European tour operators have added Lebanon to their stock of destinations, and MEA, the national airline, has staged a comeback, with a new airport to the south of the capital.

Aside from a revitalized Beirut, the country's tourist attractions include:

- Mount Lebanon, where a number of ski centres have developed only a short drive from the beach resorts of the coast. Both are mainly frequented by domestic tourists and visitors from other Arab countries such as Jordan and Saudi Arabia. Unfortunately the cedar forests which covered the mountains in biblical times have largely disappeared.
- The fertile Bekaa Valley to the east. This includes the ancient temples of Baalbek which provide an ideal setting for cultural events.

Accommodation in the Lebanon tends to be expensive, and tourism has been given little encouragement by the government, which is based on a complicated power-sharing agreement between the religious communities.

Turkey

Turkey is eager for EU membership but only 3 per cent of its territory – the region known as Eastern Thrace – is geographically part of Europe. The country is in many ways distinct from its Arab neighbours to the south, and it has affinities with both Europe and Asia, acting as a physical and cultural 'bridge' between East and West. It controls the Dardanelles and the Bosphorus, the strategic waterways linking the Aegean to the Black Sea. Turkey under the Ottoman Sultans dominated not only the Middle East but also most of North Africa, the eastern Mediterranean and the Balkan Peninsula. The heritage of the Ottoman Empire is a major part of the fascination the country holds for Western visitors. Turkish traditions, particularly in cuisine, craft industries such as carpet weaving and entertainment, help to give the country a clearly defined tourist image. Yet for many centuries prior to the arrival of the Turks from Central Asia, the region then known as Asia Minor was occupied by many earlier civilizations – those of Ancient Greece and Rome for example – and Turkey is extraordinarily rich in antiquities as a result.

The setting for tourism

Turkey is a large country by any standards, with the natural advantage of having an extensive, and for the most part, picturesque coastline along three seas – the Mediterranean, the Aegean and the Black Sea. The heartland of Turkey is less attractive, consisting of the semi-arid steppes of the Anatolian Plateau. This is separated from the fertile coastlands by a ring of mountain ranges. The climate is generally favourable for tourism, except in the mountainous north-east, which suffers from winters of almost Siberian intensity. The Black Sea coast receives a good deal of rain throughout the year, in contrast to the rest of the country.

Turkey also has the advantages of relative political stability, and an economy that is strong enough, despite rampant inflation, for its application for European Union membership to be taken seriously. This is due in no small measure to the reforms carried out by Kamal Ataturk after the abolition of the sultanate in 1923. He imposed Western institutions, the Roman alphabet and Western dress. As a result, the influence of Islam is less evident than elsewhere in the Middle East, particularly in the cities of western Turkey. However, as in other developing countries, the population is growing faster than job creation and the provision of public services. This explains the large number of Turks working in western Europe, and the growth of shantytowns (known as *gekekondu*) around Istanbul and Ankara to accommodate the vast numbers of immigrants from the rural areas.

Tourism demand and supply

Despite having much to offer the tourist, Turkey did not participate in the boom in Mediterranean beach tourism that characterized the 1970s because:

- it was expensive to reach
- the country was poorly promoted
- Turkey did not seek to enter the inclusive-tour market.

This situation changed when tourism was included in the government's Five Year Plans. Charter flights were permitted, and the country was 'discovered' by the major European tour operators. As a result, the numbers of visitors trebled during the 1980s but growth subsequently slowed as a result both of the Gulf War and also the adverse publicity about the poor standard of some accommodation in the Aegean holiday resorts of Bodrum and Kusadasi. In the early years of the twenty-first century Turkey attracted over 10 million international visitors. Germany is by far the most important generator of tourism for Turkey, followed by Russia, the Central Asian republics and the UK. Britain was a latecomer on the scene, but despite predictions to the contrary, Turkey's popularity with the British market as a value-for-money destination shows no sign of waning.

There is also a large and growing domestic market, but Turks prefer to stay with relatives rather than use the country's considerable stock of hotel and self-catering accommodation.

In the 1980s most visitors arrived by surface transport. However, change came in the 1990s, with the majority of visitors arriving by air, due to the fact that border crossings have been adversely affected by political turmoil in neighbouring countries, and new regional airports have been developed to serve the tourist areas. Istanbul, as the country's leading cultural and business centre, is the busiest gateway, while Ankara, despite being the capital since 1923, ranks far behind in terms of international traffic. Business and conference tourism is being encouraged by new convention centres in both Istanbul and Ankara. Western European holidaymakers, most of whom are on inclusive tours to the resorts of south-west Turkey, are much more likely to use the airports at Izmir, Bodrum, Dalaman and Antalya. Relatively few visitors arrive by sea, through ports such as Izmir, although these do attract substantial numbers of cruise passengers and day excursionists from the Greek Islands.

Holiday tourism is both highly seasonal and concentrated in a small part of the country, namely the south-west coastal strip. This concentration of tourism is largely the result of short-sighted planning in the 1980s when the Ministry of Tourism envisaged coastal development on a massive scale. A number of resorts in the area have already experienced most stages in the tourist area life cycle, from initial discovery by wealthy Turkish families, yachtsmen, and a few backpackers; through development by small specialist tour operators; to consolidation by large companies serving the mass market. In some resorts the environmental impact of tourism has been considerable, but elsewhere, as at Olu Deniz, famed for its beautiful beach and lagoon, development has been confined to the hills overlooking the coast. In a rare instance, development was halted altogether in the Dalyan Delta following protests by environmentalists. This shows that the Turkish government is willing to forego short-term profit in the cause of conservation, and to learn belatedly from the mistakes made by other Mediterranean destinations.

Tourism resources

South-west Turkey can be divided into the following holiday areas:

- **The Northern Aegean**, north of Izmir. This area caters mainly for domestic tourists.
- **The Southern Aegean**, between Izmir and Dalaman. The environmental and cultural impacts of mass tourism have been most evident in Marmaris, where overdevelopment and brash commercialism are rife, and at Gumbet on the Bodrum Peninsula, now easily accessible from the new airport. Although a lively resort, Bodrum itself has preserved more of its Turkish ambience, due largely to its superb setting on a bay dominated by a Crusader castle.
- **The Turquoise Coast** or 'Turkish Riviera' around the Gulf of Antalya is backed by the pine-covered Lycian and Taurus mountain ranges. The resorts of Antalya, Alanya and Side, contain many large upmarket hotels, but other resorts, such as Kalkan, lack suitable beaches and are small and less sophisticated.

Apart from the standard beach holiday, south-west Turkey can also offer a choice of cultural, special interest and activity tourism products, including:

- **Sailing holidays**. The coastline, with its many harbours, secluded coves inaccessible by road and warm sunny climate with reliable afternoon breezes is ideal for sailing. Bareboat yacht charter is available, but most holidaymakers prefer a *gulet* cruise – on a traditional wooden motor yacht, with Turkish skipper, crew and full-board arrangements.

- **Golf.** The purpose-built resort of Belek on the Gulf of Antalya claims to be Turkey's answer to the Costa del Sol.
- **Spa tourism.** The unique natural resource provided by the calcified springs at Pammukkale has been known since Roman times.
- **Activity and adventure holidays.** In the mountains close to the coastal holiday resorts, the lifestyle of the villagers has been little affected by the twentieth century. Trekking, jeep safaris and white-water rafting are offered by a number of specialist tour operators.
- **Cultural tourism.** Here the emphasis is on the ancient civilizations that flourished in this coastal region. Many of the most important sites are within a short drive of the coastal resorts:
  - Ephesus, one of the greatest cities of the Roman Empire, with its well-preserved theatre and library, is a 'must-see' attraction, but there are many other sites that are less well known, and as a result, much less crowded.
  - Troy and Pergamum (Bergama) are also firmly on the tourism circuit.
  - Other heritage sites are less accessible, being widely dispersed across the Anatolian Plateau, and necessitating a lengthy coach tour or internal flight to Ankara, Kayseri or Erzurum. The following deserve special mention:
    - the strange lunar landscapes of Cappadocia where the soft volcanic rock provided a refuge for early Christian communities, complete with underground churches and cave dwellings
    - the Armenian monasteries around Lake Van in eastern Turkey
    - the ancient monuments at Nemrut Dagh, a World Heritage Site; even in this remote area, visitor management and conservation are major issues.

The major cultural attractions for most visitors to Turkey however lie in **Istanbul**, the former capital of the Byzantine and Ottoman Empires. This city of 15 million people has become a popular short-break destination for the following reasons:

- It is a major meeting point of East and West, with two bridges across the Bosphorus literally linking Asia to Europe.
- It contains the finest achievement of Byzantine architecture – Aya Sofya (Holy Wisdom), once the largest church in Christendom, subsequently a mosque under Ottoman rule, and secularized as a museum by Ataturk.
- The Blue Mosque, with its six minarets, is one of the most outstanding examples of Islamic architecture.
- The Grand Bazaar is a 'must-see' for bargain-hunters, with over 4000 shops under one roof.
- The Topkapi Palace evokes the splendour and mystery of the Sultans, particularly the *harem* or women's quarters.
- The Cagaloglu Hamman provides the experience of a Turkish bath, another traditional institution of the Muslim world, with separate sections for men and women.

Most of Turkey still remains largely undeveloped for tourism, notably the eastern part of the Anatolia Plateau, with its harsh climate and earthquake-prone, rugged terrain. The unrest among the Kurds who inhabit much of the region has certainly been a contributory factor in discouraging tourism. The Black Sea coast, picturesque and well wooded, is mainly frequented by domestic tourists; the same also applies to the ski resorts in the mountains nearby. The south-eastern part of Turkey centring on Adana is one of the few substantial stretches of Mediterranean coastline still awaiting development, probably because agriculture and industry have been given priority.

The Arabian Peninsula

Extending between the Red Sea and the Gulf, the Arabian Peninsula offers some of the most extreme contrasts to be found in the Middle East. It mostly consists of desert landscapes, although there are mountain ranges along its western and south-eastern edges that attract some rainfall, and support a greater variety of vegetation. Saudi Arabia dominates the interior and contains most of the region's population, while the Gulf States – Kuwait, Qatar, Bahrain, the United Arab Emirates and Oman – are maritime in their location and outlook. To the south Yemen remains largely undeveloped for tourism.

The rapid development of the vast oil reserves of the countries around the Gulf has led to a tremendous growth in demand for all kinds of goods and services from a population which, a generation ago, were largely nomads and peasant farmers. It has also attracted many temporary immigrants, comprising skilled professionals from Western countries, Palestinians and a large number of labourers and domestic servants from Third World countries such as Pakistan and the Philippines, as well as from the poorer Arab countries such as Jordan and Yemen. In some of the Gulf States, expatriate workers form the majority of the population. The whole region has become an important generator of international travel, led by Saudi Arabia, and per capita expenditure on foreign travel is among the highest in the world. The major outbound flows are to the UK and France, although Egypt, Lebanon and Cyprus are also significant destinations. Outbound travel is concentrated between June and September when the summer heat is intense.

In the early 1990s spending abroad by residents of the region was estimated to be almost twice that of inbound foreign visitors, who came mainly for business reasons. This is changing with the development of the winter sun holiday market in the United Arab Emirates and Oman. Tourists have benefited from fluctuations in the business travel market after the oil boom in the 1980s, as the region's airlines – notably Gulf Air and Emirates – are anxious to fill aircraft seats, while the luxury hotels of the Gulf States also need to increase their occupancy rates. The airport infrastructure is impressive, with terminal buildings that combine traditional design with ultramodern facilities. Bahrain and Dubai are major staging points on the intercontinental routes between Europe and the Far East, and have largely replaced Beirut as banking centres for the Middle East. Surprisingly, the impact of 9/11 was less damaging for the region's airlines than for world aviation as a whole, and carriers such as Emirates and Gulf Air have prospered in the new millennium.

The Gulf States are well aware that oil resources will soon be exhausted and are using their wealth to diversify their economies, including investment in tourism-related projects. The natural assets for tourism include a number of fine beaches along the Gulf coast – although oil spills in this shallow, enclosed sea are a potential problem – and the mountains and deserts of the interior.

The United Arab Emirates

The United Arab Emirates is now a major player in international tourism, but it is Dubai, rather than the other six states of the federation, that has done most to appeal to Western tour operators. Abu Dhabi and Sharjah have concentrated on business and conference tourism; these cities are thoroughly modern in appearance and most of the traditional architecture, including the picturesque wind towers (a device for cooling buildings through evaporation), has been swept away.

Dubai offers free port status, an open skies policy to foreign airlines and, not least, a tolerance of other cultures. Dubai has retained its historic port, but has invested massively in state of the art facilities and man-made attractions for the recreational tourist, led by the Dubai Commerce and Tourism Promotion Board. These include:

- a cruise terminal
- a number of world-class golf courses in the desert (each course uses around 3 million litres of desalinated water a day)
- yacht marinas
- ultramodern shopping malls and traditional markets, such as the gold souk, appealing to bargain-hunters stopping over on intercontinental flights
- nightlife that has made Dubai 'the playground of the Middle East'
- sport tourism, including the Dubai World Cup – which showcases the Arab love of horse-racing.

More ambitious projects include the creation of two artificial resort islands, a major theme park, and an indoor winter sports centre. In contrast to these Las Vegas-style developments, four-wheel-drive expeditions into the desert, including 'wadi-bashing', appeal to Western expatriates and adventure seekers.

Oman

In contrast to Dubai, Oman can offer the tourist a more genuine experience of traditional Arab culture. The country has a long history of seafaring and traders from the port of Muscat ventured widely across the Indian Ocean. The Batinah coast to the north-east is being developed as a winter sun destination for Europeans. On the other hand the Dhofar region in the south appeals to Arabian families as a summer destination. This is the only part of the Arabian Peninsula to be affected by the Indian monsoon. Demand is concentrated in the rainy season from June to September, when temperatures are a 'cool' 30 degrees centigrade compared to a stifling 50 degrees in the interior. At the same time the monsoon brings dramatic changes to the normally parched landscape.

Saudi Arabia

As far as the West is concerned Saudi Arabia is primarily a destination for business travellers, focusing on Riyadh and Jeddah, as visas for other purposes are difficult to obtain. It is however, the destination for over two million Muslims from all over the world performing the annual *haj* or pilgrimage to the holy cities of Mecca and Medina. The *haj* is concentrated in a five-day period in Mecca during the last month of the Muslim calendar and involves a major effort in logistics and organization on the part of the Saudi authorities. Saudi Arabia has no official tourist agency at national level, but it does have a Ministry of Haji Affairs to coordinate the accommodation, catering and transport arrangements for the pilgrimage. Nevertheless security and crowd control are major problems, such that fatal accidents often occur during the climax of the rituals around the Kaaba, Islam's holiest shrine. As in other aspects of life in this fundamentalist kingdom, the *matawa* (religious police) play an important role. For many Muslims the cost of travelling to Mecca is prohibitive, but the number of pilgrims has nevertheless quadrupled since the 1960s. The Saudi government has spent a substantial part of its oil revenues on highway construction and the expansion of terminal facilities at Jeddah Airport, as the majority of pilgrims nowadays arrive on chartered flights rather than use the slow and perhaps dangerous land and sea routes.

Yemen

Yemen is much poorer than the other countries of the Arabian Peninsula and tribal traditions persist to a much greater extent. The central government in Sana'a has been ineffective in maintaining law and order in the more remote areas; in fact the negative publicity following the kidnappings of some Western tourists by dissident tribesmen seriously damaged the country's fledgling tourism industry in the late 1990s. Yet this mysterious country has much to offer the more adventurous tourist:

- A unique architectural heritage of mud-brick tower houses and palaces, particularly in Old Sana'a, Zabid and Shibam, which have been designated World Heritage Sites
- The remains of the ancient Sabaean civilization, probably the biblical Sheba (although this is disputed by Ethiopians).

The capital, situated at an altitude of 2200 metres in the northern highlands, has an attractive climate and setting. This is less true of Aden in the sweltering coastal plains of the south, which is the country's business centre.

The remote island of Socotra in the Indian Ocean is closer to Africa than any part of mainland Yemen. It offers considerable potential for diving expeditions and ecotourism; many of the plant species – such as the 'dragon trees' – are unique to the island. Like other isolated tropical islands, Socotra is highly vulnerable to the environmental impact of tourism, which needs to be carefully controlled. At present access is limited due to the infrequent scheduled services from Aden and Sana'a provided by Yemenia, the national airline, and the lack of hotel accommodation.

Iran and Iraq

Two of the most important countries in the Middle East, Iran and Iraq have exerted a strong influence on the development of tourism elsewhere in the region, while tourists have been deterred from visiting by unfavourable publicity in the Western media. The war between the two countries during the 1980s interrupted the flow of Iranian pilgrims to the Shia shrines of Karbala and Najaf, and confirmed Qom as the religious capital of Iran. The Iraq War of 2003 left that country virtually a 'no go area' for tourism for the time being.

Iraq

The major part of Iraq is made up of the fertile plains of the Tigris and Euphrates, historically known as Mesopotamia, which gave rise to one of the world's earliest civilizations – that of Sumeria, based on complex irrigation systems, in the fourth millennium BC. In more recent times Iraq has been divided culturally between the Kurdish highlands in the north, the Sunni dominated central region around Baghdad and the Shia-dominated south, which includes the city of Basra and the traditional 'Marsh Arab' communities.

Until the 1970s Iraq was one of the most prosperous countries of the Middle East. Tourism development was encouraged by a secular government, and projects such as the Habbaniya Tourist Village near Baghdad catered for wealthy foreign visitors as well as Iraqis. Prior to the Gulf War a number of archaeological sites were restored, such as Nineveh, capital of ancient Assyria, and more controversially, Babylon, as a showpiece for the Saddam regime. The long period of sanctions that followed the Gulf War halted any further growth, although Baghdad's hotels continued to attract business travellers from Russia and other countries circumventing the economic blockade.

Baghdad is predominantly a modern capital and little remains of the city of the Abbasid Caliphs that inspired the *Arabian Nights* in the ninth century. The major attraction for Western tourists is the National Museum, which contains the art treasures of Ur and other ancient cities of Mesopotamia. The threat to this heritage was highlighted by the Iraq War, but in fact the pillaging of archaeological sites is a long-standing problem.

Iran

Known as Persia until 1935, Iran is different in language, ethnicity and culture from its Arab neighbours, with a history of powerful dynasties pre-dating the introduction of Islam by many centuries. Before the 1979 revolution, which overthrew the pro-Western Shah and installed a fundamentalist Islamic regime under Ayatollah Khomeini, Iran attracted, and also generated, a significant volume of international tourism. After the revolution, Western hotel chains were expelled and tourism is now under the authority of the Ministry of Culture and Islamic Guidance – which implies the primacy of the Muslim heritage in the tourism product, and the prescription of acceptable forms of entertainment and recreation for both Iranians and foreign visitors. Despite these restrictions international tourist arrivals exceeded one million in the early years of the twenty-first century, but these were mainly from neighbouring countries, with relatively small numbers from Western Europe and even fewer from the USA. Tourism received a further setback in 2003 as a result of the earthquake which destroyed the historic citadel of Bam in the south-east of the country.

Iran is the second largest country in the Middle East after Saudi Arabia, consisting mainly of an arid central plateau surrounded by high mountain ranges, so domestic air services are an important part of the transport system. The prevalence of desert landscapes explains the Iranian reverence for irrigated gardens. Traditionally these were supplied by an intricate system of *qanats* – underground channels conveying water from the mountains to the plains.

Tehran is the modern capital and gateway to the country. Since 1979 it has experienced massive growth, partly through rural out-migration. This congested, polluted city of around 12 million inhabitants is the main generator of domestic tourism and a force for social change, with a predominantly young population wishing to express a long-suppressed demand for Western-style leisure activities.

Iran's tourism resources include:

- some of the world's finest examples of Islamic architecture, particularly in Isfahan 'the city of mosques', and Shiraz, which is also celebrated for its associations with Omar Khayyam and other poets
- the remains of the pre-Islamic Persian civilizations; the most impressive of these is Persepolis, capital of the empire of Darius and Xerxes, which was the setting for the spectacular celebrations of 2500 years of Persian monarchy staged by the last Shah in 1971
- the ski centres of the Alborz Mountains north of Tehran; these were developed prior to the 1979 revolution and cater for a growing domestic demand
- the summer resorts along the Caspian Sea, particularly Ramsar; these have a favourable climate, attractive scenery and are within easy reach of the capital
- the island of Kish in the Gulf, which has been developed as a more upmarket winter destination, but as elsewhere in Iran, with strict segregation of male and female bathers.

The position of tourism in Iran mirrors the situation in the Middle East generally. Further growth will depend upon the extent to which modernizers can prevail over hard-line fundamentalists in their efforts to revive the economy, effect social reforms and improve relations with the USA.

Summary

The countries of the Middle East are close enough to the tourist generating markets of northern Europe to have developed a sizeable tourism industry. Yet only Israel, Turkey and more recently Dubai have developed beach tourism on a scale comparable to other Mediterranean destinations. Cultural tourism is more significant in the region, but only Israel, Egypt and Turkey have attracted cultural tourists in large numbers. Saudi Arabia and the Gulf States receive a considerable volume of business tourists, and this part of the Middle East is also a major generator of outbound international tourism. Domestic tourism is also significant in most countries of the region, but is mainly VFR, rather than hotel-based.

The region's tourism products are varied, including summer and winter sun beach holidays, spas and ski resorts in the mountains, adventure holidays in the desert, religious pilgrimages, and cultural tours. The Middle East can offer many natural and man-made attractions, some of which are unique. The region's history as the setting for many civilisations over thousands of years is important, while religion continues to play an important role in everyday life.

Historically, the Middle East lies at a crossroads in world communications, where Europe, Africa and Asia meet. Transport to and within most of the region is good, and highways and airports have been provided to meet the increased demand for international travel.

There are many problems affecting the further growth of tourism. The prevailing warm dry climate, allied to demographic and economic pressures has put a severe strain on the region's scarce water supplies. Governments need to pay more attention to the conservation of the cultural as well as the natural resources on which tourism depends. However, the greatest threat is the political instability of most countries in the region, fuelled by religious fundamentalism, social and ethnic tensions, sectarianism, the unresolved conflict between Palestinians and Jews, the legacy of the Gulf War, and the war against terrorism.

Chapter 20

The tourism geography of Africa

Learning Objectives

After reading this chapter, you should be able to:

- Describe the major physical regions and climates of Africa and understand their importance for tourism.
- Appreciate the social and economic factors behind the development of tourism in the most important African destinations.
- Recognize that aside from development in North Africa and South Africa, the continent's tourism potential is largely unfulfilled.
- Appreciate the nature of the demand for inbound tourism to sub-Saharan Africa, particularly the importance of safaris.
- Describe the major international gateways and the relevant features of internal transport in Africa's major tourist regions.
- Outline the organization of tourism in the major tourist destinations of Africa.
- Be aware of the interrelationships as well as the differences between North Africa and sub-Saharan Africa.
- Demonstrate a knowledge of the tourist regions, resorts, business centres and tourist attractions of Africa and the islands of the western Indian Ocean.

Introduction

We mentioned in Chapter 19 that the countries of North Africa share many characteristics with those of the Middle East region. There are indeed major cultural and physical differences between North Africa and the rest of the continent. Physically, Morocco, Algeria and Tunisia consist largely of fold mountains that are geologically similar to those of southern Europe. Much of the scenery, with the exception of the desert zone, resembles that of Greece, Spain or southern Italy and the people are predominantly Arabs or Berbers. In contrast, most of Africa south of the Sahara consists of plateaux and block mountains, with only a narrow coastal plain separated from the interior by high escarpments. In terms of their ethnicity and culture, the emerging nations of sub-Saharan Africa are different from the Arab states of the north. For most of the twentieth century all of these countries, with the exceptions of Ethiopia and Liberia, were under colonial rule. However, this was also the experience of the countries of North Africa, which play an important role in the Organization of African Unity (OAU). Although the Sahara Desert acted as a formidable physical barrier between the countries of North Africa and those to the south, it was frequently crossed by camel caravans, allowing an exchange of goods and ideas.

The setting for tourism in Africa

The sheer size of Africa is at once an asset and a hindrance to developing a tourism industry. On the one hand, most of the continent is sparsely populated, offering wide-open spaces, an almost unique wealth of wildlife, spectacular scenery and tribal cultures that have fascinated travellers for centuries. Yet apart from North Africa, which has taken advantage of its proximity to Europe, and South Africa, with its well-developed infrastructure, the continent's tourism potential is largely untapped. This is due to the following factors:

- **Accessibility**   Before the advent of air travel, much of the interior of Africa was virtually inaccessible. Although air transport has shown substantial growth, air traffic control and airport infrastructure are deficient by Western standards, and many experts consider this is holding back the development of tourism. The same is true of surface transport. There are very few natural harbours along the coast, and even penetration up the largest rivers – the Congo or Zambezi for example – is blocked by rapids and waterfalls. Road and rail infrastructure is generally inadequate in most African countries, so that touring holidays can be a major undertaking. In the absence of adequate public transport, improvised alternatives, such as the 'bush taxis' of the Gambia and the *matatus* of Kenya, can be used by more adventurous independent travellers.
- **A low level of economic development**   Most African countries fall in the 'least developed' category, with only a few having reached the intermediate level of development. They tend to be rural in character, although the populations of the national capitals are expanding faster than the provision of jobs or public services. Levels of poverty and illiteracy generally mean that outbound travel is restricted to an elite, while the volume of domestic tourism is insignificant compared to Western countries. Although some countries do see tourism as an important source of foreign currency and a stimulus to the economy, many governments give tourism a low priority for investment compared to other economic sectors.
- **Poor organization**   There is a generally poor level of organization, particularly at the regional level. Governments also place bureaucratic obstacles in the way of

tourists, making travel between countries difficult. Education and training for the tourism sector is of a poor standard, and marketing budgets are inadequate.

- **Political instability**   Some of the world's 'trouble spots' are located in Africa, fuelled by tribal unrest, ethnic rivalries, or border disputes, as the political boundaries drawn up in the colonial era rarely correspond to natural features or tribal territories. Few African countries are therefore nation-states in the European sense. This instability has led to concern in the Western media over the physical security of tourists, and has also discouraged Western investment in the tourism industry.
- **Perceived health and safety risks**   The high incidence of AIDS, as well as insect-borne diseases such as malaria and yellow fever, is due in large measure to the inadequate infrastructure of public health services in most of Africa.
- **Sceptical investment environment**   Investors are often reluctant to invest in tourism in countries where the political climate is changeable, where a return on their investment is not guaranteed, and price inflation is not under control.

All these constraints and structural weaknesses have frustrated Africa's ability to capitalize on the growing long-haul market, and it is clear that tourism is still a fledgling industry. This is borne out by the statistics – for the whole of sub-Saharan Africa there were less than 20 million international tourist arrivals in the early years of the twenty-first century – less than international arrivals to the UK in an average year, while North Africa attracted a further 10 million. Indeed, for a continent that contains 15 per cent of the world's population and a third of the land area, it receives a small share of the tourist market, amounting to only 4 per cent. Out of more than 50 countries considered in the region, less than half have developed significant tourism industries. In the remaining countries, hotel accommodation is rarely found outside the national capital. However, there are a number of positive factors that will boost Africa's tourism in the new millennium:

- interest in African peoples and cultures
- the increasing pace and variety of tourism development
- Africa will be attractive to segments of the population in the tourism-generating markets who have both the time and the income to travel
- the growing importance of ethnic ties between Africa and Europe; there has, for example, been a considerable emigration since the 1990s from North and West Africa to Europe, and also a two-way flow of migrants between Britain and South Africa
- the growth of sport tourism, bringing together participants from many countries in the region, as shown by the Africa Cup of Nations football event and the All Africa Games
- the pursuit of free market economic policies in many African countries
- improved air access.

North Africa

In contrast to most of sub-Saharan Africa, the North African countries, with the significant exception of Libya, have developed a sizeable tourism industry, based on beach holidays and inclusive tours for the north European market. This is an extension of the resort developments around the Mediterranean coast of Europe, although the cultural setting is quite different. This region accounts for over a third of foreign tourist arrivals to the African continent, with more than half arriving from countries across the Mediterranean, namely France, Spain and Italy. Morocco was the first country to enter the market in the 1950s and both Tunisia and Algeria soon followed.

We can divide most of North Africa into three main zones:

- The fertile coastal plains, which have a Mediterranean climate.
- The Atlas mountains, which reach their greatest extent in Morocco. In relation to their resources, these highlands are quite densely populated. There are frequent snowfalls during the winter months.
- The deserts of the south where productive land is restricted to the oases. The Sahara and its peoples provide the region with its best-known tourist image, but in reality, nomadic tribes now make up only a small minority of the population, while the camel caravan has been superseded by motorized transport.

Morocco, Algeria, Tunisia and Libya have formed an important part of the Muslim world since their conquest by Arabs from the Middle East in the eighth century AD. Arabic is the official language of all four countries, and Arabs form the majority of the population, especially in the cities. However, the earlier inhabitants – the Berbers – still carry on their traditional way of life in the more remote areas. During the first half of the twentieth century, France ruled Algeria, Tunisia and the greater part of Morocco. As a result, French is the second language and some French cultural characteristics have been adopted by the educated classes of the cities. The French were also responsible for constructing a good highway system, and well-planned European-style cities. To a lesser extent, the Spanish in their zone of Morocco, and the Italians in Libya, left a similar legacy. However, the influence of the Middle East remains predominant, as evidenced by the mosques and the souks, along with the crowded *medinas* and *kasbahs* (the old Arab districts) of the cities. Traditional handicrafts – notably leather, metalwork and pottery – are important in the local economy and have been stimulated by the growth of tourism, often with government encouragement.

The main problem facing the Maghreb countries (Morocco, Algeria and Tunisia) is the 'demographic timebomb', causing acute pressure on land and water resources – half the population of about 70 million is under 21 years of age. Poverty, illiteracy and unemployment are widespread, both in the cities – which are surrounded by *bidonvilles* (shantytowns) – and in the countryside. The national economies cannot produce enough jobs to meet expectations, even for those with a Western-style education. This situation has contributed to the rise of Muslim fundamentalism in Algeria, which has so far been checked in Morocco and Tunisia. Not surprisingly, Western tourists with their relative wealth are also seen as an obvious target for exploitation by unlicensed guides, vendors and touts of every description. Tangier in Morocco is a notorious example here.

Morocco

The timeless, almost biblical, scenes that can be found in Morocco have a particular appeal. For the adventurous tourist travelling overland from Western Europe, it is the gateway to Africa. Its markets assault the senses with a medley of sights and pungent aromas, resulting in 'culture shock' for Western visitors. Its cities also contain some of the most exquisite examples of Islamic architecture. Yet this most 'oriental' of North African countries extends further west geographically than any part of the European continent, and can be reached by a three-hour flight from the cities of Western Europe. Morocco is also unique among North African countries in having been an independent kingdom for many centuries, whose power at one time extended over most of Spain and the western Sahara. It experienced only one period of foreign domination (from 1912 to 1956), when it was divided into French and Spanish protectorates. Under the rule of a strong monarchy it has remained politically stable, with the government steering a course between traditional Islam and modernization. However, Morocco's occupation of the Western Sahara has been disputed since 1975 by the Polisario guerrillas seeking independence for the former Spanish colony. This unresolved conflict has held up tourism development in the coastal desert region and soured relations with Algeria, which provides a refuge for the large number of *Sahrawis* opposed to Moroccan rule.

The heartland of Morocco is a fertile plateau separated by rugged mountain ranges from the Sahara Desert to the south and east, and the Mediterranean coast to the north. The High Atlas, rising to 4000 metres near Marrakech, is the most spectacular of these mountain ramparts. Morocco is fortunate in having an extensive coastline on both the Atlantic and the Mediterranean. The climate of the Atlantic coast is particularly favourable for tourism, due to the influence of the cool Canaries Current, which ensures that the summers are usually free of the excessive heat and dust-laden winds found elsewhere in North Africa. Winters are much warmer, drier and sunnier in southern Morocco than in the north, which explains why Agadir is promoted as a winter-sun destination whereas Tangier and the resorts along the Mediterranean coast cater for summer holidays.

Demand for tourism

Morocco received over 4 million annual tourist arrivals at the beginning of the twenty-first century, of which a third are Europeans, mainly from France, Spain, Britain and Germany. This is not surprising given the development of air-inclusive tours to Morocco and the convenient ferry links from Spain and Gibraltar. Neighbouring Algeria is also an important source of visitors. Moroccan expatriates working in Western Europe and returning for their annual holiday form a large proportion of the remaining arrivals, along with tourists from other Arab states. However, this is not reciprocated, as those Moroccans who can afford foreign travel prefer to visit Europe.

Supply of tourism

Morocco has one of the best transport systems in Africa, with tarmac highways penetrating mountains and desert, and a network of inter-city bus services, supplemented by *grands-taxis*. The national carrier, Royal Air Maroc, operates an efficient domestic air network.

Two-thirds of Morocco's accommodation is in hotels and the rest in self-catering. The French tour operator Club Méditerranée pioneered all-inclusive holiday villages on the Mediterranean coast and at Ouarzazate in the Sahara.

In the past, the Moroccan government invested heavily in tourism development, particularly in middle category and luxury hotels, so that tourism employs over half a million people. The Ministry of Tourism has the overall responsibility for the financing and development of tourism projects as well as promotion.

Following a reduction in arrivals in the first half of the 1990s, the government revised its approach to tourism. This involved the promotion of Morocco with a new image of landscapes and culture, the development of new products (such as desert tourism around Ouarzazate), quality assurance across the sector and the search for new markets. The government is now emphasizing the role of the private sector, by offering attractive incentives to developers, but ensuing that projects should be in keeping with local traditions. Two examples illustrate this policy:

- Agadir is Morocco's most popular international beach resort. The old town was destroyed by an earthquake in 1960, and a modern resort of high-rise hotels and apartment blocks soon took its place to meet the demand for accommodation. Later expansion has been more sensitively designed, in the form of low-rise developments in the traditional Moorish style.
- As part of its conservation strategy, the government has also encouraged the use of historic buildings as hotels, as shown by projects in Essaouira, formerly an important trading centre known as Mogador. Stays in *riads* – courtyard houses in the medinas of cities such as Fez and Marrakech – are increasingly popular with Western tourists.

As a result Morocco has a more upmarket, fashionable image than its rival Tunisia, but this may change, given proposals to double visitor numbers by 2010.

Tourism resources

Morocco is far more than just a beach destination. The country's resource base is varied and includes the following products:

- Two-centre holidays, combining a stay at a beach resort with sightseeing in the major cities and excursions into the countryside. For example, Agadir is the gateway to southern Morocco, and is often combined with Marrakech, perhaps the most fascinating of all Moroccan cities. Similarly the beach resorts near Casablanca could be combined with the cities of northern Morocco, but these cater mainly for the domestic market.
- More in-depth cultural tours, such as the 'Imperial Cities' circuit that combines Fez, Meknes, Rabat and Marrakech – all of which at one time have served as the capital of Morocco.
- Short city breaks in Fez and Marrakech.
- Business and conference tourism, with facilities of international standard in the modern city of Casablanca, which is Morocco's financial and commercial centre, complementing the capital, Rabat.
- Special interest holidays, including golf, painting and photography, and sport fishing off the Atlantic coast.
- Trekking, mainly in the High Atlas, which contains spectacular mountain scenery and Berber villages, apparently unchanged over the centuries. Beyond these mountains is the very different climate and landscapes of southern Morocco, where the desert is never far away. Major attractions include the oasis towns of Zagora and Ouarzazate, the gorges of the Todra and the Dades, and the distinctive fortress-villages, built of red sun-dried clay by the local Berbers;
- Skiing, for which the main centres are Ifrane in the Middle Atlas near Fez, which was originally developed by the French as a summer health resort, Oukäimeden

in the High Atlas near Marrakech and Ketama in the Rif Mountains. These cater almost exclusively for the domestic market.
- Surfing on the largely undeveloped Atlantic coast.

Whereas Agadir caters for beach tourism, the other major tourist centres of Morocco offer more possibilities for sightseeing. They include the following:

- Tangier is a popular beach resort as well as being a major gateway. For many visitors arriving by ferry or cruise ship, the medina of Tangier is their first impression of Morocco and a stressful one – due to the hordes of hustlers. From 1912 to 1956 the city had special status as an International Zone open to free trade and tolerant of alternative lifestyles, hence its enduring reputation as a centre for gay tourism.
- Tetouan was the capital of Spanish Morocco during the protectorate, and the cultural influence of Spain is still evident here and in the picturesque towns of Asilah, Chaouen and Larache. Beach tourism has developed along the Mediterranean coast near Tetouan and further east at Al Hoceima, which was badly damaged by the 2004 earthquake. The resorts suffer from the problems of seasonality and under-investment, as this part of northern Morocco has been neglected by the government for decades. Not surprisingly contraband is a major part of the local economy, involving the Berber villages of the Rif Mountains, which are difficult of access due to the rugged terrain.
- Fez, which, although its extensive medina is a World Heritage Site, is not as well known as Marrakech and has been less affected by tourism. Its main attractions are the Attarine Medrassa (one of a number of Muslim colleges), the Karaouine Mosque and the spice market. Those interested in Moroccan leather can visit the dyeworks and tanneries where medieval industrial methods are still carried on.
- Marrakech has been fashionable as a winter sun destination since the 1930s but is now mainly famous for its souks and the colourful market square known as the Djemaa el Fna, which is ideal for people-watching. Here crowds gather around entertainers such as storytellers, snake charmers, acrobats and musicians. Berber folklore features in the event attractions known as *fantasias*, which feature impressive displays of horsemanship by local tribesmen. The most attractive features of Marrakech are the gardens which provide a refuge from the extreme summer heat; those of the Mamounia Hotel are world-famous.

Tunisia

With a long history of contact with other parts of the Mediterranean, Tunisia is one of the most tolerant of the Arab states. This has been a factor in the development of the country as a holiday playground for Europeans seeking sun, sea and sand. Tunisia not only has the advantages of superb beaches and, especially in the south, a favourable winter climate, but tourism development has been encouraged and carefully managed. Compared to most other Arab states, Tunisia is politically stable, while the government has consistently applied liberal social and economic policies.

Tourism demand and supply

Tourism caters mainly for the mass market, and this is shown by the fact that about half of the 5 million annual arrivals are mostly package holidaymakers from France,

Germany and Britain, concentrated during the summer months. However, Tunisia has been successfully promoted as a winter-sun destination and this has boosted arrivals between October and March. Nevertheless, the country's dependence on the European market leaves it vulnerable to recession in the generating countries and also to the international political situation. For example, although it is geographically far from the Middle East, tourism was adversely affected by the Gulf War crisis of 1990/1991.

As you would expect in a country dependent on the mass market, the majority of visitors arrive by air. Tunis Airport mainly handles scheduled services, but most holidaymakers on inclusive tours arrive at Monastir, which was specially built to handle charter flights. La Goulette and Bizerta are the ports of arrival for cruise passengers. Tunisia's professional approach to tourism includes upgrading the welcome facilities for travellers at the major gateways.

Hotel accommodation on the coast is mostly in low-rise developments, physically separate from the local communities, designed in the traditional style and blending with the local environment. Other forms of accommodation include youth hostels and campsites. The French tour operator Club Méditerranée chose Tunisia as the location for several of its all-inclusive holiday villages.

Tourism is an important sector of the economy and government involvement is extensive. The National Ministry of the Economy formulates the policy but its day-to-day implementation is carried out by the Tunisian National Tourism Office (ONTT). Since the 1980s Tunisia has diversified the tourism product away from the sea, sun and sand image, by promoting:

- an upmarket marina and sports complex at Port El Kantaoui adjoining the city of Sousse
- a number of golf courses of world-class standard
- the Tabarka area in the north west – the 'Coral Coast' – as a scuba diving destination
- 'soft adventure' tourism in the desert south, where a number of luxury hotels are available in oasis towns such as Tozeur
- the rich cultural heritage of the country, particularly relating to the time when this part of Africa was the granary of ancient Rome and the supplier of wild beasts for the Roman arena.

Tourism resources

Most tourists prefer to spend their time on the beaches and holiday complexes of the coast, the most important being Hammanet, Monastir and Sousse. In the south, the island of Djerba with its myriad palm trees is an important winter-sun destination, while the Kerkenneh Islands offer a less sophisticated holiday product.

Tunisia is a relatively compact country, giving the holidaymaker based on the coast a wide choice of excursions, including:

- The city of Tunis, with its spacious modern boulevards, contrasting with the medieval Arab medina. The Bardo Museum has a world-renowned collection of finds from the site of Carthage, the great trading centre of ancient times, which under Hannibal challenged Rome for domination of the Mediterranean.
- The remains of the Roman cities of Dougga and El Djem – where the amphitheatre is almost as large as the Colosseum in Rome.
- The holy city of Kairouan, famous for its Great Mosque and traditional crafts, such as saddle-making and carpet-weaving.

- The troglodite community of Matmata and the oases of southern Tunisia. Although very few Tunisians are Saharan nomads, tour operators have exploited Western visitors' perceptions of the country by staging 'Bedouin feasts' that are really pseudo-events. Excursions by jeep or camel, from oasis towns such as Douz, provide a more genuine desert experience.

Algeria

In some respects Algeria is the most Westernized of the North African countries. It experienced a much longer period of French rule, and was in fact treated as part of metropolitan France. After the war of independence that ended in 1962, the FLN government established a secular, socialist-leaning state, using Algeria's considerable oil revenues to industrialize the country, expand education and redistribute wealth. Tourism was not given a high priority, and the number of arrivals was much smaller than in neighbouring Morocco and Tunisia. The situation worsened after 1991, as a result of the vicious struggle between Muslim fundamentalists and the Algerian army. In these circumstances, it has been impossible to guarantee visitor security in much of the country, including the capital.

Tourism demand and supply

Algeria received almost one million inbound arrivals in the early years of the twenty-first century; most of these are VFR tourists, as large numbers of Algerians work abroad, particularly in France, and return home for their annual summer holidays. French tourists visiting Algeria – and even more so Algerians visiting France – have been subjected to visa restrictions, as a result of the controversy over Algerian immigration. The majority of international tourists arrive by air, with the exception of Tunisians who use road or rail transport.

Algeria has five international airports and scheduled flights are operated by the major European airlines as well as Air Algerie – which also serves the extensive domestic network. Air transport is important in a country more than four times the size of France, and allows access to remote desert and mountain areas. The country has good ferry links to Marseilles in France (operated by the French Société Nationale Maritime Mediterranée – SCNM) and the Algerian state-owned shipping line. There is a very extensive road network and excellent bus services allow visitors in less troubled times to travel throughout the country and into Tunisia. Rail transport is less efficient and surface transport links with Morocco have been adversely affected by the dispute over the Western Sahara.

Even in good times, Algeria's tourism industry has suffered from an acute shortage of accommodation. This has been made worse by the need of many foreign companies to accommodate their employees in hotels, owing to the shortage of housing. At the same time, service standards are poor. The difficulty is at its worst in Algiers, where accommodating delegates attending conferences is a continual problem. Most hotel beds are located in the purpose-built tourist centres on the coast and in some of the Saharan oases.

Like other sectors of the economy, tourism is closely controlled by the state. Policy is decided by the Ministry of Tourism and Handicrafts, which, since the Millennium, has established a new tourism development agency and is embarking on a new wave of sustainable tourism development to upgrade Algeria's product.

Tourism resources

Algeria offers a diversity of natural and cultural resources to the tourist. In the extreme north, the Mediterranean coast is largely unspoilt, consisting of 1200 kilometres of small bays backed by cliffs, and scenically not very different from the Côte d'Azur. During the 1970s a number of beach resorts (Tipasa, Zeralda and Sidi Ferruch) were developed on the coast to cater for European tour operators. These were planned as self-contained towns in Arabic style, complete with well-designed souks, entertainment and sports facilities. However, the coastal lowlands – the Tell – contain 84 per cent of Algeria's population and the bulk of its industry so marine pollution is a serious problem.

Algiers itself – a metropolis of over 5 million people – is famous for its Kasbah, the fortified old town built under Ottoman rule. Despite having been declared a World Heritage Site, conservation has been neglected and its buildings are grossly overcrowded.

A series of mountain ramparts separate the coast from the Sahara, where skiing is possible during the winter months. However, much of the area, particularly the Aures Massif and Kabylie, is off-limits to tourists. The area between the two main Atlas ranges is known as the Plateau of the Shotts because of the large number of salt lakes. The true desert – and the date palms for which Algeria is famous – are reached at Laghouat, some 400 kilometres from Algiers. From here, the Trans-Saharan Highway, the most important of the desert routes, runs a further 2400 kilometres to Kano in northern Nigeria. Apart from the areas of sand dunes known as *erg*, the Algerian Sahara is scenically quite varied, including the volcanic rock formations of the Hoggar rising to 3000 metres, and eroded badlands, criss-crossed by a network of wadis. Each oasis town has a distinct character, the most interesting being those of the M'zab region, while Tamanrasset is the main centre of the 'people of the veil' – the Tuareg nomads. Prehistoric rock paintings at Ain Sefra and in the Tassili Mountains show that the Sahara once enjoyed a much wetter climate. Although UNESCO has declared these a World Heritage Site, entire frescoes have faded as a result of exposure to tourists or even been removed as part of the illicit trade in artefacts.

Libya

During the 1990s few tourists visited Libya due to the UN trade embargo, which was imposed in retaliation for the Islamic socialist regime's support of terrorist movements throughout the Middle East. Since the Iraq War the political climate has changed and scheduled air services now link Tripoli to a growing number of cities in Europe. Tourism would reduce the country's dependence on oil exports and its political isolation. Although 95 per cent of Libya is desert, vast reserves of ground water are believed to exist.

There are the following opportunities for tourism development:

- Business travel in Tripoli and Benghazi, which is open to expansion
- the longest stretch of pristine Mediterranean coastline
- important Roman remains at Leptis Magna and Sabratha (near Tripoli) and Cyrene (near Benghazi) that were systematically excavated in the 1930s by the Italians under Mussolini
- the oases of Ghadames and Ghat on the former caravan routes across the Sahara.

The prospects for tourism seem bright with the lifting of sanctions, particularly from the USA. However, there is a shortage of hotel accommodation and other facilities for Western holidaymakers.

East Africa

Tour operators regard the countries of Kenya, Tanzania and Uganda as constituting East Africa. Their tourism resources are similar, and before independence they had a measure of unity under British rule. The wider geographical region also includes the Sudan, and the countries of 'The Horn of Africa' – Ethiopia, Somalia, Eritrea and Djibouti – where tourism is still in its infancy and has been adversely affected for many years by drought and political strife. The Swahili language is widely understood throughout East Africa, while the heritage of Islam and Arab traders is evident throughout the coastal belt.

The setting for tourism

Contrasts of scenery, climate and culture are particularly evident in East Africa. Most of the region consists of an undulating plateau over 1000 metres in altitude, but it also contains the most spectacular scenery to be found anywhere on the continent. Part of the Rift Valley – a deep gash in the earth's surface extending from the Dead Sea to Lake Malawi – cuts through the region as two branches. The western branch contains Lakes Albert, Edward and Tanganyika, while the eastern branch is bounded by a high escarpment in western Kenya. The earth movements which formed the rift also raised the high mountains of volcanic origin on either side, notably Mounts Elgon, Kenya and Kilimanjaro. The valley floor is littered with a number of craters (the most famous being Ngorongoro, which is a spectacular wildlife sanctuary), and there are numerous lakes. Some of these, like Naivasha, contain fresh water and are rich in fish, whereas others – Nakuru, Magadi and Natron – have deposits of salt and soda which have attracted the attention of mineral developers as well as of conservationists who wish to protect the millions of flamingos which breed there.

Most of East Africa has a tropical wet–dry climate but, because of its position astride the Equator, the region has two dry seasons and two rainy ones. The coast is also influenced by the seasonal shift in wind direction known as the monsoon over the Indian Ocean. Altitude too has an important effect. Conditions in Nairobi at 1800 metres are ideal for Europeans, with daytime temperatures between 20 and 25 °C all year round. The main tourist seasons for East Africa's big-game areas are December to early March and July to early October as these correspond to the dry seasons when the animals are concentrated around the water-holes and the grass is short, aiding visibility. Travel is also easier then, whereas the earth roads are often impassable at the height of the rains.

East Africa contains a large variety of habitats for wildlife, ranging from the semi-deserts of northern Kenya and Somalia which support herds of antelope and gazelle to the dense rain forests of the Ruwenzori on the Uganda–Congo border which shelter the chimpanzee and gorilla. The dominant type of vegetation is thorny scrub in the drier areas, alternating with open plains or savanna where the tall grasses, dotted with umbrella-shaped acacia trees, support large herds of grazing animals and the great predators such as the lion.

Safari tourism in East Africa

Wildlife is the basis of East Africa's tourism industry. The organization of big-game hunting safaris began at the end of the nineteenth century, although the first national parks were not designated until the 1940s. Since independence, Kenya, Tanzania and Uganda have devoted large areas to wildlife conservation, either by designation as national parks, which conform to the high standards of protection laid down by the IUCN, or as game reserves. This has entailed a social cost – local communities have lost their traditional rights to these lands; for example the semi-nomadic Masai on the Kenya–Tanzania border are no longer able to graze their cattle in the Masai Mara Wildlife Reserve. The wildlife is under threat, for the following reasons:

- poaching of animals for skins, ivory and rhinoceros horn (greatly valued in both Yemen and the Far East, but for different motives)
- encroachment of the human population (growing at the rate of 3 per cent annually) on wildlife habitat; although it is poaching that receives wide publicity in the Western media, this is a more serious long-term problem. Most of the best land has already been given over to the production of cash crops for export rather than to food staples, while African farmers see wildlife as a threat to their crops, not as a resource.

The term 'safari' has come to include the following types of products:

- Budget-priced mini-bus tours of the most accessible national parks such as Amboseli and Masai Mara are based on Nairobi or one of the coastal resorts. Drivers often approach the game too closely so that tourists can get a better view. Tourists also spend most of their time looking for the 'big five' – lion, leopard, elephant, rhino and buffalo – causing bottlenecks in the process.
- In the higher price bracket, tour operators include stays in one of the government-run game lodges in the national parks. These are designed to blend in with the local environment, the most famous being 'Treetops' in the Aberdare Mountains, and Seronera in the Serengeti National Park. They offer five-star service and to an extent tourists are cut off from the realities of life in the African bush.
- Camping safaris, for example in the Tsavo National Park, are a much more authentic and sustainable alternative.
- Balloon safaris provide an ideal way to view game. However it is said that the noise from the burners frightens away game, while the back-up vehicles damage the terrain in the wet season.
- Other options include camel safaris in the remoter parts of northern Kenya; fishing expeditions to Lake Turkana; trekking and mountain climbing on Mount Kenya or Kilimanjaro; and escorted expeditions to privately owned game reserves and game ranches.

The negative impacts of safari tourism can be minimized by:

- visitor management, ensuring that tourist numbers do not exceed the carrying capacity of the area; in other words, low volume, high spending, low impact 'ecotourism' rather than mass tourism
- involvement of the local community, so that they derive tangible benefits from tourism. For example the Masai have set up *cultural bomas* – villages where they can sell their traditional crafts directly to tourists.

Kenya

Kenya is the most developed of the East African countries. Prior to independence it had a large number of white European settlers and an Asian middle class, which generated a sizeable demand for domestic tourism. Following independence in 1963 it was politically stable for decades and encouraged foreign investment in its tourism industry. The Kenyan Ministry of Tourism and Information reflects the importance placed on tourism as the major source of foreign exchange, and it enjoys private sector support from the Kenya Tourist Board, which has responsibility for promotion. Although it has pursued a policy of 'Kenyanization' replacing foreign nationals by Africans, the government in other respects has had a *'laissez-faire'* attitude toward the private sector and foreign tour operators. This is changing in response to the impact of mass tourism in the more accessible national parks and on the coast. The tourism authorities are also faced with a decline in arrivals as fears about crime in Nairobi, international terrorism (witness the bombing of a hotel in Mombasa in 2002) and political unrest have grown. Such is the problem that neighbouring countries are set to challenge Kenya's crown as the leading tourism destination in the region. This is a serious issue, as tourism represents over 10 per cent of Kenya's economy. Since the early 1990s ecotourism has been encouraged by the government's Kenya Wildlife Service (KWS), while the government's development plan has the following aims:

- to diversify the tourism product
- to attract high income, low volume tourism. Here, privately owned game ranches play an important role, as they integrate tourism, wildlife and cattle farming. Tourists can participate in activities on the ranch, while local communities benefit, with the enterprise providing jobs and funding for schools.

Tourism resources

Kenya became one of Africa's most popular destinations (approaching one million arrivals in early years of the twenty-first century), because it has a wealth of tourism resources, including some of the best-known game reserves, such as the Masai Mara, Amboseli and Tsavo, and an attractive coastline along the Indian Ocean. The capital Nairobi is a modern city, with facilities for shopping and entertainment, and good communications by air, road and rail to most of the region, making it the recognized gateway to East Africa. Most foreign tourists spend one or two nights in Nairobi, and the Kenyatta Conference Centre is a major venue for business travellers.

The old city of Mombasa, with its modern port facilities at Kilindini, and extended international airport, is the gateway to the Kenya coast. In the old port, Arab *dhows* can still be seen and the markets sell tourist curios such as Masai beadwork, wood and soapstone carvings and animal trophies. The modern resort developments near Mombasa and at Malindi attract large numbers of winter-sun package holidaymakers, mainly from Germany, Britain, Switzerland or Italy, while beaches and hotels tend to be dominated by a particular nationality. However tourism suffered a major setback in 2002 with the bombing of a hotel that was owned and mainly frequented by Israelis. Until then beach tourism had been expanding in Kenya, while visits to game reserves (except by Americans) were declining. The long white sandy beaches, and lagoons protected by an offshore coral reef, provide safe conditions for diving and other water sports. Although the underwater wildlife is protected by marine national parks at Malindi and Watamu, excessive numbers of glass bottom boats, and illegal shell collecting for the lucrative souvenir trade, have caused extensive damage to the reef. Western visitors have also caused offence to a traditional Muslim society by their dress and behaviour, and social mores are changing to the extent that sex tourism is a problem. The island of Lamu has minimized these environmental and social impacts by carefully controlling tourism. The income is used for conservation projects, so that the Swahili–Arabic heritage of this attractive resort has been retained.

Tanzania

Tanzania has a less developed tourism industry than Kenya. In part, this is due to history – until 1989 government policy encouraged African-style socialism with the state taking a major shareholding in tourism enterprises. Western-style tourism did not fit easily into this scheme and foreign companies were reluctant to invest. However, since 1990 the government has adopted a more pragmatic approach, liberalizing the tourism sector and ambitious to become a leader in this field. This has been aided by the decline in tourism in neighbouring Kenya. The Tanzania Tourist Board, created in 1992, has revitalized the sector so that it supports 27 000 jobs and generates a quarter of the country's foreign exchange. By the beginning of the twenty-first century international arrivals stood at almost half a million.

Tourism resources
Tanzania's most well known attractions lie close to the Kenyan border and this has made the task of promotion more difficult. They include:

- Africa's highest mountain – Mount Kilimanjaro
- the world famous Serengeti National Park, with its spectacular seasonal migrations of animals in search of water and grazing
- the Ngorongoro Reserve, an extinct volcanic caldera, with excellent game viewing from the crater rim.

Ironically, it is easier to reach these attractions from Nairobi than from Tanzania's former capital, Dar-es-Salaam – on the coast. This induced the government to build an airport near Arusha (Kilimanjaro International) and invest heavily in hotel complexes in that city. The enormous game reserves of southern Tanzania are underutilized as they lie off the tourism circuit and are usually reached by fly-in safaris.

Tanzania's other focus of tourist attention is the coast, particularly the islands of Zanzibar, Pemba and Mafia, where game fishing and diving are the main attractions. Zanzibar – particularly 'Stone Town' (the old trading city) – also offers major cultural attractions from the times of the Arab Sultans, but development projects for Western-style beach tourism have aroused controversy because of their social and environmental impact.

Uganda

Uganda, in contrast to Tanzania, had a flourishing tourism industry before the Amin regime brought disorder and maladministration to the country in the 1970s. Relative stability since the 1990s has led to the growth of ecotourism, based on the country's rain forest resources, which have the highest biodiversity in East Africa. Another major attraction is Murchison (Kabegera) Falls near the headwaters of the River Nile. However, the main area of tourist interest – the Queen Elizabeth National Park and the Ruwenzori Mountains – lie close to the Congolese border, and are threatened by the turmoil prevalent in Central Africa.

Entebbe is the gateway for Uganda, with ferry services across Lake Victoria linking it to Kenya and Tanzania. International tourist arrivals stood at around 200 000 at the beginning of the twenty-first century.

The other countries of East Africa

The Sudan, the largest country in Africa, is deeply divided along religious and cultural lines between the Arab-speaking, Islamic north and the black African, largely Christian south. The northern Sudan, which is largely desert, has close cultural links with Egypt and the Middle East. The Sudanese section of the River Nile is not used to any extent as a tourist route, and accommodation is severely limited outside the capital Khartoum. There are however, opportunities for diving along the Red Sea coast. Other attractions include the Dinder National Park, a major wildlife reserve near the Ethiopian border, and the volcanic highlands of Jebel Marra in the western Sudan, which provide a refuge from the extreme heat of summer.

Formerly also known as Abyssinia, **Ethiopia** has huge tourism potential and is of particular interest to cultural tourists. The heartland is a high plateau where an ancient Christian civilization has survived, isolated by mountains, deserts and often hostile Muslim neighbours. The main tourist circuit links Addis Ababa to the art treasures of Axoum, Gondar and Lalibela. There are few hotels outside the capital, which was developed as a conference venue for Africa by the last Emperor, Haile Selassie. To the east of Addis Ababa lie the game reserves of the Rift Valley and the historic Muslim city of Harar. Tourism is coordinated by the Ethiopian Tourism Commission and arrivals approached 150 000 in the early years of the twenty-first century.

Eritrea's national identity derives from half a century of Italian rule and the long struggle for independence from Ethiopia, which ended in 1993, although border disputes continue to be unresolved. The country offers two contrasting environments – the arid but sweltering Red Sea coast, and the cool, fertile highlands around Asmara. The government recognizes the importance of tourism, and plans include the restoration of the spectacular railway linking the capital to the port of Massawa, which is also the point of access for the diving sites in the Dahlak Archipelago.

Most of **Somalia** was also an Italian colony, except for the north-west which was under British control. These former divisions and bitter clan rivalries re-surfaced in the 1990s, leading to the breakdown of government authority outside Mogadishu. Yet Somalia has the advantages of a long coastline with fine beaches and potential for sport fishing, and a common language. It raises the question whether tourism can develop in a 'failed state' where part of the infrastructure – for example telecommunications – still functions in some of the areas controlled by local warlords.

With few other resources, the small ex-French colony of **Djibouti** has exploited its deepwater harbour at the entrance to the Red Sea with the view to becoming a major trading centre between Africa and the Middle East.

Southern Africa

The countries of Southern Africa recognize the importance of wildlife conservation as a major part of their tourism appeal. To counter the threats of drought, poaching and development pressures to wildlife, a number of cross-border parks have been proposed, which would allow the animals to migrate freely within their natural ecosystems. These international 'peace parks' now include the Kgadaladi Transfrontier Park in the Kalahari, involving South Africa and Botswana, and the Great Limpopo Transfrontier Park, with an area of 35 000 square kilometres, involving South Africa, Mozambique and Zimbabwe.

Most countries in the region have strong economic and cultural ties with Britain, and have succeeded in attracting visitors from the main generating markets. International air services to Southern Africa improved considerably during the 1990s. There is scope for more regional cooperation in reducing border formalities to encourage travel between the various countries, and in overseas promotion, by expanding membership of the Southern Africa Regional Tourism Council (SARTOC). However, the future growth of tourism will depend to a great extent on the continuance of political and economic stability in South Africa, which is by far the leading country in the region, accounting for 85 per cent of its GDP.

South Africa

South Africa differs from the rest of the continent in having a large number of people of European origin – over 5 million or 13 per cent of the population, while Asians and those of mixed race account for another 11 per cent. Under white rule, South Africa – particularly the Cape area with its Mediterranean climate – was often perceived as an outpost of Europe. Since the coming to power of the ANC government in 1994 attitudes have changed; the country is no longer isolated by world opinion as it was in the era of apartheid (the policy of racial segregation), and it is now taking a larger share in the development of the African continent. We can regard South Africa as a developed country rather than part of the Third World for the following reasons:

- It has an advanced economy based on vast mineral resources, with only 14 per cent of the workforce employed in agriculture (compared to 80 per cent in Kenya for example). South Africa also accounts for over half the electricity generated in the continent.
- Literacy levels are generally quite high.
- It has a well-developed infrastructure, with good air, road and rail systems.
- There are fewer health risks than in other parts of Africa – with the exception of AIDS – and malaria is confined to the Lowveld region on the eastern border.

The setting for tourism

South Africa has a warm temperate climate which is almost ideal for outdoor recreation, particularly beach tourism and water sports, as sunshine hours exceed those of most Mediterranean resorts. With the exception of the Western Cape, most of the rainfall occurs in the summer months (October to April). There are important differences in climate and landscapes between the coastal areas and the high interior plateaux – the Karoo and the Highveld, where night-time temperatures frequently fall below 0 °C during the winter months. The Drakensberg Mountains to the east form a high escarpment rising to 3000 metres, offering some of South Africa's most spectacular scenery, including the Blyde River Canyon. The Atlantic Coast north of Table Bay is less suitable for sea bathing than the Indian Ocean, as it is cooled by the cold Benguela Current, but conditions are generally favourable for surfing.

Domestic and outbound demand for tourism

Tourism is a major industry in South Africa, accounting for 8 per cent of GDP and 7 per cent of the workforce in 2000. Demand is influenced by the vast disparities in wealth, to the extent that most of the black majority continue to live in conditions of Third World poverty, without basic services in the tribal homelands or the 'townships' – the urban agglomerations adjoining Cape Town and Johannesburg. Although there has been social mobility since the ending of apartheid, with the rise of a black middle class, wealth is still concentrated in the hands of the white minority. Most black South Africans are too poor to generate an effective demand for tourism.

Domestic demand for tourism accounts for two-thirds of all tourism in South Africa – some 34 million trips in 2000. White South Africans travel widely throughout their country, and the great majority of trips are made by car, using the excellent road network. Self-catering accommodation is often used in preference to hotels. Sports events, and to a lesser extent cultural festivals, are an important motivation for travel. Although the climate is suitable for tourism for most of the year, the timing of school holidays in the Christmas and Easter periods results in a seasonal peaking of demand, which places pressures on accommodation, particularly in Durban and other resorts of the Natal coast. This is the main holiday area for South Africans, especially those from the interior provinces of Gauteng (which includes Johannesburg) and the largely Afrikaans-speaking Orange Free State and Transvaal. The Drakensberg Mountains are visited by large numbers of people from the coast during the hot, humid summers and the towns of Pietermaritzburg, Estcourt and Ladysmith have a long-established tourism industry to meet their needs. Although the mountains are sufficiently high for snow during the winter months, there is only a modest winter sports industry, based in Tiffindell near the border with Lesotho, which caters for domestic demand.

As regards outbound tourism, while the depreciation of the rand since the 1990s has made South Africa a competitively priced destination for international tourism, it has also made foreign travel much more expensive for South Africans. Considering their geographical isolation, they are well represented in the tourist arrivals for a large number of long-haul destinations, including Britain and the USA, as well as neighbouring African countries.

Inbound demand for tourism

In the apartheid era much of the inbound tourism from Britain and other European countries had been for VFR or business purposes. Since the 1990s there has been a substantial growth of interest in South Africa as a holiday destination by tour operators. Sport tourism has also played a significant role, including the hosting of the Rugby World Cup in 1995 and this is expected to increase with the hosting of the FIFA World Cup in 2010. In the early years of the twenty-first century around 6 million arrivals were recorded, including many from other African countries, notably Zimbabwe. The biggest overseas markets are the UK, Germany and the USA. As was mentioned in Chapter 12, the Netherlands accounts for only a small percentage of overseas visitors, despite the strong historical links with the first white settlers – the Afrikaaners, whose language derives from Dutch. South Africa attracts visitors with a wide range of special interests, including botanical tours and wine-tasting in the Western Cape, industrial and transport heritage – such as steam locomotives and the gold and diamond mines – and, for amateur historians, the battlefields of the Zulu and Anglo-Boer wars in KwaZulu–Natal. The ending of apartheid has also strongly influenced patterns of tourism demand. Contemporary South African culture, heritage sites commemorating the struggle for freedom and township tours are now part of the tourism product. Another niche market is health tourism, particularly cosmetic surgery, in which South Africa has the following advantages:

- a good health infrastructure, with excellent medical services and clinics
- from the viewpoint of British visitors, an English-speaking population, and a journey necessitating only a minor time change
- a weak currency, so that five-star hotels are affordable
- a range of post-treatment sightseeing opportunities.

Supply of tourism

The great majority of overseas visitors arrive on scheduled air services, as the South African government discourages charters. Johannesburg, at the hub of a network of intercontinental and regional services, is the major gateway to South Africa, followed by Cape Town. South African Airways operate most of the scheduled domestic services, with several flights a day linking the main cities. Another convenient way of seeing the country is by South African Railways. The luxury 'Blue Train' is one of the country's most famous tourist products, linking Pretoria and Cape Town and passing through some magnificent scenery on its descent from the Karoo Plateau to the coast. A large number of tours by coach or mini-bus are also available.

South Africa's tourism industry is effectively organized and marketed, within the legal framework of the 1993 Tourism Act. The continuing legacy of apartheid is reflected in the politics of tourism in South Africa with different political parties and ethnic groups (there are ten official Bantu languages for example) each having their own agendas for the sector. Policy-making is largely the responsibility of the Tourism and Environmental Affairs Ministry, which has a mission to promote sustainable development, and South African Tourism, which is charged with maintaining standards of accommodation and services, with promotion and also the development of new products. A wide range of accommodation is available, from luxury hotels to *rondavels* (African-style huts, with modern facilities) in the game reserves.

Tourism resources

Although the early white settlers wiped out much of the game they encountered, the remaining wildlife habitats have long been given a high degree of protection by the South African government. There are eleven national parks and many game reserves, most of which are small in area compared to other countries in Southern Africa. The exception – and the most popular – is the Kruger National Park located in the Lowveld along the Mozambique border, which is served by an extensive all-weather road network and well-supplied with self-catering accommodation. Prior reservation is necessary for foreign visitors, due to the heavy domestic demand. Other notable reserves – Hluhluwe and Umfolozi – are situated in KwaZulu–Natal. There are also a large number of private game reserves – such as the Sabi-Sabi adjoining the Kruger National Park – which permit hunting and the viewing of wildlife on foot as well as in open vehicles. They provide luxury chalet accommodation and most have their own airstrips.

Areas increasingly sought out by tourists from Europe include:

- **The Cape Peninsula**, where cold and warm ocean currents meet, and the hinterland of Cape Town, often considered to be the most beautiful part of South Africa. Contrasts of climate have created an extraordinary range of habitats for wildlife, and the coasts are ideal for whale watching. Cape Town, situated on one of Africa's few good natural harbours, is the country's oldest European settlement, the second largest city, and its legislative capital. This cosmopolitan city is home to many ethnic groups and cultures, and has a tolerant attitude to alternative lifestyles. The historic waterfront has been redeveloped as an international focus for retailing, restaurants and entertainment. Cape Town is dominated by the world famous landmark of Table Mountain, and there are many fine beaches, such as Camps Bay.
- Attractions in the hinterland include the vineyards of the Hex River Valley and farmhouses in the distinctive 'Cape Dutch' style of architecture. Offshore lies Robben Island, the former prison of Nelson Mandela and now a museum commemorating the struggle against apartheid.
- **The Garden Route** – the stretch of coast between Port Elizabeth and East London – offers rugged, attractive scenery, in which forest-covered mountains alternate with fertile valleys and small sandy bays. Plettenberg Bay is the best known of the many beach resorts.
- **Natal** and **Transkei** also offer resources for beach tourism. Durban is a cosmopolitan seaport as well as being a major resort, while a string of small seaside towns to the south are known as the 'Hibiscus Coast'. In contrast, the 'Wild Coast' of the Transkei is less developed. To the north of the Tugela river the principal attractions are the game reserves, and Zulu communities that have retained the traditions of a warrior nation.
- On the central plateau the main tourist centres are the cities of Johannesburg, Pretoria and Bloemfontein:
  - **Johannesburg** is South Africa's largest and most prosperous city, largely due to the gold mines of the Witwatersrand. Not surprisingly, one of its major attractions is the Gold Reef City theme park which interprets this mining heritage. Johannesburg has become a regional centre for financial services, comparable with the great cities of Europe and North America. The township of Soweto nearby is actually a city of 3 million people. It is closely identified with the apartheid struggle, and attracts the more adventurous and socially aware tourists for this reason. Some tour operators encourage visitors to interact with the local community in restaurants and *shebeens* (bars).
  - **Pretoria**, the administrative capital of South Africa, and **Bloemfontein**, its judicial capital, are centres of Afrikaaner culture, and as such form a contrast to the cosmopolitan brashness and bustle of Johannesburg.
  - **Sun City** was developed in the apartheid era as a gambling centre to rival Las Vegas, in what was then the quasi-independent state of Bophutatswana, as casinos and multi-racial entertainment were illegal in the Republic itself. In the new South Africa it continues to be a major resort, offering cabarets that attract international stars, world-class golf courses and other sports facilities, and the 'Lost City' theme park developed by a South African entrepreneur.

One of the great challenges facing the government is to balance the economic aspirations of black Africans with the need to retain white expertise and attract foreign investment, and here tourism is playing an important role. The future growth of tourism in South Africa will depend on the maintenance of political and economic stability, and the extent to which the new multi-racial 'Rainbow Nation' can offer opportunity to all ethnic groups. Throughout the 1990s levels of crime increased to become among the world's highest, particularly in Johannesburg, and the resulting insecurity is one of the biggest problems facing the country and its tourism industry.

The other countries of Southern Africa

Most of the other countries in Southern Africa are landlocked, so that their external surface transport links (and to an extent their economic fortunes) are vulnerable to the political situation in South Africa and Mozambique. The small kingdoms of Lesotho and Swaziland are particularly dependent on South Africa. Most of their visitors are South Africans, who tend to be short-stay and interested primarily in gambling in the hotel casinos of Maseru and Mbabane. Yet these countries have more to offer:

- **Lesotho** (known as 'the Roof of Africa' or 'The Kingdom in the Sky') is situated high in the Drakensberg Mountains. Apart from the impressive scenery, there are facilities for pony-trekking and even skiing (although the season is restricted to July and August). Four-wheel-drive vehicles are necessary for travel because of the rugged terrain.
- **Swaziland** (or Ngwane) is not quite as mountainous, and includes a section of the game-rich Lowveld along its boundary with Mozambique. The country's tribal traditions are among the best preserved in Africa.

Namibia and Botswana likewise have strong economic ties with South Africa, but with the advantage of direct air services from Europe to the capitals of Windhoek and Gaborone, they have been more successful in attracting overseas visitors. They are mostly made up of desert landscapes, but the Kalahari is not as arid as the Sahara and supports a surprising variety of game. Because of the vast distances and sparse population, fly-in safaris are a major element in their tourism industries.

- **Botswana** has deliberately pursued a policy of restricting tourism in the interests of conservation by keeping prices high and limiting the supply of accommodation. The main focus of tourism is the Okovango Delta, a unique wetland, created by annual flooding, which is one of Africa's most fertile habitats for wildlife.
- **Namibia** differs from its neighbour in having a long Atlantic coastline, and a large white minority of mainly German or Afrikaaner origin. The country was ruled by South Africa prior to 1990 and was a latecomer to international tourism. On offer are a large number of game reserves and some of Africa's most interesting attractions, including:
  - the Etosha Pan, which attracts great concentrations of wildlife during the dry season
  - the Fish River Canyon, a spectacular geological feature
  - the Waterberg Plateau, famous for its rock paintings – created by the nomadic San (more widely known as 'Bushmen') who were the original inhabitants of Southern Africa
  - the 'Skeleton Coast' – where the Namib Desert meets the Atlantic Ocean; fogs from the cold Benguela Current offshore sustain some unique plants and animals

although the climate is virtually rainless; this coastal area also boasts some of the world's highest sand dunes.

In contrast to Namibia, the countries of Zimbabwe, Zambia and Malawi usually receive an adequate rainfall, and since they mainly consist of highlands and plateaux rising over 1000 metres above sea level, they have a climate that is cooler than might be expected for the tropics. Under British rule the three countries were briefly united as the 'Central African Federation of Rhodesia and Nyasaland', but after 1962 they followed different paths.

Zimbabwe

Between 1964 and 1980 Zimbabwe (then known as Rhodesia) had a tourism industry serving a sizeable domestic market – essentially the dominant white community – and South Africans. There were few overseas visitors due to the economic sanctions imposed by Britain and the country's political isolation. With the coming to power of the ZANU government in 1980 Zimbabwe's independence was formally recognized by the international community. As a result, overseas visitor numbers grew rapidly, aided by political stability and the good infrastructure laid down under British rule. The Zimbabwe Tourist Authority was formed in 1996 with responsibility for promotion and development reporting to the Ministry of Environment and Tourism. However, in the early years of the twenty-first century Zimbabwe's tourism industry is in crisis, due to political unrest, unfavourable publicity in the Western media regarding the seizure of white-owned farms and the abuse of human rights, and the collapse of the economy. This has put the country's wildlife resources increasingly at risk. Despite this, the country still attracted around 2 million visitors.

Hotel accommodation is concentrated in the cities of Harare and Bulawayo – which have hosted international conferences, trade fairs and the All-Africa Games – and near the country's principal attraction – Victoria Falls, on the border with Zambia.

Zimbabwe can offer a variety of other tourism resources, including a system of national parks, which make up 12 per cent of its territory. These are administered by the Zimbabwe Parks Department, which operates a three-tier entrance fee policy. As elsewhere in Africa, the designation of the Hwange and Gonerezhou National Parks in the 1950s and 1960s involved the eviction of thousands of tribespeople from their lands, but since the 1980s government policy has changed, with local communities regaining hunting rights and becoming directly involved in ecotourism. One of the main problems facing the tourism sector is the over-commercialization of Victoria Falls compared to the under-exploitation of some of the game reserves and the scenic attractions of the Eastern Highlands. Below the waterfall the River Zambezi attracts large numbers of canoeists and white-water rafting adventure-seekers. In comparison, Lake Kariba – a vast inland sea created by the Kariba Dam in 1959 – offers few facilities.

The country's cultural heritage is also viewed differently by the white and African communities. For example, the Matapo Hills south of Bulawayo – an area of dramatic granite scenery – has been promoted to Western tourists as the burial place of Cecil Rhodes, the founder of the British colony, whose place in history is controversial. The Chinhoyi Caves, which played an important role in the independence struggle, are as yet barely exploited as a heritage attraction. On the other hand, the mysterious ruins of Great Zimbabwe are now seen as a reminder of African achievement centuries before the colonial era.

Zambia

Zambia's economy is precariously dependent on the export of copper and other minerals, and tourism is increasingly seen as a more reliable way of earning foreign exchange. The government has put a high priority on conservation – almost a third of its area is devoted to national parks and game reserves, although facilities are generally not as well developed as in Zimbabwe. In the most popular national parks – Kafue and the South Luangwa – accommodation is in thatched lodges blending in with the local habitats. The main tourist centres are Livingstone, situated close to Victoria Falls, and the capital Lusaka, which has good conference facilities.

Malawi

Malawi's main attraction is the lake of the same name, the third largest in Africa, with some of the world's best fishing, and attractive beaches along its 600 kilometre shoreline. There are good facilities for water skiing, sailing and windsurfing at the resorts of Salima and Monkey Bay. Compared to some other countries in Southern Africa, it is not rich in big game. However its undulating green plateaux and mountains are ideal for riding and trekking holidays. Since the mid-1990s a new government has liberalized the tourism sector, created a Ministry of Tourism and there has been healthy growth in international arrivals.

Angola and Mozambique

Angola and Mozambique retain some of the heritage of centuries of rule by Portugal. Independence in 1975 was soon followed by many years of civil war and the exodus of well over a million Portuguese settlers. Since the early 1990s the socialist governments of both countries have adopted a more pragmatic approach to economic development.

Mozambique had a small tourism industry before 1975, catering mainly for South Africans and Rhodesians. This was concentrated in the capital Maputo (then called Lourenço Marques), and to a lesser extent in Beira. The extensive beaches along the Indian Ocean are the country's principal tourist asset. Since the ending of the civil war there has been some development of inclusive tours, especially to the Bazaruto Islands that offer resort facilities, scuba diving and sport fishing.

Angola consists largely of a plateau averaging 1200 metres in altitude, and has a long Atlantic coastline, resulting in a cooler climate than is generally true of Mozambique. The country has great mineral wealth but the benefits have yet to filter down to the mass of the population. The hotels of the capital Luanda cater almost exclusively to business travellers, but there is tourism potential in Angola's historic ties with Brazil, and its wildlife resources.

The islands of the western Indian Ocean

To the east of the African continent lie several island groups, which are very different from the mainland in geology, flora and fauna, and where the cultures have been strongly influenced by France and Asia. All island ecosystems are vulnerable to the changes brought about by tourism and other types of development, and the wildlife resources of the Indian Ocean islands are particularly at risk:

- Pressures are most severe in Madagascar, habitat of the lemur and other unique animals.
- In Mauritius only one per cent of the original forest still survives and up to 50 per cent of the fringing coral is dead or dying.
- In the Seychelles much of the coral reef around the island of Mahe was destroyed to make way for the international airport.

Madagascar, the Comores and Réunion were formerly French colonies, whereas Mauritius and the Seychelles, although originally colonized by the French, experienced a long period of British rule.

Madagascar

Officially known as the Malagasy Republic, Madagascar stands in a class of its own, as the world's fourth largest island, with an area greater than France and a coastline 5000 kilometres in length. The country combines the red soil of Africa and the rice fields of South-East Asia, but also has landscapes that are unique, with the 'traveller's tree' as an emblematic feature. A central spine of mountains dominates the country, separating the dry savannas of the west from the lush vegetation of the east coast. Population growth and inefficient agricultural methods have caused extensive deforestation, threatening destruction of the wildlife that is Madagascar's most important tourism resource. The island is also culturally interesting with its mix of Indonesian, African and Arab ethnic groups. Other distinctive features are the elaborate tombs and funeral ceremonies based on ancestor worship.

The capital Antananarivo, located high on the central plateau, offers picturesque markets and the palaces of the Merina monarchs who ruled the country before it came under French control. However this diversity of resources has not been paralleled by a thriving tourism industry. The island is expensive to reach, and once there, surface transport is poor. The principal beach resorts, situated on the offshore islands of Nosy Be and Nosy Boraha (Ile Ste Marie), can only be reached by domestic air services. Since independence the government has given tourism a low priority, but this is changing now that relations with France and South Africa – Madagascar's largest potential markets – have improved.

The Comores

The Comores comprise four volcanic islands lying between Madagascar and Mozambique. The people are Muslims and Arabic influences are dominant in the culture. While the other islands have opted for independence, Mayotte has retained its links with France and is the most prosperous of the group.

Anjouan is the most picturesque, but Grand Comore contains the international airport and most of the few hotels. Diving and sport fishing provide the main appeal for foreign tourists, mainly wealthy Americans and Europeans, although South Africa has provided much of the investment in hotels.

Réunion

Réunion is another volcanic island, situated to the east of Madagascar. It has perhaps the most impressive scenery of any tropical island, with high mountains rising to 3000 metres within a short distance of the coast, and boasting spectacular calderas, an active volcano – the Piton de la Fournaise, and sheer lava cliffs enclosing deep canyons. There are hiking trails between the craters and good surfing off the west coast. The island's close relationship to France (it is an overseas *département*) has benefited the infrastructure and allows French tourists to take advantage of cheaper flights from Paris to the capital, St Denis. Tourism is handicapped by the proximity of Mauritius, which has much better beaches.

Mauritius

Mauritius has the advantage of direct flights from Britain and South Africa, whereas the smaller dependent island of Rodriguez is remote and much less developed. Mauritius is encircled, except to the south, by a coral reef that is responsible for the island's greatest assets – 150 kilometres of attractive coastline with calm seas ideal for water sports and white sand beaches. Mauritius is a good example of how tourism, properly handled, can benefit a small developing country. In the 1960s the island was faced with a decline for sugar, its principal export, and a seemingly inexorable pressure on resources from a rapidly growing population. Tourism (along with light industry) was seen as a solution to the grave economic situation, but the government was determined from the outset that Mauritius should be an upmarket destination. This has been achieved by:

- a ban on charter flights, while the national carrier, Air Mauritius is noted for its professionalism
- resort hotels built to high standards of design and landscaping, taking maximum advantage of the beach and lagoon setting
- hotels that use local resources, so that profits have stayed within Mauritius
- a professional Ministry of Tourism, aided by the Mauritius Tourism Promotion Authority (MTPA) created in 1996
- standards of service and cuisine that bear comparison with the best in Europe, North America and Asia.

By the early years of the twenty-first century Mauritius was attracting 600 000 international visitors, of whom approximately half came from Europe. Mauritius has the advantage of a highly skilled workforce (15 000 are employed in tourism), where the different ethnic communities – Hindus, Muslims, Chinese, Creoles (of African origin) and Europeans – live in apparent harmony. Beach resorts such as Grand Baie are the main attraction, but with the achievement of economic success, the government is giving conservation a higher priority, in a bid to attract ecotourists.

Compared to other Indian Ocean islands, the scenery of the interior is unspectacular, although there are numerous waterfalls where the central plateau of Mauritius meets the coastal plains. Away from the beaches, the main tourist centres are the multi-cultural capital St Louis, with its markets and festivals around the calendar, Curepipe with its casino and textile shops, and the Royal Botanical Gardens at

Pamplemousses. The possible disadvantages of Mauritius as a winter-sun destination for North Europeans are:

- distance
- there is high humidity and occasional cyclones from December to April
- there is little nightlife compared to more accessible destinations such as the Caribbean islands.

The Seychelles

The Seychelles are strategically located on the major shipping routes for oil tankers from the Gulf, midway between East Africa, India and Madagascar. The country has a small population and land area compared to Mauritius, but lays claim to over one million square kilometres of Indian Ocean. The islands are ecologically interesting because they contain many species of birds and plants which are unique to the Seychelles. The islands fall into two main groups:

- The main islands of Mahe, Praslin, La Digue and Silhouette are of granite formation, the possible remnants of a 'lost continent'. The combination of picturesque coves, rock formations, palm-fringed beaches and rugged mountains gives these islands a rare beauty.
- The outer islands are low-lying coral atolls. Fresh water is scarce and the islands are mostly uninhabited. The largest, Aldabra, is also the most remote and is world famous for its giant turtles.

The construction of the international airport at Mahe brought an isolated destination within reach of the main tourist-generating markets of Western Europe and South Africa, with the result that tourist arrivals increased from less than a thousand in 1970 to 140 000 in the early years of the twenty-first century. Tourism now accounts for 70 per cent of foreign exchange earnings and 30 per cent of jobs. While foreign investment in tourism is encouraged, the government has given conservation a high priority, so that only a few localities – mainly on Mahe – have been developed with low-rise hotels. However, tourism has not made the islands less vulnerable to recession in Europe than their previous dependence on agricultural exports such as cinnamon.

Standards of service and facilities in the Seychelles have in the past been compared unfavourably with those of Mauritius, as tourism was grafted on to a less developed economy and social system. As in other small developing countries tourism has caused or aggravated a number of problems, namely:

- The industry is dominated by foreign tour operators and foreign-owned hotels, so that the bulk of tourist spend does not benefit the country.
- The tourism sector has attracted workers away from agriculture, to the extent that the islands are now dependent on food imports from Europe and South Africa to meet local as well as tourist demands.
- The need to train Seychellois workers in the skills and attitudes necessary to serve affluent foreign visitors has undermined the government's policy of socialism and nation-building based on the Creole language and lifestyle. Those involved with tourism tend to be upwardly mobile, imitating Western lifestyles – the so-called 'demonstration effect'.

West Africa

We can think of West Africa as being two distinct regions:

- a southern tier of states occupying the forested coastal belt from the Gambia to Gabon
- a northern tier – the Sahel states – extending from Mauritania to Chad along the southern edge of the Sahara Desert. This region is characterized by extreme summer heat and drought, the dry season getting progressively longer the further from the Equator, so that savanna grassland gradually merges into semi-desert.

The setting for tourism

Tourism and business travel in West Africa gravitate to the coast, where commercial export-based agriculture is well developed. The climate here is characterized by sultry heat, except during the dry season – usually from December to March – when the 'harmattan' wind blows from the Sahara, drastically lowering the humidity. In Victorian times, the unhealthy reputation of the region earned it the name 'White Man's Grave'. However, conditions are by no means uniform – the coasts of Ghana and Togo, for example, are much less humid than Liberia or Equatorial Guinea.

Most of West Africa has failed to develop significant tourism industries, due to the chronic political instability affecting most countries in the region and inadequate infrastructure. Yet these countries are just within reach of the markets of Western Europe for winter-sun beach holidays. The Gambia, for example, is only six hours flying time from London, and unlike the Caribbean, it has the advantage of being in the same time zone. The Gambia's dry and sunny winter climate allows it to compete with the Canary Islands as a beach destination for the British and Scandinavians – with the extra ingredient of the chance to experience African markets and village life. Similarly, French tourists are attracted to their former colonies, especially to the beaches of Senegal, the Ivory Coast and Togo.

Apart from beach tourism West Africa can offer:

- **Ethnic tourism**   There is a large potential market for tourism among the black populations of Brazil, the Caribbean and the USA, who are mainly the descendants of West Africans brought over as slaves. The attempt by the Gambian government in the 1980s to attract Black Americans to the ancestral homeland of Alex Haley (author of *Roots*) met with some success. More tangible reminders of the slave trade can be seen in Senegal, Benin and Ghana.
- **Cultural/special interest tourism**   The contribution of West African woodcarving, textile design and dance rhythms to Western art and music is increasingly recognized. The more adventurous tourists seek out countries like Ghana, Mali and Senegal for this reason.
- **Ecotourism**   West Africa offers a considerable diversity of wildlife habitats. Gambia attracts birdwatchers to its Abuko reserve, while a rainforest project in Ghana's Kakum National Park has won acclaim from environmentalists. Game parks exist in several countries but safari tourism has not developed on any scale, because the attractions are not as well publicized as those of East and Southern Africa, and are less accessible.

- **Adventure tourism**, based on four-wheel-drive expeditions. We might consider the Paris–Dakar Rally to fall in this category, although it is a highly organized annual event involving a large logistical back-up as well as hundreds of international competitors. Although governments such as Mauritania receive revenue from film rights etc., local communities derive few benefits, as little is spent en route.

Supply of tourism

There has been some degree of cooperation among West African countries to promote tourism to the region. In 1976 the Economic Community of West African States (ECOWAS) was formed to bring together French- and English-speaking countries. The Francophone states constitute the majority and, with few exceptions, chose to retain close links with France after independence. Several countries (Côte d'lvoire, Burkina Faso, Niger, Togo and Benin) are also united by the Conseil de l'Entente whose tourism committee aims for the harmonization of entry requirements and greater uniformity in the standard of hotels. A number of West African countries have state-run hotel corporations. However, their main purpose is to attract business travellers rather than tourists, and hotel rooms are often unavailable in the major cities such as Accra due to block booking for regional conferences.

Lagos, Abidjan and Dakar are the focus of air routes into West Africa, the most important carriers being Air Nigeria, Air Afrique (which is jointly-owned by several Francophone states) and the French airline UTA. The winter-sun destinations of the Gambia, Sierra Leone and Côte d'Ivoire are encouraging charter flights to counter the high fares of scheduled airlines. Road and rail transport is geared to the commercial objectives laid down in colonial times, so that routes lead from the interior to the seaports. This inhibits travel between the countries of West Africa, but does, to some extent, allow excursions from the coastal resorts to the hinterland.

Gambia

Of the five English-speaking states, only Gambia has attracted much attention from British as well as Scandinavian tour operators. No larger than Yorkshire or Connecticut in area, the country consists of little more than a narrow strip of territory along the river Gambia, and a short stretch of Atlantic coastline where the resort facilities are concentrated. Tourism is encouraged by the government to reduce the country's dependence on groundnut exports. With the help of the World Bank, Yundum Airport has been extended, the infrastructure improved and a hotel training school established. Yet relatively few tourists venture far beyond the beaches on excursions up the river Gambia, one of the finest waterways in West Africa. Almost all the hotels are foreign-owned and many of the economic benefits of tourism are not retained, while there is concern in this traditional Muslim society about some of its social manifestations such as sex tourism and beach hustling by *bumsters*.

The military coup in 1994 severely affected tourism to Gambia with an estimated 40 per cent reduction in the number of foreign tourists. However, by the late 1990s there were around 100 000 arrivals.

Senegal

Senegal is the oldest of France's former colonies, and is a mixture of French sophistication and African traditions, best exemplified in the capital Dakar.

The island of Gorée close by has historic associations with the slave trade. In Senegal two contrasting approaches to tourism can be observed:

- French expatriates staff the Club Mediterranée village at Cap Skirring, and there is little contact with the local population; whereas
- in the *campements ruraloc intégrales* near Ziguinchor, the tourist shares the life of an African village, the accommodation being provided by a cooperative of the villagers with government support.

Côte d'Ivoire

The Ivory Coast has been more successful than most West African countries in developing its tourism industry and its economy in general. This has been due in part to a long period of stability following independence and very substantial foreign (primarily French) investment. State-owned hotels and travel companies are involved in the provision of tourist facilities, mainly along the coast east of Abidjan, where the beaches are protected by a series of lagoons from the heavy surf of the Atlantic. However, the resorts of the 'African Riviera' are expensive and beyond the reach of all but a privileged minority of the Ivorians themselves. In the interior there are a number of game parks, and the new administrative capital of Yamassoukro which boasts a cathedral second in size only to St Peter's in Rome. Abidjan remains the commercial centre of the country with good conference facilities.

Togo

Togo's capital, Lomé, has also become a leading conference destination as well as attracting tourists (many of them from other West African countries) to its beaches and entertainment facilities.

Nigeria

Nigeria is essentially a business travel destination. It is the most populous nation in Africa, with around 130 million inhabitants, and as the world's fifth largest oil producer, it should be one of the wealthiest. Income from petroleum has fuelled an enormous demand for Western consumer goods and costly development projects. It has also generated a demand for foreign travel, to the extent that Nigeria has a substantial deficit on its international travel account. However, the collapse in oil prices during the 1990s and mismanagement of the country's resources have led to a situation in which shortages of basic commodities and power failures are a fact of everyday life. There is also a shortage of hotels, especially in Lagos, which remains Nigeria's main commercial centre, although the federal capital was moved to Abuja nearer the geographical centre of the country. This was done to satisfy the four main ethnic groups – the Fulani and Hausa, who are Muslim, in the less developed north, and the mainly Christian and more business-minded Yoruba and Ibo in the southwest and south.

Responsibility for tourism development is centred in the Ministry of Culture and Tourism. For the independent traveller, the main interest of the country lies in the traditional lifestyle of Kano and other cities of northern Nigeria, while the Yoruba city of Benin is noted for the skills of its people in metalworking.

Cameroon

Nigeria's eastern neighbour Cameroon offers even more scenic variety and has been described as 'Africa in miniature'. In the Korup National Park part of the equatorial rain forest has been protected, in contrast to the unrestricted commercial logging prevalent in the Ivory Coast. Volcanic Mount Cameroon nearby is the highest mountain in West Africa. The drier northern part of the country includes extensive savannas where a number of game reserves have been designated, the most important being the Waza National Park. Yaounde, the administrative capital, and Douala, the country's commercial centre, attract a substantial volume of business travel, while the beaches of Kribi on the Gulf of Guinea are increasingly popular with tourists. More than most African countries, it is made up of a bewildering variety of tribal groups, but has the advantage that both French and English are the official languages.

The other countries of West Africa

Elsewhere in West Africa tourism is in its infancy, or has even declined since the 1980s:

- In French-speaking **Guinea** and **Benin**, along with **Guinea-Bissau** (a former Portuguese colony) tourism was for many years after independence given a low priority by their governments – apparently for ideological reasons – and these countries have only recently encouraged private enterprise.
- French-speaking **Gabon** with its great mineral wealth has seen little need to attract tourists, other than business travellers to Libreville. This thinly populated country has great potential for ecotourism, thanks to the biodiversity of its rainforests, and in 2002 this was recognized with the designation of 13 national parks. Similar conservation initiatives, funded mainly by the USA, are proposed for neighbouring countries in West and Central Africa.
- The former Spanish colony of **Equatorial Guinea** lacks the basic infrastructure for tourism. However the beautiful volcanic island of Bioko (formerly Fernando Po) has potential for beach tourism, and business travel should increase with the exploitation of the country's oil resources in the Gulf of Guinea.
- Both **Liberia** and **Sierra Leone** had tourism industries on a small scale before the outbreak of civil war in the 1990s. Liberia had strong cultural and economic ties with the USA, and its capital Monrovia was one of West Africa's leading conference venues. The former British colony of Sierra Leone, whose capital Freetown has one of Africa's finest harbours, attracted tour operators to the fine white sand beaches of the Freetown Peninsula. The unrest in both countries is partly due to the tensions between the Westernized elites of the coast and the strongly tribal societies of the interior.
- **Ghana** on the other hand made an economic recovery during the 1990s. The Ghana Tourist Board has focused attention on the 'castles' of the Gold Coast, such as Christiansborg and Elmina, where slaves were held before being transported on the infamous 'Middle Passage' to the plantations of the New World. Other attractions for the independent traveller include the rainforests of the south, the markets of Accra and the heritage of the once powerful Ashanti kingdom in the interior.

In the **Sahel states**, tourism is handicapped for the following reasons:
  ○ their landlocked situation, (with the exception of Mauritania)

○ the low level of economic development and poor infrastructure
○ there are few hotels outside the national capitals
○ political instability and ethnic strife.

In most of these countries there is a north–south divide between the Saharan nomads of the north (Moors, Tuareg and Arabs) and the black African farming communities of the south. This is particularly evident in Chad, whereas in Mauritania the Moors are clearly the dominant group, and the country has close ties to Morocco.

Yet this region has seen the rise of great African civilizations in the past. **Mali** can boast the legendary trading centre of Timbuktu which now hosts a desert music festival, and the great mosque at Djenné, which is a superb example of Sudanese mud-brick architecture. Similarly, in the **Niger Republic** the ancient Tuareg city of Agadès attracts many tourists due to its location on the main trans-Saharan Route. Compared to the Nile, the great River Niger is under-utilized as a commercial waterway and tourist route, as it is only navigable for part of the year.

There has been some development of safari tourism in **Burkina Faso**, focusing on the 'W' National Park where the country borders on Benin and Niger.

Central Africa

This region is essentially landlocked, with only a short section of coastline near the mouth of the river Congo. It includes Africa's most extensive river system and its largest area of rainforest. Most of this area is virtually inaccessible, especially during the rainy season, which prevails for most of the year near the Equator. Hotels of international standard are few, and those in the major cities – Kinshasa, Kisangani, Bangui and Brazzaville – cater for business travellers attracted by the region's vast mineral resources.

Before the outbreaks of ethnic strife between the Hutu and Tutsi that characterized the 1990s, tourism was best developed in the two small countries of **Rwanda** and **Burundi**, once called the 'Switzerland of Africa' on account of their lake and mountain scenery. The dense forests of the Kagera and Volcanoes National Parks provided a refuge for gorillas, and attracted Western tour groups for this reason. Population pressures and the devastation caused by civil war have put this resource at severe risk.

The situation is equally serious in the neighbouring **Democratic Republic of the Congo** (formerly Zaire). In the colonial era this vast country, then known as the Belgian Congo, had been a pioneer in wildlife conservation, and as a legacy 12 per cent of its territory is, in theory at least, designated as protected areas. The most important resources are:

○ the Virunga National Park which shares with neighbouring Uganda the spectacular Ruwenzori Mountains with their strange high altitude vegetation
○ the Ituri Forest, home of the Pygmies
○ two of Africa's largest lakes.

Transport on the river Congo and its tributaries is confined to small-scale local commerce, and many improvements will need to be made, to both vessels and port facilities, before this network of inland waterways is viable for international tourism.

The Atlantic islands

To the west of the African continent lie several groups of volcanic islands in the Atlantic Ocean. They are isolated from the mainstream of international trade, and tourism is handicapped by the difficulty and expense of reaching them. They include three British territories:

- **St Helena** does not have an airport, and is served only by infrequent shipping services linking Europe to South Africa. Known mainly for its associations with Napoleon, the island has potential for tourists interested in dolphin watching, game fishing and the colonial heritage.
- **Ascension** has a military airport, acting as a staging point between Britain and the Falkland Islands, but this barren island has little to attract visitors.
- **Tristan da Cunha** is stormswept, rugged and harbourless, and must rank as one of the world's most remote communities.

The prospects for tourism seem brighter in the former Portuguese colonies of Saõ Tomé and the Cape Verde Islands, which are linked by scheduled air services to Lisbon.

- **São Tomé** and its smaller neighbour **Principe** are situated on the Equator. Their main assets are the fine beaches backed by a lush setting of forests and cacao plantations.
- The **Cape Verde Islands** lie to the west of Senegal, and are climatically not very different from the Canaries. Sal has an international airport, built to serve South African Airways in the apartheid era, when the airline was prohibited for political reasons from overflying the African continent. Sal is rather barren however, and the other islands offer more attractive scenery. Mindelo on São Vicente is the most cosmopolitan town on the islands, with a cultural scene that resembles Brazil rather than West Africa. Sailing, windsurfing, diving and trekking in the mountains of Santo Antão and São Tiago, are the activities offered to visitors.

The opportunities for tourism should increase with the new airport at Praia, thereby helping the economy of the islands, which is dependent on remittances from the large numbers of Cape Verdeans working overseas.

Summary

Africa is the second largest of the continents and is rich in both natural and cultural tourism resources. Although there is a large North African tourism industry serving the mass inclusive-tour markets of Europe, sub-Saharan Africa's tourism potential is largely unfulfilled. This can be attributed to a rudimentary transport network, the generally poor organizational framework and the low level of industrial development of most African countries. Yet in such a vast continent generalizations are inappropriate; South Africa, for example has an advanced economy, a high standard of tourism organization and infrastructure, and it also generates international tourists. Some African countries have identified tourism as an area for expansion to attract foreign currency and enhance their economic position. This has been most evident in Southern Africa and some of the islands of the Indian Ocean, but most of the countries of West and Central Africa have been less successful. The tourism resources of North Africa are based on both winter and summer beach resorts with the added ingredient of a taste of Arab and Berber culture and excursions to the Sahara. East Africa's tourism resources primarily comprise the national parks and game reserves, but developments at the coast allow combined beach and safari tourism. South Africa's attractions include beaches and wildlife, as well as spectacular scenery and a warm temperate climate. In West Africa, beach tourism is important, but here, as in the rest of the continent, holidaymakers can sample the colourful everyday life of African communities.

Chapter 21

The tourism geography of South Asia

Learning Objectives

After reading this chapter you should be able to:

■ Describe the major physical features and climates of the Indian subcontinent and understand their importance for tourism.
■ Understand the importance of religion in everyday life and its effect on tourism in the region.
■ Recognize the great economic and social contrasts within the region.
■ Show that inbound tourism is being encouraged by most of the countries in the region to provide foreign exchange and employment.
■ Recognize that the tourist appeal of the Indian subcontinent for the West lies in the exotic cultures of its peoples, as well as the familiar resources of beach tourism.
■ Recognize the growing importance of the Himalayas as a tourism resource, and the potential for conflict between tourism development and conservation.
■ Demonstrate a knowledge of the tourist regions, resorts, business centres and tourist attractions of South Asia.

Introduction

Asia is the world's largest continent, and we therefore need to divide it into regions of more manageable size, made up of countries which are broadly similar in cultural terms. Three regions that are geographically part of Asia – the Central Asian republics and Siberia, and the Middle East – were described in Chapters 18 and 19. This leaves South Asia, better known as the Indian subcontinent, which the World Tourism Organization (WTO) regards as a separate world region, and South-East Asia and the Far East, which the WTO includes as part of the East Asia–Pacific region.

The governments of most Asian countries realize the importance of tourism, and many have joined organizations such as the Pacific Asia Travel Association (PATA) to promote travel to the region more effectively. From the viewpoint of the Western tourist, these countries offer interesting contrasts in landscapes and cultures, living costs are generally low, and hotel service is more personalized than in the West. On the other hand, the provision of infrastructure outside the main tourist areas is often poor. Until recently the Asian countries themselves generated few tourists, and those that did travel abroad tended to do so within the region. As the economies of Asian countries develop, so does demand for tourism, particularly in the business sector.

The setting for tourism in South Asia

Physical features

The monsoon is the defining feature of the climates of the Indian subcontinent, South-East Asia and the Far East. In summer warm, humid air from the Indian and south-west Pacific Oceans moves into southern and eastern Asia bringing heavy rainfall – the 'summer monsoon'. In winter Asia is dominated by a strong centre of high pressure from which there is a flow of air to the south and south-east. This 'winter monsoon' brings several months of clear, dry weather.

The Indian subcontinent consists of three major physical divisions:

* **The northern mountain rampart**, which separates the subcontinent from the bulk of the Asian landmass. This includes the Himalayas to the east and the Pamirs, Hindu Kush and Karakoram mountains to the west. These mountains rise to over 6000 metres and boast the world's highest summits. They also have the following important characteristics:
  ○ They act as a barrier to the movement of the very cold air masses building up over Central Asia in winter, so that the lowlands to the south enjoy a warm climate throughout the year.
  ○ They also act as a barrier to north–south communications; few roads cross the high mountain passes, and unlike the Alps, no railways penetrate the ranges. Even the pattern of air routes is affected to some extent.
  ○ Because of their altitude, the mountains themselves have a much cooler climate than the lowlands, and support a number of contrasting life zones based on differences in rainfall as well as temperature. The western Himalayas for example are much drier than those to the east – where Cherrapunji in the Assam foothills has the unenviable distinction of being one of the world's wettest places.
  ○ In relation to their resources the mountain valleys are often densely populated. The growth of tourism poses a threat to local communities already under pressure, as well as providing economic opportunity.
  ○ In the past the mountains contained a number of independent kingdoms, which were protected from outside influences by their remoteness and rugged terrain. At the present time only Bhutan, and to a lesser extent Nepal, have managed to preserve their cultural as well as political integrity. Sikkim and Ladakh have

been absorbed by India, while Tibet has been forcibly integrated into China. On the other hand, some of the ethnic groups remain essentially nomadic, ignoring the modern frontiers.

- **The Northern Plains**, through which flow the great rivers Indus, Ganges and Brahmaputra. These lowlands contain most of the historic cities and business centres of South Asia. The western part of the region has an arid climate, as shown by the Thar Desert on the India–Pakistan border. Elsewhere winter tends to be the dry season, with a large daily range of temperature. Stifling heat (with temperatures frequently exceeding 40 °C) can be expected from April to June before the onset of the summer monsoon. This provides over 90 per cent of India's water supply, so not surprisingly it has a vital influence on the landscape and the lifestyle. The arrival of the rains is one of the world's most dramatic weather events and is also remarkably predictable, starting in Kerala at the end of May, and sweeping north to reach Bombay by 5 June and Delhi by 29 June. The monsoon provides some initial relief from the excessive heat, but is soon followed by months of sweltering weather, as the high humidity negates any cooling effect the slightly lower temperatures might have.
- **Peninsular India and the islands**. This part of South Asia is dominated by the great plateau of volcanic rocks known as the Deccan and the coastal mountain ranges known as the Western and Eastern Ghats. The region has a more moderate tropical climate than the northern plains, making it a suitable winter sun destination for tourists from Europe. Coastal locations such as Goa and Kerala, as well as the island states of Sri Lanka and the Maldives in the Indian Ocean, have developed tourism industries based primarily on their beach resources.

Cultural features of South Asia

Despite the attractions of beaches and spectacular mountain scenery, the tourist appeal of South Asia is to a large extent cultural. The street life, bustling markets, colourful festivals and distinctive foods are fascinating for Western tourists, who also experience a degree of 'culture shock' on arrival. Religion has a major impact on everyday life, and the best of the cultural heritage is to be found in temples and shrines rather than secular buildings. The perceived 'other-worldliness' of countries like India and Nepal attracts many Western tourists alienated by materialism, some of whom seek spiritual guidance in religious communities or *ashrams*.

At this point some explanation of the major religions is necessary:

- **Hinduism**, with over 700 million believers, is the majority religion in India, and its rituals have profoundly influenced Indian civilization for at least three thousand years – far longer than Christianity in the West or Islam in the Middle East. The Hindu belief in *karma* and reincarnation often results in a fatalistic attitude to life that most Westerners find difficult to accept. Hindu temples are dedicated to a particular god or goddess (Brahma, Vishnu and Shiva are the most important), and are sumptuously decorated with polychrome sculptures.
- **Buddhism** also originated in northern India, but is now much more widespread in Sri Lanka, the Himalayan kingdoms, South-East Asia and the Far East. Common to all Buddhists is a belief in the importance of meditation as the path to *Nirvana* (enlightenment). Buddhist temples usually contain stylized images of the religion's founder – Gautama Siddhartha, who is venerated as the Buddha

(enlightened one). However styles of architecture vary widely – temples in Sri Lanka and Burma are quite different from those in Bhutan for example.

- **Islam** is the predominant religion in Afghanistan, Pakistan, Bangladesh and the Maldives. The Mogul Emperors imposed Islam on northern India in the sixteenth century, and were responsible for some of the world's finest Muslim architecture, including the Taj Mahal.
- **Sikhism** originally arose as a resistance to the Muslim domination of northern India. Sikhs differ from Hindus in being monotheistic, placing much less emphasis on ritual, and rejecting the rigid social distinctions or castes that have characterized traditional Indian culture. Although they number only some 18 million, based mainly in the Punjab, they play an important role in commerce and the professions.

Religious tensions also threaten the political stability of most countries in the region, and thus reduce their appeal to tourists. Differences between Muslims and Hindus in British India led to its partition into two separate countries on independence in 1947. However, this left unresolved the status of Kashmir, causing a long-running dispute between the Republic of India and Pakistan and disrupting communications between the two countries. Since the late 1990s the rise of Hindu fundamentalism in the Republic of India has posed a threat to the government's policy of secularism and religious toleration, culminating in the inter-communal massacres that occurred in Gujarat in 2002. Muslim fundamentalism has already influenced social attitudes in Afghanistan and Pakistan, where religion and politics are less clearly separated than they are in India.

Western cultural influence was largely due to the British, although the Portuguese arrived in the region much earlier. In fact, almost the whole of the Indian subcontinent was under British rule or protection during the nineteenth and early twentieth centuries, with the exception of a few small Portuguese and French enclaves such as Goa, Diu and Pondicherry. The legacy of the British *Raj* remains after independence in the widespread use of the English language and administrative framework, sporting and military traditions, an extensive railway network and a supply of mountain resorts known as hill-stations. These had provided British officials and their families, in the days before air-conditioning, with a refuge from the summer heat of the plains. These places still retain much of their colonial architecture, although they are now resorts for middle class domestic tourists. They include:

- Murree in Pakistan
- Simla in the Himalayas (the summer capital of British India)
- Ootacamund in the Nilgiri Highlands of southern India
- Nuwara Eliya in Sri Lanka.

Approaches to tourism

South Asia as a whole accounts for around one per cent of international world tourism arrivals. Over half of all tourist arrivals, and over three-quarters of receipts, are accounted for by the largest of the nine component countries of South Asia – the Republic of India. Elsewhere in much of the region tourism is of little significance, notably for Afghanistan due to political unrest rendering the country unsafe for travellers, and for Bangladesh, where more pressing economic concerns overshadow tourism development. The majority of countries have encouraged inbound tourism, and most have a positive balance on their travel account, with the notable exception of Pakistan, where outbound travel is much greater in terms of expenditure.

We can see a variety of approaches to tourism within the region including:

- stringent restriction on visitor numbers in the case of Bhutan – in contrast to neighbouring Nepal
- a policy of tourist segregation from the local communities in the Lakshadweep and the Maldive islands
- promotion of Western-style beach holidays in Goa.

India

India demands our attention for a number of reasons:

- In extent and cultural variety it is the equivalent of Europe, but with a much older civilization. There are at least 15 major languages, although Hindi is the most widely spoken. The country is a mosaic of different religions, ethnic groups and castes.
- With a population now well over a billion, India will surpass China as the world's most populous country by 2030. It has almost 20 per cent of the world's population on just 3 per cent of the world's land area, so that demographic pressures on the resource base are severe.
- Over half of India's population is under 25 years of age, 60 per cent are illiterate and the majority are living at subsistence level. Although India is a predominantly rural country, it also contains three major world cities – Delhi, Bombay and Calcutta – each with well over 10 million inhabitants, and increasing at the rate of half a million a year.
- Despite these pressures and many other socioeconomic problems, India has retained a democratic form of government since independence, although the Congress Party has been dominant in politics for most of that time. The cultural diversity of the country is recognized in the federal system of government, in which each of the 29 states and six autonomous territories has a large degree of control over its internal affairs, including tourism development.
- India is one of Asia's leading industrial nations, with technological expertise as part of its vast human resources. Bangalore and Hyderabad for example are among the world's leading centres of information technology. India also has a well-developed transport infrastructure compared to most Third World countries. On the other hand, bureaucratic controls and inertia inhibit progress.

Demand for tourism

Domestic and outbound tourism

A substantial middle class, estimated to be between 15 and 20 per cent of the population – or over 150 million people – has the means to participate in domestic tourism in India and the volumes are impressive, exceeding 200 million trips a year. Traditionally a good deal of domestic travel has been undertaken for religious reasons, as all the major faiths encourage pilgrimages to shrines or holy places.

The best known of these is the Hindu centre of Varanasi (Benares) on the river Ganges, where the *ghats* – the steps leading down to the water's edge – are the focus for ritual bathing, readings from the sacred texts by gurus and cremations. However, there are many other shrines, some in remote locations in the Himalayas and Kashmir. Often these pilgrimages entail an arduous journey, partly on foot, and embrace all classes of society, including large numbers of wandering *sadhus* (holy men). Bodhgaya is the main pilgrimage centre for Buddhists, while the Golden Temple at Amritsar is the holy place of the Sikhs. Visits to family entertainment centres and amusement parks, reflecting India's fascination with high technology, as well as stays in beach and mountain resorts, are expected to increase as incomes rise among a Western educated middle class.

Outbound tourism is much smaller in volume, but nevertheless accounted for 4 million departures a year in the early years of the twenty-first century, mainly to neighbouring countries such as Nepal. Business travel accounts for 25 per cent of these journeys. Leisure travel to countries outside South Asia should grow with the relaxation of strict foreign exchange controls imposed by the Indian government. For many years Britain has been the most popular European destination, reflecting the cultural ties between the two countries.

Inbound tourism

Despite having vast tourism potential, India received only a very small share of world tourism during the early years of the twenty-first century, amounting to some 2.5 million arrivals. Even so, tourism has shown impressive growth since 1970, when 290 000 visitors were recorded. Tourism is now India's third largest earner of foreign exchange, and provides jobs for at least 8 million people. The impact is much greater if we consider the informal sector of the economy, and the very large numbers engaged in the handicraft industries. However, a number of factors are holding back the expansion of tourism in India:

* inadequate infrastructure, especially water and power supplies
* negative publicity in the Western media; for example, outbreaks of disease and inter-communal strife, in reality confined to specific areas, are seen as affecting the whole country
* promotion of this enormous and complex country as one destination, whereas India consists of many quite different destinations and tourism products; there is a need to market specific destinations and target specific types of tourist
* the seasonal concentration of visits in the final quarter of the year, creating occupancy problems for India's hotels
* a shortage of medium-priced accommodation, particularly in Delhi
* other negative factors include air pollution in the cities during the dry season, noise, poor hygiene and harassment by beggars and street vendors.

The main generating markets for India include Britain, Germany, France, the USA, the Middle East and Japan. Many arrivals from the Middle East and Britain are in fact returning expatriates, who tend to stay with friends or relatives and make little use of tourist facilities. The average length of stay of tourists to India – at 28 days – is among the world's highest; backpackers, for example, from Europe, Australia and North America, who are including India as part of an Asian tour, spend at least 3 weeks in the country. These young budget travellers have played an important role in opening up new destinations to conventional tourism.

However the typical backpackers of the new millennium are different from their predecessors of the 1970s in that:

- they are usually following an established route pattern, staying at hostels and cheap hotels patronized by other Western budget travellers
- they are less concerned with a search for 'spiritual values'. Nowadays, an extended visit to India is seen more as an interesting way of filling the 'gap year' between college and a career.

The most popular time to visit India is from October to December when the weather is at its best, but there is a steady flow of business travellers throughout the year.

The supply of tourism

Transport

The vast majority of foreign visitors to India (other than those from neighbouring Bangladesh and Pakistan) arrive by air. Delhi and Bombay (now officially named Mumbai) are the most important gateways, and have invested heavily in improving facilities for air travellers. Calcutta and Madras (Chennai) serve the eastern and southern parts of the country. The Indian government has responded to the growth in air travel by adopting a liberal *open skies* policy, which allows foreign charter airlines to fly direct from Europe to resort areas such as Goa. Moreover the national carrier Air India has a code-sharing agreement with the American airline Continental Airways.

Only a small minority of Western tourists travel overland to India, due to the political situation in Afghanistan which has closed the historic route through the Khyber Pass, while the long-standing dispute between India and Pakistan over Kashmir places another obstacle in the way of travellers. Internal transport is less fraught with difficulties. Indian Airlines operate domestic services to over 70 destinations within the country as well as neighbouring states and new low cost carriers such as Jet Airways and Air Sahara have entered the market. India inherited from Britain the most extensive railway network in Asia, amounting to over 70 000 kilometres of track. This provides a cheaper and more interesting way of touring than by air, with express services linking all the main cities. As the system is heavily used, foreign tourists need to purchase *Indrail* passes or make prior reservations to ensure travelling in comfort and without hassle. In some areas steam locomotives are still used, as for example on the narrow-gauge Darjeeling–Himalaya railway, which is a major tourist attraction in its own right. Luxury rail products such as the 'Palace on Wheels' and the 'Royal Orient' are promoted by the India Tourism Office as a way of touring the classical sites in the north-west of the country.

India also boasts over one million kilometres of passable roads, which provide access to even remote mountain areas; however, accident levels are very high by Western standards, livestock on the road are a frequent hazard, and travel even by express bus can be a noisy and exhausting experience.

Accommodation

India's accommodation stock is extensive ranging from luxury hotels to basic hostels used by backpackers more concerned about price than fire safety standards. Modern Western-style hotels catering for both business and leisure tourists are found in all large cities and the popular tourist centres. Indian-owned chains, namely Taj, Oberoi and the state-owned India Tourism Development Corporation (ITDC), dominate this sector. More unusual types of accommodation include:

- luxury houseboats moored on Lake Dal at Srinagar, a heritage of British and Mogul rule in Kashmir
- former palaces of the Indian princes or maharajas, who were semi-independent under the British Raj, which have now been converted into 'heritage hotels', the most famous being the Lake Palace Hotel at Udaipur in Rajasthan, in a highly romantic setting
- *dak* bungalows, used primarily by government officials as rest houses but also sometimes available for overnight stays by tourists in remote areas
- hostels provided by religious organizations
- tourist bungalows providing self-catering facilities and private guesthouses, both available in resort areas; campgrounds have also been developed along the main overland routes and forest lodges are available in wildlife reserves such as the Kanha National Park.

Tourism organization

In the 1960s tourism development began to form part of the government's Five Year Plans (whose primary objective is to raise living standards) and more recently tourism has been the subject of specific 'action plans'. The Ministry of Tourism and Culture is responsible for formulating policy at cabinet level. The Ministry is supported by a number of other agencies, including:

- The India Tourism Development Corporation Ltd (ITDC) This was set up by the government in 1965 to develop infrastructure in those areas where the private sector was reluctant to invest.
- Apart from hotels the ITDC also owned resorts, restaurants and transport operations, some of which have since been privatized.
- The Tourism Finance Corporation of India, established to assist with tourism financing.
- The Indian Institute of Travel and Tourism Management (IITTM) established to set up high-quality training and education in tourism.

As well as supporting many projects through the ITDC, the government also provides financial incentives to domestic and foreign companies in the private sector. At the regional and local levels the various state and city authorities have a regulatory role, and some have set up development corporations to carry out tourism projects. In recent years, however, the public sector has not been particularly active in encouraging tourism. It is perhaps not surprising that in a country with so many pressing social and economic problems, the development of tourist facilities, which the majority of the Indian population cannot afford, is seen as a low priority.

Tourism resources

On offer is a unique blend of ancient civilizations, religious monuments, spectacular scenery, beaches, mountain resorts and wildlife reserves, that have been promoted in the West as 'Incredible India'. We can summarize the main tourism products as:

- **Cultural tourism**, usually focusing on a particular region, and taking the form of a tour circuit linking a number of sites to a gateway city.
- **Beach tourism**, at present found mainly in the states of Goa, Kerala and Tamil Nadu; little of India's 7500 kilometre-long coastline has been developed for tourism.
- **Adventure tourism**, including trekking, mountain climbing and river-running, which is mainly focused on the more accessible parts of the Himalaya region.
- **Ecotourism**. India is second only to Africa in the variety of its wildlife resources. This is perhaps surprising given the demographic pressures and the threats of increasing pollution and deforestation (only 13 per cent of the country has any type of forest cover). The first national park – Jim Corbett to the north of Delhi – was established under British rule in 1911 due to the efforts of a hunter turned conservationist. There are now some 70 national parks and 330 wildlife sanctuaries, although most are restricted in area compared to those of Africa. The federal government has effected a number of conservation measures; the most widely publicized is 'Project Tiger' which seeks to protect India's best known animal. Kanha National Park in Madhya Pradesh, the setting for Kipling's *Jungle Book*, is the best known of these game reserves. Much of the responsibility for wildlife management has devolved to the individual states. Limited funding is a problem, and issues of economic development often conflict with conservation.
- **Spa tourism** based on luxury hotels and India's tradition of yoga techniques for relaxation.

Due to its extent India is usually treated as four regions, based on the gateways of Delhi, Mumbai (Bombay), Chennai (Madras) and Calcutta.

Northern India

This region has played a major role in the history of India, and contains the best-known cultural attractions. The so-called 'Classic Triangle', a tour circuit linking the cities of Delhi, Agra and Jaipur, is the most popular route for foreign visitors.

Delhi actually consists of two cities – the old and the new. Old Delhi was the capital of the Mogul Empire, and is a maze of narrow streets, chaotic traffic and bustling bazaars. Among its Islamic monuments are the Jama Masjid Mosque and the Red Fort, once a royal palace. The British planned New Delhi as the capital of India in the closing decades of the Raj. The most important of its broad ceremonial avenues is the Rajpath linking India Gate to the President's Palace.

Agra is mainly visited for the **Taj Mahal**, the white marble mausoleum commemorating Shah Jehan's love for his favourite wife Mumtaz. This beautiful building is under threat from:

- tourist pressure, leaving in its wake litter in the gardens and even graffiti on the monument itself
- pollution – although tourism provides a livelihood for many thousands employed in the craft and service sectors, Agra is also a major industrial city. Sulphur dioxide emissions have caused a massive deterioration in the stonework.

Within easy reach of Agra are other relics of historic India:

- Fatehpur Sikri, the remains of a short lived capital of the Mogul Empire
- Orchha, which has undergone less restoration and is not as commercialized

- the temples at Khajuraho with their erotic sculptures are also a well-established part of the tour circuit.

Jaipur is the gateway to **Rajasthan**, a state which to many epitomizes India, with its colourful costumes, ethnic crafts and the palaces of the former maharajas. It also exemplifies the problems brought about by tourism in an arid region where there are few other sources of income. Some allege that conventional organized tourism does not benefit local communities as profits mainly go to the owners of 'heritage hotels', who furthermore prefer to employ immigrant Nepalis, who are prepared to accept even lower wages than the locals. On the other hand, backpackers have also been criticized for showing little respect for Hindu traditions, while the Pushkar camel market has become a commercialized tourist event. Of the tourist centres, Jaipur itself is famous for its markets and the 'Palace of the Winds', but suffers from chronic pollution and lack of investment.

Other attractions in the region include:

- Jodhpur, which gave polo to the British, is noted for its *son et lumière* performances recreating the warrior traditions of the Rajput princes.
- Udaipur is the best preserved of the Rajput cities, with a beautiful setting on Lake Pichola.
- Jaisalmer, was once a major trading centre for camel caravans crossing the Thar Desert, but is now a picturesque stop on the tourist itinerary. Income from tourism enabled the authorities to provide a piped water supply, but this together with vastly increased water consumption, has caused widespread subsidence, as the town's open drains cannot cope. As a result, many of the *havelis* (merchant houses) are in urgent need of repair.

Kashmir, with its beautiful mountain scenery and cool climate, was the favourite resort area for the Mogul rulers of India, who designed the famous Shalimar Gardens in Srinagar. The chronic dispute with Pakistan, with most of this largely Muslim state under military occupation, has deterred Western visitors, although Gulmarg was developed in the 1970s as the premier skiing and golf resort of India. On the other hand, Ladakh has become a trekking destination, offering spectacular, if barren, high mountain landscapes and a Tibetan culture which is still largely intact.

Eastern India

The Eastern India region is centred on **Calcutta**, now the capital of West Bengal. The former capital of British India is better known for its overcrowding and Mother Teresa's work among the destitute than for its cultural attractions, which actually outshine those of Delhi. Although rickshaws still feature in the traffic, Calcutta boasts India's only metro system, and its technological achievements are showcased in 'Science City'.

Within easy reach are the beach resorts of the Bay of Bengal, including Puri, which is also a major religious centre for Hindus. It is one of a number of temple-cities in the state of Orissa, the others being Konarak and Bhubaneswar. Calcutta is also the gateway to the eastern Himalayas, particularly the mountain resorts of Darjeeling and Shillong, which are noted for their tea plantations. Large areas of this sensitive frontier region are, however, tribal territories under military control, and access is restricted for security reasons.

Southern India

The Dravidian peoples of southern India are culturally distinct, and overseas trade has played an important role in the history of the region. The port of Cochin for example was noted for its trade in pepper and other spices in ancient times, and in the picturesque fishing villages Hinduism has co-existed peacefully with Christianity and other religions.

With its favourable climate, lush scenery and fine beaches, the state of Kerala is set to rival Goa as a holiday destination. A unique asset is provided by the 'backwaters', a system of canals adapted from transporting agricultural produce to recreational use. With the introduction of charter flights in 1995, Kovalam has become a major beach resort, particularly for British holidaymakers. However, this has failed to benefit the local community to the same extent as the small-scale informal tourism of earlier years, and stands in apparent contradiction to the socialist leanings of the state government.

Most of the Coromandel Coast is less attractive for tourism development, due to the heavy surf. Nevertheless, Madras has fine beaches as well as being a major cultural centre, offering the classical *kathakali* dance-dramas, adapted for a Western tourist audience. It is a good base for exploring the temples of Madurai and Kanchipuram, which are spectacular examples of Hindu architecture.

Western India

Beach tourism has developed to a greater extent in western India along the Malabar coast. The region is dominated by Bombay, India's major port and business centre, while Goa is the leading holiday destination.

Bombay is a new city by Indian standards, with many reminders of the British Raj when it was the 'gateway to India'. It is seen as a city of opportunity by rural immigrants, who pour in at the rate of a thousand a day. With little room for expansion on a narrow peninsula, the city's congestion is acute, and the contrasts between skyscrapers and grand hotels on the one hand, and the *bustees* (slums) on the other, are extreme. This may explain the dominant role of 'Bollywood' – Bombay's booming film industry – in popular culture. Apart from shopping, the city's attractions include Chowpatty Beach, with its snake charmers and other performers, the 'hanging gardens' of exclusive Malabar Hill, the Gandhi Memorial and the art collections of the Prince of Wales Museum. The ancient history of India is brought to life at the Elephanta Caves, while Bombay is a good base for visiting the Buddhist and Hindu temples of Ajanta and Ellora.

Goa's small area offers scenic variety, over 100 kilometres of fine beaches and a relaxed lifestyle. Culturally it is unique – a blend of Indian and 'Latin' influences. Carnival and both Catholic and Hindu festivals are celebrated here, while alcohol is freely available – unlike the situation elsewhere in India. Portugal ruled Goa for four and a half centuries until the Indian Army ousted it in 1961, and the Portuguese influence is evident in the architecture, music and the cuisine. The immense Baroque church of Bom Jesu in Old Goa – the former capital – contains the tomb of St Francis Xavier, the greatest of Jesuit missionaries to the East.

Western tourists are not attracted to Goa primarily for cultural or religious reasons however; since the arrival of the 'hippies' in the 1960s the focus has been on beach tourism. Nevertheless we can distinguish between different categories of visitor and a range of accommodation and services has developed to meet their needs:

- ○ Low-budget backpackers, mainly from Europe and Australia, who are stopping off in Goa as part of an extended Asian tour. They stay in cheap guesthouses in the Anjuna area, 'discovered' by the hippies of a previous generation.

- Indian domestic tourists taking seaside holidays, cultural tours and business trips, who stay at hotels in Panaji, the state capital, or other towns.
- High-income Western tourists and returning Goan expatriates, staying at luxury resort hotels on tailor-made itineraries.
- Package holidaymakers from the UK, Germany and other West European countries arriving during the winter season on direct charter flights to Goa's Dabolim Airport. They stay in three-star hotels contracted to particular tour operators. Due to the rapid growth of charters since 1987, fishing villages such as Calangute have become commercialized resorts.
- Middle class West European holidaymakers who take advantage of the cheap charter fares but who prefer to use locally owned small hotels and guesthouses.

Tourism has arguably brought economic benefits to Goa, but the state government's policy of encouraging upmarket tourism has been opposed by local non-governmental organizations (NGOs) concerned with the social and environmental issues associated with tourism development. These include:

- The diversion of scarce resources, such as water and power from agriculture to the hotel sector. It is claimed, for example, that one five-star hotel consumes as much water as five villages.
- Unlike the guesthouses and small hotels that are locally owned, the luxury hotels are linked with multi-national chains or owned by Indians from outside Goa. The state government's attempts to control the beach shacks selling food and beverages is seen as favouring the hotels at the expense of local people's livelihood.
- The expansion of tourism has resulted in a decline of traditional occupations such as fishing and cashew nut farming.
- Many Goans are offended by the association of tourism in some resort areas with Western sex and drug culture.

Goa has reached the stage in the resort life cycle where it is facing growing competition as tour operators discover more unspoiled beach locations. Backpackers, for example, are increasingly attracted to the island of Diu, another former Portuguese territory, which is much closer to the tourist attractions of Rajasthan.

The islands of India

India's island territories as yet remain largely untouched by Western style tourism, although they attract a growing number of domestic visitors. They include:

- The Lakshadweep (Laccadives) archipelago in the Indian Ocean, composed of small coral atolls similar to the Maldives further south. Bangaram is the only island open to Western tourists for diving holidays.
- The Andaman and Nicobar Islands in the Bay of Bengal, which are rugged and largely forest covered. There is potential for ecotourism and diving, but development is restricted by lack of infrastructure and the sensitive nature of relationships between mainland India and the indigenous tribes, an example of a 'Fourth World' culture which is increasingly under threat.

Pakistan

Pakistan has been less successful than India in attracting Western tourists and the sector accounts for less than one per cent of GDP. In part, this is due to the strength of

Islamic fundamentalism, security concerns, poor infrastructure and the restrictions on cross-border travel. Most of the country consists of mountain and desert landscapes, and some of the world's most difficult terrain separates Pakistan from its neighbours to the west and north. At the beginning of the twenty-first century tourist arrivals were around 500 000 a year, the most important generating countries being the UK and the USA. In addition, domestic tourism is significant, and set to grow, with an estimated 40 million trips a year.

An agency of the Ministry of Tourism, the Pakistan Tourist Development Corporation, offers a wide selection of hotels, motels and rest houses (known as *musafir khanas*) and tours operated by its subsidiary Pakistan Tours Ltd. The national airline, Pakistan International Airlines (PIA), provides a network of international and domestic services.

Although Urdu is the official language, Pakistan is made up of a number of ethnic groups and the country has been less politically stable than India. In the north west of the country, government control is only loosely exercised over the Pathans and other tribes. In the time of the Raj, this was the North West Frontier of British India, immortalized by Rudyard Kipling; nowadays it is an area rife with guns and refugees as a result of the continuing crisis in Afghanistan. For this reason, the Khyber Pass has ceased to function as an overland tourist route, although the regional capital – Peshawar – is visited by the more adventurous travellers. The majority of Pakistan's population live in the irrigated valley of the river Indus, which also contains the major tourist centres:

- Lahore is the religious and cultural centre of the country, conserving much of the heritage of the Mogul emperors of India, including its own Shalimar Gardens.
- Multan is another historic walled city, situated close to the remains of a much older civilization which flourished at Mohenjo–Daro in the third millennium BC.
- Karachi is Pakistan's largest city and major international gateway.
- Islamabad, which was deliberately planned as the capital of the new Muslim state, and the old city of Rawalpindi nearby, are mainly centres for business travel.

In the north of Pakistan, Gilgit provides facilities for skiing, trekking and mountain climbing, while adventure-seekers can follow the Karakoram Highway. This spectacular feat of engineering threads its way between some of the world's highest mountains and glaciers into China.

Sri Lanka

Formerly known as Ceylon, Sri Lanka is a large island rich in tourism resources. Its capital Colombo is well placed in relation to the air and shipping routes crossing the Indian Ocean. In the past, the island's closeness to India and fabled wealth attracted Arab traders who were followed by the Portuguese, Dutch and British. This resulted in a mix of cultures and one of the country's highest mountains – Sri Padu (Adam's Peak) is sacred to all four major religions.

Tourism demand and supply

Until the 1970s Sri Lanka had been one of the more stable countries in South Asia and the prospects for tourism seemed bright. The Ceylon Tourist Board (now the Sri Lanka Tourist Board) was established in 1966, when 19 000 visitors were received. By 1982 this had grown to over 400 000, most of whom were on air-inclusive holidays, organized by West European tour operators (the entrepreneur Freddie Laker was largely responsible for introducing Sri Lanka as a long-haul beach destination to the British market). However, there had long been tensions between the Sinhalese and the Tamil minority, who were originally brought in by the British from southern India to work in the tea plantations. During the 1980s these erupted into civil war, which rendered much of the north and east of the country off-limits to tourists, and as a result Sri Lanka lost favour with Western tour operators and visitor numbers fell dramatically. With the prospect of a lasting agreement between the government and the Tamil separatists, international tourism has now largely recovered, with arrivals approaching 400 000 in the early years of the twenty-first century.

The Ministry of Tourism has overall responsibility for the sector, while the Sri Lanka Tourist Board is responsible for promotion and market research. Although Sri Lanka has suffered from the lack of a clear tourism policy, a master plan commissioned in the 1990s provides the necessary framework for growth. The government, while encouraging foreign investment, has responded by steering development to the coastal areas close to Colombo in the west, and the port of Trincomalee in the east, in this way protecting the country's cultural and wildlife resources from the impact of tourism. The plan also stimulated a change in emphasis of tourism development to 'beach plus' products, in contrast to the sun, sand and sea formula of earlier years.

Tourism resources

Sri Lanka's tourist attractions include:

- Extensive sandy beaches along the south and west coast, although sea conditions can be rough during the period of the south-west monsoon from May to July. Here the Ceylon Tourist Board has developed resort hotels of an international standard, particularly at Bentota. The beaches on the east coast are less developed, although they are more sheltered and enjoy a drier climate.
- The 'cultural triangle' of the interior, based on the historic cities of Kandy, Anuradhapura and Polonnaruwa, each of which served at one time as capital of a powerful kingdom. The Rock Fortress at Sigiriya, rising above the northern plain, is particularly impressive, as are the remains of ancient temples, palaces and complex irrigation systems. Traditional crafts and dances continue to flourish in Kandy, which contains the 'Temple of the Tooth', a world famous Buddhist shrine.
- The wildlife resources, including the elephant orphanage at Pinnawela, and a number of national parks, such as Yala and Gal Oya in the south-east, which offer bungalow accommodation to tourists.
- Colombo is a major business and conference centre, as well as providing shopping opportunities, especially in jewellery, batik, and wood-carving.

The other countries of South Asia

Bangladesh

From 1947 to 1971 Bangladesh , formerly east Bengal, was a detached part of Pakistan, but strong cultural differences led to a war of independence. The new nation had to face severe economic and environmental problems, namely:

- It is densely populated even by Asian standards, relying on an economy dominated by agriculture, and with few industries other than textiles.
- Most of the country is low-lying and is effectively a 'waterland' after the monsoon rains. Unusually devastating floods occur when tropical cyclones from the Indian Ocean coincide with heavy monsoon rains in the eastern Himalayas.
- The country's many rivers are an obstacle to an effective road network, while ferry links are below Western standards.

Nevertheless, Bangladesh is no longer regarded as an economic 'basket case' by some Western experts, and business travel to the capital Dhaka is growing in importance. Small enterprises are expected to play a major role in any expansion of tourism. Aside from the capital, the main areas of interest for tourists are:

- the hill country of Sylhet in the north
- the vast wetland environment of the Sundarbans, formed by the deltas of the Ganges and Brahmaputra, which provides a refuge for wildlife
- Cox's Bazaar, which boasts one of the most extensive beaches in Asia, as yet little developed.

Afghanistan

In the 1970s Afghanistan was a transit area and Kabul a welcome staging point for Western tourists on the overland route to India. Since then the country's economy and infrastructure have been devastated as a result of the Soviet invasion in 1979 and civil war arising out of long-standing tribal feuds. The fundamentalist Taliban regime from 1996 to 2001 actively discouraged tourism and even destroyed much of the country's pre-Islamic heritage, such as the Buddhist monuments at Bamian. The UN intervention following 9/11 will have to bring security and much-needed improvements to the road network as pre-conditions for tourism development. Most of Afghanistan consists of arid, rugged mountains, while the climate and culture have much in common with Central Asia.

The Maldives

The Maldives is an independent republic located in the Indian Ocean, south-west of the Indian sub-continent. Geographically, the Maldives is a unique collection of 26 coral atolls, containing almost 1200 coral islands and hundreds of small sandbanks. They have little in common with the other Muslim countries of South Asia and the government has done much to encourage Western tourism, but on its own terms.

For example, the islands are strictly Islamic and no alcohol is allowed except in the resorts. Mosques are found on many islands and visitors are expected to respect the traditions of Islam in terms of modest dress when visiting the capital, Male.

Male is a small town with a few shops and restaurants, but little to attract the visitor, although it contains two-thirds of the Maldives population. However, it is the gateway to the islands through Hulhule International Airport.

The prime tourism resource of the islands is the pristine marine environment where the quality of the coral reefs and marine life is unrivalled anywhere in the world. The majority of visitors arrive in the Maldives to experience this marine environment and also for water sports. Each of the resort islands (many of which are very small) has a diving base and the resort *house reef* is commonly within wading or swimming distance from the accommodation.

The Ministry of Tourism oversees tourism development and regulates the resorts. In the late 1990s the Maldives Tourism Promotion Board was created to market the islands internationally. The islands are attempting to position themselves as the premium ecotourism destination in the world, and to diversify their markets.

Nepal

Although the Gurkhas who come from Nepal had long played an important role in the British Army, the Hindu Kingdom of Nepal was closed to the outside world until the 1950s. After its discovery by 'hippies' and overland travellers in the 1960s there was a rapid growth of tourism. However events such as 9/11, the massacre of Nepal's royal family and an on-going Maoist rebellion in the west of the country have had a severe impact, such that arrivals fell from 460 000 in 2000 to only 200 000 in 2002.

Within an area only half that of Great Britain, Nepal can offer a great variety of climates and scenery. There are three main physical divisions running east to west, namely:

- The Himalayas, which contain eight of the world's highest mountain peaks, including Everest and Annapurna, attracting trekkers, mountain climbers and adventure-seekers from many different countries.
- The foothills, including the valleys of Kathmandu and Pokhara, which contain the majority of the population. Cultural attractions abound in the form of Buddhist temples, as at Bhadgaon and Patan.
- The sub-tropical lowlands, known as the Terai, which still contain areas of jungle, including the Royal Chitwan National Park and its famous 'Tiger Tops' game lodge.
- Buddhists from all over the world are attracted to Lumbini, the birthplace of Buddha.

The Ministry of Tourism and Civil Aviation, along with the Department of National Parks and Wildlife is responsible for tourism organization, and the Nepal Tourism Board is a public/private sector partnership body. In practice, Nepal relies very much on foreign aid for tourism development, and on Indian tour operators to bring in the visitors. In the 1990s, air policy underwent a degree of liberalization allowing in other carriers to supplement Royal Nepal Airlines.

Poor access, pollution, inadequate infrastructure and frequent shortages of power and water supplies are major constraints on the growth of the tourism sector.

In addition, criticism from environmentalists about the pollution found on the mountains, and the lack of robust environmental policies (for example on timber cutting to maintain tourist lodges) may also constrain tourism growth.

Adventure trips are the mainstay of tourism in Nepal with activities including mountain climbing, river-running and mountain biking. Trekking, where tourists on foot are escorted and supplied by local porters and guides, is the most popular activity in the Himalayan zone of Nepal, accounting for over a quarter of all visitors. Nepal offers a great variety of trekking opportunities including some of the world's most spectacular scenery; the trails are well maintained and trekkers are rarely far from a village. Although new areas are being opened up to meet the demand, trekking also shows a high degree of concentration in particular areas of central and eastern Nepal, including:

- the Annapurna region west of Pokhara
- the Everest route, from Lukha to the base camp at the foot of Mount Everest.

Bhutan

This Buddhist kingdom is much smaller than Nepal in area and population as well as being more remote. The government is determined to preserve traditional lifestyles from the impact of tourism, which is therefore strictly controlled. Until recently access was restricted to a few accredited tour operators offering special interest holidays to small groups of visitors, in contrast to trekking on the Nepalese model. The government is beginning to allow some development of upmarket resort hotels, where access will be controlled by price. Culturally, Bhutan is similar to Tibet, with numerous fortified monasteries known as *dzongs* dominating the countryside.

Summary

South Asia contains comes of the world's most densely populated countries, at various stages of economic development but nevertheless poor by Western standards. Most countries in the region are developing an inbound tourism industry to earn much-needed foreign exchange and provide jobs for rapidly growing populations. The generally low level of incomes means that domestic tourism is less significant while volumes of outbound tourism are small; however both are set to increase due to the growth of a middle class, especially in India. Despite a wealth of resources, South Asia accounts for only a small percentage of world tourism.

The attractions of the region are based on the exotic cultures and landscapes, and a lifestyle in which religion plays a major role. Of particular note are the classic tour circuits in India, the beaches and gentle way of life of the Indian Ocean islands, and the spectacular scenery of the Himalayas.

Chapter 22
The tourism geography of East Asia

Learning Objectives

After reading this chapter you should be able to:

■ Describe the major physical features and climates of the region and understand their importance for tourism.
■ Recognize that the economies of the countries in the region show many contrasts, ranging from the advanced to the least developed.
■ Appreciate that outbound and domestic tourism and recreation are of growing importance to the more prosperous countries of East Asia.
■ Recognize the effect of crises such as SARS and terrorism on demand for tourism in the region.
■ Show that inbound tourism is being encouraged by most countries in the region as a source of foreign exchange and employment.
■ Recognize that the tourist appeal of East Asia is mainly cultural, although beach tourism and event attractions are growing in importance.
■ Be aware of the extent of the cultural and environmental impacts on host communities.
■ Recognize the importance of infrastructure on tourism development.
■ Demonstrate a knowledge of the tourist regions, resorts, business centres and tourist attractions of East Asia.

Introduction

East Asia consists of two distinct regions: South-East Asia, lying within the tropics, and the countries to the north, which Europeans and people from the Americas refer to as the 'Far East', although to an Australian this would seem geographically inappropriate. Most countries in East Asia have experienced rapid growth since the 1970s and have adopted Western technology without sacrificing their cultural identity, which is based on older civilizations and religions than those of the West. Economic growth has fuelled the demand for business travel, and also encouraged a significant volume of outbound leisure tourism. Demand for tourism in the region has been affected by three major events – the financial crisis of 1997/1998, the Bali bombings in 2002 and the SARS (severe acute respiratory syndrome) outbreak of 2003. In the future China will be a dominant force in outbound tourism to the rest of the world.

Domestic tourism has become increasingly significant as living standards have risen, expressed in car ownership and the purchase of leisure equipment. The more traditional patterns of travel to religious shrines and mountain resorts are changing as a growing middle class emulates Western fashions. As a result, beach resorts and theme parks, combining American and Asian motifs, are growing in popularity and outbound tourism from the region has increased. The family unit remains much stronger than in Western societies and individual freedom is less highly regarded, due to the influence of Confucian and Buddhist teachings. Cultural attitudes may mean that those employed in the service sector try to comply with unrealistic demands by Western tourists rather than lose face, leaving considerable scope for misunderstanding.

East Asia offers a wide variety of landscapes and attractions, although in most countries business and cultural tourism are more important than beach tourism. In the early years of the twenty-first century international tourist arrivals approached 100 million for East Asia as a whole. This is reflected in the impressive growth of air traffic in the region with the emergence of budget carriers and new airlines. Demographic trends – the region already contains well over a third of the world's population – the global economy and the rise of China as an economic superpower, are responsible for a rate of passenger growth which is among the world's highest. Aircraft movements suffered a temporary setback after 9/11 on the routes linking Europe and North America to the main East Asia hubs – Singapore, Tokyo, Osaka, Hong Kong, Seoul, Taipei and Bangkok. Many Asian airports are reaching the limits of their capacity and there is a flurry of airport expansion schemes and new airport plans. Only a few – notably Hong Kong's Chep Lap Kok, Singapore's Changi and Kuala Lumpur's Sepang – are equipped to handle the new breed of aircraft, seating up to 800 passengers, envisaged by the region's airlines. The airspace over the South China Sea is already one of the most congested in the world. In most countries – except for Japan, China and Vietnam – road transport plays a more important role in domestic tourism than the railway systems. However the Eastern Orient Express, linking Bangkok, Kuala Lumpur and Singapore has shown there is a market among Western tourists for luxury train services.

South-East Asia

The part of Asia extending from Burma to the Philippines was culturally influenced many centuries ago by India to the west, and China to the north. Overseas Chinese communities play an important role in the economic life of many countries in the region and indeed throughout the Pacific, but since the nineteenth century, the influence of Western Europe and the USA has become increasingly important.

During the first half of the twentieth century the whole of South East Asia – with the exception of Thailand – was under colonial rule:

- Burma (now Myanmar), Singapore, Malaysia, Brunei and Hong Kong – Britain
- Indo-China (now Vietnam, Laos and Cambodia) – France
- the Dutch East Indies and western New Guinea (now Indonesia) – the Netherlands
- East Timor and Macau – Portugal
- the Philippines was administered by the United States, having taken over from Spain after the war of 1898.

The Western powers were soon challenged by Japan, which although defeated militarily in the Second World War, has subsequently become the major economic influence in the region. After the Second World War most countries in South-East Asia suffered a good deal of political upheaval that was part of the wider struggle between the West and the Communist powers. This adversely affected the growth of tourism, which was also restricted or given a low priority by those countries with a socialist regime.

Most countries in the region have joined together to form ASEAN (Association of South East Asia Nations), which promotes cooperation in all spheres of economic activity. Although member countries compete for visitors, they each see the advantages of joint promotion aimed at the main tourist-generating markets. However, ASEAN has been less effective at coping with environmental issues, notably the severe pollution in the region.

The setting for tourism

There are wide disparities in wealth between the different countries of South-East Asia. The per capita incomes of Singapore and Brunei approach those of Western Europe, while Burma, Laos and Cambodia rank among the world's least developed nations. There are also great contrasts in economic and social development within many countries, particularly between the major cities on the one hand, and the impoverished rural communities on the other. The countries of South-East Asia also contain tribal societies, often regarded as primitive by the mainstream culture. These include:

- the hill tribes of northern Thailand
- the Montagnards of Vietnam
- the forest-dwellers of Malaysia
- the indigenous peoples of Western Papua, formerly known as Irian Jaya, in Indonesia.

Traditional cultures such as these fascinate Western tourists, but they are highly vulnerable to the negative impacts of tourism, as well as the exploitation of their environment by commercial logging and plantation agriculture.

Almost the whole of South-East Asia lies within the tropics, and experiences warm to hot weather throughout the year, with frequent but brief torrential downpours. The northern parts of the region do have a clearly defined cool dry season, while the timing and duration of the rainy season in the coastal areas of West Malaysia, Southern Thailand and Indonesia depends on their exposure to the monsoon winds; this has important consequences for beach tourism. During the colonial era, mountain resorts, similar to the hill stations of British India, were established to provide relief from the heat and humidity for the expatriate community. These are now important for domestic tourism, although their development is often hampered by poor road access. Examples include:

- Maimyo in Burma
- Cameron Highlands in West Malaysia
- Dalat in Vietnam
- Bogor in Indonesia
- Baguio in the Philippines.

More important in vying for the international tourist market are the beach resort developments on the palm-fringed coasts of the region. These are either based on established seaports (as at Penang) or have been planned on a comprehensive scale (as in the Langkawi Islands), using two examples from West Malaysia. Often such development has aroused criticism not on visual grounds (they are usually low-rise and well-designed), but on account of their impact on local communities. This is particularly the case where golf courses have been included in the resort as they make excessive demands on land and water supplies. None the less, golf tourism plays an important role in generating much-needed foreign exchange, the main sources of demand being Japan, Australia, Western Europe and the USA. Tourism within the region is being encouraged by new low cost airlines such as AirAsia, CebuPacific and Tiger Airways.

Singapore

Singapore is one of the most prosperous and stable countries in Asia, despite being a group of small islands lacking natural resources. It owes its importance to its strategic location on the shipping routes linking the Indian and Pacific oceans, which have made the city one of the world's largest seaports as well as the gateway to South-East Asia. The people are culturally diverse, with a Chinese majority, but united by the English language and a firm belief in the value of education, advanced technology and enterprise. Since independence, the government of the small island republic has encouraged foreign investment in a free market economy, but has also imposed a degree of social discipline that many Westerners would find draconian. As a result, Singapore is less plagued by squalor, car-dominated traffic and crime than most other urban societies throughout the world, and as such, can offer Western tourists a sanitized glimpse of *instant Asia*.

The country's high-profile national carrier – Singapore Airlines – is the largest in the region in terms of passenger-kilometres, and it works closely with the Singapore Tourism Board. Singapore's Stock Exchange and World Trade Centre rank among the world's most important financial institutions – not surprisingly, it has become a major conference venue and business tourism destination.

Despite the impact of SARS in the first half of 2003, Singapore attracts a large volume of inbound tourists – around 7.5 million a year during the early years of the twenty first century – but with a short length of stay. The majority are from neighbouring countries, although China is becoming an important market. Duty-free shopping accounts for a large part of the tourist spend, particularly by Western visitors, who see the city primarily as a stopover rather than as a sole destination. In an attempt to attract longer stay visitors, the government has developed a new tourism strategy by promoting niche markets such as education and health tourism. It is also emphasizing Singapore's cultural diversity, and safeguarding what remains of the old-style colonial heritage, once threatened with obliteration as a result of the drive to modernization. Such examples as the Raffles Hotel, the markets and outdoor food stalls contrast markedly with the ultra-modern shopping malls and high-rise office buildings. Singapore's attractions are primarily man-made and include:

- a number of zoos and wildlife parks
- the waterfront area of Clarke Quay, with its leisure, theatre and shopping developments
- the Suntec conference and exhibition centre
- the beach resort of Sentosa Island, which includes a number of Asian-style theme parks
- the Esplanade Centre for the performing arts, epitomizing Singapore's drive to become a cultural destination.

Singapore is compact, densely populated and low-lying, and the lack of scenic variety, together with urban pressures, generate a large volume of outbound tourism. Most of this is to neighbouring Malaysia, easily reached by the causeway to Johor, or to the beach resorts of Bintam and Batan in Indonesia's Riau archipelago which are only a short distance away by hydrofoil.

Malaysia

Like Singapore, Malaysia is a multi-cultural nation, but here the Muslim Malays are the dominant ethnic group. The country is a federation of 13 states but one party has dominated politics since independence and the nine hereditary sultans have little effective power. Malaysia also consists of two culturally distinct areas, separated by the South China Sea, namely:

- Peninsular or West Malaysia, known under British rule as Malaya, which is the southernmost peninsula of mainland Asia
- East Malaysia, consisting of the states of Sabah and Sarawak, which form part of the island of Borneo.

Unlike Singapore, Malaysia is rich in natural resources such as rubber, tin, petroleum and tropical hardwoods. These provided the basis for rapid industrialization after 1980, and a number of large-scale development projects, while rising incomes led to a considerable demand for outbound tourism. The 'Petronas Towers' dominating the skyline of Kuala Lumpur and the ultra-modern shopping malls in the capital were the products of an economic prosperity that was badly affected by the 1997/98 financial crisis. Nevertheless, the choice of Kuala Lumpur as the venue for the 1998 Commonwealth Games, the introduction of Formula One motor racing and the opening of a new international airport at Sepang, underline the importance of tourism as an earner of foreign exchange. The government has encouraged tourism through the Ministry of Culture, Arts and Tourism (MOCAT), with Tourism Malaysia responsible for promotion.

The infrastructure for tourism is efficient, including a good highway network in Peninsular Malaysia and air services operated by both the Malaysian Airline System

(MAS) and a new low fare airline 'AirAsia', which also flies internationally. At present both Malaysia's inbound and domestic tourism are performing very well with the great majority of the 13 million international arrivals from other Asian countries – over half from Singapore – and there has been considerable investment, particularly by the Japanese, in resort hotels and golf courses. However, in response to tourism growth, accommodation supply has been overestimated and occupancy rates are low.

Tourism resources

Malaysia can offer the following resources for tourism:

- the beaches of West Malaysia
- a variety of cultural attractions
- facilities for conferences and meetings including the Putra World Trade Centre and the Malaysian International Exhibition Centre
- the wildlife resources of the interior mountains and rainforests.

Most of the tourism development has taken place in **West Malaysia**. Seasonality is not a major problem, thanks to the pattern of the monsoons, which bring heavy rain to the west coast of Peninsular Malaysia between June and September, and to the east coast from November to February. Much of the west coast is low-lying, with extensive areas of mangrove swamp along the estuaries. The best beaches are found on the offshore islands, which include:

- Penang, which has retained its commercial importance as well as being a major destination for West European holidaymakers on inclusive air tours; most of the resort development has taken place around Batu Feringhi on the island's north coast
- the Langkawi Islands, which provide an ideal environment for scuba diving, but which offer much less in the way of nightlife, shopping and cultural attractions than Penang
- Pangkor and its small neighbour, Pangkor Laut, which has developed a niche market in spa tourism.

Although boasting finer beaches and attractive scenery, the east coast is less developed and the traditional Malay lifestyle is much more evident in the villages. Tioman Island and Cherating are the main resort areas.

West Malaysia's attractions also include:

- the Taman Negara National Park, covering much of the forest-covered highlands of the interior; with a huge biodiversity of species, it attracts growing numbers of ecotourists
- the Batu Caves, a major religious shrine for Hindus
- the old Portuguese trading centre of Malacca, with its colonial heritage providing a contrast to the modern capital of Kuala Lumpur
- the mountain resort of Genting Highlands, with its 'City of Entertainment', casino, golf course and funicular railway
- agro-tourism on some of the rubber plantations.

East Malaysia is much less developed, with a very limited road network, and caters mainly for adventure tourism, based on Kuching (Sarawak) and Kota Kinabalu (Sabah).

From Kuching, tourists travel up-river to visit the villages of the Dyak tribes and perhaps stay in one of the traditional longhouses. The state of Sabah boasts the highest mountain in South East Asia – Kinabalu – which attracts climbing and trekking expeditions, and some of the world's largest limestone caves.

Brunei

Brunei, which is located in the same region, derives most of its considerable wealth from petroleum, and tourism development is not a priority. Royal Brunei Airlines and the capital, Bandar Sara Begawan, cater mainly for business travellers.

Indonesia

In contrast to tiny Brunei, Indonesia is the world's largest Muslim nation, with a population approaching 250 million. It consists of a multitude of islands, of which 6,000 are inhabited, extends across three time zones, from Sumatra in the west to Papua in the east, and offers a great variety of scenery, from the rice paddies of Java and the rainforests of Kilimantan (Borneo) to the snow-capped mountains of New Guinea. The possibilities for ecotourism are indicated by the 'Wallace Line', which separates islands with Asian flora and fauna from those having species typical of Australasia. There is also a great diversity of cultures which is both a strength from the viewpoint of tourism and a challenge to the process of nation-building.

Tourism demand and supply

Indonesia has a number of socioeconomic problems that affect not just the growth of international tourism but also domestic tourism:

- The Asian financial crisis of 1997–98 affected Indonesia more severely than others in the region, with the result that the majority of the population live below the poverty line.
- The fall of the authoritarian Suharto regime destabilized the country, bringing to the surface ethnic and religious tensions, such as between the Muslim majority and the ethnic Chinese – who dominate the commercial sector – and the Christian community in the Moluccas.
- The political and economic dominance of Java, which contains almost two-thirds of the population and most of the country's industrial development. The Suharto regime attempted to relieve the acute pressures of over-population and rural poverty in Java by a policy of 'transmigration', settling farmers in the more sparsely populated islands among people of a very different cultural background, such as the Dyaks of Kilimantan and the Papuans of western New Guinea.

During the 1980s and 1990s, Indonesia experienced a very high rate of tourism growth. However, terrorist incidents – namely 'Black October', the bombing of a nightclub in the popular Balinese resort of Kuta in 2002, and the attack on an international hotel in Jakarta the following year, checked this growth. Bali alone subsequently experienced a 75 per cent fall in tourist arrivals. The crisis blighted the island's economy that had become dependent on tourism. Matters were made worse by the reaction of various Western governments, including Britain's Foreign and Commonwealth Office (FCO), advising against travel to Indonesia, in contrast to the policy of encouraging tourism to the USA after 9/11.

Nevertheless, tourism continues to be a priority for the new democratic government, with the restructured Directorate General of Tourism developing the market for conferences, exhibitions and incentive travel. Despite a government policy of spreading tourism throughout the islands, most of the growth in hotel capacity has taken place in Bintam-Batan and Bali (for leisure tourism) and in Java (mainly for business tourism, particularly in the major cities of Jakarta, Surabaya and Yogyakarta). International hotel chains dominate the accommodation sector, particularly in the mid-range and luxury categories. Although the government has moved toward a more liberal civil aviation policy, the national carrier Garuda and its subsidiaries dominate air transport.

Tourism resources

We look here at the tourism resources of those islands that are already significantly developed or have potential for growth:

- **Java** is dominated by a chain of high volcanic mountains, some of which, notably Mount Bromo in the east of the island, are still active. Over many centuries land has been brought under cultivation by an elaborate system of terracing and the island's fertility has supported a number of advanced civilizations. The most spectacular examples of this heritage are the temple at Borobodur, which is the world's largest Buddhist edifice, and the lesser-known Hindu temple at Prambunan nearby. The palaces of former sultans at Solo and Yogyakarta also attract growing numbers of cultural tourists. Although. Jakarta is primarily a major regional gateway and business centre, it does offer the leisure tourist the historic port area, formerly known as Batavia, that was the hub of the Dutch trading empire in Asia.
- **Sumatra** has an important oil industry and tourism is less developed than in Java, with Medan serving as a major business centre. The separatist uprising in Acheh province has had a negative impact on tourism in the northern part of the island. Tourism resources include the mountain scenery around Lake Toba, set amid one of the world's largest craters; the remaining rainforests that provide a refuge for the orang-utan and other threatened wildlife species; and the distinctive folklore of the Menankabau people.
- **Bali** is the best known of the holiday islands of Indonesia, with a long-established reputation as a 'tropical paradise', where a seemingly gentle, artistic people live in harmony with their environment. Balinese culture is defined by Hindu religious traditions and therefore differs from the rest of Indonesia. Bali's tourism resources include a spectacular landscape – featuring emerald-green rice terraces, hot springs and crater lakes, surfing beaches, and not least the temples and religious festivals that integrate art, music, drama and dance. Bali offers a range of accommodation – from luxury five-star hotels – concentrated in Nusa Dua – to '*homestays*' and simple beach bungalows. The opening in 1968 of an international airport at Denpasar was the catalyst for the large-scale expansion of tourism.
- **Lombok** has been the main beneficiary of government policy to spread tourism away from Bali. The two islands are roughly the same size and are superficially similar – indeed Lombok is often regarded as a less developed version of Bali, but it has a drier climate and a Muslim culture. Development is focused on the resort of Senggigi, while the offshore Gili Islands are popular with scuba divers. The authorities have set out to attract upmarket tourists with luxury hotels and the associated infrastructure including a new international airport, and improvements to ferry services, port facilities and the road network.

- The **Lesser Sunda Islands** to the east of Lombok remain largely undeveloped, but increasingly feature on the backpacker's trail, closely followed by divers and surfers. The climate is characterized by a long dry season influenced by monsoon winds from Australia, which lies not far to the south. Ecotourism has potential for growth in some of the islands, for example Komodo, which is famous for its 'dragons' (actually giant lizards).
- **Sulawesi** offers world-class diving, particularly in the north near Manado where the Benaken National Park is an outstanding example of marine conservation in a region notorious for overfishing and damage to coral reefs. Under the new government's decentralizing policies the park authorities set their own entrance fees, with the proceeds benefiting the local communities. In the mountainous interior the Toraja villages with their unique architecture and ceremonies based on ancestor worship provide the main attraction for tourists.

East Timor

East Timor gained independence from Indonesia after a long and bitter struggle in 2002. This small country's national identity derives mainly from its experience of four centuries of Portuguese colonial rule but as yet tourism plays only a minor role in the process of rebuilding the economy with United Nations and Australian assistance.

The Philippines

Like Indonesia, the Philippines is a populous island-nation containing many ethnic groups and a landscape dominated by volcanic mountains. Culturally, however, it is quite different from the other countries of South-East Asia. There are few impressive monuments from pre-colonial times, and the islands have been greatly influenced by their experience of three centuries of Spanish rule, followed by half a century of administration by the USA. The Spanish legacy of devout Roman Catholicism is evident in the churches and religious festivals culminating in Holy Week, whereas the Americans introduced the English language and sports such as baseball; the result is a culture in which Western influences and attitudes are stronger than elsewhere in Asia.

Tourism demand and supply

Tourism received a major boost under the Marcos regime in the 1970s, which hosted international events such as the Miss Universe beauty pageant, leaving Manila with a glut of luxury hotels. Since that time the emphasis by the Department of Tourism has been on planning resort clusters of international standard on a number of islands, which are linked to an international airport by boat and domestic air services. The Department's mission is to develop tourism for the economic benefit of the country and a convention and visitors bureau has been established to encourage business tourism. The main tourist markets are Japan, the USA, Taiwan, South Korea and the millions of overseas Filipinos working in many countries around the world. However, natural disasters and terrorist incidents – including the kidnapping of tourists in Mindanao (where there is a large Muslim minority and separatist movement) – have had a negative impact on arrivals and perceptions of the country, and compared to the rest of the region international arrivals are modest, at around 1.8 million a year.

Other aspects of tourism have also given cause for concern, such as damage to coral reefs and the prevalence of sex tours, particularly in Manila and Olongapo. In many areas the transport infrastructure, including roads and domestic air services, falls short of Western standards of efficiency, although ferry links between the islands have greatly improved.

Tourism resources

Tourism is concentrated mainly in the following areas:

- South Luzon, particularly in and around **Manila**. The capital's attractions include:
  - the Malacanang Palace
  - the Nayong Pilipino – an exhibition village showcasing the country's regional cultures
  - the historic district of Intramuros
  - the highly decorated *jeepneys*, which play a vital role in the city's transport system.
- A number of beach resorts, Lake Taal and the volcano of that name, and the Pagsanjan waterfalls are located within easy reach of Manila. However, one of the country's major attractions and a World Heritage Site – the rice terraces at Banaue – can only be reached by a long road journey and are much less accessible.
- The Visayas, a group of islands in the central Philippines are served by the international airport at Cebu, which has direct flights to Hong Kong, Seoul, Taipei, Singapore and Tokyo. The island of Boracay is the best known, having evolved from discovery by backpackers in the 1970s to become an upmarket destination.
- Palawan, until recently one of the more remote islands, offers world-class diving facilities and a number of small upmarket resorts that have escaped the pollution problems experienced by Boracay.
- Mindanao, much of which is still forest-covered, is developing ecotourism and has an 'ecotourism village'. Beach tourism is being developed around the cities of Davao and Zamboanga.

Thailand

Thailand (formerly known as Siam) is the only country in South-East Asia not to have experienced Western colonial rule and its monarchy has retained power and reverential status. However, Thailand has also been the country most affected by Western-style tourism. Growth has been phenomenal, from less than 500 000 international arrivals in 1970, to around 10 million in the early years of the twenty-first century, with a corresponding increase in hotel capacity. Tourism has become the country's biggest earner of foreign exchange and a major employer, but it has also exacerbated Thailand's socioeconomic problems, notably the disparities in wealth between Bangkok and the rural areas of the north and east. These problems in turn have contributed to the growth of a flourishing sex tourism industry in Bangkok and the resort of Pattaya, with damaging consequences to the country's image as a destination.

Tourism demand and supply

The Tourist Authority of Thailand (TAT) is the national body for tourism and one of the oldest in the region having been established in 1960; like other NTOs, it has responsibility for promotion, development and training. It has strategies in place to develop human resources, 'electronic tourism', events and festivals and niche markets. Thailand is one of the 'tiger economies' of Asia and economic development has seen the growth of a substantial middle class, who have the means not only to engage in domestic tourism but also to travel abroad for leisure purposes as well as for business and study.

Although there is considerable cross-border traffic between Thailand and Malaysia, the majority of international tourists arrive by air on inclusive tours and around 10 per cent are business travellers. Leisure tourists come from a wide range of generating countries, including Western Europe, North America, Japan and Australia. Bangkok's Don Muang airport is the main gateway which is served by over 40 scheduled airlines, while the north and south of the country are visited from Chiangmai and Phuket respectively. Thai International and its domestic arm, Thai Airways, operate an extensive network of air routes, while express bus and overnight rail services also link Bangkok to the major regional centres of the country.

Tourism resources

Thailand is a multi-destination country, with different areas offering sightseeing tours (there has been a substantial growth in visits to historic sites), beach tourism and adventure holidays:

- **Bangkok** is the primary destination. Despite acute traffic congestion – partly relieved by a 'skytrain' monorail system – this sprawling city has a wide range of attractions, and its Western-style hotels enjoy high occupancy rates throughout the year. Highways have replaced many of the city's canals, but the Chao Praya river, with its long-tail boats and floating markets, remains a major artery. As you might expect from a country devoted to Buddhist rituals and traditions, Bangkok is noted for its *wats* – temple-monasteries of a highly distinctive appearance – along with a multitude of lesser shrines. Shopping for Thai silk and other handicrafts is an important part of the city's appeal to Western tourists. Specific tourist attractions in Bangkok and the surrounding area include:
  - the spectacular Grand Palace, which contains the Temple of the Emerald Buddha
  - the Rose Garden Country Resort, 33 kilometres west of the capital, features cultural shows for visitors, including traditional dances, ceremonies and the distinctive Thai style of boxing
  - the nearby beach resort of Pattaya, which began as a 'rest and recreation' centre for American servicemen during the Vietnam War in the 1960s; it is noisy and over-commercialized, despite attempts by the government to clean up the environment, curb the jet skiers and tone down the exuberant nightlife offered by the bars, discotheques and massage parlours.
- Chiangmai has been developed as a counter-attraction to Bangkok in the northern part of the country, with the advantage of a cooler, less humid climate. Although the city is a major centre of Thai culture, most backpackers and Western tourists regard it as a convenient base for trekking tours among the hill tribes of the mountainous country bordering Burma and Laos, which forms part of the notorious 'Golden Triangle' of opium production. Concerted efforts by the government to crack down on the trade in narcotics carry the risk of fuelling border tensions and alienating ethnic minorities. It is also alleged that tourism does not benefit these communities but merely exploits them as a curiosity.

- Peninsular Thailand and the offshore islands in the Andaman Sea, together with those in the Gulf of Siam to the east, cater in varying degrees for beach tourism, in response to the quest, first by backpackers and later by tour operators, for 'unspoiled' holiday destinations:
  - Phuket was the first to be developed, to the extent that mass tourism has now displaced the island's traditional mining and fishing industries. Phang Nga Bay is famous for its spectacular karst limestone rock formations
  - Koh Samui is less developed and more upmarket
  - the Phi-Phi Islands are partly protected as a marine reserve, but environmentalists fear that development is inevitable, given the worldwide interest in the film *The Beach*.
- Eastern Thailand is an economically poor region, but offers wildlife for ecotourists and the remains of the ancient Khmer civilization for cultural tourists. The Tourism Authority of Thailand hopes that visitors will be attracted to a number of parks focusing on this heritage. The region is also a convenient base for excursions across the Mekong into Laos and Cambodia, where tourist accommodation is limited and expensive.

Indo-China

Until the 1990s the countries of Indo China remained on the margins of international tourism as a consequence of half a century of conflict, culminating in the Vietnam War), political isolation and instability. The socialist governments of the region gave tourism a low priority, restricting the numbers of foreign visitors and discouraging Western investment. However, they have come to realize the considerable potential of their countries for tourism and the consequent economic benefits. These countries are now in the early stages of developing a significant tourism industry, a good example of the 'involvement' stage of *the tourist area life cycle* described in Chapter 3, with Vietnam clearly in the lead.

Cambodia

Cambodia gained notoriety for the 'killing fields' of the Khmer Rouge regime in the late 1970s, but fortunately the country has a world-class attraction in the temple-city at Angkor. This was built by the powerful Khmer empire between the ninth and thirteenth centuries, but it was subsequently abandoned and covered in tropical jungle until the ruins were excavated by French archaeologists in the 1920s. By the late 1960s Angkor was attracting 45 000 visitors a year, and the nearby town of Siem Reap had a flourishing hotel and restaurant trade. Tourism has revived since 1998 after decades of conflict and neglect, but ambitious plans for hotel development near the site are regarded as inappropriate by conservationists.

The capital Phnom Penh attracts gamblers from other Asian countries, and the unacceptable face of global tourism is shown by the growth of the sex industry, exploiting a desperately poor, traumatized country, as an alternative to Thailand where the government is imposing stricter controls. According to UNICEF, much of this so-called sex tourism is in fact a modern version of the slave trade in which people traffickers supply child prostitutes to visiting paedophiles from Western Europe, Japan and the USA.

Laos

Laos (officially the Lao People's Democratic Republic) is the least developed country in South-East Asia, due largely to its mountainous and landlocked character.

The cities of Vientiane and Luang Prabang are well endowed with Buddhist temples, while the traditional, slow-paced lifestyle and prospects for ecotourism are the country's strengths as a tourist destination. However, these are largely out-weighed by the weaknesses – a poor transport infrastructure, visa restrictions and the high cost of accommodation.

Vietnam

The Western media have ensured that interest in the Vietnam War will continue long after its ending in 1975. The locations of that bitter conflict, including the Ho-Chi Minh Trail, China Beach near Danang and the Cu-Chi tunnels near Saigon that sheltered the Vietcong guerrillas from American firepower, are now on the tourist circuit.

It was not until 1994 that the USA lifted the trade embargo imposed after the Communist victory. The Vietnam National Administration of Tourism (VNAT) has implemented a national action plan for tourism and attracting foreign investment as part of a policy of gradual economic liberalization. In the early years of the twenty-first century Vietnam attracted over 2.5 million international arrivals. China, Japan and Taiwan are the most important markets, but the VNAT also aims to attract American war veterans (estimated at 2.7 million), the large numbers of overseas Vietnamese in the USA, Canada, Australia and France, and Western adventure-seekers.

Accommodation capacity increased from 13 000 hotel rooms of international standard in 1992 to 55 000 in 2000. Nevertheless, tourism development is hampered by an inadequate road system, unreliable power supplies and a bureaucracy resis-tant to change. As for the domestic market, the scale of the suppressed demand for leisure and tourism is indicated by a European bank's project for a theme park in Saigon, which will 'bring the outside world' to the Vietnamese.

Vietnam can offer a range of tourism resources including an extensive coastline, forested mountains, the Mekong and Red river deltas and a rich cultural heritage. The western highlands and the mountains of northern Tonkin have potential for ecotourism and national parks have been designated in these areas. Ha Long Bay – studded with thousands of picturesque islands – is a world-class natural attraction. Cultural tourism is mainly focused on the cities of Hanoi, Hue and Saigon:

- During the Vietnam War, Hanoi was the power base of the Communist North, and with unification it became the national capital, offering a number of show-piece attractions celebrating the country's heritage.
- Hue is located in the centre of the country and was the scene of bitter conflict during the Vietnam War. Despite this many Buddhist pagodas remain as reminders of the city's historic importance as the capital of Annam, the most important of the former kingdoms of Indo-China at the time of the French conquest.
- Saigon (Ho-Chi Minh City) was the capital of South Vietnam and is now the country's main commercial centre. Here business enterprise is flourishing to a much greater extent than in Hanoi, and the vibrant entertainment scene has revived as a result of international tourism. The French colonial influence is still evident in the architecture and restaurants, while *cyclos* (pedicabs) are a characteristic feature of the traffic.
- A number of beach resorts have developed near Saigon and are attracting Western investment.

Burma (The Union of Myanmar)

Before achieving independence, Burma was ruled as part of British India, and the government's renaming of the country, its cities and major physical features is part of a campaign of nation-building. For decades after independence, the country was isolated from the West by the government's policy of self-sufficiency; visas were difficult to obtain and tourists were not permitted to stay for more than a few days. Security was also a major problem, with uprisings by dissident ethnic groups, such as the Shans and the Karens, in the mountainous border areas. Burma is also physically isolated by high mountains to the north and east, and an inhospitable coastline of mangrove swamps and dense forests to the west.

Since the early 1990s the military regime has encouraged foreign investment in the fledgling tourism industry, primarily from Japan, and tourist arrivals have grown to around 400 000 a year. However, the way that tourism development has been carried out by the government, with apparent disregard for human rights, has raised the issue of ethical tourism. For example:

- the use of unpaid 'volunteers' (in effect, forced labour) to build infrastructure necessary for hotel development, such as much needed roads and railway improvements, and the new airport at Bassein
- the relocation of villagers to make way for tourist facilities
- the exploitation of the more 'picturesque' tribes for tour groups
- opponents of the regime, such as the democrat leader Aung San Kyi, claim that tourism revenue simply enriches those in government circles who have invested in the new hotels, and urge a Western boycott of the country; some tour operators, however, take the view that tourism can be a powerful force for liberalization and change.

Burma has much to offer both the ecotourist and the cultural tourist, including for example:

- a number of wildlife parks and sanctuaries
- the Irrawaddy (Ayayarwady) river runs through the country's heartland, providing a major transport artery, as in Kipling's time, from Rangoon (Yangon) to Mandalay. River transport is now being revitalized after decades of neglect, including luxury cruises by Eastern and Orient Express
- Rangoon boasts one of the world's most impressive Buddhist temples – the Shwe Dagon Pagoda, which is covered in gold and precious stones
- Pagan (Bagan) is renowned for its hundreds of temples, a reminder of Burma's 'golden age' during the thirteenth century
- Mandalay was the royal capital prior to British rule; the palace has been restored as a tourist attraction
- the Mergui Islands are the only part of Burma's long coastline that has potential for beach tourism and diving holidays.

The Far East/North-East Asia

The lands around the East China Sea and the Sea of Japan include some of the world's largest modern cities, as well as some of its oldest civilizations. In contrast to the tropical conditions prevalent in South-East Asia, the climate is characterized by four well-defined seasons, not unlike those of Europe and North America. Spring and autumn are the best times for visiting, as winters can be bitterly cold and summers oppressively hot and humid. Japan and South Korea have long been important destinations for the business traveller and the cultural tourist, but since the 1990s, China has emerged as a formidable competitor for the world travel market.

Japan

Japan is the leading industrial nation of Asia, with an economy based on overseas trade. Despite suffering from economic problems since the 1990s, it boasts a GDP second only to the USA, and four times greater than that of the UK. In response to the economic situation there has been a certain amount of industrial restructuring and deregulation, outbound tourism has suffered and the country has become more open to foreign investment. Nevertheless, Japan is by far the largest generator of tourists in the East Asia–Pacific Region, with a very large deficit on its international travel account.

Japan consists of four main islands located off the eastern fringe of the continent – Honshu, Hokkaido, Kyushu and Shikoku – and groups of much smaller islands, such as the Ryukyus and Iwo Jima, lying to the south. The total area of the Japanese islands is only slightly greater than the British Isles, with more than twice the population. The pressure on land resources is even more acute when we consider that over 80 per cent of the country is mountainous. Geological instability has produced the beautiful mountain landscapes of Japan – Mount Fuji is the best-known example – and the numerous hot springs, but it is also responsible for natural disasters, such as the earthquakes which devastated Kobe in 1995.

The setting for tourism

As a nation Japan has the following characteristics:

- It is remarkably homogeneous, with one language, few social divisions and no large ethnic minorities.
- It has enjoyed political stability since 1945.
- Respect for tradition co-exists with admiration for the new.
- There is a readiness to adopt the latest technological innovations.
- Society is bound by discipline and respect for authority, but leisure is seen as increasingly important.

Due to a low birth rate and high life expectancy, the Japanese population is ageing, with a higher proportion of people aged over 65 years than the USA and Western Europe; and the grey market is well catered for. There are also social trends toward a more relaxed and individualistic lifestyle, a greater emphasis on leisure and sport, and a greater readiness to adopt Western fashions. Even so, the concept of an annual holiday has only slowly been accepted in Japan, which is still largely a work-oriented society. Working hours are longer than in Europe or the USA and paid annual leave amounts to 15 days; however, Japanese workers often take only 9 days out of their full holiday entitlement out of loyalty to colleagues or to cover for illness. Holidays and leisure activities generally are frequently sponsored by large industrial corporations for their employees; however, this paternalism is not resented by most Japanese, who are prepared to accept a degree of regimentation that Westerners would find irksome.

Demand for tourism

Domestic tourism is the mainstay of the Japanese tourism market. Holiday trips are significant, accounting for the majority of trips, with business and VFR accounting for the remainder. Pilgrimages to Shinto and Buddhist shrines continue to be popular with family groups, while *onsen* (hot spring resorts) appeal more to the stressed executive at weekends. The Western influence is evident in the rapid growth of skiing, golf, baseball, water sports and visits to theme parks. The scarcity of land particularly affects demand for skiing and golf:

* Skiing is practised by some 15 million Japanese. The mountains of Northern Honshu and Hokkaido receive abundant snowfalls during the winter months, and this has encouraged the development of a large number of ski resorts. However, apart from Nagano in the Japanese Alps and Sapporo in Hokkaido, which have both hosted the Winter Olympics, few resorts approach Western standards, and overcrowding on the slopes is a major problem.
* Golf courses are few and far between and green fees are prohibitively expensive. Most would-be players are confined to multi-storey driving ranges, and real golf can only be played on overseas trips. This goes far to explaining why the Japanese are active in purchasing tourism developments overseas, and in providing Third World governments with aid for projects where golf is a major component.

Outbound tourism During the long period of Japan's self-imposed isolation from the West under the rule of the Tokugawa shoguns, outbound travel was strictly forbidden, and even after the Meiji Restoration in 1868 could only be undertaken for the purposes of business or study. After 1964 the restrictions on leisure travel were lifted, and in the late 1980s the government made a positive effort to encourage overseas travel through the 'Ten Million Programme', as a way of restructuring Japan's trade balance with the rest of the world and promoting mutual understanding. However, partly due to recent economic problems and world events, participation in outbound travel still accounts for a small percentage of the population, volumes have been depressed since 2001, and with limited holiday time available the length of stay is short, averaging eight days. Yet in the early years of the twenty-first century outbound volumes exceeded 16 million and in many countries the Japanese are the largest source of tourists; and they tend to be the biggest spenders. Over half visit destinations in Asia – mainly Taiwan, South Korea and Hong Kong; around a third go to the USA – particularly to honeymoon in Hawaii and Guam; the remainder travel to Europe or Australasia. Group travel is important, and so is *omiyake*, the customary purchase of gifts for friends, relatives and employers. Young unmarried women in their twenties – the so-called 'office ladies' – constitute a major market, particularly for the countries of Western Europe.

Inbound tourism approached 5 million visits in the early years of the twenty-first century, representing around one-third of outbound travel volumes – and the difference is even greater in terms of spend. These relative low volumes are due to Japan's distance from the traditional generating markets of Western Europe and the USA, and the country's reputation for being expensive; this is despite the country jointly hosting the Football World Cup with South Korea in 2002. One of the reasons that Japan has experienced less growth as a tourist destination than most other countries in the East Asia–Pacific region is inadequate marketing on the part of the Japan National Tourist Organization (JNTO). Business travellers account for about a quarter of incoming tourists, with the cities of Tokyo, Osaka and Nagoya as the major destinations. South Korea is the largest source of tourists, due to cultural and business ties with Japan. South-East Asia accounts for half of all visitors, with a further 10 per cent coming from the USA.

Supply of tourism

Transport   For domestic travel, road and rail is most commonly used. The northern island of Hokkaido is linked to Honshu by the world's longest rail tunnel, and bridges similarly integrate Kyushu and Shikoku with the main transport network, supplementing the ferry services. There is an extensive network of railways (20 000 kilometres), including the famous Shinkansen (bullet trains), linking Tokyo to Fukuoka, Niigata and Morioka in northern Japan. For foreign visitors, train travel is preferable to driving due to the problems of road congestion and inadequate sign-posting. Most foreign visitors arrive by air, the majority through Tokyo's Narita Airport. However, other airports are growing in importance, particularly Osaka's Kansai Airport (built on an artificial island), which has the advantage of being much closer to downtown than Narita, which is 60 kilometres from central Tokyo. Tokyo's other airport, Haneda, handles domestic flights to a large number of destinations. The busiest air routes are from South-East Asia, Hawaii and the USA. The aviation sector is dominated by two airlines – Japan Airlines and ANA – but with deregulation since 1996 they face a growing challenge from newcomers.

Accommodation   The hotel industry is driven by domestic demand, but occupancy rates for other than budget and medium-priced hotels have declined as a result of the economic problems and the resulting cutbacks in corporate entertaining by Japanese business executives. Tourists can stay in Western-style hotels or in *ryokan* – Japanese inns where the food service, bathing facilities and furnishings of *tatami* matting follow native traditions, and these are becoming increasingly popular with Western visitors. Tokyo and Osaka are the main locations for major hotel projects, some of which are financed by international chains. These tend to be very expensive, but an alternative is available for the budget traveller in the so-called *capsule hotels* – stacks of cubicles, each consisting of little more than bedspace. Subsidised family 'travel villages' and lodges are also available for the domestic market.

Organization   Responsibility for the industry lies with the Ministry of Tourism, which supervises the Japan National Tourist Organization (JNTO) whose role is to promote 'a fair and realistic image of Japan' to increase international understanding of the country, particularly among the international business community. The Japan Convention Bureau (JCB) plays a leading role in developing facilities for the important conference market.

Tourism resources

Japan's tourism resources are a unique mix of the traditional, best seen in the rural areas, and modern technology, evident in the cities and theme parks such as Tokyo Disneyland and Universal Studios Japan, while Japanese corporations such as Sony are foremost in developing visitor attractions. The highly distinctive Japanese art and architecture, miniaturized landscape gardening, the delicate skills of traditional handicrafts, the *kabuki* theatre, even karaoke bars and sumo wrestling, all these features have widespread appeal. Japan also has a unique human resource in the traditional *geishas* – skilled entertainers who still play a major role in corporate business tourism.

Despite severe pollution problems, much has been done to preserve the country's coasts, mountains and forests, including the designation of 28 national parks in the most scenic areas. However, unlike their counterparts in North America, these are scarcely wilderness areas, but contain hundreds of rural communities, such is the pressure on land and water resources. Western visitors are mainly drawn to southern Honshu – and to a lesser extent Kyushu – and to the cities, which include:

- Tokyo, which is above all a business centre, but also a city containing many temples and museums. The Ginza district includes the Stock Exchange, while leisure activities are concentrated in the Shinjuku district.
- Kyoto was for centuries until 1868 the Imperial capital of Japan, and a cultural centre which preserves the country's traditions, hundreds of shrines and temples, and gardens inspired by Zen Buddhism. However, this city of one and a half million people is no museum-piece, but a major industrial centre.
- Nikko, Nara and Ise are also religious centres, preserving much of the feudal past of Japan.
- The Inland Sea between western Honshu and Shikoku is probably the most scenic region of Japan, studded with picturesque islands and numerous Buddhist temples.
- Kyushu offers a wide variety of attractions, including:
  - theme parks such as Space World near Fukuoka
  - Huis Ten Bosch, a reproduction of a seventeenth-century Dutch city, a reminder that nearby Nagasaki, through its trade with Holland, was Japan's only contact with the West during the long period of isolation; it also provides the Japanese with a simulated European holiday experience without the trouble and expense of the real thing.
  - the Seagaia resort in Miyazaki, which contains the world's largest artificial beach and all-weather water park
  - Beppu, the most important of a number of spas based on the island's abundant geothermal resources.

Two other islands – Hokkaido and Okinawa – attract relatively few Western tourists:

- Hokkaido, with its long, bitterly cold winters and forested mountains, was settled by the Japanese in the nineteenth century. It offers space, lake and volcanic scenery, and native *Ainu* communities, now a small minority of the population. Sapporo is noted for its annual snow festival.
- Okinawa, in contrast, has a subtropical climate, and is visited by large numbers of Taiwanese tourists.

China (The People's Republic of China)

With 1.3 billion inhabitants, China accounts for over a fifth of the world's population. Since 1979, however, the government has responded to a looming demographic crisis with the one child per family policy. This has led to an uneven gender ratio of 1.2 males per female and the prospect of an ageing population.

During the twentieth century, the Chinese experienced much social and economic upheaval. The Chinese Empire under the Manchu dynasty was an autocracy that had resisted change, but it was forced into humiliating trade concessions by the

Western powers such as Britain, France and Germany. In 1911 it was replaced by a secular republic, and this was in turn overthrown by the Communist revolution of Mao Zedong, who established a totalitarian state. Following the chaos of the Cultural Revolution and Mao's demise, the government from 1978 onwards gradually moved toward a free market economy, although the Communist Party, backed up by the People's Liberation Army (PLA), remains firmly in control. Since the 1990s the rate of economic growth has been among the highest in the world, attracting foreign investment on an unprecedented scale. Some commentators believe that China is on course to become the major power of the twenty-first century and certainly it is set to dominate outbound tourism in both the East Asia region and the world in decades to come. However, China is now the world's second importer of oil along with many other raw materials, with wide implications – not just for tourism- but the world economy.

The setting for tourism

The landmass of China is equivalent in size to the USA. It contains a great range of climates from the extreme winter cold of northern Manchuria to the tropical warmth of the island of Hainan in the south. It boasts some of the world's highest mountains and plateaux, one of the most inhospitable deserts – the Takla Makan – and the world's fourth longest river – the Yangtze. Throughout history China has been prone to natural disasters on an epic scale in the form of earthquakes, floods and famines.

China has one of the world's oldest civilizations, characterized by an alphabet, a code of ethics based on the teachings of Confucius and Lao Tse, and art traditions that were already well established at the time of the Han dynasty in the second century BC.

Demand for tourism

Inbound tourism   Tourism has been encouraged by the government since 1978 as part of the campaign to make the Chinese more receptive to Western ideas and technology, and also to generate the foreign exchange needed to modernize the economy. Growth has generally been rapid, although the adverse publicity following the suppression of the pro-democracy movement in Beijing's Tiananmen Square, brought about a downturn in Western visitors in the early 1990s, and the SARS outbreak of 2003 significantly impacted upon both inbound and outbound tourism. Nevertheless, the 1997 PATA Conference was held in Beijing, highlighting the fact that China had become one of the world's leading tourist destinations, and by the early years of the twenty-first century over 30 million international tourist arrivals were recorded. The most important markets are Japan, Russia, the countries of South-East Asia and the USA, while Britain, France and Germany account for 5 per cent of arrivals. Business travel accounts for a third of inbound tourism and gravitates to the major cities of Beijing, Shanghai and Gwangzhou (Canton). This success in tourism has not been achieved without growing pains. Pricing, poor service standards and a shortage of trained personnel remain problems, as does the adjustment of a centrally planned economy to one trying to accommodate enterprise and market forces. Positive changes have taken place in the following areas:

- improvements in the transport infrastructure
- a greater choice of destinations, with more than 500 cities or areas open to visitors compared to 30 in 1982

○ a greater choice of attractions within established destinations such as Beijing and Shanghai

○ more competition between tour operators and travel agencies; in the past, group travel had been monopolized by the state-controlled China International Travel Service (CITS) which has had to improve its performance for Western tourists

○ a tenfold increase in hotel capacity between 1982 and 1999, and a much-needed improvement in standards, although most Western-style accommodation is concentrated in the major cities, notably Beijing, Guangzhou, Shanghai and the Shenzhen Special Enterprise Zone adjoining Hong Kong.

Domestic tourism has also increased rapidly since the 1990s, encouraged by the rise in living standards, and not least, by an increase in leisure time, including the introduction of the five-day working week. The Chinese now enjoy three one-week holidays, celebrating Chinese New Year, Labour Day and National Day. The volume of domestic tourism is however restricted by the low earning power of the average worker, and there are wide disparities in wealth between the interior and coastal provinces, and between those cities that have benefited most from the market economy and the outlying rural areas, where poverty and lack of opportunity have led to massive out-migration. Even so, there were estimated to be 900 million domestic trips in 2002. Family visits to Buddhist and Daoist shrines, such as the sacred mountain of Tai-Shan in Shandong province are popular, in line with tradition, but Western patterns of holiday-taking are also apparent. Beach resorts within reach of the major cities now cater for a much wider market than the Party elite. Examples include Beidahe to the north east of Beijing, and the former Treaty Ports of Wei-hai and Qingdao in the Shandong Peninsula. Western-style tourism began here in the 1920s, initially in response to the demand from European expatriates, and after the Communist revolution the accommodation was taken over for the use of the Party elite and favoured groups of industrial workers. Another example of Western fashion is the development of theme parks on the periphery of Shanghai and other major cities, but these have met with mixed success due to the low level of car ownership in China. There is now an effective demand for skiing where none existed prior to the mid-1990s. The most developed resort is Nanshan close to Beijing, where the use of snow-making machines compensates for the lack of natural snow in North China's cold but very dry winter climate. Although golf has also become an important leisure activity, other Western pastimes have proved vulnerable to changes in fashion, and many projects have failed because developers overestimated the spending power of China's middle class.

Outbound tourism was discouraged by the Chinese authorities until the 1990s, but passports are now becoming easier to obtain and travel is allowed to an increasing number of approved destinations. The growth of a middle class with the means to travel, estimated to number 400 million consumers, will ensure that China will become a major force in international tourism. In 1999 there were already 9 million visits abroad, mainly to countries with large ethnic Chinese populations in Asia, whereas Europe currently attracts less than 10 per cent of the market.

Supply of tourism

Most travel in China is by rail or air, as the road network is deficient by Western standards. The rail network, on the other hand, is the fifth largest in the world (52 000 kilometres) and offers two classes of accommodation – 'soft', recommended for Western tourists, and 'hard', for those on a budget. China has an extensive system of domestic air services, but only a few airports are, as yet, capable of handling large volumes of international traffic. Air China and a number of regional airlines compete for the growing market for air travel, while the Civil Aviation Administration of China (CAAC), which in the 1980s exercised a state monopoly of air transport, now focuses solely on its regulatory role. The CAAC has given foreign airlines more rights to use the gateway airports at Beijing, Shanghai and Gwangzhou.

Since 1984 the China National Tourism Administration has been responsible for defining overall tourism policy and overseeing its implementation, and tourism development is firmly integrated with the Five-Year Plans for the national economy. Both provincial and local authorities are now allowed considerable initiative, resulting in a flurry of master plans and investment schemes for tourism across China. The industry is represented by the China Tourism Association and the National Travel Trade Association, and is becoming more organized and professional.

Tourism resources

China is mainly famous for its age-old craft industries, traditional styles of architecture and distinctive landscapes. Since the 1980s Western fashions and styles of advertising have largely replaced the drab uniformity normally associated with Communist regimes, and traffic jams are now commonplace in cities where bicycles and pedicabs used to be the only forms of transport. However, in the headlong rush to industrialize, great damage has been inflicted on the forest and wildlife resources of the mountain areas. Air and water pollution is also widespread in the cities of eastern China, and the country's environmental record and attitude to human rights – particularly in Tibet – has aroused international concern.

In such a vast country there are considerable regional differences, in climate, landscapes and lifestyles, including cuisine.

North China, centring on the Hwang Ho river basin, was the historic cradle of Chinese civilization and the power base of the Chin and Han dynasties that were the first to unite the country. The region has a continental climate, with severe winters and hot, humid summers. Much of the region is characterized by treeless landscapes of wind-blown loess, but it has much to attract the cultural tourist, including:

- the burial place of the First Emperor at Xian, which yielded the famous terracotta warriors
- the Great Wall of China – over 3000 kilometres in length – built as a defence against the Mongol nomads to the north; the section most visited by tourists is at Badaling, reached by a 50 kilometre rail link from Beijing
- the summer resort of the Manchu dynasty at Chengde, with its gardens, palaces and pagodas
- Beijing (formerly Peking), with many reminders of its imperial past, including the Forbidden City, the former palace compound of the emperors, the Temple of Heaven and the Ming Tombs commemorating one of China's greatest dynasties. In contrast, the Great Hall of the People on Tiananmen Square symbolizes post-revolutionary China. The 2008 Olympic Games have provided the impetus for improvements to Beijing's transport and public health infrastructure. However, in the rush to modernize, many of the picturesque *hutongs* (densely packed courtyard dwellings) have been demolished to make way for faceless apartment buildings and shopping malls.

The **East Central China and Szechwan** region centres on the river Yangtze.

- Shanghai is China's largest city and owes its rise as one of the world's great seaports to trade with the West. In the 1920s when the city was dominated by foreign concessions, Shanghai was renowned for its wealth and uninhibited nightlife. The impressive skyline of the new Pudong special enterprise zone underlines the city's revival as an international business centre, while the historic waterfront area known as the Bund has been restored.
- To the west of Shanghai lie a group of historic cities that have played a major role in Chinese history as capitals or cultural centres. These include Nanjing, Hwangzhou, Wuxi, famous for its silk industry, and Suzhou, noted for its traditional Chinese gardens.
- The Yangtze provides a popular tourist route to the fertile but mountainous province of Szechwan, deep in the interior of China. The modern cruise ships and the landing stages thronged with porters typify the contrasts between the old China and the new. The highlight of the cruise is the impressive Three Gorges between Wuhan and Chongqing. This is the location for the world's largest flood control project, involving the displacement of 1.5 million people. Taming the Yangtze will prevent a repetition of the 1998 floods that claimed 4000 lives and would provide 10 per cent of China's power requirements, but critics fear that the dam will cause long-term environmental damage.

Western China comprises the autonomous regions of Sinkiang and Inner Mongolia, which are sparsely populated with mountain and desert landscapes quite unlike those of eastern China. The people are also culturally distinct from the Han Chinese. For example the Uigur speak a Turkic language, are predominantly Muslim, and have a way of life based on pastoralism. The central government in Beijing has made great efforts to improve the communications infrastructure as part of a policy of integration. Although most of the region is off-limits to tourists for military reasons, or through physical inaccessibility, hotels have been built in the oasis towns along the 'Silk Road', the overland trade route which linked North China to the Middle East centuries ago.

Tibet has special appeal as a destination:

- It is the highest and most extensive plateau on earth, for the most part above 5000 metres altitude, at the upper limits of human habitation. Lhasa, situated in a deep valley at the relatively modest altitude of 3700 metres, is one of the world's highest cities.
- The region is hemmed in by even higher mountains and was for centuries utterly remote. This physical seclusion produced a unique civilization based on a distinctive form of Buddhism. Until the Chinese takeover in 1951, Tibet was a closed society ruled by monks, with its people living in medieval conditions.
- Despite half a century of Chinese rule, the Dalai Lama still commands the loyalty of most Tibetans from his exile in Dharmasala, India, and is respected worldwide as a spiritual leader.

Improved communications by air, road and a projected rail link to Beijing are part of a strategy to bind Tibet more closely to the national economy. Development has been accompanied by a massive influx of Han Chinese who increasingly dominate the business sector, including tourism, and accelerate the process of cultural change. In Lhasa the Potala, the former palace of the Dalai Lama, is now a showpiece attraction, while a number of monasteries, out of many closed during the Cultural Revolution, have been restored. However, in encouraging international tourism, the government runs the risk that native Tibetans will be exposed to Western democratic ideas.

South China is Cantonese, rather than Mandarin-speaking, with a climate and topography offering considerable potential for ecotourism, adventure holidays and beach tourism. The major tourist centres include:

- Guilin, famous for the spectacular karst mountain scenery along the river Li that has inspired a Chinese art tradition
- Kunming, the centre for trekking tours into the hill country of Yunnan, where some 30 tribal minorities preserve much of their original culture
- Gwangzhou, the major business centre of the region, hosting two annual trade fairs in the Palace of Exhibitions which provide a showcase for the Chinese economy; in contrast, the city's markets display exotic foods and health remedies that recall an older China
- the tropical island of Hainan, which is important for domestic tourism; it has its own regional airline and is now being promoted as a winter-sun destination for the West European market.

Hong Kong and Macau

These deserve special mention because of their former status as European colonies – Hong Kong was British from 1841 to 1997, while Macau was ruled by Portugal from the mid-sixteenth century to 1999. They both consist of parts of the mainland of South China and a number of offshore islands. Hong Kong and Macau now have special status within the PRC under the government's 'one country, two systems' policy, which in effect means a *hands-off* approach to their free enterprise economics.

Hong Kong

Densely built up around its magnificent harbour, with The Peak in the background, the city of Hong Kong has one of the world's most famous skylines. As a Special Administrative Region (SAR), Hong Kong retains some of the features of British rule, including:

- free port status and a free-wheeling private enterprise economy
- border controls with the rest of China, although visa controls are being relaxed
- the Hong Kong dollar as its official currency
- English as an official language
- its own tourist authority for promotion and development – the Hong Kong Tourism Board (HKTB).

Most of Hong Kong's commercial growth has taken place since 1950, as the result of a massive influx of refugees from the PRC, liberal tax laws and its geographical location at the focus of air and shipping routes. The SAR consists of a dozen islands at the mouth of the Pearl river, the peninsula of Kowloon and the New Territories on the mainland. These are linked by an efficient transport system, including the famous Star Ferry, road tunnels and the MRT, Hong Kong's underground railway network, which carries more passengers, more efficiently, than its London counterpart.

Tourism is a significant part of the economy, accounting for over 5 per cent of GDP in 2001.

Hong Kong is one of Asia's major destinations, and is a base as well as a port of call for ocean cruises. The availability of charter flights and a well-developed business travel market have encouraged inbound tourism. This provides most of the revenue for Cathay Pacific, one of the leading airlines in the East Asia–Pacific region. The importance of Hong Kong has been enhanced by the new international airport at Chep Lap Kok. Rising educational and living standards, combined with urban pressures, make Hong Kong an important generator of tourism to the rest of the East Asia–Pacific region.

Some 40 per cent of the SAR is protected from development by country parks, providing a much-needed recreation resource for the people of Hong Kong. However, most of the beaches, such as Repulse Bay, are overcrowded on summer weekends and both airline and hotel capacities are reaching ceilings of development. Air and marine pollution are serious problems, and a massive clean-up operation will be necessary for Hong Kong to merit its name, which means 'Fragrant Harbour'.

For the foreign visitor, Hong Kong is a unique blend of Western business culture and Eastern traditions, such as *feng shui* in hotel and office developments, and *tai chi* as a popular form of recreation. There are a great variety of attractions, which include:

* shopping for consumer goods and Chinese items such as jade
* the *sampans* and floating restaurants of Aberdeen
* themed attractions such as the Sung Dynasty Village and the Middle Kingdom (showcasing China's history),
* Ocean Park and the Space Museum
* the outlying islands with their temples and peaceful countryside, providing a relief from the hectic pace of urban Hong Kong.

Macau

This Special Administrative Region lies 120 kilometres to the west of Hong Kong and consists of the city of Macau and the tiny islands of Taipa and Coloane. The Macau Government Tourist Office (MGTO) is repositioning the former colony as a destination by attempting to reduce its dependence on gambling as a source of revenue, and promoting other attractions to Western tourists. Although Macao now has its own international airport, the majority of visitors are short-stay, arriving by fast ferry from Hong Kong. Macau's main appeal lies in its blend of Chinese and Mediterranean culture. Other attractions include the Grand Prix motor race (modelled on Monaco's) and a maritime museum evoking the Portuguese heritage.

Taiwan

In 1949, following the Communist victory on the mainland, the followers of the Nationalist government of Chiang Kai Shek retreated to the island of Taiwan (then known in the West as Formosa), where they established the regime which regards itself as the legitimate Republic of China in opposition to the PRC in Beijing. Not surprisingly, relations with mainland China have tended to be difficult, but since the 1990s there have been moves toward eventual reunification, including the restoration of air and sea links and the relaxation of visa controls. Taiwan has become one of the most successful Asian economies, and despite having diplomatic relations with relatively few countries, it enjoys trading relations with many more, and business travel is of major importance. The country's political isolation has had little effect on the volume of outbound travel (over 7 million trips in the early years of the twenty-first century), resulting in a heavy deficit on the travel account as inbound arrivals only reached 2.6 million. The Tourist Bureau has responsibility for tourism nationally and is part of the Ministry of Transport and Communications.

Taiwan's main tourist markets are Japan (for golfing holidays) and the United States. The capital Taipei is a major business destination, but has little appeal to the leisure tourist apart from shopping and a number of museums, displaying Chinese art treasures. Of more importance is the island's subtropical climate, and its mountain and coastal scenery, much of which is protected in a number of national parks. Major attractions include:

- the Taroko Gorge, on the East West Highway crossing the island
- Sun Moon Lake, a favourite resort for Taiwanese holidaymakers
- the beaches of the east coast and offshore islands.

Korea

Korea occupies a mountainous peninsula lying between China and Japan. Since the Second World War the country has been divided between the Communist North, and South Korea, which has become a major industrial power under a free market economy. Since the Korean War (1950–53) an uneasy stand-off persists between North and South, long after the ending of the Cold War elsewhere.

South Korea

Like Japan, South Korea has experienced an 'economic miracle', but its tourism growth has been even more spectacular and the travel propensity of its population exceeds 66 per cent. Responsibility for tourism falls to the Korea National Tourism Organization, under the Ministry of Culture and Tourism. The main impetus was initially business tourism, but the 1988 Seoul Olympics, the Asian Games and the 2002 Football World Cup have provided the country with the opportunity to showcase its achievements and leisure tourism has followed. In the early years of the twenty-first century over 5 million international arrivals were recorded. The majority of foreign visitors are from Japan due to the cultural and business ties between the two countries. The USA is a long way behind in second place, but the American connection has been important since the Korean War. A large number of American servicemen are still stationed in the country and there is a substantial market of Korean expatriates in the USA. For Western visitors, South Korea is not as expensive or crowded as Japan, while it is less of a culture shock than China, and offers similar attractions to both.

The demand for outbound tourism was suppressed for decades after the Korean War in the interests of building up the national economy. In 1989 the travel restrictions were removed, and the country soon became one of the major generators of tourism in the East Asia–Pacific region, although the country's prosperity received a major setback with the Asian currency crisis of 1997/8. Nevertheless, over 7 million departures were recorded in 2001. Although the work ethic remains strong, domestic tourism is also significant and family visits to attractions such as the Everlands Festival World theme park are growing in popularity.

Seoul is a modern capital which preserves some heritage attractions, but tourists looking for ancient temples and traditional ambience find that Kyongyu, a former royal capital, has more to offer. Other attractions include:

- the port city of Pusan, which is also a major holiday resort
- the beaches of Cheju Island in the extreme south
- the mountainous interior, which contains a number of national parks, of which Sorak is the best known, hot spring resorts and ski centres that cater mainly for domestic demand.

North Korea (Korea DPR)

North Korea's hard-line Communist regime has discouraged international tourism, with the exception of invited groups, mainly based in the capital Pyongyang, which can be easily controlled. Strict social controls also restrict domestic travel and effectively prevent outbound tourism. However the country's chronic economic difficulties, and pressure from China, its main trading partner, may lead eventually to a liberalization of the regime. There are already signs of a rapprochement with South Korea, with the participation of teams from both countries in the 2002 Asian Games held in Pusan, and the proposals for a special economic zone to attract foreign investment on the Chinese border.

Mongolia

The former 'Outer Mongolia' emerged from obscurity and moved from Communism to a free market economy during the 1990s, following the collapse of the Soviet Union. In the thirteenth century the Mongols under Genghis Khan conquered a vast swathe of Asia from the South China Sea to the Russian steppes. In more recent times this sparsely populated and landlocked country has been overshadowed by its neighbours Russia and China, but its people still retain much of the nomadic way of life and warrior traditions, such as displays of horsemanship, archery and wrestling.

In the absence of hotels outside the capital Ulan Bator, tourists are accommodated in *gers*, the portable structures of felted material traditionally used by the nomads. Private tour companies compete with the state agency for the growing numbers of Western ecotourists. The climate is extreme, with temperatures ranging from $-40\,°C$ in winter to $+40\,°C$ in summer. Although the Gobi Desert and steppe landscapes are the dominant features, the Altai Mountains border the country to the north and there are extensive forests around Lake Hovsgol, where the reindeer, rather than the horse or the camel, has defined the traditional lifestyle.

Summary

East Asia contains some of the world's most populous countries, as well as countries at varying stages of development. The region is remote from the major tourist-generating countries of Europe and North America, but improved air transport is overcoming the friction of distance. Many countries are developing an inbound tourism industry as a source of foreign exchange and to provide jobs. Domestic tourism and recreation are now an important part of the lifestyle, due to the emergence of a middle class in the more prosperous countries. Outbound tourism is also growing, particularly from the established market of Japan and the new market of China. Business travel is important throughout the region.

Away from the more established tourist destinations, the infrastructure for tourism is of a comparatively low standard, though many countries are remedying the situation, mainly by improvements in airport facilities and the development of self-contained resort complexes.

Cultural tourism is of primary importance in the countries of the Far East, which have much to offer in the way of historic cities, temples and landscapes. It is less significant in the countries of South-East Asia where the climate favours beach tourism and where adventure travel and ecotourism increasingly play a major role. However, more needs to be done to protect natural resources and wildlife from the pollution and excessive development that has occurred in China and some of the countries of South-East Asia. Other attractions include shopping, particularly in Singapore and Hong Kong. China, the 'sleeping giant' of the region, is now becoming a major economic player on the world stage and will be a significant force in global tourism.

Chapter 23
The tourism geography of Australasia

Learning Objectives

After reading this chapter you should be able to:

■ Describe the major physical features and climates of Australasia and understand their importance for tourism.
■ Appreciate that Australia and New Zealand are socially and economically part of the developed Western world, whereas most of the Pacific islands are developing countries, and the influence these differences have on tourism patterns.
■ Recognize the importance of domestic tourism and outbound travel in Australia and New Zealand.
■ Appreciate the economic, social and environmental impacts of tourism on the native peoples and natural resources of the region.
■ Appreciate the effect of great distance from the major generating countries of the Northern Hemisphere on inbound tourism.
■ Be aware of the growing importance of ecotourism in the region, and the potential of Antarctica as one of tourism's 'last frontiers'.
■ Demonstrate a knowledge of the tourist regions, resorts, business centres and tourist attractions of Australia, New Zealand and the Pacific islands.

Introduction

Australia, New Zealand and the islands of the Pacific east of Indonesia and the Philippines form a separate geographical entity called Australasia. An alternative name – Oceania – is also appropriate as most of the constituent islands are insignificant in comparison with the vastness of the Pacific Ocean, which covers a quarter of the earth's surface and spans a distance of more than

12 000 kilometres from east to west at its widest extent. The only large landmasses are:

- Australia – often called the 'island-continent'
- New Guinea
- The two main islands of New Zealand.

The total population is small compared to that of neighbouring South-East Asia – well under 30 million – and there is generally less pressure on resources. Australia and New Zealand are economically, culturally and politically part of the developed Western world, but both countries play an important developmental role with regard to the other countries in the South Pacific region. In the northern Pacific, the islands of Hawaii are geographically part of Polynesia, but they became the 50th state of the USA in 1959 and are therefore included in Chapter 24. The rest of Australasia is economically part of the developing world, consisting mainly of island mini-states with small populations and limited land resources. Most have become politically independent only since the 1960s, while some of the smaller islands are still governed by countries lying outside the region, notably France and the USA. Yet, despite their image of paradise, there has been civil unrest in the islands, particularly Fiji and the Solomons. With the ending of the Cold War, the islands are no longer supported by the defence industries of the Western powers and must become economically more self-sufficient. For this reason, tourism and the exploitation of the islands' potentially vast marine resources increasingly play a vital role.

The Pacific Asia Travel Association (PATA) represents all the countries in the region. There are prospects for considerable growth in tourism, as the region can offer generally favourable climates, unspoiled coastal and mountain scenery, and in the main, political stability. The market potential is certainly present, with the Pacific Rim of Asia and North America an area of impressive economic growth. Since 1970, Australia and New Zealand have loosened their ties to Britain and forged closer trade links with the USA and the countries of east Asia, especially Japan. This pattern of trade has resulted in a growing volume of air traffic across the Pacific, facilitated by long-range wide-bodied jets. Air transport now plays a vital role in the economy of all the countries in the region, and the peoples of Australasia are very aviation-minded. However, these Pacific destinations are still a long way from the major tourist-generating countries – particularly those of Europe – and are therefore vulnerable to downturns in travel caused by terrorism and international crises, as well as competition from more accessible parts of the world that can offer similar attractions.

The native peoples of Australasia suffered severely as a result of Western colonization in the nineteenth century, losing most of their tribal lands and much of their culture in the process. This was particularly true of the Australian aborigines, who became a small, marginalized minority. Since the 1970s there has been a growing recognition of the value of indigenous arts, crafts and folklore as cultural resources, and native peoples not only take greater pride in their heritage, but also increasingly take an active role in the tourism industry.

Australia

For more than a century Australia, and New Zealand, have been the destinations for large numbers of emigrants, chiefly from the British Isles, but more recently from

Asian and Pacific countries. Until the 1980s Australia was not important as a holiday destination, the great majority of visitors being business or VFR travellers. In the 1980s and 1990s growth rates for inbound tourism accelerated, delivering arrivals of well over 4 million by 2002. This has in part been due to the promotional efforts of both the Australian Tourist Commission (ATC) and the Australian state governments, the showcasing of Australia for the 2000 Olympics, and competitive air fares. Tourism is now one of Australia's leading sources of foreign exchange, supporting well over half a million jobs.

Australia is the only country occupying a whole continent, with an area of 7.6 million square kilometres – comparable in size to the USA. Not surprisingly, the country has a federal system of government, similar to Canada, in which the states and the two territories – Northern Territory and Australian Capital Territory – enjoy much freedom to manage their own affairs, including the development and regulation of domestic tourism. Each state has a tourism-marketing agency and many states also have a government tourism department. At federal level, tourism began to be taken seriously in the early 1990s with a number of strategy initiatives and the appointment of a tourism minister to the cabinet. The federal Department of Tourism coordinates policy and action plans whilst the ATC is responsible for tourism marketing and is funded by the federal government with contributions from the tourism industry. Despite a very well organized tourism sector at both regional and federal level, apart from some significant destinations – Sydney, Melbourne and the Gold Coast – the organization of tourism is weak at the local level.

The setting for tourism

Physical features

Australia has great tourism potential, thanks to its warm sunny climates, unique wildlife and natural features, as well as a coastline – over 36 000 kilometres in length – which includes some of the world's finest beaches and the largest coral reef. However, most of the continent has been worn down by eons of erosion and as a result, is relatively low-lying compared to other continents, with only a few mountain ranges and inselbergs – isolated rocky outcrops rising abruptly from the surrounding plains. The main exception is the mountain system – known as the Great Dividing Range – which runs for 3600 kilometres along the eastern margin of the continent, reaching its highest point – 2200 metres – at Mount Kosciuszko. These mountain ranges separate the fertile coastal belt, where most of the cities and tourist facilities are located, from the interior. Australia can also claim to be the world's driest continent. Most of the outback – the vast, thinly populated bush country extending west of the river Darling – is desert or semi-desert, where the lakes shown on the map are usually expanses of salt and the rivers merely a succession of pools or *billabongs*.

The most interesting natural resources of Australia are the plants – mainly drought-resistant eucalyptus (or *gums*) – and the animals – marsupial species which are only native to the island-continent. Indeed, Australia has more than 2000 protected natural areas, including national parks, testament to the unique landscapes and the flora and fauna of the continent. Twelve sites are on the UNESCO World Heritage list, namely:

- Kakadu National Park in Northern Territory
- Uluru (Ayers Rock) in Northern Territory

- the Wet Tropics of north Queensland, an area of virgin rainforest
- the Great Barrier Reef off the Queensland coast
- Fraser Island – the world's largest sand island – also off the coast of Queensland
- the Central Eastern Rainforest Reserves in Queensland
- Willandra Lakes in New South Wales
- the Blue Mountains in New South Wales
- Lord Howe Island in the Tasman Sea
- Tasmanian wilderness
- Shark Bay in Western Australia
- Australian fossil mammal sites.

These landscapes provide great opportunities for tourism – tourists can prospect for gold or gemstones, go on whale or dolphin watching trips, take part in four-wheel-drive vehicle safaris that allow the more adventurous to visit remoter areas away from the all-weather roads, or try adventure sports such as abseiling and white-water rafting. The Australians are leaders in minimizing the environmental impact of these recreational activities. The ATC has the overall responsibility for monitoring the environmental impact of tourism and has initiated a number of state and federal ecotourism strategies and awards for sustainable tourism practices.

The size of Australia and its geographical location means that it experiences a wide range of climatic conditions, but no real extremes. Most of Australia, with the exception of Tasmania, lies within tropical or sub-tropical latitudes, so that winter cold is rarely a problem. The desert interior has a more extreme climate; in winter pleasantly warm days are followed by nights with temperatures dropping below 0 °C. The northernmost region of Australia around Darwin experiences a tropical monsoon type of climate with a rainy season between December and May, accompanied by high temperatures and humidity. The great majority of Australians live in the south-eastern part of the country and enjoy a warm temperate climate, which in general is ideal for outdoor recreation. However, summer temperatures frequently exceed 40 °C due to winds from the desert interior, which bring the risk of bush fires to the city. Snow is almost unknown except in Tasmania and the southern sections of the Great Dividing Range, where it provides good skiing conditions from June to September. Perhaps the best climate is around Perth in Western Australia, where summers are dry but not excessively warm due to a constant sea breeze.

Cultural features

The population of Australia exceeded 19 million in 2002 and is concentrated into a few large cities – Sydney and Melbourne account for almost 40 per cent of the population. Other major centres include Brisbane, Adelaide and Perth. Canberra is a relatively small city, though it is the federal capital. The urban character of Australia's population has an important influence on the patterns of tourism which have developed. A developed and diversified economy means that Australians enjoy a high standard of living. The ownership of motor vehicles, for example, approaches North American levels (almost 10 million passenger vehicles in 2001) and the effects are seen in suburban sprawl around the major cities. Participation in outdoor activities is high by European standards. The most popular participant sports are tennis, swimming, sailing, and surfing. Sports facilities are excellent, boosted by the Sydney Olympics in 2000, and spectator sports include football, cricket and horseracing – epitomized by the Melbourne Cup. Gambling is also popular, with casinos and clubs producing considerable revenue and attracting foreign visitors, particularly from Asia.

Demand for tourism

Domestic tourism

Each year Australians take, on average, at least two pleasure trips involving a stay away from home, and travel has become an important element of discretionary spending, increasing travel propensities. The domestic market is significant simply because of the wide range of experiences on offer in the continent, and it is the main-stay of the tourism economy. Although only a small proportion of trips cross state boundaries, partly because of the distances involved, in the early years of this century domestic travel has increased as international travel has been depressed by world events. Deregulation of domestic airlines in the early 1990s led to a lowering of air fares and boosted the domestic industry. The majority of holidays are in December and January, mostly to the beach resorts between Sydney and north Queensland. During the winter months there is a smaller but much more concentrated migration to the semi-tropical beaches of Queensland and large numbers also head for the ski slopes of the Australian Alps, while others seek the unspoiled desert scenery around Alice Springs.

Outbound tourism

Australia is the largest generator of international tourism in the Southern Hemisphere, with well over 3 million trips taken abroad in 2002. Despite their distance from other destinations, Australians feel a strong need to explore other parts of the world. The majority of Australian tourists who travel abroad are residents of the two most prosperous states, New South Wales and Victoria, which between them contain almost two-thirds of the population. Despite the high costs involved, large numbers of Australians visit Europe on holidays extending over a few weeks, during which several countries may be visited. They include a high proportion of young people combining a European tour with work experience, some travelling overland from Singapore via India and the Middle East. Other popular destinations include the USA, New Zealand and the Pacific islands such as Fiji, Vanuatu and New Caledonia. A glance at the map will show that Australia is in fact much closer to South-East Asia than it is to Europe or North America, with Indonesia being less than 1000 kilometres from Darwin. This accounts for the popularity of the beach resorts of Bali, Thailand and Malaysia, although the Bali bombings in 2002 depressed travel to Indonesia.

Inbound tourism

Only a small percentage of foreign visitors to Australia come on inclusive tours and VFR tourism is decreasing in importance from Britain and Ireland as holiday tourism becomes more important. The main inbound markets for Australia are New Zealand, North America, the UK and Asia – particularly Japan. The Japanese and North American markets were affected by 9/11 and also by the collapse of Ansett – Australia's second airline. The Japanese are predominantly in the younger age groups and are mainly attracted to the resorts of the Queensland coast. The Americans, on the other hand, are generally older with a high propensity to travel; they feel an affinity with the pioneering spirit of Australia and are most likely to take a touring holiday. A growing number of tourists come from China, Singapore, Hong Kong and other Asian countries, and many of these are in the student category. Such has been the turnaround in demand for tourism that Australia now runs a surplus on its travel account and tropical destinations such as Cairns and the Whitsunday Islands are taking market share from places such as Fiji.

Supply of tourism

The tourism industry in Australia caters in the main for the large domestic demand, and until the 1980s little attention was paid to the needs of foreign visitors. Until quite recently, service standards were indifferent, partly because of the egalitarian attitudes prevalent in the country. Change has come about partly as a result of the influx of large numbers of emigrants from Southern and Eastern Europe, and, to a lesser extent, from Asia. These 'New Australians' have expanded the range of entertainments and restaurants on offer in their adopted cities and greatly improved standards in Australia's 5000-plus hotels.

The great majority of foreign visitors to Australia arrive in Sydney or Melbourne and few travel beyond New South Wales or Queensland to take advantage of lower domestic fares. This is despite attempts to spread arrivals to other gateways such as Cairns – where Qantas's new holiday airline is based. Deregulation of the domestic airlines in 1991 attracted new airlines to Australia, but none succeeded until the arrival of Virgin Blue in 2001. In that year more services were developed and air fares fell – such that domestic air movements stood at 57 million in 2001. Airports across Australia are also being privatized and upgraded. Surface transport in such a vast, sparsely populated country can be problematic; travel across the continent from Perth to Sydney (3300 kilometres) involves a 2-hour time change and a journey by train or bus lasting three days. Despite its length (40 000 kilometres) the Australian rail system is not a viable alternative to flying as the network is incomplete and interrupted by changes of gauge at state boundaries. An exception is the Indian Pacific Express which allows direct travel from Sydney to Perth. Dedicated tourism rail services are also being developed and include the Great South Pacific Express between Sydney and Cairns, and The Ghan between Adelaide and Darwin.

Tourism resources

New South Wales

Tourism in New South Wales is dominated by its capital, **Sydney**. Sydney has arguably a better climate, a more spectacular setting and a more varied nightlife than its rival Melbourne. The city has developed around one of the world's finest harbours and the beaches of the Pacific are within easy reach by hydrofoil or ferry. Sydney's attractions include:

- the famous suspension bridge across the harbour, which can now be ascended by visitors; harbour-side attractions such as the Sydney Opera House, the ferry terminal at Circular Quay, shopping, restaurants and hotels on the harbour side and revitalized areas such as 'The Rocks' with art galleries and specialist shopping
- Darling Harbour, which has been revitalized with the Sydney Aquarium, the Maritime and Powerhouse Museums, and an IMAX Cinema
- heritage sites and buildings around Sydney Harbour, such as Fort Dennison and the Quarantine Station where emigrants first landed, now converted into a hotel

○ many cultural attractions, such as the Art Gallery of New South Wales and a range of museums

○ districts such as Paddington and Kings Cross with their distinctive lifestyles.

The best known of Sydney's beaches is Bondi, with its superb conditions for surfing; but since the strong tidal surges can be dangerous many families prefer the more sheltered beaches of Port Jackson or the small seaside resort of Manly with its Oceanworld attraction. Sydney's hosting of the 2000 Olympics gave tourism a major boost and involved the building of 14 new hotels, improving the transport infrastructure, and the provision of new sports facilities.

Recreational areas within easy reach of the city include:

• the Snowy Mountains with ski resorts such as Thredbo and Perisher
• the gorges of the Hawkesbury river
• the Hunter Valley vineyards
• the Blue Mountains, a scenic area of forested ridges, caves and waterfalls; cable-cars and a funicular railway provide access from the resort of Katoomba to a variety of viewpoints.

Queensland

From Sydney a scenic coastal route leads northwards into Queensland, which is predominantly a destination for beach tourism. The route passes through resorts such as Newcastle, Coffs Harbour, Port Stephens, Port Macquarie, Byron Bay (a famous surfing beach) and the rainforest in the Dorrigo National Park. The area 50 kilometres south of Brisbane, known as the **Gold Coast**, is one of the most popular holiday regions for Australians, but also caters for international visitors, particularly the Japanese. The coast is a highly developed 70-kilometre-long strip of resorts with Surfer's Paradise at its heart. Much of the development is badly planned and commercialized with many high-rise hotels. The area is the site of both sporting events and a number of major theme parks, reminiscent of Florida:

○ Seaworld
○ Warner Brothers Movie World
○ Wet 'n Wild waterpark
○ Dreamworld (a Disney-type park).

Lamington National Park in the hinterland of the Gold Coast is well known for its birdlife.

Brisbane, the state capital, received a boost to tourism in 1988 by hosting Expo, and the site has been redeveloped as the Southbank Parklands – a cultural and park area on the south bank of the Brisbane river. The city has a spectacular setting on the river where *CityCat* catamarans ferry visitors and commuters, and offers a range of cultural venues, museums and galleries.

Close to the coast near Brisbane is Fraser Island – the world's largest barrier island composed of sand deposits. Other offshore islands are both recreational areas for Queenslanders and also good locations for dolphin and whale watching. To the north of Brisbane, the **Sunshine Coast** has excellent beaches stretching from Caloundra to Rainbow Beach. One resort – Noosa Heads – has specialized in fine dining. In the hinterland are the Noosa and Cooloola national parks.

One of Australia's unique tourist attractions, the **Great Barrier Reef**, begins 350 kilometres north of Brisbane and extends northwards for 2000 kilometres to Cape York. The reef provides opportunities for scuba diving that are unequalled elsewhere, but there are fears that global warming and the 'crown of thorns' starfish are damaging the coral. Between the reef and the coast lies an enormous sheltered lagoon dotted with hundreds of islands. Some of these have been developed as exclusive holiday resorts with marinas, golf courses and other sports facilities, while others cater more for campers. Examples include:

○ Hamilton Island in the Whitsunday group, which has its own jetport with flights from Brisbane.
○ Green Island, specializing in eco-friendly tourism.
○ Great Keppel Island, which is predominantly for young travellers.
○ Bedarra, which specializes in honeymooners.

Pollution and over-fishing are problems on the more popular islands with consequent danger to the reef ecosystem; to remedy this some areas have been designated as nature reserves. The ports of the Queensland coast, notably Cairns, Townsville and Port Douglas are the starting point of excursions to the Reef and offshore islands by boat and helicopter. Cairns is now an important gateway, particularly for Asian visitors, and is a booming resort city offering a range of hotels and a casino. Inland, sugar plantations, the rainforests of the Daintree National Park and the Atherton Tableland provide the main interest away from the coastal resorts. The Kurunda Skyrail provides a 7.5 kilometre ride over the rainforest canopy, with the Tjapukai Aboriginal Cultural Park at its foot. From Cairns northwards to Cape York lie the excellent and largely deserted white beaches of the **Marlin Coast**.

Victoria

Victoria experiences more variable weather conditions than other states of mainland Australia, with rural tourism playing a more important role. The capital of Victoria – **Melbourne** – rivals Sydney as the commercial capital of the country, with a more conservative, less flamboyant lifestyle. The city has as wide a range of retailing, restaurants, cultural and sporting attractions and is almost as cosmopolitan as Sydney, with large Italian and Greek communities. Melbourne has a range of sporting venues, such as the Melbourne Cricket Ground (MCG) and Albert Park, where the Australian Formula One Grand Prix is held; however it is the Melbourne Cup – not only a sporting event but a fashion show – that attracts most interest. The city has its own beach resort at St Kilda and is conveniently placed for touring the vineyards of the Yarra river.

Other tourism resources accessible from Melbourne include:

• the Victorian Alps – a popular region for walking, skiing (in resorts such as Mount Buller) and white water rafting
• the Great Ocean Road drive along the picturesque Victoria coast, with rock features such as the Twelve Apostles
• Phillip Island, with its burrowing penguins
• the Gippsland Lake District
• reminders of Victoria's nineteenth-century mining heritage, with 'living museums' recreating the 1850s Gold Rush and Beechworth – associated with Ned Kelly, Australia's most famous outlaw
• old-style steamboat trips on the Murray river, an important commercial waterway before the coming of the railways.

Australian Capital Territory

Canberra is the capital of Australia and is spaciously planned in a beautiful lakeland setting near the Snowy Mountains. It cannot compare in vitality to Sydney or

Melbourne, but boasts major cultural attractions, including the National Gallery and Museum, as well as national institutions such as the Australian Institute of Sport and Parliament House.

Tasmania

The small island-state of Tasmania lies to the south of the mainland, across the Bass Strait. It can be reached by ferry or fast catamaran from Melbourne or by air to Launceston or Hobart. With its mild oceanic climate and perpetually green country-side, Tasmania contrasts with the rest of Australia and has its own flora and fauna – such as the Tasmanian Devil. The small resorts along the north coast (such as Stanley) are not unlike those of England's West Country, and are particularly attractive for senior citizens escaping the summer heat and more hurried lifestyle on the mainland. Inland there is mountain and lake scenery in the Cradle Mountain – Lake St Clair National Park and the Cataract Gorge, a spectacular ravine popular for adventure sports. The southwest of the island receives the heaviest rainfall in Australia and is covered by barely explored rainforest. The Tasmanian Wilderness Railway – once used for transporting minerals – has been restored as a 30-kilometre journey through virgin wilderness. The island has a range of heritage attractions such as the Port Arthur historic site, a reminder of Australia's most notorious penal settlement.

Western Australia

The largest and most thinly populated of the states, Western Australia suffers as a destination due to its great distance from the more popular tourist regions of the east coast, but is nevertheless developing markets based on ecotourism, adventure tourism and its mining heritage. Perth is a green, spacious city close to good surfing beaches (such as Scarborough and Margaret River) fronting the Indian Ocean, while Fremantle gained wide publicity by hosting the America's Cup yacht race and now has a maritime museum. The city has a variety of attractions, including the Perth Mint, Cultural Centre and gemstone shopping in the suburbs. Perth is also a good base for exploring the Outback including:

- the Punululu/Bungle Bungle National Park, with its multi-coloured rock formations
- the even more remote Kimberley region, over 2000 kilometres north of Perth, a wilderness of sandstone gorges, transformed during the rainy season into a riot of vegetation and cascading waterfalls; the El Questro wilderness park provides a variety of accommodation for tourists
- Kalgoorlie and Coolgardie with their gold mining heritage.

  Attractions along the coast include:

- Shark Bay which is renowned for its marine wildlife, including the dolphins of Monkey Mia that interact freely with visitors, but this situation could change if tourist numbers become excessive
- Exmouth, on the **Coral Coast**, which is the base for exploring the Ningaloo Reef
- Broome, famous for its former pearl diving industry, and now an upmarket beach resort.

South Australia

Most of South Australia is desert country, but in contrast, Adelaide, the 'Festival City', has a very English ambience in a parkland setting. Adelaide is close to the coastal resort of Glenelg, the vineyards of the Clare and Barossa Valleys and the scenic Flinders Mountains with the Flinders Chase National Park. Further afield is Kangaroo Island, and the opal mining town of Coober Pedy, deep in the outback where visitors can stay in the Desert Caves Hotel, built underground like most dwellings in this community to avoid the extreme desert heat.

Northern Territory

The Stuart Highway links Australia's southern city of Adelaide with the northern city of Darwin. Darwin is the only city of any size in the 'Top End', with a limited range of attractions but it is used as a base for exploring the region's tourism resources. These include Australia's tropical northlands with their game-rich grasslands and reserves on which the Australian aborigines continue their traditional lifestyle. In the Tiwi Islands it is possible for visitors to interact with the aborigines. There are a number of significant tourism areas accessible to Darwin:

- The Kakadu National Park is probably the most popular attraction in this region. It was the setting for the *Crocodile Dundee* film and has rich wetland wildlife.
- Litchfield National Park is closer to Darwin, famous for wildlife, aborigine rock art and the Gagudju Crocodile Hotel – so called because of its design.
- Arnhemland is a large unspoilt wetland area under aborigine management where visitor numbers are strictly controlled by a permit system.

Further south lies the **red heart** of Australia, an area of spinifex desert, salt lakes and strange rock formations such as the Olgas/Kata Tjuta and the more famous Ayers Rock/Uluru. The only town in the region, **Alice Springs**, offers a range of attractions such as:
   ○ the Telegraph Station, a reminder of the city's pioneering role
   ○ the Alice Springs Cultural Precinct showcasing the history of central Australia
   ○ the School of the Air Outback Radio Service
   ○ the base of the Flying Doctor Service.
However, Alice Springs owes its importance as a tourist centre more to its function as the gateway to the Uluru National Park and its prime attraction – **Ayers Rock** (**Uluru** in the local aborigine language). This has achieved internal recognition as an icon of Australia, due to its unique character as the world's largest monolith – it measures 9 kilometres in circumference and 300 metres in height – and the way the rock changes colour at sunrise and sunset. Ayers Rock became much more accessible with the opening of an airport and purpose-built resort at Yulara in the 1980s. This provides a range of accommodation from budget camping to the five-star Ayers Rock Resort Hotel. Guided tours of the Rock and the surrounding area interpret aborigine culture and legends of the Dreamtime, and visitors can sample 'bush tucker' – the natural foods of the outback. Nevertheless, the ever-growing number of visitors raises a number of issues regarding the future of tourism in the area, namely:
   ○ sustainability – burgeoning demand may exhaust ground water supplies, already under pressure from the cattle industry; although the Yulara resort is built to an aesthetically high standard, it is difficult to justify air-conditioning and swimming pools as being compatible with ecotourism
   ○ the potential for conflict between tourists and the host community – Ayers Rock is a sacred site for the aboriginal people, but to most tourists it is a photo-opportunity and an objective to be climbed, albeit with difficulty; many aborigines regard this as an act of desecration.

New Zealand

Although New Zealand shares cultural similarities with Australia, including a love of sport and the outdoor life, and a certain informality of outlook, it is different in many other respects, both in terms of its physical geography and culture.

The setting for tourism

New Zealand is separated from Australia by the Tasman Sea – 1900 kilometres wide and often stormy. New Zealand is scenically very different from its big neighbour, boasting volcanoes, glaciers and fjords among its natural attractions, which have gained world-wide attention as the backdrop for the filming of the *Lord of the Rings* trilogy. The native flora and fauna is also quite unlike that of Australia. Much of this, including the unique flightless birds, was threatened with extinction as a result of the introduction of new species by Europeans in the process of clearing 'the bush' for farmland. New Zealand was among the first countries to establish national parks on the American model, to conserve what remained of the natural heritage. There continues to be a widespread interest in environmental issues, such as opposition to the French nuclear testing in the South Pacific.

Physical features

Most of New Zealand is hilly or mountainous and the country's greatest tourist asset is the beauty and variety of its scenery. The two large islands that make up the bulk of New Zealand offer quite different environments. Much of the North Island consists of a volcanic plateau, while the South Island is dominated by a range of high fold mountains, the Southern Alps, which contain glaciers, snowfields and a fjord coastline.

New Zealand favours the more active types of outdoor recreation, with its equable temperatures and pollution-free atmosphere. Although the islands enjoy more sunshine than the British Isles, sunshine is not guaranteed, and the range of latitude occupied by the islands means that while Auckland has a subtropical climate, at Invercargill 1600 kilometres further south the temperatures more closely resemble those experienced in the western islands of Scotland. This puts domestic tourism at a disadvantage compared to Australia's Gold Coast, Bali and the islands of the Pacific. The mountains in both the North and South Islands are high enough to receive heavy snowfalls, the skiing season lasting from July to October.

Cultural features

New Zealand's cultural heritage includes an export-oriented pastoral economy and a nineteenth-century gold-rush – in Westland – reminiscent of the Australian experience. However, New Zealand was colonized by the British with free settlers, in contrast to the convict origins of most of the Australian states. The indigenous Maori people had a highly developed, if warlike, culture derived from their homeland in Polynesia. They now account for some 12 per cent of the population and their cultural heritage, expressed in crafts and dances, forms an important ingredient in New Zealand's tourist appeal. The Maori have become more fully integrated into the mainstream culture than the native peoples of Australia, although the incidence of unemployment and other social problems in Maori communities is higher than the national average.

Tourism demand and supply

The New Zealand government was one of the first to recognize the importance of tourism, setting up an official tourist organization as far back as 1901. Tourism now is a significant export earner and foreign visitor arrivals in the early twenty-first century exceeded 2 million a year, compared to only 100 000 in 1970. This growth has been achieved in spite of the remoteness of this small island nation from the world's major trade routes and centres of population, by successful promotion and development of the country's resources, and clever exploitation of the islands as the setting for the *Lord of the Rings* films. Tourism New Zealand works closely with the private sector to attract the more adventurous type of tourist who is interested in scenery, meeting people and the outdoor life. New Zealand can offer the unique resource of uncrowded countryside, with a population of only 4 million occupying an area comparable in size to the British Isles.

Three-quarters of New Zealand's population live in North Island, and of these, 40 per cent are concentrated in the country's largest city, Auckland. The standard of living is high, with motor vehicle ownership approaching Australian levels, although cars and other consumer goods have to be imported. The economy is dependent on the export of primary products such as meat and wool, but the service sector, including tourism, is becoming increasingly important. Nevertheless, despite the distances that must be covered, and the high cost of air fares, New Zealanders have a high propensity to travel abroad, and with much the same preferences regarding destinations as the Australians. About half of all overseas visits are to Australia, with the encouragement of cheap air fares.

A much greater number of New Zealanders take annual summer holidays in their own country, mostly during the six weeks from mid-December to the end of January. Since this coincides with the peak period of arrival for foreign visitors, there is considerable pressure on hotel rooms in most resort areas. Motels are the type of accommodation most favoured by domestic holidaymakers, although caravanning, camping and youth hostelling are also popular, and many families also own, or share, a second home at the coast.

Most tourism enterprises in New Zealand are small businesses catering mainly for domestic demand. However, foreign visitors are often attracted to remote and sparsely populated rural areas, where it has been uneconomic for the private sector to develop resort facilities of international standard. In the past, the government intervened by financing the Tourist Hotel Corporation to operate quality hotels in scenic locations. Since the 1980s the international hotel chains have developed large hotels in the main resorts, catering mainly for the inclusive tour market; whilst luxurious lodges cater for the top end of the independent traveller market. Farm-stays are also available throughout New Zealand, providing welcome income to the agricultural sector.

Australia provides around one-third of incoming tourists, followed by North Americans, many of whom are interested in hunting and fishing holidays. East Asian countries such as Japan and South Korea are also significant source markets. The Japanese are interested in New Zealand not only as a destination for skiing holidays, when the Northern Hemisphere season has ended, but also for other types of outdoor activities. The UK market has stayed fairly constant at around 10 per cent of arrivals since the 1950s, but its composition has changed, with fewer British visitors falling into the VFR category, and an increasing number opting to purchase tailor-made holidays rather than inclusive tours.

New Zealand's transport system is well developed. The mountainous topography has encouraged the widespread use of domestic air services connecting the main cities – Auckland, Wellington, Christchurch and Dunedin – and the resort areas. Specially equipped light aircraft bring the Southern Alps within easy reach of tourists, while hiking trails and scenic mountain highways are used by the more adventurous. Rail transport has declined, except on a few scenic routes. A network of bus services provides access to most parts of the country, while the Wellington–Picton ferry service across Cook Strait acts as a vital link between the North and South Islands.

Auckland and Wellington serve as important gateways to the South Pacific region and are major centres for business travel.

Tourism resources

New Zealand has an extensive resource base for sightseeing, ecotourism and adventure tourism, which includes some unusual, if not risky, extreme sports such as jet-boating, parapenting and bungee jumping, as well as sea kayaking and white-water rafting. Beach tourism, catering mainly for domestic demand, is well developed on the east coast of North Island, with resorts such as Hastings and Napier. Auckland, Rotorua and Wellington are the major tourist centres in **North Island**, catering for the bulk of the international demand.

* **Auckland**, attractively sited between two harbours, is known as 'The City of Sails', and was the venue of the 1999/2000 America's Cup yacht race. Auckland is the centre for touring the sub-tropical north of the country with its kauri forests, surfing beaches and opportunities for game fishing.
* **Rotorua** is situated in the volcanic plateau in the centre of North Island, which contains some of the world's most unusual scenery, including the Pohutu geyser, and Mount Tongariro – which is still active. Rotorua became a resort in the late nineteenth century when it was fashionable to bathe in the hot springs. It is also the centre of traditional Maori culture as interpreted for tourists. Although tourism provides employment for Maori entertainers and craftsmen, most of the business enterprises are owned by *pakehas* (white New Zealanders), resulting in fewer economic benefits to local communities.
* **Wellington**, the capital of New Zealand, has a harbour setting reminiscent of San Francisco and a range of cultural attractions. The city is convenient for visiting the vineyards of the Marlborough Sounds area of South Island, New Plymouth with its rugby football museum, and the beaches of Hawkes Bay, where Napier is noted for its Art Deco architecture – the legacy of reconstruction following the 1931 earthquake.

South Island was the setting for much of the filming of *The Lord of the Rings*. The Mount Cook National Park boasts New Zealand's highest mountain and the Tasman Glacier, one of the largest in the South Hemisphere outside Antarctica. In the Westland National Park glaciers flow almost to the sea amid dense evergreen forests. Ecotourists are particularly attracted to Fiordland, a barely explored wilderness which is the nation's largest national park. One of its most spectacular features is Milford Sound, which can be reached by boat, or overland on a popular hiking trail. Another important centre for ecotourism is Kaikoura, a Maori community not far from Christchurch, which has become world famous for whale watching. In contrast to Rotorua, tourism enterprises are operated by local people, who claim exclusive use of marine resources, in a bid to discourage competition by white New Zealanders. Other important tourist centres include:

- **Christchurch** – the international gateway to South Island and a garden city with a reputation as the most English city in New Zealand. It is now attempting to diversify this image by promoting the scenic attractions and ski resorts of the Southern Alps, which are within easy reach. The city's Canterbury Museum focuses on Antarctica, a reminder that Christchurch has been the point of departure for many expeditions to the 'white continent'.
- **Queenstown** on Lake Wakatipu has two tourist seasons, as a ski resort in winter and as a centre for mountain climbing, hiking and a whole range of activity holidays in summer. Queenstown's entertainment scene is also extensive, attracting young people from all over New Zealand.

The Pacific islands

The 'South Sea islands' image of blue lagoons, palm-fringed coral beaches, lush scenery and hospitable islanders has a powerful appeal to would-be escapists from the industrialized societies of the West. So far, the great distances separating the Pacific islands from the tourist-generating countries has prevented the development of mass tourism, based on sun, sand and sea – the islands only account for 0.15 per cent of world arrivals! The exceptions are Hawaii and, to a lesser extent, Fiji. There is little demand for domestic or outbound tourism, and most of the arrivals at airports in many of the islands are returning emigrants visiting their families.

Most of the Pacific islands have a tropical humid climate, characterized by abundant rainfall and strong solar radiation, with air and sea temperatures averaging well above 20 °C throughout the year. Sea breezes mitigate the heat and humidity, especially in Polynesia, but tropical storms are frequent during the rainy season and can cause widespread damage. The larger islands are generally of volcanic origin, mountainous and covered with luxuriant vegetation, with fringing coral reefs along the coast. The smaller islands are mostly coral atolls, low-lying and consisting of little more than a narrow strip of sand, almost enclosing what may be an extensive lagoon.

Inter-island distances are great compared to the Caribbean, making it difficult to visit more than a few countries in one itinerary, while the absence of inter-line agreements between the various national airlines adds to the cost of travel. In the past, shipping services connected the islands, but these have long been in decline. However, most governments in the region recognize that, given their limited financial resources, some degree of international cooperation is necessary. The South Pacific Tourism Organization (SPTO) plays an important role in promoting most countries in the region. Investment for the development of facilities has to come mainly from external sources of capital, not only in the West but also increasingly in Asian countries such as Japan and South Korea. Hotel accommodation is generally of a high standard, designed in sympathy with the environment and local building traditions. The main problems are a lack of infrastructure, especially poor roads, and an insufficiently skilled local workforce.

As with the Caribbean, it is a mistake to stereotype the Pacific islands as offering similar tourism products. In fact, we need to distinguish three culturally distinct regions, namely:

- **Micronesia** in the western Pacific, lying to the east of the Philippines
- **Melanesia**, with its darker skinned peoples, in the south-west Pacific
- **Polynesia**, roughly forming a triangle drawn between Hawaii, Fiji and Easter Island, and covering a vast expanse in the centre of the Pacific Ocean.

Micronesia

The thousands of small islands that make up Micronesia total less than 3000 square kilometres in area, scattered over 8 million square kilometres of ocean. With the exception of the Marianas, which are volcanic and mountainous, most of the islands are coral atolls, with the former British colony of Kiribati claiming the world's largest atoll – Christmas Island. Following Japan's defeat in the Second World War most of the region was ruled by the USA, until the islands gained independence in the early 1990 as four separate republics, namely:

- the Northern Marianas, including Saipan
- Palau
- the Federal Republic of Micronesia (formerly the Caroline Islands)
- the Marshall Islands, including Majuro.

Micronesia's main tourism resources are the beaches and lagoons that are ideal for sailing and diving. Palau boasts some of the world's best dive sites, including the Truk Lagoon, scene of a major naval battle in the Second World War. Here the wrecks of numerous Japanese ships and aircraft have been transmuted into colourful artificial reefs.

Guam is the most developed tourism destination in Micronesia. It was acquired by the USA from Spain in 1898, continues to be administered as a United States territory and, offering more attractions and facilities than the other islands, receives a large number of tourists. There are important American military bases on some of the other islands, and United States aid is crucial in the development of infrastructure projects such as airports and harbours. As a result, tourism has grown rapidly, although as yet it has made little impact on the more remote islands. The USA, Japan and South Korea provide the majority of tourists to Micronesia, some of whom are ex-servicemen and their families revisiting the battlefields of the Second World War.

Melanesia

Melanesia mainly consists of fairly large, mountainous and densely forested islands. In fact, commercial logging has become a major earner of foreign exchange, but the rapid depletion of the forest cover could have a serious effect on the islands' wildlife, water supplies and offshore coral reefs. Melanesia includes the following destinations:

- **Papua–New Guinea** – the second largest country of Australasia, boasting its highest mountains, its largest area of rainforest and a great variety of wildlife, including the bird of paradise. Pidgin-English, as elsewhere in the western Pacific, has become the means of communication in a country where there are some 400 different tribes. With surface transport poor or non-existent, domestic air services play an essential role, and most tribes, especially those in the central highlands, have moved from the Stone Age to the Jet Age within a generation. Outside the capital, tourist facilities are few, but a number of tour circuits have been established based on Port Moresby and Mount Hagen in the central highlands.

- **New Caledonia** offers more sophisticated facilities and an attractive coastline, protected by a barrier reef. The capital of this French territory, Nouméa, has been styled with some exaggeration, as 'the Paris of the Pacific'. The island attracts substantial numbers of tourists from Australia and Japan.

- **Vanuatu** comprises the volcanic islands known prior to independence as the New Hebrides, when they were ruled jointly by Britain and France. This unique arrangement did little to encourage the development of the country, although the legacy of bilingualism has probably been an advantage for tourism. Vanuatu also earns considerable revenue from its status as a tax haven and flag of convenience. Tourist facilities have developed based on water sports and 'safaris' to native villages. Pentecost Island is celebrated for the ritual in which young tribesmen leap from towers with a jungle vine securing their ankles. It may be that bungee jumping, developed as a commercial activity in New Zealand, originated in Vanuatu.

- The **Solomon Islands** receive relatively few tourists, in part due to political instability, and there is a lack of facilities outside Guadalcanal and the capital Honiara; however the islands do offer some of the world's best dive sites.

Polynesia

Polynesia arguably contains the most attractive islands of the Pacific, offering a climate in which malaria and other tropical diseases are largely absent, lush scenery, and a culture in which music, dance and seafaring play major roles. The various island groups are separated by vast expanses of ocean, but the Moahi (Polynesians) long ago developed the double-hulled outrigger canoe and the navigation skills to make long voyages.

Tourism has developed most on those islands acting as staging points on the trans-Pacific air and shipping routes. This is particularly true of Hawaii and Fiji and, to a lesser extent, of Tahiti and Samoa. At the other extreme the most remote islands – such as Pitcairn (of 'Mutiny on *The Bounty*' fame) lack airports and, moreover, are served by very infrequent shipping services. Cruise ships call at an increasing number of Pacific islands, but this can be a mixed blessing. As in the Caribbean, the economic benefits of cruising compared to long-stay hotel tourism have been questioned, while the arrival of a thousand Western visitors can cause considerable disruption to a small, unsophisticated island community. Apart from Hawaii, the more important destinations of Polynesia include:

- **French Polynesia**, often referred to as Tahiti, after the most important island, which contains the capital Papeete and, along with its neighbour Moaréa, the bulk of the tourist accommodation. However, there are actually five separate archipelagos, spread out over 4 million square kilometres of ocean. Since their discovery by Europeans in the eighteenth century, the islands have captured the Western imagination, inspiring artists such as Gauguin, writers and film-makers. Islands such as Moaréa and Bora Bora are exceptionally beautiful, and essentially unspoiled compared to Tahiti itself, offering a landscape of mountain peaks, waterfalls, forests and sheltered lagoons. Much of the development is in the form of *fare*, Polynesian-style bungalows built on stilts over the waters of a lagoon. The promotion board – Tahiti Tourisme – has been successful in attracting large numbers of Americans, Japanese and Australian visitors, while Club Mediterranée operate villages on Mooréa and Bora Bora. Although the beach and water sports are the main attraction, horse riding and mountain trekking are also encouraged. Tourism has helped to revive the traditional dances and handicrafts such as pareo-weaving, but at the same time has undermined the integrity of the native culture. Although French Polynesia is a very expensive destination to visit, few hotels are profitable due to high labour costs. Most supplies are imported, and the economy is heavily dependent on huge subsidies from France – referred to locally as *atomic rent* on account of the French government's nuclear tests in the Tuamotu Islands.

- **Fiji**, as an ex-British colony, has a different appeal. The country consists of over a hundred inhabited islands and contains two distinct ethnic groups – the native Fijians and the descendants of Hindu immigrants from India brought in under British rule to work the sugar plantations. Although ethnic tensions have contributed to civil unrest which causes temporary downturns in tourism, multiculturalism is also one of Fiji's assets as a destination. Most of the population live on the large volcanic island of Viti Levu, which contains the capital Suva – also the hub for domestic air services and a major port for cruise ships – and the international airport at Nandi. Fiji's national airline, Air Pacific, provides an extensive network of services throughout the region, with direct flights to Los Angeles, Tokyo and a number of cities in Australia and New Zealand. Resort development has mainly taken place along the drier west coast and the 'Coral Coast' to the south, which offers fine beaches and water sports facilities. Entertainment is mainly geared to Australians and New Zealanders, who are the most important tourist markets. Fiji's cultural attractions, which include fire-walking and war dances, are of secondary importance to the beaches and duty-free shopping.

- The islands of **Samoa** are divided administratively between the USA and a now independent former British colony. American Samoa centres on the important harbour of Pago-Pago. Western Samoa offers a more traditional lifestyle, where much of the tourist accommodation in the form of beach *fales* with an open veranda and thatched roof, operated by local families and located in village communities. Most of the tourist attractions, including waterfalls and the former home of the great writer Robert Louis Stevenson, are located on the island of Upolu.

- **Tonga** is also traditional in character, and is the only Pacific island group to have retained a native monarchy. Most of the visitors arrive by cruise ship, but since the expansion of the airport in the early 1990s, the numbers of long-stay tourists have been steadily increasing. Tonga provides opportunities for surfing and other water sports, and a mix of accommodation that includes resort villages and guest houses.

- The **Cook Islands** have encouraged tourism to the extent that it now dominates the economy and the native culture, particularly on the main island – Rarotonga – which is often visited by cruise ships.

- **Easter Island** is geographically the most remote of all Pacific destinations. However, scheduled air services cross the 4000 kilometres of ocean separating the island from mainland Chile (to which it belongs), and provide a link to Tahiti, which lies an equivalent distance to the west. Visitors are attracted by the mysterious giant statues or *moai* that stand as mute reminders of a vanished civilization. It is now thought that the people of Rapa Nui who built these monuments some centuries ago exploited the resources of the island to the point of ecological collapse. The legacy is a treeless landscape that is very different from other Pacific islands.

Tourism, along with other aspects of Western consumer society, has been a mixed blessing to the Pacific islands. Most islanders have lost their skills for self-sufficiency in agriculture and fishing and have come to rely heavily on imported foods, with a negative effect on dietary standards. The native culture had in any case been under severe pressure for two centuries from Western missionaries, traders and administrators imposing their value systems. Governments in the region see tourism as almost their only chance of raising living standards and reducing the dependence of the islands on world markets for their exports of copra and other products. Tourism has helped to revive the folklore of the islanders and provide new markets for their traditional handicrafts. However, much of the spending by tourists fails to benefit the local economy as it does not stay in the islands. Most of the hotels are owned by foreign companies, and considerable imports of food and drink have to be made to meet tourist requirements. Unless the development of tourism is carefully planned with regard to carrying capacity, further damage is likely to be inflicted on the traditional culture of the islands and the fragile marine environment that is their primary resource. The latter is already under threat from the effects of climate change. Global warming might well result in a massive die-off of corals over large areas of the Pacific and the inundation of low-lying atolls through rising sea levels and storm surges, while ozone depletion could affect the food chain of the oceans, with disastrous consequences.

Antarctica

Antarctica differs from other parts of the world in having no indigenous communities to be affected by tourism. In the 1970s the 'white continent' was tourism's last frontier; now there are guidebooks to the Antarctic and the number of tourists arriving during the summer months of December, January and February exceeds the resident population of scientists and support personnel at the research stations. Tourists are attracted by the unique wildlife, awe-inspiring glacial scenery and the heritage of polar explorers such as Amundsen, Scott and Shackleton; yet, aside from outer space, Antarctica is probably the most hostile environment known to mankind. Over 98 per cent of its 14 million square kilometres of land surface (larger than Australia or Europe) is permanently ice-covered. Because of its high altitude, the interior of Antarctica is extremely cold and very dry, while the coast is swept by pitiless winds.

Unlike the Arctic, which is divided among a number of countries, the Antarctic south of latitude 60 degrees is effectively a 'no-man's land'. Under the terms of the 1959 Antarctic Treaty, the territorial claims made by seven of the signatory governments are in abeyance, so that the region acts as a vast laboratory for international cooperation in scientific research. Environmental protection is given priority, and there is a moratorium on mineral exploitation.

As a tourist destination Antarctica differs from the northlands surrounding the Arctic Ocean in that it is much less accessible. Antarctica is separated from the nearest populated lands in the Southern Hemisphere by vast expanses of stormy ocean in the latitudes known as the 'Roaring Forties', the 'Furious Fifties' and the 'Screaming Sixties', and is moreover ringed by a barrier of pack-ice for most of the year. It is therefore unlikely that Antarctica was visited by man before its discovery by American, British and Russian explorers in the early nineteenth century. Permanent scientific bases have only been established since the 1940s. No international air routes cross the southern polar regions. Travel from the major tourist-generating countries is expensive and time-consuming, involving up to two days of air travel, plus a sea voyage lasting from two to ten days from the nearest ports in South America, South Africa, Australia and New Zealand.

Although they are usually regarded by tour operators and travel writers as one entity, we should distinguish between the sub-Antarctic islands of the Southern Ocean, and the continent of Antarctica with its offshore islands and vast ice shelves:

- The **sub-Antarctic islands** lie close to the Antarctic Convergence, where the cold surface water spreading outwards from the continent meets warmer water from the north. The milder climatic conditions allow for more variety of plant and animal life than in Antarctica itself, and the islands' resources were exploited in the nineteenth century by whalers, sealers and even would-be colonizers. Some of the islands feature on cruise itineraries, such as South Georgia (a British territory), Macquarie Island (Australian) and the Auckland and Campbell Islands (which belong to New Zealand). There are fewer visitors to the French Southern and Antarctic Territories (TAAF), which include Kerguelen Island with its spectacular fjord and mountain scenery.
- The **continent of Antarctica** is now thought to be two geologically distinct landmasses beneath the 2500 metre-thick icecap, separated by the Transantarctic Mountains. West Antarctica includes the most accessible part of the continent – the Antarctic Peninsula – which is only 1000 kilometres from Cape Horn in South America. East Antarctica includes the 'Far Side' of the continent which is remote even from Australia and New Zealand.

Tourism, as distinct from government-sponsored expeditions (which never carried paying passengers), began in the late 1950s with the first charter flights from Chile and New Zealand; the first Lindblad cruise followed in 1966. However, it was not until an Antarctic Treaty conference in 1977 that tourism received official attention. Throughout the 1990s tourism grew rapidly, exceeding 12 000 arrivals in the 2000–2001 summer season. This growth is largely due to the following factors:

- there is increased competition between tour operators offering cruises to Antarctica
- since the collapse of the Soviet Union, Russia's scientific institutes have been eager to lease their ice-breaker ships at bargain rates to Western tour operators; this has opened up previously inaccessible areas, such as the Ross Sea, to cruising, and made it possible to circumnavigate Antarctica in a single season
- advances in cold weather technology have also made it possible to promote the interior of Antarctica as well as the coastal fringe for adventure tourism.

We can distinguish between the following types of tourism:

- land-based, with air support; tourists stay in tents or at a scientific base
- overflights

- sea-based, where the ship provides the accommodation and all other facilities; visits from cruise ships account for the great majority of tourist arrivals in the Antarctic.

Land-based tourism

Compared to the Arctic regions of North America, there is a lack of ground facilities for commercial aircraft. Although the research stations are served by an elaborate infrastructure of aircraft, supply ships and fuel depots, this is very costly to maintain, and most governments are reluctant to support tourism ventures because of the health and safety issues involved, and the possible disruption to scientific programmes. However, between 1984 and 1993 Chile actively promoted air-inclusive tours to its base on King George Island in the South Shetlands, and more recently Russia has attempted a similar venture. Russia needs the hard currency, while Chile and Argentina have used tourism to bolster their long-standing (and conflicting) territorial claims to this sector of Antarctica. A few specialist tour operators fly adventure-seeking clients to the interior of the continent for mountain climbing in the Vinson Massif, kite-skiing and even sky diving at the South Pole! Blue ice landing strips are used where the icecap has been swept clear of snow, and skidoos provide ground transportation.

Overflights

In the 1970s overflying Antarctica was popular in New Zealand, until an Air New Zealand Boeing 747 crashed on Mount Erebus, killing all on board. In 1994 a Melbourne-based company resumed flight-seeing tours from Australian cities, and by 2001 over 10 000 passengers had viewed the spectacular icefalls and glaciers of the Transantarctic Mountains from the air.

Sea-based tourism

This includes a few expeditions by private yacht, but cruising is far more significant, with most of the ships carrying between 40 and 150 passengers. The west coast of the Antarctic Peninsula and the South Shetland Islands is the most visited area, since it has a milder climate than the rest of Antarctica, is relatively close to the ports of Punta Arenas and Ushuaia in South America, and cruise itineraries can include the Falklands and South Georgia. Zodiac landing craft carry tourists ashore to visit penguin rookeries, geological curiosities such as Deception Island (a volcanic caldera) and historic whaling sites. Visits to research stations are also on the cruise itinerary; tourists are usually welcome, providing a break in routine for base personnel and (in the case of the stations run by less wealthy countries) some much-needed revenue.

A smaller number of cruises, originating mainly in Australia and New Zealand, undertake the long voyage to the Ross Sea, which is geographically much closer to the South Pole than the Antarctic Peninsula. Here the attractions include:

- Cape Evans – with its relics of Scott's ill-fated expedition to the South Pole
- the US McMurdo Base (the largest in Antarctica)
- the Mount Erebus volcano
- the Ross Ice Barrier.

The ice-free 'Dry Valleys' of the interior – said to be the nearest thing on Earth to the landscape of Mars – can be reached by on-board helicopters.

The impacts of tourism

Tourism in Antarctica is an outstanding example of cooperation between the various stakeholders, which include:

- the commercial sector, represented by the International Association of Antarctic Tour Operators (IAATO)
- the IUCN and the governments that are signatories to the Antarctic Treaty and the 1991 Madrid Protocol on Environmental Protection, and not least
- the tourists themselves.

Cruise operators to Antarctica generally subscribe to strict codes of conduct. Passengers during their few hours ashore are kept under constant surveillance, for their own safety, and to minimize contamination and disturbance to wildlife. However, despite the vast extent of the region, tourists follow established routes and are concentrated in a relatively few sites during the short summer season; and many believe this has an adverse effect on the breeding patterns of seals and penguins. Emissions from the outboard motors of the zodiacs pollute the water, while not all cruise ships dispose of waste in accordance with environmental guidelines. Nevertheless, land-based tourism represents a much greater threat to the environment, if we consider the impact already made by the permanent scientific research stations. Tourism currently accounts for less than one per cent of all person-days logged in Antarctica compared to more than 99 per cent for base personnel, who arguably do much more damage. Ironically it was the negative publicity generated by returning cruise passengers about the garbage at one American base that forced the authorities to clean up their act.

It is not just the growth in the numbers of tourists that threatens the environment, but the changing nature of the demand. The typical Antarctic cruise passenger is predominantly from the older age groups and is content with a passive role as an ecotourist, seeing Antarctica from a distance and responding positively to the restrictions imposed by tour operators. The future is likely to see a growth in adventure tourism, attracting younger visitors who may show less concern for the environment and their own safety.

Summary

Australasia is located mainly in the Southern Hemisphere, and consists of Australia, New Zealand and a large number of relatively small islands separated by wide expanses of ocean. The 'tyranny of distance' from the rest of the world is now being overcome by the development of air transport, but the distance from the major tourist-generating countries of the Northern Hemisphere has prevented the region from becoming a major holiday destination.

Australia and New Zealand clearly belong to the affluent West, while most of the Pacific islands have more in common with the developing countries of the Third World. The tourism industries of Australia and New Zealand have primarily developed to satisfy demand from their own populations, and incoming tourism is not nearly as significant or as vital to the economy as it is to the smaller, poorer islands of the Pacific.

Australasia is primarily a destination area for those travelling for recreational rather than cultural reasons, although ecotourism is of growing importance in most of these countries and in the new destination of Antarctica. The climates of Australasia are generally favourable, and there is less population pressure on available resources than is the case elsewhere. Environments such as the Australian Outback, the Great Barrier Reef, the Southern Alps of New Zealand and the atolls of the South Pacific offer a range of opportunities for adventure holidays. Another factor favouring the development of tourism is the political stability prevailing in most of the region, creating good conditions for investment.

Chapter 24
The tourism geography of North America

Learning Objectives

After reading this chapter you should be able to:

■ Describe the major physical features and climates of North America and understand their importance for tourism.
■ Appreciate the scale and characteristics of domestic tourism in the USA and Canada.
■ Understand the importance of the USA and Canada as tourist-generating countries.
■ Appreciate the significance of the conservation movement in North America and the importance of the national park system in particular to tourism.
■ Be aware of the cultural diversity of the USA and Canada.
■ Recognize the importance of transport in the development of the tourism industry.
■ Demonstrate a knowledge of the tourist regions, resorts, business centres and tourist attractions of North America.

Introduction

Although the World Tourism Organization treats the Americas – North and South – as one region, the two continents need to be investigated separately in view of their extent and the striking differences between North and South America, particularly in terms of ecology and culture. In our definition North America excludes Mexico, which we treat as part of Latin America in Chapter 25, but includes Hawaii.

Both the United States and Canada boast a wealth of natural resources in a vast physical setting. Although the contribution of the native peoples is increasingly recognized, both countries are predominantly 'nations of immigrants', who have blended to produce a distinct North American culture. The English language is dominant, despite being challenged by Spanish in Florida and the south-western USA, and by French in parts of Canada. Both countries have developed democratic federal structures of government and legal systems largely inherited from Britain. They are informal and competitive in their outlook, and share similar attitudes to business enterprise and the freedom of the individual. This has favoured an innovatory approach to leisure activities and tourism, especially in visitor management, marketing and merchandising.

In the early years of the twenty-first century North America received about 10 per cent of the world's international tourist arrivals and accounted for almost a quarter of the world's hotel capacity. From a visitor's point of view the size of the continent is important – extending over eight time zones and including most of the world's climates – but equally important is the rich variety of landforms and ecosystems. The western part of North America is dominated by high mountain chains, including the spectacular scenery of the Rockies and the Sierra Nevada. Near the eastern seaboard rise the forested Appalachians, much lower in altitude than the Rockies. Between these two mountain systems lie vast interior plains, drained by great rivers such as the Mississippi and its tributaries in the south, and by the St Lawrence, Athabasca and Mackenzie in the north.

The climate of North America is largely determined by relief and tends to be more extreme than similar latitudes in Western Europe, with warmer summers and colder winters. In winter Arctic winds penetrate far to the south, and occasionally bring freezing temperatures to the Gulf coast and northern Florida. Yet in summer most of the continent is open to tropical airstreams originating in the Gulf of Mexico, so that humidity tends to be high in the eastern half of the United States. Along the western seaboard high mountain ranges intercept moisture-bearing winds from the Pacific Ocean, bringing heavy rainfall to coastal areas, which also experience much milder temperatures than the interior and eastern seaboard. Most of the western USA however has a dry climate, due to its situation in the 'rain shadow' of the mountain barriers. The most important climatic divide is between the Frostbelt, consisting of Canada and the northern states of the USA, and the Sunbelt, stretching from California to the Carolinas. This has far-reaching social and economic implications in that industry and population as well as tourism increasingly gravitate from the northern states, with their declining industries and cold winters, to more attractive environments in the south and west.

Compared to the rest of the world, North Americans have been profligate in their use of natural resources, favoured by low energy costs. This has not encouraged sustainable forms of development, as shown by the dominance of the motor-car and the prevalence of urban sprawl. Nevertheless the USA and Canada are very much involved with issues of environmental protection. Despite the fact that the great majority of the population live in cities, the unsettled wilderness is very much part of the national heritage in both countries, and determined efforts have been made to save areas of unique scenery from development. The United States was the first country in the world to designate a system of national parks, starting with Yellowstone in 1872; Banff in the Canadian Rockies followed in 1885. Such areas are owned and managed by the federal government with the objectives of conservation and providing access for outdoor recreation. Most of the services required by tourists are however operated by the private sector on a concession basis. The national parks are widely regarded as a major North American contribution to world tourism, and a role model for good practice in both landscape and wildlife conservation and interpretation. However, national parks tend to be resource-oriented and they are mostly located in areas distant from the major centres of population. Closer to urban areas, this has led to the development of recreation areas that are more user-orientated, providing a range of facilities, such as the state parks in the USA and some of the provincial parks in Canada.

North America also offers a host of man-made attractions celebrating its achievements in science, technology and the arts. Canada and the United States are 'young nations' compared to those of Europe, while their cities are undergoing a continual process of renewal and reinvention, so that historical buildings are few. Those that have survived tend to be associated with celebrities or important events in the process of nation-building. They have been carefully restored, or in some cases reconstructed, as heritage attractions, with costumed guides and craft workers interpreting the lifestyle of the past – Colonial Williamsburg in Virginia is an outstanding example. This, like many others, operates as a non-profit-making trust. Theme parks on the other hand, along with a great number of smaller attractions, are part of the much larger private sector of the tourism industry.

Big cities play a major role in the cultural life of the USA and Canada, with significant museums, theatres and art galleries. There are 35 such 'metropolitan areas' with populations exceeding one million in the USA, and another three in Canada. As population centres, they generate most of the demand for holiday travel, and as commercial centres, they attract a considerable amount of business travel. The convention (conference) industry plays an important role, with city governments competing to increase market share with ever-more impressive facilities. However, from the viewpoint of tourists from Europe, relatively few North American cities are attractive in themselves. The pattern of high-rise central business districts, commercial strip development along the highways and low-density suburbs is repeated throughout the continent. A number of cities have attempted to regenerate their run-down inner city areas, with projects aimed at attracting the leisure shopper and tourist. Many visitors from Europe and Asia find the out-of-town shopping malls more appealing, although they are no longer as unique to North America as they were in the 1980s.

The United States

The period since 1918 has been called the 'American Century', during which the United States has consistently been one of the world's leading generators of international tourism, especially long-haul travel. With its wealth of national resources and technical know-how, the USA boasts the world's largest economy, and since the collapse of the Soviet Union it has become the only superpower. Although there is a tendency toward cultural homogeneity, regional differences persist. Each of the 50 constituent states is self-governing to a large extent, and Americans retain a strong attachment to their home state. United States territory also extends beyond the North American continent to the islands of the Caribbean – specifically Puerto Rico and the US Virgin Islands – (see Chapter 25), and to the Pacific – Guam and American Samoa (which we described in Chapter 23).

The USA is also one of the world's leading destinations, with tourism accounting for 6 per cent of the gross domestic product, and employing 7.9 million people. In contrast to some other sectors of the economy the tourism industry is made up largely of small- and medium-sized enterprises, and these have contributed substantially to the high rate of economic growth and job creation that the country has enjoyed since its recovery from the 1980s recession. Nevertheless, the promotion of tourism has generally been weak at the federal level of government. This is primarily due to two factors:

- the belief in free enterprise with the minimum of government interference
- the division of responsibilities between the federal government in Washington and the state governments.

It was not until 1981 that the United States Travel and Tourism Administration (USTTA) was set up to coordinate federal government policies regarding tourism and to promote the country more effectively abroad. The demise of the USTTA means that the USA enters the new millennium without an overall tourism strategy or tourist information service for the whole country. In the absence of government backing, a trade association – the Travel Industry Association of America (TIA) – carries out a promotional and research role. However since what is now known as '9/11' (the terrorist attacks of 11 September 2001), the federal government has re-appraised the role of tourism, as well as giving emergency support to the airlines. An extended credit scheme and tax relief are available to small- and medium-sized business enterprises in a bid to boost domestic tourism. Most states and many large cities do have some kind of official body concerned with tourism, although these vary considerably in their effectiveness. This has led a number of state governments to combine their resources to promote a particular region on the international stage.

Demand for tourism

Inbound tourism

Inbound tourism continued to grow steadily over the last two decades of the twentieth century, to exceed 50 million arrivals by the year 2000, but then falling back to 45 million as a result of 9/11. Canadians make up half of the total, in addition to many more day-visitors. Other important markets are Mexico (high volume but low spend), Japan and the countries of Western Europe. The number of tourists from Europe fluctuates with the strength of the dollar and the level of air fares. The UK is by far the most important generator of demand, followed by Germany and France. Japanese visitors are growing in number and tend to spend more per capita than Europeans, Canadians and Mexicans, although this market has been severely impacted by 9/11.

Outbound and domestic tourism

Only around 20 per cent of the US travel market involves trips to foreign countries. Almost 85 per cent of Americans have never travelled outside their own continent and only a minority own passports (which they do not require for travel to Canada or Mexico). There is seemingly a huge untapped market for overseas travel. However, national tourism organizations in Europe and elsewhere are aware that the US market is lucrative but volatile, notoriously sensitive to any hint of unrest in a particular region. Indeed, 9/11 severely depressed the US outbound market, which fell from almost 61 million trips in 2000, to 58 million in 2001.

Although overseas travel by Americans has grown steadily over recent decades, most of the outbound tourism is to Canada and Mexico. Much of this is business travel, stimulated by the success of the North American Free Trade Agreement

(NAFTA) to which the three countries belong. Trips to Canada tend to be short-stay and undertaken mainly by car, whereas visits to Mexico tend to be of longer duration and involve air travel to the destination. The Caribbean attracts a large number of leisure tourists, including a major share of the growing cruise market.

An important constraint on the demand for tourism is the limited leisure time available to most Americans of working age. The USA is an affluent but 'leisure poor' society compared to most European countries, and predictions made in the 1970s of a 'leisure boom' have not materialized. Since that decade productivity has trebled but the amount of leisure time has been reduced substantially over the same period, despite the introduction of flexible working hours. Thanks to 'downsizing' and the resulting job insecurity Americans are working harder than before. For example:

- the average working week in the USA is 43 hours, compared to 38 hours in the UK
- workers in the USA on average have 19 days of paid annual leave (including public holidays) compared to 24 days for their counterparts in Europe
- in the USA leave is negotiated with the employer as part of the contract; many employers have reduced leave entitlement or have encouraged flexitime
- a third of American workers only take half or less of their full leave entitlement
- employers and the corporate culture at the workplace often frown upon the practice of taking two weeks paid holiday all at once.

This means that although 70 per cent of American households still take a holiday away from home, for middle-income families this tends increasingly to be in the form of short weekend breaks rather than a long summer vacation. There continues to be peak in demand for domestic holidays in the months of July and August, so that beaches are generally deserted before Memorial Day in late May and after Labor Day in early September. Thanksgiving in late November is the time when family reunions, often involving long-distance air and car travel, are almost obligatory.

Compared to Britain, the annual beach holiday is not dominant as a motivation for leisure travel, and is much more likely to be sacrificed as a luxury in the event of a recession. Other travel motivators include:

- visits to **theme parks**, often involving at least one overnight stay
- **sport tourism** – the USA boasts some of the world's largest sporting venues and has hosted the Olympic Games four times, although the 1995 football World Cup was less successful in attracting tourists, with hoteliers reporting lower occupancy rates than expected; soccer has only a limited following in the USA compared to the huge interest in the Super Bowl and the World Series (the major events in the American football and baseball calendars), not to mention basketball
- **shopping tours** – shopping malls and factory discount outlets cooperate in marketing campaigns to attract the out-of-state visitor
- **health tourism** to spas (meaning facilities offering the latest medical and beauty treatments rather than mineral springs) have become increasingly popular as an antidote to stress
- the opportunity to participate in a wide range of **outdoor recreational activities**, such as fishing, golf, sailing and skiing; there is also a growing demand for the purchase of second homes (often a lakeside cabin), campervans (motor caravans) and off-the-road recreational vehicles.

A feature of the long school vacation is the popularity of **summer camps**, often in a semi-wilderness setting, where parents send their children to participate in a wide range of activities under expert supervision. Summer camps began in the late nineteenth century as a way of giving the children of inner-city families a healthy outdoor experience, but they have long since catered for the demand from affluent middle class parents (Löfgren, 1999).

Supply of tourism

In the public sector a number of organizations are involved with the supply of recreational resources at the federal level of government. These include:

- the National Park Service, the Fish and Wildlife Service and the Bureau of Land Management, which come under the jurisdiction of the Department of the Interior
- the United States Forest Service, which is part of the Department of Agriculture.

The National Park Service (NPS) was set up in 1916, taking responsibility for a range of protected areas, variously designated as National Parks, National Recreation Areas and National Monuments (which are usually specific sites rather than large areas). Most of the national parks are located in the western states, and can be visited in practice only by private transport – making them inaccessible to the inner city populations of the north-east. Nevertheless, the number of visitors to the national parks trebled between 1960 and 1994 and by 2002 exceeded 420 million. This has caused the following problems:

- Popular attractions and campgrounds in the most visited parks regularly reach their capacity at peak holiday times.
- Traffic on access routes and on roads within the parks has also risen considerably.
- Footpath erosion is severe in the most visited areas, while vegetation and wildlife have been disturbed by trail bikes, hiking off the designated trails and careless behaviour by campers.

Measures to curb car use in a few of the most popular parks, namely Yosemite, the Grand Canyon and Zion, have met with some success. However, given the size and physical configuration of most national parks, it is difficult to implement 'park and ride' schemes and circular bus tours.

The Forest Service is responsible for the National Forest system, where the emphasis is on multiple-use management, including grazing, watershed control and wildlife conservation as well as forestry and recreation. Some 17 per cent of National Forest land is classified as 'wilderness areas' under a 1964 Act of Congress prohibiting road building and other development, for the benefit of backpackers and canoeists seeking unspoiled nature and physical challenge.

The coastline of the United States provides a more accessible and popular resource, particularly the beaches of Southern California, the Gulf of Mexico and the Eastern seaboard from Cape Cod to Florida. Off the Atlantic coast is the world's longest series of barrier islands, acting as natural sand breakwaters, that form parallel to a low-lying coastal plain. Miami Beach and Atlantic City are the best-known examples of resort development on such offshore islands. Unfortunately these resources are threatened by over-development and by rising sea levels, not to mention the occasional hurricane sweeping up from the Caribbean.

Many coastal communities have built sea walls as protection from destructive waves, but these merely accelerate erosion elsewhere. Others, like Miami Beach, have called upon the United States Army Corps of Engineers to carry out beach re-nourishment, using sand dredged from other locations. Nevertheless, the best long-term solution is for the state governments to introduce land use management regulations in the coastal zone.

In the private sector the theme park is dominant, with over 320 million visitors annually. Although its antecedents can be found in the amusement parks, seaside piers and fairgrounds of nineteenth century Europe, the theme park is an American invention and has reached its fullest expression in the USA. Old-style amusement parks such as New York's Coney Island found it difficult to compete with other forms of entertainment, and are mainly places for young people to meet, rather than being regarded as suitable destinations for family outings (Chubb and Chubb, 1981). Theme parks fulfil this function, and differ from the old-style amusement parks in the following ways:

- Development is planned around a single theme, with the rides, shows, shopping and catering facilities promoted as a coordinated set of attractions.
- Location is all-important – they are market-oriented attractions. Theme parks are built between major cities and near motorway interchanges so that as large a population as possible lives within a 160-kilometre radius.
- There is an all-inclusive admission charge.
- Theme parks are imaginatively landscaped. Millions of dollars are spent on maintenance, upgrading facilities and on new rides and shows using the latest technology.
- Theme parks are staffed by young people who are well motivated and trained to provide a high standard of service.

Theme parks require massive capital investment and are therefore owned by large corporations with interests in television, the film industry, or – in the case of Busch Gardens, Florida – a major brewing company. The Disney theme parks are world-class destinations in their own right. Walt Disney must certainly be regarded as one of the greatest innovators in leisure and tourism. In 1955 he opened his first theme park – Disneyland – at Anaheim, near Los Angeles on a 60-hectare site developed around five themed areas. Disneyland's success encouraged a sprawl of development in its vicinity. To avoid a repetition, the second theme park – Walt Disney World (WDW) – was constructed on 1000 hectares of swampland in central Florida, over which Disney had complete planning control. It is a self-contained destination with its own transport system, hotels and facilities for a wide range of outdoor activities. In the blueprint for Epcot, Disney even envisaged the urban community of the future. Disney theme parks aim to insulate the visitor from the world of reality by means of:

- the Disney corporate ethos; where staff are known as 'cast members'
- the concepts of 'imagineering' and 'animatronics', using the cutting edge of technology
- a sophisticated infrastructure, that is concealed from the visitor, and the use of non-polluting transport modes within the park.

The Disney theme parks provide a clean, safe and wholesome environment for families, but some would argue that the experience is too sanitized and that too much control is exercised over visitors and staff.

In contrast to the large theme parks such as Six Flags and Disneyland, there are a vast number of small-town attractions, each striving to boost the local economy. Some showcase aspects of the American heritage, notably achievements in sport, industry and entertainment, while others attempt to replicate the cultures of Europe and Asia in the New World. Many of these attractions lack authenticity or an appropriate setting.

Transport

Transport in the USA is highly developed, as you might expect from a nation constantly on the move. The following characteristics are worth emphasizing:

- the private car is the dominant transport mode for all types of journeys
- domestic air services are widely used
- public transport, except in some major cities, is poorly developed.

The United States has the highest car ownership in the world, with the number of motor vehicles in some states exceeding the resident population. Well over 80 per cent of holiday trips are taken by car. Although the internal combustion engine was not an American invention, it was largely due to Henry Ford that ownership of an automobile was brought within reach of people on modest incomes. As a result, by 1930 there were 23 million cars registered in the USA, whereas in Europe similar levels were not reached until the late 1950s. Demand from vehicle manufacturers and motorists led to much-needed road improvements, such as the legendary Route 66 from Chicago to Los Angeles. Scenic routes or *parkways*, such as the Skyline Drive in the Blue Ridge Mountains of Virginia, were designed in the 1930s to encourage sightseeing by car. From the late 1950s onwards some of the older highways – including Route 66 – were superseded by the Interstate Highway system, financed very largely by the federal government. This provided a nationwide motorway network – 69 000 kilometres in length – linking most of the major cities, and resulted in a threefold increase in the number of kilometres travelled by car between 1950 and 1980. Motoring in the USA is subject to fewer inconveniences than elsewhere in the world and fuel costs are relatively low. However the American love affair with the car has had an adverse environmental impact, including:

- pollution – despite strict regulations on motor vehicle emissions
- visual blight – with large areas given over to parking lots
- urban sprawl – which in turn necessitates ever-lengthening journeys to work, shopping and recreational facilities.

Since the early 1990s even cities as wedded to the car as Los Angeles and Miami have realized that road-building alone cannot solve traffic congestion, and they have invested heavily in rapid transit schemes.

Air transport accounts for some 10 per cent of holiday trips, and most medium-sized towns in the USA have an airport within easy reach by car. Air fares are relatively cheap, largely due to competition between the airlines. After 1978, when the civil aviation industry was deregulated, routes were organized on a 'hub and spoke' system, with a few major airports handling the bulk of the traffic. As a result of deregulation many small airlines came into service, but some old-established carriers failed to adjust to the new conditions. The largest casualty was undoubtedly Pan-Am, which had largely pioneered intercontinental air services before the

Second World War. The airlines that have clearly emerged as front-runners include United, American, Delta and Continental, while Denver, Chicago, Atlanta and Dallas have developed as major hubs. All airlines have had to cope with the impact of 9/11, which has threatened the financial viability of many of America's 'icon' airlines. A large number of regional carriers, often code-sharing with one of the major airlines, provide feeder services.

Public transport by road and rail compares unfavourably with the situation in most other developed countries. The major bus company – Greyhound – does provide an extensive network of intercity services, as well as inclusive tours and bargain fares for foreign tourists. Nevertheless coach travel (in its British rather than American meaning) accounts for less than 3 per cent of the domestic market and is widely regarded as downmarket. The train provides a more stylish alternative. To a large extent the railways made America, but in the 1950s passenger services declined as a result of competition from the airlines and the private car. They might have disappeared altogether from the long distance routes had not the federal government intervened in 1970 with the introduction of Amtrak, a semi-public corporation that operates passenger trains over the network of a dozen private railroad companies. Amtrak has upgraded rolling stock, in some cases introducing double-decker 'superliners' for scenic viewing. Historic routes have been revived, such as the 'Empire Builder' which takes 46 hours to cover the 3500 kilometres from Chicago to Seattle. The introduction of high-speed trains is however inhibited by the cost of upgrading track; also much of the network is single-track, with precedence given to freight trains. Amtrak has achieved most success in the densely populated 'north-east corridor' linking Newport News in Virginia with Boston via Washington, Philadelphia and New York City. This is by far the most important route, accounting for 50 per cent of Amtrak's revenue, and competing effectively with the airlines for the lucrative business market. Elsewhere in the USA, train services, where they exist, tend to be infrequent. This situation may change as Americans become more aware of the safety and environmental issues posed by growing congestion on the highways, at airport terminals and in the airways. Congress is reluctant to further subsidize Amtrak's investment programme, as politicians are inclined to take the short-term view of reducing public spending.

Accommodation

Americans have long demanded high standards of convenience in their accommodation, resulting in the concept of the hotel in holiday destinations as a 'resort', a self-contained leisure complex. Across North America, the supply of accommodation is closely linked to patterns of transport. In the largest cities hotels are most numerous in the 'downtown' areas or CBDs. Elsewhere the distribution tends to be peripheral, with hotels clustering around an airport or located in the commercial strip developments fanning out along the main highways, alongside restaurants and other businesses. The first motels developed in the 1930s as family enterprises offering fairly basic accommodation. From the 1950s, following the example of the 'Holiday Inns' chain, the trend was to go more upmarket with facilities such as swimming pools, and toward standardization of the product in terms of service and décor. Hotels themselves have become increasingly innovative, with such features as the atrium lobby pioneered by Regency Hyatt, and the concept of theming, which is best seen in Las Vegas, to appeal to niche markets. Bed and breakfast in private homes is a growing sector, although it has a more upmarket image than its British counterpart, particularly in New England where much of the accommodation is in restored colonial buildings. Apartments in condominiums, campsites and trailer parks for recreational vehicles are a major part of the accommodation sector.

Tourism resources

The north-east

The north-eastern states constitute the most densely populated and one of the most visited parts of the country, including the four major gateway cities of Boston, New York, Philadelphia and Washington. The urbanized belt – 'Megalopolis' – extending from Boston to Washington, contains over 45 million inhabitants and has excellent transport facilities in the form of road, rail and shuttle air services. In contrast, there are large areas of forested wilderness in the mountains of the northern Appalachians.

New England is probably the most interesting region in the USA from a historical standpoint. In the seventeenth century it was occupied by English settlers who were Puritans seeking freedom to practise their religious beliefs. What came to be known as the 'Yankee' traits of hard work, thrift and ingenuity were forged in the struggle to wrest a livelihood from a harsh environment of cold winters and infertile soils. This explains the importance in the region's history of fishing, whaling, overseas trade and manufacturing industry. New England played a crucial role in the struggle for independence from British rule in the 1770s, notably the 'Boston Tea Party' and the battle of Lexington. The region has a strong cultural tradition, as shown by the international reputation of its universities – particularly Yale, Harvard and the Massachusetts Institute of Technology – and it has produced many famous writers. Since the mid-nineteenth century New England has become a multi-cultural society as a result of further immigration, particularly from Ireland and Italy.

The rural interior is noted for its forested mountains and picturesque villages of clapboard houses grouped around a wooden church; two of the most visited examples are Sturbridge and Pittsfield in western Massachusetts. Many of the farms have long been abandoned and are now used as weekend or summer retreats by city dwellers. In the fall (autumn) the brilliant foliage displays attract crowds of weekend visitors, particularly to the state of Vermont. During the snowy winters skiing is a major activity, particularly at Bretton Woods and Mount Washington Valley in New Hampshire, and at Stowe in Vermont.

The coast is equally appealing. In the state of Maine it is rugged, deeply indented and backed by a sparsely populated hinterland of rivers and forests; sailing, fishing and canoeing are popular activities. Further south there are many fine beaches and a number of historic seaports. Tourists are particularly attracted to the following areas:

- **The Cape Cod** peninsula, with its extensive sand dunes. Summer resorts such as Hyannisport cater for wealthy second-home owners, while ferries connect to the islands of Nantucket and Martha's Vineyard. At Plymouth there is a 'living museum' commemorating the original settlement of the Pilgrim Fathers in 1620.
- **Newport, Rhode Island** was once the exclusive summer resort for America's millionaires. It is now a major yachting centre and a popular venue for music festivals.
- **Salem** is mainly visited because of its association with the witch trials of 1692, an example of Puritan intolerance.
- **New Bedford** and **Mystic** are historic seaports associated with the nineteenth-century whaling industry.

- **Boston** is a major North American city that has retained its compact character and mellow brick buildings, although these are often overshadowed by examples of modern architecture such as Government Center. The 'Freedom Trail' commemorates Boston's role in America's struggle for independence.

The **Middle Atlantic region** is less easily defined. Even in colonial times it was settled by immigrants from a variety of origins, including English Quakers, Irish Catholics, Dutch, Germans and Scandinavians. The mountainous interior, which forms part of the Appalachians, the beach resorts of Long Island, New Jersey, and the Delmarva Peninsula east of Chesapeake Bay, are mainly visited by domestic tourists. The attractions of most interest to foreign tourists are to be found in the big cities, for example:

- **New York** is the largest city of North America, with over 15 million people living in the metropolitan area. The terrorist attacks of 9/11 on the World Trade Center have highlighted the city's international profile and it is one of the world's top ten destinations. Tourism is of major importance to the city's economy, generating about 25 billion dollars in revenue and supporting 282 000 jobs. Although it is not an administrative capital, New York is the nation's primary city in almost every other respect. It is for example the USA's leading financial centre and conference venue, with more hotel beds than any other city. It is also a major centre for fashion and the arts. New York City boasts world-class cultural attractions such as the Metropolitan Opera House and Carnegie Hall, while the Madison Square Garden, Shea Stadium and Flushing Meadows are among the country's top sport venues. New York has an international role as the seat of the United Nations Assembly, but transactions in Wall Street have an even greater impact on the global economy.

  New York City owes a great deal to its historic role as the major port of entry to the USA, with the advantages of a deepwater harbour and access via the Hudson river to the interior of North America. Until the 1960s the Statue of Liberty was, for most immigrants and visitors, their first sight of the New World. Part of the historic waterfront of Manhattan Island has been regenerated with visitor attractions such as the Intrepid Sea–Air–Space Museum and South Street Seaport. Manhattan is one of the Western world's most densely populated areas, and along with Brooklyn and Queens, the most cosmopolitan, with ethnic neighbourhoods and a range of restaurants that is probably unrivalled. Many tourist attractions cluster to the south and east of Central Park, including the best known skyscrapers in 'midtown', 'Museum Mile', the Broadway Theatre District, and the shops along Fifth Avenue. 'Downtown' Manhattan – the oldest part of New York – contains the Stock Exchange, Chinatown, the artistic quarter of Greenwich Village and the site of the 'Twin Towers', known as 'Ground Zero'.

- **Philadelphia**, the fourth largest city in the United States, is regarded as the birthplace of the nation, witnessing the Declaration of Independence (1776) and the ratification of the US Constitution (1788). Independence Hall, the Liberty Bell and Congress Hall are reminders of the early history of America. It is a major sports venue and cultural centre, while Penn's Landing is a maritime heritage attraction.

- **Baltimore** is another large seaport whose Inner Harbor development provides an excellent example of a decayed waterfront area being transformed into a high class tourist attraction. However, unlike Philadelphia it is a staging point rather than a tourist destination.

- **Washington, DC** has a unique appeal, as the capital of the United States. It was planned as such at the beginning of the nineteenth century, with wide avenues lined with neo-classical buildings and attractive parks. The most important feature is the Mall, extending from the Lincoln Memorial to the Capitol housing the American Congress; grouped nearby are other important public buildings such as the White House, the Smithsonian museums and the National Gallery of Art. Tourism is second only to the government as an employer. Security was tightened following 9/11, but this has not deterred domestic tourists, who are motivated by patriotic solidarity. The federal government and various international agencies such as the World Bank generate a considerable volume of business travel. The capital is served by two international airports – Dulles International and Washington-Baltimore. Washington lacks the skyscrapers and entertainment facilities of New York, but it is growing in importance as a major cultural centre, with venues such as the Kennedy Center for the Performing Arts. The district of Georgetown is noted for its boutiques and restaurants. The American pattern of wide separation of home and workplace is evident, with relatively few government employees living in the central city – the District of Columbia – as compared to the sprawling suburbs in Maryland and Virginia.

The **Northern Appalachians** constitute the rural hinterland of the cities of the Eastern Seaboard. They are made up of forested mountain ridges, narrow river valleys and rolling hill country. In parts of West Virginia and Pennsylvania the landscape has been blighted by coal mining and heavy industry, leaving behind polluted rivers. On the other hand, there are widespread opportunities for field sports, white-water rafting (mainly in West Virginia) and skiing during the winter months.

- **'Upstate' New York** boasts a variety of scenic attractions, providing a contrast to the bustle of New York City. These include the Finger Lakes, and the Adirondack Mountains, which contain extensive wilderness areas as well as Lake Placid, venue for the 1980 Winter Olympics. The Catskills have long been popular as a resort area for New Yorkers. The Hudson Valley, with its vineyards, historic mansions and wooded scenery, has been called 'the Rhineland of North America'. Two tourist centres in New York State deserve special mention – the festival town of Woodstock, and Rochester, where George Eastman made photography accessible to a mass market. The state's most famous attraction – although half of it lies in Canada – is Niagara Falls. Since the nineteenth century a variety of facilities have been provided for viewing the spectacle, but some of the development, particularly on the American side, is excessively commercialized and inappropriate for the setting.
- **Pennsylvania** offers the Pocono and Allegheny Mountains, the Civil War battlefield of Gettysburg, and Lancaster County, famous for its Amish communities of German origin who have rejected technological progress. The Amish have accepted tourism on their own terms, but nevertheless the influx of visitors poses a threat to their traditional way of life.

The **coastal resorts** include the Hamptons on Long Island, Atlantic City and Cape May in New Jersey, and Ocean City in Maryland. Although some resorts aimed for exclusivity, Atlantic City in particular was the creation of the railroad and developed to meet the needs of the growing numbers of industrial workers. In the 1920s the resort achieved fame for its event attractions, such as the Miss America beauty pageant. After the Second World War fashions changed as alternative destinations such as Florida became more accessible, and Atlantic City entered a long period of stagnation. The resort's fortunes revived in the late 1970s, following the decision of the state government to legalize gambling. Its casinos now attract more visitors than those of Las Vegas, although their length of stay tends to be much shorter. Atlantic City's other main attraction is the elevated boardwalk (promenade) along the beach.

The South

The South is the most distinctive region of the USA, although its boundaries are difficult to define. Many regard the Ohio river and the Mason–Dixon Line separating Virginia from Pennsylvania as the northern limit. We can regard the South as being distinguished by these features:

- A climate that is characterized by long sultry summers, short mild winters and abundant rainfall.
- The importance given by Southerners to the American Civil War (1861–1865), in which the Confederacy, made up of 11 slave-holding states was defeated in its attempts to secede from the Union.
- The presence of a large Black minority, who for a century after the Civil War continued to suffer from many forms of discrimination.
- A lifestyle which is more traditional, family-orientated and religion-based than other regions of the USA. The strength of fundamentalist Christianity explains the use of the term 'Bible Belt' for much of the region.
- An economy in which areas of dynamic growth and prosperity – the so-called 'New South' – contrast with pockets of rural poverty.

The heritage of the period before the Civil War, often highly romanticized, is an important part of the South's appeal for tourists, usually focusing on the plantation houses of the former slave-owners. Of wider significance is the contribution the region has made to literature and popular music, including jazz, country and western, rhythm and blues, gospel etc. The South is also well endowed with recreational resources, which include:

- large areas of forest, particularly in the Southern Appalachians
- the wetlands of the coastal plains, such as the Okefonokee Swamp in southern Georgia, and the *bayous* of the Mississippi Delta, that provide a unique refuge for wildlife
- a number of large man-made lakes providing facilities for water sports; these are a legacy of the hydro-electric power projects carried out by the federal government to boost the region's economy, following President Roosevelt's New Deal in the 1930s
- the abundance of golf courses, particularly in the hilly, well-wooded Piedmont zone between the Appalachians and the coastal plains. Pinehurst in North Carolina and Augusta in Georgia are the most popular golfing resorts
- the barrier islands of the Atlantic and Gulf coasts provide many fine beaches; some have been developed as resorts – Hilton Head Island is one example – while others such as Cape Hatteras and Cumberland Island are preserved from development by federal and state governments.

We can divide the South for tourism purposes into a number of sub-regions, starting with Virginia.

Virginia was the first English colony in the New World. It played a major role in the struggle for independence – George Washington and Jefferson were both Virginians. During the American Civil War, Richmond, less than 200 kilometres from Washington DC, was the capital of the Confederacy. Not surprisingly, heritage attractions play an important role. They include:

- George Washington's home at Mount Vernon
- the Civil War battlefield site at Fredericksburg
- 'the Historic Triangle', consisting of Jamestown – site of the first English settlement; Yorktown and Williamsburg, the capital of Virginia in colonial times. Of these Williamsburg is the most popular, and it has become a role model for similar attractions in other countries, due to its meticulous attention to detail
- the western part of the state includes the scenic Blue Ridge Mountains and the Shenandoah Valley National Park; all of these attractions are within easy reach of Washington.

The **south-east** consists of Georgia and the Carolinas, three states that have shown remarkable economic growth since the 1950s.

- **Atlanta** is the main conference venue of the south-east, with its modern hotels and excellent communications. As a major hub its airport has overtaken Chicago in terms of domestic traffic and is growing in importance as an international gateway – one of the main reasons it was chosen as the venue for the 1996 Olympics. As a major centre for finance and broadcasting, Atlanta is a symbol of the 'New South'. The city also has important associations with Martin Luther King and the Civil Rights movement of the 1960s. Other attractions include 'Underground Atlanta' – a project to revive the decaying inner city; the 'World of Coca-Cola' museum celebrating the city's best-known product; and Stone Mountain – reputedly the world's largest granite monolith.
- The seaports of **Savannah** and **Charleston** have based their tourism industries on the heritage of the Old South. Charleston attracts a large number of foreign as well as domestic tourists to its well-preserved *ante-bellum* (pre-Civil War) mansions, with garden tours being especially popular. Strict zoning regulations ensure that the tourist facilities are kept separate from the historic district of Old Charleston.

The **Southern Appalachians**, a series of forest-covered ranges separated by deep valleys, rise to the north of Georgia and to the west of North Carolina, accounting for most of Tennessee and Kentucky. In the more remote mountain valleys the persistence of craft industries is a legacy of the old pioneering days. Gatlinburg and Cherokee, on the fringes of the much-visited Smoky Mountains National Park, are examples of rural communities that have exploited this heritage. To the west of the mountains lie the fertile Nashville Basin and the 'Bluegrass Country' of Kentucky – an area noted for its bourbon distilleries and equestrian sports. Kentucky also boasts the world's most extensive cave system in the Mammoth Cave National Park. In Tennessee, Nashville and Memphis rank among the most important tourist centres in the South:

- **Nashville** is widely regarded as the 'capital' of the country and western music industry. This is showcased in the Grand Old Opry auditorium and a number of theme parks in the area, but many find that the clubs and bars in 'Music Row' provide a more authentic experience.

- Memphis is particularly rich in musical traditions, focusing on the historic district of Beale Street, known as the 'birthplace of the blues'. However, the most popular attraction is undoubtedly Graceland, visited by Elvis Presley fans from all over the world.

The **Deep South** usually refers to the states of Alabama, Mississippi and Louisiana, where Southern traditions are strongest. Tourism is of particular importance to Louisiana, where the economy has been affected by the fall in oil prices. The cultural heritage of French and Spanish rule is a major part of its appeal, especially the spicy cuisine.

- **New Orleans** is a major port on the Mississippi river and ranks among the five most popular cities visited by foreign and well as American tourists. Much of the city lies below river level, and is protected by high artificial banks or *levees*. Tourists are mainly attracted to the historic core of the city, known as the Vieux Carré or the French Quarter, focused on Bourbon Street and St Louis Cathedral. New Orleans has a long-established reputation for entertainment and gambling, but its tourism industry is also firmly based on conventions and sporting events. The city's fame as the birthplace of jazz appeals to many tourists, and the annual Mardi Gras carnival is one of the USA's most popular event attractions. The Mississippi's historical role as a major transport artery is recalled in the stern-wheeler steamboats that are now used for short river cruises.
- Other tourist centres include Lafayette for visiting 'Cajun country', Natchez, famed for its pre-Civil War plantation houses, and the beach resorts of Gulfport and Biloxi.

The **Ozarks** in Arkansas and southern Missouri are similar in many respects to the Appalachians. Tourism centres on the spa resort of Hot Springs and the small town of Branson, which boasts no less than 40 theatres featuring big-name performers in the music industry. This success is difficult to explain in resource terms, but it is clearly demand-led, with most of the 7 million annual visitors arriving from other parts of the South and the Mid-West.

Florida

Although the northern part of the state – particularly the 'Panhandle' west of Tallahassee – is typically 'Southern', most of Florida is quite different from the rest of the South, in the following ways:

- Its tourism industry is on a different scale, with a constant flow of visitors all year round.
- Retired people from the northern states make up a high percentage of its population.
- The influx of Cuban immigrants to southern Florida since 1960 has made Miami a largely Spanish-speaking city and effectively the financial centre of Latin America.

Florida is among the world's leading holiday destinations, with an annual income from tourism exceeding Spain's receipts from its foreign visitors. Orlando alone receives over 35 million visitors a year as the world's 'theme park capital'. At the beginning of the twentieth century Florida was largely wilderness, one of the least developed and most sparsely populated regions of the USA. Tourism was to change all that, along with the development of large-scale agriculture and the aerospace industry after the Second World War. The population grew from 2.7 million in 1950 to almost 13 million in the late 1990s. This growth has put enormous pressure on the water resources and fragile eco-systems of the Florida Peninsula, which is low-lying and of limestone formation.

The great majority of Florida's visitors are Americans, mainly from the states east of the Mississippi, and Canadians. Overseas tourists come mainly from Latin American countries and from Western Europe, where the UK is the leading market for air-inclusive holidays. Florida's success can be attributed to its subtropical climate, a coastline of white sandy beaches, and not least, to a major investment by the private sector in sports facilities, theme parks and other man-made attractions. Florida is readily accessible, with domestic air services to all parts of the USA and three international airports – Miami, Orlando and Tampa. The main east coast highway (US 1) brings the Atlantic coast resorts within the reach of the family motorist living in the cities of the Eastern Seaboard.

Florida originated as a winter destination for wealthy Americans in the 1890s, with the opening of hotels in the old Spanish town of St Augustine. By the 1920s, with the extension of the railroad, Palm Beach (catering exclusively for the wealthy) and Miami Beach (for those a little less affluent) had been established on barrier islands off the Atlantic coast. Since the 1950s, with the vast improvement in road and air transport, Florida has broadened its appeal to become a summer destination within reach of the majority of Americans. However the southern third of the state has retained its image as a winter haven for Northerners and Canadians, and this is reflected in lower hotel prices during the summer months. Large numbers of foreign visitors have invested in holiday and retirement homes, but with the visa restrictions imposed following 9/11, travel arrangements are less flexible, and this could have an adverse effect on Florida's tourism and real estate industries.

The city of Miami (as distinct from Miami Beach) is primarily a business centre with a population of well over 2 million. Miami Airport is the major gateway to the Caribbean islands and the countries of Central and South America, while the port of Miami is the base for most Caribbean cruises.

In the south-east of Florida a string of resorts have developed, the most important are:

- **Fort Lauderdale**, known as the 'Venice of Florida', with its extensive marina facilities; during the spring vacation the resort caters for an influx of fun-seeking college students
- **Miami Beach**, which, with its concentration of high-rise accommodation, suffered from a period of stagnation in the 1960s and 1970s with an ageing clientele and falling property values; it has since restored its Art Deco hotels, reclaimed its beachfront and re-invented its image as a centre of fashion
- the **Florida Keys** – a chain of coral islands to the south of Miami – provide ideal opportunities for scuba diving; Key West, with its Hemingway associations, is the most developed tourist centre.

The development of tourism on such a large scale has created problems. Many hotels and condominiums have been built so close to the sea that the beaches have been badly eroded, while a great deal of the best recreational land has been bought up as sites for private homes. The demand for water by large-scale agriculture and the residents of Greater Miami has endangered the unique wetland ecosystem of the Everglades.

The south-west of Florida along the Gulf coast is much less developed, with the exception of the Tampa Bay area. The most important resorts are St Petersburg – one of America's largest retirement centres, Sarasota, and Clearwater, each catering for different markets. Further south, Naples and Fort Myers provide less expensive self-catering accommodation.

The beaches of the northern Gulf coast cater for summer visitors from Alabama and Georgia rather than foreign tourists, with Panama City being the clear favourite. Other important recreational resources in this part of Florida are the hundreds of crystal-clear freshwater springs underlying the surface. Some of these have been developed as secondary attractions, a notable example being Weeki Wachee Springs with its 'mermaid show'.

Central Florida is the fastest growing tourism area, thanks largely to the success of **Disneyworld** since its opening in 1971. In 2002 this theme park complex was estimated to receive over 40 million visitors a world record for any attraction. The success of Disneyworld has encouraged other leisure projects. The main impact has been on Orlando – a medium-sized town noted only for its citrus industry prior to 1971, but now a major international gateway. The other major attraction in Central Florida is the NASA space research centre at Cape Canaveral.

The Mid-West

In marked contrast, this region, with its cold winters and hot humid summers, is a tourist-generating area and a zone of passage rather than a destination. Lying to the west of the Appalachians and south of the Great Lakes, the Mid-West is one of the world's most productive agricultural areas. From the air, the landscape from Iowa to Ohio appears like a huge chessboard, with fields, roads and settlements laid out on a regular grid pattern. Further north in Wisconsin, Minnesota and Michigan, the scenery is much more diverse with innumerable lakes and landforms resulting from past glaciation, and large areas of forest. The Great Lakes themselves are a major attraction; there are fine beaches along the southern shores of Lakes Michigan and Huron, while Lake Superior, the largest and deepest, has a shoreline of spectacular cliffs. The state of Michigan has a well-established tourism industry based on these resources. The resorts cater mainly for the demand from the region's cities, notable examples being Lake Geneva, 30 kilometres from Chicago, and Kensington, which serves Detroit. In winter large areas of northern Minnesota and northern Wisconsin are set aside for snowmobile trails, while Upper Michigan provides facilities for skiing.

Some of the cities of the Mid-West are important cultural as well as business centres:

- **Detroit** remains the world's leading city for motor vehicle manufacturing, although it suffered severely from the recession in the 1980s and became a byword for urban decay. At nearby Dearborn, Henry Ford revolutionized transport and tourism with the Model T, and later founded Greenfield Village as an open-air museum of small-town America prior to the advent of the automobile.
- **Cleveland** offers the Rock n' Roll Hall of Fame, mainly because this industrial city boasts some of the largest audiences for this type of music; an example of an attraction based on demand.
- **Chicago** can claim to be the transportation centre of the USA and is its second largest city. O'Hare Airport is one of the world's busiest, the city is a major rail

terminal and despite its distance from the sea it is also a port – thanks to the St Lawrence Seaway. Chicago is renowned for its architectural achievements – particularly those associated with Frank Lloyd Wright and Mies Van de Rohe. Its many cultural attractions include the Museum of Science and Industry and the Art Institute. As a commercial centre it has excellent facilities for conventions and trade fairs. The city is also a major sports venue and its recreational facilities include 24 kilometres of public beaches, yacht marinas and parks along the shores of Lake Michigan. The popular perception of Chicago however owes more to its reputation for gangsterism in the Prohibition era of the 1920s and early 1930s, an image which the city has tended to downplay although it appeals to many visitors.

- Indianapolis, with its motor racing circuit; Dayton, Ohio – famous in aviation history as the home town of the Wright brothers; Milwaukee and its breweries; and St Louis – 'the gateway to the West' – each has a particular appeal for tourists.

The West

The West is defined by American geographers as the part of the USA lying beyond the 100th meridian, where the climate becomes too dry in most years to support arable farming and ranching is more significant. Most of this vast region is sparsely populated and its appeal for tourism is based on the 'great outdoors', and the heritage of the frontier. This has been evoked in countless 'western' movies, which have also made the extraordinary landscapes of the region familiar to millions. The West also contains the great majority of the Indian reservations – tribal lands set aside by treaty with the federal government – where the Native American way of life continues to flourish. Indian handicrafts are much in demand, and Indian traditions have influenced white Americans seeking alternative, more holistic lifestyles. Tourist accommodation is available on some reservations, while a few Indian nations have taken advantage of their special status in relation to federal and state law to open gambling casinos. Tourism may prove to be a threat as well as an opportunity to communities already under pressure, with levels of unemployment and alcohol abuse well above the national average.

Tourism ranks as the most important employer in four western states – Colorado, Nevada, New Mexico and Wyoming – and is in second place in five others. Because of its extent we need to divide the West into a number of sub-regions as follows:

- The **High Plains**, stretching from Oklahoma to North Dakota. This was the setting of the 'dustbowl' of the 1930s, and the region is often afflicted by extreme weather events such as tornadoes. It is for the most part relatively featureless. One major exception is the granite Black Hills of South Dakota that rise abruptly from the surrounding prairies. The famous sculptures of Mount Rushmore are located in this area, along with the Crazy Horse Memorial commemorating the Indian resistance led by the Sioux chief of that name. Another tourist attraction is the former mining town of Deadwood – notorious in 'Wild West' mythology. Further south in Nebraska the Scotts Bluff National Monument was one of the landmarks on the trail of the covered wagons that carried millions of pioneers westward during the nineteenth century.
- The **Rocky Mountains** form a barrier 2000 kilometres in length, 500 kilometres wide and reach a height of 4000 metres. They are in fact a series of ranges separated by a number of enclosed basins. Winters provide dry 'powder' snow for

skiing in the mountains of Idaho – where Sun Valley was developed in the 1930s – and in Colorado, where Aspen, Vail and other resorts became established in the 1950s. These are easily reached from the gateway city of Denver. Aspen in particular has a fashionable reputation and hosts an all-year programme of cultural events. Wyoming boasts two world-class national parks – the Tetons, with their glaciated landscapes, and the better-known Yellowstone which contains many remarkable geothermal features. A touring circuit 237 kilometres in length provides access to the popular sites – the Yellowstone Falls, Mammoth Hot Springs and Old Faithful, the most famous of the 200 or so geysers. These parks also provide a refuge for wildlife, notably bears, buffalo, antelope, elk and beaver. The National Parks Service has aroused controversy by introducing wolves to Yellowstone, and using controlled forest fires to create a more balanced ecosystem. Further to the north, Montana is less visited. It contains a number of old mining towns, forests and ranchlands, and the lake and mountain scenery of the Glacier National Park.

- The **south-west** is distinguished by its cultural heritage as well as its climates and scenery. The whole of this region, along with Texas and California, was once part of the Spanish Empire and later Mexico, before its acquisition by the United States in 1848. Most of the South-west is desert 'basin and range' country with a sparse cover of sage brush and mesquite vegetation, or consists of high plateaus dissected by deep gorges or canyons. The tourist appeal of the region is based on these features:
  - The warm, dry, sunny climate that has long attracted winter visitors and a growing number of retired people to cities such as Phoenix and Tucson. Health tourism is particularly important in Arizona, with its many spa facilities.
  - The facilities for water-based recreation, unusual in a desert region, in Lakes Powell, Mead and Havasu. These lakes were created by the damming of the Colorado river in the 1930s for power generation and irrigation projects.
  - Dude ranches, providing the tourist with accommodation, riding expeditions and the opportunity to sample the cowboy lifestyle. Many communities also hold rodeos, where professionals display the horsemanship and other traditional skills associated with cattle ranching.
  - A wealth of scenic attractions, including Monument Valley – a much photographed group of *mesas* (flat topped landforms formed by erosion) and the lesser-known Bryce and Zion Canyons in Utah. The most visited attraction, however, is the world-famous **Grand Canyon** in Arizona. Here the Colorado river has cut a gorge almost 2000 metres deep in the sedimentary rocks of the Colorado Plateau. The vast majority of the Canyon's 5 million annual visitors, arriving by car, coach and train, do not stray far from the tourist facilities on the South Rim. Flight-seeing tours give some idea of the immensity of the Canyon, but for a true appreciation it needs to be explored on foot or by mule, camping overnight. Another alternative is to take part in one of the white-water rafting expeditions organized by tour operators.
  - The Indian heritage with archaeological excavations at Canyon de Chelly and the Mesa Verde National Park that provide evidence of an advanced culture centuries before the arrival of the Spanish missionaries and colonizers. The contrasts between the Hopi and Navajo illustrate the diversity of Native American culture today. The Navajo's lifestyle is semi-nomadic, based on stock-raising, and their reservation occupies an area the size of Belgium. The Hopi live in *pueblos*, permanent farming communities where religious ceremonial

continues to play an essential role. To respect these traditions, tourism needs to be carefully managed.

○ The heritage of the 'Wild West'. In the late nineteenth century the region's rich mineral resources supported thriving mining communities, which have now become 'ghost towns'. Some of these have been restored, notably Tombstone in Arizona, scene of the shoot-out at the OK Corral.

○ **Las Vegas** – 'the total leisure experience'. The tourism industry of Nevada is a special case, thanks to this state's liberal attitudes to marriage and divorce and above all to gambling, which elsewhere in the USA was illegal for most of the twentieth century. At the same time, the state authorities have exercised some control over the gambling industry, which is often associated with sleaze and organized crime. There are two major centres – Reno, which is more accessible from San Francisco, and Las Vegas, by far the most popular, which is easily reached by car from Los Angeles. Its airport – McCarran International – is linked to all major cities in the USA and a growing number of foreign countries. Despite its desert location, Las Vegas has developed rapidly since the 1940s, sustained by power generated from the Boulder Dam on the Colorado river. It is now a major city of half a million inhabitants attracting 36 million visitors in 2000, where activity is centred on The Strip, a 6-kilometre long boulevard flanked by casinos and large hotels. The enormous revenues from the casinos have made Las Vegas the 'world's entertainment capital'. Since the 1990s Americans can gamble in many places outside Nevada, but the city has re-invented itself as a family resort, with massive investment in theme parks, shopping malls and museums, while also going upmarket with luxury hotels and golf courses. Some see in Las Vegas the tourism of the future, in which themed hotels provide a virtual, risk-free substitute for a real destination or an imagined past. The first themed hotel was Caesar's Palace in the 1960s based on Ancient Rome (as interpreted by Hollywood). Since then, advances in technology have made it possible to replicate a volcanic eruption (The Mirage), a naval battle (Treasure Island) and a foreign destination (Venice).

Two other tourist centres in the south-west deserve specific mention, both very different in character from Las Vegas:

• **Santa Fe** is the historic capital of New Mexico, with a well-preserved Spanish-Indian heritage of adobe buildings and traditional handicrafts. Large numbers of artists have been attracted to the city and nearby Indian communities such as Taos.

• **Salt Lake City** is both a business and religious centre, where the Church of Latter Day Saints or Mormon Church plays a dominant role (as a consequence most of Utah is 'dry' – meaning an alcohol-free zone). Visitors are attracted to the Mormon Tabernacle and the Family History Library, which contains the world's largest collection of genealogical records. The Wasatch Mountains provide first class ski facilities, Salt Lake City having been chosen as the venue for the 2002 Winter Olympics. The Great Salt Lake has been used for attempts on the world land speed record.

Texas

For historical reasons, the 'Lone Star State' is as much part of the South as it is of the West, while its closeness to Mexico is reflected in its food, architecture and music. Texas has a booming economy that has generated a considerable volume of business travel to its major cities. Dallas is a major financial and distribution centre, while the neighbouring city of Fort Worth takes pride in its cattle industry heritage. Houston is noted for its oil and aero-space industries, where the major attractions are the Space Center, the Astrodome – the world's largest covered sports facility – and the Astroworld theme park. The fine beaches of the Gulf coast are within easy reach, notably those of Galveston and Padre Island. Other tourist centres include Austin, the state capital with an important music-recording industry, and San Antonio, which celebrates its 'Latin' traditions. This city's best known tourist attraction is the Alamo, the old Spanish mission that played a major role in the Texan struggle for independence from Mexico. The Paseo del Rio (Riverwalk) is a fine example of a major event attraction – the 1968 Hemisfair Spanish American Exposition – providing the impetus for inner city regeneration.

California and the far west

The West Coast, particularly California, is much more populated, cosmopolitan and dynamic in its outlook than the interior. It faces the other countries of the Pacific Rim and is at the cutting edge of the new technology – 'Silicon Valley' around San Jose and the Boeing plant outside Seattle are just two examples. Since 1849, when gold was discovered near Sacramento, Americans have regarded California as the land of opportunity. It has long been the richest state, with a population that is extraordinarily mobile even by American standards. The 'Golden State' is renowned for its warm, sunny climate and the remarkable variety of its scenery. This includes lush farmlands, forests of giant redwood and sequoia, strange volcanic landforms, and the high peaks of the Sierra Nevada – contrasting dramatically with Death Valley, one of the lowest, driest and hottest locations on Earth. All these, and a wealth of man-made attractions, explain why California is the primary holiday destination for Americans, and one of the most popular states for foreign tourists. Even so, tourism is less important to the Californian economy than the engineering industries and agriculture, unlike the situation in Florida, where tourism is the main source of income.

There are important differences in climate between the Pacific coast, which is cooled by the California Current, and the Central Valley east of the Coast Ranges, where summer temperatures frequently exceed 40 °C. Northern California also has a generally cooler and wetter climate than the south, where conditions are ideal for outdoor recreation. Nevertheless California has its share of environmental problems. These include:

- the earthquakes associated with the San Andreas Fault and other lines of weakness in the Earth's crust; these destroyed San Francisco in 1906 and threatened Los Angeles in 1998
- the devastating fires that occur in summer in the dry *chaparral* scrub, and the equally destructive floods and landslides affecting slopes cleared for development
- the severe air pollution in Los Angeles, which occupies a valley hemmed in by mountains
- the demands for water that may not be sustainable in the long term

Tourism in California is mainly concentrated in the following areas:

Los Angeles 'LA' is not so much a city as a sprawling conurbation covering an area of 2000 square kilometres and consisting of no less that 82 separate local authorities and many ethnic communities. It is held together by the most extensive freeway network in the USA, and this provides the only practical way of visiting the dispersed attractions. Los Angeles has grown to prominence on the basis successively of the citrus industry, oil, motion pictures, aerospace and music recording. The city's tourism industry was given a major boost by the 1984 Olympic Games. With the San Bernardino Mountains and the Mojave Desert at its backdoor, and with an extensive shoreline along the Pacific, Los Angeles offers a wide range of recreational opportunities. The beach resorts of Santa Monica and Venice Beach have been trend-setters in leisure fashions, epitomizing the Californian obsession with youth and physical fitness. Southern California can claim to be the birthplace of the American theme park, the best known being Disneyland, but in this respect it now suffers by comparison with Florida. The glamorous image of Hollywood is a major draw for visitors, and some of the film studios have been transformed into tourist attractions. Even the desert interior has been affected by tourism by its closeness to Los Angeles, and in some areas trail bikes and 'dune buggies' have had a severe environmental impact. One of the most important resorts of Southern California is Palm Springs, an oasis of golf courses in the midst of the Mojave Desert.

San Francisco The 'City on the Bay' is very different from Los Angeles. It is relatively compact, with a good public transport system, and is widely regarded as the most scenic and 'European' of all North American cities. San Francisco has also acquired a reputation for tolerance of lifestyles that do not conform to the mainstream culture; it played a prominent role in the 'hippy' movement of the 1960s – centred on the district of Haight-Ashbury – and it has attracted a large gay community. The city developed after the 1849 Gold Rush as a major seaport on one of the world's finest natural harbours. Much of the waterfront is now devoted to tourism, restaurants and entertainment, notably at Fisherman's Wharf. Other major attractions include the largest Chinese community in North America, the famous 'cable cars' (actually nineteenth-century trams), a flourishing theatre and arts scene, and the Golden Gate Bridge spanning the entrance to the harbour. The cold current offshore deterred would-be escapers from Alcatraz Island, and results in San Francisco having the lowest summer temperatures of any major city in the USA, often accompanied by coastal fog. Within easy reach of San Francisco are:

- the exclusive beach resorts of Carmel and Monterey
- the wine-producing area of the Napa Valley, including the spa town of Calistoga
- the ski resorts around Lake Tahoe and the Sierra Nevada mountains
- the Yosemite National Park with its spectacular waterfalls and sheer granite cliffs; Yosemite Valley is crammed to capacity at summer weekends
- the redwood forests to the north of San Francisco, reached by a scenic coastal highway.

San Diego is the third gateway city to California, lying close to the Mexican border. The city is primarily a naval port, but visitors are attracted by an ideal climate and the excellent beaches such as those of La Jolla, with facilities for sailing and sport fishing.

Santa Barbara deserves special mention, out of the many beach resorts of Southern California, for its attractive Spanish-style architecture. The city originated – like so many others in California – as a Spanish mission. However, its buildings are not relics from colonial times but the result of a deliberate planning initiative following an earthquake in 1925.

The north-west

The other states of the Far West – Oregon and Washington – have been less affected by tourism. In fact the environmentally conscious state government of Oregon has severely limited development along its coastline. The unspoiled national scenery provides the main appeal for tourists. Outstanding attractions include:

- Crater Lake, a perfect example of a volcanic caldera
- the Olympic National Park, an area of heavy rainfall that supports dense temperate rain forests
- the Mount Rainier National Park, which boasts large numbers of glaciers, lakes and waterfalls; this forms part of the Cascades Range, which includes a number of active volcanos such as Mount St Helens.

Portland and Seattle are the gateway cities to the north-west. Seattle has the advantage of an attractive coastal setting. One of its main landmarks is the Space Needle, erected for the 1962 World Fair. Seattle is also the main gateway to Alaska for visitors by sea.

Alaska

As much of Alaska lies within the Arctic Circle, it is climatically distinct from the rest of the USA and is isolated from the 'lower 48' states by some of Canada's most difficult mountain terrain. Only the narrow Bering Strait – ice covered in winter – separates it from Siberia on the other side of the International Date Line. In fact Alaska was purchased from the Tsar of Russia in 1867, and the Orthodox cathedral in Sitka evokes the Russian heritage. To most Americans, Alaska is the 'last frontier' – a wilderness image that has persisted since the 1898 Gold Rush. The gruelling Iditarod dog sled rally from Anchorage to Nome is an annual reminder of those pioneering days. Nowadays air transport is crucial to this sparsely settled state, and Alaska's main external links are also by air. Its major city, Anchorage, lies on the trans-polar route from Europe to Japan.

Alternative ways of reaching Alaska are:

- the Alcan Highway, over 2000 kilometres in length and constructed during the Second World War from Edmonton to Fairbanks, remains the only practical overland route from Canada
- the Alaska Marine Highway System operates ferry services linking Prince Rupert in British Columbia to the coastal communities of southern Alaska, including Juneau, the state capital.

In most of Alaska the climate is a major constraint on tourism development. The south-east of Alaska has the greatest tourism potential, offering spectacular fjords, rugged mountain scenery and some of the largest glaciers in the Northern Hemisphere. The climate here is relatively mild but excessively rainy. A sheltered coastal waterway – the Inside Passage – provides a route for summer cruises operating out of Long Beach, San Francisco and Seattle. The rapid expansion of cruise tourism has brought problems to the small coastal communities in the form of overcrowding and marine pollution – a sensitive issue since the 1989 *Exxon Valdez* oil spill disaster.

Elsewhere in Alaska ecotourism and adventure tourism are growing in popularity, bringing some economic benefit to the native Indian, Aleut and Inupiat (Eskimo) communities. However wilderness areas such as the Arctic National Wildlife Refuge (Anwar) are under threat from proposals to expand the oil industry, already well established at Prudhoe Bay. With less than a million people inhabiting an area the size of western Europe, the majority of Alaskans are not opposed to development, and some resent what they see as interference by environmentalists from the 'lower 48'.

The Denali National Park – boasting North America's highest mountain – is already experiencing visitor pressure despite its rigorous sub-arctic climate and lack of tourist facilities. This is because Denali can be accessed by road and rail from Anchorage, whereas other natural attractions, such as the volcanic landscapes of Katmai National Park, are even more remote, and as a result, much less visited.

Hawaii

The location of the Hawaiian Islands in mid-Pacific, 4000 kilometres south-west of California, sets them apart from the rest of the USA as a destination. Hawaii received more than 6 million visitors in the early years of the twenty-first century, of whom two-thirds were Americans from the mainland. The Japanese market is much smaller in volume but highly significant in terms of visitor spend. Hawaii has become one of the world's best-known holiday destinations on the basis of the climate, superb volcanic scenery and surfing beaches of the islands, and their Polynesian heritage, romanticized by the Hollywood film industry. These resources have become accessible to the North American mass market through cheap domestic air fares and competitive tour pricing.

Oahu is the most visited of the islands, and most of the tourism development has been concentrated there. It contains 75 per cent of the population, the naval base of Pearl Harbor and the state capital, Honolulu, which is the gateway to the islands. It is also a major city which has become increasingly important as a business centre for trade between North America and the East Asia–Pacific region. Honolulu's world famous Waikiki Beach, backed by scores of high-rise hotels, extends for three kilometres to the cliffs of Diamond Head, an extinct volcanic crater. The 'North Shore' (the north-west coast of Oahu) offers some of the best conditions for surfing (the sport was in fact invented by the native Hawaiians).

Since the 1960s the state government, increasingly concerned about the undesirable impacts of mass tourism on Oahu, has encouraged quality development projects on the other major islands. Maui contains the Haleakala National Park with its impressive volcanic scenery and the former whaling port of Lahaina. Kauai is particularly renowned for its lush landscapes, exemplified by the Fern Grotto at Wailua, the Waimea Canyon and the beaches at Hanalei (the location for 'Bali Hai' in the film *South Pacific*). The 'Big Island' of Hawaii (from which the state takes its name) offers great climatic and scenic variety, due to the effect of the high volcanic peaks of Mauna Loa and Mauna Kea on the prevailing trade winds. Hilo on the windward side of the island receives heavy rainfall, whereas Kona on the west coast is much drier. Frequent volcanic eruptions have created a lunar landscape of craters and lava caves in the south-eastern part of the island, in contrast to the rainforests, coffee plantations and cattle ranches elsewhere. Molokai and Lanai are islands as yet little influenced by tourism and sparsely populated Niihau has rejected it altogether.

Canada

Canada is second only to the Russian Federation in area, and is larger than the United States, but has only a tenth of its population. Climatic factors, such as the chilling effect of Hudson Bay and the Labrador Current, largely explain why the great majority of Canadians occupy a narrow belt of territory lying within 200 kilometres of the United States border. Tourism is also unevenly distributed, with most foreign visitors shunning the prairies of central Canada, concentrating their attention on Vancouver and the Rockies in the west, and Toronto or Montreal in the south-east. In economic and cultural terms Canada tends to be overshadowed by its powerful neighbour, and this together with a more northerly location, has resulted in an image problem.

About 80 per cent of this vast country is classified as wilderness, mainly coniferous forest or tundra, and Canada boasts some of the world's largest lakes and 15 per cent of its freshwater resources. Not surprisingly the promotional literature highlights the unspoiled scenery and the great outdoors; but since most Canadians are city dwellers, the 'Discover Our True Nature' campaign also emphasizes the sophistication of Canada's cities, contrasting the traditional appeal of Quebec with the contemporary attractions of Montreal. Canada's separate identity is demonstrated by its political institutions, strict gun control laws and by a number of heritage attractions commemorating French and British rule, including resistance to United States expansion in the War of 1812. However, Canada's quest for national unity is made problematic by the existence of two official languages, representing two different cultural traditions.

Demand for tourism

Domestic and international tourism together account for 5 per cent of Canada's gross domestic product and around 10 per cent of employment. As early as 1929 tourism was a major earner of foreign exchange, and in 1934 the Canadian Travel Bureau was established under the Department of Commerce to carry out promotion abroad. However it is only since the late 1960s that the federal government in Ottawa has become directly involved. Marketing is carried out by the Canadian Tourism Commission (CTC), created in 1995 as a partnership between the federal government and the domestic travel industry. The governments of the ten provinces and the three territories are also involved in product development and overseas promotion with all levels of government in Canada having tourism responsibilities.

Inbound tourism

The majority of Canada's 20 million foreign tourists come from the United States, and less than 10 per cent arrive from European countries. Americans also account for the large volume of excursionists, whose numbers fluctuate according to differences in prices on either side of the border and the strength of the two currencies. This does leave Canadian tourism vulnerable to a downturn in the US economy. The great majority of American tourists arrive by car, return frequently and are attracted mainly by the recreational facilities of the Canadian countryside. Canada's cities are also perceived to be safe compared to those of the USA, the language and culture are familiar, and crossing the world's longest undefended border is an easy matter for Americans. Overseas visitors tend to spend much more per head than the Americans, the leading markets being the UK, France, Germany and Japan, although overseas markets have declined in the wake of 9/11, whereas the American market has increased. Most overseas visitors arrive by air at Toronto or Montreal, and almost half of these stay primarily with friends and relatives.

Outbound and domestic tourism

The Canadian winter partly explains why Canadians have a high propensity to travel outside their own country, with around one-third of the population taking a trip abroad in any one year. This, combined with a high travel frequency, results in a massive deficit in Canada's international travel account. The American border states of New York, Vermont, Michigan and Washington are the most visited destinations. Florida is also popular with Canadians, particularly in winter, with many retired people spending several months either there or in Hawaii. This exodus of 'snowbirds' may well increase with the general ageing of the population, while the open skies agreement between the US and Canadian governments will favour a greater use of the airlines rather than travel by private car. Other destinations include Mexico, the Caribbean islands, Europe and East Asia. Most of the expenditure on foreign travel, especially to Europe, is generated by the more prosperous and urbanized provinces, such as Ontario, British Columbia and Manitoba.

As in the United States, domestic tourism is far larger than inbound or outbound tourism. British Columbia and Prince Edward Island are the destinations most favoured by Canadian holidaymakers.

Supply of tourism

Canada does not have such a wide range of resources for recreation as the USA, since it lies entirely outside the warm climate zone. Foreign tourists are attracted to the country's mountains, lakes and forests rather than its extensive coastline. Most of the national parks are situated in the more scenic western part of Canada. The Canadian Pacific Railway (CPR) was largely instrumental in their creation specifically as tourist attractions – hence the luxury hotels at such locations as Banff and Lake Louise in the Rockies. The national parks, together with a large number of National Historic Sites (NHS), are administered by a federal agency – Parks Canada. Each of the provinces and territories has an agency responsible for the conservation of natural resources, with a remit for recreation and tourism. The provincial parks are widely distributed, and while some provide a variety of recreational facilities, others are less developed than the national parks.

The severity and length of winter – even most of southern Canada is snow-covered for at least three months of the year – is a constraint on tourism development. Canadians invented the snowshoe and snowmobile, and regard winter as a time for participation in a wide range of recreation activities. Snowmobile trails thread the countryside, and many ski resorts have developed to meet domestic demand within reach of all the major cities. Snowfall is heavier in southern Quebec than in the Prairies, where temperatures are lower. Some of the resorts in the Laurentian Mountains of Quebec and the Canadian Rockies attract a growing international market. Canadian cities are well equipped to meet the challenges of winter, and in some, underground shopping centres provide full protection from the weather.

Summers, at least in southern and western Canada, are warm enough for a wide range of outdoor activities, including beach tourism and water sports. Transport and equipment for fishing and hunting trips is provided by specialist outfitters in even the most remote areas of Canada. Boating and canoeing are especially popular in the many lakes and rivers of the Canadian Shield – the vast expanse of forest lying to the north of the Great Lakes and the St Lawrence river. Canada's waterways played a crucial role in the early development of the country. Unlike the French *voyageurs* and the Hudson Bay fur traders, today's canoeists have the advantage of lightweight equipment. The old canoe trails form the basis for a system of 'heritage rivers'. This is a good example of cooperation between the public and private sector in resource management; stakeholders include the federal government, provincial or territorial governments, the local communities – especially those of the 'First Nations' or native Indians, and tour operators. The activities of the users – anglers, campers and ecotourists as well as canoeists – are carefully monitored to avoid environmental damage.

Transport

In most of Canada winter poses problems for vehicles and road maintenance. As in the USA, the railways played a major role in opening up the western part of the country to settlement, and the scenic mountain areas to tourism. After the 1950s they faced severe competition from domestic air services. In 1972 the passenger services of the CPR and the state-owned Canadian National Railways (CNR) were combined under the banner of VIA Rail, an independent Crown corporation that is subsidized by the federal government. By the late 1980s scheduled train services had been drastically reduced on most routes with the exception of the Toronto– Montreal corridor. VIA Rail still provides a trans-continental service, but at a frequency of only three trains a week in either direction; however sightseeing tours by train are available in the Rocky Mountains in the summer months. The great majority of domestic trips are now undertaken by private car. Most of the major cities, from Vancouver to Halifax, are linked to the world's longest national road – the Trans-Canada Highway. Domestic air travel is dominated by Air Canada, which ranks as one of the world's leading airlines. There are a number of regional carriers and air charter companies serving the vast areas that are virtually inaccessible by surface transport.

Tourism resources

Ontario

Ontario accounts for over half of Canada's industrial production, and has a number of cities, apart from Toronto and Ottawa, that rank as major business centres. It is the most visited province, containing Canada's largest English-speaking city, and is easily reached by road from New York in the south and Michigan to the west. It has a third of Canada's hotel capacity and offers a wide range of accommodation, including the popular holiday homes known as 'cabins' or 'cottages'. Many of these are located in the Muskoka Lakes area north of Toronto. Most of the population of Ontario is concentrated in the fertile peninsula lying between three of the Great Lakes – Huron, Erie and Ontario. Relatively few live in the Canadian Shield to the north of Lake Superior – a vast area of granite outcrops separated by lakes and *muskeg* (swamps), and covered with forests of spruce and fir.

- **Toronto** is Canada's most cosmopolitan city, with a vibrant nightlife and cultural scene – a far cry from its staid reputation in the 1950s, when it was known as 'Toronto the Good'. Attractions include Ontario Place – a major waterfront recreation area; the CN Tower; the Ontario Science Centre – one of the first inter-active museums; and the Hockey Hall of Fame, celebrating Canada's national game.
- **Ottawa** as the federal capital attracts sightseers to its impressive Gothic-style Parliament Buildings, the National Gallery of Canada and other important museums.

- The **Niagara** area includes not only the famous waterfalls, but also the resort of Niagara-on-the-Lake, famous for its theatre festival, and a popular wine route.
- **Stratford** is famed throughout North America as a theatrical centre.
- **Kingston** is important for its historical associations and as a base for visiting the scenic Thousand Islands.
- **Georgian Bay** and the **Algonquin Provincial Park** offer large areas of unspoiled lake and forest scenery on the southern edge of the Canadian Shield.

Quebec

Quebec Province is culturally distinct from the rest of Canada – an island of French-speakers in an English-speaking continent. Until the 1960s it was predominantly rural and traditional in outlook, but since that time there has been rapid economic growth, based largely on the province's huge resources of hydro-electric power. The great majority of the population live in a relatively narrow strip bordering the St Lawrence river. The influence of Catholicism remains strong, as shown by the popularity of pilgrimages to the shrine of St Anne de Beaupré.

- **Montreal** is Canada's largest city and the world's second largest French-speaking metropolis, with restaurants and *boites de chanson* (nightclubs) to match those of Paris. It vies with Toronto as the gateway to Canada, with two international air-ports – Dorval and Mirabel – and is a port on the St Lawrence Seaway linking the Atlantic to the Great Lakes. This has made Montreal a major financial centre. The 1967 World Exposition and the 1976 Olympic Games did much to improve the city's transport and recreation facilities. This includes Le Souterrain – an under-ground shopping area served by an efficient metro system, centred on Place Ville-Marie.
- **Quebec City** is less cosmopolitan than Montreal and its historic core has preserved the ambience of eighteenth-century France. Most of the tourist attractions are in the fortified Upper Town, which is dominated by the Chateau Frontenac, a *grand hotel* built by the Canadian Pacific Railway. Quebec is also famous throughout Canada for the ice sculptures and exuberance of its Winter Carnival.
- Downstream from Quebec City are two scenic areas: the fjord-like Saguenay river – increasingly popular for whale watching – and the picturesque Gaspé Peninsula, with its fishing villages.
- Ski resorts in Quebec Province include Mont Tremblant in the Laurentian Mountains and Mount Orford in the Notre Dame Range.

The Atlantic provinces

The provinces along the Atlantic seaboard of Canada are relatively poor, due to the decline of traditional industries such as fishing. International tourism is handi-capped by the region's peripheral location and an indifferent climate.

- **Newfoundland**, consisting of the island of that name and the coast of Labrador, typifies these conditions. The climate is influenced by the cold Labrador Current – the Atlantic coast is called 'Iceberg Alley'. This results in the late arrival of spring, frequent fogs and a short, cool summer. Scores of small fishing villages cling to the rocky coastline, where ecotourism in the form of bird watching and whale watching may provide an alternative livelihood. Newfoundland is the nearest part of North America to Europe and this was significant in the early days of transatlantic communications; in the pre-jet era Gander Airport near St Johns was an important staging point, and as 9/11 showed, it continues to play an important role as a diversionary airport. Coastal shipping services are a lifeline for many isolated communities.

- **St Pierre and Miquelon** are two small islands off the south coast of Newfoundland, all that remains of France's once vast territories in North America. As such they have curiosity appeal, attracting American and Canadian day-visitors on shopping trips.
- **Prince Edward Island**, the smallest of the three Maritime Provinces, enjoys a warmer climate and a flourishing tourism industry, although this caters mainly for the domestic market. The island's resources include fine sandy beaches, attractive countryside, golf courses and its literary associations – the town of Cavendish is the setting for *Anne of Green Gables*. The island is now linked to the mainland by the Confederation Bridge.
- **Nova Scotia** offers a variety of coastal scenery, and an interesting French and Scottish cultural heritage. Tourism is based on a number of touring routes such as Evangeline Trail, but some communities might well benefit from a greater influx of long-stay visitors. The capital Halifax is a major seaport with a marine heritage that includes its association with the *Titanic*. Louisbourg on Cape Breton Island is a former French fortress that has been restored as a 'living history' attraction.
- **New Brunswick** is less orientated toward the sea, although the Bay of Fundy is famous for its tides. The extensive forests and rivers of the interior attract hunters, anglers and canoeists.

The prairie provinces

The heartland of Canada consists of two provinces – Manitoba and Saskatchewan – that are mainly known for their vast wheat-growing prairies. Winters are comparable with those of Siberia, but Lake Winnipeg is a major focus for water sports during the short hot summers. Further north the prairies give way to forests, where fly-in camps and lodges provide accommodation for anglers. Although the scenery may be low-key, the region is culturally diverse, with large communities of Ukrainians, Germans and Icelanders that have retained the traditions of their homelands. Winnipeg is the main business and cultural centre of the region, followed by Regina, home of that world famous national institution, the Royal Canadian Mounted Police.

The isolated community of Churchill on Hudson Bay (it can only be reached by air, or train from Winnipeg) is an example of how ecotourism can revive a local economy. A one-time fur trading post and grain-exporting port, it is now visited by tourists in summer for whale watching, and in October to view polar bears from the safety of 'tundra buggies' – four-wheel drive all-terrain vehicles.

The west

The provinces of Alberta and British Columbia offer some of the most spectacular scenery and wildlife to be found in North America. The Rocky Mountains contain no less than seven of Canada's national parks. Most of the tourism development is on the **Alberta** side, including the following:

- **Banff National Park** is the most popular area, attracting 4 million visitors a year, mainly in the months of July and August. It contains two world famous resorts – Banff and Lake Louise. Banff was originally developed as a spa by the CPR on the basis of its hot springs and attracted a wealthy international clientèle in the early part of the twentieth century. With the development of skiing after the Second World War it became an all-year resort, with a winter sports season lasting from November to May. It is now a major urban centre with attractions, restaurants, golf courses and other facilities that often seem inappropriate to the setting and the national park ethos. Banff also offers major cultural events, such art and film festivals.

- **Jasper National Park** lies close to the Yellowhead Pass, the route across the Rockies followed by the CNR. Major attractions include the Columbia Icefield and Maligne Lake, both superb examples of glacial scenery. Outside the park boundaries, heli-skiing and heli-hiking allow access to the most remote mountain areas.

- **Calgary** is the gateway to the Canadian Rockies. It is also the centre for the ranching industry of south-western Alberta, hence the significance of the 'Stampede' – a world famous event attraction celebrating the cowboy lifestyle. The winter climate of this area is often affected by warm, dry *chinook* winds – similar to the *föhn* of the Alps – that can raise temperatures by as much as 25 °C. This would be disastrous for the ski resort operations were it not for the availability of computerized snow-making systems covering most of the pistes. Waterton Lakes near Calgary was the venue for the 1988 Winter Olympics.

- **Edmonton** has long been regarded as the gateway to the Canadian North. Its modern prosperity is largely based on the oil industry, and the city boasts the largest shopping mall in North America – Edmonton West – offering a range of themed attractions.

- The arid landscapes of the **Alberta Badlands** are unlike any other part of Canada. They are noted for their dinosaur fossil beds and the landforms resulting from wind erosion known as *hoodoos*.

The coastal region of **British Columbia** offers many attractions, including:

- a climate characterized by the mildest winters of Canada – with temperatures 20 °C higher than in Labrador at the same latitude – and in the south, warm summers with abundant sunshine

- a spectacular coastline backed by mountains, deeply indented with fjords and with many offshore islands

- diverse ecosystems, including the rainforests of Vancouver Island, and rivers teeming with salmon

- the Indian heritage: the abundance of natural resources allowed the Haida of the Queen Charlotte Islands and other coastal tribes to develop a sophisticated culture which was severely disrupted by contact with Europeans, but the totem pole survives as the best known example of native skills.

The main tourist centres are Vancouver and Victoria:

- **Vancouver** is Canada's third largest city and a major gateway to the East Asia–Pacific Region. This makes the city particularly appealing for visitors from Japan, Hong Kong and other Asian countries. The superb natural setting means that sailing, golf and skiing can be enjoyed on the same day.

- **Victoria**, on Vancouver Island is a major holiday resort and retirement area, with a strong English ambience that makes it appealing to American tourists from the West Coast.

The interior of British Columbia comprises high mountain ranges, broad plateaux, and deep, canyon-like valleys. The climate is much drier than the coast, with cold winters but very warm summers. This is particularly true of the sheltered Okanagan Valley, where sailing and water skiing are popular at the lake resorts of Penticton and Kelowna. On the Fraser river visitors can experience white-water rafting or pan for gold near former mining towns. Excellent winter sports facilities are available in the Selkirk Mountains at Kimberley, and at Kamloops, the heart of British Columbia's cattle-ranching country.

The north

Although Canadians living in southern Ontario perceive James Bay, Labrador and northern Quebec as being part of the North, the region is generally defined as comprising the Yukon, the North-West Territories and Nunavut, which lie north of 60 degrees latitude.

- **The Yukon Territory** is more accessible than other parts of the Canadian North, and although winters are just as severe, summers are much warmer than in Nunavut. The Yukon's tourism industry is mainly based on the heritage of the 1898 Gold Rush, Canada's equivalent of the 'Wild West' – at Dawson City and Whitehorse. The Kluane National Park provides limited facilities for adventure tourism.
- **The North-West Territories** (NWT) have substantial indigenous communities, belonging to the Dene Indian and Inuit (Eskimo) cultures. Although there is road access to Yellowknife, and to Inuvik on the Mackenzie delta, most of the NWT is suitable only for expeditions. The problems caused by even a limited amount of tourism are becoming evident in the region's main natural attraction – the Nahanni National Park Reserve. This World Heritage Site includes the spectacular Virginia Falls and an extensive karst limestone system – unusual in such high latitudes. Although this remote area is only accessible by air, it is already experiencing severe impacts, resulting from the growth of white-water rafting on the South Nahanni river.
- **Nunavut** covers most of the Canadian Arctic, and was created by the federal government in 1999 specifically for the Inuit people. Visits to the region are part of the growing ecotourism movement and this is a sector in which Inuit guides and outfitters, with their intimate knowledge of the country, are playing an important role, sustaining both their economy and culture. Nunavut's rigorous climate, the vast distances between the few settlements and the forbidding terrain are obstacles to tourism development and discourage independent travel. The resource base includes:
  - the spectacular glaciated mountain and fjord scenery of Baffin Island, culminating in the Auyuittuq National Park
  - the pristine lakes and rivers of the Barren Lands, the tundra plains extending from Hudson Bay north-westwards to the Arctic Ocean
  - the marine wildlife of Hudson Bay and Lancaster Sound
  - Inuit handicrafts based on their hunting traditions.

Greenland (Kalaallit Nunaat)

A permanent ice cap thousands of metres thick covers 84 per cent of Greenland, so that the mainly Inuit population live in scattered communities along the western and south-eastern coasts. To the north, a barrier of pack ice prevents circumnavigation of the world's largest island.

A self-governing Danish territory, Greenland has shunned incorporation in the European Union, but its economy remains highly dependent on Denmark. Greenland is more accessible by air services from Copenhagen and Iceland than from Canada, although this may change, with Greenlanders seeking closer links with their Inuit neighbours in Nunavut.

Greenland's main tourism resource is its fjord and mountain scenery, culminating in Disko Bay, where glaciers reach the sea to spawn a myriad icebergs (the ice here is claimed to be the world's purest). Narsarsuaq in the extreme south is the main focus for activities such as hiking and mountain climbing, while the ruins of Viking farms and churches are evidence of climate change during the past millennium. Prospects for tourism development are limited by the high costs of accommodation and transport. Even in summer, the coastal ferries and the system of air services (mainly using helicopters) are likely to be disrupted by a sudden deterioration in weather conditions, including fogs and strong winds.

Summary

North America is a vast continent of scenic and climatic contrasts. With the exception of northern Canada and Greenland it is highly developed economically. Urban landscapes, lifestyles, transport systems and tourist facilities are broadly similar throughout both the United States and Canada, and there is a considerable volume of travel between the two countries. The main problem for the overseas visitor is the great distances involved, but this has been largely overcome by excellent highways and an extensive network of air services, with rail transport now playing only a minor role. Tourist facilities have been developed mainly to serve the enormous domestic market, and it is only recently that federal, state and provincial governments have become directly involved in encouraging inbound tourism. North Americans spend heavily on travel abroad, with the result that Canada continues to have a large deficit on its international travel account. However, 9/11 has changed travel patterns markedly. Overseas visitors to the United States and Canada are attracted mainly to the cities for broadly cultural reasons, and there is a large VFR market. However, Florida is regarded mainly as a beach and theme park destination. Both the United States and Canada have realized the importance of conservation and their state-controlled national parks and forest reserves are probably the world's finest. The native peoples of North America, marginalized in the past, are now taking a more active share in tourism development. The private sector of tourism is very much larger than the state sector, and is responsible for all profit-making enterprises; sports facilities and theme parks are particularly important.

Chapter 25
The tourism geography of Latin America and the Caribbean

Learning Objectives

After reading this chapter you should be able to:

■ Describe the major physical features and climates of Latin America and the Caribbean, and understand their importance for tourism.
■ Appreciate the significance of tourism to the economies of the Caribbean islands.
■ Appreciate the cultural heritage of Latin America and the Caribbean.
■ Recognize the importance of adequate infrastructure and political stability in encouraging tourism development.
■ Recognize the potential for ecotourism in many of the countries of the region.
■ Appreciate the importance of cruise tourism in the Caribbean.
■ Demonstrate a knowledge of the tourist regions, resorts, business centres and tourist attractions of Latin America and the Caribbean.

Introduction

Latin America is a cultural entity consisting of 19 Spanish-speaking countries and Portuguese-speaking Brazil, as a result of colonization by Europeans from the Iberian Peninsula. Most of the Caribbean islands, along with Belize and the Guianas on the mainland, were colonized later by the British, the Dutch and the French. Nevertheless the countries south of the US border share many cultural and economic features, and can be considered a single region. The European colonists imported slaves from Africa to provide labour, and their descendants contribute a major ingredient to the cultural mix, particularly in Brazil and the Caribbean. The total population of Latin America and the Caribbean is well over 500 million and includes two of the world's mega-cities – São Paulo, with almost 20 million inhabitants, and Mexico City, which is approaching 22 million inhabitants. Most of the region is Roman Catholic, and religious festivals play an important role in the culture. Some of the Commonwealth Caribbean islands are strongly Protestant, while evangelical movements are challenging the dominance of the Roman Catholic Church in parts of Latin America.

Most Latin American and Caribbean countries are at the intermediate stage of economic development, with a few reaching the 'drive to maturity'. During the 1990s governments throughout the region adopted free market and privatization policies in place of the protectionism of earlier decades, to stimulate economic growth. However, most countries remained dependent on the export of minerals or cash crops. With the new millennium most of Latin America is experiencing an economic malaise more severe in its impact than the Asian currency crisis of 1997/98. Some blame this on globalization, but much can be attributed to excessive borrowing by the public sector. Governments have been forced to adopt austerity measures and divert a high proportion of their resources to repay huge debts to foreign creditors. If anything, social inequalities have increased since 2000, with over half the region's population living below the poverty line. There are usually great disparities in wealth between the major cities, that resemble those of Europe or North America, and the more remote rural areas where pre-industrial lifestyles persist. Rural poverty in turn has led to a massive exodus to the cities, where most migrants live in crime-ridden shanty towns on the periphery, deprived of basic services.

At the beginning of the twenty-first century the region accounted for about 10 per cent of the world total of international tourist arrivals. Patterns of tourism do vary widely, with major differences between the countries of the mainland and the smaller Caribbean islands. Latin America includes four of the world's biggest spenders on international travel – Brazil, Mexico, Argentina and Venezuela – as well as some major destinations, while in a few countries tourism is in its infancy. We can make the following generalizations about tourism in the region:

- The wealthier socioeconomic groups often prefer to travel abroad, particularly to the USA, rather than take holidays in their own countries.
- Visitors from other countries in the region, usually short stay, make up the bulk of arrivals.
- The USA provides the majority of tourists from outside the region to Mexico, Central America and the Caribbean, but some South American countries attract a large proportion of their tourists from Europe.
- Tourism is much less significant as a source of foreign exchange in South America than it is to the Caribbean islands.
- The region's airlines have suffered as a result of 9/11. They were already struggling against competition from US carriers, which now account for two-thirds of the Latin American market for international air travel. Unlike their North American competitors, they can count on little support from their governments, and few are able to meet the stringent safety standards now required by the US government in the aftermath of 9/11.

There is a great variety of tourism resources in a region which is greater in latitudinal extent than either North America or Africa. Products include beach tourism in the Caribbean islands and Mexico, adventure travel and ecotourism in the mountains and forests of the interior, and cultural tourism in the Andes of South America and the 'Maya Route' of Central America.

The Caribbean islands

Physical features

The islands of the Caribbean form a chain, extending for some 4000 kilometres from Florida to the northern coast of South America. The Caribbean Sea is almost enclosed, and has been called, with some justification, 'the American Mediterranean'. However, it is warmer and less polluted than its Old World counterpart, with a greener coastline and finer beaches.

The islands are generally healthier than most tropical destinations. The north-east trade winds moderate the rather high temperatures and humidity, bringing heavy rainfall to the windward coasts; this means that locations on the sheltered side of a mountainous island, and low-lying islands generally, have a much drier climate, as evidenced by cacti and other drought-resistant vegetation. The best time for visiting the Caribbean is from December through to April when the weather is pleasantly warm, sunny and relatively dry. This has long been the high season for winter sun-seekers, arriving mainly from North America. Summer temperatures are appreciably higher and there is a greater probability of rain. Hotel prices are generally lower in summer, and this attracts a younger, less affluent type of holidaymaker, including many from Europe. In fact the Caribbean is no longer primarily a winter destination, as over 60 per cent of its visitors now arrive during the summer months. From July to November there is the risk of hurricanes occurring in some parts of the region, and these tropical storms can cause immense damage to the tourism infrastructure of the islands and the Caribbean coast of Central America.

While climatic conditions are fairly uniform throughout the region, there are considerable differences between the landscapes of the various islands. There are also great disparities in size – from tiny Saba, with little over a thousand inhabitants, to Cuba, which is comparable in area and population to a medium-sized country in Europe. The Greater Antilles – Cuba, Hispaniola, Puerto Rico and Jamaica – could be described as 'continents in miniature'. The smaller islands or Lesser Antilles tend to fall into two categories:

- the 'low islands' of limestone formation; these are scenically less interesting, but boast fine beaches of white coral sand
- the 'high islands' of volcanic origin in the eastern Caribbean; these are mountainous and often densely forested, but have fewer beaches and a wetter climate, while rugged terrain makes road building and airport expansion difficult. There have been few volcanic eruptions in recent centuries – Mont Pelée in Martinique (1902) and Montserrat (1995–97) are notable exceptions – but there are significant geothermal resources in most of these islands.

Cultural features

The islands are a mosaic of different races, languages and religions, with a cultural heritage resulting from successive phases of European colonization, namely:

- **The age of discovery** The arrival of the Spanish under Columbus had a fatal impact on the native Amerindians, particularly the Arawak of the Greater Antilles, and few traces of their culture remain. The Caribs of the eastern Caribbean put up a longer resistance, and a small community still survive in Dominica.

- **The age of piracy** The buccaneers of the seventeenth century used the smaller islands abandoned by the Spanish as bases for their expeditions, which were directed mainly against the Spanish treasure fleets from Mexico and South America.
- **The plantation era** The plantation economy developed in the eighteenth century when sugar was a valuable commodity, and the islands a prize to be acquired by even minor European powers, such as Denmark (the US Virgin Islands) and Sweden (St Barts). In the course of the next century slavery was abolished, but the legacy of the plantation is still evident in the attitude of many Afro-Caribbeans toward tourism.

Development of tourism in the Caribbean

English is the most widely spoken language in the Caribbean, and this, together with proximity to the USA, has been a factor encouraging the development of tourism. The region is, however, highly fragmented politically. Even the Commonwealth Caribbean consists of no less than ten independent island-nations and five British colonies, but there is an increasing awareness of the advantages of cooperation in the fields of tourism planning and promotion. Most of the remaining islands retain close links with France, the Netherlands and the United States. Cuba, the Dominican Republic and Puerto Rico have strong cultural ties with Spain and the other Spanish-speaking countries of Latin America. There has been some progress toward economic integration through Caricom (the Caribbean Community), while the Caribbean Tourism Organization (CTO) carries out joint promotion with member countries in Europe and North America.

Most of the Caribbean islands are over-populated in relation to their limited resources for economic development. Tourism is encouraged by most governments in the region who perceive that beaches, sunshine and scenery are more marketable assets than sugar or bananas. Since 1997 agriculture has become even less profitable, as islands are no longer guaranteed a market for their produce in the European Union, thanks to the ruling of the World Trade Organization. Tourism has the advantage of creating jobs in a region where unemployment is high, where emigration is no longer an alternative and where manufacturing industry is generally not viable. Tourism is now the major earner of foreign exchange, the fastest-growing sector of the economy, contributing 20 per cent of the region's GDP, and a major employer, accounting for over a third of the workforce in many of the islands.

Since 1985, the Caribbean's hotel capacity has grown rapidly, exceeding 40 000 rooms in 2002. However the region is highly dependent on the North American market, which supplies the majority of all staying visitors and over 90 per cent of cruise passengers, and is therefore vulnerable to the affects of recession in the USA. Most national currencies are tied to the US dollar, and resort accommodation is designed and priced to meet North American expectations. Foreign tour operators also tend to regard the islands as offering an interchangeable holiday product, disregarding the considerable cultural differences that exist within the Caribbean and national aspirations.

The dependence on tourism does mean that the islands are highly vulnerable to negative publicity on crime. Much of this is linked to drug-running, since the Caribbean Sea lies between some of the world's major suppliers and the world's largest market for narcotics. The many harbours and airfields are difficult to patrol effectively, with under-resourced police forces helping the US Coast Guard to intercept the traffickers. This is another area where greater cooperation between island governments would be an advantage.

An island's success as a tourist destination depends to a large extent on its accessibility to air and shipping services. Inter-island ferry services tend to be less reliable than air transport, making 'island hopping' problematic. There are many small regional airlines in the Caribbean but only a few international airports with the capacity to handle a large volume of long-haul traffic. Barbados, for example, acts as a regional hub, providing services to the less developed islands such as St Vincent and Dominica. The vital air links to North America and Europe are dominated by airlines based outside the Caribbean, although BWIA (the national airline of Barbados and Trinidad) and Air Jamaica are gaining a larger share of the market.

Tourism in the Caribbean has had negative as well as positive impacts on host communities. This is particularly true of two holiday types which have been encouraged by most governments as a means of maximizing income from visitors, namely cruising and all-inclusives.

- **Cruising** The Caribbean has maintained its position as the world's most popular cruise destination, due largely to competitive pricing by the shipping lines, aimed particularly at middle-income groups in the USA. Cruising has shown a faster rate of growth than land-based tourism, from less than a million passengers in the early 1980s to almost 5 million at the beginning of the twenty-first century, while the ships boast a far higher occupancy rate than most resort hotels. In winter the Caribbean has unrivalled natural advantages, but in summer it faces strong competition from other destinations, leading some cruise lines to reposition their vessels in Alaskan or Mediterranean waters. Both the number of ships and their overall size is increasing, with the largest accommodating more than 2500 passengers and over a thousand crew. Size is an advantage for cruise operators in terms of yield, while stricter environmental and safety regulations also discourage the use of smaller, older vessels. Although providing terminal facilities is costly for island governments, an equivalent number of staying tourists would require a much greater investment in hotel building. Nevertheless the economic benefits of attracting the multi-billion dollar cruise market have been disputed, and there are also negative environmental and cultural impacts (Pattullo, 1996). We can summarize the objections to cruising as follows:
  ○ cruise lines offer unfair competition to Caribbean hoteliers, as they pay little in the way of taxes to island governments
  ○ cruise lines provide few employment and business opportunities to island communities. They source most of their food requirements from outside the Caribbean, claiming that local farmers cannot provide supplies to the quantity or quality required
  ○ cruising is high-volume but low-spend tourism as the increasingly sophisticated on-board facilities for shopping, leisure and gambling mean there is less incentive for passengers to spend in the ports of call; duty-free goods – most of which have to be imported – account for half the spend ashore, which puts the smaller, less developed islands at a disadvantage
  ○ the sheer volume of passengers is difficult for some communities to handle, given the limited number of taxis and buses available
  ○ cruising is 'convenience travel'; in contrast to the Mediterranean and other cruise destinations, the Caribbean attracts 'sun and fun' holidaymakers rather than those interested in sightseeing, while the ship is often promoted as the

primary attraction; with just a few hours ashore, passengers receive only a stereotyped impression of the Caribbean, and the commercialization of the ports of call can be demeaning to both the visitors and the host community
  ○ cruise ships generate an enormous amount of waste, and island governments are ill-equipped to carry out clean-up operations on the scale required.

The eventual inclusion of Cuba in cruise itineraries may put some of the smaller islands at a disadvantage.

- **All-inclusive resorts** Although Club Méditerranée pioneered the all-inclusive principle in their villages in the French islands of Martinique and Guadeloupe, the idea did not spread to the rest of the Caribbean until the late 1980s, following the example of the Sandals group in Jamaica. All-inclusives have the following advantages:
  ○ for tourists, they offer value for money holidays, as there is no need to budget for 'extras' such as drinks and the use of sports facilities
  ○ for tour operators they boost profits by stimulating sales
  ○ for the hoteliers they improve occupancy rates, allowing more staff to be employed year-round.

On the other hand, all-inclusives have been accused of widening social divisions between the tourists, who see little need to venture beyond the security of the hotels, and the host community. Also most are owned by multi-nationals, which reduces their benefits to the local economy.

Other forms of tourism allow more of the visitor spend to be retained locally, by encouraging linkages with suppliers in the islands. They include:

- **Yachting** Whereas only a small number of harbours in the Caribbean can accommodate 100 000 tonne cruise ships, yachtsmen from Europe and North America have an almost unlimited choice of natural anchorages. Purpose-built marinas are available in many islands, providing facilities for both bareboat charter and crewed vessels. Nautical tourists are predominantly from the upper-income groups, but tend to be more informal in their dealings with local people than their counterparts in the luxury resort hotels.
- **Diving** Some of the world's finest coral reefs fringe the Caribbean islands. The invention of the self-contained underwater breathing apparatus (scuba) in the 1950s revolutionized diving and opened up a new frontier for tourism. With more than 5 million practitioners in the USA alone, scuba diving is one of the world's fastest growing sports, and divers are among those campaigning against the depletion of the reef ecosystem by overfishing and marine pollution. A number of resorts provide facilities for divers, but the best sites tend to be in areas which can only be accessed by 'live-aboards', boats specially designed and chartered for diving expeditions.
- **Ecotourism** Columbus was the first European visitor to describe the Caribbean islands, with their profusion of colourful plant and bird life, as a 'paradise on earth'. Although the original forest cover has long since disappeared on most of the low islands, the Greater Antilles and volcanic Windward Islands retain much to attract nature lovers.
- **Cultural and heritage tourism** Most Caribbean islands can offer an interesting colonial heritage and a vibrant contemporary culture, expressed particularly in music and dance (most 'Latin' rhythms are in fact Caribbean in origin), and to a lesser extent in the visual arts. The colourful Carnivals staged by many islanders,

and other event attractions – such as *Reggae Sunsplash* in Jamaica, *Junkanoo* in the Bahamas, *Cropover* in Barbados, and *'Pirates Week'* in the Cayman Islands – are showcases of national identity, giving tourists the opportunity to interact with the host community.

Tourism resources

We will now look in more detail at the resources for tourism offered by some of the islands, starting with the English-speaking countries of the Commonwealth Caribbean.

The Bahamas

Of the 700 islands that make up the Bahamas, only 14 are inhabited. Poor soils and a lack of surface water mean that only 5 per cent of the land is suitable for agriculture, forcing the islanders to find alternative sources of income. Nassau became fashionable as a winter destination for wealthy Americans in the late nineteenth century, but it was not until the 1960s, in the aftermath of the Cuban Revolution, that mass tourism developed. Proximity to Miami has ensured that the Bahamas are the most popular ports of call for cruise ships, including a number of private islands, where passengers are free of the unwelcome attentions of the beach vendors and hustlers prevalent in many Caribbean resorts. Most of the hotels and other facilities are concentrated on two islands:

- **New Providence** contains the capital Nassau, and the resort areas of Paradise Island – which boasts casinos and the Atlantis Hotel and leisure complex among its attractions – and Cable Beach, lined with expensive hotels.
- **Grand Bahama** offers two purpose-built resorts – Freeport and Lucaya – based on golf, duty-free shopping and gambling.

In contrast, the 'Family' or 'Out Islands' are less developed, but provide for a range of outdoor activities and low impact ecotourism. Abaco has a long-established boat-building industry and is a yachting centre; Eleuthera and Bimini are noted for game fishing, while the exceptionally clear waters around Andros are ideal for scuba diving.

The Turks and Caicos Islands

These islands to the south of the Bahamas are flat and rather arid, but upmarket tourism has developed on Providenciales, which offers fine beaches and world class diving, and is easily accessible from the USA.

Bermuda

We feel justified in including Bermuda as part of the Caribbean in view of the cultural and physical similarities. Nevertheless you should be aware that this small British colony is situated in the North Atlantic, much closer to North Carolina than to the Bahamas.

A group of interlinked coral islands, Bermuda offers world-class beaches of pink sand, facilities for sailing and diving, as well as golf, cycling and riding among its attractions. Bermuda was originally developed as a winter resort for wealthy

Americans from New York and Boston, but since beach tourism became fashionable summer has been the preferred season. The islands have retained their exclusive appeal, primarily by careful resource management. For example:

- hotel capacity is limited to 10 000 bedspaces
- cruise arrivals are restricted, to protect the hotel sector from competition and Hamilton's shopping and port facilities from congestion
- the environment is safeguarded by a ban on rental cars and roadside advertising.

To reduce its dependence on beach tourism Bermuda is also promoting its naval heritage and music festival scene.

Jamaica

Jamaica, located in the centre of the Caribbean, is the largest of the English-speaking islands, with a more diversified economy and a higher international profile than most countries in the region. Elite tourism was well established before the Second World War, with writers such as Ian Fleming taking up residence near Port Antonio. However, large-scale development did not take place until the 1960s. Jamaica's image has since been damaged by internal political strife and drug-related crime. The government has countered the effect of negative publicity with infrastructural improvements, event attractions and currency devaluation to attract foreign visitors, while domestic tourism has also been encouraged. Outside Kingston, which is a major business centre for the Caribbean, most of the hotel development is concentrated along the north coast, at Montego Bay, Ocho Rios – a major port of call for cruise ships – and Negril. Here the fine beaches are backed by forest-covered mountains, the best known attractions being Dunns River Falls near Ocho Rios and rafting on the Rio Grande near Port Antonio. Jamaica can offer excellent sports facilities, particularly at Negril, which was developed in the 1970s to cater for the younger, more active type of holidaymaker. Much of the accommodation is in all-inclusives, but most of these are Jamaican-owned. Market segmentation is evident, with different hotels catering for young singles seeking a hedonistic lifestyle, couples and families with young children. Jamaica can also offer the following alternatives to beach tourism:

- ecotourism in the Blue Mountains and the karst limestone Cockpit Country based on small resorts such as Discovery Bay and Mandeville
- the colonial heritage, including the great houses built by wealthy plantation owners, the old pirate stronghold of Port Royal in Kingston harbour and the Seville Heritage Park
- contemporary West Indian culture, particularly the musical legacy of Bob Marley.

The Cayman Islands

These small islands lying to the west of Jamaica are the best known of a number of Caribbean territories that provide offshore financial services to the international business community. Grand Cayman is also a developed upmarket holiday destination, while the islands offer world class diving, including the 'drop-off' known as Bloody Bay Wall off Little Cayman.

The Leeward Islands and the Windward Islands

The islands of the eastern Caribbean fall into two major groups:

- the Leeward Islands, clustering around Antigua
- the Windward Islands to the south, forming a chain from Dominica to Grenada.

The two groups share a common currency – the East Caribbean dollar – and belong to the Organization of Eastern Caribbean States (OECS).

Antigua is the most developed of the Leeward Islands, with an international airport handling direct flights from London and North America, as well as a network of regional services. Most of the island is low-lying and suffers from chronic water shortages, and has few natural attractions other than a coastline indented with coves and harbours, and boasting many fine beaches. Tourism dominates the economy of this small island-nation and, with tourist arrivals greatly outnumbering the resident population, has been a mixed blessing. For example:

- most jobs in tourism are low status, with managerial posts usually filled by expatriates;
- Antiguans have been criticized for their attitude to service work
- Antiguan popular culture has been stereotyped to meet tourist expectations
- the island's ecosystems have been damaged by beachfront development.

Antigua offers a major heritage attraction in English Harbour, an attractive yachting centre where Nelson's Dockyard is a reminder of the island's former importance to the British navy.

The other Leeward Islands can offer a greater variety of scenery than Antigua, and have not embraced mass tourism to the same extent, retaining a mix of small hotels, inns and guest houses. **Anguilla**, with its pink and white sand beaches, **Nevis** and **Montserrat** are small-scale upmarket destinations reflecting a more traditional Caribbean lifestyle. **St Kitts** in its Frigate Bay development has sought the middle-income market, particularly from Canada, and the island is a venue for a number of cultural events such as music festivals.

St Lucia is the most developed of the Windward Islands, and for many visitors it represents the ideal holiday destination. Fine beaches of coral sand, as at Marigot Bay, contrast with the mountainous interior. The twin peaks of volcanic origin known as the Pitons must rank among the most spectacular attractions of the Caribbean and provide St Lucia with a unique selling point (USP) which few other islands can offer. However the international airport is inconveniently located at the southern tip of the island in relation to the capital Castries. Tourism developed rapidly during the 1990s and most of the resort hotels are now all-inclusives.

Dominica was a latecomer to tourism, with its lack of beaches, rainy climate and relative inaccessibility. The island has set out to attract nature-loving tourists to its mountainous interior, which offers pristine rainforest, waterfalls, sulphur springs and a 'boiling lake' of volcanic origin. Accommodation is in small hotels and guest houses that are locally owned and managed, with strong linkages to the island's farms and craft industries. However tourism growth in the 1990s – including a tenfold increase in cruise passenger arrivals – has put the more accessible sites under severe pressure. Some would agree that cruise tourism on this scale is incompatible with ecotourism, and that Dominica's unique appeal as the 'nature island of the Caribbean' is at risk.

Ecotourism and adventure tourism have also been promoted by the governments of **St Vincent** and Grenada, on the basis of similar resources. **Grenada**, known as the 'Spice Island of the Caribbean', does have the attraction of white sand beaches, coral reefs and the fine harbour of St Georges, which is a major yachting centre. The chain of small coral islands known as the Grenadines are well developed for tourism, with a number of small resorts catering for divers and yachtsmen, while **Mustique** is famous as a hideaway for celebrities.

Barbados

Barbados is the easternmost of the Caribbean islands, with a long-established tourism industry. This is one of the few destinations in the region where British visitors outnumber those of North American origin, and the legacy of over three centuries of uninterrupted British rule is evident. The appeal of Barbados lies in its countryside – 'the garden of the West Indies', its sporting attractions, notably cricket, and the superb beaches. Most of the resort development is on the west coast near the capital Bridgetown, where land prices are among the highest in the world, fuelled by the influx of 'new money'. The rugged east coast, exposed to the Atlantic surf, is protected from development. Tourism has to compete with other land uses in this small, densely populated island. To meet the challenge, the government has an effective coastal zone management plan to prevent beach erosion, and is reducing the country's dependence on fossil fuels by encouraging solar energy use. The tourist authorities have tried to maintain the exclusive appeal of Barbados while at the same time encouraging middle-income holidaymakers on air-inclusive charters.

Trinidad and Tobago

The large island of Trinidad lies outside the hurricane belt close to the mainland of South America. It has a fairly developed economy based on petroleum, and a vibrant culture in which Asian as well as African and European influences are evident. The capital, Port of Spain, is an important regional gateway and business centre. The collapse of oil prices in the 1990s has induced the government to place more emphasis on tourism. Trinidad is famed for its steel bands, calypso singers and limbo dancers, and its Carnival must rank as one of the most spectacular event attractions in the Caribbean. The island also boasts a geological curiosity – Pitch Lake – and the Caroni Swamp with its wildlife resources. The much smaller island of Tobago offers a more relaxed lifestyle than Trinidad and an environment that is better suited to beach tourism and water sports.

The Virgin Islands

This cluster of islands is divided between Britain and the USA. The **US Virgin Islands** have the advantage of free access to sources of investment in the USA, and in the case of St Thomas, frequent air and shipping services from the US mainland. The port of Charlotte Amalie is thronged with American cruise passengers seeking duty-free shopping bargains. St John's marine resources have been given National Park status. The **British Virgin Islands** (BVI) are much less developed in terms of hotel capacity, and although Tortola and Virgin Gorda are on the cruise circuit they receive far fewer visitors than St Thomas. The sheltered waters between the islands provide an ideal environment for flotilla sailing.

The French Antilles

The former French colonies of Martinique and Guadeloupe have opted for closer association with France, as overseas *départements*, instead of independence. This has advantages in guaranteeing a higher standard of living than their Commonwealth

Caribbean neighbours, and frequent flights to and from Paris. The influence of French culture is apparent in the cuisine and architecture, and the islands cater mainly for French holidaymakers. Of the two main islands, **Martinique** is scenically the more attractive, with its volcanic peaks and lush vegetation, and Fort de France is one of the most sophisticated cities in the Caribbean. **Guadeloupe** is less popular as a destination, despite the fine beaches along its eastern coast. The outlying island of St Barts (St Barthelémy) has become a 'jet-set' resort.

The Netherlands Antilles (NA) and Aruba

Six Caribbean islands are associated with the Netherlands and are regarded by the World Tourism Organization as separate destinations:

- Saba, St Eustatius and St Maarten are situated among the Leeward Islands. Of these St Maarten (St Martin) is by far the most developed, and it is a major port of call for cruise ships. Part of the appeal lies in the fact that this small island is divided between the Netherlands and France, so that the visitor has the choice of shopping in Philipsburg or Marigot (on the French side).
- The southern group, known as the 'ABC Islands' (Aruba, Bonaire and Curaçao), lie close to the South American mainland and speak a language – Papamiento – which is a mixture of Dutch and Spanish. Their arid landscapes also mark them out from other Caribbean islands. The main attraction to tourists lies in the excellent beaches, facilities for water sports and duty-free shopping. Aruba has set out to attract the mass market in the USA with casinos and non-stop entertainment, whereas Bonaire is mainly known for its diving resources. Curaçao's capital – Willemstad – offers picturesque canals and Dutch-style buildings, and this island appeals to visitors from Europe and South America as well as the USA.

Hispaniola and Puerto Rico

The Dominican Republic and Puerto Rico – along with Cuba – share a heritage from the time of the Spanish Empire in the Americas. During the twentieth century they followed very different political paths, and this has affected the type of tourism that has developed.

Puerto Rico, not yet a state, although a former US territory, is associated with the USA as a self-governing commonwealth. With the advantage of ready access to markets and sources of finance in the USA, a large manufacturing and service sector has developed in an island that, prior to 1950, was one of the poorest in the Caribbean. The capital San Juan is a major business centre and one of the main gateways to the Caribbean. With a number of beaches within easy reach, it is also an important holiday destination with hotel accommodation geared to a clientele that is 80 per cent North American. Another major source of visitors is the large number of Puerto Ricans resident on the US mainland, but these usually fall into the VFR category. Puerto Rico's major attractions include:

- Old San Juan, the fortified colonial city, showcasing the Spanish heritage
- El Yunque National Park, an area of rainforest in the eastern highlands
- cultural events such as the Pablo Casals music festival.

The large island of **Hispaniola** is divided on cultural as well as political lines between the Spanish-speaking Dominican Republic and French Creole-speaking Haiti, where African influences are predominant. Between 1980 and 1995 the fledgling tourism industry of the two countries took a very different course; the Dominican

Republic experienced a phenomenal rate of tourism growth, to become the most popular holiday destination in the Caribbean, while arrivals in Haiti declined considerably during the same period.

The **Dominican Republic** has been much more successful in attracting foreign investment in a bid to become a low-cost beach destination catering primarily for West Europeans. The country is served by a large number of charter airlines, with international airports at Puerto Plata, Punta Cana and Santo Domingo. Development is mainly in tourist enclaves on the 'Amber Coast' in the north and in the south-east, with all-inclusives dominating the accommodation sector. However tourism growth has tended to outstrip the provision of adequate infrastructure, and the country's vulnerability to the mass market was shown in 1997, when British tour operators dropped it from their programmes following a health scare. The Dominican Republic's cultural attractions are largely overlooked by most tourists, apart from an introduction to sensual *merengue* rhythms, but the country has much to offer besides fine beaches, golf and water sports. The Ministry of Tourism stresses the key role of the capital, Santo Domingo, in the Spanish conquest of the Americas; the city boasts the first cathedral in the New World and other early sixteenth-century buildings. This was given further emphasis in 1992, with the inauguration of the controversial Faro a Colón (Columbus Lighthouse) commemorating the great explorer's achievement. The interior offers scope for adventure tourism with a landscape that includes the highest mountain in the Caribbean, rainforest and desert. Although there are ten national parks, conservation measures are largely ineffective, and there is a shortage of quality accommodation away from the coastal resorts.

Haiti has suffered more than other Caribbean destinations from misgovernment, political instability and negative publicity – including an AIDS scare in the early 1980s and an ongoing reputation as the poorest country in the Western Hemisphere. Haitian emigrants provide much of the labour for tourism developments in the English speaking Caribbean, and this has led to social problems, as in the Turks and Caicos Islands. Population pressures have resulted in ecological disaster, and only 2 per cent of the original forest cover now remains. All this has tended to overshadow the fact that Haiti was the first country in the region to win independence from colonial rule, and the skills of its people in painting and handicrafts. The rituals of voodoo – an alternative African religion – also attract the more intrepid type of tourist. However hotel accommodation is in short supply outside the capital Port-au-Prince and Cap Haitien in the north. The latter is visited for the remarkable citadel built by Henri Cristophe, one of the leaders in the war of independence against the French. Cruise ships on the eastern Caribbean circuit tend to use the private island of Labadee, with its fine beaches, in preference to calling at Port-au-Prince or Cap Haitien – yet another example of 'enclave tourism'.

Cuba

Cuba, with the only centrally planned economy in the Western Hemisphere, is a unique destination and merits special attention. Separated from the USA by only the 150 kilometre wide Florida Strait, this large island is far more than a beach destination and can appeal to a wider range of markets than most Caribbean countries. It has a vibrant Spanish and African cultural heritage, and Cuban dance rhythms – notably salsa – have done much to promote the country's image in Europe. The on-going United States blockade has resulted in a '1950s time-warp' with American cars of that era still in use on the streets of Havana. At the same time Cuba has a high reputation for health care, and this attracts visitors seeking medical treatment.

Tourism has gone through the following phases, in response to political changes:

- **'Elite tourism'**   From 1902 until 1959 Cuba's economy was controlled by United States interests. Tourism was concentrated, as it is today, in Havana and the beach resort of Varadero, which largely developed in the 1920s with American capital. Havana was renowned for its uninhibited nightlife and casinos, catering for a wealthy and predominantly American clientèle. In the 1950s Cuba was the leading destination of the Caribbean.
- **'Socialist tourism'**   Following Fidel Castro's revolution in 1959, Cuba lost 80 per cent of its international tourist market as a result of the trade and travel embargo imposed by the United States government. Castro turned to the USSR for economic aid, and tourism subsequently followed a similar pattern to the countries of Eastern Europe, with the state ownership of hotels, an emphasis on social tourism for the domestic market including Young Pioneer Camps, and cultural exchanges with other members of the Eastern bloc. Visitors from Western countries were largely restricted to group tours, organized by specialist tour operators who were broadly in sympathy with the regime and its achievements in education and health care.
- **Incipient mass tourism**   During the 1980s the government modified its attitude to international tourism. Joint ventures between Cubanacán, the state-owned tour operator, and foreign companies, such as the Spanish Meliá group, were encouraged, with the aim of expanding and modernizing the hotel sector. Cuba became popular as a low-cost winter-sun destination for Canadians. With the collapse of the Soviet Union, Cuba was deprived of cheap oil imports and a guaranteed market for its sugar, so that tourism was increasingly seen as a lifeline for the economy. Cuba is now offered as a package holiday destination by the leading tour operators of Western Europe, and the US dollar has become the only acceptable currency for most transactions involving tourists. Small business enterprises are allowed to participate in the tourism sector, such as the *paladares* (restaurants in private homes).

Tourist arrivals grew from 30 000 in the late 1970s to approach 2 million in the early years of the twenty-first century. Around half come from Europe, whilst North America accounts for a much smaller percentage of tourists, mainly Canadians – although a surprising number of US citizens find ways of getting round the embargo. Foreign visitors are mainly concentrated in tourist enclaves such as Varadero – located on a sandpit with restricted access and which has its own international airport – and Cayo Largo, a beach resort that has been developed on a small offshore island. Tourism receipts now exceed those from sugar exports, but the net gain to the economy is much less, due to the need to import materials that Cuban industry and agriculture cannot provide, and the repatriation of profits by foreign investors. Tourism developers also have to cope with a deteriorating infrastructure – including power cuts, poor roads and inadequate public transport – and an inefficient bureaucracy. On the other hand, Cuba has one of the best educated workforces in Latin America.

Cuba's resource base includes extensive sandy beaches, coral islands for scuba diving and picturesque mountain scenery. The best known scenic area is the Sierra Maestra in the south-east of the island. The province of Pinar del Rio is closer to Havana and, as the main tobacco-growing area, supplies Cuba's most famous export. Heritage attractions include the colonial cities of Trinidad and Santiago de Cuba.

The latter is almost 1000 kilometres from Havana, and is best reached by air rather than the unreliable rail service.

Havana can offer performing arts, museums, galleries and other cultural attractions comparable with those of Europe, and is arguably the most sophisticated city in the Caribbean region. Old Havana boasts some of the finest colonial architecture in the Americas, and as a World Heritage Site is undergoing extensive restoration. One of Havana's biggest attractions is the Tropicana floorshow, a relic of pre Revolution Cuba that has been revived primarily for tourists.

The future of tourism in Cuba depends on improved relations with the USA and a peaceful transition to a more liberal regime. An intensification of the US embargo, by extending it to third parties – as threatened by the Helms–Burton Act – could discourage foreign investment. Even controlled Western-style tourism could undermine socialist principles, by creating divisions in Cuban society between those with access to dollars – in effect those in direct contact with tourists – and the 95 per cent of the population who are paid entirely in almost worthless Cuban pesos. Sex tourism, which was rife in pre-1959 Havana, and prohibited after the Revolution, is once more on the increase as a consequence. Closer contact with Western tourists can only add to the demand for greater freedom for Cubans.

Mexico

The heartland of Mexico is a high plateau – the Meseta Central – separated by the mountain barriers of the Sierra Madre from the tropical coastlands to the east and west. To the north are semi-desert landscapes similar to those of the south-western USA, whereas central and southern Mexico, along with the countries of Central America, forms part of the much more diverse region known to anthropologists as Meso-America. Here differences in altitude result in three major climate zones, namely:

- the *tierra caliente* or tropical zone up to 1000 metres
- the *tierra templada* or sub-tropical zone between 1000 and 2000 metres where warm climate crops such as coffee and avocados are cultivated; most of the health resorts favoured by better-off Mexicans are located in this zone
- the *tierra fria* or 'cold' zone above 2000 metres, where nights are chilly, especially during the dry season, although daytime temperatures are generally warm throughout the year; some of the largest cities, including Mexico City, are located in this zone.

Mexico is the second largest economy in Latin America and the world's most populous Spanish-speaking country. Unlike most countries in the region it has experienced political stability since the 1920s, after one of the few revolutions to bring about lasting social and economic change. The Revolutionary party (PRI) had a near monopoly of political power until the Presidential elections in 2000, when the more conservative Nationalist party (PAN) won control. The nationalist and socialist aspirations of the Mexican Revolution remain largely unfulfilled, in part due to Mexico's situation in the economic shadow of the USA. Moreover Mexico's impressive economic development scarcely keeps pace with rapid population growth, and there are regional disparities in wealth distribution. This has caused a massive flow of emigration – much of it illegal – to the USA, where the economic opportunities are so much greater. Mexico's membership of NAFTA has opened up the economy to foreign investment, and stimulated business travel to and from the United States and Canada.

Mexico's appeal to North Americans is partly based on its beaches and sunny winter climate, but the cultural contrasts which the country offers to the USA are equally important. Although the majority of Mexicans are *mestizos* (of mixed Spanish and Amerindian origins), the Indian heritage, as expressed in cuisine, folklore and handicrafts, is regarded as central to the national identity. There is a contradiction here, as the majority of present-day Indians are socially and geographically marginalized in the poorer southern states. The most significant features of this rich cultural heritage are:

- The impressive remains of advanced Indian civilizations which flourished in Mexico before the Spanish conquest. The best known of these are Teotihuacán and Tula in central Mexico, and the cities of the Mayas in Yucatán and Chiapas in the south. These form part of the Ruta Maya tourist circuit, which also takes in neighbouring Belize, Honduras and Guatemala.
- The legacy of the Spanish colonial period, particularly the numerous Baroque churches, and picturesque towns such as Quéretaro, Morelia, San Miguel Allende and Guanajuato in central Mexico. These are associated with the Mexican struggle for independence, and have been meticulously preserved. Most of the colonial *haciendas* (country estates) on the other hand were destroyed during the Mexican Revolution (1910–1920). Other legacies of Spanish rule, such as the bullfight and the fiestas of the Catholic Church, continue to flourish in the popular culture.
- The artistic legacy of the Mexican Revolution, as expressed by painters such as Frida Kahlo (now a feminist icon), Diego Rivera and many others noted for their mural paintings celebrating Mexican folk traditions and the pre-conquest civilizations.

Tourism demand and supply

Mexico is one of the world's leading travel destinations, attracting around 20 million foreign tourists in the early years of the twenty-first century, with tourism supporting 1.7 million jobs and contributing over 8 per cent of GDP. However the tourism industry is highly dependent on the United States and Canadian markets; less than 5 per cent of visitors originate from other countries, and this leaves it vulnerable to 'shocks' to tourism demand such as 9/11.

While traditional Mexico provides the tourist image, modern Mexico – particularly the wealthier northern states – has adopted many aspects of the lifestyle of the USA. A substantial middle class generates a considerable demand for domestic tourism and for international travel – despite a number of economic crises that have resulted in the devaluation of the peso against foreign currencies. The majority of Mexicans do not have sufficient disposable income to take holiday trips. There is some development of social tourism, including holiday villages for industrial workers such as those employed by PEMEX, the state-owned petroleum corporation.

In an attempt to improve the economic situation the federal government has given tourism a prominent role in national planning since the 1950s. Foreign developers are encouraged to participate in large hotel projects that will stimulate job creation, especially in the less developed regions. There is a strong Ministry of Tourism (SECTUR) that is responsible for policy-making. The federal government has also taken a direct role in tourism development through the FUNATUR funding agency. This has been responsible for a number of comprehensively planned resorts such as Ixtapa on the Pacific coast and Cancún.

As in most Latin American countries, domestic air services and long distance bus travel are more important than rail transport. The major cities are linked by modern highways to the USA, but east–west communications are less adequate. Water supplies and sanitation are defective in many rural areas, falling far short of those considered acceptable in the United States.

Tourism resources

Mexico can offer a great variety of colourful traditions – showcased by the Ballet Folklórico in the capital – as well as contrasting landscapes. We can divide the country into the following tourist regions.

The north and west

The northern part of Mexico contains large areas of desert, similar to those across the US border in Arizona. The most visited tourist centres are the towns along the border, particularly Tijuana. Spending by United States visitors in these border towns has accounted for over half of Mexico's receipts from tourism; such visitors are however cost-conscious and numbers vary according to the strength of the dollar against the peso. Also liberal attitudes to gambling and sex tourism are a less important motivator for young Americans now that such attractions are widely available nearer home. Monterey is the major city of northern Mexico, rivalling the capital as a business centre.

The **peninsula of 'Baja'** (Lower California) in the north-west is largely desert, but the beaches and game fishing attract large numbers of Californians from north of the border, thanks to an excellent highway running the length of the peninsula. Ensenada and La Paz have become major tourist centres, while the federal government has developed purpose-built resorts at Loreto and Los Cabos.

The **'Mexican Riviera'** further south has a tropical climate with a long dry season corresponding to winter in the USA. This has made this stretch of Pacific coast popular with North Americans as a winter-sun destination and retirement area. Acapulco is the most important centre, with good air and road communications to Mexico City. The historic seaport is now overshadowed by a vast agglomeration of hotels and condominiums surrounding the famous bay. Other resorts have developed from fishing ports, such as Puerto Vallarta and Mazatlán.

The Gulf coast of Mexico, with its more humid climate, is less popular as a holiday area, but offers the historic port of Veracruz among its many cultural attractions.

Central Mexico

The area richest in cultural attractions is the southern part of the Meseta Central, which is dominated by volcanoes such as Popocatepetl. These include the archaeological sites and colonial cities mentioned earlier, and many others such as Puebla, noted for fine ceramics, and Taxco, which grew rich on its silver mining industry. All of these are easily reached from the capital.

- **Mexico City** is the world's fastest-growing metropolis with 22 million inhabitants at the dawn of the new millennium, although this growth has been accompanied by severe air pollution and acute traffic congestion. Whilst few traces remain of the Aztec city of Tenochtitlán, the central square or Zócalo, with the cathedral and Presidential Palace, occupies the site of its most important temples. The capital's attractions include:

○ the National Museum of Anthropology, celebrating the achievements of the Aztecs and other Indian civilizations
○ the Basilica of Guadalupe, one of the world's most visited shrines
○ the floating gardens of Xochimilco, popular for Sunday excursions; this is all that remains of the lake that once surrounded the former Aztec city, but the attraction is increasingly threatened by a lowering of the water table.

Southern Mexico and Yucatán

Southern Mexico, particularly the states of Chiapas and Oaxaca, is also noted for its Indian heritage. Along with the Yucatán Peninsula, this region forms part of the area covered by the *Mundo Maya* (World of the Maya) tourism development plan, which also embraces four Central American countries – Belize, El Salvador, Guatemala and Honduras. This is an example of regional cooperation between governments, tour operators and the local communities, with the aim of achieving sustainable development. There are also plans for an 'ecological corridor' giving more adequate protection to the rich biodiversity of southern Mexico and Central America.

Tourism is mainly focused on the fine beaches of the Yucatán Peninsula facing the Caribbean. The interior of Yucatán is a low limestone plateau dotted with *cenotes* (sinkholes) that have yielded much archaeological evidence of the ancient Maya civilization. The region was isolated from the rest of Mexico until the 1970s, when the federal government improved the infrastructure and developed facilities, notably at Cancún. This part of Mexico can be included in the western Caribbean cruise circuit and also has the advantage of greater proximity by air to Miami and the cities of the eastern USA. Cancún is a good example of 'enclave tourism', a self-contained 'mega-resort' where holidaymakers and conference delegates have little contact with the indigenous Maya population. South of Cancún, development is taking place along the so-called Mayan Riviera, but on a smaller scale and with more respect for traditional values. The hinterland, with its impressive Mayan cities of Uxmal and Chichen Itza, is of more interest for cultural tourists.

Central America

Central America is the mountainous neck of land linking the continents of North and South America. The region is prone to natural disasters such as earthquakes, volcanic eruptions and hurricanes, and also has a reputation for political instability. It consists of three main physical divisions:

• the coastal lowlands along the Caribbean, often densely forested, and sparsely inhabited by ethnic minorities, including some English-speaking communities
• the central volcanic highlands, that contain the majority of the population and much of the cultural heritage
• the Pacific coast, which has better beaches and a drier climate than the Caribbean lowlands.

Central America consists of six Spanish-speaking republics and English-speaking Belize, which is culturally and economically part of the Commonwealth Caribbean. Few air services link the region directly to Europe, and the majority of tourists – other than those from neighbouring countries – come from the United States. Most of these use air transport, especially from Miami, rather than the Pan-American highway system. Much of the region – notably Guatemala, El Salvador and Nicaragua – has only recently recovered from a long period of violent political strife, and this has held back the development of tourism. During the 1990s Central America experienced a higher growth rate in tourist arrivals than either the Caribbean or South America, but from a very low base. Costa Rica and Belize have concentrated on the development of ecotourism while in Guatemala cultural tourism is dominant, but other countries in the region have been arguably less successful in defining their tourism product. In most of these countries the capital city is not a major destination in itself, except for business travellers.

Tourism resources

Guatemala
There is a legacy of ethnic division between the *Ladinos* (Spanish-speakers), who are the dominant group, and the Amerindian majority, who still live in traditional communities where the value systems are quite different. Guatemala has great scenic and cultural diversity for such a small country, and this is its strength as a tourist destination. Attractions include:

- The colonial heritage, based mainly on Antigua, the former capital, which has become an important centre for Spanish-language tuition.
- Traditional culture – each Amerindian community has its own distinctive costume, which makes their markets exceptionally colourful, the best-known example being that of Chichicastenango in the northern highlands; also, ancient Mayan beliefs coexist with the Catholicism introduced by the Spanish.
- The volcanic mountain scenery around Lake Atitlán.
- The Tikal National Park in the Petén rainforest, protecting one of the most important Maya sites in Central America. This city, with its stepped pyramid-temples and ceremonial plazas was abandoned to the jungle centuries before the Spanish conquest, and was only rediscovered in the nineteenth century.

Belize
Belize can also claim large tracts of pristine forest, important Mayan sites and the world's second largest barrier reef. The policy of the government is to encourage 'community-based ecotourism' but also to use it as a means of earning foreign exchange to finance economic development. In other words, Belize is an excellent example of how a country can use the notion of sustainability to promote the development of new types of tourism (Mowforth and Munt, 1998). Much of the tourism industry is owned by expatriates, mostly US citizens, and although some reefs have been designated as marine reserves, others are likely to develop as exclusive resorts.

El Salvador
The country has few ecological resources, as it is the most densely populated in Latin America, and one of the most developed, with a large industrial sector. Its spas

and beach resorts cater mainly for the domestic market and the large number of Salvadorean emigrants in the USA. El Salvador has been at the forefront in attempts at regional economic cooperation, including Grupo TACA – a consortium of five national airlines.

Honduras

Honduras is better known for the banana plantations around San Pedro Sula than for tourism. The interior is rugged mountain country, making air transport almost essential. The country is one of the poorest in Latin America and its plans for economic development were dealt a heavy blow by Hurricane 'Mitch' in 1998. The Bay Islands offer diving facilities, while Copán is an important Maya site.

Nicaragua

The international spotlight fell on Nicaragua in the 1980s, when the USA sought to bring down the left-wing Sandinista regime through economic sanctions and support for the 'Contra' rebels. The present government has given generous tax breaks to foreign investors, and the country is becoming a retirement haven for US citizens, following the examples of Costa Rica and Honduras. Nicaragua's attractions include:

- the spectacular scenery of Lake Nicaragua, studded with volcanic islands
- the cities of Granada and León with their fine colonial heritage.

There is some small-scale development of beach tourism along the Pacific coast, catering mainly to middle class visitors from other parts of Central America.

Costa Rica

Costa Rica has a well-developed infrastructure and accommodation sector, and unlike other countries in the region has a long-established reputation for democracy and political stability. This small country is the meeting-point of North American and South American eco-systems, and is exceptionally rich in species of orchids, birds and butterflies.

Since the 1960s the government has developed a system of national parks that cover about a quarter of the country, protecting its most precious natural asset – its forests. Despite serious under-funding, this is the resource base for a tourism industry that relies heavily on the country's biodiversity and its scenic attractions.

The accommodation sector is for the most part locally owned, and on a small scale, even in the capital San José. It caters to a large extent for the backpacker market. San José also attracts 'health tourists' from the USA – mainly from older age groups – with its low cost medical services. There is also some beach tourism around the Gulf of Nicoya. However the development of golf courses in this area has been criticized by environmentalists as being incompatible with Costa Rica's image as destination for ecotourism and 'soft adventure'. The problem is that the government, like so many others throughout Latin America, needs a higher yield type of tourism to service the country's large foreign debt. The growth of cruise tourism to the Pacific port of Puntarenas is also likely to have an impact on some of the country's more accessible national parks.

Panama

The country owes much of its importance as a tourist destination to the famous Canal, which passed from United States to Panamanian control at the end of 1999, along with the surrounding territory known as the Canal Zone. Some 40 to 50 ships pass through the Canal each day. The locks at Gatún, where the Canal crosses the Continental Divide, must count as one of the world's major feats of engineering. The city of Panama, with its mixture of high-rise modern buildings and Asian bazaars, is a major centre of international commerce, encouraged by the country's liberal banking laws and use of the dollar as the national currency. The free port of Colón, at the western (Caribbean) end of the Canal is another important trading centre. However Panama has yet to realize its full potential as 'the crossroads of the Americas', due to the jungles of Darien only 200 kilometres to the east. These pose a formidable barrier to the completion of the Pan-American highway system and any projected route must respect the land claims of the local Amerindian tribes.

Panama's holiday attractions mainly lie in the offshore islands. Of these the Pearl Islands have received the most attention from tour operators. The most important of these – Contadora – is a luxury resort and conference venue. The San Blas Islands are noted for game fishing, but here the local Kuna Indians have kept development at arm's length – tourism has to be on their terms.

It is likely that the former Canal Zone will be developed to yield maximum revenue, with marinas, hotels and timeshare apartments. The Canal itself is too restricted for the largest cruise ships, and a third set of locks will be needed to increase capacity – but this could have an adverse environmental impact, affecting water supplies to the city of Panama. In contrast ecotourism is being encouraged in other parts of the country, along with projects to restore the old Spanish seaport of Portobelo – a reminder that the isthmus was an important transit corridor for trade centuries before the opening of the Canal.

South America

South America receives around 2.5 per cent of the world's international tourist arrivals. The high cost of air fares and the lack of charter flights partly explains why this continent remains a destination for the wealthy or adventurous traveller. There is also a shortage of suitable hotels for the inclusive-tour market. Long-term planning and investment in the tourism industry have been discouraged by political instability and inflation.

Climatic conditions, dense vegetation and rugged terrain have been a great obstacle to road and railway construction in many areas. In the west, the Andes – the world's longest mountain range, and second only to the Himalayas in altitude – pose a formidable barrier. Most of South America lies within the tropics, and the continent includes the world's largest rainforest in the Amazon Basin. Water transport is still widely used wherever there are navigable rivers – such as the Amazon and the Paraná – but the shipping services are usually slow and uncomfortable. Transport infrastructure is gradually improving with the expansion of the Pan-American highway network and the development of internal air services. Rail systems in South America tend to be rudimentary, but some of the world's most spectacular lines are to be found in the Andes, and these have become tourist attractions in their own right.

A number of countries in South America are undergoing rapid industrialization, with a resulting increase in business travel from Europe and the USA. As regards the holiday market, national tourist offices in South American countries are generally underfunded, so that overseas promotion has been left to the national airlines or to specialist tour operators in the tourist-generating countries. Closer international cooperation, as among the Andean Pact countries and those belonging to MERCOSUR, should facilitate travel within the region and bring about more effective tourism promotion.

Brazil

Brazil occupies almost half of South America and is a leading member of MERCOSUR. Unlike most Latin American countries, Brazil has a well-defined image, based on its beaches, the Rio de Janeiro carnival and the Amazon rainforest. The country is comparable in size to the USA – spanning three time zones – and is the world's fifth most populous country, with 175 million inhabitants, mainly concentrated along the Atlantic seaboard. Brazilians are essentially the result of a fusion of three cultures – Portuguese, African and Amerindian. Since the nineteenth century the country has also attracted many millions of immigrants from all over the world, but it has arguably been more successful than the USA in blending different races and cultures.

Brazil's market potential for tourism is closely linked to the development of the economy, now the largest in Latin America. Growth was particularly rapid during the 1990s as a result of currency reform and privatization initiatives, but was checked by the near collapse of the economy in 2000. It remains to be seen whether the 'boom and bust' cycle, so evident in the past, can be solved. Most of the country's industrial wealth is concentrated in the Rio de Janeiro–São Paulo–Belo Horizonte triangle, while other regions, notably the north-east, remain poor and underdeveloped.

Demand for tourism

The near collapse of the economy in 2000 made Brazil a cheap country to visit and inbound arrivals increased to 4.8 million. Brazil received more visitors from European countries than from the United States. Business travel is strong and inbound arrivals are seasonal, with January and February seeing the greatest tourist activity coinciding with the carnival season – which also happens to be the hottest and most humid time of the year in most of Brazil.

The economic circumstances of the country in the early years of the twenty-first century kept many Brazilians at home, boosting domestic travel to 45 million trips. Under the country's labour laws employees are guaranteed a 48-hour week and an annual paid holiday of 20 days, but many are excluded from becoming tourists by low incomes, especially in the rural areas. However recreational facilities are provided by the state governments in city areas, while the beaches are freely available to rich and poor alike. Domestic tourists tend to use small hotels and campgrounds, or stay with friends and relatives. Currently internal travel is very road-based (the majority of tourism trips) due to the high cost of air transport. However, this may change as a result of competition between the airlines and domestic tour operators. Brazilians are far more interested in beach holidays than in trips to the Amazon, as the beach occupies a central place in the nation's hedonistic lifestyle. Television through the popular *tele-novelas* (soap operas) plays an important role in opening up new coastal areas for the domestic market. Brazil's economic situation since 2000 has meant that overseas travel is expensive and the market reduced significantly in 2001 to 2.6 million trips, leading to the collapse of Brazil's major travel agency company in 2001.

Supply of tourism

The vast size of Brazil poses a major problem for overland transport, especially during the rainy season from December to May. The Amazon and its tributaries provide 20 000 kilometres of navigable waterways, but these are far from the major populated areas and port facilities are inadequate. The national transport strategy is to construct a number of major highways through the rainforest to improve access to the Amazon and eventually link up with the road system of neighbouring countries. However, the road network has not opened up the interior for development to the extent the government envisaged; rather it has facilitated rural out-migration, and contributed to the decline of Brazil's antiquated railway system.

On the other hand, Brazil's internal air network is well-developed, with nine international airports and hundreds of airfields allowing access to even the most remote areas. Services are provided by the national airline VARIG and its subsidiaries. VARIG also plays a major role in overseas promotion. There is a frequent shuttle service between São Paulo and Rio de Janeiro for business travellers.

Tourism development since the 1960s has been the responsibility of Embratur, a federal government agency that reports to the Ministry of Sport and Tourism. Special incentives apply to the regional development areas in the north-east and Amazonia, which are the responsibility of two other federal agencies – Sudene and Sudam respectively.

There was considerable investment by state governments and the private sector throughout the 1990s in hotels and leisure complexes. The federal government is investing in training for those employed in the tourism sector, along with improvements in infrastructure and more effective marketing as the government recognizes the central importance of tourism for the economy.

Tourism resources

Brazil has five tourist regions, each offering a different appeal.

Amazonia forms the major part of the world's greatest river basin, that covers 5 million square kilometres and contains 20 per cent of the planet's freshwater resources. The region's rainforests hold a fascination for foreign visitors as an ecological resource threatened with destruction. This is a good example of a change in perception, contrasting with the earlier view of the Amazon as the 'green hell' vividly described by Colonel Fawcett and other explorers. In Brazil itself there is a growing environmental movement, following the Rio Summit in 1992, to prevent further exploitation of the region for large-scale cattle grazing, mining and road-building. Most tourists arrive by air at Manaos or Belem. Both cities have fine buildings dating from the rubber boom of the 1890s, particularly Manaos with its magnificent opera house. After a long period of decline, the city has been revitalized with its development as a free port. Santarem, at the confluence of the Amazon and the Tapajoz, is another important tourist centre. Ecotourists seeking a closer encounter with the rainforest are accommodated in a number of lodges, some of which are built in the tree canopy, while others use 'floatels' moored at the river bank. Sustainable tourism is aimed for in the following ways:

- by restricting lodge capacity to a small number of guests
- by keeping facilities simple, using solar power and local food supplies wherever possible, and dispensing with air-conditioning

- by maintaining remoteness, with the journey from, say, Manaos being undertaken by boat and canoe rather than by air
- visits to Indian villages are controlled by FUNAI, the Indian Protection Agency; tourists are taken to visit local families but no family is visited regularly, so minimizing impact.

As a result of these policies the natural resources are protected and the quality of the experience for the visitor is also maintained.

The **north-east** consists of a fertile coastal belt and the semi-arid scrublands of the *sertão* or backlands, an area often described as the 'Triangle of Thirst'. This is a poverty-stricken region that has traditionally exported millions of rural migrants to the cities of southern Brazil. Unlike Amazonia, the coast is very popular with Brazilians, as it offers many fine beaches. Former fishing villages are 'discovered' and then cease to be fashionable in the never-ending quest for the 'perfect beach'. The coast is the subject of a tourism development programme, resulting from an agreement between the state governments of the region and the Inter-American Development Bank (IDB). International hotel groups have moved in, particularly along the 'Golden Coast' south of Recife, creating tourist enclaves. In contrast, accommodation is in short supply and often substandard in the sertão, which has an important place in Brazilian folklore as former bandit country.

The major tourist centres of the north-east include:

- Salvador de Bahia, famed for its attractive colonial architecture, and as the birthplace of the samba, hosting a carnival that rivals Rio's
- Fortaleza, noted for its fine beaches
- Recife, the international gateway to the region, known as the 'Venice of Brazil' on account of its many waterways.

The **centre-west** is Brazil's underdeveloped heartland, although it received a major boost in the 1960s with the establishment of Brasilia as the new federal capital. Most of the region consists of savanna grassland, with extensive wetlands near the Paraguayan border. This area, known as the Pantanal, is rich in wildlife that had previously co-existed with cattle ranching. This unique environment is now under threat from the activities of poachers, the expansion of agriculture, and projects to improve navigation on the rivers Paraná and Paraguay. The government-sponsored National Environment Agency has designated a number of natural reserves in the region, but these are under-funded. In contrast, Brasilia is noted for its freeways and the futuristic architecture of Oscar Niemeyer, epitomized by the Palace of Congress.

The **south** is the only region of Brazil to experience a temperate climate, with occasional frosts during the winter months. It is home to many migrants from Europe, including a large German-speaking community. Florianopolis is a popular beach resort for domestic tourists and well-off Paraguayan visitors, while Curitiba is one of the most progressive cities in the Americas. The major attraction for foreign tourists is Iguacú Falls on the border with Argentina. This is actually a series of cataracts three times larger than Niagara. Walkways have been built in the Garganta de Diablo gorge at the edge of the biggest waterfall. The resort of Foz de Iguacú has good communications by air and is a major conference venue.

The **south-east** receives the most foreign tourists, largely because it contains **Rio de Janeiro**. This is one of the world's great tourist cities, for the following reasons:

- the spectacular beauty of its setting, on one of the world's finest harbours, backed by the granite peaks of Sugarloaf, and Corcovado, with its famous statue of Christ the Redeemer
- some 80 kilometres of fine sandy beaches, the best known being Copacabana and the more fashionable Ipanema; these are ideal for people-watching (but not for bathing due to the heavy Atlantic surf)
- the uninhibited dance rhythms and extravagant costume parades of the Rio Carnival, one of the greatest shows on Earth.

To complement these resources the city has a good transport infrastructure, including two major airports, and world-class hotels that are concentrated in the Copacabana area.

The coastline between Rio and Santos, backed by the lush mountain scenery of the Serra do Mar, has been designated for major tourism development. A number of beach resorts are increasingly popular with foreign visitors, such as Buzios, Angra dos Reis and Sepetiba. However, development poses a threat to the Atlantic rainforests, already under severe pressure. The interior of this part of Brazil also has much to attract the cultural tourist, including the picturesque colonial town of Ouro Preto, which grew rich from the silver and diamond mining boom of the eighteenth century. Business travellers gravitate to the big modern cities of Belo Horizonte and São Paulo.

São Paulo has diversified from coffee production to become one of the world's great manufacturing and financial centres during the twentieth century. The city typifies the contrasts that exist in Brazil between private wealth and social deprivation; it has South America's highest car ownership and a major pollution problem. Nevertheless, Brazil's largest city can offer an arts and music scene to rival that of Rio de Janeiro.

Northern South America

We could include the northern countries of South America as part of the Caribbean region; in fact Venezuela and Surinam belong to the CTO while Guyana and Surinam are members of Caricom. Colombia and Venezuela share an extensive coastline on the Caribbean, and the cities of Cartagena and Caracas feature prominently on some cruise itineraries. Guyana, Surinam and French Guiana have cultural similarities with the West Indies and retain close links with Britain, the Netherlands and France respectively. Moreover, the music of the tropical coastlands of Colombia, Venezuela and the Guianas is African rather than Amerindian in origin.

Colombia

Colombia has the dubious distinction of being the country most threatened by terrorism, while the prevalence of drug-related crime has made Bogotá one of the world's most dangerous cities. Kidnappings are a feature of the long-running conflict between the army, paramilitaries and Marxist guerrillas – notably the FARC – that afflicts large areas of the country. This negative publicity overshadows the progress in industrial development and the fact that Colombia is the world's chief exporter of coffee and emeralds. The national airline – AVIANCA – was among the first to pioneer domestic air services in the Western Hemisphere; this was largely in response to the difficult topography. Colombia is compartmentalized by the Andes which here form a triple chain of mountains, acting as a formidable barrier to east–west communication. Not surprisingly, small regional airlines, often employing robust DC3 aircraft that can use short runways – are the lifeline for many communities.

Tourism development is the responsibility of the Corporación Nacional de Turismo (CNT) which has built a network of *paradors* along the main tourist routes. Most visitors arrive overland from Ecuador and Venezuela, attracted by shopping bargains. Promotion is mainly aimed at the US market, although growing numbers of tourists are coming from Germany and France.

Although Colombia has an extensive share of the Amazon rainforest and a long Pacific coastline, factors of climate, accessibility and security determine that the most popular tourist area is the Caribbean coast, where tropical beaches are backed by the snow-capped mountains of the Sierra Nevada. The beach resort of Santa Marta and the historic seaport of Cartagena de Indias – the key fortress of the 'Spanish Main' in colonial times – offer vibrant *cumbia* rhythms and beauty pageants among their attractions. The islands of San Andrés and Providencia attract domestic tourists with duty-free shopping.

In the interior of Colombia, Medellín and Cali are major business centres, while the main tourist attractions are smaller cities such as Popayán, located in beautiful mountain valleys, that still retain much of their Spanish colonial heritage. Bogotá is noted for its Gold Museum, a collection of artefacts from the pre-conquest Indian civilizations, while San Agustín is one of the largest archaeological sites in the Americas.

Venezuela

As a major oil producer, Venezuela enjoyed the highest per capita income of any Latin American country prior to the fall in oil prices in the early 1990s. Middle class Venezuelans travelled abroad in large numbers, particularly to Miami, leaving a substantial deficit in the international travel account. The subsequent financial crisis has led the government to impose strict exchange controls and take a greater interest in encouraging inbound tourism. Venezuela has the reputation of being an expensive destination, despite the devaluation of the bolivar against foreign currencies. In contrast to the situation in other South American destinations, most of Venezuela's visitors do not come from neighbouring countries, but from Europe and the United States. About half are visiting for business reasons and many are VFR tourists – the result of substantial immigration from Spain and Italy. The private car is the dominant mode for domestic tourism, thanks to cheap petrol and an excellent highway network. Air transport is facilitated by a large number of airports throughout the country, and VIASA, the national carrier is one of South America's leading airlines.

Hotel capacity is mainly concentrated in the capital and the beach resorts of the Caribbean coast. Timeshare apartments are an important part of the accommodation sector, particularly for domestic tourists.

Venezuela's tourism resources include:

- The capital **Caracas**, one of South America's great cities and a major gateway to the continent. It is primarily a business destination, but it does have historic significance as the birthplace of Simon Bolivar, who liberated six South American countries from Spanish rule.

- The beach resorts of the Caribbean, the most important being Porlamar on the island of Margarita, and Puerto La Cruz.
- A section of the Andes, including the colonial city of Mérida, which also boasts the world's highest cableway.
- The vast grasslands known as the Llanos, and the Guiana Highlands south of the River Orinoco, offer many possibilities for ecotourism. Fly-in camps in this remote, sparsely populated region provide a base for exploring the strange landscapes of the *tepuys* – sheer-sided, flat-topped mountains that inspired Conan Doyle's *'Lost World'* – and viewing the world's highest waterfall, Angel Falls.

The Guianas

In Guyana, Surinam and French Guiana tourism is in its infancy. Throughout the Guianas there is a contrast between the low-lying coast, with its plantation economy, and the forested interior, where Amerindian tribes maintain their traditional way of life. The majority of the population live on the coast and are mainly of African or Asian origin. The lack of beaches and poor infrastructure means that ecotourism is often the only viable form of tourism. A coastal highway linking the three countries was only completed in 1998, while the rivers and internal air services provide the only access to the interior.

- **Guyana** has some of South America's finest rivers and one of its highest waterfalls – Kaieteur – as yet unexploited as a tourist attraction. The few hotels are found mainly in Georgetown, and elsewhere forest lodges provide accommodation. The Rupununi region in the south-west of the country is an example of sustainable development, integrating ecotourism and forest management for the benefit of the local Indian communities.
- **Surinam** has strong cultural and business ties with the Netherlands, but tourism has been handicapped by political instability.
- **French Guiana** benefits from direct flights between Paris and Cayenne, due to its status as an overseas *département* of France, and as the base for the European Space Agency's 'Ariane' programme. The country is better known for its former role as a penal colony, including the infamous 'Devil's Island'.

The Andean republics

Peru, Ecuador and Bolivia share a similar physical environment, dominated by the Andes mountains, and a similar cultural heritage, in which the Amerindian influence is more prominent than elsewhere in South America. The region consists of three major physical divisions, namely:

- the Pacific coastal lowlands of Ecuador and Peru, where there is some development of beach tourism
- the High Andes – actually two mountain chains separated by a series of intermontane basins and high plateaux; here cultural tourism and more recently, adventure tourism are important
- the forested lowlands to the east of the Andes, forming part of the vast Amazon Basin, where ecotourism is being developed.

The majority of the attractions are to be found in the Andes, where there is a great variety of climates and landscapes due to differences in altitude. The arrangement of zones is similar to that of Mexico, but there are also extensive areas above 4000 metres altitude, known as *puna*, where the climate is bleak and dry, or as *páramo*, where it is cold and damp year-round. Although *soroche* (mountain sickness) is a distinct possibility due to the altitude, climbers from all over the world are attracted to the challenge of peaks such as Chimborazo, Huascarán and Illimani, while the spectacular scenery attracts growing numbers of trekkers from Europe and North America. There is also much to interest the cultural tourist. Intricate cultivation terraces on steep mountainsides, and the remains of temples and fortresses bear witness to the achievements of the Incas who ruled this part of South America prior to the Spanish conquest. The Amerindian influence is also evident in the artistic heritage of the colonial period in cities such as Quito, Cuzco and Sucre, and in the folklore and plaintive music of the Andes.

Due to the difficult terrain, road transport in the Andean republics is inadequate. However air travel within the region has been facilitated since the early 1990s under the terms of the Andean Pact. Accommodation varies widely in quality, standards of service and cost. There is a large informal sector of hostels, often with very basic facilities, that cater for the backpacker market.

Peru

Peru is the largest of the Andean republics and has the most developed tourism industry. Its capital Lima is the major gateway to the region. Since 1990 tourism has grown rapidly as a result of greater political and economic stability and the demise of the 'Shining Path' terrorist movement. However, Peru continues to have many social problems, not least the marginalization of its Indian rural communities.

Tourists from Western Europe and the United States each account for about a quarter of all arrivals. Peru appeals both to the luxury tour market, which has proved resilient to the effects of recession, and to the young traveller on a budget who sees the country as an adventure destination. The Peruvian government has been involved in developing tourism with the Ministerio de Comercio Exterior y Turismo coordinating agencies such as Enturperu – now privatized – which runs a chain of hotels, and COPESCO which is concerned with restoring historic sites. Tourism promotion is carried out by Promperu, with private sector backing. Most of the hotel capacity is concentrated in Lima and Cuzco – which is close to the major archaeological sites. The government's open skies policy has attracted foreign air-lines, including European carriers. The rail system – primarily developed for con-veying minerals from the Andes to coastal ports – is important for tourism, as it includes the highest narrow-gauge railway in the world (from Callao to Huancayo – reaching 4800 metres), and the line from Cuzco to Machu Picchu – Peru's best-known tourist attraction.

Most of the tourist attractions of Peru are located in the Andes, although Lima is the usual starting-point for cultural tours. The Peruvian capital is less appealing to foreign visitors than **Cuzco**, which is said to be the oldest continuously inhabited city in the Americas. Here Spanish buildings have been erected on Inca foundations. Cuzco and the 'sacred valley' of the Urubamba provide the best examples of the heritage of this advanced Indian civilization. These include:

- the Inca fortresses of Sacsahuamán and Ollantaytambo, built of intricate masonry without the use of mortar or iron tools
- the 'lost city' of **Machu Picchu**, abandoned for centuries in the forest and redis-covered by an American archaeologist in 1911. During the late 1990s the site

attracted 300 000 visitors a year, some arriving by helicopter, the majority making the journey by rail and road along the Urubamba Valley. Some 20 per cent of visitors followed the 'Inca Trail' – one of the world's most famous trekking routes, originally used by Indian couriers and llama pack trains. This popularity has had a negative impact in the form of widespread erosion, discarded toilet paper and other refuse; and damage from illegal campfires. In 2000 the authorities closed the trail to all but authorized trekking companies employing local guides and porters. Some argue that the ban on independent hikers, most of whom are environmentally aware, is indiscriminate. Another controversial measure is the replacement of the buses that take tourists from the hotels to the site by a high capacity cableway.

Alternative attractions to Cuzco and Machu Picchu include:

- the attractive city of Arequipa with its colonial architecture and the nearby Colca Canyon
- the Callejón de Huaylas in the north of the country with its spectacular mountain scenery
- Lake Titicaca on the border with Bolivia, at almost 4000 metres altitude, the world's highest navigable body of water.

The Peruvian coast is mainly desert, although fogs are a feature of the climate of Lima and El Niño episodes bring about dramatic changes. The capital has many cultural attractions as a reminder of its historic role as the power base for Spanish rule of South America. The region's beaches now feature on the international surfing circuit. The coastal desert has yielded many relics of ancient Indian civilizations, epitomized by the mysterious Nazca Lines, a heritage increasingly at risk from treasure seekers and the illicit trade in pre-Columbian artefacts.

Ecuador

Ecuador has many natural advantages as a tourist destination, containing a range of attractions within a relatively compact area. Although CETUR, the national tourism organization, has done much to promote the country, Peru is better known for Indian handicrafts, and few people realize that 'Panama hats' are actually made in Ecuador. Ecotourism is the largest growth market, and 17 per cent of the country has national park status. However conservation is threatened by under-funding and the lack of trained guides. The Cotopaxi National Park, centred on South America's most famous volcano, is under pressure from tourism development. Visitor arrivals to Ecuador have grown steadily to around 600 000 at the turn of the century, but many of these are low-spending backpackers who perceive the country to be a safe destination compared to others in the region. Visitors from the United States far outnumber those from Europe. The holiday options available include stays on colonial-style *haciendas* in the Sierra, the Andean region of Ecuador.

Within the Sierra are the series of intermontane valleys known as the 'Avenue of the Volcanoes'. An attractive countryside, framed by mountains and eucalyptus trees, along with picturesque Indian markets, explain the Sierra's appeal. The cities have a rich cultural heritage, especially the following which are both World Heritage Sites:

- **Quito**, known as 'the city of eternal spring', is celebrated for the number of Baroque churches and convents in its historic centre. However the capital is suffering from

runaway growth, air pollution and the consequences of the economic crisis that has afflicted Ecuador since the early 1990s.
- **Cuenca**, Ecuador's third largest city has similar cultural attractions, but fewer social and environmental problems.

Domestic tourists gravitate to spas such as Baños or to the beach resorts of the Pacific coast, which also attract large numbers of holidaymakers from Colombia and Peru. The coastal lowlands offer a very different environment to the Sierra, with a plantation economy geared to export markets. The important seaport of Guayaquil is Ecuador's main business centre.

Ecuador's section of the Amazon Basin is known as the Oriente, an area of rainforest that was undeveloped prior to the discovery of oil in the 1960s. Adventure tourism, including canoeing on the river Napo, is organized by tour operators based in Quito, who also promote the region for ecotourism. However, much of this so-called ecotourism is merely another form of exploitation that fails to benefit the local Indian communities. One exception is the Cuyabeno Reserve, which is partly under the control of the Secoya tribe. Here tourist groups are limited in numbers, and sustainable forms of transport and accommodation are used. However the region's ecosystems continue to be under threat from oil spillages and its native people from diseases against which they have little resistance.

The **Galápagos Islands**, situated in the Pacific Ocean some 1000 kilometres west of Guayaquil, despite their remoteness are probably the best known part of Ecuador and generate much of the country's revenue from tourism. They are volcanic and rather barren, but the unique wildlife is a world-class attraction for ecotourists, and this has been given international recognition as a World Heritage Site and Biosphere Reserve. Most of the animals have no fear of human beings, as there are no natural predators. Although the islands are situated on the Equator, penguins and sea lions flourish alongside tropical species, due to the cold ocean currents offshore. The best-known animals are the giant tortoises and marine iguanas, with 14 distinct species on the different islands. This provided the inspiration for Darwin's theory of evolution by natural selection, and the value of the islands as a 'living laboratory' has long been recognized. About 97 per cent of the Galápagos is designated as a national park, and stringent regulations are in force to protect the wildlife from the impact of tourists. However, this unique environment faces a more insidious threat from the growing numbers of Ecuadorian settlers from the mainland. As a result, introduced plant and animal species may soon outnumber those native to the islands.

Bolivia

Tourism in Bolivia is handicapped by the country's land-locked situation, inadequate communications and a poorly developed accommodation sector. Yet the country has as great a variety of landscapes as any in South America, including vast salt lakes in the south-west, lush subtropical valleys on the northern flanks of the Andes and tropical rainforests, swamps and savannas in the eastern part of the country. The Altiplano, at an average altitude of 4000 metres, is Bolivia's heartland – a bleak plateau characterized by intense sunshine during the day and sub-zero temperatures for much of the year at night. The majority of the population are Amerindian, speaking the Quechua and Aymara languages rather than Spanish. The mysterious ruins of Tiahuanaco near Lake Titicaca are a reminder of an Indian civilization that flourished here many centuries before the Incas.

Mining was historically the basis for Bolivia's economy, as shown by the Baroque architecture of the city of Potosí. This was made possible by the rich mines of the mountain known as the Cerro Rico overlooking the city, and the backbreaking labour of untold millions of Indians. Bolivia also boasts the world's highest capital city and international airport – La Paz – and what surely must be the world's highest ski resort nearby. With its upper slopes at the breathtaking altitude of 5500 metres, Chacaltaya is suitable only for skiers who are fully acclimatized!

Temperate South America

Argentina, Chile, Uruguay and Paraguay are in the part of South America lying outside the tropics. Due to its triangular shape, tapering toward Antarctica, this region is known as the 'Cono Sur' (Southern Cone) by Spaniards and Latin Americans. Distance from the main generating countries in both Europe and North America has been a major disadvantage for the development of international tourism. Nevertheless – with the exception of Paraguay – these countries share a relatively high level of economic development and educational attainment. Since the nineteenth century they have attracted large numbers of immigrants from Europe – particularly Italy and Germany – as well as Spain, and this has strongly influenced the culture, while the Indian heritage is less evident than elsewhere in Latin America. Tourism industries are well established, and there is a substantial middle class providing a large domestic market.

Paraguay

Paraguay is an enigma; one of the poorest, least developed and least publicized countries in the Western Hemisphere. Despite having a central location in South America, it is an isolated 'backwater', with few border crossings. Paraguay is also the only nation in Latin America where an Indian language – *Guaraní* – has the same official status as Spanish. West of the River Paraguay lies the Gran Chaco, an expanse of scrubland characterized by drought, extreme summer heat and occasional winter cold associated with the *Pampero* winds from the south. Not surprisingly the great majority of the population live in the eastern part of the country that is also scenically much more attractive. An important part of Paraguay's appeal lies in the music and handicrafts of the Guaraní people, a legacy of the Jesuit missions that flourished here in colonial times. Paraguay's membership of MERCOSUR provides access to funding from the wealthier South American countries for much-needed infrastructural improvements. At present there are few hotels outside the capital Asunción and the border town of Ciudad del Este – which has developed largely as a result of the Itaipú Dam project, and which offers shopping bargains to Argentinian and Brazilian visitors. Prospects for ecotourism are limited by poor infrastructure and lack of promotion.

Uruguay

Uruguay's position as a small country between two big neighbours – Argentina and Brazil – and its reputation for political stability, explains why it has become an important venue for international conferences. Almost half the population live in the capital Montevideo, which is said to be the safest big city in Latin America. Uruguay is best known for sport (it was the first country to host the football World Cup, in 1930), but it also shares much of the cultural heritage of Argentina, including gauchos and tango rhythms. The *estancias* or country estates in the interior are developing agro-tourism in response to the fall in beef and wool prices on the world market. Uruguay's main tourist asset however is 500 kilometres of fine beaches. Punta del Este is one of South America's most important holiday resorts, attracting the 'jet set' to its casinos, luxury hotels, boutiques and sports facilities between December and February. Other resorts along the Atlantic coast cater for large numbers of domestic tourists of modest means and Argentinians. The flow of tourists between Argentina and Uruguay should increase substantially once the planned fixed link across the Rio de la Plata between Buenos Aires and the historic town of Colonia del Sacramento becomes a reality.

Argentina

Traditionally Argentina has looked towards Europe rather than the rest of South America for trade and cultural inspiration. The financial crisis of 2001 devastated the middle class and dealt a severe blow to the country's self-image. Yet the country has vast natural resources, including cheap energy supplies and the fertile farmlands of the Pampas. These resources made Argentina one of the world's richest countries prior to the Second World War, when Buenos Aires was known as the 'Paris of South America', but much of this wealth was squandered as a result of the social and economic projects of the Perón regime, and the decades of political strife that followed. One of the country's main problems is outdated infrastructure – most of the road and railway system was built in the early twentieth century; another is the imbalance between Buenos Aires – which has a disproportionate share of the wealth and population – and the provinces, which are deprived of political and financial influence despite a federal system of government.

Until the 1980s incoming tourism was of little importance to the country's economy and better-off Argentinians spent as much on travel abroad – particularly to neighbouring Chile, Uruguay and Brazil. With the economic collapse of the country, inbound tourism is a now an important earner of foreign exchange and employs over 10 per cent of the workforce. Hotel accommodation is mainly concentrated in Buenos Aires and the second city of Argentina, Córdoba, but there is a tendency for new projects to be located in outlying regions such as the Andes. Domestic air services are improving as a result of privatization, but the same cannot be said of the Argentinian rail network, once one of the largest in the world. It now carries only a small volume of passenger traffic compared to road or air transport. The National Tourism Secretariat have promoted Buenos Aires both as a destination in its own right and as the gateway to the rest of Argentina. The latter role is problematic, due to the great distances separating the capital from the main tourist regions in outlying parts of the country.

- The **north-east** offers a spectacular part of Iguazú Falls and former Jesuit missions that are now World Heritage Sites.
- The **north-west** is characterized by landscapes similar to those of neighbouring Bolivia; In the cities of Salta and Jujuy the colonial heritage of Spain is much more evident than in Buenos Aires.
- The **west** includes the vineyards around Mendoza, the important ski resort of Las Leñas in the foothills of the Andes, and the Argentine Lake District around San Carlos de Bariloche, which is both a summer and winter resort for domestic tourists. Here the Andes form a formidable barrier between Argentina and Chile. The only major route linking the two countries is over the Uspallata Pass, with its

famous statue of 'Christ of the Andes'. Nevertheless, cross-border traffic forms a large percentage of the tourist arrivals in both countries.

- **Patagonia** extends from the Rio Negro south to Tierra del Fuego. This vast, sparsely settled region lies in the rain shadow of the Southern Andes and is mostly a wind-swept semi-desert. Here ecotourism is growing in popularity based on the wildlife resources of the Valdés Peninsula and the mountain, lake and glacier scenery of Los Glaciares National Park. All terrain vehicles provide access for tour groups reaching as far south as Ushuaia, Argentina's gateway to Antarctica.

The Pampas are the heartland of Argentina, but these featureless grasslands are of little interest to foreign visitors, except as the setting for the gaucho (cattleman), who plays an important role in national folklore. Some of the *estancias* do provide visitors with accommodation, an *asado* (barbecue), as well as displays of horsemanship and other traditional skills.

In contrast, **Buenos Aires** is a cosmopolitan city displaying architectural styles from France, Italy, Spain and Britain. The waterfront district known as La Boca was the birthplace of the tango, while the Teatro de Colón rivals Milan's La Scala as one of the world's great opera houses. The beaches of Mar del Plata offer relief from the city's humid summers. As a result of the economic crisis, Buenos Aires, formerly an expensive city, has become a 'bargain-basement' for North American tourists.

Chile

Chile must rank as one of the world's most remote destinations. It is a narrow expanse of territory between the world's largest ocean and the Andes, and further isolated by the world's driest desert – the Atacama – to the north. As part of the 'Pacific Ring of Fire', the country is prone to devastating earthquakes. Yet Chile is one of the most successful economies in Latin America, with a good infrastructure. Tourism is a major growth sector, promoted by SERNATUR, the national tourist organization.

The latitudinal extent of the country results in striking differences in climate between the north and the south. Most of the population is concentrated in the central region, which enjoys a Mediterranean climate.

- The desert **north** was the setting for an important mining industry for nitrates and copper in the early part of the twentieth century, which brought prosperity to cities like Antofagasta. Many former mining communities have since become 'ghost towns' amid a landscape of geysers, salt lakes and sand dunes. There has been some development of beach tourism around ports such as Iquique, and ecotourism in the Lauca National Park.
- **Central** Chile can be compared to California, with a fertile central valley lying between the Pacific coastal ranges and higher mountains to the east. Here Santiago is one of the major gateways to South America. The ski resorts of Portillo and Los Nevados are within easy reach, and these attract skiers from the USA during the Northern Hemisphere summer. The vineyards of the Maipo Valley provide Chile's best-known export. The Pacific coast offers fine beaches, although heavy surf and strong currents discourage bathing. Viña del Mar is Chile's major beach resort and is also an important cultural centre. Valparaiso has a similar setting to that of San Francisco, but its prosperity declined with the opening of the Panama Canal, and the port needs urban regeneration.

- The **Lakes Region** around Temuco has a cooler, wetter climate that supports extensive forests of Araucaria pine. It boasts some of the world's most spectacular lake and mountain scenery, culminating in the active volcano of Osorno. The region is also the homeland of a substantial Indian minority that has been in dispute with the government over land rights since the return of democracy to Chile in the 1990s. Puerto Montt is the gateway to southern Chile with shipping services and the Carretera Austral road link.
- The **Far South** is one of South America's most challenging environments. It is a wilderness of fjords, evergreen beech forests and glaciers, with a cold, damp and windy climate. Nevertheless, ecotourism and adventure tourism are being developed in this region. Summer cruises navigate the more sheltered inner channels. This has led to a revival in the fortunes of Punta Arenas, which lost most of its former importance as a seaport on world shipping routes with the opening of the Panama Canal. The Torres del Paine National Park near Puerto Natales contains some of the most spectacular peaks in the Andes.
- Chile also owns **Easter Island**, which we described as part of Polynesia in Chapter 23.

The Falkland Islands

The Falklands are a group of islands in the South Atlantic some 500 kilometres east of Patagonia. Since 1833 they have been a British colony, but Argentina has a long-standing claim to the territory it calls 'Las Malvinas', and has also been in dispute with Britain over South Georgia and the sector of Antarctica lying to the south of Cape Horn. In scenery, climate and lifestyle the islands more closely resemble the Scottish Hebrides than mainland South America. The wildlife – including penguins and sea mammals – is representative of the sub-Antarctic zone, and is of great interest to ecotourists. The opening in 1985 of a modern airport near Port Stanley made the islands much more accessible to Europe, but they remain a remote and expensive destination.

Summary

The countries of the Western Hemisphere south of the United States border form a cultural entity consisting of three distinct geographical regions. Of these, the Caribbean is the most important from the viewpoint of inbound tourism and it is the world's premier cruise destination. The English language is widespread throughout the islands, while the Iberian culture and languages are dominant on the mainland. Broadly speaking, the Caribbean islands cater mainly for 'recreational' tourism, whereas the traditional lifestyles and historic sites of Mexico, Central America and South America appeal more to 'cultural' tourists. Ecotourism is growing in importance, particularly in the more remote areas of Central and South America, but it has often failed to benefit the indigenous communities.

The USA dominates the market for Caribbean travel although the Dominican Republic, Jamaica and Barbados have achieved wider appeal as destinations due to their accessibility by air and shipping services. On the Latin American mainland Mexico is clearly the most visited destination, due again to its proximity to the USA. Despite having spectacular scenery Central and South America have been much less successful. This is partly due to political instability and the inadequacy of the infrastructure. However, countries such as Peru and Brazil are benefiting from the growing popularity of long-haul holidays. Business travel is also likely to increase to those countries which are undergoing rapid economic development, such as Brazil.

Although incomes are generally low throughout Latin America and the Caribbean, domestic tourism is significant and there is a considerable demand for outbound tourism to Europe and the USA from a growing middle class.

The future geography of travel and tourism

Introduction

The early years of the twenty-first century have witnessed severe shocks to the tourism system – the terrorist attacks on New York and Washington on '9/11', foot and mouth disease in the UK, terrorist bombings in holiday resorts and the Iraq War. These events emphasize the fact that we cannot manage tourism if we do not understand how it reacts to change. Making predictions is fraught with problems, especially with a sector as fickle as tourism; but if we are successfully to manage tourism in the future, that is what we must do. This means identifying the drivers of future trends, recognizing that while some forces of change such as demographics and technology are already clearly evident, others have yet to emerge. We therefore set out to identify the key trends and issues that will reshape the geography of travel and tourism through the twenty-first century under the following headings:

- changing markets
- changing destinations
- developments in transport and the tourism sector
- globalization and the new world order.

Common to each of these themes are other agents of change such as technology, the search for sustainability in tourism, and changes in consumer behaviour. These trends are interlinked and are combining to accelerate the pace of change. For example, tourists are increasingly knowledgeable and sophisticated, and can now be catered for by a tourism sector that is firmly embracing marketing strategies, facilitated by technological developments such as the Internet and mobile commerce – where the mobile phone becomes the medium for guiding and visitor information. At the same time, the sector is becoming truly global as larger organizations operate across different cultures and time zones. In combination with continued shifts in the world economic and political situation, these trends will influence tourism flows, as new generators and new destinations emerge. Underlying all of these trends are two imperatives. First, the pressure for sustainable development will ensure that destinations are better planned and managed, and will show more concern for their environment and host community than did their earlier counterparts. This is supported by international conferences such as the 2002 World Summit for Sustainable Development in Johannesburg, and the WTO's global code of tourism ethics. Second, since 9/11 much of the tourism sector has been in crisis. There is a real imperative to develop crisis management response strategies covering all sectors of the tourism industry to anticipate future 'shocks' to the system and ensure that tourism can recover from any future crises.

One of our consistent themes is that we can only understand tourism if we recognize the inter-relationships between the various elements in the system. This is equally true in attempting to understand the future. Here the concept of 'product markets' is helpful; these recognize the relationship between the changing demands of tourists and the need to develop tourism products to meet their needs. For example, we know that the 'new tourist' demands low impact tourism, active involvement and environmentally and socially acceptable tourism – hence the development of ecotourism products. At the same time there is a trend towards greater market segmentation and the development of a vast range of different products to meet specialized demands.

Markets

Patterns of demand

There is no doubt that in the past 50 years a wave of leisure and travel has broken across the globe pushing the frontier of tourism further outward as more and more people have enjoyed access to travel. This trend will continue as demand for both domestic and international tourism expands in this century. Indeed, as early as the year 2010 international arrivals will exceed one billion. However, forecasters also suggest that both demand and supply side constraints may slow the growth of tourism:

- On the demand side, some countries are reaching ceilings of airport capacity and available leisure time that will constrain further growth. The WTO study on leisure time, for example, has shown that leisure is under threat from the pressures of changing work practices, technology and competition.
- On the supply side, the threat of terrorism, political instability, ethnic strife, health risks and capacity ceilings in transport infrastructure may discourage tourism growth in some areas.

There is no doubt that the distribution of tourism by the year 2020 will therefore be different from that of the early years of this century. The countries of the East Asia and Pacific (EAP) region are emerging as important generators of tourism and as major tourist destinations. China in particular will become a major generator of both domestic and outbound tourism, changing the nature of travel across the globe. The EAP region will rival Europe and North America in its significance for tourism. To some extent, the success of the EAP region is at the expense of Europe's traditional dominance. Europe's share of international tourism will continue to erode as more long-haul destinations grow in popularity. The principal long-term factors affecting demand for tourism are demographic changes, the amount of leisure and holiday time available, consumer preferences and the economic performance of the main tourism-generating countries. In the short term, as well as the potentially drastic impact of wars and further terrorist incidents, other factors such as relative prices and exchange rates affecting the cost of travel and effective marketing and promotion will also be important. Although forecasters say that long-haul travel will continue to increase, short-haul travel – especially to neighbouring countries – will still account for a very high proportion of international trips. Business tourism will remain an important segment of the market but it is probable that developments in communications – such as video-conferencing and videophones – may reduce the need, at least in the West. The evidence here is inconclusive, suggesting that unless travel becomes prohibitively expensive, face-to-face meetings will remain an important reason for business tourism in some cultures at least.

Changing market demands

While there is no doubt that social and economic trends will encourage the growth of tourism, the nature of the market will change, with consequent implications for the type of development at the destination. The tourists of tomorrow will be more discerning, seeking a quality experience and, in the developed world, increasingly drawn from an older age group. They may subscribe to the principles of sustainable development, but they also know their rights and, as an empowered group, will complain and seek compensation if their travel experience is disappointing. Demographic changes can be forecast to an extent – we know, for example, that as the baby boom generation ages there will be a large 'grey tourism' market. Yet it is conceivable that larger families may become fashionable in the West and this, along with the consequences of massive migration from the Third World, would increase fertility rates and halt further population decline. It is also difficult to track the influence of changing values among the travelling public. For example, motivations for travel are moving away from passive sunlust towards active participation and curiosity about other cultures. As everyday life and work becomes safer, more predictable and less physically demanding, there will be a greater demand, at least in the youth market, for extreme sports, 'hard adventure' and other high-risk activities. More leisure should be available through flexible working practices, sabbaticals, study leave and early retirement. However, if the USA is any guide, the corporate work-place could become the chief provider of recreation opportunities for many employees, thus blurring the boundaries between work and leisure. Lifestyle changes such as the growing numbers of 'singletons' (young single person households) and 'downshifting' – where an individual changes from a highly paid, high pressure job to one with less income but more free time – will have an impact on the demand for tourism. Travel will also be tailor-made to suit other groups in society such as single parents. Intensive marketing research on consumer preferences, allied to technology, will increasingly allow more sophisticated market segmentation of tourists, so that product development can be engineered to deliver quality experiences. Use of the Internet is already allowing modularization of the elements of travel packages so that consumers can put together their own holidays and trade direct with suppliers: an innovation with significant implications for the way travel has traditionally been distributed. As a consequence, travel intermediaries are re-inventing their role in the tourism system in order to survive. In short, tourism is becoming less passive and less dominated by the mass market, and more geared to active involvement, individual preferences and direct purchase of tailor-made products.

Destinations

Hand-in-hand with market changes is the realization by tourism developers that destinations are unique, special and fragile places and have to be carefully managed if they are to retain their appeal. The destination of the future will use sustainability and product differentiation, based on a unique selling proposition (USP) to remain competitive. Attitudes on the part of both consumers and suppliers are changing as the result of pressure from the environmentalist movement, media exposure of bad practices and a more mature tourism industry. Sustainability has been publicized through high profile conferences such as the 2002 World Summit for Sustainable Development, by initiatives from representative bodies for the industry such as the World Travel and Tourism Council (WTTC), and by tour operators themselves. In particular, the realization of the negative impacts of tourism upon host environments, societies and developing economies has prompted the search for alternative forms of tourism – such as ecotourism – and a critical attitude towards mass tourism (although we must recognize that mass tourism will remain a very substantial part of the market). Sustainable tourism ensures that the tourism sector is sympathetic to host environments and societies. An increasing number of public agencies are drawing up guidelines for the reduction of tourism impacts and there is no doubt that the consumer of the future will shun destinations that are not 'environmentally sound'. In essence, we are seeing a move towards the responsible development and consumption of tourism through:

- more local control of tourism development, as recommended by the Agenda 21 initiatives of the Rio Earth Summit and the World Summit for Sustainable Development in Johannesburg in 2002

- translation of the *principles* of sustainability into *practice* through codes of conduct, accreditation schemes, eco-labelling, best practice guidelines and industry self regulation
- pro-active adoption of professional approaches to the integrated management of visitors, traffic and resources at tourist destinations, instead of reacting to problems as they arise
- use of marketing and information management to influence the behaviour of visitors at destinations
- initiatives such as the WTO's drive to use tourism as an agent of poverty alleviation, and its global code of tourism ethics
- an enhanced awareness of the impacts of tourism.

It is perhaps inevitable that these ideas will find more fertile ground in the developed world than in most developing countries, where the short-term imperatives of obtaining foreign exchange and job creation will still dominate and may eclipse the longer-term objectives of sustainable development. Destinations are responding to these demands in a variety of ways:

- Resource-based destinations, i.e. those based on elements of the natural or cultural heritage, are adopting sophisticated planning, management and interpretive techniques to provide both a welcome and a rewarding experience for the tourist, while at the same time ensuring protection of the resource itself. It is felt that once tourists understand why a destination is significant they will want to protect it. Protection here may be not only in terms of changed behaviour but also through *enhancive sustainability* initiatives where the visitor 'leaves the destination in a better condition than before'. These initiatives include:
  ○ 'visitor payback' where visitors become financial supporters of a site
  ○ voluntary 'eco-taxes' to protect and repair tourist destinations suffering environmental and social damage
  ○ new products such as 'working holidays' to 'clean up' degraded destinations.
- Good planning and management of the destination lies at the heart of providing the tourism consumer of the future with a high-quality experience. To achieve this, it may be that tourists of the future will have to accept increasingly restricted viewing times at popular sites, comply with destination 'codes of conduct', be content with replicas of the real thing (as at the caves of Altamira and Lascaux), or even a 'virtual' substitute in cyberspace using computer technology.
- As resource-based destinations come under increased pressure, we are seeing greater emphasis on purpose-built, demand-led attractions that merge tourism and entertainment. The trend to more frequent trips taken closer to home will demand 'synthetic' attractions such as artificial ski slopes and those which combine leisure, entertainment, retailing, accommodation and quality catering in a single setting. The emergence of totally enclosed and controlled tourist environments such as theme parks, mega-cruise ships and vacation islands will be promoted as a 'market-oriented' alternative to the real, and increasingly fragile, 'resource-based', non-reproducible attractions of natural, historic or cultural destinations. Such artificial settings have many advantages and can provide the safe and secure environment sought by most tourists – already destinations such as Dubai, Las Vegas and Alton Towers are bringing these trends to life.

In the future destinations will be affected by climate change, with rising sea levels creating problems for coastal resorts, the erosion of the ozone layer modifying the traditional beach holiday to 'beach plus' tourism, and the generally more volatile weather conditions worldwide affecting the profitability of the sector. There is also a real threat that climate change will destroy some tourism icons, such as Australia's Great Barrier Reef and the Alpine glaciers. But a more insidious threat could be posed by the growth of tourism itself. In the 1950s the polar regions and the Himalayas were the ultimate frontier for tourism; nowadays they are exposed to the assault of thousands of adventure-seeking tourists, and climbers have to 'book' Everest several years in advance. Having visited most of the world's wild places and cultural sites, the well-heeled tourist is seeking new horizons and challenges. The frontiers of tourism will therefore expand ever outwards, with new destinations being created under the oceans and in space. In fact we know less about the ocean depths (or for that matter what lies beneath the Earth's crust) than we do about the surface of the Moon or Mars. The development of submersibles capable of withstanding the immense pressures would enable tourists to view the *Titanic* wreck site and the strange life-forms of the ocean floor. On the continental shelves projects for undersea hotels are already under way. Yet it is space that is much more likely to appeal to the imagination of future tourists.

Virtual reality (VR) sparks controversy between futurists – some argue that it will never replace the real experience of travel, whilst others foresee the home becoming the centre for all leisure activities – a total immersive cave or experience chamber – with VR discs available for tourism destinations as 'tasters', the ultimate replacement for the travel brochure or DVD. In some respects, this is the perfect form of tourism as the destination receives a royalty for the disc, but receives none of the negative impacts of tourists actually on site. Similarly, the would-be tourist could view a historic building from any angle, and also receive the sensory experience of a destination – for example, the sounds, humidity and aromas of the rainforest, but without irksome transport delays or the risk of crime and disease. Crude versions of virtual destinations already exist and clearly the diversion of visitor pressure away from the real thing is important. Of course we are then faced with the question: 'Does VR represent tourism in the true sense?'

Space is the real new destination of the future, and simulated space travel experiences and tours of space research centres are already popular. Although NASA first landed astronauts on the Moon in 1969, space tourism – as distinct from space travel for scientific or military reasons – did not become a reality until 2001, when an American millionaire visited the International Space Station as a paying passenger on a Russian space mission. Space tourism has been defined as the 'taking of short pleasure trips in low earth orbit by members of the public' (Collins and Ashford, 1998), implying that interplanetary voyages in outer space are ruled out for the foreseeable future. Tourism in near space is already technically feasible, but is prohibitively expensive because of the high cost of launches and the fact that space vehicles are not yet truly 're-usable'. This situation is likely to change as a result of international competition for the 'X Prize' – a US$10 million award to any entrepreneur who can build a commercially viable spacecraft. Incidents such as the *Columbia* shuttle disaster in 2002 mean that passenger safety will be a real issue for space tourism; however, space-planes would pose a much lower risk than the existing space shuttles that use ballistic missile technology (Ashford, 2003). Health risks are perhaps less significant. The condition of weightlessness, due to zero gravity in space, offers recreational opportunities as well as challenges to would-be tourists. Long-term health issues such as a loss in bone density, as well as exposure to cosmic and solar radiation, are unlikely to affect tourists – as distinct from astronauts or crew members – on a sub-orbital flight lasting only a few hours, but those staying at a 'space hotel' would need to have adequate protection.

Developments in transport

We have already touched on some of the future developments in transport (see Table 5.1). These are notoriously difficult to predict, and forecasts made in the 1950s have proved to be inaccurate 40 years later. Technology and changing business practices will have a major impact on transport systems. The hydrogen fuel-cell has been hailed as the answer to our energy problems, but as of now the production of hydrogen results in as much pollution as the burning of fossil fuels. However, by mid-century hydrogen should replace petroleum as the main source of motive power.

In civil aviation long-haul airline operations will be characterized by the use of aircraft larger than the present 'jumbos', with a capacity for as many as 700 passengers. The application of space technology will enable these aircraft to achieve hypersonic speeds and a much greater range, so that the flying time between London and Sydney could be reduced to two hours, without stops for re-fuelling. For short-haul operations the use of VTOL (vertical take-off and landing aircraft) would provide more flexibility. The trend toward deregulation will continue across the world. In the USA and Europe deregulation has already led to domination of the market by a few major airlines and the forging of strategic alliances, a trend which is emerging in other sectors of the tourism industry. In such an environment competitive advantage will not come from government protection. On regional and short-haul flights 'budget' airlines will compete on the basis of Internet reservations, ticketless travel procedures and 'no frills' service. The major airlines will concentrate on hub and spoke operations. Airlines based at a 'hub' airport in a prime geographical location will coordinate their schedules, enabling travellers to make onward connections between flights on routes radiating from the central hub. This gives the hub airline a strong competitive edge and leads to a system of 'fortress hubs', keeping out newcomers. However this could result in some communities having less choice in their travel arrangements than was the case hitherto.

Although VTOL aircraft and giant versions of seaplanes could eventually take some of the pressure, airports will need to be built on a major scale to cope with the anticipated growth in air traffic; this will be greatest in the East Asia–Pacific region. Local communities and environmentalists from different countries will launch coordinated protest campaigns through the Internet, but these will largely be ineffective. However, governments, particularly in the West, will increasingly be faced with the dilemma of balancing the benefits of economic growth against the environmental damage. Government policies favouring airport expansion can be criticized for the following reasons:

- the predicted growth rate for air traffic is based on the rapid increase since the 1970s, but the demand for air travel will slow down as the market matures
- the growth in demand for cheap air travel cannot be sustained indefinitely as the true cost in environmental terms is not borne by the airline or the passenger.

In surface transport the desire for personal mobility will have to be reconciled with the need for an efficient form of mass transit, that truly responds to public demand. Throughout the world car ownership is growing inexorably as suppressed demand becomes expressed demand as a result of economic growth and democratic structures of government. Even in the USA the market has not reached saturation, as the demand for sports utility vehicles (SUVs) has shown. We can expect developments in automotive technology to make driving safer and more environmentally acceptable, including satellite navigation systems and improved fuel efficiency. We can be sure that the car of the future will be quite different from the vehicle that has evolved with the internal combustion engine in the course of the twentieth century, but until the infrastructure is in place, cars powered by hydrogen or electricity will be slow to capture the market. Highway networks will continue to develop around the world and the capacity of busy routes could be greatly increased with the use of computer-controlled guideways; this will make motoring safer but at the cost of the driver's independence.

As the century unfolds, it is likely that car use will decline for inter-city travel and for trips within large cities for the following reasons:

- The development of high speed inter-city rail links could result in the train being preferred over the car – or air transport – for journeys of less than 500 kilometres due to the following:
  - congestion on the roads and airways
  - the train is perceived as a 'greener' form of travel
  - a range of new rail-based leisure and business tourism products will be developed
  - the application of innovative technology, such as magnetic levitation or repulsion in which the train 'flies' above a track at speeds of up to 500 kilometres/ hour; this will transform the image of rail travel and bring it firmly into the twenty first century.
- Within the world's major cities rapid transit systems will reduce car use, as is now occurring in Asia.

On the world's oceans high-speed vessels and passenger-carrying submarines will be developed. Mega-cruise ships carrying 5000 passengers will cater for the mass market, possibly with 'satellite' vessels for diving and shore excursions. A variety of much smaller ships would provide nature-based cruises to island destinations such as the Galápagos, linking up with local hotels on a 'cruise and stay' programme. Some experts predict that the tourists of the future where appropriate will stay in prefabricated mobile 'pods' which can be set up in the most remote locations, such as Antarctica, with minimal impact on the environment.

The tourism sector

As the tourism market matures, the sector is striving for acceptability not only in terms of environmental practices such as auditing and total quality management, but also business ethics and social responsibility as short-term, profit-driven operations become less acceptable. The added pressures of a global downturn in business caused by global events have complicated this agenda. There will be an increasing consideration for all stakeholders involved in the business, including the well-being of the destination and its residents. For example, it makes increasing commercial sense for tour operators to invest in destinations and their facilities as evidenced by the 'Tour Operator's Initiative for Sustainable Tourism Development' representing

25 companies worldwide, whilst the accommodation sector is developing environmentally sound units such as eco-lodges.

In response to these trends, the tourism sector is rapidly becoming more professional and embracing developments in technology. Indeed, technology is being employed to improve the management of tourism businesses and has allowed the industry to move towards a marketing philosophy of anticipating consumer needs and ensuring that they can be supplied. Technology facilitates this through 'database marketing' allowing direct contact with the consumer. The Internet and computer reservation systems (CRS) are particularly important here. Use of the Internet, combined with a more knowledgeable tourist market, is driving the emergence of a growing number of independent travellers who bypass intermediaries in the tourism distribution chain. Suppliers will target their products more closely to the desires of their customers and, increasingly, new tourist destinations will be created.

Globalization and the New World Order

The tourism sector does not operate in a vacuum and is affected by globalization which is the trend for markets and production to become inter-dependent worldwide, regardless of government policies in any particular country. Smeral (1998) has identified the key drivers of globalization in tourism as:

- the adoption of free trade agreements, removing barriers to international transactions
- computer and communications technology encouraging 'e-business'
- worldwide-acting suppliers utilizing CRS and global distribution systems (GDS); examples here include the major airlines, hotel chains and tour operators, as well as their strategic alliance partners in the supply chain
- decreasing costs of international travel allowing access to most markets in the world
- increasing levels of income in the generating countries, allied to the 'new tourist' who is experienced and discerning
- the emergence of 'new' destinations, fuelling the demand for more international travel.

The consequences of globalization for the tourism sector include:

- standard procedures and quality control (as in the accommodation sector); there are concerns that this could result in a worldwide homogenization of tourism products
- increased competition
- head office decisions on marketing and technology in the larger companies
- forging of strategic alliances (as in the airlines sector)
- adoption of global brands (American Express, Sheraton Disney etc.)
- changing management approaches
- adoption of new ways of doing business, such as use of e-mail and the Internet (already effectively used by budget airlines)

- adoption of global distribution systems and yield management
- more difficult trading conditions for small and medium-sized tourism enterprises (SMTEs).

On this latter point, there is scope in tourism for both the large organization and the small independent operator supplying niche markets. However, the medium-sized enterprises have neither the power of the large firms, nor the opportunities to specialize and will therefore struggle to survive in a globalizing sector. In fact, the competitive dominance of larger corporations in tourism will continue through their strict quality control and global branding which is designed to reduce the perceived risk of a tourism purchase. This has implications for tourism destinations that may become increasingly dependent upon decisions made by such corporations. Nonetheless, we must never lose sight of the fact that tourism will continue to be delivered at a destination by local employees, within the context of a local culture.

The future of tourism cannot be divorced from political events and trends. Initiatives at different geographical scales are changing the world order and these will impact upon tourism. At the national level, a major shift has been the way that the role of government in tourism has changed since 9/11. Until then the trend had been for tourism to be seen as a private sector activity and governments were gradually withdrawing support and subsidy. However, with the impact of 9/11 potentially devastating whole tourism economies and national airlines, the public sector's role has revived, with assistance to businesses through state funding and rescue packages, as well as the coordination and promotion of tourism at ministerial level.

At the international level, tourism in the future will be facilitated by the free trade agreements under the umbrella of the General Agreement on Trade in Services (GATS) signed in 1994. GATS is based on the principle that free market forces are the best means of providing consumers with the best products at the best prices. The role of GATS is controversial, since:

- on the one hand supporters of GATS point to the elimination of barriers to tourism growth, removing restrictions on hiring staff from other countries, establishment of management operations and franchises in other countries, easier transfers of currency and other payments; but
- on the other hand, opponents of GATS maintain that freedom for companies to operate where they wish, to hire non-local staff and to franchise their products flies in the face of the development of sustainable tourism, as there will be few controls on the activities of companies in the tourism sector.

There are two opposing trends to the world order implied by GATS:

- First, the formation of a number of trading blocs across the globe as country groupings come together in economic alliances is evident. Notable examples are the North American Free Trade Agreement (NAFTA), the creation of the European Union (EU) under the 1992 initiative, the Association of South East Asian nations (ASEAN), and Mercado del Cono Sur (MERCOSUR) covering most of South America.
- Second, regional and national politics are also at variance with the spirit of GATS. The rise of regionalism and a search for cultural identity – particularly amongst ethnic minorities – has led to conflict in some parts of the world (as in the regions

of the former Yugoslavia), but elsewhere the trend is less sinister. In the midst of this contradiction 'city states' are emerging as major tourist destinations, whether it be as cultural centres, or simply competing with others to stage mega-events such as the Olympic Games or the soccer World Cup.

As the millennium unfolds, the new world order and the global tourism industry will continue to be threatened by terrorism. This, along with natural disasters, epidemics and inter-communal violence, will particularly affect developing countries who can ill-afford the loss of foreign exchange. It is likely that tourists themselves will be a primary target for terrorists rather than being incidental victims. Security efforts after 9/11 have concentrated on protecting air travellers, but as the *Achille Lauro* incident showed as long ago as 1985, and the Madrid atrocity in 2004, cruise ships and rail terminals can be vulnerable to attack. The effect of 9/11 and subsequent disasters has been to tighten security and immigration procedures, and for crisis and risk management plans to be developed for many destinations and the tourism sector generally. Crisis and risk management recognizes that we must be prepared for man-made and natural disasters and lays down a response pattern to such events. The most significant risks are determined, and strategies implemented to deal with them. Although international organizations will be important, as the World Health Organization showed by its role in containing the SARS epidemic, the onus will be on individuals, private businesses and governments to be vigilant concerning future crises, but not to the extent of being risk-averse.

Discussion

A number of commentators have attempted to synthesize the trends identified above. Poon suggests that the future will see a flexible, segmented, customized and diagonally integrated tourism sector rather than the mass-market, rigid, standardized and packaged tourism of the 1970s (see Figure 26.1). Poon (1989, p. 92) identifies the key trends leading to this new tourism as:

- the diffusion of a system of new information technologies in the tourism industry
- deregulation of the airline industry and financial services
- the negative impact of mass tourism on host countries
- the movement away from sunlust to sun-plus tourism
- environmental pressures
- technology
- competition
- changing consumer tastes.

There is no doubt that the maturing and changing tourist market will have major implications for the geography of travel and tourism. This will manifest itself in changing patterns of tourism around the world as new destinations emerge and older ones decline. The nature of the impact at the destination will increasingly depend on the type of tourism, and those charged with planning for the industry will respond more positively to visitors' needs and desires. Above all, the challenge for this century will be the balancing of the environmental and social impacts of

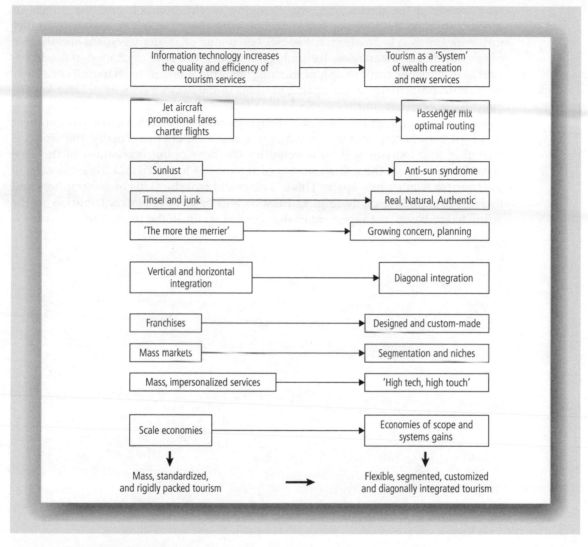

Figure 26.1 International tourism in metamorphosis

Source: Poon, in Cooper, 1989

tourism against its perceived economic gains. It is here that geography will continue to play a valuable role in providing us with:

- a holistic approach to tourism
- the specialized knowledge needed to plan and manage low-impact tourism.

Summary

The future geography of travel and tourism will be influenced by a number of inter-related trends. These can be summarized as the changing tourism marketplace, new trends at the destination, the changing world situation and the effects of globalization on the tourism sector. In line with these forces for change are other influences such as technology, consumer behaviour, crisis management and the rise of environmental awareness. Technology is forcing the pace of change in the transport sector, mobile commerce and the Internet. This is linked to changing consumer behaviour, particularly in the ageing markets of the developed world. Here knowledgeable, discerning tourists are seeking independent travel and active involvement. Destinations will respond through positive planning, concern for the environment and host community, and by providing a quality experience. Finally, the world is changing and tourism will be affected by the developing economies of the East Asia–Pacific region, the rising number of signatories to GATS and the expansion of the tourism frontier into space. There is no doubt that the skills of geographers and their understanding of these global issues will be a valuable contribution to the 'knowledge-based' management of the tourism sector in the twenty-first century.

References

Ashford, D. (2003) *Spaceflight Revolution*. Imperial College Press.

Ashworth, G. J. and Tunbridge, J. E. (1990) *The Tourist-Historic City*. Belhaven.

Bramwell, W. and Lane, B. (1994) *Rural Tourism and Sustainable Rural Development*. Channel View Publications.

Butler, R. W. (1980) The concept of a tourist area cycle of evolution. *Canadian Geographer*, 24 (1).

Chubb, M. and Chubb, H. (1981) *One Third Of Our Time: An Introduction To Recreation Behavior and Resources*. John Wiley and Sons.

Clawson, M. and Knetsch, J. (1966) *The Economics of Outdoor Recreation*. Johns Hopkins University Press.

Cleverdon, R. (1979) *The Economic and Social Impact of Tourism on Developing Countries*. Economist Intelligence Unit.

Cohen, E. (1972) Toward a sociology of international tourism. *Social Research*, 39 (1), 164–183.

Collins, P. and Ashford, D. (1998) Space tourism. *Ada Astronautica* 17 (4), 421–431.

Cooper, C., Gilbert, D., Fletcher, J., Shepherd, R. and Wanhill, S. (1998) *Tourism Principles and Practice*. Pearson.

Davidson, R. (1994) *Business Travel*. Addison, Wesley and Longman.

Faulks, R. W. (1990) *The Principles of Transport*, 4th edn. McGraw-Hill.

Graburn, N. (1976) *Ethnic and Tourist Arts: Cultural Expressions from the Fourth World*. University of California Press.

Gray, H. P. (1970) *International Travel – International Trade*. Heath Lexington Books.

Hatch, D. (1985) *Weather Around the World*. Amsterdam.

Kotler, S., Makens, J. and Bowen, D. (2003) *Marketing for Hospitality and Tourism*. Prentice Hall.

Lansing, J. B. (1960) *The Changing Travel Market*. Institute for Social Research.

Lavery, P. (ed.) (1971) *Recreational Geography*. David & Charles.

Lee, D. and Lemons, H. (1949) Clothing for global man. *Geographical Review*, 39, 181–213.

Leiper, N. (1979) The framework of tourism. *Annals of Tourism Research*, 6 (4), 390–407.

Löfgren, O. (1999) *On Holiday: A History of Vacationing*. University of California Press.

Mathieson, A. and Wall, G. (1982) *Tourism: Economic, Physical and Social Impacts*. Longman.

Mill, R. C. and Morrison, A. (1985) *The Tourism System*. Prentice Hall.

Mowforth, M. and Munt, I. (1998) *Tourism and Sustainability*. Routledge.

Newsome, D., Moore, S. A. and Dowling, R. K. (2002) *Natural Area Tourism*. Channelview.

Patullo, P. (1996) *Last Resorts: The Cost of Tourism in the Caribbean*. Cassell.

Poon, A. (1989) Competitive strategies for a 'New Tourism', in C. Cooper (ed.), *Progress in Tourism, Recreation and Hospitality Management* I. Belhaven, pp. 91–102.

Rostow, W. W. (1959) *The Stages of Economic Growth*. Cambridge University Press.

Smeral, E. (1998) The impact of globalization on small to medium sized enterprises. *Tourism Management*, 19 (4), 371–380.

Smith, V. L. (1978) *Hosts and Guests: The Anthropology of Tourism*. Blackwell.

Swarbrooke, J. (1995) *The Development and Management of Visitor Attractions*. Butterworth-Heinemann.

Terjung, W. H. (1966) Physiological climates of the coterminous United States: a bioclimatological classification based on man. *Annals of the Association of American Geographers*, 56, 141–179.

Trewartha, G. (1954) *An Introduction to Climate*, 3rd edn. McGraw-Hill.

Ullman, E. (1980) *Geography as Spatial Interaction*. University of Washington Press.

Waugh, D. (1995) *Geography: An Integrated Approach*. Nelson.

Williams, A. V. and Zelinsky, W. (1970) On some patterns in international tourist flows. *Economic Geography*, 46 (4), 549–567.

World Tourism Organization (1995) *Global Tourism Forecasts to the Year 2000 and Beyond*. WTO.

World Tourism Organization (1998) *Tourism Highlights 1997*. WTO.

World Tourism Organization (2003) *Global Code of Ethics for Tourism*. WTO.

A compendium of worldwide destination sources

Since the first two editions of *The Geography of Travel and Tourism* the volume of tourism literature has expanded rapidly, not only in terms of academic texts, journals and case studies but also media coverage of tourism destinations now provides a rich source of material. This is in the form of television and radio documentaries, video travelogues, newspaper supplements and specialist travel magazines.

But perhaps the greatest innovation in source material has come from the World Wide Web. The Web is now a major source of information about tourism and destinations. The Web is somewhat disorganized and lacks any form of information quality control, but the official tourism sites in particular provide instant access to countries, cities and resorts unparalleled five years ago. Other sites are now available that provide destination accounts, photographs and statistics. Because we feel that this is such a valuable source for everyone reading this book, we have provided a comprehensive list of the website addresses of national tourist organizations of the major tourism countries in the world. In addition, the companion website to the book provides a comprehensive listing of travel and tourism websites, including search engines.

This compendium is designed to list the key sources available in the subject area on a systematic basis and so provides the first port of call for an assignment, lecture or presentation. We have organized the compendium to cover the following key sources:

- books relevant to the chapters in this book
- reports, dictionaries, yearbooks and encyclopedias
- abstracting services
- statistical sources
- tourism journals
- website addresses of national tourism organizations.

Books: Part one   The elements of the geography of travel and tourism

Chapter 1   Introduction to the geography of tourism

Ashworth, G. (1984) *Recreation and Tourism*. Bell & Hyman.

Bull, A. (1998) *The Economics of Travel and Tourism*. Longman.

Burkhart, A. J. and Medlik, S. (1991) *Tourism, Past, Present and Future*. Heinemann.

Burns, P. M. and Holden, A. (1995) *Tourism: A New Perspective*. Prentice Hall.

Callaghan, P. (1989) *Travel and Tourism*. Business Educational.

Coltman, M. (1989) *Introduction to Travel and Tourism*. Van Nostrand Reinhold.

Cooper, C. P., Fletcher, J., Gilbert, D. and Wanhill, S. (1998) *Tourism Principles and Practice*. Addison Wesley Longman.

De Kadt, E. (1979) *Tourism: Passport to Development*. Oxford University Press.

Dumazedier, J. (1967) *Towards a Society of Leisure*. Free Press.

Gee, C. Y., Choy, D. J. L. and Makens, J. C. (1997) *The Travel Industry*. Van Nostrand Reinhold.

Glyptis, S. (1993) *Leisure and the Environment*. Wiley.

Goeldner, C. R. and Ritchie, J. R. B. (2004) *Tourism: Principles, Practices, Philosophies*. John Wiley

Hall, C. M. and Page, S. (2002) *The Geography of Tourism and Recreation*. Routledge.

Holloway, C. (1994) *The Business of Tourism*. Addison Wesley Longman.

Horner, S. and Swarbrooke, J. (2003) *International Cases in Tourism Management*. Elsevier Butterworth-Heinemann.

Howell, D. W. (1993) *Passport: An Introduction to the Travel and Tourism Industry*. South Western.

Hudman, L. E. (1980) *Tourism: A Shrinking World*. Wiley.

Hudman, L. E. and Jackson, R. H. (1999) *The Geography of Travel and Tourism*. Delmar.

Ioannides, D. and Debbage, K. G. (1998) *The Economic Geography of the Tourist Industry*. Routledge.

Kelly, J. R. (1990) *Leisure*. Prentice Hall.

Leiper, N. (1990) *The Tourism System*. Massey University Press.

Likorish, L. and Jenkins, C. L. (1997) *An Introduction to Tourism*. Butterworth-Heinemann.

Lundberg, D. E. (1975) *The Tourist Business*. Van Nostrand Reinhold.

Lundberg, D. E., Stavenga, M. H. and Krishanmoorthy, M. (1995) *Tourism Economics*. Wiley.

Matley, I. M. (1976) *The Geography of International Tourism*. Association of American Geographers Resource Paper 76 1, Washington, DC.

Medlik, S. (1995) *Managing Tourism*. Butterworth-Heinemann.

Mercer, D. (1980) *In Pursuit of Leisure*. Sorret.

Mill, R. C. (1990) *Tourism: The International Business*. Prentice Hall.

Mill, R. C. and Morrison, A. (1992) *The Tourism System: An Introductory Text*. Prentice Hall.

Page, S. (2003) *Tourism Management: Managing for Change*. Elsevier Butterworth-Heinemann.

Page, S., Brunt, P., Busby, G. and Connell, J. (2001) *Tourism. A Modern Synthesis*. Thomson Learning.

Pearce, D. (1995) *Tourism Today: A Geographical Analysis*. Longman.

Poon, A. (1993) *Tourism, Technology and Competitive Strategies*. CAB.

Ryan, C. (2003) *Recreational Tourism*. Channelview.

Sharpley, R. (1994) *Tourism, Tourists and Society*. Elm.

Shaw, G. and Williams, A. (1994) *Critical Issues in Tourism*. Blackwell.

Sinclair, T. and Stabler, M. (1991) *The Tourism Industry: An International Analysis*. CAB.

Sinclair, T. and Stabler, M. (1997) *The Economics of Tourism*. Routledge.

Theobald, W. F. (1994) *Global Tourism: The Next Decade*. Butterworth-Heinemann.

Towner, J. (1994) *An Historical Geography of Recreation and Tourism*. Belhaven.

Tribe, J. (1995) *The Economics of Leisure and Tourism: Environments, Markets and Impacts*. Butterworth-Heinemann.

Turner, L. and Ash, J. (1975) *The Golden Hordes: International Tourism and the Pleasure Periphery*. Constable.

Vellas, F. and Becherel, L. (1995) *International Tourism*. Macmillan.

Wahab, S. (1993) *Tourism Management*. Tourism International Press.

Weaver, D. and Lawton, L. (2002) *Tourism Management*. John Wiley.

Williams, S. (2003) *Tourism, Critical Concepts in the Social Sciences*. Routledge.

Williams, S. (1998) *Tourism Geography*. Routledge.

Witt, S., Brooke, M. Z. and Buckley, P. J. (1995) *The Management of International Tourism*. Unwin Hyman.

Chapter 2   The geography of demand for tourism

Baron, R. (1989) *Travel and Tourism Data: A Comprehensive Research Handbook*. Euromonitor.

Butler, R. W. and Pearce, D. G. (1993) *Tourism Research*. Routledge.

Crotts, J. C. and Van Raaij, W. F. (1993) *Economic Psychology of Travel and Tourism*. Haworth Press.

Davidson, R. (1994) *Business Travel*. Addison Wesley Longman.

Frechtling, D. (2001) *Forecasting Tourism Demand*. Elsevier Butterworth-Heinemann.

Ioannides, D. and Debbage, K. G. (1998) *The Economic Geography of the Tourist Industry*. Routledge.

Jennings, G. (2001) *Tourism Research*. John Wiley

Iso-Ahola, S. E. (1980) *The Social Psychology of Leisure and Recreation*. W. C. Brown.

Lennon, J. J. (2003) *Tourism Statistics*. Allen and Unwin.

MacCannell, D. (1976) *The Tourist: A New Theory of the Leisure Class*. Macmillan.

Pearce, D. and Butler, R. (1993) *Tourism Research: Critiques and Challenges*. Routledge.

Pearce, P. L. (1982) *The Social Psychology of Tourist Behaviour*. Pergamon.

Poon, A. (1993) *Tourism, Technology and Competitive Strategies*. CAB.

Ritchie, J. R. B. and Goeldner, C. R. (1994) *Travel, Tourism and Hospitality Research: A Handbook for Managers and Researchers*. Wiley.

Ross, G. F. (1996) *The Psychology of Tourism*. Hospitality Press.

Ryan, C. (2002) *The Tourist Experience*. Continuum.

Ryan, C. (1995) *Researching Tourist Satisfaction: Issues, Concepts and Problems*. Routledge.

Smith, S. L. J. (1983) *Recreation Geography*. Longman.

Smith, S. L. J. (1996) *Tourism Analysis: A Handbook*. Addison Wesley Longman.

Witt, S. and Witt, C. (1991) *Modelling and Forecasting Demand in Tourism*. Academic Press.

World Tourism Organization (1999) *Changes In Leisure Time*. WTO.

Chapter 3 The geography of resources for tourism

Special interest tourism

Bowden, G., McDonnell, I., Allen, J. and O'Toole, W. (2001) *Events Management*. Elsevier Butterworth-Heinemann.

Clift, M. C., Luongo, M. and Callister, C. (2002) *Gay Tourism*. Continuum.

Fladmark, M. (1995) *Cultural Tourism*. Dunhead.

Font, X. and Tribe, J. (1999) *Forest Tourism and Recreation*. CABI.

Getz, D. (1997) *Event Management and Event Tourism*. Cognizant.

Getz, D. (1991) *Festivals, Special Events and Tourism*. Van Nostrand Reinhold.

Goddie, P., Price, M. and Zimmerman, F. M. (1999) *Tourism and Development in Mountain Regions*. CABI.

Goldblatt, J. (2001) *Special Events*. John Wiley.

Hall, C. M. and Sharples, L. (2003) *Food Tourism Around the World*. Elsevier Butterworth-Heinemann.

Hall, C. M., Sharples, L., Cambourne, B. and Macionis, N. (2002) *Wine Tourism Around the World*. Elsevier Butterworth-Heinemann.

Hall, C. M. (1992) *Hallmark Tourist Events: Impacts, Management, Planning*. Belhaven Press.

Hinch, T. and Higham, J. (2003) *Sports Tourism Development*. Channelview.

Hudson, S. (2003) *Sport and Adventure Tourism*. Haworth.

Law, C. (2002) *Urban Tourism*. Continuum.

Lennon, J. and Foley, M. (2000) *Dark Tourism: The Attraction of Death and Disaster*. Continuum.

McCabe, V., Poole, B., Weeks, P. and Leiper, N. (2000) *The Business and Management of Conventions*. John Wiley.

Murphy, P. (1997) *Quality Management in Urban Tourism*. Wiley.

Page, S. (1994) *Urban Tourism*. Routledge.

Page, S. and Getz, D. (1997) *The Business of Rural Tourism*. International Thomson Press.

Richards, G. (2001) *Cultural Attractions and European Tourism*. CABI.

Rogers, T. (2003) *Conferences and Conventions: A Global Industry*. Elsevier Butterworth-Heinemann.

Shackley, M. (1996) *Wildlife Tourism*. Thomson International Business Press.

Sharpley, R. and Sharpley, J. (1997) *Rural Tourism: An Introduction*. International Thomson Press.

Swarbrooke, J. and Horner, S. (2001) *Business Travel and Tourism*. Elsevier Butterworth-Heinemann.

Swarbrooke, J., Beard, C., Leckie, S. and Pomfret, G. (2003) *Adventure Tourism. The New Frontier*. Elsevier Butterworth-Heinemann.

Weed, M. and Bull, C. (2003) *Sports Tourism*. Elsevier Butterworth-Heinemann.

Weiler, B. and Hall, C. M. (1992) *Special Interest Tourism*. Wiley.
World Tourism Organization (2002) *Sport and Tourism*. WTO.
Yeoman, I., Robertson, M., Ali-knight, J., Drummond, S. and McMahon-Beattie, U. (2003) *Festival and Events Management*. Elsevier Butterworth-Heinemann.

Planning and management

Ashworth, G. and Dietvorst, A. (1995) *Tourism and Spatial Transformations: Implications for Policy and Planning*. CAB.
Eagles, P. F. J. and McCool, S. (2002) *Tourism in National Parks and Protected Areas: Planning and Management*. CABI.
Fyall, A., Garrod, B. and Leask, A. (2002) *Managing Visitor Attractions: New Directions*. Elsevier Butterworth-Heinemann.
Gearing, S. E., Swart, W. W. and Var, T. (eds) (1976) *Planning for Tourism Development*. Praeger
Gunn, C. and Var, T. (2002) *Tourism Planning*. Routledge.
Gunn, C. A. (1997) *Vacationscape: Designing Tourist Regions*. Van Nostrand Reinhold.
Hall, C. M. (1994) *Tourism and Politics*. Wiley.
Hall, C. M. and Jenkins, J. M. (1994) *Tourism and Public Policy*. Routledge.
Hawkins, D. E., Shafer, E. L. and Rovelstadt, J. M. (1980) *Tourism Planning and Development Issues*. George Washington University Press.
Inskeep, E. (1991) *Tourism Planning: An Integrated Planning and Development Approach*. Van Nostrand Reinhold.
Inskeep, E. (1993) *National and Regional Planning: Methodologies and Case Studies*. WTO/Routledge.
Inskeep, E. and Kallenberger, M. (1992) *An Integrated Approach to Resort Development*. WTO.
Jeffries, D. (2001) *Governments and Tourism*, Elsevier Butterworth-Heinemann.
Johnson, P. and Thomas, B. (1992) *Perspectives on Tourism Policy*. Mansell.
Jubenville, A., Twight, D. W. and Becker, R. H. (1987) *Outdoor Recreation Management Theory and Applications*. Venture.
Lawson, F. (1995) *Hotels and Resorts: Planning, Design and Refurbishment*. Butterworth-Heinemann.
Lawson, F. R. and Baud-Bovy, M. (1998) *Tourism and Recreation: Handbook of Planning and Design*. Architectural Press.
Pearce, D. (1989) *Tourist Development*. Longman.
Pearce, D. (1992) *Tourist Organizations*. Longman.
Pearce, D. G. and Butler, R. W. (2001) *Contemporary Issues in Tourism Development*. Routledge.
Sharpley, R. and Telfer, D. (2002) *Tourism and Development*. Channelview.
Swarbrooke, J. (2001) *The Development and Management of Visitor Attractions*. Elsevier Butterworth-Heinemann.

Heritage tourism

Ashworth, G. J. and Tunbridge, J. E. (1990) *The Tourist-Historic City*. Belhaven.
Boniface, P. and Fowler, P. (1993) *Heritage and Tourism in the Global Village*. Routledge.
Drummond, S. and Yeoman, I. (2000) *Quality Issues in Heritage Visitor Attractions*. Elsevier Butterworth-Heinemann.
Hall, C. M. and McArthur, S. (1998) *Integrated Heritage Management*. The Stationery Office.
Harrison, R. (1994) *Manual of Heritage Management*. Butterworth-Heinemann.

Herbert, D. (1992) *Heritage Sites: Strategies for Marketing and Development*. Gower.
Shackley, M. (2000) *Visitor Management: Case Studies from World Heritage Sites*. Elsevier Butterworth-Heinemann.
Shackley, M. (2001) *Managing Sacred Sites*. Continuum.
World Tourism Organization (1999) *Tourism at World Heritage Sites*. WTO.

Risk and safety

Bierman, D. (2003) *Restoring Destinations in Crisis*. Allen and Unwin.
Keller, P. (2003) *Crisis Management in the Tourism Industry*. Elsevier Butterworth-Heinemann.
Pizam, A. and Mansfield, Y. (1996) *Tourism, Crime and International Security Issues*. Wiley.
Wilks, J. and Page, S. (2003) *Managing Tourist Health and Safety in the New Millennium*. Elsevier Butterworth-Heinemann.
World Tourism Organization (1996) *Tourist Safety and Security: Practical Measures for Destinations*, WTO.
World Tourism Organization (1998) *Handbook on Natural Disaster Reduction in Tourist Areas*. WTO.

Ecotourism

Boo, E. (1990) *Ecotourism: The Potentials and Pitfalls*. World Wildlife Fund.
Cater, E. and Lowman, G. (1994) *Ecotourism*. Wiley.
Fennell, D. A. (2003) *Ecotourism*. Routledge.
Garrod, B. and Wilson, J. (2003) *Marine Ecotourism*. Channelview.
Wearing, S. and Neil, J. (1999) *Ecotourism*. Elsevier Butterworth-Heinemann.
Weaver, D. (2001) *The Encyclopaedia of Ecotourism*. CABI.
Weaver, D. (1998) *Ecotourism in the Less Developed World*. CABI.
Weaver, D. (2002) *Ecotourism*, John Wiley.
World Tourism Organization (2001) *Sustainable Development of Ecotourism: A Compilation of Good Practices*, WTO.
World Tourism Organization (2003) *Sustainable Development of Ecotourism: A Compilation of Good Practices in SMEs*. WTO.

Sustainability

Aitchison, C., Macleod, N. E. and Shaw, S. E. (2001) *Leisure and Tourism Landscapes*. Routledge.
Boissevain, J. (1996) *Coping with Tourists: European Reaction to Mass Tourism*. Berghahn Books.
Bramwell, B. (2003) *Coastal Mass Tourism*, Channelview.
Bramwell, W. and Lane, B. (1994) *Rural Tourism and Sustainable Rural Development*. Channel View Publications.
Bramwell, W., Henry, I., Jackson, G., Prat, A., Richards, G. and Van Der Straaten, J. (1996) *Sustainable Tourism Management: Principles and Practice*. Tilburg University Press.
Briguglio, L. (1995) *Sustainable Tourism*. Cassell.
Brown, F. (2000) *Tourism Reassessed: Blight or Blessing?* Elsevier Butterworth-Heinemann.
Butler, R. and Hinch, T. (1996) *Tourism and Indigenous Peoples*. International Thomson Business Press.

Butler, R., Hall, C. M. and Jenkins, J. (1998) *Tourism and Recreation in Rural Areas*. Wiley.

Coccosis, H. and Nijcamp, P. (1995) *Sustainable Tourism Development*. Avebury.

Cooper, C. and Wanhill, S. (1997) *Tourism Development: Environmental and Community Issues*. Wiley.

Craig-Smith, S. (1994) *Learning to Live with Tourism*. Addison Wesley Longman.

Croall, J. (1995) *Preserve or Destroy: Tourism and the Environment*. Calousie Gulbenkian/Tourism Concern.

Eber, S. (1995) *Beyond the Green Horizon: Principles of Sustainable Tourism*. Tourism Concern.

Edington, J. M. and Edington, M. A. (1990) *Ecology, Recreation and Tourism*. Cambridge University Press.

Farrell, B. H. (1987) *Tourism and the Physical Environment*. Pergamon.

Forsyth, T. (1996) *Sustainable Tourism: Moving from Theory to Practice*. World Wildlife Fund/Tourism Concern.

Hall, D. and Richards, G. (2003) *Tourism and Sustainable Community Development*. Routledge.

Harris, R. and Leiper, N. (1995) *Sustainable Tourism: An Australian Perspective*. Butterworth-Heinemann.

Harris, R., Griffin, T. and Williams, P. (2002) *Sustainable Tourism*. Elsevier Butterworth-Heinemann.

Harrison, L. and Husbands, W. (1996) *Practising Responsible Tourism*. Wiley.

Holden, A. (2000) *Environment and Tourism*. Routledge.

Hunter, C. and Green, H. (1995) *Tourism and Environment: A Sustainable Relationship?* Routledge.

Jenner, P. and Smith, C. (1995) *Tourism Industry and the Environment*. Economist Intelligence Unit.

Krippendorf, J. (1987) *The Holiday Makers: Understanding the Impact of Leisure and Travel*. Heinemann.

MacCannell, D. (1992) *Empty Meeting Grounds*. Routledge.

Mason, P. and Mowforth, M. (1995) *Codes of Conduct in Tourism*. Occasional Papers in Geography, University of Plymouth.

Mason, P. (2003) *Tourism Impacts: Planning and Management*. Elsevier Butterworth-Heinemann.

Mathieson, A. and Wall, G. (1989) *Tourism: Economic, Physical and Social Impacts*. Longman.

Middleton, V. T. C. and Hawkins, R. (1998) *Sustainable Tourism: A Marketing Perspective*, Elsevier Buttterworth-Heinemann.

Mowforth, M. (2003) *Tourism and Sustainability*. Routledge.

Mowforth, M. and Munt, I. (1998) *Tourism and Sustainability*. Routledge.

Murphy, P. E. (1991) *Tourism: A Community Approach*. Methuen.

Newsome, D., Moore, S. and Dowling, R. (2001) *Natural Area Tourism*. Channelview.

Organization for Economic Co-operation and Development (OECD) (1981) *Case Studies of the Impact of Tourism on the Environment*. OECD.

Pearce, D. and Butler, R. (1995) *Change in Tourism: People, Places, Processes*. Routledge.

Price, M. (1996) *People and Tourism in Fragile Environments*. Wiley.

Schyvens, R. (2002) *Tourism for Development: Empowering Communities*, Prentice Hall.

Smith, V. L. (1989) *Hosts and Guests*. University of Pennsylvania Press.

Smith, V. and Brent, M. (2003) *Hosts and Guests Revisited*. Cognizant.

Smith, V. L. and Eadington, W. R. (1995) *Tourism Alternatives: Potential Problems in the Development of Tourism*. University of Pennsylvania Press.

Swarbrooke, J. (1999) *Sustainable Tourism Management*. CABI.
World Tourism Organization (1993) *Sustainable Tourism Development: Lessons for Local Planners*. WTO.
World Tourism Organization (2000) *Sustainable Development of Tourism: A Compilation of Good Practices*. WTO.
World Tourism Organization (2002) *Tourism and Poverty Alleviation*. WTO.
World Tourism Organization (2002) *Sustainable Tourism in Protected Areas*. WTO.

Destination management

Ashworth, G. and Goodall, B. (1990) *Marketing Tourism Places*. Routledge.
Cole, G. (2003) *Managing the Tourist Destination*. Allen and Unwin.
Davidson, R. and Maitland, R. (1997) *Tourism Destinations*. Hodder & Stoughton.
Goodall, B. and Ashworth, G. (1988) *Marketing in the Tourism Industry: The Promotion of Destination Regions*. Croom Helm.
Heath, E. and Wall, G. (1992) *Marketing Tourism Destinations: A Strategic Planning Approach*. Wiley.
Howie, F. (2002) *Managing the Tourist Destination*. Continuum.
Laws, E. (1995) *Tourist Destination Management: Issues, Analysis and Policies*. Routledge.
Lickorish, L. J. (1991) *Developing Tourism Destinations, Policies and Perspectives*. Longman.
Ritchie, J. R. B. and Crouch, G. I. (2003) *The Competitive Destination*. CABI.

Chapter 4   Climate and tourism

Hatch, D. (1989) *Weather around the World*. Amsterdam.
Henson, R. (2002) *The Rough Guide to Weather*. Rough Guides.
Morgan, M. and Moran, J. (1997) *Weather and People*. Prentice Hall.
Pearce, E. A. and Smith, C. G. (1990) *The World Weather Guide*. Hutchinson.
Trewartha, G. (1954) *An Introduction to Climate*. McGraw-Hill.
World Tourism Organization (2003) *Climate Change and Tourism*. WTO.

Chapter 5   The geography of transport for travel and tourism

Ashford, N. (1991) *Airport Operations*. Addison Wesley Longman.
Blackshaw, C. (1992) *Aviation Law and Regulation*. Addison Wesley Longman.
British Airways (annual) *Environmental Report*. BA.
Cartwright, R. and Baird, C. (1999) *Development and Growth of the Cruise Industry*. Elsevier Butterworth-Heinemann.
Cole, S. (1987) *Applied Transport Economics*. Kogan Page.
Doganis, R. (1992) *The Airport Business*. Routledge.
Doganis, R. (2001) *The Airline Business in the Twenty First Century*. Routledge.
Doganis, R. D. (1985) *Flying Off Course: The Economics of International Airlines*. Allen & Unwin.
Faulks, R. W. (1992) *The Geography of Transport for Tourism*. Ian Allan.
Gialloreto, L. (1988) *Strategic Airline Management*. Addison Wesley Longman.
Graham, A. (2003) *Managing Airports: An International Perspective*. Elsevier Butterworth-Heinemann.

Graham, B. (1995) *Geography and Air Transport*. Wiley.

Hanlon, P. (1995) *Global Airlines: Competition in a Transnational Industry*. Butterworth-Heinemann.

Hanlon, P. (1999) *Global Airlines*. Elsevier Butterworth-Heinemann.

Lumsden, L. M. and Page, S. (2004) *Tourism and Transport*. Elsevier Butterworth-Heinemann.

Miller, J. C. and Sawers, P. (1988) *The Technical Development of Modern Aviation*. Routledge.

Page, S. (1999) *Transport and Tourism*. Pearson Education.

Peisley, T. (2003) *Global Changes in the Cruise Industry 2003–2010*. Seatrade Communications.

Shaw, S. (1990) *Airline Marketing and Management*. Pitman.

Wheatcroft, S. (1994) *Aviation and Tourism Policies: Balancing the Benefits*. Routledge/WTO.

Books: Part two   The regional geography of travel and tourism in the world

General

Burton, R. (1995) *Travel Geography*. Addison Wesley Longman.

Conlin, M. V. and Baum, T. (1995) *Island Tourism*. Wiley.

Drakakis-Smith, G. and Lockhart, D. (1997) *Island Tourism: Trends and Prospects*. Pinter.

Harrison, D. (2002) *Tourism in the Less Developed World*. CABI.

Harrison, D. (1994) *Tourism and the Less Developed Countries*. Wiley.

Robinson, H. (1976) *A Geography of Tourism*. Macdonald & Evans.

Taylor, M. (annual) *World Travel Atlas*. Columbus Press.

Europe

Barke, M., Towner, J. and Newton, M. T. (1996) *Tourism in Spain: Critical Issues*. CAB.

Cronin, M. and O'Connor, B. (2003) *Irish Tourism*. Channelview.

Davidson, R. (1998) *Travel and Tourism in Europe*. Addison Wesley Longman.

Drakakis-Smith, G. and Lockhart, D. (1997) *Island Tourism: Trends and Prospects*. Pinter.

Hall, D. (1991) *Tourism and Economic Development in Eastern Europe and the Soviet Union*. Belhaven.

Horner, S. and Swarbrooke, J. (1996) *Marketing Tourism, Leisure and Hospitality in Europe*. International Thomson Business Press.

Montanaria, A. and Williams, A. (1995) *European Tourism: Regions, Spaces and Restructuring*. Wiley.

Pompl, W. and Lavery, P. (1993) *Tourism in Europe: Structures and Developments*. CAB.

Williams, A. M. and Shaw, G. J. (1991) *Tourism and Economic Development: Western European Experiences*. Belhaven.

Asia

Hall, C. M. and Page, S. (2000) *Tourism in South East Asia: Issues and Cases*. Elsevier Butterworth-Heinemann.

Hernmann, E., Hitchcock, M. J., King, V. T. and Parnwell, M. (1992) *Tourism in South East Asia*. Routledge.

Hitchcock, M., King, V. T. and Parnwell, J. G. (1993) *Tourism in South East Asia*. Routledge.

Lew, A., Yu, L., Guangrui, Z. and Ap, J. (2003) *Tourism in China*. Haworth.

Richter, L. K. (1989) *The Politics of Tourism in Asia*. University of Hawaii Press.

Africa

Dieke, P. (2000) *The Political Economy of Tourism Development in Africa*. Cognizant.

Gamble, W. P. (1989) *Tourism and Development in Africa*. Murray.

Australasia (Oceania)

Bauer, T. (2001) *Tourism in the Antarctic*. Haworth.

Hall, C. M. (1994) *Tourism in the Pacific Rim*. Longman.

Hall, C. M. (1997) *Introduction to Tourism in Australia*. Longman.

Hall, C. M. and Johnston, M. (1995) *Polar Tourism*. Wiley.

Harrison, D. (2003) *Pacific Island Tourism*. Cognizant.

Jackson, I. (1989) *An Introduction to Tourism in Australia*. Hospitality Press.

King, B. (1989) *Tourism Marketing in Australia*. Hospitality Press.

Opperman, M. (1998) *Pacific Rim Tourism*, CABI.

Americas

Duval, D. T. (2003) *Tourism in the Caribbean*. Routledge.

Farrell, B. H. (1982) *Hawaii: The Legend that Sells*. University of Hawaii Press.

Gayle, D. J. (1993) *Tourism Marketing and Management in the Caribbean*. Routledge.

Pattullo, P. (1996) *Last Resorts: The Cost of Tourism in the Caribbean*. Cassell.

Santana, G. (2001) *Tourism in South America*. Haworth.

Reports, dictionaries, yearbooks and encyclopedias

In addition to books, journals and trade press coverage of worldwide destinations, there are a number of useful sources to be found in consultants' reports (including those on line such as www.euromonitor.com), tourism dictionaries, yearbooks and encyclopedias. Some of the key sources include:

Collin, P. H. (1994) *Dictionary of Hotels, Tourism and Catering Management*. P. H. Collin.

Cooper, C. and Lockwood, A. (1989) *Progress in Tourism, Recreation and Hospitality Management*, vols 1–6. Belhaven and John Wiley.

Economic Intelligence Unit publications.

Euromonitor publications.

Europa Publications (annual) *The Europa World Yearbook*. Europa Publications.

INSIGHTS, English Tourist Board.

Jafari, J. (2000) *The Encyclopedia of Tourism*. Routledge.

Khan, M., Olsen, M. and Var, T. (1993) *Encyclopedia of Hospitality and Tourism*. Van Nostrand Reinhold.

Medlik, S. (1993) *Dictionary of Transport, Travel and Hospitality*. Butterworth-Heinemann.

Paxton, J. (annual) *The Statesman's Yearbook*. Macmillan.

Ritchie, J. R. B. and Hawkins, D. (annual) *World Travel and Tourism Review*, vols 1–3. CAB.

Seaton, A., Wood, R., Dieke, P. and Jenkins, C. (eds) (1994) *Tourism: the State of the Art: The Strathclyde Symposium*. Wiley.

Witt, S. F. and Mountinho, L. (1995) *Tourism Marketing and Management Handbook*. Student edn. Prentice Hall.

World Bank (annual) *The World Bank Atlas*. Washington, DC.

Abstracting services

Using electronic searching and abstracting services is a very effective way of searching the available literature and a great way to begin an assignment or presentation. The key services include:

Articles in Tourism (monthly) Universities of Bournemouth, Oxford Brookes and Surrey.

International Tourism and Hospitality Data Base CD-ROM. The Guide to Industry and Academic Resources. Wiley.

Leisure, Recreation and Tourism Abstracts (quarterly) CAB.

The Travel and Tourism Index. Brigham Young University Hawaii Campus.

Tour CD – Leisure Recreation and Tourism on CD-ROM.

Statistical sources

There is still a limited range of sources that draw together tourism statistics and trends. None the less the WTO's increasingly user-friendly reports are well worth consulting for both global and regional trends – but beware the distinctions between travellers, tourists and day visitors in the tables. The key sources are:

Organization for Economic Co-operation and Development (annual) *Tourism Policy and International Tourism in OECD Member Countries*. OECD.

Pacific Asia Travel Association (PATA) (annual) *Annual Statistical Report*. PATA.

World Tourism Organization (annual) *Compendium of Tourism Statistics*. WTO.

World Tourism Organization (annual) *Yearbook of Tourism Statistics*. WTO.

World Tourism Organization (monthly) *World Tourism Barometer*, WTO.

World Tourism Organization (1994) *Recommendations on Tourism Statistics*. WTO.

World Tourism Organization (1999) *Tourism Market Trends*, 6 vols. WTO.

World Tourism Organization (2001) *Tourism 2020 Vision – Global Forecast and Profiles of Market Segments*. WTO.

World Tourism Organization (2001) *Tourism Forecasts*, 6 vols. WTO.

Journals

The growth in tourism journals has brought with it a rich source of case study and statistical material. In addition, the geographical and leisure journals are increasingly publishing tourism-related papers. Journals with content relevant to the geography of travel and tourism include:

Annals of Leisure Research
Annals of Tourism Research
ASEAN Journal of Hospitality and Tourism
Asia Pacific Journal of Tourism Research
Australian Journal of Hospitality Management
Current Issues in Tourism
e-Review of Tourism Research (http://ertr.tamu.edu)
Event Management
Festival Management and Event Tourism
Hospitality and Tourism Educator
International Journal of Contemporary Hospitality Management
International Journal of Hospitality Management
International Journal of Hospitality and Tourism Administration
International Journal of Service Industry Management
International Journal of Tourism Research
Journal of Air Transport Geography
Journal of Air Transport Management
Journal of Convention and Exhibition Management
Journal of Ecotourism
Journal of Hospitality and Leisure Marketing
Journal of Hospitality, Leisure, Sport and Tourism
Journal of Hospitality and Tourism Research
Journal of Leisure Research
Journal of Sport Tourism
Journal of Sustainable Tourism
Journal of Teaching in Travel and Tourism
Journal of Tourism and Cultural Change
Journal of Tourism Studies
Journal of Travel and Tourism Marketing
Journal of Travel Research
Journal of Travel and Tourism Research
Journal of Vacation Marketing
Leisure Futures, Henley Centre for Forecasting
Leisure Sciences
Leisure Studies
Managing Leisure
Pacific Tourism Review
Progress in Tourism and Hospitality Research
Scandinavian Journal of Hospitality and Tourism
Service Industries Journal
The Tourist Review
Tourism Analysis

Tourism and Hospitality Research
Tourism Culture and Communication
Tourism Economics
Tourism Geographies
Tourism in Focus
Tourism Management
Tourism Recreation Research
Tourism, Culture and Communication
Tourist Studies
Travel and Tourism Analyst
World Leisure and Recreation Association Journal

World wide web (WWW) site addresses of national tourism organizations

The World Wide Web is now a rich source of material for anyone researching the geography of travel and tourism. Destinations, organizations, companies and individuals provide millions of Web pages containing material and information that was previously only available by contacting the organization concerned. It is worth mentioning that this source of information needs to be used with care, as there is no quality control of much of the material that is available on the Web. The companion website for this book provides an annotated list of useful travel and tourism websites. It is the aim of this section of the compendium to provide the reader with a list of the official tourism sites of governments and tourist boards, where these exist for each country in the world. This is a good source of initial information about a country, and, as well as providing excellent destination information, many sites have Web pages of interest for professionals working in the industry and students giving statistics and useful material about planning, marketing and policy for tourism in the country concerned. None the less, even within Europe, the quality of the websites is variable – the official site for Hungary for example is excellent, providing comprehensive tourism information for the professional as well as the traveller, whilst the site for Poland is not as satisfactory.

At the time of writing, these addresses were correct, but you must remember that they may change and you will need to use a search engine to find the new address. The companion website to this book provides hints about searching the World Wide Web.

Country	Website
Algeria	http://www.mta.gov.dz/
Andorra	http://www.turisme.ad
Angola	http://www.angola.org/
Anguilla	http://net.ai/
Antigua and Barbuda	http://www.interknowledge.com/ antigua-barbuda/
Argentina	http://www.sectur.gov.ar/
Aruba	http://www.interknowledge.com/aruba

Australia	http://www.australia.com
Austria	http://www.austria-tourism.at/
Bahamas	http://www.interknowledge.com/bahamas/
Bangladesh	http://www.bangladesh.com
Barbados	http://barbados.org/
Belgium	http://www.visitbelgium.com/
Belize	http://www.travelbelize.org/
Bermuda	http://www.bermudatourism.com
Bhutan	http://www.tourisminbhutan.com
Bolivia	http://www.bolivia.com/noticias/tourismo.asp
Bonaire	http://www.interknowledge.com/bonaire/ index.html
Brazil	http://www.embratur.gov.br/
Bulgaria	http://mi.government.bg/eng/tur/pol/ orgs.html
Cambodia	http://www.tourismcambodia.com
Cameroon	http://www.compufix.demon.co.uk/camweb/
Canada	http://www.visitcanada.com
Cayman Islands	http://www.caymanislands.ky
Chile	http://www.turismochile.cl
China	http://www.chinatour.com
Colombia	http://www.presidencia.gov.co/
Costa Rica	http://www.tourism-costarica.com
Croatia	http://www.vlada.hr/
Cuba	http://www.cubaweb.cu/
Curacao	http://www.interknowledge.com/curacao/
Cyprus	http://www.cyprustourism.org/
Czech Republic	http://czechtourism.com
Denmark	http://www.visitdenmark.com
Ecuador	http://www.ecuador.us
Egypt	http://www.egypttourism.org/
Estonia	http://www.tourism.ee/
Ethiopia	http://www.ethiopia.ottawa.on.ca/tourism.htm
Falkland Islands	http://www.tourism.org.fk/
Federated States of Micronesia	http://fsmgov.org/
Fiji	http://www.BulaFiji.com
Finland	http://www.finland-tourism.com
France	http://www.maison-de-la-france.fr
French Guiana	http://www.guyanetourisme.com/
Gabon	http://www.tourisme-gabon.com
Gambia	http://www.gambiatourism.info
Georgia	http://www.parliament.ge/TOURISM
Germany	http://www.germany-tourism.de/
Gibraltar	http://www.gibraltar.gi/tourism/

Greece   http://www.greektourism.gr
Greenland   http://www.greenland-guide.dk
Grenada   http://www.interknowledge.com/grenada/
Guadeloupe   http://www.antilles-info-tourisme.com/
                        guadeloupe/
Guam   http://www.visitguam.org/
Guatemala   http://www.visitguatemala.com
Guyana   http://www.turq.com/guyana.html

Hawaii   http://www.hawaii.gov/tourism/
Honduras   http://www.turq.com/honduras.html
Hong Kong   http://www.hkta.org
Hungary   http://www.hungarytourism.hu/

Iceland   http://www.icetourist.is/
India   http://www.tourindia.com/
Indonesia   http://tourismindonesia.com
Iran   http://www.itto.org/
Ireland   http://www.ireland.travel.ie
Isle of Man   http://www.isle-of-man.com/
Israel   http://www.infotour.co.il
Italy   http://www.enit.it/

Jamaica   http://www.visitjamaica.com/
Japan   http://www.jnto.go.jp/
Jersey   http://www.jtourism.com
Jordan   http://www.jordanembassyus.org

Kenya   http://www.bwanazulia.com/kenya/
Korea (South)   http://www.knto.or.kr

Laos P.D.R   http://www.mekongcenter.com
Lebanon   http://www.Lebanon-tourism.gov.lb
Liechtenstein   http://www.news.li/touri/index.htm
Luxembourg   http://www.etat.lu/tourism

Macau   http://www.macautourism.gov.mo/login.html
Macedonia   http://www.tarm.org.mk
Malaysia   http://tourism.gov.my/
Maldives   http://www.visitmaldives.com/intro.html
Malta   http://www.tourism.org.mt/
Martinique   http://www.martinique.org/
Mauritius   http://www.mauritius.net/
Mexico   http://www.mexico-travel.com/
Micronesia   http://www.visit-fsm.org/
Monaco   http://www.monaco.mc/monaco/guide_en.html
Mongolia   http://www.mongoliatourism.gov.mn/
Morocco   http://www.tourisme-marocain.com
Myanmar   http://www.myanmartourism.com

Namibia	http://www.namibiatourism.co.uk
Nepal	http://www.visitnepal.com
Netherlands	http://www.visitholland.com/
New Zealand	http://www.purenz.com
Nicaragua	http://www.intur.gob.ni/
Nigeria	http://www.nigeria-tourism.net
Northern Ireland	http://www.nitb.com
Norway	http://www.tourist.no
Palau	http://www.visit-palau.com/
Palestine	http://www.pna.org
Panama	http://www.panamainfo.com/
Papua New Guinea	http://www.pngtourism.org.pg
Peru	http://www.peruonline.net
Philippines	http://www.tourism.gov.ph/
Poland	http://www.polandtour.org
Portugal	http://www.portugal.org
Puerto Rico	http://www.gotopuertorico.com
Romania	http://www.turism.ro/
Russian Federation	http://www.interknowledge.com/russia/index.html
Saba	http://www.turq.com/saba/
Saint-Pierre-et-Miquelon	http://www.saint-pierre-et-miquelon.com
Scotland	http://www.travelscotland.co.uk
Senegal	http://www.earth2000.com
Serbia	http://www.serbia.sr.gov.yu
Seychelles	http://www.seychelles.com/
Singapore	http://www.visitsingapore.com
Slovakia	http://www.scar.sk
Slovenia	http://www.slovenia-tourism.si
South Africa	http://www.environment.gov.za/
Spain	http://www.tourspain.es
Sri Lanka	http://www.lanka.net/ctb/
St Barthelemy	http://www.st-barths.com/
St Eustatius	http://www.turq.com/statia/
St Kitts & Nevis	http://www.interknowledge.com/stkitts-nevis/
St Lucia	http://www.st-lucia.com/
St Maarten	http://www.st-maarten.com/
St Martin	http://www.interknowledge.com/st-martin
St Vincent & The Grenadines	http://www.turq.com/stvincent
Sudan	http://www.sudan.net/
Sweden	http://www.visit-sweden.com
Switzerland	http://www.switzerlandtourism.ch/
Syria	http://www.syriatourism.org
Taiwan	http://www.tbroc.gov.tw/
Tanzania	http://www.tanzania-web.com
Thailand	http://www.tourismthailand.org

Tibet	http://www.tibet-tour.com/
Trinidad and Tobago	http://www.visittnt.com/
Tunisia	http://www.tourismtunisia.com/
Turkey	http://www.turkey.org/
Turks & Caicos	http://www.interknowledge.com/turks-caicos
Uganda	http://www.uganda.co.ug/tour.htm
United Kingdom	http://www.visitbritain.com/
USA	http://www.tinet.ita.doc.gov/
Uruguay	http://www.turismo.gub.uy
US Virgin Islands	http://www.usvi.net/
Vanuatu	http://www.vanuatu.net.vu/
Venezuela	http://www.venezlon.demon.co.uk
Vietnam	http://www.vn-tourism.com/index.htm
Wales	http://www.visitwales.com
Western Samoa	http://www.visitsamoa.com
Yemen	http://www.yementourism.com
Zambia	http://www.africa-insites.com/zambia/
Zanzibar	http://www.zanzibar.net/zautalii/index.html
Zimbabwe	http://www.zimbabwetourism.co.zw/ defaulta.htm

Selective place name index

Subject index